FOUNDATIONS OF COMPUTER SCIENCE

FOUNDATIONS OF
COMPUTER SCIENCE

BEHROUZ FOROUZAN AND
FIROUZ MOSHARRAF

COURSE TECHNOLOGY
CENGAGE Learning™

Australia • Brazil • Japan • Korea • Mexico • Singapore • Spain • United Kingdom • United States

COURSE TECHNOLOGY
CENGAGE Learning™

**Foundations of Computer Science,
Second Edition**
Behrouz Forouzan and Firouz Mosharraf

Publishing Director: Linden Harris

Content Project Editor: Alison Walters

Head of Manufacturing: Jane Glendening

Production Controller: Tom Relf

Marketing Manager: Jason Bennett

Cover design: Landsky, UK

Text design: WordMongers Ltd, UK

For product information and technology assistance,
contact **emea.info@cengage.com**.

For permission to use material from this text or product,
and for permission queries,
email **clsuk.permissions@cengage.com**.

British Library Cataloguing-in-Publication Data
A catalogue record for this book is available from the British Library.

ISBN: 978-1-84480-700-0

Cengage Learning EMEA
Cheriton House, North Way, Andover, Hampshire, SP10 5BE, United Kingdom

Cengage Learning products are represented in Canada by Nelson Education Ltd.

For your lifelong learning solutions, visit
www.cengage.co.uk

Purchase your next print book, e-book or e-chapter at
www.CengageBrain.co.uk

Printed by Seng Lee Press, Singapore
5 6 7 8 9 10 – 12 11 10

To my wife, Faezeh.

Behrouz

To my wife, Ellie.

Firouz

Contents

Preface

Computers play a large part in our everyday lives and will continue to do so in the future. Computer science is a young discipline that is evolving and progressing. Computer networks have connected people from far-flung points of the globe. Virtual reality is creating three-dimensional images that amaze the eyes. Space exploration owes part of its success to computers. Computer-created special effects have changed the movie industry. Computers have played important roles in genetics.

This book is designed for a CS0 course based on the recommendations of the Association of Computing Machinery (ACM). It covers all areas of computer science in breadth.

Pedagogical features

Several features of this book not only make it unique, but make it easier for beginners to understand.

Concepts

Throughout the book, we have tried to emphasize the concept rather than the mathematical model. We believe an understanding of the concept leads to an understanding of the model.

Visual approach

A brief examination of the book will show that our approach is very visual. There are nearly 400 figures. While this tends to increase the length of a book, figures aid understanding of the text.

Algorithms

Tens of algorithms have been added to the new edition to make the student familiar with problem solving and programming.

UML

Throughout the book we have used UML diagrams to make students familiar with this tool, which is becoming the de facto standard in the industry.

Key points

These are denoted by an 'i' icon in the margin, as shown below, and are summaries of summaries. These are the points that students need to use as revision for exam aids.

Computers store positive and negative numbers differently.

Examples

Whenever appropriate we have used examples to demonstrate the concept and the mathematical model.

End-of-chapter material

The end material of each chapter contains four parts: recommended reading, key terms, summary, and practice set.

Recommended reading This section gives a list of books recommended for that chapter. These lists can also be used for reference.

Key terms This provides a list of the important terms introduced in the chapter. Every key term is defined in the glossary.

Summary The summaries contain a concise overview of all the key points of the chapter. They are bulleted for readability.

Practice sets Each practice set contains three parts: review questions, multiple-choice questions, and exercises.

❑   Review questions test understanding of key points and concepts of the chapter.

❑   Multiple-choice questions are designed to test understanding of the materials.

❑   Exercises are designed to see if students can apply the concepts and formulas.

Glossary

A glossary of all key terms and acronyms is included at the end of the book.

Solutions to practice sets

Solutions to the review questions, multiple-choice questions, and exercises are available online at http://www.cengage.co.uk/forouzan.

Instructional materials

PowerPoint presentations of all figures and highlighted points, in addition to the solutions of all review questions, multiple-choice questions, and exercises, are available online at http://www.cengage.co.uk/forouzan.

Changes in the new edition

The reader will notice the difference between the first and the second edition by the number of pages. This is caused by revised material, rewritten material, new material, and combined material.

Revised material

Chapters 2, 3, 4, 5, 7, 9, and 10 have been revised based on the recommendations of the reviewers for this edition. Most of the exercises at the ends of the chapters have also been revised and augmented.

Rewritten material

Chapters 6, 10, and 16 have been rewritten.

New material

Chapter 18 (Artificial Intelligence) is new for this edition. There are also four new appendices: Appendix E (Boolean Algebra and Logic Circuits), Appendix F (Examples of Programs in C, C++, and Java), Appendix G (Mathematical Review), and Appendix H (Error Detection and Correction).

Combined or replaced material

Appendix A and B of the first edition have been combined into a new Appendix A. Appendix C (Flow Charts) has been replaced by a new Appendix B (UML). Appendix F (Discrete Cosine Transform) is now part of the new Appendix G (Mathematical Review).

Acknowledgments

No text of this scope can be developed without the support of many people. This is especially true for this book.

Peer reviewers

To anyone who has not been through the process, the value of peer reviews cannot be appreciated enough. Writing a book rapidly becomes a myopic process. The important guidance of reviewers who can stand back and view the text as a whole cannot be measured. We would especially like to acknowledge the contributions of the reviewers for the second edition: John Newman, University of Wales, Steve Maybank, Birbeck College, Mario Kolberg, University of Stirling, Colin Price, University of Worcester, Boris Cogan, London Metropolitan University, Thomas Mandl, University of Hildesheim, Daphne Becker, University of South Africa, Lubna Fekry Abdulhai and Osama Abulnaja, King Abdulaziz University, and Katie Atkinson, University of Liverpool.

People at Cengage Learning

Our thanks also go to people at Cengage Learning, Allie, Matthew and Gaynor, and also to Steve Rickaby of Wordmongers for all his care and attention to the manuscript.

Our family

Last, and most obviously not least, is the support of our families and friends. While the authors suffer through the writing process, families and friends suffer through their absence. We can only hope that as they view the final product, they feel that their sacrifices were worth it.

1 Introduction

The phrase *computer science* has a very broad meaning today. However, in this book, we define the phrase as "issues related to the computer". This introductory chapter first tries to find out what a computer is, then investigates other issues directly related to computers. We look first at the **Turing model** as a mathematical and philosophical definition of computation. We then show how today's computers are based on the **von Neumann model**. The chapter ends with a brief history of this culture-changing device… the computer.

Objectives

After studying this chapter, the student should be able to:

❑ Define the Turing model of a computer.

❑ Define the von Neumann model of a computer.

❑ Describe the three components of a computer: hardware, data, and software.

❑ List topics related to computer hardware.

❑ List topics related to data.

❑ List topics related to software.

❑ Discuss some social and ethical issues related to the use of computers.

❑ Give a short history of computers.

1.1 TURING MODEL

The idea of a universal computational device was first described by Alan Turing in 1937. He proposed that all computation could be performed by a special kind of a machine, now called a *Turing machine*. Although Turing presented a mathematical description of such a machine, he was more interested in the philosophical definition of computation than in building the actual machine. He based the model on the actions that people perform when involved in computation. He abstracted these actions into a model for a computational machine that has really changed the world.

Data processors

Before discussing the Turing model, let us define a computer as a **data processor**. Using this definition, a computer acts as a black box that accepts input data, processes the data, and creates output data (Figure 1.1). Although this model can define the functionality of a computer today, it is too general. In this model, a pocket calculator is also a computer (which it is, in a literal sense).

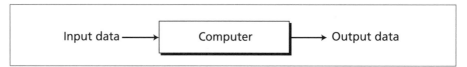

Figure 1.1   A single purpose computing machine

Another problem with this model is that it does not specify the type of processing, or whether more than one type of processing is possible. In other words, it is not clear how many types or sets of operations a machine based on this model can perform. Is it a specific-purpose machine or a general-purpose machine?

This model could represent a specific-purpose computer (or processor) that is designed to do a single job, such as controlling the temperature of a building or controlling the fuel usage in a car. However, computers, as the term is used today, are *general-purpose* machines. They can do many different types of tasks. This implies that we need to change this model into the Turing model to be able to reflect the actual computers of today.

Programmable data processors

The Turing model is a better model for a general-purpose computer. This model adds an extra element to the specific computing machine: the *program*. A **program** is a set of instructions that tells the computer what to do with data. Figure 1.2 shows the Turing model.

In the Turing model, the **output data** depends on the combination of two factors: the **input data** and the program. With the same input data, we can generate different outputs if we change the program. Similarly, with the same program, we can generate different outputs if we change the input data. Finally, if the input data

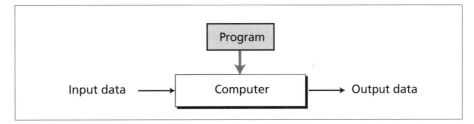

Figure 1.2   A computer based on the Turing model: programmable data processor

and the program remain the same, the output should be the same. Let us look at three cases.

Same program, different input data

Figure 1.3 shows the same sorting program with different input data. Although the program is the same, the outputs are different, because different input data is processed.

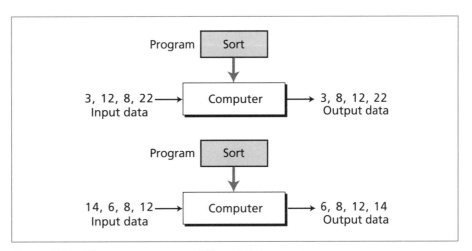

Figure 1.3   The same program, different data

Same input data, different programs

Figure 1.4 shows the same input data with different programs. Each program makes the computer perform different operations on the input data. The first program sorts the data, the second adds the data, and the third finds the smallest number.

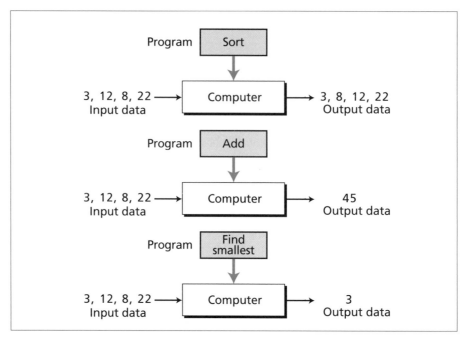

Figure 1.4   The same data, different programs

Same input data, same program

We expect the same result each time if both input data and the program are the same, of course. In other words, when the same program is run with the same input data, we expect the same output.

The universal Turing machine

A *universal Turing machine*, a machine that can do any computation if the appropriate program is provided, was the first description of a modern computer. It can be proved that a very powerful computer and a universal Turing machine can compute the same thing. We need only provide the data and the program—the description of how to do the computation—to either machine. In fact, a universal Turing machine is capable of computing anything that is computable.

1.2   VON NEUMANN MODEL

Computers built on the Turing universal machine store data in their memory. Around 1944–1945, John von Neumann proposed that, since program and data are logically the same, programs should also be stored in the memory of a computer.

Four subsystems

Computers built on the **von Neumann model** divide the computer hardware into four subsystems: memory, arithmetic logic unit, control unit, and input/output (Figure 1.5).

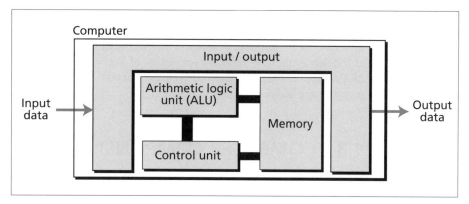

Figure 1.5   The von Neumann model

Memory

Memory is the storage area. This is where programs and data are stored during processing. We discuss the reasons for storing programs and data later in the chapter.

Arithmetic logic unit

The **arithmetic logic unit (ALU)** is where calculation and logical operations take place. For a computer to act as a data processor, it must be able to do arithmetic operations on data (such as adding a list of numbers). It should also be able to do logical operations on data, as we will see in Chapter 4.

Control unit

The **control unit** controls the operations of the memory, ALU, and the input/output subsystem.

Input / output

The input subsystem accepts input data and the program from outside the computer, while the output subsystem sends the results of processing to the outside world. The definition of the input/output subsystem is very broad: it also includes secondary storage devices such as disk or tape that store data and programs for processing. When a disk stores data that results from processing, it is considered an output device: when data is read from the disk, it is considered an input device.

The stored program concept

The von Neumann model states that the program must be stored in memory. This is totally different from the architecture of early computers in which only the data was stored in memory: the programs for their tasks were implemented by manipulating a set of switches or by changing the wiring system.

The memory of modern computers hosts both a program and its corresponding data. This implies that both the data and programs should have the same format, because they are stored in memory. In fact, they are stored as *binary* patterns in memory—a sequence of 0s and 1s.

Sequential execution of instructions

A program in the von Neumann model is made of a finite number of **instructions**. In this model, the control unit fetches one instruction from memory, decodes it, then executes it. In other words, the instructions are executed one after another. Of course, one instruction may request the control unit to jump to some previous or following instruction, but this does not mean that the instructions are not executed sequentially. Sequential execution of a program was the initial requirement of a computer based on the von Neumann model. Today's computers execute programs in the order that is most efficient.

1.3 COMPUTER COMPONENTS

We can think of a computer as being made up of three components: computer hardware, data, and computer software.

Computer hardware

Computer hardware today has four components under the von Neumann model, although we can have different types of memory, different types of input/output subsystems, and so on. We discuss computer hardware in more detail in Chapter 5.

Data

The von Neumann model clearly defines a computer as a data processing machine that accepts the input data, processes it, and outputs the result.

Storing data The von Neumann model does not define how data must be stored in a computer. If a computer is an electronic device, the best way to store data is in the form of an electrical signal, specifically its presence or absence. This implies that a computer can store data in one of two states.

Obviously, the data we use in daily life is not just in one of two states. For example, our numbering system uses digits that can take one of ten states (0 to 9). We cannot (as yet) store this type of information in a computer: it needs to be changed to another system that uses only two states (0 and 1). We also need to be able to process other types of data (text, image, audio, video). These also cannot be stored in a computer directly, but need to be changed to the appropriate form (0s and 1s).

In Chapters 3, we will learn how to store different types of data as a binary pattern, a sequence of 0s and 1s. In Chapter 4, we show how data is manipulated, as a binary pattern, inside a computer.

Organizing data Although data should be stored in only one form inside a computer, a binary pattern, data outside a computer can take many forms. In addition, computers (and the notion of data processing) have created a new field of study known as *data organization*, which asks the question: can we organize our data into different entities and formats before storing it inside a computer? Today, data is not treated as a flat sequence of information. Instead, data is organized into small units, small units are organized into larger units, and so on. We will look at data from this point of view in Chapters 11–14.

Computer software

The main feature of the Turing or von Neumann models is the concept of the *program*. Although early computers did not store the program in the computer's memory, they did use the concept of programs. *Programming* those early computers meant changing the wiring systems or turning a set of switches on or off. Programming was therefore a task done by an operator or engineer before the actual data processing began.

Programs must be stored

In the von Neumann model programs are stored in the computer's memory. Not only do we need memory to hold data, but we also need memory to hold the program (Figure 1.6).

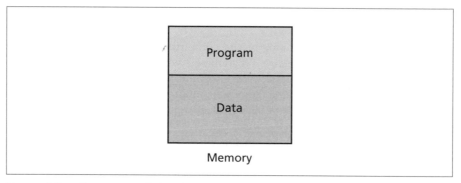

Figure 1.6   Program and data in memory

A sequence of instructions

Another requirement of the model is that the program must consist of a sequence of instructions. Each instruction operates on one or more data items. Thus, an instruction can change the effect of a previous instruction. For example, Figure 1.7 shows a program that inputs two numbers, adds them, and prints the result. This program consists of four individual instructions.

> 1. Input the first number into memory.
> 2. Input the second number into memory.
> 3. Add the two together and store the result in memory.
> 4. Output the result.
>
> ## Program

Figure 1.7   A program made of instructions

We might ask why a program must be composed of instructions. The answer is reusability. Today, computers do millions of tasks. If the program for each task was an independent entity without anything in common with other programs, programming would be difficult. The Turing and von Neumann models make programming easier by defining the different instructions that can be used by computers. A programmer can then combine these instructions to make any number of programs. Each program can be a different combination of different instructions.

Algorithms

The requirement for a program to consist of a sequence of instructions made programming possible, but it brought another dimension to using a computer. A programmer must not only learn the task performed by each instruction, but also learn how to combine these instructions to do a particular task. Looking at this issue differently, a programmer must first solve the problem in a step-by-step manner, then try to find the appropriate instruction (or series of instructions) to implement those steps. This step-by-step solution is called an **algorithm**. Algorithms play a very important role in computer science and are discussed in Chapter 8.

Languages

At the beginning of the computer age there was only one computer language, *machine language*. Programmers wrote instructions (using binary patterns) to solve a problem. However, as programs became larger, writing long programs using these patterns became tedious. Computer scientists came up with the idea of using symbols to represent binary patterns, just as people use symbols (words) for commands in daily life. Of course, the symbols used in daily life are different than those used in computers. So the concept of **computer languages** was born. A natural language such as English is rich and has many rules to combine words correctly: a computer language, on the other hand, has a more limited number of symbols and also a limited number of words. We will study computer languages in Chapter 9.

Software engineering

Something that was not defined in the von Neumann model is **software engineering**, which is the design and writing of *structured programs*. Today it is not acceptable just to write a program that does a task: the program must follow strict rules and principles. We discuss these principles, collectively known as *software engineering*, in Chapter 10.

Operating systems

During the evolution of computers, scientists became aware that there was a series of instructions common to all programs. For example, instructions to tell a computer where to receive data and where to send data are needed by almost all programs. It is more efficient to write these instructions only once for the use of all programs. Thus the concept of the **operating system** emerged. An operating system originally worked as a manager to facilitate access to the computer's components by a program, although today operating systems do much more. We will learn about them in Chapter 7.

1.4 HISTORY

In this section we briefly review the history of computing and computers. We divide this history into three periods.

Mechanical machines (before 1930)

During this period, several computing machines were invented that bear little resemblance to the modern concept of a computer.

❑ In the 17th century, Blaise Pascal, a French mathematician and philosopher, invented Pascaline, a mechanical calculator for addition and subtraction operations. In the 20th century, when Niklaus Wirth invented a structured programming language, he called it Pascal to honor the inventor of the first mechanical calculator.

❑ In the late 17th century, German mathematician Gottfried Leibnitz invented a more sophisticated mechanical calculator that could do multiplication and division as well as addition and subtraction. It was called Leibnitz' Wheel.

❑ The first machine that used the idea of storage and programming was the Jacquard loom, invented by Joseph-Marie Jacquard at the beginning of the 19th century. The loom used punched cards (like a stored program) to control the raising of the warp threads in the manufacture of textiles.

❑ In 1823, Charles Babbage invented the Difference Engine, which could do more than simple arithmetic operations—it could solve polynomial equations too. Later, he invented a machine called the Analytical Engine that, to some extent, parallels the idea of modern computers. It had four components: a mill (corresponding to a modern ALU), a store (memory), an operator (control unit), and output (input/output).

❑ In 1890, Herman Hollerith, working at the US Census Bureau, designed and built a programmable machine that could automatically read, tally, and sort data stored on punched cards.

The birth of electronic computers (1930–1950)

Between 1930 and 1950, several computers were invented by scientists who could be considered the pioneers of the electronic computer industry.

Early electronic computers

The early computers of this period did not store the program in memory—all were programmed externally. Five computers were prominent during these years:

❑ The first special-purpose computer that encoded information electrically was invented by John V. Atanasoff and his assistant Clifford Berry in 1939. It was called the ABC (Atanasoff Berry Computer) and was specifically designed to solve a system of linear equations.

❑ At the same time, a German mathematician called Konrad Zuse designed a general-purpose machine called Z1.

❑ In the 1930s, the US Navy and IBM sponsored a project at Harvard University under the direction of Howard Aiken to build a huge computer called Mark I. This computer used both electrical and mechanical components.

❑ In England, Alan Turing invented a computer called Colossus that was designed to break the German Enigma code.

❏ The first general-purpose, totally electronic computer was made by John Mauchly and J. Presper Eckert and was called ENIAC (Electronic Numerical Integrator and Calculator). It was completed in 1946. It used 18,000 vacuum tubes, was 100 feet long by 10 feet high, and weighed 30 tons.

Computers based on the von Neumann model

The preceding five computers used memory only for storing data, and were programmed externally using wires or switches. John von Neumann proposed that the program and the data should be stored in memory. That way, every time we use a computer to do a new task, we need only change the program instead of rewiring the machine or turning hundreds of switches on and off.

The first computer based on von Neumann's ideas was made in 1950 at the University of Pennsylvania and was called EDVAC. At the same time, a similar computer called EDSAC was built by Maurice Wilkes at Cambridge University in England.

Computer generations (1950–present)

Computers built after 1950 more or less follow the von Neumann model. They have become faster, smaller, and cheaper, but the principle is almost the same. Historians divide this period into generations, with each generation witnessing some major change in hardware or software (but not in the model).

First generation

The first generation (roughly 1950–1959) is characterized by the emergence of commercial computers. During this time, computers were used only by professionals. They were locked in rooms with access limited only to the operator or computer specialist. Computers were bulky and used vacuum tubes as electronic switches. At this time, computers were affordable only by big organizations.

Second generation

Second-generation computers (roughly 1959–1965) used transistors instead of vacuum tubes. This reduced the size of computers, as well as their cost, and made them affordable to small and medium-size corporations. Two high-level programming languages, FORTRAN and COBOL (see Chapter 9), were invented and made programming easier. These two languages separated the programming task from the computer operation task. A civil engineer, for example could write a FORTRAN program to solve a problem without being involved in the electronic details of computer architecture.

Third generation

The invention of the **integrated circuit** (transistors, wiring, and other components on a single chip) reduced the cost and size of computers even further. *Minicomputers* appeared on the market. Canned programs, popularly known as *software packages*, became available. A small corporation could buy a package, for example for accounting, instead of writing its own program. A new industry, the software industry, was born. This generation lasted roughly from 1965 to 1975.

Fourth generation

The fourth generation (approximately 1975–1985) saw the appearance of *microcomputers*. The first desktop calculator, the Altair 8800, became available in 1975. Advances in the electronics industry allowed whole computer subsystems to fit on a single circuit board. This generation also saw the emergence of computer networks (see Chapter 6).

Fifth generation
This open-ended generation started in 1985. It has witnessed the appearance of laptop and palmtop computers, improvements in secondary storage media (CD-ROM, DVD and so on), the use of multimedia, and the phenomenon of virtual reality.

1.5 SOCIAL AND ETHICAL ISSUES

Computer science has created some peripheral issues, the most prevalent of which can be categorized as social and ethical issues.

Social issues

Computers have created some controversy. We introduce some of these arguments here.

Dependency
Computer science has definitely changed our society. Based on some surveys, more than half of the households in the US use a computer to access the Internet. Does this mean that a society in which the majority of people have access to a computer is considered a *better* society? Some people think that the use of computers is inevitable in everyone's life: life is more difficult without it, while others think that computers have created a kind of dependency. The latter group think that this new dependency, like others, makes people's lives more difficult.

Social justice
Social justice is another issue we often hear about. The advocates of this issue argue that using computers at home is a luxury that not all people can afford. The cost of a computer, peripheral devices, and a monthly charge for Internet access is an extra burden on low-income people. This means that computers have created a service only for middle or high-income people, while low-income people are deprived of it. The opponents of this idea argue that the same issue was applied when other modern communication services were created, such as telephone and television. This group argue that, with the advance of technology, one day everyone will be able to afford a computer and access to the Internet.

Digital divide
The concept of a **digital divide** covers both the issues of dependency and social justice discussed above. The concept divides society into two groups: those who are electronically connected to the rest of society and those who are not. Someone in the first group communicates with people in the group through e-mail and uses the Internet for business and entertainment. Someone in the second group uses "snail mail" and the telephone for communication, and enjoys sitting in a cinema to see a movie instead of downloading it from a cable network. This digital divide is gradually disappearing in industrial countries, but experts believe that it will stay for a long time in developing countries.

Ethical issues

Computers have created some ethical issues. We introduce some of these here.

Privacy

Computers allow communication between two parties to be done electronically. However, much needs to be done to make this type of communication private. Society is paying a high price for private electronic communication. Network security (Chapter 16) may create this type of privacy, but it needs effort and costs a lot.

Copyright

Another ethical issue in a computerized society is copyright: who owns data? The Internet has created opportunities to share ideas, but has also brought a further ethical issue: electronic copyright.

Computer crime

Like any innovation, computers and information technology have created new types of crime. Hackers have been able to access many computers in the world and have stolen a lot of money. Virus creators design new viruses to be sent through the Internet and damage the information stored in computers. Although there are many anti-virus programs in use today, society is paying a high price for this type of crime, which did not exist before the computer and Internet era.

1.6   COMPUTER SCIENCE AS A DISCIPLINE

With the invention of computers, a new discipline has evolved: *computer science*. Like any other discipline, computer science has now divided into several areas. We can divide these areas into two broad categories: *system areas* and *applications areas*. System areas cover those areas that are directly related to the creation of hardware and software, such as *computer architecture, computer networking, security issues, operating systems, algorithms, programming languages*, and *software engineering*. Applications areas cover those that are related to the *use* of computers, such as *databases* and *artificial intelligence*. This book is a breadth-first approach to all these areas. After reading the book, the reader should have enough information to select the desired area of specialty.

1.7   OUTLINE OF THE COURSE

After this introductory chapter, the book is divided into five parts.

Part I: Data representation and operation

This part includes Chapters 2, 3, and 4. Chapter 2 discusses number systems, how a quantity can be represented using symbols. Chapter 3 discusses how different data is stored inside the computer. Chapter 4 discusses some primitive operations on *bits*.

Part II: Computer hardware

This part includes Chapters 5 and 6. Chapter 5 gives a general idea of computer hardware, discussing different computer organizations. Chapter 6 shows how individual computers are connected to make computer networks, and *internetworks* (internets). In particular, this chapter explores some subjects related to the Internet and its applications.

Part III: Computer software

This part includes Chapters 7, 8, 9, and 10. Chapter 7 discusses operating systems, the system software that controls access to the hardware by users—either human or application programs. Chapter 8 shows how problem solving is reduced to writing an algorithm for the problem. Chapter 9 takes a journey through the list of contemporary programming languages. Finally, Chapter 10 is a review of software engineering, the engineering approach to the development of software.

Part IV: Data organization and abstraction

This part complements Part I. In computer science, *atomic* data is collected into records, files, and databases. Data *abstraction* allows the programmer to create abstract notions about data. Part IV includes Chapters 11, 12, 13, and 14. Chapter 11 discusses data structures, collecting data of the same or different types under one category. Chapter 12 discusses abstract data types. Chapter 13 shows how different file structures can be used for different purposes. Finally, Chapter 14 discusses databases.

Part V: Advanced topics

Part V gives an overview of advanced topics, topics that students of computer science will encounter later in their education. This part covers Chapters 15, 16, 17, and 18. Chapter 15 discusses data compression, which is prevalent in today's data communications. Chapter 16 explores some issues to do with security, which is becoming more and more important when we communicate over insecure channels. Chapter 17 discusses the theory of computation: what can and cannot be computed. Finally Chapter 18 gives some idea of artificial intelligence, a topic with day-to-day challenges in computer science.

1.8 RECOMMENDED READING

For more details about the subjects discussed in this chapter, the following books are recommended:

- ❏ Schneider G M and Gersting J L: *Invitation to Computer Science*, Boston, MA: Course Technology, 2004
- ❏ Dale N and Lewis J: *Computer Science Illuminated*, Sudbury, MA: Jones and Bartlett, 2004
- ❏ Patt Y and Patel S: *Introduction to Computing Systems*, New York: McGraw-Hill, 2004

1.9   KEY TERMS

This chapter has introduced the following key terms, which are listed here with the pages on which they first occur:

algorithm 8	arithmetic logic unit (ALU) 5
computer languages 8	control unit 5
data processor 2	digital divide 11
input data 2	instruction 5
integrated circuit 10	memory 5
operating system 8	output data 2
program 2	software engineering 8
Turing model 1	von Neumann model 5

1.10   SUMMARY

- The idea of a universal computational device was first given by Alan Turing in 1937. He proposed that all computation can be performed by a special kind of a machine, now called a Turing machine.
- The von Neumann model defines a computer as four subsystems: memory, arithmetic logic unit, control unit, and input/output. The von Neumann model states that the program must be stored in memory.
- We can think of a computer as made up of three components: computer hardware, data, and computer software.

- The history of computing and computers can be divided into three periods: the period of mechanical machines (before 1930), the period of electronic computers (1930–1950), and the period that includes the five modern computer generations.
- Computer science has created some peripheral issues, the most prevalent of which can be categorized as social and ethical issues.
- With the invention of computers a new discipline has evolved, *computer science*, which is now divided into several areas.

1.11   PRACTICE SET

Review questions

1. Define a computer based on the Turing model.
2. Define a computer based on the von Neumann model.
3. What is the role of a program in a computer that is based on the Turing model?
4. What is the role of a program in a computer based on the von Neumann model?
5. What are the various subsystems of a computer?

6. What is the function of the memory subsystem in a computer?
7. What is the function of the ALU subsystem in a computer?
8. What is the function of the control unit subsystem in a computer?
9. What is the function of the input/output subsystem in a computer?
10. Briefly describe the five generations of computers.

Multiple-choice questions

11. The _____ model is the basis for today's computers.
    a. Leibnitz
    b. von Neumann
    c. Pascal
    d. Charles Babbage

12. In a computer, the _____ subsystem stores data and programs.
    a. ALU
    b. input/output
    c. memory
    d. control unit

13. In a computer, the _____ subsystem performs calculations and logical operations.
    a. ALU
    b. input/output
    c. memory
    d. control unit

14. In a computer, the _____ subsystem accepts data and programs and sends processing results to output devices.
    a. ALU
    b. input/output
    c. memory
    d. control unit

15. In a computer, the _____ subsystem serves as a manager of the other subsystems.
    a. ALU
    b. input/output
    c. memory
    d. control unit

16. According to the von Neumann model, _____ stored in memory.
    a. only data is
    b. only programs are
    c. data and programs are
    d. (none of the above)

17. A step-by-step solution to a problem is called _____.
    a. hardware
    b. an operating system
    c. a computer language
    d. an algorithm

18. FORTRAN and COBOL are examples of _____.
    a. hardware
    b. operating systems
    c. computer languages
    d. algorithms

19. A 17th-century computing machine that could perform addition and subtraction was the _____.
    a. Pascaline
    b. Jacquard loom
    c. Analytical Engine
    d. Babbage machine

20. _____ is a set of instructions in a computer language that tells the computer what to do with data.
    a. An operating system
    b. An algorithm
    c. A data processor
    d. A program

21. _____ is the design and writing of a program in structured form.
    a. Software engineering
    b. Hardware engineering
    c. Algorithm development
    d. Instructional architecture

22. The first electronic special-purpose computer was called _____.
    a. Pascal
    b. Pascaline
    c. ABC
    d. ENIAC

23. One of the first computers based on the von Neumann model was called _____.
    a. Pascal
    b. Pascaline
    c. ABC
    d. EDVAC

24. The first computing machine to use the idea of storage and programming was called _____.
    a. the Madeline
    b. EDVAC
    c. the Babbage machine
    d. the Jacquard loom

25. _____ separated the programming task from computer operation tasks.
    a. Algorithms
    b. Data processors
    c. High-level programming languages
    d. Operating systems

Exercises

26. Explain why a computer cannot solve a problem for which there is no solution outside the computer.

27. If a small cheap computer can do the same thing as a large expensive computer, why do people need to have a large one.

28. Do some research and find out whether the Pascaline calculator is a computer according to the Turing model.

29. Do some research and find out whether Leibnitz's Wheel is a computer according to the Turing model.

30. Do some research and find out whether the Jacquard Loom is a computer according to the Turing model.

31. Do some research and find out whether Babbage's Analytical Engine is a computer according to the von Neumann model.

32. Do some research about the ABC computer and find out whether this computer followed the von Neumann model.

33. Do some research and find out in which computer generation keyboards originated.

34. Do some research and find out in which computer generation printers originated.

35. According to the von Neumann model, can the hard disk of today be used as input or output? Explain.

36. A programming language has ten different instructions. How many five-instruction programs can be written in this language if no instruction is repeated? How many seven-instruction programs?

37. Which is more valuable today to an organization: hardware, software, or data?

2 Number Systems

This chapter is a prelude to Chapters 3 and 4. In Chapter 3 we will show how data is stored inside the computer. In Chapter 4 we will show how logic and arithmetic operations are performed on data. This chapter is a preparation for understanding the contents of Chapters 3 and 4. Readers who know about number systems can skip this chapter and move on to Chapter 3 without loss of continuity. Note that the number systems discussed in this chapter are "paper and pencil representations": we show how these numbers are stored in a computer in Chapter 3.

Objectives

After studying this chapter, the student should be able to:

❏ Understand the concept of number systems.

❏ Distinguish between nonpositional and positional number systems.

❏ Describe the decimal system (base 10).

❏ Describe the binary system (base 2).

❏ Describe the hexadecimal system (base 16).

❏ Describe the octal system (base 8).

❏ Convert a number in binary, octal, or hexadecimal to a number in the decimal system.

❏ Convert a number in the decimal system to a number in binary, octal, and hexadecimal.

❏ Convert a number in binary to octal and vice versa.

❏ Convert a number in binary to hexadecimal and vice versa.

❏ Find the number of digits needed in each system to represent a particular value.

2.1   INTRODUCTION

A **number system** (or numeral system) defines how a number can be represented using distinct symbols. A number can be represented differently in different systems. For example, the two numbers $(2A)_{16}$ and $(52)_8$ both refer to the same quantity, $(42)_{10}$, but their representations are different. This is the same as using the words *cheval* (French) and *equus* (Latin) to refer to the same entity, a horse.

As we use symbols (characters) to create words in a language, we use symbols (digits) to represent numbers. However, we know that the number of symbols (characters) in any language is limited. We need to repeat characters and combine them to create words. It is the same for numbers: we have a limited number of symbols (digits) to represent numbers, which means that the digits need to be repeated.

Several number systems have been used in the past and can be categorized into two groups: positional and non-positional systems. Our main goal is to discuss the positional number systems, but we also give examples of non-positional systems.

2.2   POSITIONAL NUMBER SYSTEMS

In a **positional number system**, the position a symbol occupies in the number determines the value it represents. In this system, a number represented as:

$$\pm (S_{k-1} \ldots S_2\, S_1\, S_0.\, S_{-1}\, S_{-2} \ldots S_{-l})_b$$

has the value of:

$$n = \pm\ \ S_{k-1} \times b^{k-1} + \ldots + S_1 \times b^1 + S_0 \times b^0\ \ +\ \ S_{-1} \times b^{-1} + S_{-2} \times b^{-2} + \ldots + S_{-l} \times b^{-l}$$

in which S is the set of symbols, b is the **base** (or **radix**), which is equal to the total number of the symbols in the set S, and S_i is the symbol in position *i*. Note that we have used an expression that can be extended from the right or from the left. In other words, the power of b can be 0 to $k - 1$ in one direction and -1 to $-l$ in the other direction. The terms with non-negative powers of b are related to the integral part of the number, while the terms with negative power of b are related to the fractional part of the number. The ± sign shows that the number can be either positive or negative. We will study several positional number systems in this chapter.

The decimal system (base 10)

The first positional number system we discuss in this chapter is the **decimal system**. The word *decimal* is derived from the Latin root *decem* (ten). In this system the base b = 10 and we use ten symbols to represent a number. The set of symbols is S = {0, 1, 2, 3, 4, 5, 6, 7, 8, 9}. As we know, the symbols in this system are often referred to as **decimal digits** or just digits. In this chapter, we use ± to show that a number can be positive or negative, but remember that these signs are not stored in computers—computers handle the sign differently, as we discuss in Chapter 3.

Computers store positive and negative numbers differently.

In the decimal system, a number is written as:

$$\pm (S_{k-1} \ldots S_2\, S_1\, S_0 . S_{-1}\, S_{-2} \ldots S_{-l})_{10}$$

but for simplicity, we often drop the parentheses, the base, and the plus sign (if the number is positive). For example, we write the number $+(552.23)_{10}$ as 552.23—the base and plus signs are implicit.

Integers

An **integer** (an integral number with no fractional part) in the decimal system is familiar to all of us—we use integers in our daily life. In fact, we have used them so much that they are intuitive. We represent an integer as $\pm\ S_{k-1} \ldots S_1\, S_0$. The value is calculated as:

$$N = \pm \quad S_{k-1} \times 10^{k-1} + S_{k-2} \times 10^{k-2} + \ldots + S_2 \times 10^2 + S_1 \times 10^1 + S_0 \times 10^0$$

in which S_i is a digit, $b = 10$ is the base, and k is the number of digits.

Another way to show an integer in a number system is to use **place values**, which are powers of 10 (10^0, 10^1, ... 10^{k-1}) for decimal numbers. Figure 2.1 shows an integer in the decimal system using place values.

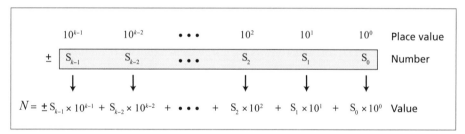

Figure 2.1 Place values for an integer in the decimal system

Example 2.1

The following shows the place values for the integer $+224$ in the decimal system.

	10^2	10^1	10^0	Place value
	2	2	4	Number
$N = +$	2×10^2	$+\ 2 \times 10^1$	$+\ 4 \times 10^0$	Value

Note that the digit 2 in position 1 has the value 20, but the same digit in position 2 has the value 200. Also note that we normally drop the plus sign, but it is implicit.

Example 2.2

The following shows the place values for the decimal number −7508. We have used 1, 10, 100, and 1000 instead of powers of 10.

	1000		100		10		1	Place value
	7		5		0		8	Number
N = −	$(7 \times 1000$	+	5×100	+	0×10	+	$8 \times 1)$	Value

Maximum value

Sometimes we need to know the maximum value of a decimal integer that can be represented by k digits. The answer is $N_{max} = 10^k - 1$. For example, if $k = 5$, then the maximum value is $N_{max} = 10^5 - 1 = 99{,}999$.

Reals

A **real** (a number with a fractional part) in the decimal system is also familiar. For example, we use this system to show dollars and cents ($23.40). We can represent a real as $\pm\ S^{k-1} \ldots S_1\ S_0 \cdot S_{-1} \ldots\ S_{-l}$. The value is calculated as:

Integral part	Fractional part
$R = \pm\quad S_{k-1} \times 10^{k-1} + \ldots + S_1 \times 10^1 + S_0 \times 10^0\quad +$	$S_{-1} \times 10^{-1} + \ldots + S_{-l} \times 10^{-l}$

in which S_i is a digit, b = 10 is the base, k is the number of digits in the integral part, and l is the number of digits in the fractional part. The decimal point we use in our representation separates the fractional part from the integral part.

Example 2.3

The following shows the place values for the real number +24.13.

	10^1		10^0		10^{-1}		10^{-2}	Place value
	2		4	•	1		3	Number
R = +	$(2 \times 10$	+	4×1	+	1×0.1	+	$3 \times 0.01)$	Value

The binary system (base 2)

The second positional number system we discuss in this chapter is the **binary system**. The word *binary* is derived from the Latin root *bini* (or two by two). In this system the base b = 2 and we use only two symbols, S = {0, 1}. The symbols in this system are often referred to as **binary digits** or **bits** (binary digit). As we will see in Chapter 3, data and programs are stored in the computer using binary patterns, a string of bits. This is because the computer is made of electronic switches that can have only two states, on and off. The bit 1 represents one of these two states and the bit 0 the other.

Integers

We can represent an integer as ± $(S_{k-1} \dots S_1 \, S_0)_2$. The value is calculated as:

$$N = \pm\; S_{k-1} \times 2^{k-1} + S_{k-2} \times 2^{k-2} + \dots + S_2 \times 2^2 + S_1 \times 2^1 + S_0 \times 2^0$$

in which S_i is a digit, b = 2 is the base, and k is the number of bits. Another way to show a binary number is to use place values (2^0, 2^1, ... 2^{k-1}). Figure 2.2 shows a number in the binary number system using place values:

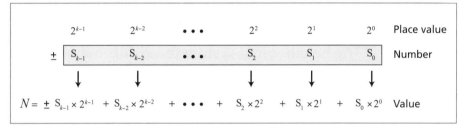

Figure 2.2   Place values for an integer in the binary system

Example 2.4

The following shows that the number $(11001)_2$ in binary is the same as 25 in decimal. The subscript 2 shows that the base is 2.

2^4	2^3	2^2	2^1	2^0	Place value
1	1	0	0	1	Number
$N = 1 \times 2^4$	$+\;1 \times 2^3$	$+\;0 \times 2^2$	$+\;0 \times 2^1$	$+\;1 \times 2^0$	Decimal

Note that the equivalent decimal number is $N = 16 + 8 + 0 + 0 + 1 = 25$.

Maximum value

The maximum value of a binary integer with k digits is $N_{max} = 2^k - 1$. For example, if $k = 5$, then the maximum value is $N_{max} = 2^5 - 1 = 31$.

Reals

A real—a number with an optional fractional part—in the binary system can be made of k bits on the left and l bits on the right, ± $(S^{k-1} \dots S_1 \, S_0 \cdot S_{-1} \dots S_{-l})_2$. The value can be calculated as:

Integral part   ·   Fractional part

$$R = \pm \quad S_{k-1} \times 2^{k-1} + \dots + S_1 \times 2^1 + S_0 \times 2^0 \quad + \quad S_{-1} \times 2^{-1} + \dots + S_{-l} \times 2^{-l}$$

in which S_i is a digit, b = 2 is the base, k is the number of bits to the left, and l is the number of bits to the right of the decimal point. Note that k starts from 0, but l starts from −1. The highest power is $k - 1$ and the lowest power is $-l$.

Example 2.5

The following shows that the number $(101.11)_2$ in binary is equal to the number 5.75 in decimal.

2^2	2^1	2^0		2^{-1}	2^{-2}	Place value
1	0	1	•	1	1	Number
R = 1×2^2	+ 0×2^1	+ 1×2^0	+	1×2^{-1}	+ 1×2^{-2}	Value

Note that the value in the decimal system is $R = 4 + 0 + 1 + 0.5 + 0.25 = 5.75$.

The hexadecimal system (base 16)

Although the binary system is used to store data in computers, it is not convenient for representation of numbers outside the computer, as a number in binary notation is much longer than the corresponding number in decimal notation. However, the decimal system does not show what is stored in computer as binary directly— there is no obvious relationship between the number of bits in binary and the number of decimal digits. Conversion from one to the other is not fast, as we will see shortly.

To overcome this problem, two positional systems were devised: hexadecimal and octal. We first discuss the **hexadecimal system**, which is more common. The word *hexadecimal* is derived from the Greek root *hex* (six) and the Latin root *decem* (ten). To be consistent with decimal and binary, it should really have been called *sexadecimal*, from the Latin roots *sex* and *decem*. In this system the base b = 16 and we use sixteen symbols to represent a number. The set of symbols is S = {0, 1, 2, 3, 4, 5, 6, 7, 8, 9, A, B, C, D, E, F}. Note that the symbols A, B, C, D, E, F (uppercase or lowercase) are equivalent to 10, 11, 12, 13, 14, and 15 respectively. The symbols in this system are often referred to as **hexadecimal digits**.

Integers   We can represent an integer as $\pm S_{k-1} \dots S_1 S_0$. The value is calculated as:

$$N = \pm S_{k-1} \times 16^{k-1} + S_{k-2} \times 16^{k-2} + \dots + S_2 \times 16^2 + S_1 \times 16^1 + S_0 \times 16^0$$

in which S_i is a digit, b = 16 is the base, and k is the number of digits.

Another way to show a hexadecimal number is to use place values (16^0, 16^1, ... 16^{k-1}). Figure 2.3 shows a number in the hexadecimal number system using place values.

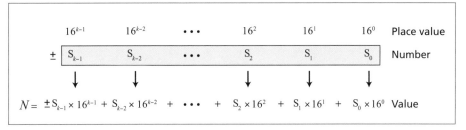

Figure 2.3 Place values for an integer in the hexadecimal system

Example 2.6

The following shows that the number $(2AE)_{16}$ in hexadecimal is equivalent to 686 in decimal.

16^2	16^1	16^0	Place value
2	A	E	Number
N = 2×16^2 +	10×16^1 +	14×16^0	Value

Maximum value

The maximum value of a hexadecimal integer with k digits is $N_{max} = 16^k - 1$. For example, if $k = 5$, then the maximum value is $N_{max} = 16^5 - 1 = 1,048,575$.

Reals

Although a real number can be also represented in the hexadecimal system, it is not very common. We leave this as an exercise.

The octal system (base 8)

The second system that was devised to show the equivalent of the binary system outside the computer is the **octal system**. The word *octal* is derived from the Latin root *octo* (eight). In this system the base b = 8 and we use eight symbols to represent a number. The set of symbols is S = {0, 1, 2, 3, 4, 5, 6, 7}. The symbols in this system are often referred to as **octal digits**.

Integers

We can represent an integer as ± $S_{k-1} \ldots S_1 S_0$. The value is calculated as:

$$N = \pm S_{k-1} \times 8^{k-1} + S_{k-2} \times 8^{k-2} + \ldots + S_2 \times 8^2 + S_1 \times 8^1 + S_0 \times 8^0$$

in which S_i is a digit, b = 8 is the base, and k is the number of digits.

Another way to show an octal number is to use place values $(8^0, 8^1, \ldots 8^{k-1})$. Figure 2.4 shows a number in the octal number system using place values.

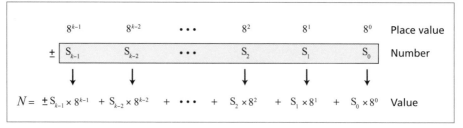

Figure 2.4   Place values for an integer in the octal system

Example 2.7

The following shows that the number $(1256)_8$ in octal is the same as 686 in decimal.

	8^3	8^2	8^1	8^0	Place value
	1	2	5	6	Number
N =	1×8^3	$+ \quad 2 \times 8^2$	$+ \quad 5 \times 8^1$	$+ \quad 6 \times 8^0$	Value

Note that the decimal number is $N = 512 + 128 + 40 + 6 = 686$.

Maximum value

The maximum value of an octal integer with k digits is $N_{max} = 8^k - 1$. For example, if $k = 5$, then the maximum value is $N_{max} = 8^5 - 1 = 32767$.

Reals

Although a real number can be also represented in the octal system, it is not very common. We leave this as an exercise.

Summary of the four positional systems

Table 2.1 shows a summary of the four positional number systems discussed in this chapter.

Table 2.1   Summary of the four positional number systems

System	Base	Symbols	Examples
Decimal	10	0, 1, 2, 3, 4, 5, 6, 7, 8, 9	2345.56
Binary	2	0, 1	$(1001.11)_2$
Octal	8	0, 1, 2, 3, 4, 5, 6, 7	$(156.23)_8$
Hexadecimal	16	0, 1, 2, 3, 4, 5, 6, 7, 8, 9, A, B, C, D, E, F	$(A2C.A1)_{16}$

Table 2.2 shows how the number 15 is represented with two digits in decimal, four digits in binary, two digits in octal, and only one digit in hexadecimal. The hexadecimal representation is definitely the shortest.

Table 2.2 Comparison of numbers in the four systems

Decimal	Binary	Octal	Hexadecimal
0	0	0	0
1	1	1	1
2	10	2	2
3	11	3	3
4	100	4	4
5	101	5	5
6	110	6	6
7	111	7	7
8	1000	10	8
9	1001	11	9
10	1010	12	A
11	1011	13	B
12	1100	14	C
13	1101	15	D
14	1110	16	E
15	1111	17	F

Conversion

We need to know how to convert a number in one system to the equivalent number in another system. Since the decimal system is more familiar than the other systems, we first show how to covert from any base to decimal. Then we show how to convert from decimal to any base. Finally, we show how we can easily convert from binary to hexadecimal or octal and vice versa.

Any base to decimal conversion

This type of conversion is easy and fast. We multiply each digit with its place value in the source system and add the results to get the number in the decimal system. Figure 2.5 shows the idea.

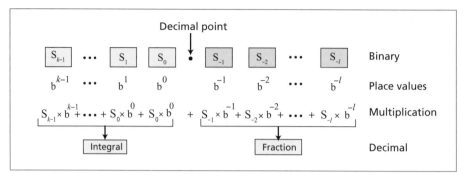

Figure 2.5   Converting other bases to decimal

Example 2.8

The following shows how to convert the binary number $(110.11)_2$ to decimal: $(110.11)_2 = 6.75$.

Binary	1		1		0	•	1		1
Place value	2^2		2^1		2^0		2^{-1}		2^{-2}
Partial result	4	+	2	+	0	+	0.5	+	0.25

Decimal: 6.75

Example 2.9

The following shows how to convert the hexadecimal number $(1A.23)_{16}$ to decimal.

Hexadecimal	1		A	•	2		3
Place value	16^1		16^0		16^{-1}		16^{-2}
Partial result	16	+	10	+	0.125	+	0.012

Decimal: 26.137

Note that the result in the decimal notation is not exact, because $3 \times 16^{-2} = 0.01171875$. We have rounded this value to three digits (0.012). In other words, $(1A.23)_{16} \approx 26.137$. When we convert a number in decimal to hexadecimal, we need to specify how many digits we allow to the right of the decimal point.

Example 2.10

The following shows how to convert $(23.17)_8$ to decimal.

Octal	2		3	•	1		7
Place value	8^1		8^0		8^{-1}		8^{-2}
Partial result	16	+	3	+	0.125	+	0.109

Decimal: 19.234

This means that $(23.17)_8 \approx 19.234$ in decimal. Again, we have rounded up 7×8^{-2} = 0.109375.

Decimal to any base

We can convert a decimal number to its equivalent in any base. We need two procedures, one for the integral part and one for the fractional part.

Converting the integral part

The integral part can be converted using repetitive division. Figure 2.6 shows the UML diagram for the process. We use UML diagrams through the book. For those readers not familiar with UML diagrams, please see Appendix B.

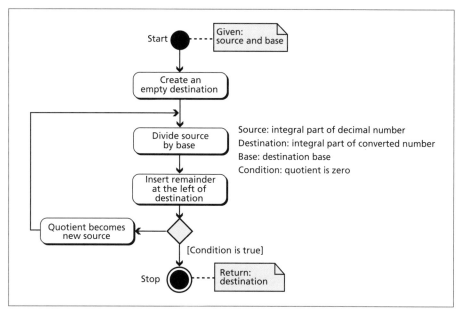

Figure 2.6   Converting the integral part of a number in decimal to other bases

We call the integral part of the decimal number the *source* and the integral part of the converted number the *destination*. We first create an empty destination. We then repeatedly divide the source to get the quotient and the remainder. The remainder is inserted to the left of the destination. The quotient becomes a new source. Figure 2.7 shows the how the destination is made with each repetition.

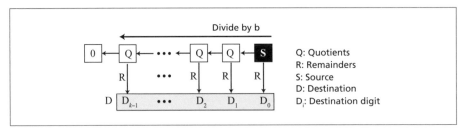

Figure 2.7   Converting the integral part of a number in decimal to other bases

We use Figure 2.7 below to illustrate the process manually with some examples.

Example 2.11
The following shows how to convert 35 in decimal to binary. We start with the number in decimal, we move to the left while continuously finding the quotients and the remainder of division by 2. The result is $35 = (100011)_2$.

0	←	1	←	2	←	4	←	8	←	17	←	35	Decimal
		↓		↓		↓		↓		↓		↓	
		1		0		0		0		1		1	Binary

Example 2.12
The following shows how to convert 126 in decimal to its equivalent in the octal system. We move to the right while continuously finding the quotients and the remainder of division by 8. The result is $126 = (176)_8$.

0	←	1	←	15	←	126	Decimal
		↓		↓		↓	
		1		7		6	Octal

Example 2.13
The following shows how we convert 126 in decimal to its equivalent in the hexadecimal system. We move to the right while continuously finding the quotients and the remainder of division by 16. The result is $126 = (7E)_{16}$.

0	←	7	←	126	Decimal
		↓		↓	
		7		E	Hexadecimal

Converting the fractional part

The fractional part can be converted using repetitive multiplication. We call the fractional part of the decimal number the *source* and the fractional part of the converted number the *destination*. We first create an empty destination. We then repeatedly multiply the source to get the result. The integral part of the result is inserted to the right of the destination, while the fractional part becomes the new source. Figure 2.8 shows the UML diagram for the process.

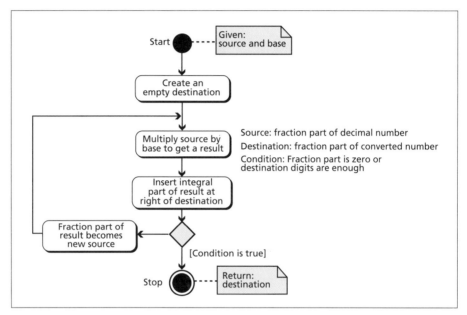

Figure 2.8   Converting the fractional part of a number in decimal to other bases

Figure 2.9 shows how the destination is made in each repetition. We use the figure to illustrate the process manually with some examples.

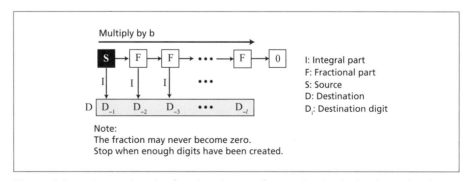

Figure 2.9   Converting the fractional part of a number in decimal to other bases

Example 2.14

Convert the decimal number 0.625 to binary.

Solution

Since the number 0.625 has no integral part, the example shows how the fractional part is calculated. The base here is 2. Write the decimal number at the left corner. Multiply the number continuously by 2 and record the integral and fractional part of the result. The fractional part moves to the right, and the integral part is recorded under each operation. Stop when the fractional part is 0 or there are enough bits. The result is $(0.101)_2$.

Decimal	0.625	→	0.25	→	0.50	→	0.00
	↓		↓		↓		
Binary •	1		0		1		

Example 2.15

The following shows how to convert 0.634 to octal using a maximum of four digits. The result is $0.634 = (0.5044)_8$. Note that we multiply by 8 (base octal).

Decimal	0.634	→	0.072	→	0.576	→	0.608	→	0.864
	↓		↓		↓		↓		
Octal •	5		0		4		4		

Example 2.16

The following shows how to convert 178.6 in decimal to hexadecimal using only one digit to the right of the decimal point. The result is $178.6 = (B2.9)_{16}$. Note that we divide or multiply by 16 (base hexadecimal).

Decimal	0	←	11	←	178		0.6	→	0.6
			↓		↓		↓		
Hexadecimal			B		2	•	9		

Example 2.17

An alternative method for converting a small decimal integer (usually less than 256) to binary is to break the number as the sum of numbers that are equivalent to the binary place values shown:

Place value	2^7	2^6	2^5	2^4	2^3	2^2	2^1	2^0
Decimal equivalent	128	64	32	16	8	4	2	1

Using this table, we can convert 165 to binary $(10100101)_2$ as shown below:

Decimal 165 =	128	+	0	+	32	+	0	+	0	+	4	+	0	+	1
Binary	1		0		1		0		0		1		0		1

Example 2.18
A similar method can be used to convert a decimal fraction to binary when the denominator is a power of two:

Place value	2^{-1}	2^{-2}	2^{-3}	2^{-4}	2^{-5}	2^{-6}	2^{-7}
Decimal equivalent	$1/2$	$1/4$	$1/8$	$1/16$	$1/32$	$1/64$	$1/128$

Using this table, we convert $27/64$ to binary $(0.011011)_2$ as shown below:

$$\text{Decimal } 27/64 = \quad 16/64 \quad + \quad 8/64 \quad + \quad 2/64 \quad + \quad 1/64$$
$$1/4 \quad + \quad 1/8 \quad + \quad 1/32 \quad + \quad 1/64$$

Aligning these fractions according to decimal equivalent values:

Decimal $27/64$ =	0	+	$1/4$	+	$1/8$	+	0	+	$1/32$	+	$1/64$
Binary	0		1		1		0		1		1

Number of digits
We often need to know the number of digits before converting a number from decimal to other bases. In a positional number system with base b, we can always find the number of digits of an integer using the relation $k = \lceil \log_b N \rceil$, in which $\lceil x \rceil$ means the smallest integer greater than or equal to x (it is also called the *ceiling* of x), and N is the decimal value of the integer. For example, we can find the required number of bits in the decimal number 234 in all four systems as follows:

a. In decimal: $k_d = \lceil \log_{10} 234 \rceil = \lceil 2.37 \rceil = 3$, which is obvious.

b. In binary: $k_b = \lceil \log_2 234 \rceil = \lceil 7.8 \rceil = 8$. This is true because $234 = (11101010)_2$

c. In octal: $k_o = \lceil \log_8 234 \rceil = \lceil 2.62 \rceil = 3$. This is true because $234 = (352)_8$

d. In hexadecimal $k_h = \lceil \log_{16} 234 \rceil = \lceil 1.96 \rceil = 2$. This is true because $234 = (EA)_{16}$

See Appendix G for information on how to calculate $\log_b N$ if your calculator does not include logs to any base.

Binary–hexadecimal conversion

We can easily change a number from binary to hexadecimal and vice verse. The reason for this is that there is a relationship between the two bases: four bits in binary is one digit in hexadecimal. Figure 2.10 shows how this conversion can be done.

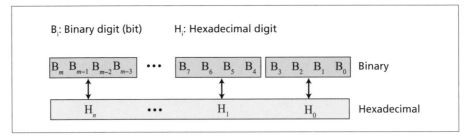

Figure 2.10   Binary to hexadecimal and hexadecimal to binary conversion

Example 2.19

Show the hexadecimal equivalent of the binary number $(10011100010)_2$.

Solution

We first arrange the binary number in 4-bit patterns: 100 1110 0010. Note that the leftmost pattern can have one to four bits. We then use the equivalent of each pattern shown in Table 2.2 on page 25 to change the number to hexadecimal: $(4E2)_{16}$.

Example 2.20

What is the binary equivalent of $(24C)_{16}$?

Solution

Each hexadecimal digit is converted to 4-bit patterns: $2 \rightarrow 0010$, $4 \rightarrow 0100$, and $C \rightarrow 1100$. The result is $(001001001100)_2$.

Binary–octal conversion   We can easily convert a number from binary to octal and vice versa. The reason is that there is an interesting relationship between the two bases: three bits is one octal digit. Figure 2.11 shows how this conversion can be done.

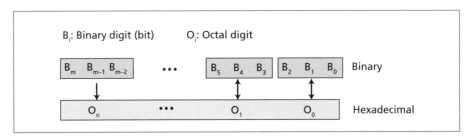

Figure 2.11   Binary to octal and octal to binary conversion

Example 2.21

Show the octal equivalent of the binary number $(101110010)_2$.

Solution

Each group of three bits is translated into one octal digit. The equivalent of each 3-bit group is shown in Table 2.2 on page 25. The result is $(562)_8$.

Example 2.22
What is the binary equivalent of $(24)_8$?

Solution
Write each octal digit as its equivalent bit pattern to get $(010100)_2$.

Octal–hexadecimal conversion

It is not difficult to convert a number in octal to hexadecimal or vice versa. We can use the binary system as the intermediate system. Figure 2.12 shows an example.

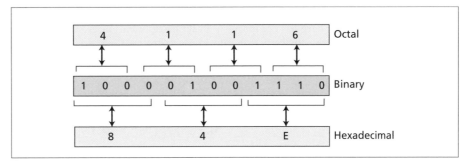

Figure 2.12   Octal to hexadecimal and hexadecimal to octal conversion

The following illustrates the process:

❑   To convert from octal to hexadecimal, we first convert the number in the octal system to binary. We then rearrange the bits in groups of four bits to find the hexadecimal equivalent.

❑   To convert from hexadecimal to octal, we first convert the number in the hexadecimal system to binary. We then rearrange the bits in groups of three to find the octal equivalent.

Number of digits

In conversion from one base to another, we often need to know the minimum number of digits we need in the destination system if we know the maximum number of digits in the source system. For example, if we know that we use at most six decimal digits in the source system, we want to know the minimum number of binary digits we need in the destination system. In general, assume that we are using k digits in base b_1 system. The maximum number we can represent in the source system is $b_1^k - 1$. The maximum number we can have in the destination system is $b_2^x - 1$. Therefore, $b_2^x - 1 \geq b_1^k - 1$. This means $b_2^x \geq b_1^k$, which means:

$$x \geq k \times (\log b_1 / \log b_2) \qquad \text{or} \qquad x = \lceil k \times (\log b_1 / \log b_2) \rceil$$

Example 2.23
Find the minimum number of binary digits required to store decimal integers with a maximum of six digits.

Solution

$k = 6$, $b_1 = 10$, and $b_2 = 2$. Then $x = \lceil k \times (\log b_1 / \log b_2) \rceil = \lceil 6 \times (1 / 0.30103) \rceil = 20$. The largest six-digit decimal number is 999,999 and the largest 20-bit binary number is 1,048,575. Note that the largest number that can be represented by a 19-bit number is 524287, which is smaller than 999,999. We definitely need twenty bits.

2.3   NONPOSITIONAL NUMBER SYSTEMS

Although nonpositional number systems are not used in computers, we give a short review here for comparison with positional number systems. A **nonpositional number system** still uses a limited number of symbols in which each symbol has a value. However, the position a symbol occupies in the number normally bears no relation to its value—the value of each symbol is fixed. To find the value of a number, we add the value of all symbols present in the representation. In this system, a number is represented as:

$$S_{k-1} \ldots S_2 \, S_1 \, S_0 \bullet S_{-1} \, S_{-2} \ldots S_{-l}$$

and has the value of:

	Integral part		Fractional part
$n = \pm$	$S_{k-1} + \ldots + S_1 + S_0$	$+$	$S_{-1} + S_{-2} + \ldots + S_{-l}$

There are some exceptions to the addition rule we just mentioned, as shown in Example 2.24.

Example 2.24

Roman numerals are a good example of a nonpositional number system. This system was invented by the Romans and was used until the sixteenth century in Europe. It is still used in sports events, clock dials and other applications. This number system has a set of symbols S = {I, V, X, L, C, D, M}. The values of each symbol is shown in Table 2.3

Table 2.3   Values of symbols in the Roman number system

Symbol	I	V	X	L	C	D	M
Value	1	5	10	50	100	500	1000

To find the value of a number, we need to add the value of symbols subject to specific rules:

1. When a symbol with a smaller value is placed after a symbol having an equal or larger value, the values are added.

2. When a symbol with a smaller value is placed before a symbol having a larger value, the smaller value is subtracted from the larger one.

3. A symbol S_1 cannot come before another symbol S_2 if $S_1 \leq 10 \times S_2$. For example, I or V cannot come before C.

4. For large numbers a bar is placed above any of the six symbols (all symbols except I) to express multiplication by 1000. For example, $\overline{V} = 5,000$ and $\overline{M} = 1,000,000$.

5. Although Romans used the word *nulla* (nothing) to convey the concept of zero, Roman numerals lack a zero digit in their system.

The following shows some Roman numbers and their values.

III	→	1 + 1 + 1	=	3
IV	→	5 − 1	=	4
VIII	→	5 + 1 + 1 + 1	=	8
XVIII	→	10 + 5 + 1 + 1 + 1	=	18
XIX	→	10 + (10 −1)	=	19
LXXII	→	50 + 10 + 10 + 1 + 1	=	72
CI	→	100 + 1	=	101
MMVII	→	1000 + 1000 + 5 + 1 + 1	=	2007
MDC	→	1000 + 500 + 100	=	1600

2.4 RECOMMENDED READING

For more details about the subjects discussed in this chapter, the following books are recommended:

- Stalling, W: *Computer Organization and Architecture*, Upper Saddle River, NJ: Prentice Hall, 2000.
- Mano M: *Computer System Architecture*, Upper Saddle River, NJ: Prentice Hall, 1993
- Null L and Lobur J: *Computer Organization and Architecture*, Sudbury, MA: Jones and Bartlett, 2003
- Brown S and Vranesic Z: *Fundamentals of Digital Logic with Verilog Design*, New York: McGraw-Hill, 2003

2.5 KEY TERMS

This chapter has introduced the following key terms, which are listed here with the pages on which they first occur:

base 18	binary digit 20
binary system 20	bit 20
decimal digit 18	decimal system 18
hexadecimal digit 22	hexadecimal system 22
integer 19	nonpositional number system 34
number system 18	octal digit 23
octal system 23	place value 19
positional number system 18	radix 18
real 20	Roman number system 34

2.6 SUMMARY

- A number system (or numeral system) is a system that uses distinct symbols to represent a number.

- In a positional number system, the position a symbol occupies in the number determines the value it represents. Each position has a place value associated with it.

- A nonpositional number system uses a limited number of symbols in which each symbol has a value. However, the position a symbol occupies in the number normally bears no relation to its value: the value of each symbol is normally fixed.

- In the decimal system, the base b = 10 and we use 10 symbols to represent numbers. The symbols in this system are often referred to as *decimal digits* or just *digits*.

- In the binary system, the base b = 2 and we use only two symbols to represent numbers. The symbols in this system are often referred to as *binary digits* or *bits*.

- In a hexadecimal system, the base b = 16 and we use sixteen symbols to represent numbers. The symbols in this system are often referred to as *hexadecimal digits*.

- In an octal system, the base b = 8 and we use eight symbols to represent numbers. The symbols in this system are often referred to as *octal digits*.

- We can convert a number in any system to decimal. We multiply each digit with its place value in the source system and add the result to get the number in the decimal system.

- We can convert a decimal number to its equivalent in any base using two different procedures, one for the integral part and one for the fractional part. The integral part needs repeated division and the fraction part needs repeated multiplication.

- Conversion from the binary system to the hexadecimal system and from the hexadecimal system to the binary system is very easy, because four bits in the binary system are represented as one digit in the hexadecimal system.

- Conversion from the binary system to the octal system and from the octal system to the binary system is very easy, because three bits in the binary system are represented as one digit in the octal system.

2.7 PRACTICE SET

Review questions

1. Define a number system.
2. Distinguish between positional and nonpositional number systems.
3. Define the base or radix in a positional number system. What is the relationship between a base and the number of symbols in a positional number system?
4. Explain the decimal system. Why is it called *decimal*? What is the base in this system?
5. Explain the binary system. Why is it called *binary*? What is the base in this system?
6. Explain the octal system. Why is it called *octal*? What is the base in this system?
7. Explain the hexadecimal system. Why is it called *hexadecimal*? What is the base in this system?
8. Why is it easy to convert from binary to hexadecimal and vice versa?
9. How many bits in the binary system are represented by one digit in the hexadecimal system?
10. How many bits in the binary system are represented by one digit in the octal system?

Multiple-choice questions

11. The base of the decimal number system is ____.
    a. 2
    b. 8
    c. 10
    d. 16
12. The base of the binary number system is ____.
    a. 2
    b. 8
    c. 10
    d. 16
13. The base of the octal number system is ____.
    a. 2
    b. 8

c. 10
d. 16

14. The base of the hexadecimal number system is ____.
    a. 2
    b. 8
    c. 10
    d. 16
15. When converting a decimal integer to base b, we repeatedly _____ by b.
    a. divide
    b. multiply
    c. neither a nor b
    d. both a and b
16. When converting a decimal fraction to base b, we repeatedly _____ by b.
    a. divide
    b. multiply
    c. neither a nor b
    d. both a and b
17. Which of the following representations is erroneous?
    a. $(10111)_2$
    b. $(349)_8$
    c. $(3AB)_{16}$
    d. 256
18. Which of the following representations is erroneous?
    a. $(10211)_2$
    b. $(342)_8$
    c. $(EEE)_{16}$
    d. 145
19. Which of the following representations is erroneous?
    a. $(111)_2$
    b. $(346)_8$
    c. $(EEG)_{16}$
    d. 221

20. Which of the following representations is erroneous?
    a. $(110)_2$
    b. $(141)_8$
    c. $(EF)_{16}$
    d. 22A

21. Which of the following is equivalent to 12 in decimal?
    a. $(1110)_2$
    b. $(C)_{16}$
    c. $(15)8$
    d. None of the above

22. Which of the following is equivalent to 24 in decimal?
    a. $(11000)_2$
    b. $(1A)_{16}$
    c. $(31)_8$
    d. None of the above

Exercises

23. Convert the following binary numbers to decimal without using a calculator, showing your work:
    a. $(01101)_2$
    b. $(1011000)_2$
    c. $(011110.01)_2$
    d. $(111111.111)_2$

24. Convert the following hexadecimal numbers to decimal without using a calculator, showing your work:
    a. $(AB2)_{16}$
    b. $(123)_{16}$
    c. $(ABB)_{16}$
    d. $(35E.E1)_{16}$

25. Convert the following octal numbers to decimal without using a calculator, showing your work:
    a. $(237)_8$
    b. $(2731)_8$
    c. $(617.7)_8$
    d. $(21.11)_8$

26. Convert the following decimal numbers to binary without using a calculator, showing your work:

a. 1234
b. 88
c. 124.02
d. 14.56

27. Convert the following decimal numbers to octal without using a calculator, showing your work:
    a. 1156
    b. 99
    c. 11.4
    d. 72.8

28. Convert the following decimal numbers to hexadecimal without using a calculator, showing your work:
    a. 567
    b. 1411
    c. 12.13
    d. 16.5

29. Convert the following octal numbers to hexadecimal without using a calculator, showing your work:
    a. $(514)_8$
    b. $(411)_8$
    c. $(13.7)_8$
    d. $(1256)_8$

30. Convert the following hexadecimal numbers to octal without using a calculator, showing your work:
    a. $(51A)_{16}$
    b. $(4E1)_{16}$
    c. $(BB.C)_{16}$
    d. $(ABC.D)_{16}$

31. Convert the following binary numbers to octal without using a calculator, showing your work:
    a. $(01101)_2$
    b. $(1011000)_2$
    c. $(011110.01)_2$
    d. $(111111.111)_2$

32. Convert the following binary numbers to hexadecimal without using a calculator, showing your work:
    a. $(01101)_2$
    b. $(1011000)_2$
    c. $(011110.01)_2$
    d. $(111111.111)_2$

33. Convert the following decimal numbers to binary using the alternative method discussed in Example 2.17, showing your work:
    a. 121
    b. 78
    c. 255
    d. 214

34. Change the following decimal numbers into binary using the alternative method discussed in Example 2.18, showing your work:
    a. $3\,^5/_8$
    b. $12\,^3/_{32}$
    c. $4\,^{13}/_{64}$
    d. $12\,^5/_{128}$

35. In a positional number system with base b, the largest integer number that can be represented using k digits is $b^k - 1$. Find the largest number in each of the following systems with *six* digits.
    a. Binary
    b. Decimal
    c. Hexadecimal
    d. Octal

36. Without converting, find the minimum number of digits needed in the destination system for each of the following cases:
    a. Five-digit decimal number converted to binary.
    b. Four-digit decimal converted to octal.
    c. Seven-digit decimal converted to hexadecimal.

37. Without converting, find the minimum number of digits needed in the destination system for each of the following cases:
    a. 5-bit binary number converted to decimal.
    b. Three-digit octal number converted to decimal.
    c. Three-digit hexadecimal converted to decimal.

38. The following table shows how to rewrite a fraction so the denominator is a power of two (1, 4, 8, 16, and so on).

Original	New	Original	New
0.5	$^1/_2$	0.25	$^1/_4$
0.125	$^1/_8$	0.0625	$^1/_{16}$
0.03125	$^1/_{32}$	0.015625	$^1/_{64}$

However, sometimes we need a combination of entries to find the appropriate fraction. For example, 0.625 is not in the table, but we know that 0.625 is 0.5 + 0.125. This means that 0.625 can be written as $^1/_2 + ^1/_8$, or $^5/_8$.

Change the following decimal fractions to a fraction with a power of 2.
    a. 0.1875
    b. 0.640625
    c. 0.40625
    d. 0.375

39. Using the results of the previous problem, change the following decimal numbers to binary numbers.
    a. 7.1875
    b. 12.640625
    c. 11.40625
    d. 0.375

40. Find the maximum value of an integer in each of the following cases:
    a. $b = 10, k = 10$
    b. $b = 2, k = 12$
    c. $b = 8, k = 8$
    d. $b = 16, k = 7$

41. Find the minimum number of required bits to store the following integers:
    a. less than 1000
    b. less than 100,000
    c. less than 64
    d. less than 256

42. A number less than b^k can be represented using k digits in base b. Show the number of digits needed in each of the following cases.
    a. Integers less than 2^{14} in binary
    b. Integers less than 10^8 in decimal
    c. Integers less than 8^{13} in octal
    d. Integers less than 16^4 in hexadecimal

43. A common base used on the Internet is b = 256. We need 256 symbols to represent a number in this system. Instead of creating this large number of symbols, the designers of this system have used decimal numbers to represent a symbol: 0 to 255. In other words, the set of symbols is S = {0, 1, 2, 3, ..., 255}. A number in this system is always in the format $S_1.S_2.S_3.S_4$ with four symbols and three dots that separate

the symbols. The system is used to define Internet addresses (see Chapter 6). An example of an address in this system is 10.200.14.72, which is equivalent to $10 \times 256^3 + 200 \times 256^2 + 14 \times 256^1 + 72 \times 256^0 = 180{,}883{,}016$ in decimal. This number system is called *dotted decimal notation*.

Find the decimal value of each of the following Internet addresses:

a. 17.234.34.14

b. 14.56.234.56

c. 110.14.56.78

d. 24.56.13.11

44. Internet addresses described in the previous problem are also represented as patterns of bits. In this case, 32 bits are used to represent an address, eight bits for each symbol in dotted decimal notation. For example, the address 10.200.14.72 can also be represented as 00001010 11001000 00001110 01001000.

Show the bit representation of the following Internet addresses:

a. 17.234.34.14

b. 14.56.234.56

c. 110.14.56.78

d. 24.56.13.11

45. Write the decimal equivalent of the following Roman numbers:

a. XV

b. XXVII

c. VLIII

d. MCLVII

46. Convert the following decimal numbers to Roman numbers:

a. 17

b. 38

c. 82

d. 999

47. Find which of the following Roman numerals are not valid:

a. MMIM

b. MIC

c. CVC

d. VX

48. Mayan civilization invented a positional vigesimal (base 20) numeral system, called the *Mayan numeral system*. They use base 20 probably because they used both their fingers and toes for counting. This system has 20 symbols that are constructed from three simpler symbols. The advanced feature of the system is that it has a symbol for zero, which is a shell. The other two symbols are a circle (or a pebble) for one and a horizontal bar (or a stick) for five. To represent a number greater than nineteen, numerals are written vertically. Search the Internet to answer the following: what are the decimal numbers 12, 123, 452, and 1256 in the Mayan numeral system?

49. Babylonian civilization is credited for developing the first positional numeral system, called the *Babylonian numeral system*. They inherited the Sumerian and Akkadian numeral system and developed it into positional sexagesimal system (base 60). This base is still used today for times and angles. For example, one hour is 60 minutes and one minute is 60 seconds: similarly, one degree is 60 minutes and one minute is 60 seconds. As a positional system with base b requires b symbols (digits), we expect a positional sexagesimal system to require 60 symbols. However, the Babylonians did not have a symbol for zero, and produced the other 59 symbols by stacking two symbols, those for one and ten. Search the Internet to answer the following questions:

a. Express the following decimal numbers in Babylonian numerals: 11291, 3646, 3582.

b. Mention problems that might arise from not having a symbol for 0. Find how the Babylonian numeral system addresses the problem.

3

Data Storage

As discussed in Chapter 1, a computer is a programmable data processing machine. Before we can talk about processing data, we need to understand the nature of data. In this chapter we discuss different data types and how they are stored inside a computer. In Chapter 4, we show how data is manipulated inside a computer.

Objectives

After studying this chapter, the student should be able to:

- ❏ List five different data types used in a computer.
- ❏ Describe how different data is stored inside the computer as bit patterns.
- ❏ Describe how integers are stored in a computer using unsigned format.
- ❏ Describe how integers are stored in a computer using sign-and-magnitude format.
- ❏ Describe how integers are stored in two's complement format.
- ❏ Describe how reals are stored in a computer using floating-point format.
- ❏ Describe how text is stored in a computer using one of the various encoding systems.
- ❏ Describe how audio is stored in a computer using sampling, quantization, and encoding.
- ❏ Describe how images are stored in a computer using raster and vector graphics schemes.
- ❏ Describe how video is stored in a computer as a representation of images changing in time.

3.1 DATA TYPES

Data today comes in different forms including numbers, text, audio, image, and video (Figure 3.1).

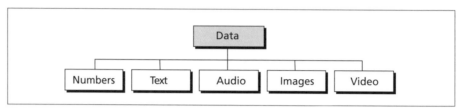

Figure 3.1   Different types of data

People need to be able to process many different types of data:

❑ An engineering program uses a computer mainly to process numbers: to do arithmetic, to solve algebraic or trigonometric equations, to find the roots of a differential equation, and so on.

❑ A word processing program, on the other hand, uses a computer mainly to process text: justify, move, delete, and so on.

❑ A computer also handles audio data. We can play music on a computer and can records sound as data.

❑ An image processing program uses a computer to manipulate images: create, shrink, expand, rotate, and so on.

❑ Finally, a computer can be used not only to show movies, but also to create the special effects seen in movies.

> **The computer industry uses the term "multimedia" to define information that contains numbers, text, images, audio, and video.**

Data inside the computer

All data types are transformed into a uniform representation when they are stored in a computer and transformed back to their original form when retrieved. This universal representation is called a *bit pattern*, as discussed shortly.

Bits

A **bit (binary digit)** is the smallest unit of data that can be stored in a computer and has a value of 0 or 1. A bit represents the state of a device that can take one of two states. For example, a *switch* can be on or off. A convention can be established to represent the "on" state as 1 and the "off" state as 0, or vice versa. In this way, a switch can store one bit of information. Today, computers use various two-state devices to store data.

Bit patterns

To represent different types of data, we use a **bit pattern**, a sequence, or as it is sometimes called, a *string of bits*. Figure 3.2 shows a bit pattern made up of sixteen bits. It is a combination of sixteen 0s and 1s. This means that if we need to store a bit pattern made of sixteen bits, we need sixteen electronic switches. If we need to store 1000 bit patterns, each sixteen bits long, we need 16,000 switches, and so on. By tradition a bit pattern with eight bits is called a **byte**. Sometimes the term **word** is used to refer to a longer bit pattern.

1 0 0 0 1 0 1 0 1 1 1 1 1 1

Figure 3.2   A bit pattern

As Figure 3.3 shows, a piece of data belonging to different data types can be stored as the same pattern in the memory.

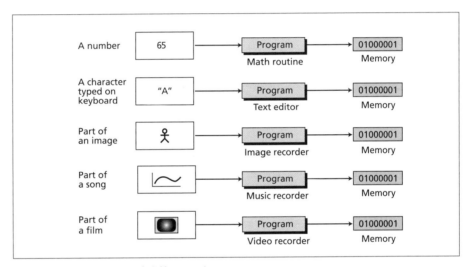

Figure 3.3   Storage of different data types

If we are using a text editor (a word processor), the character A typed on the keyboard can be stored as the 8-bit pattern 01000001. The same 8-bit pattern can represent the number 65 if we are using a mathematical routine. In the same way, the same pattern can represent part of an image, part of a song, or part of a scene in a film. The computer's memory stores all of them without recognizing what type of data they represent.

Data compression

To occupy less memory space, data is normally compressed before being stored in the computer. Data compression is a very broad and involved subject, so we have dedicated the whole of Chapter 15 to it.

Data compression is discussed in Chapter 15.

Error detection and correction

Another issue related to data is the detection and correction of errors during transmission or storage. We discuss this issue briefly in Appendix H.

Error detection and correction is discussed in Appendix H.

3.2 STORING NUMBERS

A number is changed to the binary system before being stored in the computer's memory, as described in Chapter 2. However, there are still two issues that need to be handled:

1. How to store the sign of the number.
2. How to show the decimal point.

There are several ways to handle the sign issue, discussed later in this chapter. For the decimal point, computers use two different representations: fixed-point and floating-point. The first is used to store a number as an integer—without a fractional part, the second is used to store a number as a real—with a fractional part.

Storing integers

Integers are whole numbers (numbers without a fractional part). For example, 134 and –125 are integers, whereas 134.23 and –0.235 are not. An integer can be thought of as a number in which the position of the decimal point is fixed: the decimal point is to the right of the least significant (rightmost) bit. For this reason, **fixed-point representation** is used to store an integer, as shown in Figure 3.4. In this representation the decimal point is assumed but not stored.

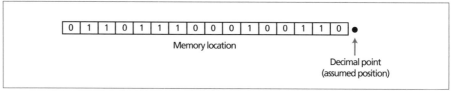

Figure 3.4   Fixed point representation of integers

However, a user (or a program) may store an integer as a real with the fractional part set to zero. This may happen, for example, if an integer is too large to be stored in the size defined for an integer. To use computer memory more efficiently, unsigned and signed integers are stored inside the computer differently.

> **An integer is normally stored in memory using fixed-point representation.**

Unsigned representation

An **unsigned integer** is an integer that can never be negative and can take only 0 or positive values. Its range is between 0 and positive infinity. However, since no computer can possibly represent all the integers in this range, most computers define a constant called the *maximum unsigned integer*, which has the value of $(2^n - 1)$ where n is the number of bits allocated to represent an unsigned integer.

Storing unsigned integers

An input device stores an unsigned integer using the following steps:

❏ The integer is changed to binary.

❏ If the number of bits is less than n, 0s are added to the left of the binary integer so that there is a total of n bits. If the number of bits is greater than n, the integer cannot be stored. A condition referred to as *overflow* will occur, which we discuss later.

Example 3.1

Store 7 in an 8-bit memory location using unsigned representation.

Solution

First change the integer to binary, $(111)_2$. Add five 0s to make a total of eight bits, $(00000111)_2$. The integer is stored in the memory location. Note that the subscript 2 is used to emphasize that the integer is binary, but the subscript is not stored in the computer.

Change 7 to binary	→						1 1	1
Add five bits at the left	→	0 0	0 0	0	1	1	1	

Example 3.2

Store 258 in a 16-bit memory location.

Solution

First change the integer to binary $(100000010)_2$. Add seven 0s to make a total of sixteen bits, $(0000000100000010)_2$. The integer is stored in the memory location.

Change 258 to binary	→							1 0 0 0 0 0 0 1 0								
Add seven bits at the left	→	0 0 0 0 0 0 0 1 0 0 0 0 0 0 1 0															

Retrieving unsigned integers

An output device retrieves a bit string from memory as a bit pattern and converts it to an unsigned decimal integer.

Example 3.3

What is returned from an output device when it retrieves the bit string 00101011 stored in memory as an unsigned integer?

Solution

Using the procedure shown in Chapter 2, the binary integer is converted to the unsigned integer 43.

Overflow

Due to size limitations—the allocated number of bits—the range of integers that can be represented is limited. In an n-bit memory location we can only store an unsigned integer between 0 and $2^n - 1$. Figure 3.5 shows what happens if we try to store an integer that is larger than $2^4 - 1 = 15$ in a memory location that can only hold four bits. This situation, called **overflow**, happens when, for example, we have stored the integer 11 in a memory location and then try to add 9 to the integer. The minimum number of bits we need to represent the decimal 20 is five bits. In other words, $20 = (10100)_2$, so the computer drops the leftmost bit and keeps the rightmost four bits $(0100)_2$. People are surprised when they see that the new integer is printed as 4 instead of 20. Figure 3.5 shows why this happens.

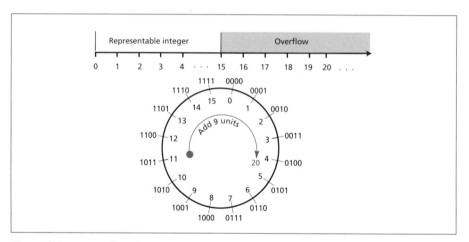

Figure 3.5   Overflow in unsigned integers

Applications of unsigned integers

Unsigned integer representation can improve the efficiency of storage because we do not need to store the sign of the integer. This means that the entire bit allocation can be used for storing the number. Unsigned integer representation can be used whenever we do not need negative integers. The following lists some cases:

❑ *Counting.* When we count, we do not need negative numbers. We start counting from 1 (sometimes 0) and go up.

❑ *Addressing.* Some computer programs store the address of a memory location inside another memory location. Addresses are positive integers starting from 0 (the first memory location) and going up to an integer representing the total memory capacity. Here again, we do not need negative integers—unsigned integers can easily do the job.

❑ *Storing other data types.* Other data types (text, images, audio, and video), as we will discuss shortly, are stored as bit patterns, which can be interpreted as unsigned integers.

Sign-and-magnitude representation

Although the sign-and-magnitude format is not commonly used to store integers, this format is used to store part of a real number in a computer, as described in the next section. For this reason we briefly discuss this format here. In this method, the available range for unsigned integers (0 to $2^n - 1$) is divided into two equal subranges. The first half represents positive integers, the second half, negative integers. For example, if n is 4, the range is 0000 to 1111. This range is divided into two halves: 0000 to 0111 and 1000 to 1111 (Figure 3.6). The bit patterns are then assigned to negative and positive integers. Note that the negative numbers appear to the right of the positive numbers, which is contrary to conventional thinking about positive and negative numbers. Also note that we have two 0s: positive zero (0000) and negative zero (1000).

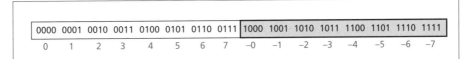

0000	0001	0010	0011	0100	0101	0110	0111	1000	1001	1010	1011	1100	1101	1110	1111
0	1	2	3	4	5	6	7	–0	–1	–2	–3	–4	–5	–6	–7

Figure 3.6   Sign-and-magnitude representation

Storing an integer in sign-and-magnitude format requires one bit to represent the sign (0 for positive, 1 for negative). This means that in an 8-bit allocation, we can only use seven bits to represent the absolute value of the number (number without the sign). Therefore, the maximum positive value is one half the unsigned value. The range of numbers that can be stored in an n-bit location is $-(2^{n-1} -1)$ to $+ (2^{n-1} -1)$. In an n-bit allocation, the leftmost bit is dedicated to store the sign (0 for positive, 1 for negative).

In sign-and-magnitude representation, the leftmost bit defines the sign of the integer. If it is 0, the integer is positive. If it is 1, the integer is negative.

Example 3.4

Store +28 in an 8-bit memory location using sign-and-magnitude representation.

Solution

The integer is changed to 7-bit binary. The leftmost bit is set to 0. The 8-bit number is stored.

Change 28 to 7-bit binary			0	0	1	1	1	0	0
Add the sign and store	**0**	0	0	1	1	1	0	0	

Example 3.5

Store –28 in an 8-bit memory location using sign-and-magnitude representation.

Solution

The integer is changed to 7-bit binary. The leftmost bit is set to 1. The 8-bit number is stored.

Change 28 to 7-bit binary			0	0	1	1	1	0	0
Add the sign and store	**1**	0	0	1	1	1	0	0	

Example 3.6

Retrieve the integer that is stored as 01001101 in sign-and-magnitude representation.

Solution

Since the leftmost bit is 0, the sign is positive. The rest of the bits (1001101) are changed to decimal as 77. After adding the sign, the integer is +77.

Example 3.7

Retrieve the integer that is stored as 10100001 in sign-and-magnitude representation.

Solution

Since the leftmost bit is 1, the sign is negative. The rest of the bits (0100001) are changed to decimal as 17. After adding the sign, the integer is –17.

Overflow in sign-and-magnitude representation

Like unsigned integers, signed integers are also subjected to overflow. However, in this case, we may have both positive and negative overflow. Figure 3.7 shows both positive and negative overflow when storing an integer in sign-and-magnitude representation using a 4-bit memory location. Positive overflow occurs when we try to store a positive integer larger than 7. For example, assume that we have stored integer 5 in a memory location and we then try to add 6 to the integer. We expect the result to be 11, but the computer's response is –3. The reason is that if we start from 5 on a circular representation and go six units in the clockwise direction, we end up at –3. A positive overflow wraps the integer back to the range.

A negative overflow can happen when we try to store a integer that is less than –7, for example if we have stored the integer –5 in a memory and try to subtract 7 from it. We expect the result to be –12, but the computer's response is +6. The reason is that if we start from –5 on a circular representation and go seven units in the counterclockwise direction, we end up at +6.

There are two 0s in sign-and-magnitude representation: +0 and −0.

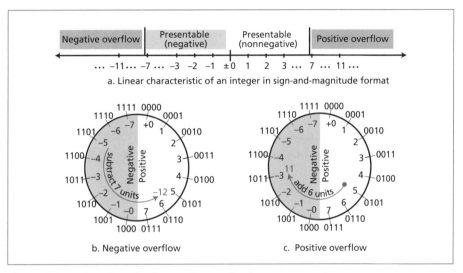

Figure 3.7   Overflow in sign-and-magnitude representation

Applications of sign-and-magnitude representation

Sign-and-magnitude representation is not used to store integers. However, it is used to store parts of real numbers, as we will see shortly. In addition, sign-and-magnitude representation is often used when we quantize an analog signal, such as audio.

Two's complement representation

Almost all computers use **two's complement** representation to store a signed integer in an n-bit memory location. In this method, the available range for an unsigned integer of (0 to $2^n - 1$) is divided into two equal subranges. The first subrange is used to represent nonnegative integers, the second half to represent negative integers. For example, if n is 4, the range is 0000 to 1111. This range is divided into two halves: 0000 to 0111 and 1000 to 1111. The two halves are swapped to be in agreement with the common convention of showing negative integers to the left of positive integers. The bit patterns are then assigned to negative and nonnegative (zero and positive) integers, as shown in Figure 3.8.

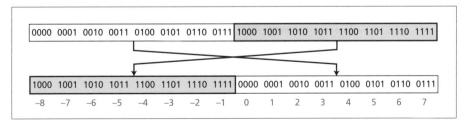

Figure 3.8   Two's complement representation

Although the sign of the integer affects every bit in the binary integer stored, the first (leftmost) bit determines the sign. If the leftmost bit is 0, the integer is nonnegative: if the leftmost bit is 1, the integer is negative.

> **In two's complement representation, the leftmost bit defines the sign of the integer. If it is 0, the integer is positive. If it is 1, the integer is negative.**

Two operations

Before we discuss this representation further, we need to introduce two operations. The first is called *one's completing* or *taking the one's complement of an integer*. The operation can be applied to any integer, positive or negative. This operation simply reverses (flips) each bit. A 0-bit is changed to a 1-bit, a 1-bit is changed to a 0-bit.

Example 3.8

The following shows how we take the one's complement of the integer 00110110.

Original pattern	0	0	1	1	0	1	1	0
After applying one's complement operation	1	1	0	0	1	0	0	1

Example 3.9

The following shows that we get the original integer if we apply the one's complement operations twice.

Original pattern	0	0	1	1	0	1	1	0
One's complementing once	1	1	0	0	1	0	0	1
One's complementing twice	0	0	1	1	0	1	1	0

The second operation is called *two's completing* or *taking the two's complement* of an integer in binary. This operation is done in two steps. First, we copy bits from the right until a 1 is copied, Then, we flip the rest of the bits.

Example 3.10

The following shows how we take the two's complement of the integer 00110100.

Original integer	0	0	1	1	0	1	0	0
	↓	↓	↓	↓	↓	↓	↓	↓
Two's complementing once	1	1	0	0	1	1	0	0

Example 3.11

The following shows that we always get the original integer if we apply the two's complement operation twice.

Original integer	0 0 1 1 0 1 0 0
	↓ ↓ ↓ ↓ ↓ ↓ ↓ ↓
Two's complementing once	1 1 0 0 1 1 0 0
	↓ ↓ ↓ ↓ ↓ ↓ ↓ ↓
Two's complementing twice	0 0 1 1 0 1 0 0

An alternative way to take the two's complement of an integer is to first take the one's complement and then add 1 to the result (see Chapter 4 for binary addition).

Storing an integer in two's complement format

To store an integer in two's complement representation, the computer follows the steps below:

❑ The integer is changed to an *n*-bit binary.

❑ If the integer is positive or zero, it is stored as it is: if it is negative, the computer takes the two's complement of the integer and then stores it.

Retrieving an integer in two's complement format

To retrieve an integer in two's complement representation, the computer follows the steps below:

❑ If the leftmost bit is 1, the computer applies the two's complement operation to the integer. If the leftmost bit is 0, no operation is applied.

❑ The computer changes the integer to decimal.

Example 3.12

Store the integer 28 in an 8-bit memory location using two's complement representation.

Solution

The integer is positive (no sign means positive), so after decimal to binary transformation no more action is needed. Note that five extra 0s are added to the left of the integer to make it eight bits.

Change 28 to 8-bit binary	0 0 0 1 1 1 0 0

Example 3.13

Store −28 in an 8-bit memory location using two's complement representation.

Solution

The integer is negative, so after changing to binary, the computer applies the two's complement operation on the integer.

Change 28 to 8-bit binary									0	0	0	1	1	1	0	0
									↓	↓	↓	↓	↓	↓	↓	↓
Apply two's complement operation									1	1	1	0	0	1	0	0

Example 3.14

Retrieve the integer that is stored as 00001101 in memory in two's complement format.

Solution

The leftmost bit is 0, so the sign is positive. The integer is changed to decimal and the sign is added.

Leftmost bit is 0. The sign is positive	0	0	0	0	1	1	0	1
Integer changed to decimal								13
Sign is added (optional)								+13

Example 3.15

Retrieve the integer that is stored as 11100110 in memory using two's complement format.

Solution

The leftmost bit is 1, so the integer is negative. The integer needs to be two's complemented before changing to decimal.

Leftmost bit is 1. The sign is negative	1	1	1	0	0	1	1	0
	↓	↓	↓	↓	↓	↓	↓	↓
Apply two's complement operation	0	0	0	1	1	0	1	0
Integer changed to decimal								26
Sign is added								−26

A very interesting point about two's complement is that there is only one zero in this representation. In sign-and-magnitude representation, there are two zeros (+0 and −0).

There is only one zero in two's complement notation.

Overflow in two's complement notation

Like other representations, integers stored in two's complement format are also subject to overflow. Figure 3.9 shows both positive and negative overflow when storing a signed integer in a 4-bit memory location. Positive overflow occurs when we try to store a positive integer larger than 7. For example, assume that we have stored an integer value 5 in a memory location and we then try to add 6 to the integer. We expect the result to be 11, but the computer's response is –5. The reason is if we start from 5 on the circular representation and move six units in the clockwise direction, we end up at –5. The positive overflow wraps the integer back to the range.

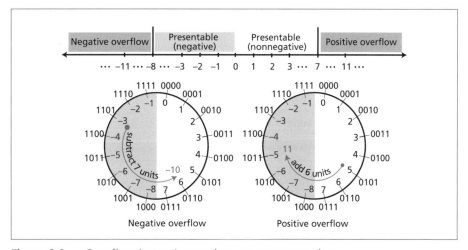

Figure 3.9   Overflow in two's complement representation

A negative overflow can happen when we try to store a integer that is less than –8, for example if we have stored –3 and try to subtract 7 from it. We expect the result to be –10, but the computer's response is +6. The reason is that if we start from –3 on a circular representation and go seven units in the counterclockwise direction, we end up at +6.

Applications of two's complement notation

Two's complement representation is the standard representation for storing integers in computers today. In the next chapter we will see why this is the case when we see the simplicity of operations using two's complement.

Comparison of the three systems

Table 3.1 shows a comparison between unsigned, two's complement, and sign-and-magnitude integers. A 4-bit memory location can store an unsigned integer between 0 and 15, and the same location can store two's complement signed integers between –8 and +7. It is very important that we store and retrieve an integer in the same format. For example, if the integer 13 is stored in signed format, it needs to be retrieved in signed format: the same integer is retrieved as −3 in two's complement format.

Table 3.1 Summary of integer representations

Contents of memory	Unsigned	Sign-and-magnitude	Two's complement
0000	0	0	+0
0001	1	1	+1
0010	2	2	+2
0011	3	3	+3
0100	4	4	+4
0101	5	5	+5
0110	6	6	+6
0111	7	7	+7
1000	8	−0	−8
1001	9	−1	−7
1010	10	−2	−6
1011	11	−3	−5
1100	12	−4	−4
1101	13	−5	−3
1110	14	−6	−2
1111	15	−7	−1

Storing reals

A **real** is a number with an integral part and a fractional part. For example, 23.7 is a real number—the integral part is 23 and the fractional part is 7/10. Although a fixed-point representation can be used to represent a real number, the result may not be accurate or it may not have the required precision. The next two examples explain why.

Example 3.16

In the decimal system, assume that we use a fixed-point representation with two digits at the right of the decimal point and fourteen digits at the left of the decimal point, for a total of sixteen digits. The precision of a real number in this system is lost if we try to represent a decimal number such as 1.00234: the system stores the number as 1.00.

Example 3.17

In the decimal system, assume that we use a fixed-point representation with six digits to the right of the decimal point and ten digits to the left of the decimal point, for a total of sixteen digits. The accuracy of a real number in this system is lost if we try to represent a decimal number such as 236154302345.00. The system stores the number as 6154302345.00: the integral part is much smaller than it should be.

> **Real numbers with very large integral parts or very small fractional parts should not be stored in fixed-point representation.**

Floating-point representation

The solution for maintaining accuracy or precision is to use **floating-point representation**. This representation allows the decimal point to *float*: we can have different numbers of digits to the left or right of the decimal point. The range of real numbers that can be stored using this method increases tremendously: numbers with large integral parts or small fractional parts can be stored in memory. In floating-point representation, either decimal or binary, a number is made up of three sections, as shown in Figure 3.10.

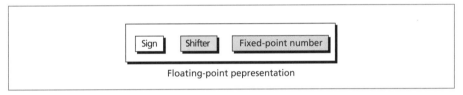

Figure 3.10   The three parts of a real number in floating-point representation

The first section is the sign, either positive or negative. The second section shows how many places the decimal point should be shifted to the right or left to form the actual number. The third section is a fixed-point representation in which the position of the decimal is fixed.

> **A floating point representation of a number is made up of three parts: a sign, a shifter, and a fixed-point number.**

Floating-point representation is used in science to represent very small or very large decimal numbers. In this representation, which is called *scientific notation*, the fixed-point section has only one digit to the left of the decimal point and the shifter is the power of 10.

Example 3.18

The following shows the decimal number 7425,000,000,000,000,000,000.00 in scientific notation (floating-point representation).

Solution

Actual number	→	+	7,425,000,000,000,000,000,000.00
Scientific notation	→	+	7.425×10^{21}

The three sections are the sign (+), the shifter (21), and the fixed-point part (7.425). Note that the shifter is the exponent. We can easily see the advantage of this. Even if we just want to write the number on a piece of paper, the scientific notation is shorter and takes less space. The notation uses the concept of floating-point because the position of the decimal point, which is near the right-hand end in the example, has moved 21 digits to the left to make the fixed-point part of the number. Some programming languages and calculators shows the number as +7.425E21 because the base 10 is understood and does not need to be mentioned.

Example 3.19

Show the number −0.0000000000000232 in scientific notation.

Solution

We use the same approach as in the previous example—we move the decimal point after the digit 2, as shown below:

Actual number	→	−	0.0000000000000232
Scientific notation	→	−	2.32×10^{-14}

Note that the exponent is negative here because the decimal point in 2.32 needs to move to the left (fourteen positions) to form the original number. Again, we can say that the number in this notation is made of three parts: sign (−), the real number (2.32), and the negative integer (−14). Some programming languages and calculators show this as −2.32E−14.

Similar approaches have been used to represent very large or very small numbers (both integers and reals) in binary, to be stored in computers.

Example 3.20

Show the number $(101001000000000000000000000000000.00)_2$ in floating-point format.

Solution

We use the same idea, keeping only one digit to the left of the decimal point.

Actual number	→	+	$(101001000000000000000000000000000.00)_2$
Scientific notation	→	+	1.01001×2^{32}

Note that we don't have to worry about all those 0s at the right of the rightmost 1, because they are not significant when we use the real $(1.01001)_2$. The exponent is shown as 32, but it is actually stored in the computer in binary, as we will see shortly. We have also shown the sign as positive, but it would be stored as one bit.

Example 3.21

Show the number $-(0.00000000000000000000000101)_2$ in floating-point format.

Solution

We use the same idea, keeping only one non-zero digit on the left-hand side of the decimal point.

Actual number	$\rightarrow$ $-$	$(0.00000000000000000000000101)_2$
Scientific notation	$\rightarrow$ $-$	1.01×2^{-24}

Note that exponent is stored as a negative binary in the computer.

Normalization To make the fixed part of the representation uniform, both the scientific method (for the decimal system) and the floating-point method (for the binary system) use only one non-zero digit to the left of the decimal point. This is called **normalization**. In the decimal system this digit can be 1 to 9, while in the binary system it can only be 1. In the following, d is a non-zero digit, x is a digit, and y is either 0 or 1.

Decimal	$\rightarrow$	$\pm$	d.xxxxxxxxxxxxxx Note: d is 1 to 9 and each x is 0 to 9
Binary	$\rightarrow$	$\pm$	1.yyyyyyyyyyyyyy Note: each y is 0 or 1

Sign, exponent, and mantissa After a binary number is normalized, only three pieces of information about the number are stored: sign, exponent, and mantissa (the bits to the right of the decimal point). For example, +1000111.0101 becomes:

+	2^6	$\times$	1.0001110101
+	6		0001110101
↑	↑		↑
Sign	Exponent		Mantissa

> **Note that the point and the bit 1 to the left of the fixed-point section are not stored—they are implicit.**

Sign

The sign of the number can be stored using 1 bit (0 or 1).

Exponent

The exponent (power of 2) defines the shifting of the decimal point. Note that the power can be negative or positive. The **Excess** representation (discussed later) is the method used to store the exponent.

Mantissa

The **mantissa** is the binary integer to the right of the decimal point. It defines the precision of the number. The mantissa is stored in fixed-point notation. If we think of the mantissa and the sign together, we can say this combination is stored as an integer in sign-and-magnitude format. However, we need to remember that it is not an integer—it is a fractional part that is stored like an integer. We emphasize this point because in a mantissa, if we insert extra 0s to the *right* of the number, the value will not change, whereas in a real integer if we insert extra 0s to the *left* of the number, the value will not change.

> **The mantissa is a fractional part that, together with the sign, is treated like an integer stored in sign-and-magnitude representation.**

The Excess system

The mantissa can be stored as an unsigned integer. The exponent, the power that shows how many bits the decimal point should be moved to the left or right, is a signed number. Although this could have been stored using two's complement representation, a new representation, called the Excess system, is used instead. In the Excess system, both positive and negative integers are stored as unsigned integers. To represent a positive or negative integer, a positive integer (called a *bias*) is added to each number to shift them uniformly to the non-negative side. The value of this bias is $2^{m-1} - 1$, where m is the size of the memory location to store the exponent.

Example 3.22

We can express sixteen integers in a number system with 4-bit allocation. Using one location for 0 and splitting the other fifteen (not quite equally) we can express integers in the range of –7 to 8, as shown in Figure 3.11. By adding seven units to each integer in this range, we can uniformly translate all integers to the right and make all of them positive without changing the relative position of the integers with respect to each other, as shown in the figure. The new system is referred to as *Excess-7*, or biased representation with biasing value of 7.

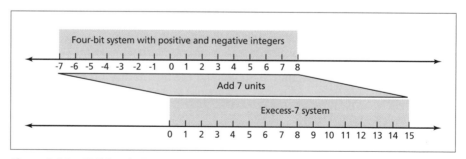

Figure 3.11   Shifting in Excess representation

The advantage of this new representation compared to that before the translation is that all integers in the Excess system are positive, so we don't need to be concerned about the sign when we are comparing or doing operations on the integers. For 4-bit allocation, the bias is $2^{4-1} - 1 = 7$, as we expected.

IEEE standards

The Institute of Electrical and Electronics Engineers (IEEE) has defined several standards for storing floating-point numbers. We discuss the two most common ones here, single precision and double precision. These formats are shown in Figure 3.12. The numbers above the boxes are the number of bits for each field.

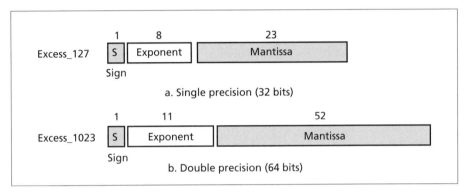

Figure 3.12   IEEE standards for floating-point representation

Single precision format uses a total of 32 bits to store a real number in floating-point representation. The sign occupies one bit (0 for positive and 1 for negative), the exponent occupies eight bits (using a bias of 127), the mantissa uses 23 bits (unsigned number). This standard is sometimes referred to as **Excess_127** because the bias is 127.

Double precision format uses a total of 64 bits to store a real number in floating-point representation. The sign occupies one bit, the exponent occupies eleven bits (using a bias of 1023), and the mantissa uses 52 bits. The standard is sometimes referred to as **Excess_1023** because the bias is 1023. Table 3.2 summarizes the specification of the two standards.

Table 3.2   Specifications of the two IEEE floating-point standards

Parameter	Single precision	Double precision
Memory location size (number of bits)	32	64
Sign size (number of bits)	1	1
Exponent size (number of bits)	8	11
Mantissa size (number of bits)	23	52
Bias (integer)	127	1023

Storage of IEEE standard floating point numbers

A real number can be stored in one of the IEEE standard floating-point formats using the following procedure, with reference to Figure 3.12:

1. Store the sign in S (0 or 1).
2. Change the number to binary.
3. Normalize.
4. Find the values of E and M.
5. Concatenate S, E, and M.

Example 3.23

Show the Excess_127 (single precision) representation of the decimal number 5.75.

Solution

a. The sign is positive, so S = 0.
b. Decimal to binary transformation: $5.75 = (101.11)_2$.
c. Normalization: $(101.11)_2 = (1.0111)_2 \times 2^2$.
d. E = 2 + 127 = 129 = $(10000001)_2$, M = 0111. We need to add nineteen zeros at the right of M to make it 23 bits.
e. The presentation is shown below:

0	10000001	01110000000000000000000
S	E	M

The number is stored in the computer as 01000000101110000000000000000000.

Example 3.24

Show the Excess_127 (single precision) representation of the decimal number −161.875.

Solution

a. The sign is negative, so S = 1.
b. Decimal to binary transformation: $161.875 = (10100001.111)_2$.
c. Normalization: $(10100001.111)_2 = (1.0100001111)_2 \times 2^7$.
d. E = 7 + 127 = 134 = $(10000110)_2$ and M = $(0100001111)_2$.
e. Representation:

1	10000110	01000011110000000000000
S	E	M

The number is stored in the computer as 11000011010000111100000000000000.

Example 3.25

Show the Excess_127 (single precision) representation of the decimal number
−0.0234375.

Solution

a. S = 1 (the number is negative).

b. Decimal to binary transformation: $0.0234375 = (0.0000011)_2$.

c. Normalization: $(0.0000011)_2 = (1.1)_2 \times 2^{-6}$.

d. $E = -6 + 127 = 121 = (01111001)_2$ and $M = (1)_2$.

e. Representation:

1	01111001	10000000000000000000000
S	E	M

The number is stored in the computer as 10111100110000000000000000000000.

Retrieving numbers stored in IEEE standard floating point format

A number stored in one of the IEEE floating-point formats can be retrieved using the following method:

1. Find the value of S, E, and M.
2. If S = 0, set the sign to positive, otherwise set the sign to negative.
3. Find the shifter (E −127).
4. Denormalize the mantissa.
5. Change the denormalized number to binary to find the absolute value.
6. Add the sign.

Example 3.26

The bit pattern $(11001010000000000111000100001111)_2$ is stored in memory in Excess_127 format. Show what the value of the number is in decimal notation.

Solution

a. The first bit represents S, the next eight bits, E, and the remaining 23 bits, M.

S	E	M
1	10010100	00000000111000100001111

b. The sign is negative.

c. The shifter = E − 127 = 148 − 127 = 21.

d. Denormalization gives us $(1.00000000111000100001111)_2 \times 2^{21}$.

e. The binary number is $(1000000001110001000011.11)_2$.

f. The absolute value is 2,104,378.75.

g. The number is −2,104,378.75.

Overflow and underflow

In the case of floating point numbers, we can have both an overflow and **underflow**. Figure 3.13 shows the ranges of floating-point representations using 32-bit memory locations (Excess_127). This representation cannot store numbers with very small or very large absolute values. An attempt to store numbers with very small absolute values results in an underflow condition, while an attempt to store numbers with very large absolute values results in an overflow condition. We leave the calculation of boundary values (+largest, −largest, +smallest, and −smallest) as exercises.

Storing zero

You may have noticed that a real number with an integral part and the fractional part set to zero, that is, 0.0, cannot be stored using the steps discussed above. To handle this special case, it is agreed that in this case the sign, exponent, and the mantissa are set to 0s.

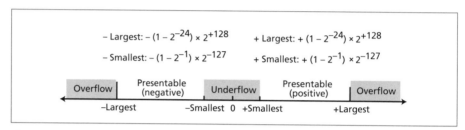

Figure 3.13   Overflow and underflow in floating-point representation of reals

Truncation errors

When a real number is stored using floating-point representation, the value of the number stored may not be exactly as we expect it to be. For example, assume we need to store the number:

$$(1111111111111111.11111111111)_2$$

in memory using Excess_127 representation. After normalization, we have:

$$(1.111111111111111111111111111)_2$$

This means that the mantissa has 26 1s. This mantissa needs to be truncated to 23 1s. In other words, what is stored in the computer is:

$$(1111111111111111.11111111)_2$$

with the three 1s at the right of the fractional part truncated. The difference between the original number and what is retrieved is called the **truncation error**. This type of error is very important in areas in which very small or very large number are used, such as calculations in the space industry. In such cases we need to use larger memory locations and other presentations. The IEEE defines other standards with larger mantissas for these purposes.

3.3 STORING TEXT

A section of **text** in any language is a sequence of symbols used to represent an idea in that language. For example, the English language uses 26 symbols (A, B, C,..., Z) to represent uppercase letters, 26 symbols (a, b, c, ..., z) to represent lowercase letters, ten symbols (0, 1, 2, …, 9) to represent numeric characters (not actual numbers—numbers are treated separately, as we explained in the previous section), and symbols (., ?, :, ; , …, !) to represent punctuation. Other symbols such as blank, newline, and tab are used for text alignment and readability.

We can represent each symbol with a bit pattern. In other words, text such as "CATS", which is made up from four symbols, can be represented as four *n*-bit patterns, each pattern defining a single symbol (Figure 3.14).

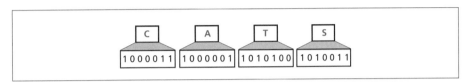

Figure 3.14   Representing symbols using bit patterns

Now the question is: how many bits are needed in a bit pattern to represent a symbol in a language? It depends on how many symbols are in the set used for the language. For example, if we create an imaginary language that uses only English uppercase letters, we need only 26 symbols. A bit pattern in this language needs to represent at least 26 symbols.

For another language, such as Chinese, we may need many more symbols. The length of the bit pattern that represents a symbol in a language depends on the number of symbols used in that language. More symbols mean a longer bit pattern.

Although the length of the bit pattern depends on the number of symbols, the relationship is not linear: it is logarithmic. If we need two symbols, the length is one bit ($\log_2 2$ is 1). If we need four symbols, the length is two bits ($\log_2 4$ is 2). Table 3.3 shows the relationship. A bit pattern of two bits can take four different forms: 00, 01, 10, and 11. Each of these forms can represent a symbol. In the same way, a bit pattern of three bits can take eight different forms: 000, 001, 010, 011, 100, 101, 110, and 111.

Table 3.3   Number of symbols and bit pattern length

Number of symbols	Bit pattern length	Number of symbols	Bit pattern length
2	1	128	7
4	2	256	8
8	3	65,536	16
16	4	4,294,967,296	32

Codes   Different sets of bit patterns have been designed to represent text symbols. Each set is called a **code**, and the process of representing symbols is called *coding*. In this section, we explain the common codes.

ASCII

The **American National Standards Institute (ANSI)** developed a code called **American Standard Code for Information Interchange (ASCII)**. This code uses seven bits for each symbol. This means that $2^7 = 128$ different symbols can be defined in this code. The full bit patterns for ASCII code are included in Appendix A. Today ASCII is part of Unicode, which is discussed next.

Unicode

A coalition of hardware and software manufacturers have designed a code called **Unicode** that uses 32 bits and can therefore represent up to $2^{32} = 4,294,967,296$ symbols. Different sections of the code are allocated to symbols from different languages in the world. Some parts of the code are used for graphical and special symbols. A brief set of Unicode symbols is listed in Appendix A. ASCII is part of Unicode today.

Other codes

Other codes have been developed during the last few decades. Most of these codes have been made less common with the advent of Unicode. We leave the exploration of these codes as an exercise.

3.4 STORING AUDIO

Audio is a representation of sound or music. Audio, by nature, is different than the numbers or text we have discussed so far. Text is composed of countable entities (characters): we can count the number of characters in text. Text is an example of **digital** data. In contrast, audio is not countable. Audio is an entity that changes with time—we can only measure the intensity of the sound at each moment. When we discuss storing audio in computer memory, we mean storing the intensity of an audio signal, such as the signal from a microphone, over a period of time: one second, one hour.

Audio is an example of **analog** data. Even if we are able to measure all its values in a period of time, we cannot store these in the computer's memory, as we would need infinite number of memory locations. Figure 3.15 shows the nature of an analog signal, such as audio, that varies with time.

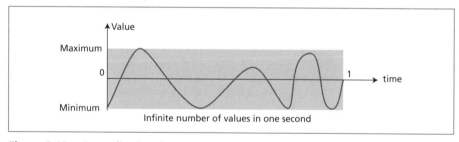

Figure 3.15   An audio signal

Sampling

If we cannot record all the values of an audio signal over an interval, we *can* record some of them. **Sampling** means that we select only a finite number of points on the analog signal, measure their values, and record them. Figure 3.16 shows that selection of ten samples from the signal: we can then record these values to represent the analog signal.

Sampling rate

The next logical question is, how many samples do we need in each second to be able to retrieve a replica of the original signal? The number of samples depends on the maximum number of changes in the analog signal. If the signal is smooth, we need less samples: if the signal is changing rapidly, we need more samples. It has been shown that a **sampling rate** of 40,000 samples per second is good enough to reproduce an audio signal.

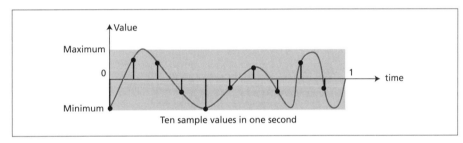

Figure 3.16   Sampling an audio signal

Quantization

The value measured for each sample is a real number. This means that we can store 40,000 real values for each one-second sample. However, it is simpler to use an unsigned integer (a bit pattern) for each sample. **Quantization** refers to a process that rounds the value of a sample to the closest integer value. For example, if the real value is 17.2, it can be rounded down to 17: if the value is 17.7, it can be rounded up to 18.

Encoding

The next task is **encoding**. The quantized sample values need to be encoded as bit patterns. Some systems assign positive and negative values to samples, some just shift the curve to the positive part and assign only positive values. In other words, some systems use an unsigned integer to represent a sample, while others use signed integers to do so. However, the signed integers don't have to be in two's complement, they can be sign-and-magnitude values. The leftmost bit is used to represent the sign (0 for positive values and 1 for negative values), and the rest of the bits are used to represent the absolute values.

Bit per sample

The system needs to decide how many bits should be allocated for each sample. Although in the past only eight bits were assigned to sound samples, today 16, 24 or even 32 bits per sample is normal. The number of bits per sample is sometimes referred to as the **bit depth**.

Bit rate   If we call the bit depth or number of bits per sample B, the number of samples per second, S, we need to store S × B bits for each second of audio. This product is sometimes referred to as **bit rate**, R. For example, if we use 40,000 samples per second and 16 bits per each sample, the bit rate is R = 40,000 × 16 = 640,000 bits per second = 640 kilobits per second.

Standards for sound encoding

Today the dominant standard for storing audio is **MP3** (short for *MPEG Layer 3*). This standard is a modification of the **MPEG** (Motion Picture Experts Group) compression method used for video. It uses 44,100 samples per second and 16 bits per sample. The result is a signal with a bit rate of 705,600 bits per second, which is compressed using a compression method that discards information that cannot be detected by the human ear. This is called *lossy* compression, as opposed to loss-less compression: see Chapter 15.

3.5 STORING IMAGES

Images are stored in computers using two different techniques: *raster graphics* and *vector graphics*.

Raster graphics

Raster graphics (or **bitmap graphics**) is used when we need to store an analog image such as a photograph. A photograph consists of analog data, similarly to audio information: the difference is that the intensity (color) of data varies in space instead of in time. This means that data must be sampled. However, sampling in this case is normally called **scanning**. The samples are called **pixels** (which stands for *picture elements*). In other words, the whole image is divided into small pixels where each pixel is assumed to have a single intensity value.

Resolution   Just like audio sampling, in image scanning we need to decide how many pixels we need to record for each square or linear inch. The scanning rate in image processing is called **resolution**. If the resolution is sufficiently high, the human eye cannot recognize the discontinuity in reproduced images.

Color depth   The number of bits used to represent a pixel, its **color depth**, depends on how a pixel's color is handled by different encoding techniques. The perception of color is how our eyes respond to a beam of light. Our eyes have different types of *photoreceptor* cells: some respond to the three primary colors red, green, and blue (often called **RGB**), while others merely respond to the intensity of light.

True-Color

One of the techniques used to encode a pixel is called **True-Color**, which uses 24 bits to encode a pixel. In this technique, each of the three primary colors (RGB) are represented by eight bits. Since an 8-bit pattern can represent a number between 0 to 255 in this technique, each color is represented by three decimal numbers between 0 to 255. Table 3.4 shows the three values for some of the colors in this technique.

Table 3.4   Some colors defined in True-Color

Color	Red	Green	Blue	Color	Red	Green	Blue
Black	0	0	0	Yellow	255	255	0
Red	255	0	0	Cyan	0	255	255
Green	0	255	0	Magenta	255	0	255
Blue	0	0	255	White	255	255	255

Note that the True-Color scheme can encode 2^{24} or 16,776,216 colors. In other words, the color intensity of each pixel is one of these values.

Indexed color

The True-Color scheme uses more than 16 million colors. Many applications do not need such a large range of colors. The **indexed color**—or **palette color**—scheme uses only a portion of these colors. In this scheme each application selects a few (normally 256) colors from the large set of colors and indexes them, assigning a number between 0 and 255 to each selected color. This is similar to the way in which an artist might have a great many colors in their studio, but at each moment use only a few on their palette. Figure 3.17 illustrates the idea of indexed color.

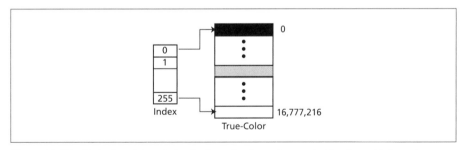

Figure 3.17   Relationship of the indexed color scheme to the True-Color scheme

The use of indexing reduces the number of bits required to store a pixel. For example, in the True-Color scheme 24 bits are needed to store a single pixel. The index color scheme normally uses 256 indexes, which needs only eight bits to store the same pixel. For example, a high-quality digital camera uses almost three million pixels for a 3 × 5 inch photo. The following shows the number of bits that need to be stored using each scheme:

True-Color:	3,000,000	×	24	=	72,000,000
Indexed-Color:	3,000,000	×	8	=	24,000,000

Standards for image encoding   Several de facto standards for image encoding are in use. **JPEG** (Joint Photographic Experts Group) uses the True-Color scheme, but compresses the image to reduce the number of bits (see Chapter 15). **GIF** (Graphic Interchange Format), on the other hand, uses the indexed color scheme.

Vector graphics

Raster graphics has two disadvantages: the file size is big and rescaling is troublesome. To enlarge a raster graphics image means enlarging the pixels., so the image looks ragged when it is enlarged. The **vector graphic** image encoding method, however, does not store bit patterns for each pixel. An image is decomposed into a combination of geometrical shapes such as lines, squares, or circles. Each geometrical shape is represented by a mathematical formula. For example, a line may be described by the coordinates of its endpoints, and a circle may be described by the coordinates of its center and the length of its radius. A vector graphic image is made up from a series of commands that defines how these shape should be drawn.

When the image is to be displayed or printed, the size of the image is given to the system as an input. The system rescales the image to the new size and uses the same formulae to draw the image. In this case, each time an image is drawn, the formulae are reevaluated. For this reason, vector graphics are also called *geometric modeling* or *object-oriented graphics*.

For example, consider a circle of radius r. The main pieces of information a program needs to draw this circle are:

❑   The radius r and equation of a circle.

❑   The location of the center point of the circle.

❑   The stroke line style and color.

❑   The fill style and color.

When the size of the circle is changed, the program changes the value of the radius and recalculates the information to draw the circle again. Rescaling does not change the quality of the drawing.

Vector graphics is not suitable for storing the subtleties of photographic images. JPEG or GIF raster graphics provide much better and more vivid pictures. Vector graphics *is* suitable for applications that use mainly geometric primitives to create images. It is used in applications such as FLASH, and to create TrueType (Microsoft, Apple) and PostScript (Adobe) fonts. Computer-aided design (CAD) also uses vector graphics for engineering drawings.

3.6 STORING VIDEO

Video is a representation of images (called *frames*) over time. A movie consists of a series of frames shown one after another to create the illusion of motion. In other words, video is the representation of information that changes in space (single image) and in time (a series of images). So, if we know how to store an image inside a computer, we also know how to store video: each image or frame is transformed into a set of bit patterns and stored. The combination of the images then represents the video. Today video is normally compressed. In Chapter 15 we discuss MPEG, a common video compression technique.

3.7 RECOMMENDED READING

For more details about the subjects discussed in this chapter, the following books are recommended:

- ❏ Halsall F: *Multimedia Communication*, Boston, MA: Addison Wesley, 2001
- ❏ Koren I: *Computer Arithmetic Algorithms*, Natick, MA: A K Peters, 2001
- ❏ Long B: *Complete Digital Photography*, Hignham, MA: Charles River Media, 200
- ❏ Mano M: *Computer System Architecture*, Upper Saddle River, NJ: Prentice Hall, 1993
- ❏ Miano, J: *Compressed Image File Formats*, Boston, MA: Addison Wesley, 1999

3.8 KEY TERMS

This chapter has introduced the following key terms, which are listed here with the pages on which they first occur:

American National Standards Institute (ANSI) 64	American Standard Code for Information Interchange (ASCII) 64
analog 64	audio 64
binary digit 42	bit 42
bit depth 66	bit pattern 42
bit rate 66	bitmap graphic 66
byte 43	code 63
color depth 66	digital 64
encoding 65	Excess representation 58
Excess_1023 59	Excess_127 59
fixed-point representation 44	floating-point representation 55
Graphic Interchange Format (GIF) 68	indexed color 67
Joint Photographer Expert Group (JPEG) 68	mantissa 58
MP3 66	MPEG 66

3.9 SUMMARY

- Data comes in different forms, including numbers, text, audio, image, and video. All data types are transformed into a uniform representation called a *bit pattern*.

- A number is changed to the binary system before being stored in computer memory. There are several ways to handle the sign. There are two ways to handle the decimal point: fixed-point and floating-point.

- An integer can be thought of as a number in which the position of the decimal point is fixed: the decimal point is at the right of the least significant bit. An unsigned integer is an integer that can never be negative.

- One of the methods used to store a signed integer is the sign-and-magnitude format. In this format, the leftmost bit is used to show the sign and the rest of the bits define the magnitude. Sign and magnitude are separated from each other.

- Almost all computers use the *two's complement representation* to store a signed integer in an *n*-bit memory location. In this method, the available range for unsigned integers is divided into two equal subranges. The first half is used to represent non-negative integers, the second half is used to represent negative integers. In two's complement representation, the leftmost bit defines the

sign of the integer, but sign and magnitude are not separated from each other.

- A *real* is a number with an integral part and a fractional part. Real numbers are stored in the computer using *floating-point representation*. In floating-point representation a number is made up of three sections: a sign, a shifter, and a fixed-point number.

- A piece of text in any language is a sequence of symbols. We can represent each symbol with a bit pattern. Different sets of bit patterns (codes) have been designed to represent text symbols. A coalition of hardware and software manufacturers have designed a code called *Unicode* that uses 32 bits to represent a symbol.

- Audio is a representation of sound or music. Audio is analog data. We cannot record an infinite number of values in an interval, we can only record some samples. The number of samples depends on the maximum number of changes in the analog signal. The values measured for each sample is a real number. *Quantization* refers to a process that rounds up the sample values to integers.

- Storage of images is done using two different techniques: *raster graphics* and *vector graphics*. Raster graphics are used when we need to store an analog image such as a photograph. The image is scanned (sampled) and pixels are stored. In the vector graphic method, an image is decomposed into a combination of geometrical shapes such as lines, squares, or circles. Each geometrical shape is represented by a mathematical formula.

- Video is a representation of images (called *frames*) in time. A movie is a series of frames shown one after another to create the illusion of continuous motion. In other words, video is the representation of information that changes in space (single image) and in time (a series of images).

3.10 PRACTICE SET

Review questions

1. Name five types of data that a computer can process.
2. How is bit pattern length related to the number of symbols the bit pattern can represent?
3. How does the bitmap graphic method represent an image as a bit pattern?
4. What is the advantage of the vector graphic method over the bitmap graphic method? What is the disadvantage?
5. What steps are needed to convert audio data to bit patterns?
6. Compare and contrast the representation of positive integers in unsigned, sign-and-magnitude format, and two's complement format.
7. Compare and contrast the representation of negative integers in sign-and-magnitude and two's complement format.
8. Compare and contrast the representation of zero in sign-and-magnitude, two's complement, and Excess formats.
9. Discuss the role of the leftmost bit in sign-and-magnitude, and two's complement, formats.
10. Answer the following questions about floating-point representations of real numbers:
    a. Why is normalization necessary?
    b. What is the mantissa?
    c. After a number is normalized, what kind of information does a computer store in memory?

Multiple-choice questions

11. A byte consists of _____ bits.
    a. 2
    b. 4
    c. 8
    d. 16
12. In a set of 64 symbols, each symbol requires a bit pattern length of _____ bits.
    a. 4
    b. 5
    c. 6
    d. 7
13. How many symbols can be represented by a bit pattern with ten bits?
    a. 128
    b. 256
    c. 512
    d. 1024
14. If the ASCII code for E is 1000101, then the ASCII code for e is _____. Answer the question without consulting the ASCII table.
    a. 1000110
    b. 1000111
    c. 0000110
    d. 1100101
15. A 32-bit code called _____ represents symbols in all languages.
    a. ANSI
    b. Unicode
    c. EBCDIC
    d. Extended ASCII
16. An image can be represented in a computer using the _____ method.
    a. bitmap graphic
    b. vector graphic
    c. Excess system
    d. a or b

17. In the _____ graphic method of representing an image in a computer, each pixel is assigned a bit pattern.
    a. bitmap
    b. vector
    c. quantized
    d. binary

18. In the _____ graphic method of representing an image in a computer, the image is decomposed into a combination of geometrical figures.
    a. bitmap
    b. vector
    c. quantized
    d. binary

19. In the _____ graphic method of representing an image in a computer, rescaling of the image creates a ragged or grainy image.
    a. bitmap
    b. vector
    c. quantized
    d. binary

20. When we want to store music in a computer, the audio signal must be _____.
    a. sampled
    b. quantized
    c. coded
    d. all of the above

21. If the leftmost bit in _____ number representation is zero, then the decimal number is non-negative.
    a. two's complement
    b. floating point
    c. Excess system
    d. both a and b

22. If the leftmost bit in _____ number representation is 1, then the decimal number is negative.
    a. two's complement
    b. floating point
    c. Excess system
    d. both a and b

23. Which number representation method is often used to store the exponential value of a fractional part?
    a. unsigned integers

    b. two's complement
    c. Excess system
    d. none of the above

24. In an Excess conversion, we _____ the bias number to the number to be converted.
    a. add
    b. subtract
    c. multiply
    d. divide

25. When a fractional part is normalized, the computer stores the _____.
    a. sign
    b. exponent
    c. mantissa
    d. all of the above

26. The precision of the fractional part of a number stored in a computer is defined by the _____.
    a. sign
    b. exponent
    c. mantissa
    d. any of the above

27. The combination of sign and mantissa of a real number in IEEE standard floating point format is stored as an integer in the _____ representation
    a. unsigned
    b. sign-and-magnitude
    c. two's complement
    d. none of the above

Exercises

28. How many distinct 5-bit patterns can we have?

29. In some countries vehicle license plates have two decimal digits (0 to 9). How many distinct plates can we have? If the digit 0 is not allowed on the license plate, how many distinct plates can we have?

30. Redo Exercise 29 for a license plate that has two digits followed by three uppercase letters (A to Z).

31. A machine has eight different cycles. How many bits are needed to represent each cycle?

32. A student's grade in a course can be A, B, C, D, F, W (withdraw), or I (incomplete). How many bits are needed to represent the grade?

33. A company has decided to assign a unique bit pattern to each employee. If the company has 900 employees, what is the minimum number of bits needed to create this system of representation? How many patterns are unassigned? If the company hires another 300 employees, should it increase the number of bits? Explain your answer.

34. If we use a 4-bit pattern to represent the digits 0 to 9, how many bit patterns are wasted?

35. An audio signal is sampled 8,000 times per second. Each sample is represented by 256 different levels. How many bits per second are needed to represent this signal?

36. Change the following decimal numbers to 8-bit unsigned integers.
    a. 23
    b. 121
    c. 34
    d. 342

37. Change the following decimal numbers to 16-bit unsigned integers.
    a. 41
    b. 411
    c. 1234
    d. 342

38. Change the following decimal numbers to 8-bit two's complement integers.
    a. −12
    b. −145
    c. 56
    d. 142

39. Change the following decimal numbers to 16-bit two's complement integers.
    a. 102
    b. −179
    c. 534
    d. 62,056

40. Change the following 8-bit unsigned numbers to decimal.
    a. 01101011
    b. 10010100
    c. 00000110
    d. 01010000

41. Change the following 8-bit two's complement numbers to decimal.
    a. 01110111
    b. 11111100
    c. 01110100
    d. 11001110

42. The following are two's complement binary numbers. Show how to change the sign of the number.
    a. 01110111
    b. 11111100
    c. 01110111
    d. 11001110

43. If we apply the two's complement operation to a number twice, we should get the original number. Apply the two's complement operation to each of the following numbers and see if we can get the original number.
    a. 01110111
    b. 11111100
    c. 01110100
    d. 11001110

44. Normalize the following binary floating point numbers. Explicitly show the value of the exponent after normalization.
    a. 1.10001
    b. $2^3 \times 111.1111$
    c. $2^{-2} \times 101.110011$
    d. $2^{-5} \times 101101.00000110011000$

45. Convert the following numbers in 32-bit IEEE format.
    a. $-2^0 \times 1.10001$
    b. $+2^3 \times 1.111111$
    c. $+2^{-4} \times 1.01110011$
    d. $-2^{-5} \times 1.01101000$

46. Convert the following numbers in 64-bit IEEE format:
    a. $-2^0 \times 1.10001$
    b. $+2^3 \times 1.111111$
    c. $+2^{-4} \times 1.01110011$
    d. $-2^{-5} \times 1.01101000$

47. Convert the following numbers in 32-bit IEEE format.
    a. 7.1875
    b. –12.640625
    c. 11.40625
    d. –0.375

48. The following are sign-and-magnitude binary numbers in an 8-bit allocation. Convert them to decimal.
    a. 01110111
    b. 11111100
    c. 01110100
    d. 11001110

49. Convert the following decimal integers to sign-and-magnitude with 8-bit allocation.
    a. 53
    b. –107
    c. –5
    d. 154

50. One method of representing signed numbers in a computer is one's complement representation. In this representation, to represent a positive number, we store the binary number. To represent a negative number, we apply the one's complement operation to the number. Store the following decimal integers to one's complement with 8-bit allocation.
    a. 53
    b. –107
    c. –5
    d. 154

51. The following are one's complement binary numbers in an 8-bit allocation. Convert them to decimal (see Exercise 50).
    a. 01110111
    b. 11111100
    c. 01110100
    d. 11001110

52. If we apply the one's complement operation to a number twice, we should get the original number. Apply the one's complement operation twice to each of the following numbers and see if you can get the original number (see Exercise 50).
    a. 01110111
    b. 11111100

c. 01110100
d. 11001110

53. An alternative method to find the two's complement of a number is to first take the one's complement of the number (see Exercise 50) and then add 1 to the result. (Adding binary integers is explained in Chapter 4). Try both methods using the following numbers. Compare and contrast the results.
    a. 01110111
    b. 11111100
    c. 01110100
    d. 11001110

54. The equivalent of one's complement (see Exercise 50) in the binary system is nine's complement in the decimal system ($1 = 2 – 1$ and $9 = 10 – 1$). With n-digit allocation, we can represent nine's complement numbers in the range of:

$$– [(10^n/2) – 1] \quad \text{to} \quad + [(10^n/2 – 1)]$$

The nine's complement of a number with n digit allocation is obtained as follows. If the number is positive, the nine's complement of the number is itself. If the number is negative, we subtract each digit from 9. Answer the following questions for three-digit allocation:
    a. What is the range of the numbers we can represent using nine's complement?
    b. In this system, how can we determine the sign of a number?
    c. Do we have two zeros in this system?
    d. If the answer to c. is yes, what is the representation for +0 and –0?

55. Assuming three-digit allocation, find the nine's complement of the following decimal numbers (see Exercise 54):
    a. +234
    b. +560
    c. –125
    d. –111

56. The equivalent of two's complement in the binary system is ten's complement in the decimal system (in the binary system, 2 is the base, in the decimal system, 10 is the base). Using

n-digit allocation, we can represent numbers in the range of:

$$-(10^n/2) \quad \text{to} \quad +(10^n/2 - 1)$$

in ten's complement format. The ten's complement of a number with *n*-digit allocation is obtained by first finding the nine's complement of the number (as described in Exercise 54) and then adding 1 to the result. Answer the following questions for three-digit allocation.

   a. What is the range of the numbers we can represent using ten's complement?

   b. In this system, how can we determine the sign of a number?

   c. Do we have two zeros in this system?

   d. If the answer to c. is yes, what is the representation for +0 and −0?

57. Assuming three-digit allocation, find the ten's complement of the following decimal numbers. (The information for doing this problem is presented in Exercise 56).

   a. +234

   b. +560

   c. −125

   d. −111

58. The equivalent of one's complement (Exercise 50) in the binary system is fifteen's complement in the hexadecimal system (1 = 2 − 1 and 15 = 16 − 1). Read the explanation provided for Exercise 54 to answer the following questions:

   a. What range of numbers can we represent with three-digit allocation in fifteen's complement?

   b. Explain how the fifteen's complement of a number is obtained in the hexadecimal system.

   c. Do we have two zeros in this system?

   d. If the answer to c. is yes, what is the representation for +0 and −0?

59. Assuming three-digit allocation, find the fifteen's complement of the following hexadecimal numbers (see Exercise 58):

   a. +B14

   b. +FE1

   c. −1A

   d. −1E2

60. The equivalent of two's complement in the binary system is sixteen's complement in the hexadecimal system. Read the explanation provided for Exercise 56 to answer the following questions.

   a. What range of numbers can we represent with three-digit allocation in sixteen's complement?

   b. Explain how a sixteen's complement of a number is obtained in the hexadecimal system.

   c. Do we have two zeros in this system?

   d. If the answer to c. is yes, what is the representation for +0 and −0?

61. Assuming three-digit allocation, find the sixteen's complement of the following hexadecimal numbers (see Exercise 60):

   a. +B14

   b. +FE1

   c. −1A

   d. −1E2

4

Operations on Data

In Chapter 3 we showed how to store different types of data in a computer. In this chapter, we show how to operate on data stored in a computer. Operations on data can be divided into three broad categories: logic operations, shift operations, and arithmetic operations.

Objectives

After studying this chapter, the student should be able to:

❑ List the three categories of operations performed on data.

❑ Perform unary and binary logic operations on bit patterns.

❑ Distinguish between logic shift operations and arithmetic shift operations.

❑ Perform logic shift operations on bit patterns.

❑ Perform arithmetic shift operations on integers stored in two's complement format.

❑ Perform addition and subtraction on integers stored in two's complement format.

❑ Perform addition and subtraction on integers stored in sign-and- magnitude format.

❑ Perform addition and subtraction operations on reals stored in floating-point format.

❑ Understand some applications of logical and shift operations such as setting, unsetting, and flipping specific bits.

4.1   LOGIC OPERATIONS

In Chapter 3 we discussed the fact that data inside a computer is stored as patterns of bits. **Logic operations** refer to those operations that apply the same basic operation on individual bits of a pattern, or on two corresponding bits in two patterns. This means that we can define logic operations at the bit level and at the pattern level. A logic operation at the pattern level is n logic operations, of the same type, at the bit level where n is the number of bits in the pattern.

Logic operations at bit level

A bit can take one of the two values: 0 or 1. If we interpret 0 as the value *false* and 1 as the value *true*, we can apply the operations defined in **Boolean algebra** to manipulate bits. Boolean algebra, named in honor of George Boole, belongs to a special field of mathematics called *logic*. Boolean algebra and its application to building logic circuits in computers are briefly discussed in Appendix E. In this section, we show briefly four bit-level operations that are used to manipulate bits: NOT, AND, OR, and XOR.

> **Boolean algebra and logic circuits are discussed in Appendix E.**

Figure 4.1 shows the symbols for these four bit-level operators and their truth tables. A **truth table** defines the values of the output for each possible input or inputs. Note that the output of each operator is always one bit, but the input can be one or two bits.

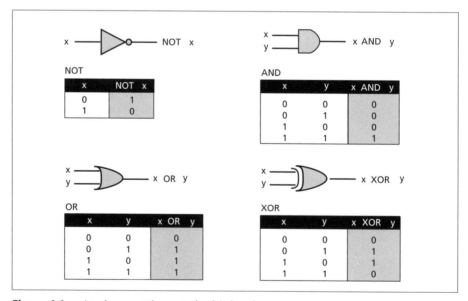

Figure 4.1   Logic operations at the bit level

NOT

The **NOT operator** is a unary operator: it takes only one input. The output bit is the complement of the input. If the input is 0, the output is 1, if the input is 1, the output is 0. In other words, the NOT operator flips its input. The truth table of the NOT operator has only two rows because the single input can be either 0 or 1: two possibilities.

AND

The **AND operator** is a binary operator: it takes two inputs. The output bit is 1 if both inputs are 1s and the output is 0 in the other three cases. The truth table of the AND operator has four rows because, with two inputs, there are four possible input combinations.

A property

One interesting point about the AND operator is that if a bit in one input is 0, we do not have to check the corresponding bit in the other input: we can quickly conclude that the result is 0. We use this property when we discuss the application of this operator in relation to a bit pattern.

For x = 0 or 1   x AND 0 → 0   and   0 AND x → 0

OR

The **OR operator** is a also a binary operator: it takes two inputs. The output bit is 0 if both inputs are 0s and the output is 1 in the other three cases. The truth table of the OR operator has also four rows. The OR operator is sometimes called the *inclusive-or operator* because the output is 1 not only when one of the inputs is 1, but also when both inputs are 1s. This is in contrast to the operator we introduce next.

A property

One interesting point about the OR operator is that if a bit in one input is 1, we do not have to check the corresponding bit in the other input: we can quickly conclude that the result is 1. We use this property when we discuss the application of this operator in relation to a bit pattern.

For x = 0 or 1   x OR 1 → 1   and   1 OR x → 1

XOR

The **XOR operator** (pronounced "exclusive-or") is also a binary operator like the OR operator, with only one difference: the output is 0 if both inputs are 1s. We can look at this operator in another way: the output is 0 when both inputs are the same, and the output is 1 when the inputs are different.

Example 4.1

In English we use the conjunction "or" sometimes to means an inclusive-or, and sometimes to means an exclusive-or.

    a. The sentence "I wish to have a car *or* a house" uses "or" in the inclusive sense—I wish to have a car, a house, or both.

    b. The sentence "Today is either Monday or Tuesday" uses "or" in the exclusive sense—today is either Monday or Tuesday, but it cannot be both.

Example 4.2

The XOR operator is not actually a new operator. We can always simulate it using the other three operators. The following two expressions are equivalent

> **x XOR y ↔ [x AND (NOT y)] OR [(NOT x) AND y]**

The equivalence can be proved if we make the truth table for both.

A property

A property of XOR is that if a bit in one input is 1, the result is the complement of the corresponding bit in the other input. We use this property when we discuss the application of this operator in relation to a bit pattern.

> **For x = 0 or 1   1 XOR x → NOT x   and   x XOR 1 → NOT x**

Logic operations at pattern level

The same four operators (NOT, AND, OR, and XOR) can be applied to an *n*-bit pattern. The effect is the same as applying each operator to each individual bit for NOT and to each corresponding pair of bits for the other three operators. Figure 4.2 shows these four operators with input and output patterns.

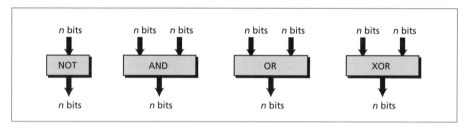

Figure 4.2   Logic operators applied to bit patterns

Example 4.3

Use the NOT operator on the bit pattern 10011000.

Solution

The solution is shown below. Note that the NOT operator changes every 0 to 1 and every 1 to 0.

NOT	1	0	0	1	1	0	0	0	Input
	0	1	1	0	0	1	1	1	Output

Example 4.4

Use the AND operator on the bit patterns 10011000 and 00101010.

Solution

The solution is shown below. Note that only one bit in the output is 1, where both corresponding inputs are 1s.

	1	0	0	1	1	0	0	0	Input 1
AND	0	0	1	0	1	0	1	0	Input 2
	0	0	0	0	1	0	0	0	Output

Example 4.5

Use the OR operator on the bit patterns 10011001 and 00101110.

Solution

The solution is shown below. Note that only one bit in the output is 0, where both corresponding inputs are 0s.

	1	0	0	1	1	0	0	1	Input 1
OR	0	0	1	0	1	1	1	0	Input 2
	1	0	1	1	1	1	1	1	Output

Example 4.6

Use the XOR operator on the bit patterns 10011001 and 00101110.

Solution

The solution is shown below. Compare the output in this example with the one in Example 4.5. The only difference is that when the two inputs are 1s, the result is 0 (the effect of exclusion).

	1	0	0	1	1	0	0	1	Input 1
XOR	0	0	1	0	1	1	1	0	Input 2
	1	0	1	1	0	1	1	1	Output

Applications   Four logic operations can be used to modify a bit pattern.

Complementing

The only application of the NOT operator is to complement the whole pattern. Applying this operator to a pattern changes every 0 to 1 and every 1 to 0. This is sometimes referred to as a one's complement operation. Example 4.3 shows the effect of complementing.

Unsetting specific bits

One of the applications of the AND operator is to **unset** (force to 0) specific bits in a bit pattern. The second input in this case is called a **mask**. The 0-bits in the mask unset the corresponding bits in the first input: the 1-bits in the mask leave the corresponding bits in the first input unchanged. This is due to the property we mentioned for the AND operator: if one of the inputs is 0, the output is 0 no matter what the other input is. Unsetting the bits in a pattern has many applications. For example, if an image uses only one bit per pixel (a black and white image), then we can make a specific pixel black using a mask and the AND operator.

Example 4.7

Use a mask to unset (clear) the five leftmost bits of a pattern. Test the mask with the pattern 10100110.

Solution
The mask is 00000111. The result of applying the mask is:

		1	0	1	0	0	1	1	0	Input
AND		0	0	0	0	0	1	1	1	Mask
		0	0	0	0	0	1	1	0	Output

Note that the three rightmost bits remain unchanged, while the five leftmost bits are unset (changed to 0) no matter what their previous values.

Setting specific bits

One of the applications of the OR operator is to **set** (force to 1) specific bits in a bit pattern. Again we can use a mask, but a different one. The 1-bits in the mask set the corresponding bits in the first input, and the 0-bits in the mask leave the corresponding bits in the first input unchanged. This is due to the property we mentioned for the OR operator: if one of the inputs is 1, the output is 1 no matter what the other input is. Setting the bits in a pattern has many applications. For example, if an image uses only one bit per pixel (a black and white image), then we can make a specific pixel white using a mask and the OR operator.

Example 4.8

Use a mask to set the five leftmost bits of a pattern. Test the mask with the pattern 10100110.

Solution
The mask is 11111000. The result of applying the mask is:

		1	0	1	0	0	1	1	0	Input
OR		1	1	1	1	1	0	0	0	Mask
		1	1	1	1	1	1	1	0	Output

Flipping specific bits

One of the applications of the XOR operator is to flip (complement) specific bits in a bit pattern. Again we can use a mask, but a different one. The 1-bits in the mask flip the corresponding bits in the first input, and the 0-bits in the mask leave the corresponding bits in the first input unchanged. This is due to the property we mentioned for the XOR operator: if one of the inputs is 1, the output is the complement of the corresponding bit. Note the difference between the NOT operator and the XOR operator. The NOT operator complements all the bits in the input, while the XOR operator complements only the specific bits in the first input as defined by the mask.

Example 4.9

Use a mask to flip the five leftmost bits of a pattern. Test the mask with the pattern 10100110.

Solution

The mask is 11111000. The result of applying the mask is:

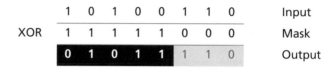

		1	0	1	0	0	1	1	0	Input
XOR		1	1	1	1	1	0	0	0	Mask
		0	1	0	1	1	1	1	0	Output

4.2 SHIFT OPERATIONS

Shift operations move the bits in a pattern, changing the positions of the bits. They can move bits to the left or to the right. We can divide shift operations into two categories: logical shift operations and arithmetic shift operations.

Logical shift operations

A **logical shift operation** is applied to a pattern that does not represent a signed number. The reason is that these shift operations may change the sign of the number that is defined by the leftmost bit in the pattern. We distinguishes two types of logical shift operations, as described below.

Logical shift

A logical right shift operation shifts each bit one position to the right. In an *n*-bit pattern, the rightmost bit is lost and a 0 fills the leftmost bit. A logical left shift operation shifts each bit one position to the left. In an *n*-bit pattern, the leftmost bit is lost and a 0 fills the rightmost bit. Figure 4.3 shows the logical right shift and logical left shift operations for an 8-bit pattern.

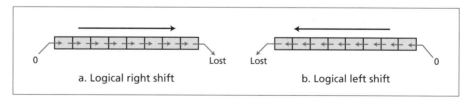

Figure 4.3   Logical shift operations

Example 4.10

Use a logical left shift operation on the bit pattern 10011000.

Solution
The solution is shown below. The leftmost bit is lost and a 0 is inserted as the right-most bit.

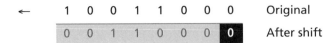

| ← | 1 | 0 | 0 | 1 | 1 | 0 | 0 | 0 | Original |
| | 0 | 0 | 1 | 1 | 0 | 0 | 0 | **0** | After shift |

Circular shift

A **circular shift operation** (or **rotate operation**) shifts bits, but no bit is lost or added. A circular right shift (or *right rotate*) shifts each bit one position to the right. The rightmost bit is circulated and becomes the leftmost bit. A circular left shift (or *left rotate*) shifts each bit one position to the left. The leftmost bit circulates and become the rightmost bit. Figure 4.4 shows the circular shift left and circular shift right operations.

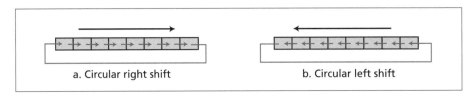

a. Circular right shift   b. Circular left shift

Figure 4.4   Circular shift operations

Example 4.11

Use a circular left shift operation on the bit pattern 10011000.

Solution
The solution is shown below. The leftmost bit is circulated and becomes the right-most bit.

| 1 | 0 | 0 | 1 | 1 | 0 | 0 | 0 | Original |
| 0 | 0 | 1 | 1 | 0 | 0 | 0 | **1** | After shift |

Arithmetic shift operations

Arithmetic shift operations assume that the bit pattern is a signed integer in two's complement format. Arithmetic right shift is used to divide an integer by two, while arithmetic left shift is used to multiply an integer by two (discussed later). These operations should not change the sign (leftmost) bit. An arithmetic right shift retains the sign bit, but also copies it into the next right bit, so that the sign is preserved. An arithmetic left shift discards the sign bit and accepts the bit to the left of the sign bit as the sign. If the new sign bit is the same as the previous one, the operation is successful, otherwise an overflow or underflow has occurred and the result is not valid. Figure 4.5 shows these two operations.

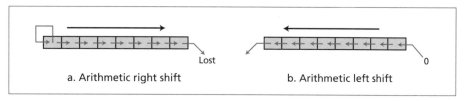

Figure 4.5   Arithmetic shift operations

Example 4.12

Use an arithmetic right shift operation on the bit pattern 10011001. The pattern is an integer in two's complement format.

Solution

The solution is shown below. The leftmost bit is retained and also copied to its right neighbor bit.

1	0	0	1	1	0	0	1	Original
1	1	0	0	1	1	0	0	After shift

The original number was –103 and the new number is –52, which is the result of dividing –103 by 2 truncated to the smaller integer.

Example 4.13

Use an arithmetic left shift operation on the bit pattern 11011001. The pattern is an integer in two's complement format.

Solution

The solution is shown below. The leftmost bit is lost and a 0 is inserted as the rightmost bit.

1	1	0	1	1	0	0	1	Original
1	0	1	1	0	0	1	0	After shift

The original number was –39 and the new number is –78. The original number is multiplied by two. The operation is valid because no underflow occurred.

Example 4.14

Use an arithmetic left shift operation on the bit pattern 01111111. The pattern is an integer in two's complement format.

Solution

The solution is shown below. The leftmost bit is lost and a 0 is inserted as the rightmost bit.

0	1	1	1	1	1	1	1	Original
1	1	1	1	1	1	1	0	After shift

The original number was 127 and the new number is –2. Here the result is not valid because an overflow has occurred. The expected answer $127 \times 2 = 254$ cannot be represented by an 8-bit pattern.

Example 4.15

Combining logic operations and logical shift operations gives us some tools for manipulating bit patterns. Assume that we have a pattern and we need to use the third bit (from the right) of this pattern in a decision-making process. We want to know if this particular bit is 0 or 1. The following shows how we can find out.

	h	g	f	e	d	c	b	a	Original
	0	h	g	f	e	d	c	b	One right shift
	0	0	h	g	f	e	d	c	Two right shifts
AND	0	0	0	0	0	0	0	1	Mask
	0	0	0	0	0	0	0	c	Result

We shift the pattern two bits to the right so that the target bit moves to the right-most position. The result is then ANDed with a mask which has one 1 at the left-most position. The result is a pattern with seven 0s and the target bit at the rightmost position. We can then test the result: if it is an unsigned integer 1, the target bit was 1, whereas if the result is an unsigned integer 0, the target bit was 0.

4.3 ARITHMETIC OPERATIONS

Arithmetic operations involve adding, subtracting, multiplying, and dividing. We can apply these operations to integers and floating-point numbers.

Arithmetic operations on integers

All arithmetic operations such as addition, subtraction, multiplication, and division can be applied to integers. Although multiplication (division) of integers can be implemented using repeated addition (subtraction), the procedure is not efficient. There are more efficient procedures for multiplication and division, such as Booth procedures, but these are beyond the scope of this book. For this reason, we only discuss addition and subtraction of integers here.

Addition and subtraction for two's complement integers

We first discuss addition and subtraction for integers in two's complement representation, because it is easier. As we discussed in Chapter 3, integers are normally stored in two's complement format. One of the advantages of two's complement representation is that there is no difference between addition and subtraction. When the subtraction operation is encountered, the computer simply changes it to an addition operation, but makes two's complement of the second number. In other words:

$$A - B \leftrightarrow A + (\overline{B} + 1) \quad \text{where } ((\overline{B} + 1)) \text{ means the two's complement of B}$$

This means that we only need to discuss addition. Adding numbers in two's complement is like adding the numbers in decimal: we add column by column, and if there is a carry, it is added to the next column. However, the carry produced from the last column is discarded.

We should remember that we add integers column by column. In each column, we have either two bits to add if there is no carry from the previous column, or three bits to add if there is a carry from the previous column. The number of 1s in each column can be zero, one, two, or three. The following table shows the sum and carry (C).

Table 4.1 Carry and sum resulting from adding two bits

Column	Carry	Sum	Column	Carry	Sum
Zero 1s	0	0	Two 1s	1	0
One 1	0	1	Three 1s	1	1

Now we can show the procedure for addition or subtraction of two integers in two's complement format (Figure 4.6). Note that we use the notation $(\overline{X} + 1)$ to mean two's complement of X. This notation is very common in literature because $\overline{X}$ denotes the one's complement of X. If we add 1 to the one's complement of an integer, we get its two's complement.

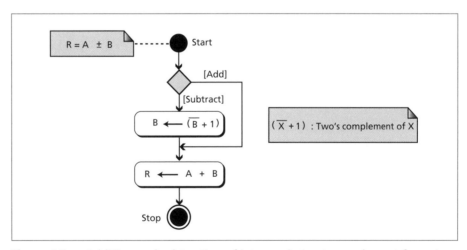

Figure 4.6   Addition and subtraction of integers in two's complement format

The procedure is as follows:

1. If the operation is subtraction, we take the two's complement of the second integer. Otherwise, we move to the next step.
2. We add the two integers.

Example 4.16

Two integers A and B are stored in two's complement format. Show how B is added to A.

$$A = (00010001)_2 \quad B = (00010110)_2$$

Solution

The operation is adding. A is added to B and the result is stored in R.

	1								Carry
	0	0	0	1	0	0	0	1	A
+	0	0	0	1	0	1	1	0	B
	0	0	1	0	0	1	1	1	R

We check the result in decimal: $(+17) + (+22) = (+39)$.

Example 4.17

Two integers A and B are stored in two's complement format. Show how B is added to A.

$$A = (00011000)_2 \quad B = (11101111)_2$$

Solution

The operation is adding. A is added to B and the result is stored in R.

1	1	1	1	1					Carry
	0	0	0	1	1	0	0	0	A
+	1	1	1	0	1	1	1	1	B
	0	0	0	0	0	1	1	1	R

Checking the result in decimal, $(+24) + (-17) = (+7)$.

Example 4.18

Two integers A and B are stored in two's complement format. Show how B is subtracted from A.

$$A = (00011000)_2 \quad B = (11101111)_2$$

Solution

The operation is subtracting. A is added to $(\overline{B} + 1)$ and the result is stored in R.

	1								Carry
	0	0	0	1	1	0	0	0	A
+	0	0	0	1	0	0	0	1	$(\overline{B} + 1)$
	0	0	1	0	1	0	0	1	R

Checking the result in decimal, $(+24) - (-17) = (+41)$.

Example 4.19

Two integers A and B are stored in two's complement format. Show how B is subtracted from A.

$$A = (11011101)_2 \quad B = (00010100)_2$$

Solution

The operation is subtracting. A is added to $(\overline{B} + 1)$ and the result is stored in R.

	1	1	1	1	1	1			Carry
		1	1	0	1	1	1	0	1	A
+	1	1	1	0	1	1	0	0	$(\overline{B} + 1)$
	1	1	0	0	1	0	0	1	R

Note that the last carry is discarded. Checking the result in decimal, $(-35) - (+20) = (-55)$.

Example 4.20

Two integers A and B are stored in two's complement format. Show how B is added to A.

$$A = (01111111)_2 \quad B = (00000011)_2$$

Solution

The operation is adding. A is added to B and the result is stored in R.

	1	1	1	1	1	1	1		Carry
	0	1	1	1	1	1	1	1	A
+	0	0	0	0	0	0	1	1	B
	1	0	0	0	0	0	1	0	R

We expect the result to be $127 + 3 = 130$, but the answer is -126. The error is due to overflow, because the expected answer $(+130)$ is not in the range -128 to $+127$.

> When we do arithmetic operations on numbers in a computer, we should remember that each number and the result should be in the range defined by the bit allocation.

Addition or subtraction for sign-and-magnitude integers

Addition and subtraction for integers in sign-and-magnitude representation looks very complex. We have four different combination of signs (two signs, each of two values) for addition, and four different conditions for subtraction. This means that we need to consider eight different situations. However, if we first check the signs, we can reduce these cases, as shown in Figure 4.7.

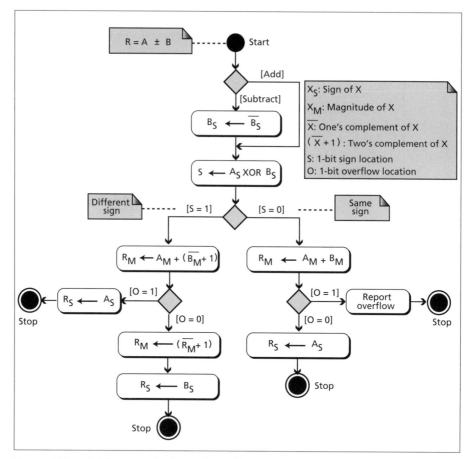

Figure 4.7   Addition and subtraction of integers in sign-and-magnitude format

Let us first explain the diagram:

1. We check the operation. If the operation is subtraction, we change the sign of the second integer (B). This means we now only have to worry about addition of two signed integers.

2. We apply the XOR operation to the two signs. If the result (stored in temporary location S) is 0, it means that the signs are the same (either both signs are positive or both are negative).

3. If the signs are the same, $R = \pm (A_M + B_M)$. We need to add the magnitude and the sign of the result is the common sign. So, we have:

$$R_M = (A_M) + (B_M) \quad \text{and} \quad R_S = A_S$$

where the subscript M means magnitude and subscript S means sign. In this case, however, we should be careful about the overflow. When we add the two magnitudes, an overflow may occur that must be reported and the process aborted.

4. If the signs are different, $R = \pm (A_M - B_M)$. So we need to subtract B_M from A_M and then make a decision about the sign. Instead of subtracting bit by bit, we take the two's complement of the second magnitude (B_M) and add them. The sign of the result is the sign of the integer with larger magnitude.

    a. It can be shown that if $A_M \geq B_M$, there is an overflow and the result is a positive number. Therefore, if there is an overflow, we discard the overflow and let the sign of the result be the sign of A.

    b. It can be shown that if $A_M < B_M$, there is no overflow, but the result is a negative number. So if there is no overflow, we make the two's complement of the result and let the sign of the result be the sign of B.

Example 4.21

Two integers A and B are stored in sign-and-magnitude format (we have separated the sign from the magnitude for clarity). Show how B is added to A.

$$A = (0\ 0010001)_2 \quad B = (0\ 0010110)_2$$

Solution

The operation is adding: the sign of B is not changed. Since $S = A_S$ XOR $B_S = 0$, $R_M = A_M + B_M$ and $R_S = A_S$. There is no overflow.

	No overflow			1					Carry
A_S	**0**		0	0	1	0	0	0	1	A_M
B_S	**0**	+	0	0	1	0	1	1	0	B_M
R_S	**0**		0	1	0	0	1	1	1	R_M

Checking the result in decimal, $(+17) + (+22) = (+39)$.

Example 4.22

Two integers A and B are stored in sign-and-magnitude format. Show how B is added to A.

$$A = (0\ 0010001)_2 \quad B = (1\ 0010110)_2$$

Solution

The operation is adding: the sign of B is not changed. $S = A_S$ XOR $B_S = 1$; $R_M = A_M + (\overline{B}_M + 1)$. Since there is no overflow, we need to take the two's complement of R_M. The sign of R is the sign of B.

	No overflow								Carry
A_S	**0**		0	0	1	0	0	0	1	A_M
B_S	**1**	+	1	1	0	1	0	1	0	$(\overline{B}_M + 1)$
			1	1	1	1	0	1	1	R_M
R_S	**1**		0	0	0	0	1	0	1	$R_M = \overline{(R_M + 1)}$

Checking the result in decimal, $(+17) + (-22) = (-5)$.

Example 4.23

Two integers A and B are stored in sign-and-magnitude format. Show how B is subtracted from A.

$$A = (1\ 1010001)_2 \quad B = (1\ 0010110)_2$$

Solution

The operation is subtracting: $B_S = \overline{B}_S$. $S = A_S$ XOR $B_S = 1$, $R_M = A_M + (\overline{B}_M + 1)$. Since there is an overflow, the value of R_M is final. The sign of R is the sign of A.

			Overflow →	1								Carry
A_S	1				1	0	1	0	0	0	1	A_M
B_S	1		+		1	1	0	1	0	1	0	$(\overline{B}_M + 1)$
R_S	1				0	1	1	1	0	1	1	R_M

Checking the result in decimal, $(-81) - (-22) = (-59)$.

Arithmetic operations on reals

All arithmetic operations such as addition, subtraction, multiplication, and division can be applied to reals stored in floating-point format. Multiplication of two reals involves multiplication of two integers in sign-and-magnitude representation. Division of two reals involves division of two integers in sign-and-magnitude representations. Since we did not discuss the multiplication or division of integers in sign-and-magnitude representation, we will not discuss the multiplication and division of reals, and only show addition and subtraction for reals.

Addition and subtraction of reals

Addition and subtraction of real numbers stored in floating-point numbers is reduced to addition and subtraction of two integers stored in sign-and-magnitude (combination of sign and mantissa) after the alignment of decimal points. Figure 4.8 shows a simplified version of the procedure (there are some special cases that we have ignored).

The simplified procedure works as follows:

1. If any of the two numbers (A or B) is zero, we let the result be 0 and stop.
2. If the operation is subtraction, we change the sign of the second number (B) to simulate addition.
3. We denormalize both numbers by including the hidden 1 in the mantissa and incrementing the exponents. The mantissa is now treated as an integer.
4. We then align the exponents, which means that we increment the lower exponent and shift the corresponding mantissa until both have the same exponent. For example, if we have:

$$1.11101 \times 2^4 + 1.01 \times 2^2$$

We need to make both exponents 4:

$$1.11101 \times 2^4 + 0.0101 \times 2^4$$

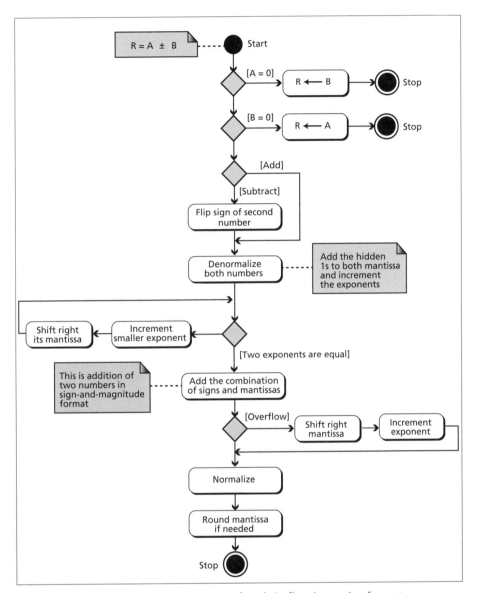

Figure 4.8   Addition and subtraction of reals in floating-point format

5. Now, we treat the combination of the sign and mantissa of each number as an integer in sign-and-magnitude format. We add these two integers, as explained earlier in this chapter.

6. Finally, we normalized the number again to 1.000111×2^5.

Example 4.24

Show how the computer finds the result of $(+5.75) + (+161.875) = (+167.625)$.

Solution

As we saw in Chapter 3, these two numbers are stored in floating-point format, as shown below, but we need to remember that each number has a hidden 1 (which is not stored, but assumed).

	S	E	M
A	0	10000001	0111000000000000000000000
B	0	10000110	0100001111000000000000000

The first few steps in the UML diagram (Figure 4.8) are not needed. We move to denormalization and denormalize the numbers by adding the hidden 1s to the mantissa and incrementing the exponent. Now both denormalized mantissas are 24 bits and include the hidden 1s. They should be stored in a location that can hold all 24 bits. Each exponent is incremented.

	S	E	Denormalized M
A	0	10000010	101110000000000000000000
B	0	10000111	101000011110000000000000

Now we need to align the mantissas. We need to increment the first exponent and shift its mantissa to the right. We change the first exponent to $(10000111)_2$, so we need to shift the first mantissa right by five positions.

	S	E	Denormalized M
A	0	10000111	000001011100000000000000
B	0	10000111	101000011110000000000000

Now we do sign-and-magnitude addition, treating the sign and the mantissa of each number as one integer stored in sign-and-magnitude representation.

	S	E	Denormalized M
R	0	10000111	101001111010000000000000

There is no overflow in the mantissa, so we normalize.

	S	E	M
R	0	10000110	0100111101000000000000000

The mantissa is only 23 bits, no rounding is needed. E = $(10000110)_2$ = 134 M = 0100111101. In other words, the result is $(1.0100111101)_2 \times 2^{134-127}$ = $(10100111.101)_2$ = 167.625.

Example 4.25

Show how the computer finds the result of $(+5.75) + (-7.0234375) = -1.2734375$.

Solution

These two numbers can be stored in floating-point format, as shown below:

	S	E	M
A	0	10000001	01110000000000000000000
B	1	10000001	11000001100000000000000

Denormalization results in:

	S	E	Denormalized M
A	0	10000010	101110000000000000000000
B	1	10000010	111000001100000000000000

Alignment is not needed (both exponents are the same), so we apply addition operation on the combinations of sign and mantissa. The result is shown below, in which the sign of the result is negative:

	S	E	Denormalized M
R	1	10000010	001010001100000000000000

Now we need to normalize. We decrement the exponent three times and shift the denormalized mantissa to the left three positions:

	S	E	M
R	1	01111111	010001100000000000000000

The mantissa is now 24 bits, so we round it to 23 bits.

	S	E	M
R	1	01111111	01000110000000000000000

The result is $R = -2^{127-127} \times 1.0100011 = -1.2734375$, as expected.

4.4 RECOMMENDED READING

For more details about the subjects discussed in this chapter, the following books are recommended:

❑   Mano M: *Computer System Architecture*, Upper Saddle River, NJ: Prentice Hall, 1993

❑   Null L and Lobur J: *Computer Organization and Architecture*, Sudbury, MA: Jones and Bartlett, 2003

❑   Stalling, W: *Computer Organization and Architecture*, Upper Saddle River, NJ: Prentice Hall, 2000.

4.5 KEY TERMS

This chapter has introduced the following key terms, which are listed here with the pages on which they first occur:

AND operation 79	arithmetic operation 86
arithmetic shift operation 84	Boolean algebra 78
circular shift operation 84	logic operation 78
logical shift operation 83	mask 81
NOT operation 79	OR operation 79
rotate operation 84	set 81
truth table 78	unset 81
XOR operation 79	

4.6 SUMMARY

• Operations on data can be divided into three broad categories: logic operations, shift operations, and arithmetic operations. Logic operations refer to those operations that apply the same basic operation to individual bits of a pattern or to two corresponding bits in two patterns. Shift operations move the bits in the pattern. Arithmetic operations involve adding, subtracting, multiplying, and dividing.

• The four logic operators discussed in this chapter (NOT, AND, OR, and XOR) can be used at the bit level or the pattern level. The NOT operator is a unary operator, while the AND, OR, and XOR operators are binary operators.

• The only application of the NOT operator is to complement the whole pattern. One of the applications of the AND operator is to unset (force to 0) specific bits in a bit pattern. One of the applications of the OR operator is to set (force to 1) specific bits in a bit pattern. One of the applications of the XOR operator is to flip (complement) specific bits in a bit pattern.

• Shift operations move the bits in the pattern: they change the positions of the bits. We can divide shift operations into two categories: logical shift operations and arithmetic shift operations. A logical shift operation is applied to a pattern that does not represent a signed number. Arithmetic shift operations assume that the bit pattern is a signed integer in two's complement format.

• All arithmetic operations such as addition, subtraction, multiplication, and division can be applied to integers. Integers are normally stored in two's complement format. One of the advantages of two's complement representation is that there is no difference between addition and subtraction. When the subtraction operation is encountered, the computer simply changes it to an addition operation, but forms the two's complement of the second number. Addition and subtraction for integers in sign-and-magnitude representation looks very complex. We have eight situations to consider.

- All arithmetic operations such as addition, subtraction, multiplication, and division can be applied to reals stored in floating-point format. Addition and subtraction of real numbers stored in floating-point numbers is reduced to addition and subtraction of two integers stored in sign and magnitude after the alignment of decimal points.

4.7   PRACTICE SET

Review questions

1. What is the difference between an arithmetic operation and a logical operation?
2. What happens to the carry from the leftmost column in the addition of integers in two's complement format?
3. Can n, the bit allocation, equal 1? Why, or why not?
4. Define the term *overflow*.
5. In the addition of floating-point numbers, how do we adjust the representation of numbers with different exponents?
6. What is the difference between a unary operation and a binary operation?
7. Name the logical binary operations.
8. What is a truth table?
9. What does the NOT operator do?
10. When is the result of an AND operator true?
11. When is the result of an OR operator true?
12. When is the result of an XOR operator true?
13. Mention an important property of the AND operator discussed in this chapter.
14. Mention an important property of the OR operator discussed in this chapter.
15. Mention an important property of the XOR operator discussed in this chapter.
16. What binary operation can be used to set bits? What bit pattern should the mask have?
17. What binary operation can be used to unset bits? What bit pattern should the mask have?
18. What binary operation can be used to flip bits? What bit pattern should the mask have?
19. What is the difference between logical and arithmetic shifts?

Multiple-choice questions

20. _____ is an arithmetic bit operation.
    a. The exclusive OR
    b. The unary NOT
    c. Subtraction
    d. All of the above
21. _____ is a logical bit operator.
    a. The exclusive OR
    b. The unary NOT
    c. The binary AND
    d. All of the above
22. The _____ method of integer representation is the most common method for storing integers in computer memory.
    a. sign-and-magnitude
    b. one's complement
    c. two's complement
    d. unsigned integers
23. In two's complement addition, if there is a final carry after the leftmost column addition, _____.
    a. add it to the rightmost column
    b. add it to the leftmost column
    c. discard it
    d. increase the bit length

24. For an 8-bit allocation, the smallest decimal number that can be represented in two's complement form is _____.
    a. −8
    b. −127
    c. −128
    d. −256

25. For an 8-bit allocation, the largest decimal number that can be represented in two's complement form is _____.
    a. 8
    b. 127
    c. 128
    d. 256

26. In two's complement representation with a 4-bit allocation, we get _____ when we add 1 to 7.
    a. 8
    b. 1
    c. −7
    d. −8

27. In two's complement representation with a 4-bit allocation, we get _____ when we add 5 to 5.
    a. −5
    b. −6
    c. −7
    d. 10

28. If the exponent in Excess_127 is binary 10000101, the exponent in decimal is _____.
    a. 6
    b. 7
    c. 8
    d. 9

29. If we are adding two numbers, one of which has an exponent value of 7 and the other an exponent value of 9, we need to shift the decimal point of the smaller number _____.
    a. one place to the left
    b. one place to the right
    c. two places to the left
    d. two places to the right

30. The binary _____ operator takes two inputs to produce one output.
    a. AND

    b. OR
    c. XOR
    d. all of the above

31. The unary _____ operator inverts its single input.
    a. AND
    b. OR
    c. NOT
    d. XOR

32. For the binary _____ operator, if the input is two 0s, the output is 0.
    a. AND
    b. OR
    c. XOR
    d. all of the above

33. For the binary _____ operator, if the input is two 1s, the output is 0.
    a. AND
    b. OR
    c. XOR
    d. all of the above

34. For the binary AND operation, only an input of _____ gives an output of 1.
    a. two 0s
    b. two 1s
    c. one 0 and one 1
    d. any of the above

35. For the binary OR operation, only an input of _____ gives an output of 0.
    a. two 0s
    b. two 1s
    c. one 0 and one 1
    d. any of the above

36. We use a bit pattern called a _____ to modify another bit pattern.
    a. mask
    b. carry
    c. float
    d. byte

37. To flip all the bits of a bit pattern, make a mask of all 1s and then _____ the bit pattern and the mask.
    a. AND
    b. OR

c. XOR

d. NOT

38. To unset (force to 0) all the bits of a bit pattern, make a mask of all 0s and then _____ the bit pattern and the mask.

a. AND

b. OR

c. XOR

d. NOT

39. To set (force to 1) all the bits of a bit pattern, make a mask of all 1s and then _____ the bit pattern and the mask.

a. AND

b. OR

c. XOR

d. NOT

Exercises

40. Show the result of the following operations:

a. NOT $(99)_{16}$

b. NOT $(FF)_{16}$

c. NOT $(00)_{16}$

d. NOT $(01)_{16}$

41. Show the result of the following operations:

a. $(99)_{16}$ AND $(99)_{16}$

b. $(99)_{16}$ AND $(00)_{16}$

c. $(99)_{16}$ AND $(FF)_{16}$

d. $(FF)_{16}$ AND $(FF)_{16}$

42. Show the result of the following operations:

a. $(99)_{16}$ OR $(99)_{16}$

b. $(99)_{16}$ OR $(00)_{16}$

c. $(99)_{16}$ OR $(FF)_{16}$

d. $(FF)_{16}$ OR $(FF)_{16}$

43. Show the result of the following operations:

a. NOT $[(99)_{16}$ OR $(99)_{16}]$

b. $(99)_{16}$ OR $[NOT (00)_{16}]$

c. $[(99)_{16}$ AND $(33)_{16}]$ OR $[(00)_{16}$ AND $(FF)_{16}]$

d. $(99)_{16}$ OR $(33)_{16}$ AND $[(00)_{16}$ OR $(FF)_{16}]$

44. We need to unset (force to 0) the four leftmost bits of a pattern. Show the mask and the operation.

45. We need to set (force to 1) the four rightmost bits of a pattern. Show the mask and the operation.

46. We need to flip the three rightmost and the two leftmost bits of a pattern. Show the mask and the operation.

47. We need to unset the three leftmost bits and set the two rightmost bits of a pattern. Show the masks and operations.

48. Use the shift operation to divide an integer by 4.

49. Use the shift operation to multiply an integer by 8.

50. Use a combination of logical and shift operations to extract the fourth and fifth bits of an unsigned integer.

51. Using an 8-bit allocation, first convert each of the following integers to two's complement, do the operation, and then convert the result to decimal.

a. 19 + 23

b. 19 – 23

c. –19 + 23

d. –19 – 23

52. Using a 16-bit allocation, first convert each of the following numbers to two's complement, do the operation, and then convert the result to decimal.

a. 161 + 1023

b. 161 – 1023

c. –161 + 1023

d. –161 –1023

53. Which of the following operations creates an overflow if the numbers and the result are represented in 8-bit two's complement representation?

a. 11000010 + 00111111

b. 00000010 + 00111111

c. 11000010 + 11111111

d. 00000010 + 11111111

54. Without actually doing the calculation, can we tell which of the following creates an overflow if the numbers and the result are in 8-bit two's complement representation?

   a. 32 + 105
   b. 32 − 105
   c. −32 + 105
   d. −32 − 105

55. Show the result of the following operations assuming that the numbers are stored in 16-bit two's complement representation. Show the result in hexadecimal notation.

   a. $(012A)_{16} + (0E27)_{16}$
   b. $(712A)_{16} + (9E00)_{16}$
   c. $(8011)_{16} + (0001)_{16}$
   d. $(E12A)_{16} + (9E27)_{16}$

56. Using an 8-bit allocation, first convert each of the following numbers to sign-and-magnitude representation, do the operation, and then convert the result to decimal.

   a. 19 + 23
   b. 19 − 23
   c. −19 + 23
   d. −19 − 23

57. Show the result of the following floating-point operations using IEEE_127—see Chapter 3.

   a. 34.75 + 23.125
   b. −12.625 + 451.00
   c. 33.1875 − 0.4375
   d. −344.3125 − 123.5625

58. In which of the following situations does an overflow never occur? Justify the answer.

   a. Adding two positive integers.
   b. Adding one positive integer to a negative integer.
   c. Subtracting one positive integer from a negative integer.
   d. Subtracting two negative integers.

59. What is the result of adding an integer to its one's complement?

60. What is the result of adding an integer to its two's complement?

5 Computer Organization

In this chapter we discuss the organization of a stand-alone computer. We explain how every computer is made up of three subsystems. We also show how a simple, hypothetical computer can run a simple program to perform primitive arithmetic or logic operations.

Objectives

After studying this chapter, the student should be able to:

❑ List the three subsystems of a computer.

❑ Describe the role of the central processing unit (CPU) in a computer.

❑ Describe the fetch-decode-execute phases of a cycle in a typical computer.

❑ Describe the main memory and its addressing space.

❑ Distinguish between main memory and cache memory.

❑ Define the input/output subsystem.

❑ Understand the interconnection of subsystems and list different bus systems.

❑ Describe different methods of input/output addressing.

❑ Distinguish the two major trends in the design of computer architecture.

❑ Understand how computer throughput can be improved using pipelining.

❑ Understand how parallel processing can improve the throughput of computers.

We can divide the parts that make up a computer into three broad categories or subsystem: the central processing unit (CPU), the main memory, and the input/output subsystem. The next three sections discusses these subsystems and how they are connected to make a standalone computer. Figure 5.1 shows the three subsystems of a standalone computer.

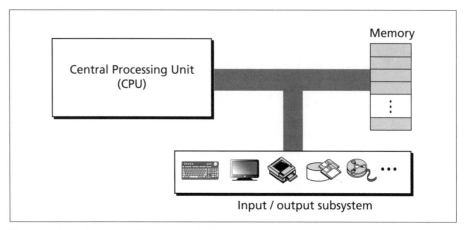

Figure 5.1   Computer hardware (subsystems)

5.1   CENTRAL PROCESSING UNIT

The **central processing unit (CPU)** performs operations on data. In most architectures it has three parts: an arithmetic logic unit (ALU), a control unit, and a set of registers, fast storage locations (Figure 5.2).

The arithmetic logic unit (ALU)

The **arithmetic logic unit (ALU)** performs logic, shift, and arithmetic operations on data.

Logic operations

We discussed several logic operations, such as NOT, AND, OR, and XOR, in Chapter 4. These operations treat the input data as bit patterns and the result of the operation is also a bit pattern.

Shift operations

We discussed two groups of shift operations on data in Chapter 4: logical shift operations and arithmetic shift operations. Logical shift operations are used to shift bit patterns to the left or right, while logical arithmetic operations are applied to integers. Their main purpose is to divide or multiply integers by two.

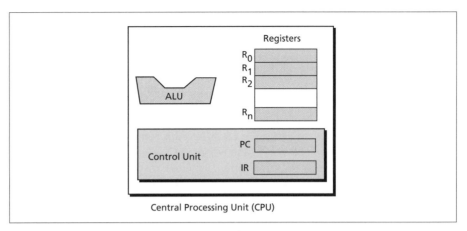

Figure 5.2 Central processing unit (CPU)

Arithmetic operation

We discussed some arithmetic operations on integers and reals in Chapter 4. We mention that some operations can be implemented more efficiently in hardware.

Registers

Registers are fast stand-alone storage locations that hold data temporarily. Multiple registers are needed to facilitate the operation of the CPU. Some of these registers are shown in Figure 5.2.

Data registers

In the past computers had only a few data registers to hold the input data and the result of the operations. Today, computers use dozens of registers inside the CPU to speed up their operations, because complex operations are done using hardware instead of software. These require several registers to hold the intermediate results. Data registers are named R_1 to R_n in Figure 5.2.

Instruction registers

Today computers store not only data, but also programs, in their memory. The CPU is responsible for fetching instructions one by one from memory, storing them in the **instruction register** (register IR in Figure 5.2), decoding them, and executing them. We will discuss this issue later in the chapter.

Program counter

Another common register in the CPU is the **program counter** (PC in Figure 5.2). The program counter keeps track of the instruction currently being executed. After execution of the instruction, the counter is incremented to point to the address of the next instruction in memory.

The control unit

The third part of any CPU is the control unit. The **control unit** controls the operation of each subsystem. Controlling is achieved through signals sent from the control unit to other subsystems.

5.2 MAIN MEMORY

Main memory is the second major subsystem in a computer (Figure 5.3). It consists of a collection of storage locations, each with a unique identifier, called an *address*. Data is transferred to and from memory in groups of bits called *words*. A word can be a group of 8 bits, 16 bits, 32 bits, or 64 bits (and growing). If the word is 8 bits, it is referred to as a *byte*. The term "byte" is so common in computer science that sometimes a 16-bit word is referred to as a 2-byte word, or a 32-bit word is referred to as a 4-byte word.

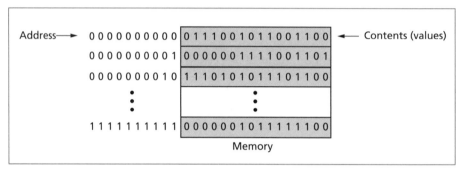

Figure 5.3   Main memory

Address space

To access a word in memory requires an identifier. Although programmers use a name to identify a word (or a collection of words), at the hardware level each word is identified by an address. The total number of uniquely identifiable locations in memory is called the **address space**. For example, a memory with 64 kilobytes and a word size of 1 byte has an address space that ranges from 0 to 65,535.

Table 5.1 shows the units used to refer to memory. Note that the terminology is misleading: it approximates the number of bytes in powers of 10, but the actual number of bytes is in powers of 2. Units in powers of 2 facilitates addressing.

Table 5.1   Memory units

Unit	Exact number of bytes	Approximation
kilobyte	2^{10} (1024) bytes	10^3 bytes
megabyte	2^{20} (1,048,576) bytes	10^6 bytes
gigabyte	2^{30} (1,073,741,824) bytes	10^9 bytes
terabyte	2^{40} bytes	10^{12} bytes

Addresses as bit patterns   Because computers operate by storing numbers as bit patterns, a memory address is also represented as a bit pattern. So if a computer has 64 kilobytes (2^{16}) of memory with a word size of 1 byte, we need a bit pattern of 16 bits to define an address. Recall from Chapter 3 that addresses can be represented as unsigned integers (we do not have negative addresses). In other words, the first location is referred to as address 0000000000000000 (address 0), and the last location is referred to as address 1111111111111111 (address 65535). In general, if a computer has N words of memory, we need an unsigned integer of size $\log_2 N$ bits to refer to each memory location.

> **Memory addresses are defined using unsigned binary integers.**

Example 5.1

A computer has 32 MB (megabytes) of memory. How many bits are needed to address any single byte in memory?

Solution
The memory address space is 32 MB, or 2^{25} ($2^5 \times 2^{20}$). This means that we need $\log_2 2^{25}$, or 25 bits, to address each byte.

Example 5.2

A computer has 128 MB of memory. Each word in this computer is eight bytes. How many bits are needed to address any single word in memory?

Solution
The memory address space is 128 MB, which means 2^{27}. However, each word is eight (2^3) bytes, which means that we have 2^{24} words. This means that we need $\log_2 2^{24}$, or 24 bits, to address each word.

Memory types

Two main types of memory exist: RAM and ROM.

RAM

Random access memory (RAM) makes up most of the main memory in a computer. In a random access device, a data item can be accessed randomly—using the address of the memory location—without the need to access all data items located before it. However, the term is confusing, because ROM can also be accessed randomly. What distinguishes RAM from ROM is that RAM can be read from and written to. The CPU can write something to RAM and later overwrite it. Another characteristic of RAM is that it is *volatile*: the information (program or data) is lost if the computer is powered down. In other words, all information in RAM is erased if you turn off the computer or if there is a power outage. RAM technology is divided into two broad categories: SRAM and DRAM.

SRAM

Static RAM (SRAM) technology uses traditional *flip-flop gates* (see Appendix E) to hold data. The gates hold their state (0 or 1), which means that data is stored as long as the power is on and there is no need to refresh memory locations. SRAM is fast but expensive.

DRAM

Dynamic RAM (DRAM) technology uses capacitors, electrical devices that can store energy, for data storage. If a capacitor is charged, the state is 1, if it is discharged, the state is 0. Because a capacitor loses some of its charge with time, DRAM memory cells need to be refreshed periodically. DRAMs are slow but inexpensive.

ROM

The contents of **read-only memory (ROM)** are written by the manufacturer, and the CPU can read from, but not write to, ROM. Its advantage is that it is *nonvolatile*—its contents are not lost if you turn off the computer. Normally, it is used for programs or data that must not be erased or changed even if you turn off the computer. For example, some computers come with ROM that holds the *boot program* that runs when we switch on the computer.

PROM

One variation of ROM is **programmable read-only memory (PROM)**. This type of memory is blank when the computer is shipped. The user of the computer, with some special equipment, can store programs on it. When programs are stored, it behaves like ROM and cannot be overwritten. This allows a computer user to store specific programs in PROM.

EPROM

A variation of PROM is **erasable programmable read-only memory (EPROM)**. It can be programmed by the user, but can also be erased with a special device that applies ultraviolet light. To erase EPROM memory requires physical removal and reinstallation of the EPROM.

EEPROM

A variation of EPROM is **electrically erasable programmable read-only memory (EEPROM)**. EEPROM can be programmed and erased using electronic impulses without being removed from the computer.

Memory hierarchy

Computer users need a lot of memory, especially memory that is very fast and inexpensive. This demand is not always possible to satisfy—very fast memory is usually not cheap. A compromise needs to be made. The solution is hierarchical levels of memory (Figure 5.4). The hierarchy is based on the following:

❑ Using a very small amount of costly high-speed memory where speed is crucial. The registers inside the CPU are of this type.

❑ Using a moderate amount of medium-speed memory to store data that is accessed often. *Cache memory*, discussed next, is of this type.

❑ Using a large amount of low-speed memory for data that is accessed very often. Main memory is of this type.

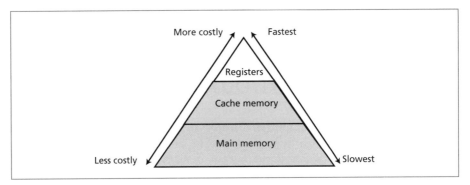

Figure 5.4 Memory hierarchy

Cache memory

Cache memory is faster than main memory but slower than the CPU and its registers. Cache memory, which is normally small in size, is placed between the CPU and main memory (Figure 5.5).

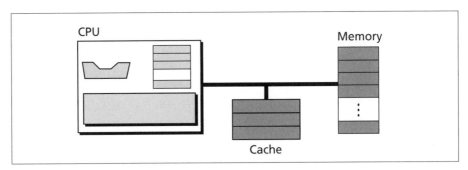

Figure 5.5 Cache memory

Cache memory at any time contains a copy of a portion of main memory. When the CPU needs to access a word in main memory, it follows this procedure:

1. The CPU checks the cache.
2. If the word is there, it copies the word: if not, the CPU accesses main memory and copies a block of memory starting with the desired word. This block replaces the previous contents of cache memory.
3. The CPU accesses the cache and copies the word.

This procedure can expedite operations: if the word is in the cache, it is accessed immediately. If the word is not in the cache, the word and a whole block are copied to the cache. Since it is probable that the CPU, in its next cycle, will need to access the words following the first word, the existence of the cache speeds processing.

We might wonder why cache memory is so efficient despite its small size. The answer lies in the "80–20 rule". It has been observed that most computers typically spend 80 percent of their time accessing only ·20 percent of the data. In other words, the same data is accessed over and over again. Cache memory, with its high speed, can hold this 20 percent to make access faster at least 80 percent of the time.

5.3   INPUT/OUTPUT SUBSYSTEM

The third major subsystem in a computer is the collection of devices referred to as the **input/output (I/O) subsystem**. This subsystem allows a computer to communicate with the outside world, and to store programs and data even when the power is off. Input/output devices can be divided into two broad categories: nonstorage and storage devices.

Nonstorage devices

Nonstorage devices allow the CPU/memory to communicate with the outside world, but they cannot store information.

Keyboard and monitor

Two of the more common nonstorage input/output devices are the keyboard and the monitor. The **keyboard** provides input, the **monitor** displays output and at the same time echoes input typed on the keyboard. Programs, commands, and data are input or output using strings of characters. The characters are encoded using a code such as ASCII (see Appendix A). Other devices that fall in this category are *mice*, *joysticks*, and so on.

Printer

A **printer** is an output device that creates a permanent record. A printer is a nonstorage device because the printed material cannot be entered directly into a computer again unless someone retypes or scans it.

Storage devices

Storage devices, although classified as I/O devices, can store large amounts of information to be retrieved at a later time. They are cheaper than main memory, and their contents are nonvolatile—that is, not erased when the power is turned off. They are sometimes referred to as *auxiliary storage devices*. We can categorize them as either magnetic or optical.

Magnetic storage devices

Magnetic storage devices use magnetization to store bits of data. If a location is magnetized, it represents 1, if not magnetized, it represents 0.

Magnetic disks

A **magnetic disk** consists of one or more disks stacked on top of each other. The disks are coated with a thin magnetic film. Information is stored on and retrieved from the surface of the disk using a **read/write head** for each magnetized surface of the disk. Figure 5.6 shows the physical layout of a magnetic disk drive and the organization of a disk.

❑   **Surface organization.** To organize data stored on the disk, each surface is divided into **tracks**, and each track is divided into **sectors** (Figure 5.6). The

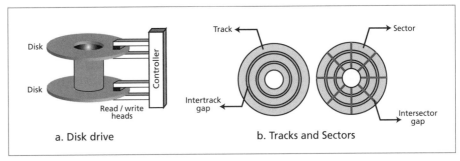

Figure 5.6 A magnetic disk

tracks are separated by an **intertrack gap**, and the sectors are separated by an **intersector gap**.

❑ **Data access**. A magnetic disk is considered a random access device. In a random access device, a data item can be access randomly without the need to access all other data items located before it. However, the smallest storage area that can be accessed at one time is a sector. A block of data can be stored in one or more sectors and retrieved without the need to retrieve the rest of the information on the disk.

❑ **Performance**. The performance of a disk depends on several factors, the most important being the rotational speed, the seek time, and the transfer time. The **rotational speed** defines how fast the disk is spinning. The **seek time** defines the time to move the read/write head to the desired track where the data is stored. The **transfer time** defines the time to move data from the disk to the CPU/memory.

Magnetic tape

Magnetic tape comes in various sizes. One common type is half- inch plastic tape coated with a thick magnetic film. The tape is mounted on two reels and uses a read/write head that reads or writes information when the tape is passed through it. Figure 5.7 shows the mechanical configuration of a magnetic tape drive.

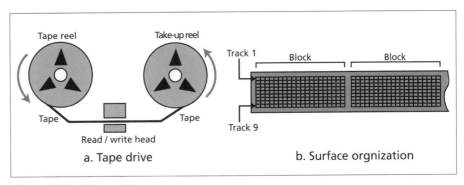

Figure 5.7 Magnetic tape

❑ **Surface organization**. The width of the tape is divided into nine tracks, each location on a track storing 1 bit of information. Nine vertical locations can store 8 bits of information related to a byte plus a bit for error detection (Figure 5.7).

❑ **Data access**. A magnetic tape is considered a sequential access device. Although the surface may be divided into blocks, there is no addressing mechanism to access each block. To retrieve a specific block on the tape, we need to pass through all the previous blocks.

❑ **Performance**. Although magnetic tape is slower than a magnetic disk, it is cheaper. Today, people use magnetic tape to back up large amounts of data.

Optical storage devices

Optical storage devices, a relatively recent technology, use laser light to store and retrieve data. The use of optical storage technology followed the invention of the compact disk (CD) used to store audio information. Today, the same technology—slightly improved—is used to store information in a computer. Devices that use this technology include CD-ROMs, CD-Rs, CD-RWs, and DVDs.

CD-ROMs

Compact disk read-only memory (CD-ROM) disks use the same technology as the audio CD, originally developed by Phillips and Sony for recording music. The only difference between these two technologies is enhancement: a CD-ROM drive is more robust and checks for errors. Figure 5.8 shows the steps involved in creating and using a CD-ROM.

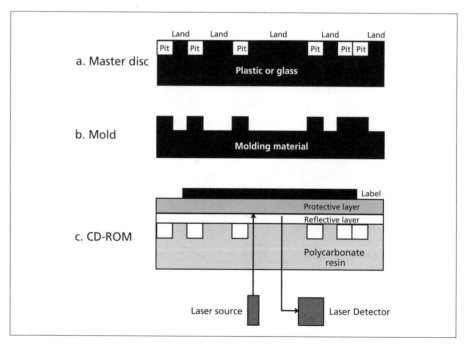

Figure 5.8   Creation and use of CD-ROMs

❑ **Creation**. CD-ROM technology uses three steps to create a large number of discs:

a. A **master disk** is created using a high-power infrared laser that creates bit patterns on coated plastic. The laser translates the bit patterns into a sequence of **pits** (holes) and **lands** (no holes). The pits usually represent 0s and the lands usually represent 1s. However, this is only a convention, and it can be reversed. Other schemes use a transition (pit to hole or hole to pit) to represent 1, and a lack of transition to represent 0.

b. From the master disk, a mold is made. In the mold, the pits (holes) are replaced by bumps.

c. Molten **polycarbonate resin** is injected into the mold to produce the same pits as the master disk. A very thin layer of aluminum is added to the polycarbonate to provide a reflective surface. On top of this, a protective layer of lacquer is applied and a label is added. Only this last step needs to be repeated for each disk.

❑ **Reading**. The CD-ROM is read using a low-power laser beam. The beam is reflected by the aluminum surface when passing through a land. It is reflected twice when it encounters a pit, once by the pit boundary and once by the aluminum boundary. The two reflections have a destructive effect, because the depth of the pit is chosen to be exactly one-fourth of the beam wavelength. In other words, the sensor installed in the drive detects more light when the location is a land and less light when the location is a pit, so can read what was recorded on the original master disk and copied to the CD-ROM.

❑ **Format**. CD-ROM technology uses a different format than magnetic disk (Figure 5.9). The format of data on a CD-ROM is based on:

a. A block of 8-bit data transformed into a 14-bit symbol using an error-correction method called Hamming code.

b. A frame made up from 42 symbols (14 bits/symbol).

c. A sector made up from 98 frames (2352 bytes).

❑ **Speed**. CD-ROM drives come in different speeds. Single speed is referred to as 1x, double speed 2x, and so on. If the drive is single speed, it can read up to 153,600 bytes per second. Table 5.2 shows the speeds and their corresponding data rates.

Table 5.2 CD-ROM speeds

Speed	Data rate	Approximation
1x	153,600 bytes per second	150 KB/s
2x	307,200 bytes per second	300 KB/s
4x	614,400 bytes per second	600 KB/s
6x	921,600 bytes per second	900 KB/s

Table 5.2   CD-ROM speeds (continued)

Speed	Data rate	Approximation
8x	1,228,800 bytes per second	1.2 MB/s
12x	1,843,200 bytes per second	1.8 MB/s
16x	2,457,600 bytes per second	2.4 MB/s
24x	3,688,400 bytes per second	3.6 MB/s
32x	4,915,200 bytes per second	4.8 MB/s
40x	6,144,000 bytes per second	6 MB/s

❑ **Application**. The expense involved in creating a master disk, mold, and the actual disk can be justified if there are a large number of potential customers. In other words, this technology is economical if the discs are mass produced.

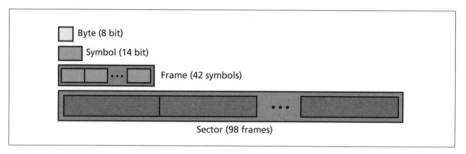

Figure 5.9   CD-ROM format

CD-R

Clearly, CD-ROM technology is justifiable only if the manufacturer can create a large number of disks. On the other hand, the **compact disk recordable (CD-R)** format allows users to create one or more disks without going through the expense involved in creating CD-ROMs. It is particularly useful for making backups. You can write once to CD-R disks, but they can be read many times. This is why the format is sometimes called **write once, read many (WORM)**.

❑ **Creation**. CD-R technology uses the same principles as CD-ROM to create a disk (Figure 5.10). The following lists the differences:

a. There is no master disk or mold.

b. The reflective layer is made of gold instead of aluminum.

c. There are no physical pits (holes) in the polycarbonate: the pits and lands are only simulated. To simulate pits and lands, an extra layer of dye, similar to the material used in photography, is added between the reflective layer and the polycarbonate.

d. A high-power laser beam, created by the CD burner of the drive, makes a dark spot in the dye, changing its chemical composition, which simulates a pit. The areas not struck by the beam become lands.

❑ **Reading**. CD-Rs can be read by a CD-ROM or a CD-R drive. This means that any differences should be transparent to the drive. The same low-power laser beam passes in front of the simulated pits and lands. For a land, the beam reaches the reflective layer and is reflected. For a simulated pit, the spot is opaque, so the beam cannot be reflected back.

❑ **Format and speed**. The format, capacity, and speed of CD-Rs are the same as CD-ROMs.

❑ **Application**. This technology is very attractive for the creation and distribution of a small number of disks. It is also very useful for making archive files and backups.

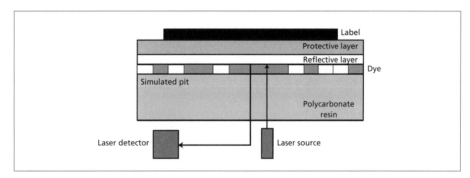

Figure 5.10   Making a CD-R

CD-RW

Although CD-Rs have become very popular, they can be written to only once. To overwrite previous materials, a new technology allows a new type of disk called **compact disk rewritable (CD-RW)**. It is sometimes called an *erasable optical disk*.

❑ **Creation**. CD-RW technology uses the same principles as CD-R to create the disk (Figure 5.11). The following lists the differences:

a. Instead of dye, the technology uses an alloy of silver, indium, antimony, and tellurium. This alloy has two stable states: crystalline (transparent) and amorphous (nontransparent).

b. The drive uses high-power lasers to create simulated pits in the alloy (changing it from crystalline to amorphous).

❑ **Reading**. The drive uses the same type of low-power laser beam as CD-ROM and CD-R to detect pits and lands.

❑ **Erasing**. The drive uses a medium-power laser beam to change pits to lands. The beam changes a location from the amorphous state to the crystalline state.

❑ **Format and speed**. The format, capacity, and speed of CD-RWs are the same as CD-ROMs.

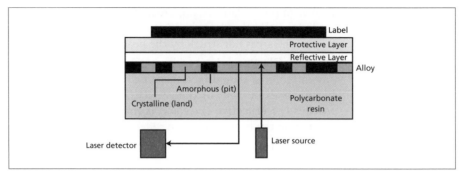

Figure 5.11   Making a CD-RW

❑ **Application**. The technology is definitely more attractive than CD-R technology. However, CD-Rs are more popular for two reasons. First, blank CD-R discs are less expensive than blank CD-RW discs. Second, CD-Rs are preferable in cases where the created disk must not be changed, either accidentally or intentionally.

DVD

The industry has felt the need for digital storage media with even higher capacity. The capacity of a CD-ROM (650 MB) is insufficient to store video information. The latest optical memory storage device on the market is called a **digital versatile disk (DVD)**. It uses a technology similar to CD-ROM, but with the following differences:

a. The pits are smaller: 0.4 microns in diameter instead of the 0.8 microns used in CDs.

b. The tracks are closer to each other.

c. The beam is a red laser instead of infrared.

d. DVDs use one to two recording layers, and can be single-sided or double-sided.

❑ **Capacity**. These improvements result in higher capacities (Table 5.3).

Table 5.3   DVD capacities

Feature	Capacity
Single-sided, single-layer	4.7 GB
Single-sided, dual-layer	8.5 GB
Double-sided, single-layer	9.4 GB
Double-sided, dual-layer	17 GB

❑ **Compression**. DVD technology uses MPEG (see Chapter 15) for compression. This means that a single-sided, single-layer DVD can hold 133 minutes of video at high resolution. This also includes both audio and subtitles.

❑ **Application**. Today, the high capacity of DVDs attracts many applications that need to store a high volume of data.

5.4 SUBSYSTEM INTERCONNECTION

The previous sections outlined the characteristics of the three subsystems (CPU, main memory, and I/O) in a stand-alone computer. In this section, we explore how these three subsystems are interconnected. The interconnection plays an important role because information needs to be exchanged between the three subsystems.

Connecting CPU and memory

The CPU and memory are normally connected by three groups of connections, each called a **bus**: data bus, address bus, and control bus (Figure 5.12).

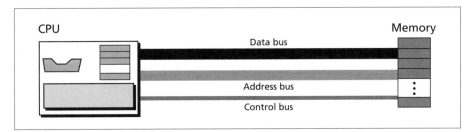

Figure 5.12   Connecting CPU and memory using three buses

Data bus

The **data bus** is made of several connections, each carrying 1 bit at a time. The number of connections depends on the size of the word used by the computer. If the word is 32 bits (4 bytes), we need a data bus with 32 connections so that all 32 bits of a word can be transmitted at the same time.

Address bus

The **address bus** allows access to a particular word in memory. The number of connections in the address bus depends on the address space of the memory. If the memory has 2^n words, the address bus needs to carry n bits at a time. Therefore, it must have n connections.

Control bus

The **control bus** carries communication between the CPU and memory. For example, there must be a code, sent from the CPU to memory, to specify a read or write operation. The number of connections used in the control bus depends on the total number of control commands a computer needs. If a computer has 2^m control actions, we need m connections for the control bus, because m bits can define 2^m different operations.

Connecting I/O devices

I/O devices cannot be connected directly to the buses that connect the CPU and memory because the nature of I/O devices is different than the nature of CPU and memory. I/O devices are electromechanical, magnetic, or optical devices, whereas the CPU and memory are electronic devices. I/O devices also operate at a much slower speed than the CPU/memory. There is a need for some sort of intermediary to handle this difference. Input/output devices are therefore attached to the buses through **input/output controllers** or interfaces. There is one specific controller for each input/output device (Figure 5.13).

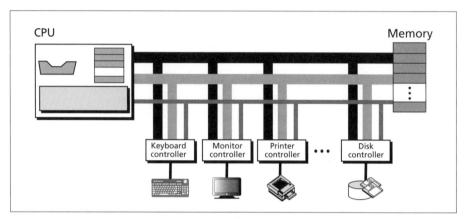

Figure 5.13   Connecting I/O devices to the buses

Controllers   Controllers or interfaces bridge the gap between the nature of the I/O device and the CPU and memory. A controller can be a serial or parallel device. A serial controller has only one data wire, while a parallel controller has several data connections so that several bits can be transferred at a time.

Several kinds of controllers are in use. The most common ones today are SCSI, FireWire, and USB.

SCSI

The **small computer system interface (SCSI)** was first developed for Macintosh computers in 1984. Today it is used in many systems. It has a parallel interface with 8, 16, or 32 connections. The SCSI interface provides a daisy-chained connection, as shown in Figure 5.14. Both ends of the chain must be connected to a special device called a *terminator*, and each device must have a unique address (target ID).

FireWire

IEEE standard 1394 defines a serial interface commonly called **FireWire**. It is a high-speed serial interface that transfers data in packets, achieving a transfer rate of up to 50 MB/sec, or double that in the most recent version. It can be used to connect up to 63 devices in a daisy chain or a tree connection (using only one connection). Figure 5.15 shows the connection of input/output devices to a FireWire controller. There is no need for termination as there is for SCSI.

USB

Universal Serial Bus (USB) is a competitor for FireWire. Although the nomenclature uses the term *bus*, USB is a serial controller that connects both low and high-speed

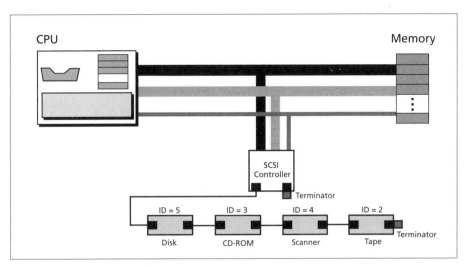

Figure 5.14 SCSI controller

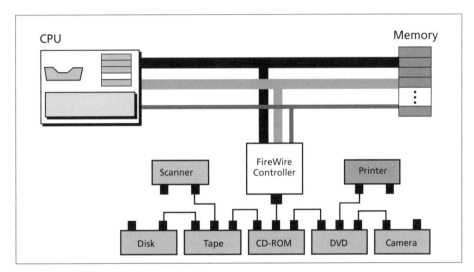

Figure 5.15 FireWire controller

devices to the computer bus. Figure 5.16 show the connection of the USB controller to the bus and the connection of devices to the controller.

Multiple devices can be connected to a USB controller, which is also referred to as a *root hub*. USB-2 (USB Version 2.0) allows up to 127 devices to be connected to a USB controller using a tree-like topology with the controller as the root of the tree, hubs as the intermediate nodes, and the devices as the end nodes. The difference between the controller (root hub) and the other hubs is that the controller is aware of the presence of other hubs in the tree, but other hubs are passive devices that simply pass the data.

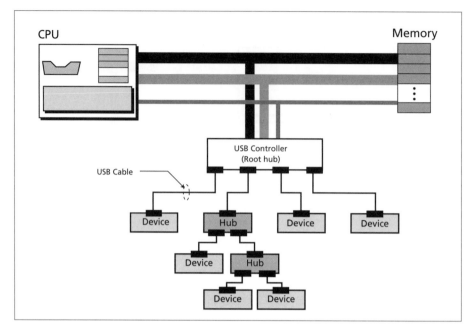

Figure 5.16 USB controller

Devices can easily be removed or attached to the tree without powering down the computer. This is referred to as *hot-swappable*. When a hub is removed from the system, all device and other hubs connected to it are also removed.

USB uses a cable with four wires. Two wires (+5 volts and ground) are used to provide power for low-power devices such as keyboards or mice. A high-power device needs to be connected to a power source. A hub get its power from the bus and can provide power for low-power devices. The other two wires (twisted together to reduce noise) are used to carry data, addresses, and control signals. USB uses two different connectors: A and B. The A connector (downstream connector) is rectangular and is used to connect to the USB controller or the hub. The B connector (upstream connector) is close to square and is used to connect to the device. Recently two new connectors, mini A and mini B, have been introduced that are used for connecting to small devices and laptop computers.

USB-2 provides three data transfer rates: 1.5 Mbps (megabits per second), 12 Mbps, and 480 Mbps. The low data rate can be used with slow devices such as keyboards and mice, the medium data rate with printers, and the high data rate with mass storage devices.

Data is transferred over USB in packets (see Chapter 6). Each packet contains an address part (device identifier), a control part, and part of the data to be transmitted to that device. All devices will receive the same packet, but only those devices with the address defined in the packet will accept it.

Addressing input/output devices

The CPU usually uses the same bus to read data from or write data to main memory and I/O device. The only difference is the instruction. If the instruction refers to a word in main memory, data transfer is between main memory and the CPU. If the instruction identifies an I/O device, data transfer is between the I/O device and the CPU. There are two methods for handling the addressing of I/O devices: isolated I/O and memory-mapped I/O.

Isolated I/O

In the **isolated I/O** method, the instructions used to read/write memory are totally different than the instructions used to read/write I/O devices. There are instructions to test, control, read from, and write to I/O devices. Each I/O device has its own address. The I/O addresses can overlap with memory addresses without any ambiguity because the instruction itself is different. For example, the CPU can use a command "Read 101" to read from memory word 101, and it can use a command "Input 101" to read from I/O device 101. There is no confusion, because the read command is for reading from memory and the input command is for reading from an I/O device (Figure 5.17).

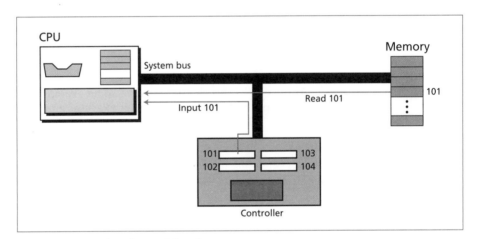

Figure 5.17   Isolated I/O addressing

Memory-mapped I/O

In the **memory-mapped I/O** method, the CPU treats each register in the I/O controller as a word in memory. In other words, the CPU does not have separate instructions for transferring data from memory and I/O devices. For example, there is only one "Read" instruction. If the address defines a word from memory, the data is read from that word. If the address defines a register from an I/O device, the data is read from that register. The advantage of the memory-mapped configuration is a smaller number of instructions: all the memory instructions can be used by I/O devices. The disadvantage is that part of the memory address space is allocated to registers in I/O controllers. For example, if we have five I/O controllers and each has four registers, 20 addresses are used for this purpose. The size of the memory is reduced by 20 words. Figure 5.18 shows the memory-mapped I/O concept.

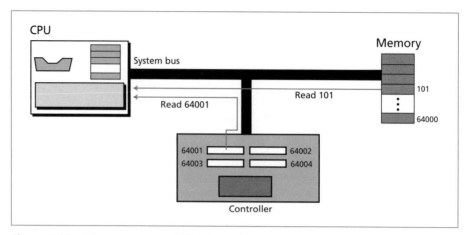

Figure 5.18   Memory-mapped I/O addressing

5.5 PROGRAM EXECUTION

Today, general-purpose computers use a set of instructions called a *program* to process data. A computer executes the program to create output data from input data. Both the program and the data are stored in memory.

> **At the end of this chapter we give some examples of how a hypothetical simple computer executes a program.**

Machine cycle

The CPU uses repeating **machine cycles** to execute instructions in the program, one by one, from beginning to end. A simplified cycle can consist of three phases: *fetch*, *decode*, and *execute* (Figure 5.19).

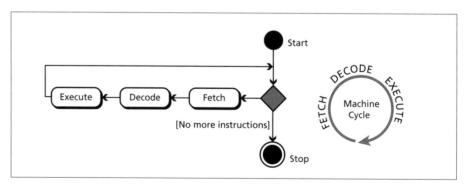

Figure 5.19   The steps of a cycle

Fetch

In the **fetch** phase, the control unit orders the system to copy the next instruction into the instruction register in the CPU. The address of the instruction to be copied is held in the program counter register. After copying, the program counter is incremented to refer to the next instruction in memory.

Decode

The second phase in the cycle is the **decode** phase. When the instruction is in the instruction register, it is decoded by the control unit. The result of this decode step is the binary code for some operation that the system will perform.

Execute

After the instruction is decoded, the control unit sends the task order to a component in the CPU. For example, the control unit can tell the system to load (read) a data item from memory, or the CPU can tell the ALU to add the contents of two input registers and put the result in an output register. This is the **execute** phase.

Input/output operation

Commands are required to transfer data from I/O devices to the CPU and memory. Because I/O devices operate at much slower speeds than the CPU, the operation of the CPU must be synchronized with the I/O devices somehow. Three methods have been devised for this synchronization: programmed I/O, interrupt-driven I/O, and direct memory access (DMA).

Programmed I/O

In the **programmed I/O** method, synchronization is very primitive: the CPU waits for the I/O device (Figure 5.20).

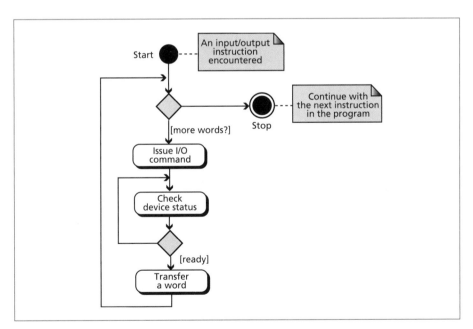

Figure 5.20   Programmed I/O

The transfer of data between the I/O device and the CPU is done by an instruction in the program. When the CPU encounters an I/O instruction, it does nothing else until the data transfer is complete. The CPU constantly checks the status of the I/O device: if the device is ready to transfer, data is transferred to the CPU. If the device is not ready, the CPU continues checking the device status until the I/O device is ready. The big issue here is that CPU time is wasted by checking the status of the I/O device for each unit of data to be transferred. Note that data is transferred to memory after the input operation, while data is transferred from memory before the output operation.

Interrupt-driven i/O

In the **interrupt-driven I/O** method, the CPU informs the I/O device that a transfer is going to happen, but it does not test the status of the I/O device continuously. The I/O device informs (interrupts) the CPU when it is ready. During this time, the CPU can do other jobs such as running other programs or transferring data from or to other I/O devices (Figure 5.21).

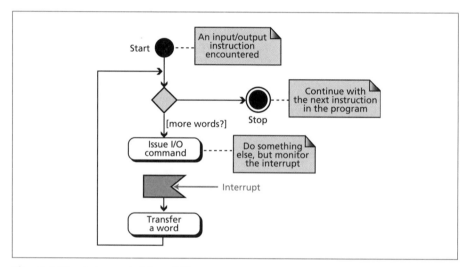

Figure 5.21   Interrupt-driven I/O

In this method, CPU time is not wasted—the CPU can do something else while the slow I/O device is finishing a task. Note that, like programmed I/O, this method also transfers data between the device and the CPU. Data is transferred to memory after the input operation. While data is transferred from memory before the output operation.

Direct memory access (DMA)

The third method used for transferring data is **direct memory access (DMA)**. This method transfers a large block of data between a high-speed I/O device, such as a disk, and memory directly without passing it through the CPU. This requires a DMA controller that relieves the CPU of some of its functions. The DMA controller has registers to hold a block of data before and after memory transfer. Figure 5.22 shows the DMA connection to the data, address and control buses.

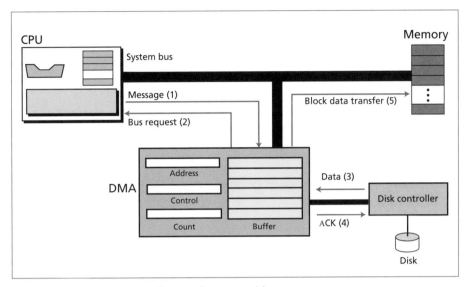

Figure 5.22   DMA connection to the general bus

Using this method for an I/O operation, the CPU sends a message to the DMA. The message contains the type of transfer (input or output), the start address of the memory location, and the number of bytes to be transferred. The CPU is then available for other jobs (Figure 5.23).

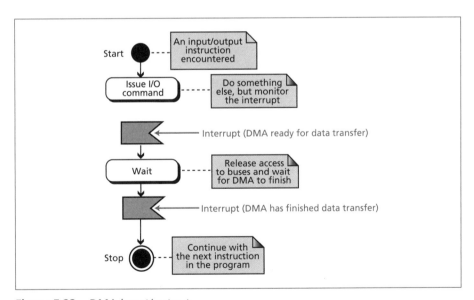

Figure 5.23   DMA input/output

When ready to transfer data, the DMA controller informs the CPU that it needs to take control of the buses. The CPU stops using the buses and lets the controller use them. After data transfer directly between the DMA and memory, the CPU continues its normal operation. Note that, in this method, the CPU is idle for a time. However, the duration of this idle period is very short compared to other methods—the CPU is idle only during the data transfer between the DMA and memory, not while the device prepares the data.

5.6   DIFFERENT ARCHITECTURES

The architecture and organization of computers has gone through many changes in recent decades. In this section we discuss some common architectures and organizations that differ from the simple computer architecture we discussed earlier.

CISC

CISC (pronounced *sisk*) stands for **complex instruction set computer (CISC)**. The strategy behind CISC architectures is to have a large set of instructions, including complex ones. Programming CISC-based computers is easier than in other designs because there is a single instruction for both simple and complex tasks. Programmers therefore do not have to write a set of instructions to do a complex task.

The complexity of the instruction set makes the circuitry of the CPU and the control unit very complicated. The designers of CISC architectures have come up with a solution to reduce this complexity: programming is done on two levels. An instruction in machine language is not executed directly by the CPU—the CPU performs only simple operations, called *microoperations*. A complex instruction is transformed into a set of these simple operations and then executed by the CPU. This necessitates the addition of a special memory called *micromemory* that holds the set of operations for each complex instruction in the instruction set. The type of programming that uses microoperations is called *microprogramming*.

One objection to CISC architecture is the overhead associated with microprogramming and access to micromemory. However, proponents of the architecture argue that this compensates for smaller programs at the machine level. An example of CISC architecture can be seen in the Pentium series of processors developed by Intel.

RISC

RISC (pronounced *risk*) stands for **reduced instruction set computer**. The strategy behind RISC architecture is to have a small set of instructions that do a minimum number of simple operations. Complex instructions are simulated using a subset of simple instructions. Programming in RISC is more difficult and time-consuming than in the other design because most of the complex instructions are simulated using simple instructions.

Pipelining

We have learned that a computer uses three phases of *fetch*, *decode*, and *execute* for each instruction. In early computers, these three phases needed to be done in series for each instruction. In other words, instruction *n* needs to finish all of these phases before instruction *n* + 1 can start its own phases. Modern computers use a technique called **pipelining** to improve the **throughput** (the total number of instructions performed in each period of time). The idea is that if the control unit can do two or three of these phases simultaneously, the next instruction can start before the previous one is finished. Figure 5.24.a shows how three consecutive instructions are handled in a computer that uses no pipelining. Figure 5.24.b shows how pipelining can increase the throughput of the computer by allowing different types of phases belonging to different instructions to be done simultaneously. In other words, when the CPU is performing the decode phase of the first instruction, it can also perform the fetch phase of the second instruction. The first computer can perform on average nine phases in the specific period of time, while the pipelined computer can perform 24 phases in the same period of time. If we assume that each phase uses the same amount of time, the first computer has done 9/3 = 3 instructions while the second computer has done 24/3 = 8 instructions. The throughput is therefore increased 8/3 or 266 percent.

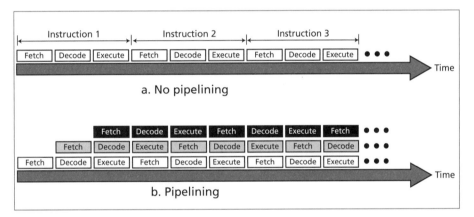

Figure 5.24 Pipelining

Of course, pipelining is not as easy as this. There are some problems, such as when a jump instruction is encountered. In this case, the instruction in the *pipe* should be discarded. However, new CPU designs have overcome most drawbacks. Some new CPU designs can even do several fetch cycles simultaneously.

Parallel processing

Traditionally a computer had a single control unit, a single arithmetic logic unit, and a single memory unit. With the evolution in technology and the drop in the cost of computer hardware, today we can have a single computer with multiple control units, multiple arithmetic logic units and multiple memory units. This idea is referred to as *parallel processing*. Like pipelining, parallel processing can improve throughput.

Parallel processing involves many different techniques. A general view of parallel processing is given by the taxonomy proposed by M. J. Flynn. This taxonomy divides the computer's organization (in terms of processing data) into four categories, as shown in Figure 5.25. According to Flynn, parallel processing may occur in the data stream, the instruction stream, or both.

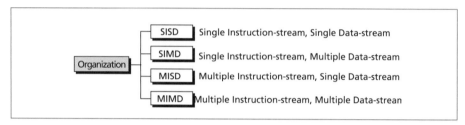

Figure 5.25   A taxonomy of computer organization

SISD organization

A **single instruction-stream, single data-stream (SISD)** organization represents a computer that has one control unit, one arithmetic logic unit, and one memory unit. The instructions are executed sequentially and each instruction may access one or more data item in the data stream. Our simple computer introduced earlier in the chapter is an example of SISD organization. Figure 5.26 shows the concept of configuration for an SISD organization.

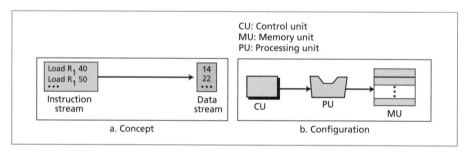

Figure 5.26   SISD organization

SIMD organization

A **single instruction-stream, multiple data-stream (SIMD)** organization represents a computer that has one control unit, multiple processing units, and one memory unit. All processor units receive the same instruction from the control unit, but operate on different items of data. An array processor that simultaneously operates on an array of data belongs to this category. Figure 5.27 shows the concept and implementation of an SIMD organization.

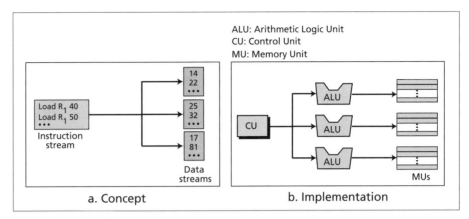

Figure 5.27 SIMD organization

MISD organization

A **multiple instruction-stream**, **single data-stream (MISD)** architecture is one in which several instructions belonging to several instruction streams simultaneously operate on the same data stream. Figure 5.28 shows the concept, but it has never been implemented.

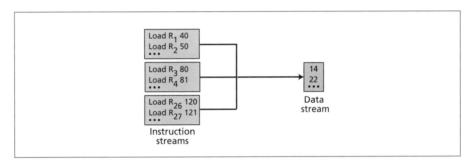

Figure 5.28 MISD organization

MIMD organization

A **multiple instruction-stream**, **multiple data-stream (MIMD)** architecture is one in which several instructions belonging to several instruction streams simultaneously operate on several data streams (each instruction on one data stream). Figure 5.29 shows the concept and implementation. MIMD organization is considered as a true parallel processing architecture by some experts. In this architecture several tasks can be performed simultaneously. The architecture can use a single shared memory or multiple memory sections.

Parallel processing has found some applications, mostly in the scientific community, in which a task may take several hours or days if done using a traditional computer architecture. Some examples of this can be found in multiplication of very large matrices, in simultaneous processing of large amounts of data for weather prediction, or in space flight simulations.

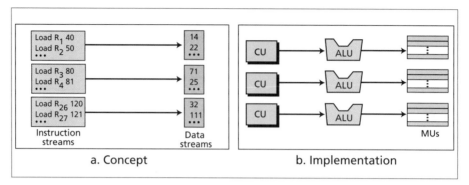

Figure 5.29   MIMD organization

5.7   A SIMPLE COMPUTER

To explain the architecture of computers as well as their instruction processing, we introduce a simple (unrealistic) computer, as shown in Figure 5.30. Our simple computer has three components: CPU, memory, and an input/output subsystem.

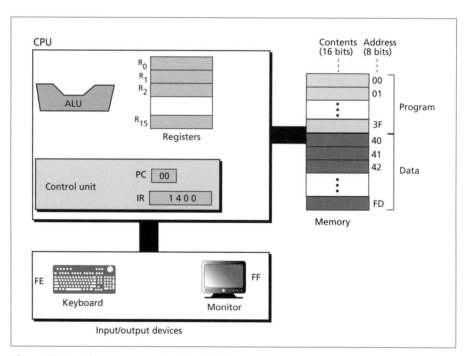

Figure 5.30   The components of a simple computer

CPU

The CPU itself is divided into three sections: data registers, arithmetic logic unit (ALU), and the control unit.

Data registers

There are sixteen 16-bit data registers with hexadecimal addresses $(0, 1, 2,..., F)_{16}$, but we refer to them as R_0 to R_{15}. In most instructions, they hold 16-bit data, but in some instructions they may hold other information.

Control unit

The control unit has the circuitry to control the operations of the ALU, access to memory, and access to the I/O subsystem. In addition, it has two dedicated registers: program counter and instruction register. The program counter (PC), which can hold only eight bits, keeps track of which instruction is to be executed next. The contents of the PC points to the address of the memory location of the main memory that holds the next program instruction. After each machine cycle the program counter is incremented by one to point to the next program instruction. The instruction register (IR) holds a 16-bit value which is the encoded instruction for the current cycle.

Main memory

The main memory has 256 16-bit memory locations with binary addresses $(00000000 \text{ to } 11111101)_2$ or hexadecimal addresses $(00 \text{ to } FD)_{16}$. The main memory holds both data and program instructions. The first sixty-four locations $(00 \text{ to } 3F)_{16}$ are dedicated to program instructions. Program instructions for any program are stored in consecutive memory locations. Memory locations $(40 \text{ to } FD)_{16}$ are used for storing data.

Input/output subsystem

Our simple computer has a very primitive input/output subsystem. The subsystem consists of a keyboard and a monitor. Although we show the keyboard and monitor in a separate box in Figure 5.30, the subsystem is part of the memory address-wise. These devices have memory-mapped addresses, as discussed earlier in the chapter. We assume that the keyboard (as the input device) and monitor (as the only output device) act like memory locations with addresses $(FE)_{16}$ and $(FF)_{16}$ respectively, as shown in the figure. In other words, we assume that they behave as 16-bit registers that interact with the CPU as a memory location would. These two devices transfer data from the outside world to the CPU and vice versa.

Instruction set

Our simple computer is capable of having a set of sixteen instructions, although we are using only fourteen of these instructions. Each computer instruction consists of two parts: the operation code (*opcode*) and the *operand(s)*. The opcode specifies the type of operation to be performed on the operand(s). Each instruction consists of sixteen bits divided into four 4-bit fields. The leftmost field contains the opcode and the other three fields contains the operand or address of operand(s), as shown in Figure 5.31. The instruction are listed in Table 5.4 on page 131.

Note that not every instruction requires three operands. Any operand field not needed is filled with $(0)_{16}$. For example, all three operand fields of the halt instruction, and the last field of the move and NOT instructions, are filled with $(0)_{16}$. Also note that a register address is described by a single hexadecimal digit and thus uses a single field, but a memory location is described by two hexadecimal digits and uses two fields.

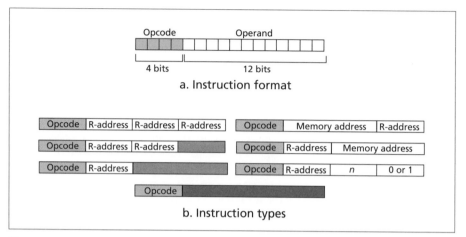

Figure 5.31   Format and different instruction types

There are two add instructions: one for adding integers (ADDI) and one for adding floating point numbers (ADDF). The simple computer can take input from a keyboard if we use address $(FE)_{16}$ as the second operand of the LOAD instruction. Similarly, the computer sends output to the monitor if we use the address $(FF)_{16}$ as the first operand of the STORE instruction. If the third operand of the ROTATE instruction is 0, the instruction circularly rotates the bit pattern in R to the right n places: if the third operand is 1, it rotates it to the left. We have also included one increment (INC) and one decrement (DEC) instruction.

Processing the instructions

Our simple computer, like most computers, uses machine cycles. A cycle is made of three phases: *fetch*, *decode*, and *execute*. During the *fetch* phase, the instruction whose address is determined by the PC is obtained from the memory and loaded into the IR. The PC is then incremented to point to the next instruction. During the *decode* phase, the instruction in IR is decoded and the required operands are fetched from the register or from memory. During the *execute* phase, the instruction is executed and the results are placed in the appropriate memory location or the register. Once the third phase is completed, the control unit starts the cycle again, but now the PC is pointing to the next instruction. The process continues until the CPU reaches a HALT instruction.

Table 5.4 List of instructions for the simple computer

Instruction	Code d_1	Operands d_2	d_3	d_4	Action
HALT	0				Stops the execution of the program
LOAD	1	R_D	M_S		$R_D \leftarrow M_S$
STORE	2	M_D		R_S	$M_D \leftarrow R_S$
ADDI	3	R_D	R_{S1}	R_{S2}	$R_D \leftarrow R_{S1} + R_{S2}$
ADDF	4	R_D	R_{S1}	R_{S2}	$R_D \leftarrow R_{S1} + R_{S2}$
MOVE	5	R_D	R_S		$R_D \leftarrow R_S$
NOT	6	R_D	R_S		$R_D \leftarrow \overline{R_S}$
AND	7	R_D	R_{S1}	R_{S2}	$R_D \leftarrow R_{S1}$ AND R_{S2}
OR	8	R_D	R_{S1}	R_{S2}	$R_D \leftarrow R_{S1}$ OR R_{S2}
XOR	9	R_D	R_{S1}	R_{S2}	$R_D \leftarrow R_{S1}$ XOR R_{S2}
INC	A	R			$R \leftarrow R + 1$
DEC	B	R			$R \leftarrow R - 1$
ROTATE	C	R	n	0 or 1	Rot_n R
JUMP	D	R		n	IF $R_0 \neq R$ then PC = n, otherwise continue

Key: R_S, R_{S1}, R_{S2}: Hexadecimal address of source registers
R_D: Hexadecimal address of destination register
M_S: Hexadecimal address of source memory location
M_D: Hexadecimal address of destination memory location
n: hexadecimal number
d_1, d_2, d_3, d_4: First, second, third, and fourth hexadecimal digits

An example

Let us show how our simple computer can add two integers A and B and create the result as C. We assume that integers are in two's complement format. Mathematically, we show this operation as:

$$C = A + B$$

To solve this problem with the simple computer, it is necessary for the first two integers to be held in two registers (for example, R_0 and R_1) and the result of the operation to be held in a third register (for example R_2). The ALU can only operate on the data that is stored in data registers in the CPU. However, most computers, including our simple computer, have a limited number of registers in the CPU. If the number of data items is large and they are supposed to stay in the computer for the duration of the program, it is better to store them in memory and only bring them to the registers temporarily. So we assume that the first two integers are stored in memory locations $(40)_{16}$ and $(41)_{16}$ and the result should be stored in memory location $(42)_{16}$. This means that two integers need to be loaded into the CPU and the result needs to be stored in the memory. Therefore, a simple program to do the simple addition needs five instructions, as shown below:

1. Load the contents of M_{40} into register R_0 ($R_0 \leftarrow M_{40}$).
2. Load the contents of M_{41} into register R_1 ($R_1 \leftarrow M_{41}$).
3. Add the contents of R_0 and R_1 and place the result in R_2 ($R_2 \leftarrow R_0 + R_1$).
4. Store the contents R_2 in M_{42} ($M_{42} \leftarrow R_2$).
5. Halt.

In the language of our simple computer, these five instructions are encoded as:

Code	Interpretation			
$(1040)_{16}$	1: LOAD	0: R_0	40: M_{40}	
$(1141)_{16}$	1: LOAD	1: R_1	41: M_{41}	
$(3201)_{16}$	3: ADDI	2: R_2	0: R_0	1: R_1
$(2422)_{16}$	2: STORE	42: M_{42}		2: R_2
$(0000)_{16}$	0: HALT			

Storing program and data

To follow the von Neumann model, we need to store the program and the data in memory. We can store the five-line program in memory starting from location $(00)_{16}$ to $(04)_{16}$. We already know that the data needs to be stored in memory locations $(40)_{16}$, $(41)_{16}$, and $(42)_{16}$.

Cycles

Our computer uses one cycle per instruction. If we have a small program with five instructions, we need five cycles. We also know that each cycle is normally made up of three steps: *fetch, decode, execute*. Assume for the moment that we need to add $161 + 254 = 415$. The numbers are shown in memory in hexadecimal is, $(00A1)_{16}$, $(00FE)_{16}$, and $(019F)_{16}$.

Cycle 1

At the beginning of the first cycle (Figure 5.32), the PC points to the first instruction of the program, which is at memory location $(00)_{16}$. The control unit goes through three steps:

1. The control unit *fetches* the instruction stored in memory location $(00)_{16}$ and puts it in the IR. After this step, the value of the PC is incremented.
2. The control unit *decodes* the instruction $(1040)_{16}$ as $R_0 \leftarrow M_{40}$.
3. The control unit *executes* the instruction, which means that a copy of the integer stored in memory location $(40)_{16}$ is loaded into register R_0.

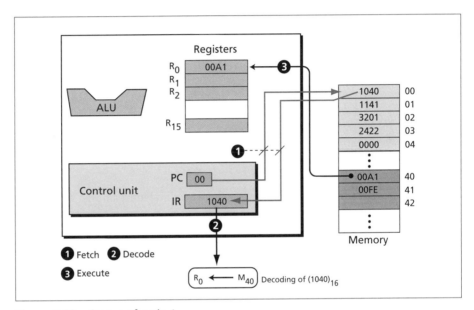

Figure 5.32   Status of cycle 1

Cycle 2

At the beginning of the second cycle (Figure 5.33), the PC points to the second instruction of the program, which is at memory location $(01)_{16}$. The control unit goes through three steps:

1. The control unit *fetches* the instruction stored in memory location $(01)_{16}$ and puts it in the IR. After this step, the value of the PC is incremented.
2. The control unit *decodes* the instruction $(1141)_{16}$ as $R_1 \leftarrow M_{41}$.
3. The control unit *executes* the instruction, which means that a copy of integer stored in memory location $(41)_{16}$ is loaded into register R_1.

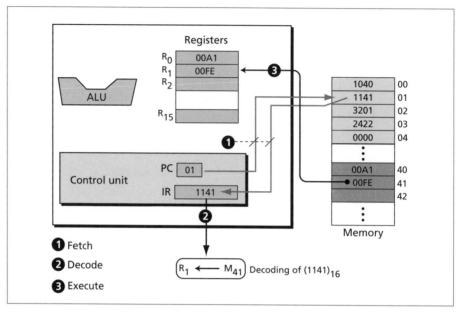

Figure 5.33   Status of cycle 2

Cycle 3

At the beginning of the third cycle (Figure 5.34), the PC points to the third instruction of the program, which is at memory location $(02)_{16}$. The control unit goes through three steps:

1. The control unit *fetches* the instruction stored in memory location $(02)_{16}$ and puts it in the IR. After this step, the value of the PC is incremented.
2. The control unit *decodes* the instruction $(3201)_{16}$ as $R_2 \leftarrow R_0 + R_1$.
3. The control unit *executes* the instruction, which means that the contents of R_0 is added to the content of R_1 (by the ALU) and the result is put in R_2.

Cycle 4

At the beginning of the fourth cycle (Figure 5.35), the PC points to the fourth instruction of the program, which is at memory location $(03)_{16}$. The control unit goes through three steps:

1. The control unit *fetches* the instruction stored in memory location $(03)_{16}$ and puts it in the IR. After this step, the value of the PC is incremented.
2. The control unit *decodes* the instruction $(2422)_{16}$ as $M_{42} \leftarrow R_2$.
3. The control unit *executes* the instruction, which means a copy of integer in register R_2 is stored in memory location $(42)_{16}$.

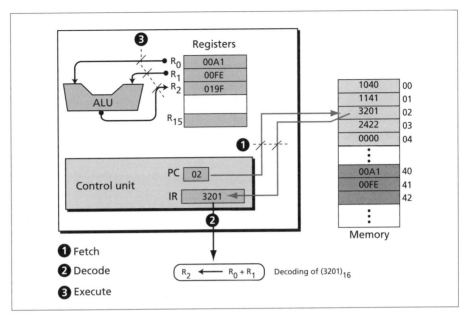

Figure 5.34 Status of cycle 3

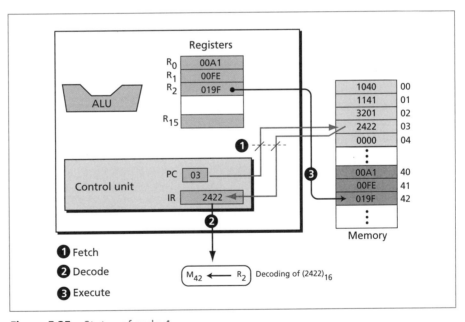

Figure 5.35 Status of cycle 4

Cycle 5

At the beginning of the fifth cycle (Figure 5.36), the PC points to the fifth instruction of the program, which is at memory location $(04)_{16}$. The control unit goes through three steps:

1. The control unit *fetches* the instruction stored in memory location $(04)_{16}$ and puts it in the IR. After this step, the value of the PC is incremented.

2. The control unit *decodes* the instruction $(0000)_{16}$ as Halt.

3. The control unit *executes* the instruction, which means that the computer stops.

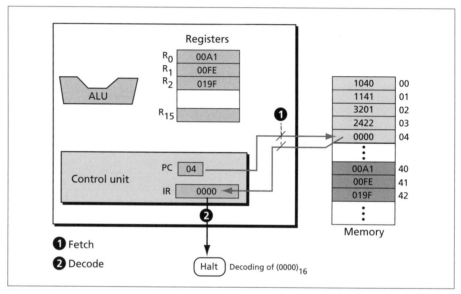

Figure 5.36   Status of cycle 5

Another example

In the previous example we assumed that the two integers to be added were already in memory. We also assumed that the result of addition will be held in memory. You may ask how we can store the two integers we want to add in memory, or how we use the result when it is stored in the memory. In a real situation, we enter the first two integers into memory using an input device such as keyboard, and we display the third integer through an output device such as a monitor. Getting data via an input device is normally called a *read* operation, while sending data to an output device is normally called a *write* operation. To make our previous program more practical, we need modify it as follows:

1. Read an integer into M_{40}.

2. $R_0 \leftarrow M_{40}$.

3. Read an integer into M_{41}.

4. $R_1 \leftarrow M_{41}$.

5. $R_2 \leftarrow R_0 + R_1$.

6. $M_{42} \leftarrow R_2$.

7. Write the integer from M_{42}.

8. Halt.

There are many ways to implement input and output. Most computers today do direct data transfer from an input device to memory and direct data transfer from memory to an output device. However, our simple computer is not one of them. In our computer we can simulate read and write operations using the LOAD and STORE instructions. Furthermore, LOAD and STORE read data input to the CPU and write data from the CPU. We need two instruction to read data into memory or write data out of memory. The read operation is:

$R \leftarrow M_{FE}$ Because the keyboard is assumed to be memory location $(FE)_{16}$

$M \leftarrow R$

The write operation is:

$R \leftarrow M$

$M_{FF} \leftarrow R$ Because the monitor is assumed to be memory location $(FF)_{16}$

You may ask why, if the operations are supposed to be done in the CPU, do we transfer the data from the keyboard to the CPU, then to the memory, then to the CPU for processing? Could we directly transfer data to the CPU? The answer is that we can do this for this small problem, but we should not do it in principle. Think what happens if we need to add 1000 numbers or sort 1,000,000 integers. The number of registers in the CPU is limited (it may be hundreds in a real computer, but still not enough).

> **The input operation must always read data from an input device into memory: the output operation must always write data from memory to an output device.**

With this in mind, the program is coded as:

1	$(1FFE)_{16}$	5	$(1040)_{16}$	9	$(1F42)_{16}$
2	$(240F)_{16}$	6	$(1141)_{16}$	10	$(2FFF)_{16}$
3	$(1FFE)_{16}$	7	$(3201)_{16}$	11	$(0000)_{16}$
4	$(241F)_{16}$	8	$(2422)_{16}$		

Operations 1 to 4 are for input and operations 9 and 10 are for output. When we run this program, it waits for the user to input two integers on the keyboard and press the enter key. The program then calculates the sum and displays the result on the monitor.

Reusability One of the advantages of a computer over a non-programmable calculator is that we can use the same program over and over. We can run the program several times and each time enter different inputs and obtain a different output.

5.8 RECOMMENDED READING

For more details about the subjects discussed in this chapter, the following books are recommended:

❑ Englander I: *The Architecture of Computer Hardware and Systems Software*, Hoboken, NJ: Wiley, 2003

❑ Mano M: *Computer System Architecture*, Upper Saddle River, NJ: Prentice Hall, 1993

❑ Null L and Lobur J: *Computer Organization and Architecture*, Sudbury, MA: Jones and Bartlett, 2003

❑ Hamacher C, Vranesic Z, and Zaky S: *Computer Organization*, New York: McGraw-Hill, 2002

❑ Warford S: *Computer Systems*, Sudbury, MA: Jones and Bartlett, 2005

❑ Ercegovac M, Lang T, and Moreno J: *Introduction to Digital Systems*, Hoboken, NJ: Wiley, 1998

❑ Cragon H: *Computer Architecture and Implementation*, Cambridge: Cambridge University Press, 2000

❑ Stallings W: *Computer Organization and Architecture*, Upper Saddle River, NJ: Prentice Hall, 2002

5.9 KEY TERMS

This chapter has introduced the following key terms, which are listed here with the pages on which they first occur:

address bus 115	address space 104
arithmetic logic unit (ALU) 102	bus 115
cache memory 107	central processing unit (CPU) 102
compact disk read-only memory (CD-ROM) 110	compact disk rewritable (CD-RW) 113
complex instruction set computer (CISC) 124	control bus 115
control unit 103	data bus 115
decode 121	digital versatile disk (DVD) 114
direct memory address (DMA) 122	dynamic RAM (DRAM) 106
electronically erasable programmable read-only memory (EEPROM) 106	erasable programmable read-only memory (EPROM) 106
execute 121	fetch 121

5.10   SUMMARY

- The parts that make up a computer can be divided into three broad categories or subsystems: the central processing unit (CPU), the main memory, and the input/output subsystem.

- The central processing unit (CPU) performs operations on data. It has three parts: an arithmetic logic unit (ALU), a control unit, and a set of registers. The arithmetic logic unit (ALU) performs logic, shift, and arithmetic operations on data. Registers are fast stand-alone storage locations that hold data temporarily. The control unit controls the operation of each part of the CPU.

- Main memory is a collection of storage locations, each with a unique identifier called the *address*. Data is transferred to and from memory in groups of bits called *words*. The total number of uniquely identifiable locations in memory is called the *address space*. Two types of memory are available: random access memory (RAM) and read-only memory (ROM).

- The collection of devices referred to as the input/output (I/O) subsystem allows a computer to communicate with the outside world and to store programs and data even when the power is off. Input/output devices can be divided into two broad categories: nonstorage and storage devices. Nonstorage devices allow the CPU/memory to communicate with the outside world. Storage devices can store large amounts of information to be retrieved at a later time. Storage devices are categorized as either magnetic or optical.

- The interconnection of the three subsystems of a computer plays an important role, because information needs to be exchanged between these subsystems. The CPU and memory are normally connected by three groups of connections, each called a *bus*: data bus, address bus, and control bus. Input/output devices are attached to the buses through an *input/output controller* or interface. Several kinds of controllers are in use. The most common ones today are SCSI, FireWire, and USB.

- There are two methods of handling the addressing of I/O devices: isolated I/O and memory-mapped I/O. In the isolated I/O method, the instructions used to read/write to and from memory are different than the instructions used to read/write to and from input/output devices. In the memory-mapped I/O method, the CPU treats each register in the I/O controller as a word in memory.

- Today, general-purpose computers use a set of instructions called a *program* to process data. A computer executes the program to create output data from input data. Both the program and the data are stored in memory. The CPU uses repeating machine cycles to execute instructions in the program, one by one, from beginning to end. A simplified cycle can consist of three phases: *fetch*, *decode*, and *execute*.

- Three methods have been devised for synchronization between I/O devices and the CPU: programmed I/O, interrupt-driven I/O, and direct memory access (DMA).

- The architecture and organization of computers have gone through many changes during recent decades. We can divide computers architecture into two broad categories: CISC (complex instruction set computers) and RISC (reduced instruction set computers).

- Modern computers use a technique called *pipelining* to improve their throughput. The idea is to allow the control unit to perform two or three phases simultaneously, which means that processing of the next instruction can start before the previous one is finished.

- Traditionally, a computer had a single control unit, a single arithmetic logic unit, and a single memory unit. Parallel processing can improve throughput by using multiple instruction streams to handle multiple data streams.

5.11   PRACTICE SET

Review questions

1. What are the three subsystems that make up a computer?

2. What are the components of a CPU?

3. What is the function of the ALU?

4. What is the function of the control unit?

5. What is the function of main memory?

6. Define RAM, ROM, SRAM, DRAM PROM, EPROM, and EEPROM.

7. What is the purpose of cache memory?

8. Describe the physical components of a magnetic disk.

9. How are the surfaces of a magnetic disk and magnetic tape organized?

10. Compare and contrast CD-R, CD-RW, and DVD.

11. Compare and contrast SCSI, FireWire and USB controllers.

12. Compare and contrast the two methods for handling the addressing of I/O devices.

13. Compare and contrast the three methods for handling the synchronization of the CPU with I/O devices.

14. Compare and contrast CISC architecture with RISC architecture.

15. Describe pipelining and its purpose.

16. Describe parallel processing and its purpose.

Multiple-choice questions

17. The _____ is a computer subsystem that performs operations on data.
    a. CPU
    b. memory
    c. I/O hardware
    d. none of the above

18. _____ is a stand-alone storage location that holds data temporarily.
    a. An ALU
    b. A register
    c. A control unit
    d. A tape drive

19. _____ is a unit that can add two inputs.
    a. An ALU
    b. A register
    c. A control unit
    d. A tape drive

20. A register in a CPU can hold _____.
    a. data
    b. instructions
    c. program counter values
    d. all of the above

21. A control unit with five wires can define up to _____ operations.
    a. 5
    b. 10
    c. 16
    d. 32

22. A word is _____ bits.
    a. 8
    b. 16
    c. 32
    d. any of the above

23. If the memory address space is 16 MB and the word size is 8 bits, then _____ bits are needed to access each word.
    a. 8
    b. 16
    c. 24
    d. 32

24. The data in _____ is erased if the computer is powered down.
    a. RAM
    b. ROM
    c. a tape drive
    d. a CD-ROM

25. _____ is a memory type with capacitors that need to be refreshed periodically.
    a. SRAM
    b. DRAM
    c. ROM
    d. all of the above

26. _____ is a memory type with traditional flip-flop gates to hold data.
    a. SRAM
    b. DRAM
    c. ROM
    d. all of the above

27. There are _____ bytes in 16 Terabytes.
    a. 2^{16}
    b. 2^{40}
    c. 2^{44}
    d. 2^{56}

28. _____ can be programmed and erased using electronic impulses but can remain in a computer during erasure.
    a. ROM
    b. PROM
    c. EPROM
    d. EEPROM

29. _____ is a type of memory in which the user, not the manufacturer, stores programs that cannot be overwritten.
    a. ROM
    b. PROM
    c. EPROM
    d. EEPROM

30. Main memory in a computer usually consists of large amounts of _____ speed memory.
    a. high
    b. medium
    c. low
    d. any of the above

31. A _____ is a storage device to which the user can write information only once.
    a. CD-ROM
    b. CD-R
    c. CD-RW
    d. all of the above

32. A _____ is a storage device that can undergo multiple writes and erasures.
    a. CD-ROM
    b. CD-R
    c. CD-RW
    d. all of the above

33. The smallest storage area on a magnetic disk that can be accessed at one time is a _____.
    a. track
    b. sector
    c. frame
    d. head

34. If the memory has 2^{32} words, the address bus needs to have _____ wires.
    a. 8
    b. 16
    c. 32
    d. 64

35. A control bus with eight wires can define _____ operations.
    a. 8
    b. 16
    c. 256
    d. 512

36. A _____ controller is a high-speed serial interface that transfers data in packets.
    a. SCSI
    b. USB
    c. FireWire
    d. both b and c

37. The three steps in the running of a program on a computer are performed in the specific order _____.
    a. fetch, execute, and decode
    b. decode, execute, and fetch
    c. fetch, decode, and execute
    d. decode, fetch, and execute

38. In the _____ method for synchronizing the operation of the CPU with an I/O device, the I/O device informs the CPU when it is ready for data transfer.
    a. programmed I/O
    b. interrupt-driven I/O
    c. DMA
    d. isolated I/O

39. In the _____ method for synchronizing the operation of the CPU with an I/O device, the CPU is idle until the I/O operation is finished.
    a. programmed I/O
    b. interrupt-driven I/O
    c. DMA
    d. isolated I/O

40. In the _____ method for synchronizing the operation of the CPU with an I/O device, a large block of data can be passed from an I/O device to memory directly.
    a. programmed I/O
    b. interrupt-driven I/O
    c. DMA
    d. isolated I/O

Exercises

41. A computer has 64 MB (megabytes) of memory. Each word is 4 bytes. How many bits are needed to address each single word in memory?

42. How many bytes of memory are needed to store a full screen of data if the screen is made of 24 lines with 80 characters in each line? The system uses ASCII code, with each ASCII character stored as a byte.

43. An imaginary computer has sixteen data registers (R0 to R15), 1024 words in memory, and 16 different instructions (add, subtract, and so on). What is the minimum size of an instruction in bits if a typical instruction uses the following format: *Instruction M R2*.

44. If the computer in Exercise 43 uses the same size of word for data and instructions, what is the size of each data register?

45. What is the size of the instruction register in the computer in Exercise 43?

46. What is the size of the program counter in the computer in Exercise 43?

47. What is the size of the data bus in the computer in Exercise 43?

48. What is the size of the address bus in the computer in Exercise 43?

49. What is the minimum size of the control bus in the computer in Exercise 43?

50. A computer uses isolated I/O addressing. Its memory has 1,024 words. If each controller has 16 registers, how many controllers can be accessed by this computer?

51. A computer uses memory-mapped I/O addressing. The address bus uses 10 lines (10 bits). If memory is made up of 1,000 words, how many four-register controllers can be accessed by the computer?

52. Using the instruction set of the simple computer in Section 5.7, write the code for a program that performs the following calculation:

$$D \leftarrow A + B + C$$

A, B, C, and D are integers in two's complement format. The user types the value of A, B, and, C, and the value of D is displayed on the monitor.

53. Using the instruction set of the simple computer in Section 5.7, write the code for a program that performs the following calculation:

$$B \leftarrow A + 3$$

A and 3 are integers in two's complement format. The user types the value of A and the value of B is displayed on the monitor. (Hint: use the increment instruction.)

54. Using the instruction set of the simple computer in Section 5.7, write the code for a program that performs the following calculation:

$$B \leftarrow A - 2$$

A and 2 are integers in two's complement format. The user types the value of A and the value of B is displayed on the monitor. (Hint: use the decrement instruction.)

55. Using the instruction set of the simple computer in Section 5.7, write the code for a program that adds n integers typed on the keyboard and displays their sum. You need first to type the value of n. (Hint: use decrement and jump instructions and repeat the addition n times.)

56. Using the instruction set of the simple computer in Section 5.7, write the code for a program that accepts two integers from the keyboard. If the first integer is 0, the program increment the second integer, and if the first integer is 1, the programs decrement the second integer. The first integer must be only 0 or 1 otherwise the program fails. The program displays the result of the increment or decrement.

6
Computer Networks

The development of the personal computer has brought about tremendous changes for business, industry, science, and education. A similar revolution has occurred in networking. Technological advances are making it possible for communication links to carry more and faster signals. As a result, services are evolving to allow use of this expanded capacity. Research in this area has resulted in new technologies. One goal is to be able to exchange data such as text, audio, and video from all parts of the world. We want to access the Internet to download and upload information quickly and accurately and at any time.

Objectives
After studying this chapter, the student should be able to:

❑ Describe network criteria, physical structures, and categories of networks.

❑ Distinguish an internet from the Internet.

❑ Describe the TCP/IP protocol suite as the network model in the Internet.

❑ Define the layers in the TCP/IP protocol suite and their relationship.

❑ Discuss the client-server architecture of the Internet.

❑ Describe the three early applications of the Internet: electronic mail, file transfer, and remote login.

❑ Understand the World Wide Web as the most common application of the Internet and its components.

❑ Distinguish between three Internet document types: static, dynamic, and active.

❑ List other Internet applications, such as videoconferencing, group discussion, and chat.

6.1   INTRODUCTION

A **network** is a combination of hardware and software that sends data from one location to another. The hardware consists of the physical equipment that carries signals from one point in the network to another. The software consists of instructions that make the services that we expect from a network possible.

Network criteria

A network must be able to meet a number of criteria. The most important of these are performance, reliability, and security.

Performance

Performance can be measured in many ways, including transit time and response time. Transit time is the amount of time required for a message to travel from one device to another. Response time is the elapsed time between an enquiry and a response. The performance of a network depends on a number of factors, including the number of users, the type of transmission medium, the capabilities of the connected hardware, and the efficiency of the software.

Reliability

In addition to accuracy of delivery, network **reliability** is measured by the frequency of failure, the time it takes to recover from a failure, and the network's robustness in a catastrophe.

Security

Network **security** issues include protecting data from unauthorized access, damage and change, and implementing policies and procedures for recovery from breaches and data losses. We discuss security in Chapter 16.

Physical structures

Before discussing networks, we need to define some network attributes.

Type of connection

A network consists of two or more devices connected through links. A link is a communications pathway that transfers data from one device to another. For visualization purposes, it is simplest to imagine any link as a line drawn between two points. For communication to occur, two devices must be connected in some way to the same link at the same time. There are two possible types of connections: point-to-point and multipoint.

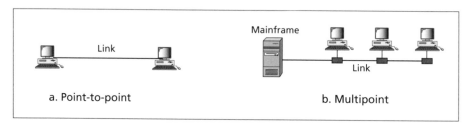

Figure 6.1   Types of connections: point-to-point and multipoint

A **point-to-point connection** provides a dedicated link between two devices, and the entire capacity of the link is reserved for transmission between these two devices. A **multipoint connection** (also called **multidrop connection**) is one in which more than two specific devices share a single link. In a multipoint environment, the capacity of the channel is shared, either spatially or temporally.

Physical topology

The term *physical topology* refers to the way in which a network is laid out physically. Two or more devices connect to a link: one or more links form a topology. The topology of a network is the geometric representation of the relationship of all the links and devices (usually called **nodes**) to one another. There are four possible basic topologies: mesh, star, bus, and ring (see Figure 6.2).

In a **mesh topology**, every device has a dedicated point-to-point link to every other device. In a **star topology**, each device has a dedicated point-to-point link only to a central controller, usually called a **hub**. A **bus topology** uses a multipoint link. One long cable, called the *bus*, acts as a **backbone** to link all the devices in a network. Nodes are connected to the bus cable by drop lines and taps (connectors). In a **ring topology**, each device has a dedicated point-to-point connection with only the two devices on either side of it. A signal is passed along the ring in one direction, from device to device, until it reaches its destination. Each device in the ring incorporates a repeater. When a device receives a signal intended for another device, its repeater regenerates the bits and passes them along.

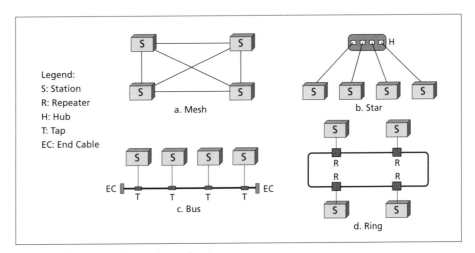

Figure 6.2 Four physical topologies

Each topology has its own advantages and disadvantages. A mesh guarantees that each connection can carry its own data load, eliminating traffic problems. It is also robust in the sense that if one link becomes unusable, it does not incapacitate the entire network. The main disadvantages of a mesh topology are related to the amount of cabling and the number of input/output ports required.

A ring is relatively easy to install and reconfigure. In addition, fault isolation is simplified. However, a break in the ring (such as a disabled station) can disable the entire network. This weakness can be solved by using a dual ring or a switch capable of closing off the break. Ring topology was prevalent when IBM introduced its local-area network Token Ring. Today, the need for higher-speed networks has made this topology less popular.

A bus topology can be installed easily. Backbone cable can be laid along the most efficient path, then connected to the nodes by drop lines of various lengths. However, a fault or break in the bus cable stops all transmission, even between devices on the same side of the problem section.

Today the most common topology in high-speed local-area networks is a star. A star topology is less expensive than a mesh topology, but has most of the advantages of the latter. One big disadvantage of a star topology is the dependency of the whole topology on one single point, the hub. If the hub goes down, the whole system is dead. However, the low cost of a star topology and ease of installation and scalability has made the star topology the only common topology.

Categories of networks

Today networks can be divided into three broad categories: local-area networks (LANs), wide-area networks (WANs), and metropolitan area networks (MANs). The category into which a network falls is determined by its size. A LAN normally covers a small area, a WAN can be worldwide, while a MAN covers a small city or town.

Local area networks

A **local area network (LAN)** is usually privately owned and links the devices in a single office, building, or campus (see Figure 6.3). Depending on the needs of an organization and the type of technology used, a LAN can be as simple as two PCs and a printer in someone's home office, or it can extend throughout a company and include audio and video peripherals. Currently, LAN size is limited to a few kilometers.

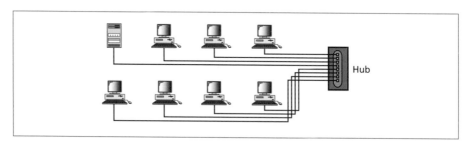

Figure 6.3   An isolated LAN connecting eight computers to a hub

LANs are designed to allow resources to be shared between personal computers or workstations. The resources to be shared can include hardware, such as a printer, software, such as an application program, or data. A common example of a LAN found in many business environments links a workgroup of task-related computers, for example, engineering workstations or accounting PCs. One of the computers may be given a large-capacity disk drive and may become a server to clients. Software can be stored on this central server and used by the whole group. In this example, the size of the LAN may be determined by licensing restrictions on the number of users per copy of software, or by restrictions on the number of users licensed to access the operating system.

Wide area networks

A **wide area network (WAN)** provides long-distance transmission of data, images, audio, and video information over large geographic areas that may comprise a country, a continent, or even the whole world. A WAN can be as complex as the backbones that connect the Internet or as simple as a dial-up line that connects a home computer to the Internet. A point-to-point WAN is normally a single line connection between two devices such as a dial-up line or a cable line. A backbone WAN is a complex network operated by a service provider and normally connects Internet service providers (ISPs) (see Figure 6.4).

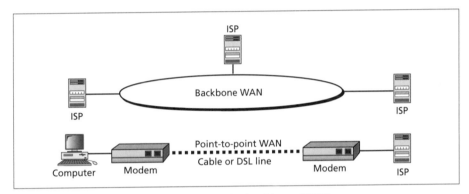

Figure 6.4   A point-to-point WAN and a backbone WAN

Metropolitan area networks

A **metropolitan area network (MAN)** is a network with a size between a LAN and a WAN. It normally covers the area inside a town or a city. It is designed for customers who need high-speed connectivity, normally to the Internet, and has endpoints spread over a city or part of city. A good example of a MAN is that part of a telephone company's network that can provide a high-speed DSL line to the customer. Another example is the cable network that was originally designed for cable television, but today can also be used for high-speed data connection to the Internet.

An internet

Today, it is very rare to see a network in isolation: networks are connected to one another. When two or more networks are connected, they become an **internetwork**, or an **internet** (lowercase "i"). Figure 6.5 shows an example of an internet.

In other words, a network is a group of connected communicating devices such as computers and printers, while an internet is two or more networks that can communicate with each other. In Figure 6.5 we have seven LANs and two WANs. Each LAN is a local network connecting computers, printers, and other devices inside a

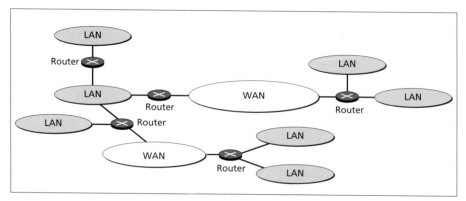

Figure 6.5   An internet made of WANs, LANs, and routers

building or a campus. The WANs are either point-to-point (a leased line, for example) or a backbone operated by a network service provider. The **routers** are connecting devices that route the *packets* (messages) travelling through the internet.

The Internet

The most notable internet is the Internet (uppercase "I"), a collaboration of hundreds of thousands of interconnected networks. Private individuals, as well as various organizations such as government agencies, schools, research facilities, corporations, and libraries in more than 100 countries use the Internet. Millions of people are users.

It is difficult to give an accurate representation of the Internet, because it is continually changing—new networks are being added and networks of defunct organizations removed. Today most end users who want an Internet connection use the services of **Internet service providers (ISPs)**. An ISP is an organization with one or more *servers* (high capacity computers) that are connected to the Internet through high-speed links. Individual Internet users or small companies can be connected to the servers of a local ISP by establishing a service contract and paying a fee. There are international service providers, national service providers, regional service providers, and local service providers. The Internet today is run by private companies, not the government. Figure 6.6 shows a conceptual (but not geographic) view of part of the Internet.

The Internet has revolutionized many aspects of our daily lives. It has affected the way we do business as well as the way we spend our leisure time. Count the ways you've used the Internet recently. Perhaps you've sent electronic mail (e-mail) to a business associate, paid a utility bill, read a newspaper from a distant city, or looked up a local movie schedule—all by using the Internet. Or maybe you researched a medical topic, booked a hotel reservation, chatted with a colleague, or comparison-shopped for a car. The Internet is a communication system that has brought a wealth of information to our fingertips and organized it for our use.

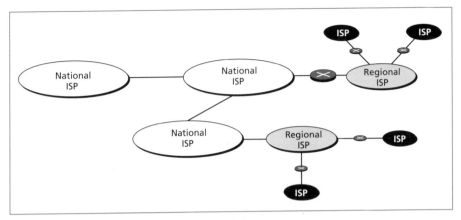

Figure 6.6   Hierarchical organization of the Internet

6.2   TCP/IP PROTOCOL SUITE

We can compare the task of networking to the task of solving a math problem with a computer. The fundamental job of solving the problem with a computer is done by computer hardware. However, this is a very tedious task if only hardware is involved. We would need switches for every memory location to store and manipulate data. The task is much easier if software is available. At the highest level, a program can direct the problem-solving process: the details of how this is done by the actual hardware can be left to the layers of software that are called by the higher levels.

Compare this to a service provided by a computer network. For example, the task of sending an e-mail from one place in the world to another can be broken down into several tasks, each performed by a layer. Each layer uses the services of a lower layer. At the lowest layer, a signal, or a set of signals, is sent from the source computer to the destination computer.

To divide the services required to perform a task, the Internet has created a set of rules called *protocols*. These allow different local and wide area networks, using different technologies, to be connected together and carry a message from one point to another. The set, or *suite*, of protocols that controls the Internet today is referred to as the **TCP/IP protocol suite**. The abbreviations (TCP and IP) will become clear as we explain different protocols.

The original TCP/IP protocol suite was defined as having four layers: host-to-network (or link), internet (network), transport, and application. However, the TCP/IP protocol suite today is normally considered as a five-layer model, as shown in Figure 6.7.

Figure 6.8 shows the layers involved when a message is sent from device A to device B. As the message travels from A to B, it may pass through many routers. Routers use only the first three layers.

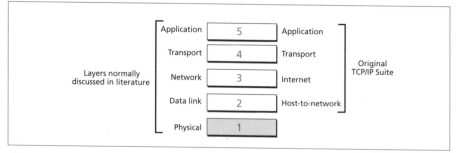

Figure 6.7   The TCP/IP protocol suite

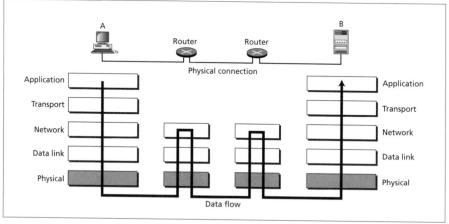

Figure 6.8   The interaction between layers in the TCP/IP protocol suite

Within a single machine, each layer calls on the services of the layer immediately below it. Layer 3, for example, uses the services provided by layer 2 and provides services for layer 4.

6.3 LAYERS

This section briefly describes the function of each layer in the TCP/IP protocol suite. We show how a message travels through the different layers until it reaches the physical layer and is sent by the transmission media.

Application layer

The **application layer** enables a user, whether human or software, to access the network. It provides support for services such as electronic mail, remote file access and transfer, browsing the World Wide Web, and so on. Later in this chapter we discuss some common applications of the Internet. The application layer is the only layer seen by most users of the Internet.

> **The application layer is responsible for providing services to the user.**

Client-server architecture

Although there are two architectures (designs) that allow two application programs, running on two remote computers, to communicate with each other, **client-server architecture** is more common. The other architecture, **peer-to-peer architecture**, is becoming popular, but we only discuss client-server architecture in this chapter. In client-server architectures, each application is made up of two separate but related programs: a *client* program and a *server* program. The server program must be running all the time: the client program can be run only when needed. This implies that the computer on which the server program is running must be on all the time, while the computer that runs the client program may also only be on when needed. In practice, the computer that runs the server program is referred to as the *server* and the computer that runs the client program is referred to as the *client* (Figure 6.9).

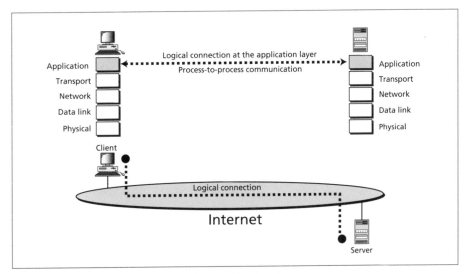

Figure 6.9   Communication at the application layer

The communication between a client program and a server program is referred to as **process-to-process communication**, because a running program in this architecture is called a **process**. In Figure 6.9 the server process is the server program that is running all the time waiting to receive a request from a client process.

The user (human or software) that needs the services of the server process runs the dormant client program (changing it to a client process) and lets the client process request the service, which will be responded to by the server process. Note that when a server process is running many client processes can request services and obtain responses.

Application-layer address

When a client needs to send a request to a server, it needs the server application-layer address. Although the number of Internet applications is limited, the number of sites that run a server for a specific application is huge. For example, there are many sites that run an HTTP (defined later) server, and HTTP clients can access these sites to browse or download information stored at the site. To identify one particular HTTP site, the client uses a **Uniform Resource Locator (URL)**. For example, to access the publisher of this book, the user needs to use the URL *http://www.cengage.co.uk*. As we will see later, the server application-layer address is not used for delivery of messages, it only helps the client to find the actual address of the server computer. Note that a client site needs no identification at the application layer because it is not a service provider—it only receives services. Different sites will have different application-layer addresses, although they may be running the same server type (for example, HTTP).

The address at the application layer cannot be used to send a message. The client needs the actual address of the server in the network. The situation is similar to sending a letter to a person if we only know their name. The post office cannot deliver a letter based only on the name of the recipient: the actual address is needed. The application layer address can help the client to find the actual address of the server in the network. Each computer in the network has an address, called a *logical address* or *IP address*, as we see shortly.

The server application-layer address can help the client to find the **IP address** of the server computer. The client process should already know the address of a **domain name server (DNS)**. These servers, which are spread over the Internet, each have a directory that matches domain names to IP addresses. The client prepares and sends a message to a DNS server and asks for the actual IP address of the desired server. After receiving the response, the client server knows the IP address of the desired server. Figure 6.10 shows the idea. In the figure, d_5 is the application-layer address and d_3 is the network-layer or IP address.

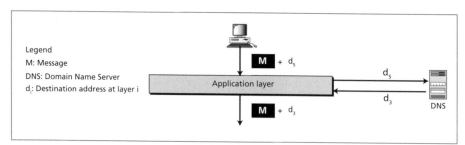

Figure 6.10   Addresses at the application layer

Transport layer

The **transport layer** is responsible for **process-to-process delivery** of the entire message: logical communication is created between the transport layer of the client and the server computer. In other words, although physical communication is between two physical layers (through many possible links and routers), the two application layers consider the transport layer as the agent that takes responsibility for delivering the messages. Figure 6.11 shows the logical connection between the two transport layers through the Internet.

> **The transport layer is responsible for the logical delivery of a message between client and server processes.**

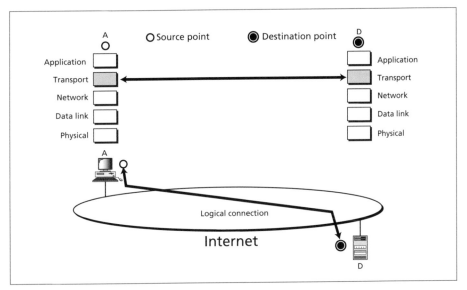

Figure 6.11 Communication at the transport layer

Transport-layer addresses (port numbers)

The IP address of the server is necessary for communication, but more is required. The server computer may be running several processes at the same time, for example an FTP server process and an HTTP server process. When the message arrives at the server, it must be directed to the correct process. We need another address for server process identification, called a **port number**. An analogy may help here. Assume that everyone in a community lives in apartment buildings. To send a message to a specific person, we need to know both the building address and the apartment number. The IP address is similar to the building address, and the port address is similar to apartment number. Server port numbers are well-known: most computers have a file that gives server port addresses, while the client port number can be temporarily assigned by the computer running the client process. However, the Internet restricts the range of temporary port numbers to avoid infringing the range of well-known port addresses (Figure 6.12). In the figure, d_4 is the well-known port number and s_4 is the temporary port number.

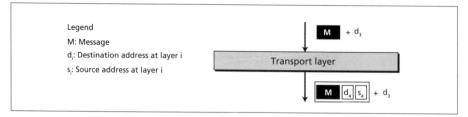

Figure 6.12   Addresses at the transport layer

Multiplexing and demultiplexing

One of the duties of the transport layer is **multiplexing** and **demultiplexing**. To continue with our analogy, in large cities where people live in big apartment buildings, the mailman cannot collect the mail from each individual tenant and cannot deliver mail to each individual tenant. This duty is normally taken by a concierge. The concierge collects outgoing mail from tenants and delivers them to the mailman (multiplexing), and distributes incoming mail to the tenants after it has arrived (demultiplexing). The transport layer does the same for the different processes, collecting outgoing messages from processes and distributing incoming messages to processes. The transport layer uses port numbers (similar to the apartment numbers used by the concierge or apartment manager) to do the multiplexing and demultiplexing.

This implies that port numbers should be unique in a computer. Server processes use well-known port numbers, but client processes use temporary port numbers that are assigned by the transport layer.

Congestion control

The transport layer carries out **congestion control**. The underlying networks that physically carry the packets may become congested with traffic. This may cause the network to drop—lose—some packets. Some protocols use a buffer for each process. The messages are stored in the buffer before being sent. If the transport layer detects that there is congestion in the network, it slows transmission. This is similar to the effect of traffic lights installed at highway junctions in some countries. Only one car is allowed to pass the lights with each green signal: if there is traffic in the junction, the interval between green lights increases.

Flow control

The transport layer also carries out flow control. The transport layer at the sender site can monitor the transport layer at the receiver site to check that the receiver is not overwhelmed with received packets. This is achieved if the system uses acknowledgment from the receiver. The receiver can acknowledge receipt of each, or a group of, packets to allow the sender to check that the receiver is not overwhelmed.

Error control

During a message's journey it can be corrupted, lost, duplicated, or received out of order. The sending transport layer is responsible for ensuring that the message is received correctly by the destination transport layer. The acknowledgment system described above can also provide error control. The transport layer can keep a copy of the message in a buffer (temporary storage) until it receives acknowledgement from the receiver that the packet has arrived uncorrupted and in the right order. If no acknowledgment arrives in due time, or a negative acknowledgment arrives (denoting the packet is corrupted), the sender resends the packet. To be able to check the ordering of packets, the transport layer can add a sequence number to the packet and an acknowledgement number to the acknowledgment.

Transport layer protocols

During the life of the TCP/IP protocol suite three transport layer protocols have been designed: UDP, TCP, and SCTP.

UDP

The **User Datagram Protocol (UDP)** is the simplest of all three protocols. UDP does multiplexing and demultiplexing (by adding source and destination ports to the packet). It also does a type of error control by adding a checksum (see Appendix H) to the packet. Error control in this case is only a "yes or no" procedure—the receiver recalculates the checksum to see if an error has occurred during transmission. If the receiver concludes that the packet is corrupted, it silently drops the packet without warning the sender to resend it. UDP is not a perfect protocol, but it is useful in some circumstances when other duties are not required of the transport layer, or are already carried out by the application layer. UDP, however, being simple, has the advantage of being fast. UDP is also more efficient: it carries less information overhead than other protocols. Some application programs prefer to use UDP because they either do flow and error control themselves, or need a fast and efficient response. An example of this is the DNS server discussed before. UDP is also suitable for applications whose timing is more important than accuracy. For example, when we are dealing with real-time transmission of video on the Internet, it is important that all packets that form an image arrive on time, and if a small number of packets are lost or corrupted, the viewer cannot detect a small and transient error in the image.

UDP is referred to as a **connectionless protocol** because it does not provide a logical connection between packets belonging to a single message. Each packet is an individual entity in UDP, due to the lack of sequence numbers. This service is similar to that provided by the regular mail system. Assume you need to send a set of ordered packets to a destination: the post office cannot guarantee that they are delivered in the requested order. Each packet, as far as the post office is concerned, is an individual entity with no relationship to other packets.

TCP

Transmission Control Protocol (TCP) is a protocol that supports all the duties of a transport layer. However, it is not as fast and as efficient as UDP. TCP uses sequence numbers, acknowledgment numbers, and checksums. It also uses buffers at the sender's site. This combination of provisions provides multiplexing, demultiplexing, flow control, congestion control, and error control.

TCP is referred to as a **connection-oriented protocol** because it provides a logical connection between the two transport layers: one at the source, the other at the destination. The use of sequence numbers maintains a connection: if a packet arrives out of order or lost, it will be resent. The transport layer at the receiver does not deliver the out of sequence packet to the application process, but holds all packets in a message until they are received in the correct order.

Although TCP is a perfect transport-layer protocol for data communication, it is not suitable for real-time transmission of audio or video. If a packet is lost, TCP needs to resend it, which destroys the synchronization of packets.

SCTP

Stream Control Transmission Protocol (SCTP) is a new protocol that is designed for new services expected from the Internet, such as Internet telephony and video streaming. This protocol combines the advantages of both UDP and TCP. Like UDP, it is suitable for real-time transmission of audio and video, but like TCP, it provides error and flow control.

The network layer

The **network layer** is responsible for the source-to-destination (computer-to-computer or host-to-host) delivery of a packet, possibly across multiple networks (links). The network layer ensures that each packet gets from its point of origin to its final destination.

> **The network layer is responsible for the delivery of individual packets from the source host to the destination host.**

The services expected from a network layer are similar to the services mentioned above for a "perfect" transport layer, with the exception of multiplexing/demultiplexing. In other words, a network layer protocol should provide congestion, flow and error control. However, this does not happen in the Internet, as we will see shortly.

Network-layer addresses

The packet travelling from the client to the server and the packet returning from the server need a network-layer address. The server address is provided by the server, as discussed above, while the client address is known by the client computer. Figure 6.13 shows the idea. In addition, the network layer uses its routing table to find the logical address of the next hop (router), which is passed to the data link layer. This logical address (n_3) is needed by the data link layer to find the data link layer address of the next router.

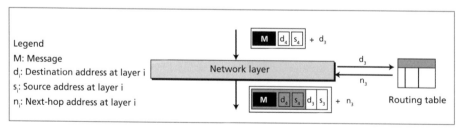

Figure 6.13   Addresses at the network layer

Routing

The network layer has a specific duty: **routing**. Routing means determination of the partial or total path of a packet. As the Internet is a collection of networks (LANs,

WANs, and MANs), the delivery of a packet from its source to its destination may be a combination of several deliveries: a source-to-router delivery, several router-to-router deliveries, and finally a router-to-destination delivery.

We can again compare the delivery of a packet on the Internet to the delivery of a letter using the regular postal service. Imagine that a letter is to go from a small town in California to a small town in Florida. The sender drops the letter at the post office of the town in California (the first router). The local post office collects the letter and sends it to the main post office in Los Angeles (a router). The letter is probably delivered to Los Angeles airport (another router). The postal airplane delivers the letter to Miami airport (another router). The letter then is delivered to the main post office in Miami (another router). The letter is then sent to the local post office of the destination town (the final router). Finally it will be delivered to the recipient of the letter.

This is probably the normal scenario. But what happens if, due to bad weather, the postal airplane cannot fly from Los Angeles to Miami? The office at Los Angeles airport (acting as a router) may decide to choose another route. The letter might be sent to New York. After arrival, it could be carried to the Miami main post office by road. Note that in this case the source and destination addresses of the letter remain the same, but the route is changed. The post office router at Los Angeles airport decides that the best route at this moment, although probably longer, is via New York.

Note that in both scenarios, the source and destination address of the letter (as written on it) remain the same: the only thing that is changed is the route. The route is selected based on the destination address and the available best paths. For example, in the second scenario, when the letter arrives at Los Angeles airport, the post office sends it by air to New York, not Miami.

The situation is the same with routing in the network layer. When a router receives a packet, it consults its routing table to determine the best route for the packet to reach its final destination. The routing table provides the IP address of the next router. When the packet reaches the next router, a new decision is made. In other words, the routing decision is made at each router.

Figure 6.14 shows the route of a packet from source to destination through some networks. The source is computer A, the destination is computer D. When the packet arrives at router R1, this router selects router R4 (instead of R3) as the next router (probably WAN 1 is either down or congested). Router R4 selects router R5 as the next router. Finally the packet is delivered to its destination, computer D. Note that the routers use only the first three layers of the TCP/IP protocol suite: they do not need the transport layer, which is responsible for the end-to-end delivery.

How does a router update its routing table? This is done by other protocols, *routing protocols*. A routing protocol sends its own messages to all routers on the Internet to update them about routes. Several routing protocols are used on the Internet, such as RIP, OSPF, and BGP, but a discussion of these is beyond the scope of this chapter.

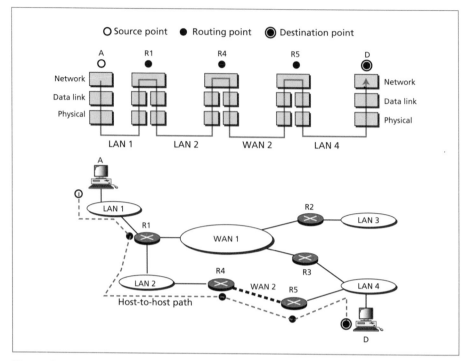

Figure 6.14   Routing at the network layer

Network layer protocols

The TCP/IP protocol suite supports one main protocol (IP) and several auxiliary protocols to help IP to perform its duties.

IP

In the TCP/IP protocol suite, the main protocol at the network layer is **Internet Protocol (IP)**. The current version is IPv4 (version 4) although IPv6 (version 6) is also in use, though not ubiquitously. IPv4 is responsible for the delivery of a packet from the source computer to the destination computer. For this purpose, every computer and router in the world is identified by a 32-bit IP address, which is presented in **dotted decimal notation**. The notation divides the 32-bit address into four 8-bit sections and writes each section as a decimal number between 0 and 255 with three dots separating the sections. For example, an IPv4 address 00001010 00011001 10101100 00001111 is written as 10.25.172.15 in dotted decimal notation.

At a message's source the IPv4 protocol adds the source and destination IP addresses to the packet passed from the application. The packet is then ready for its journey. However, the actual delivery is done by the data link and physical layer, as described shortly.

The address range of IPv4 (32 bits) can define up to 2^{32} (more than 4 billion) different devices. However, the way in which addresses have been allocated in the past has created *address depletion*. Several remedies have been designed to solve this problem, but experts foresee an imminent change in the structure of IP addresses. The ultimate solution is IPv6 (partially in use today) in which the address is made up from 128 bits.

IP provides a **best-effort service**. It does not guarantee that packets will arrive error-free or in the order intended by the sender. It does not even guarantee that any packet is delivered: a packet may be lost for ever. Although this looks superficially like a terrible service, we can see that the Internet is working and doing its job. The situation is the same as the basic service offered by the post office. If we use the normal services offered by the post office, it does not guarantee that our letters will be received by the destination, but the system works almost all the time. If we need a guaranteed delivery, we can use other services offered by the post office, such as certified mail or a return receipt. The situation is the same with the Internet. Although IP is unreliable, an application can use the services of a reliable transport protocol, such as TCP, or implement error control itself to complement the service provided by IP.

Auxiliary protocols

Internet Protocol uses other auxiliary protocols to compensate for its deficiencies to some extent. Internet Control Message Protocol (ICMP) can be used to report a limited number of errors to the source computer. For example, if a router drops a packet because of congestion, ICMP can send a packet to the source to warn it of the congestion. ICMP can also be used to check the status of nodes in the Internet.

Internet Group Management Protocol (IGMP) can be used to add *multicasting* capability to IP. IP per se is a *unicast* protocol: one source, one destination. Multicasting enables IP to do multicasting: one source, many destinations. Other auxiliary protocols are used in the network layer, such as Address Resolution Protocol (ARP) and Reverse Address Resolution Protocol (RARP), that give other help to IP, but we must leave the discussion of these protocols to textbooks devoted to networking.

Data link layer

As we saw in the previous section, the network layer packet may pass through several routers in its journey from its source to its destination. Carrying the packet from one node to another (where a node can be a computer or a router) is the responsibility of the **data link layer**.

In our previous analogy, after the post office at Los Angeles airport decides that the letter should go to the post office at New York airport, the letter is delivered to the crew of the corresponding aircraft. Note however that the crew is only responsible for carrying the letter from Los Angeles to New York. The letter is probably put in a bag or a box with a label such as "from Los Angeles to New York".

The situation is the same on the Internet. In Figure 6.15, after the source decides that the packet should be sent to router R1 (the only possible router in this case), it encapsulates the packet in a **frame** and adds the link-layer address of router R1 in the packet's header as the destination address, and the link-layer address of computer A as the source address, then sends the packet. Every device connected to LAN 1 receives the frame, but only R1 opens it, because it recognizes its data-link layer address. This procedure is repeated between R1 and R4, between R4 and R5, and between R5 and D. Note that the reason we show separate boxes for the data-link and physical layers in the upper part of the diagram is because each network (LAN and WAN) may operate under different protocols with different address or frame formats.

The data-link layer is responsible for node-to-node delivery of frames.

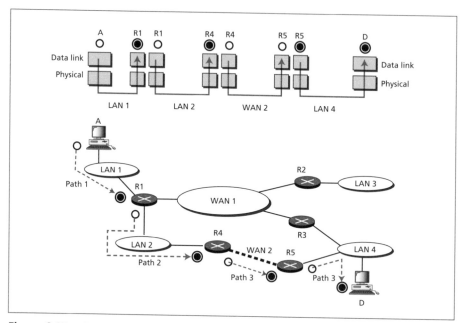

Figure 6.15 Communication at the data-link layer

Data-link layer addresses

Two questions that come to mind are how computer A knows the data-link layer address of router R1, or router R1 knows the data-link layer address of router R4. A device can find the data-link address of another device either statically or dynamically. In the static method, a device can create a table with two columns and store the network-layer link-layer addresses pairs. In the dynamic method, a device can broadcast a special packet containing the IP address of the next device and ask the neighbor with this IP address to send back its link address. Figure 6.16 shows the idea of data-link layer. In the figure, the data-link layer uses a static or dynamic process to find the data-link layer address of the next hop (router).

Unlike IP addresses, addresses at the data-link layer cannot be universal. Each data-link protocol may have a different address format and size. The Ethernet protocol, the most prevalent local area network in use today, uses a 48-bit address,

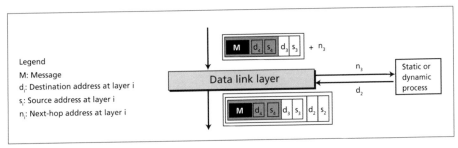

Figure 6.16   Addresses at the data-link layer

which is normally written in hexadecimal format (grouped in six sections, each with two hexadecimal digits) as shown below:

07:01:02:11:2C:5B

Data-link layer addresses are often called **physical addresses** or **media access control (MAC) addresses**.

Error and flow control

Some data-link layer protocols use error control and flow control at the data-link layer. The procedure is the same as we discussed for the transport layer. However, it is implemented only between the outgoing point of a node and the incoming point of another node. This means that, for example, errors are checked several times, but none of the error checking covers errors that may happen inside a router. There may be no error from the outgoing port of router R1 to the incoming port of router R2, but what if the error happens within either of the routers? This is the reason why we need error control at the transport layer: to check the error from end to end.

Physical layer

The **physical layer** coordinates the functions required to carry a bit stream over a physical medium. Although the data-link layer is responsible for moving a frame from one node to another, the physical layer is responsible for moving the individual bits that make up the frame to the next node. In other words, the unit of transfer in the data link layer is a frame, while the unit of transfer in the physical layer is a bit. Each bit in the frame is transformed to an electromagnetic signal and propagated through the physical medium (wireless or cable). Note that there is no need for addressing in the physical layer: the propagation is broadcast. The signal sent from a device is received by other devices that are connected to the sending device by some means as long as there is no filtering to filter out the signal. For example, in a local area network, when a signal is sent by a computer or a router, all other computers and routers will receive it. Figure 6.17 shows the concept of the physical layer.

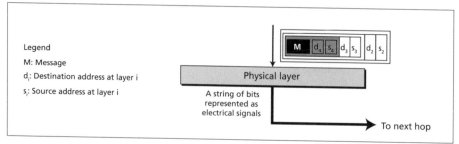

Figure 6.17   Duty of the physical layer

Summary of layers

Figure 6.18 summarizes the duties of each layer in the TCP/IP protocol and the addresses involved in each layer.

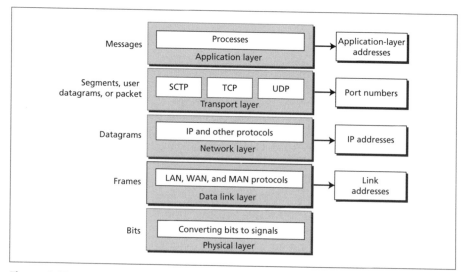

Figure 6.18   Four level of addressing in the Internet

The figure shows the unit of data in each layer. In the application layer, processes exchange messages. At the transport layer, the unit of data is referred to as a *segment* (TCP), a *user datagram* (UDP), or a packet (SCTP). At the network layer, the unit of data is referred to as a datagram. At the data-link layer, the unit of data is referred to as a frame. Finally, in the physical layer, the unit of data is a bit.

Figure 6.19 shows another aspect of the various layers: **encapsulation**. In the figure, D5 denotes the data unit at layer 5, D4 denotes the data unit at layer 4, and so on. The process starts at layer 5 (the application layer), then moves from layer to layer in descending, sequential order. At each layer, a **header**, or possibly a **trailer**, can be added to the data unit. Commonly, the trailer is added only at layer 2. When the formatted data unit passes through the physical layer (layer 1) it is changed into an electromagnetic signal and transported via a physical link.

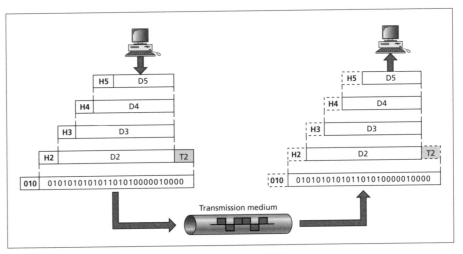

Figure 6.19   An exchange using the TCP/IP model

Upon reaching its destination, the signal passes into layer 1 and is transformed back into digital form. The data units then move back up through the layers. As each block of data reaches the next higher layer, the headers and trailers attached to it at the corresponding sending layer are removed, and actions appropriate to that layer are taken. By the time it reaches layer 5, the message is again in a form appropriate for the application and is made available to the recipient.

Note that the relationship between data units in the layers is not one-to-one. In other words, a message in layer 5 may not be necessarily encapsulated in a single segment in layer 4. In TCP, a message in layer 5 is divided into several sections and each section is encapsulated in one segment. In UDP, however, each message is encapsulated in one user datagram. This means that the messages delivered to UDP must be small enough to fit in one user datagram. The situation is the same when a segment or user datagram is encapsulated in a datagram (layer 4). A datagram in the network layer may also be split into several frames in the data link layer.

6.4   INTERNET APPLICATIONS

The main task of the Internet is to provide services for users. Among the most popular applications are electronic mail, remote login, file transfer, and accessing the World Wide Web (WWW). We briefly discuss these applications in this section.

e-mail

Let us first discuss **electronic mail (e-mail)**. Ironically, this first application that we discuss in this section cannot be supported by one client process and one server process. The reason is that e-mail is the exchange of messages between two entities. Although the sender of the e-mail can be a client program, the receiver cannot be the corresponding server, because that implies that the receiver must let their computer run all the time, as they do not know when an e-mail will arrive. For this purpose, e-mail architecture is designed as shown in Figure 6.20.

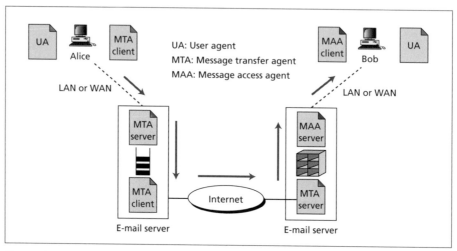

Figure 6.20   E-mail architecture

Assume that Alice is working in an organization that runs an e-mail server: every employee is connected to the e-mail server through a LAN. Alternatively, Alice could be connected to the e-mail server of an ISP through a WAN (telephone line or cable). Bob is also in one of the above two situations. The administrator of the e-mail server at Alice's site has created a queuing system that sends e-mail messages to the Internet one by one. The administrator of the e-mail server at Bob's site has created a mailbox for every user connected to the server: the mailbox holds the received messages until they are retrieved by the recipient. When Alice needs to send a message to Bob, she invokes a **user agent (UA)** program to prepare the message. She then uses another program, a **message transfer agent (MTA)**, to send the message to the mail server at her site. Note that the MTA is a client/server program with the client part installed on Alice's computer and the server part installed on the mail server. The application program that does the job of the MTA client and server is called **Simple Mail Transfer Protocol (SMTP)**. The message received at the mail server at Alice's site is queued with all other messages: each goes to its corresponding destination. In Alice's case, her message goes to the mail server at Bob's site. A client/server MTA is responsible for the e-mail transfer between the two servers. When the message arrives at the destination mail server, it is stored in Bob's *mailbox*, a special file that holds the message until it is retrieved by Bob. When Bob needs to retrieve his messages, including the one sent by Alice, he invokes another program, a **message access agent (MAA)**. The MAA is also designed as a client/server program with the client part installed on Bob's computer and the server part installed on the mail server.

There are several important points about the architecture of the e-mail system:

❑   Sending an e-mail from Alice to Bob is a store-and-retrieve activity. Alice can send an e-mail today: Bob, being busy, may check his e-mail three days later. During this time the e-mail is stored in Bob's mailbox on the server until it is retrieved.

❑   The main communication between Alice and Bob is through two application programs: the MTA client on Alice's computer and the MAA client on Bob's computer.

❑   The MTA client program is a *push* program: the client pushes (uploads) the message when Alice needs to send it. The MAA client program is a *pull* program: the client pulls (downloads) messages when Bob is ready to retrieve his e-mail.

❑   Alice and Bob cannot communicate directly using an MTA client at the sender site and an MTA server at the receiver site. This requires that the MTA server is running all the time, because Bob does not know when a message will arrive. This is not practical, because Bob probably turns off his computer when he does not need it.

Mail access protocols   Stored e-mail remains on the mail server until it is retrieved by the recipient through an access protocol. Currently two e-mail access protocols are in common use: Post Office Protocol, Version 3 (POP3) and Internet Mail Access Protocol (IMAP).

POP

Post Office Protocol (POP) is simple but limited in functionality. The client POP software is installed on the recipient's computer and the server POP software is installed on the e-mail server.

Mail access starts with the client when the user needs to download their received e-mail from their mailbox on the mail server. The client (user agent) sends the user name and password to access the mailbox. The user can then list and retrieve the e-mail messages one by one.

POP has several deficiencies:

❑   It does not allow the user to organize e-mail on the server.

❑   The user cannot have different folders on the server, although of course the user can create folders on their own computer.

❑   POP does not allow the user to check the contents of their e-mail before downloading it.

IMAP

A second popular mail access protocol, **Internet Mail Access Protocol (IMAP)**, can handle these deficiencies. IMAP, although similar to POP, has more features and is more powerful and complex. IMAP provides the following extra functions. Users can:

❑   Check an e-mail header prior to downloading.

❑   Search the contents of their e-mail prior to downloading.

❑ Partially download e-mail. This is especially useful if the user has limited capacity and the e-mail volume is large.

❑ Create, delete, or rename mailboxes on the e-mail server.

❑ Create a hierarchy of mailboxes in a folder for e-mail storage.

Addresses

An e-mail handling system must have a unique addressing system to deliver mail. The addressing system used by SMTP consists of two parts: a *local part* and a *domain name*, separated by an @ sign (see Figure 6.21).

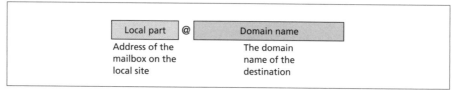

Figure 6.21   E-mail address composition

Local part

The local part defines the name of a special file, the user's *mailbox*, where all of the e-mail received for a user is stored for retrieval by the user's agent.

Domain name

The second part of the address is a name assigned to an IP address (a connection to the Internet). An organization usually selects one or more hosts to receive and send e-mail. The name assigned to each mail server, the **domain name**, comes from a universal naming system called the *domain name system* (DNS).

Multipurpose Internet Mail Extension (MIME)

As its name implies, SMTP is a simple mail transfer protocol. Its simplicity, however, comes with a price. SMTP can send messages only in NVT (*network virtual terminal*) 7-bit ASCII format. It cannot be used for languages that are not supported by 7-bit ASCII characters, such as French, German, Hebrew, Russian, Chinese, and Japanese. Also, it cannot be used to send binary files, video or audio data.

Multipurpose Internet Mail Extension (MIME) is a supplementary protocol that allows non-ASCII data to be sent through SMTP. MIME is not an e-mail protocol and cannot replace SMTP, it is only an extension to SMTP.

MIME transforms non-ASCII data at the sender's site into NVT ASCII data and delivers it to the client SMTP to be sent through the Internet. The server SMTP at the receiving side receives the NVT ASCII data and delivers it to MIME to be transformed back to the original data.

We can think of MIME as a set of software functions that transforms non-ASCII data into ASCII data and vice versa (see Figure 6.22).

File Transfer Protocol (FTP)

File Transfer Protocol (FTP) is the standard mechanism for one of the most common tasks on the Internet, copying a file from one computer to another.

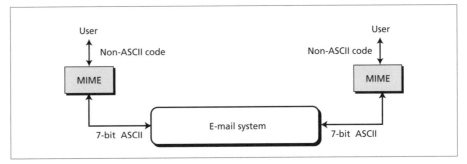

Figure 6.22   Multipurpose Internet Mail Extension (MIME)

Although file transfer from one system to another seems simple and straightforward, some problems must be dealt with first. For example, two systems may use different file naming conventions. Two systems may also have different ways to represent text and data, or different directory structures. All of these problems have been solved by FTP with a very simple and elegant approach.

FTP differs from other client-server applications in that it establishes two connections between the hosts. One connection is used for data transfer, the other for control information (commands and responses). Separation of commands and data transfer makes FTP more efficient. The control connection uses very simple rules of communication. We need to transfer only a line of command or a line of response at a time. The data connection, on the other hand, needs more complex rules due to the variety of data types transferred.

Figure 6.23 shows the basic model for FTP. The client has three components: the user interface, the client control process, and the client data transfer process. The server has two components: the server control process and the server data transfer process. The control connection is made between the control processes. The data connection is made between the data transfer processes.

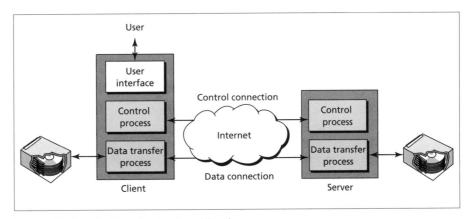

Figure 6.23   File Transfer Protocol (FTP)

The control connection remains open during the entire interactive FTP session, while the data connection is opened and then closed for each file transferred. It opens each time commands that involve transferring files are used, and it closes after the file is transferred. The two FTP connections, control and data, use different strategies and different port numbers.

Closed and open FTP

Sites that run FTP servers to allow users to access files use one of two strategies: a site is either closed or open to the public. A closed FTP site allows only specific users to access files: access is controlled by the user account and password and the general public are not allowed to access files at such sites.

An open FTP site allows anyone to access files. These sites offer **anonymous FTP**. Users can use *anonymous* as the user name and *guest* as the password. User participation in this system is very limited. Some sites allow anonymous users only a subset of commands. For example, most sites allow users to copy files, but do not allow navigation through the file system.

There are occasions when we need simply to copy a file without the need for all of the functionalities of FTP. **Trivial File Transfer Protocol (TFTP)** is designed for these types of file transfer. It makes a single connection and transfers a small file quickly. However, this application is not universally available.

Remote login – TELNET

The main task of the application layer is to provide services for users. For example, users want to be able to run different application programs at a remote site and create results that can be transferred to their local site. One way to satisfy these demands is to create different client-server application programs for each desired service. Programs such as file transfer programs (FTP and TFTP), e-mail (SMTP), and so on are already available. However, it would be impossible to write a client-server program for each specific application.

TELNET is a general-purpose client-server program that lets a user access any application program on a remote computer. In other words, it allows the user to log onto a remote computer. After logging on, a user can use the services available on the remote computer and transfer the results back to the local computer.

TELNET is an abbreviation for *terminal network*. TELNET enables the establishment of a connection to a remote system in such a way that the local terminal appears to be a terminal connected directly to the remote system.

Local login

When a user logs onto a local time-sharing system, it is called *local login*. As the user types at a terminal or a workstation running a terminal emulator, the keystrokes are accepted by the terminal driver. The terminal driver passes the characters to the operating system. The operating system, in turn, interprets the combination of characters and invokes the desired application program or utility (see Figure 6.24).

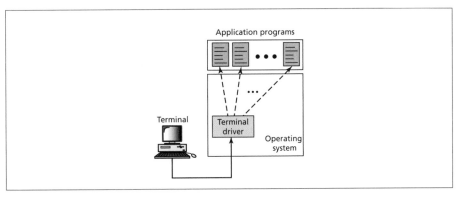

Figure 6.24 Local login

Remote login The mechanism for remote login is not as simple as local login. The operating system may assign special meanings to special characters. For example, in UNIX some combinations of characters have special meanings, such as the combination of the control character with the character "z" to mean "suspend", the combination of the control character with the character "c" to mean abort, and so on. Whereas these special situations do not create any problems in local login, because the terminal emulator and the terminal driver know the exact meaning of each character or combination of characters, they may create problems in remote login. For example, which process should interpret special characters: the client or the server?

When a user wants to access an application program or utility located on a remote machine, they perform a remote login. Here the TELNET client and server programs come into use. The user sends the keystrokes to the terminal driver, where the local operating system accepts them but does not interpret them. The ASCII characters are then sent to the TELNET client, which transforms each character into a character in a universal character set called *network virtual terminal* (NVT) characters and delivers them to the local TCP/IP stack. At the server site, the TELNET server transforms each NVT character back to ASCII and then delivers it to a pseudo-terminal driver (see Figure 6.25).

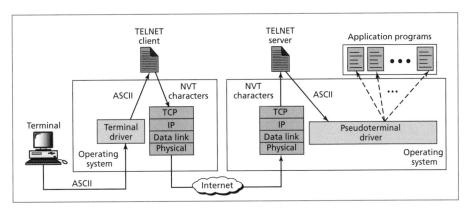

Figure 6.25 Remote login

The World Wide Web (WWW)

The **World Wide Web (WWW)**, or just "the web", is a repository of linked information spread all over the world. The WWW has a unique combination of flexibility, portability, and user-friendly features that distinguish it from other services provided by the Internet. The WWW today is a distributed client-server service in which a client using a browser can access a service using a server. However, the service provided is distributed over many locations, called *web sites*.

The idea of the World Wide Web started in 1989 at the European Particle Physics Laboratory in Geneva, Switzerland. Tim Berners-Lee needed to create a large database for physics research, which he found impossible to do using a single computer. The obvious solution was to let each piece of information be stored on an appropriate computer and let the computers be linked together through hypertext. In 1993, the University of Illinois, under the supervision of Marc Andreessen, created the first graphical browser, called Mosaic. In 1994, Andreessen and some colleagues started Netscape. Another widely used browser is Microsoft Explorer.

Hypertext and hypermedia

The WWW uses the concept of *hypertext* and *hypermedia*. In a hypertext environment, information is stored in a set of documents that are connected together using the concept of *links*. An item can be associated with another document using a link. The reader who is browsing through the document can move to other documents by choosing (clicking) on the items that are linked to other documents. Figure 6.26 shows the concept of hypertext.

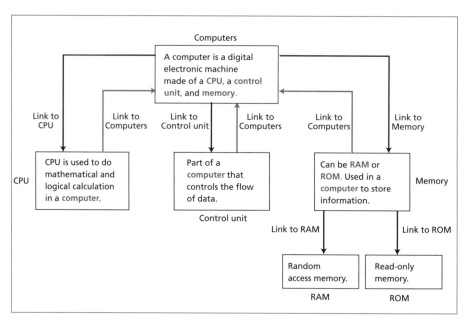

Figure 6.26 Hypertext

There are five documents in this hypothetical example: *Computers*, *CPU*, *Memory*, *ROM*, and *RAM*. A user who is browsing the Computer document can click on the

CPU link to find information about CPUs. A user who is browsing in the CPU document can click on the computer link to read more about computers. All five documents are somehow linked together.

Whereas hypertext documents contain only text, hypermedia documents can contain pictures, graphics, and sound. A unit of hypertext or hypermedia available on the web is called a *page*. The main or root page for an organization or an individual is known as a *home page*.

Components of the WWW

To use the WWW we need three components: a browser, a web server, and a protocol called Hypertext Transfer Protocol (HTTP).

Browser

A variety of vendors offer commercial browsers that interpret and display a web document, and all of them use nearly the same architecture. Each browser usually consists of three parts: a controller, client programs, and interpreters. The controller receives input from the keyboard or the mouse and uses the client programs to access the document. After the document has been accessed, the controller uses one of the interpreters to display the document on the screen. The client program can be one of the protocols described previously, such as FTP or TELNET, but it is usually HTTP. The interpreter handles the languages used today on the Internet, such as HTML or Java (see Figure 6.27).

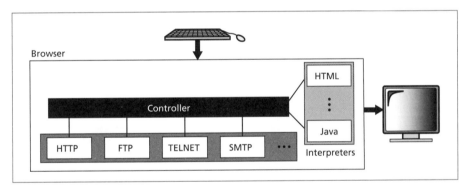

Figure 6.27   Browser structure

Server

The server stores all pages belonging to a web site.

Hypertext Transfer Protocol (HTTP)

Hypertext Transfer Protocol (HTTP) is a protocol used mainly to access data on the World Wide Web. The protocol transfers data in the form of plain text, hypertext, audio, video, and so on. It is called Hypertext Transfer Protocol because its efficiency allows its use in a hypertext environment and enables rapid jumps from one document to another.

The idea of HTTP is very simple. A client sends a request, which looks like e-mail, to the server. The server sends the response, which looks like an e-mail reply, to the client. The request and response messages carry data in the form of a letter with a MIME-like format.

The commands from the client to the server are embedded in a text-based request message. The contents of the requested file or other information are also embedded in a text-based response message.

Figure 6.28 illustrates an HTTP transaction between the client and server. The client initializes the transaction by sending a request message. The server replies by sending a response.

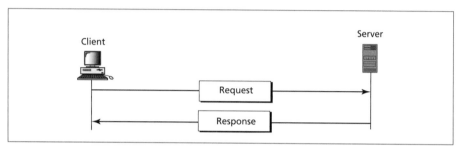

Figure 6.28   HTTP transaction

Addresses

A client that wants to access a document needs an address. To facilitate the access of documents distributed throughout the world, HTTP uses the concept of *locators*. The uniform resource locator (URL) is a standard for specifying any kind of information on the Internet. The URL defines four things: method, host computer, port, and path (see Figure 6.29).

Figure 6.29   URL structure

The *method* is the protocol used to retrieve the document, for example, HTTP. The *host* is the computer on which the information is located, although the name of the computer can be an alias. Web pages are usually stored on computers, and computers are given alias names that usually begin with the characters "www." This is not mandatory, however, as any name can be given to the computer that hosts the web page.

The URL optionally can contain the port number of the server. If the port is included, it is inserted between the host and the path, and it should be separated from the host name by a colon.

The *path* is the pathname of the file where the information is located. Note that the path can itself contain slashes that, in the UNIX operating system, separate the directories from the subdirectories and files.

Static documents

The documents on the WWW can be grouped into three broad categories: static, dynamic, and active. This categorization is based on the time at which the contents of the documents are determined. **Static documents** are fixed-content documents that are created and stored on a server. The client can only get a copy of the document. In other words, the contents of the file are determined when the file is created, not when it is used. Of course, the contents of the server can be changed, but the user cannot change them. When a client accesses the document, a copy of the document is sent. The user can then use a browser to display the document.

HTML

Hypertext Markup Language (HTML) is a language for creating web pages. The term *markup language* comes from the book publishing industry. Before a book is typeset and printed, a copy editor reads the manuscript and puts marks on it. Let us clarify the idea with an example. To make part of a text display in boldface with HTML, we put beginning and ending boldface tags (marks) in the text. The two tags <B> and </B> are instructions for the browser. When the browser sees these marks, it knows that the text between them must be set in boldface. A markup language such as HTML allows us to embed formatting instructions in the file itself. The instructions are included with the text. In this way, any browser can read the instructions and format the text according to the specific computer on which the browser runs.

We might ask why we do not use the formatting capabilities of word processors to create and save formatted text. The answer is that different word processors use different techniques or procedures for formatting text. For example, imagine that a user creates formatted text on a Macintosh and stores it in a web page. Another user who uses an IBM computer would not be able to receive the web page, because the two computers use different formatting procedures. HTML lets us use only ASCII characters for both the main text and the formatting instructions. In this way, every computer can receive the whole document as an ASCII document. The main text is the data, and the formatting instructions can be used by the browser to format the data.

A web page is made up of two parts: the head and the body. The head is the first part of a web page. The head contains the title of the page and other parameters that the browser will use. The actual contents of a page are in the body, which includes the text and the tags. Whereas the text is the actual information contained in a page, the tags define the appearance of the document. Figure 6.30 shows the format of an HTML document.

When a browser encounters the document shown on the left of the figure, something similar to what is shown on the right is displayed. Of course, the real format, such as title, font size, or indention depends on the browser.

Another interesting tag category is the image tag. Such nontextual information as digitized photos or graphic images is not a physical part of an HTML document. But we can use an image tag to point to the file containing the photo or image. The

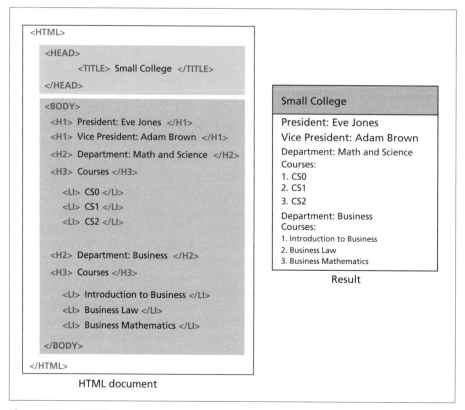

Figure 6.30   HTML example

image tag defines the address (URL) of the image to be retrieved. It also specifies how the image should be inserted after retrieval.

A third interesting category is the hyperlink tag, which is needed to link documents together. Any item (word, phrase, paragraph, or image) can refer to another document through a mechanism called an *anchor*. An anchor is defined by <A ... > and </A> tags, and the anchored item uses the URL to refer to another document. When the document is displayed, the anchored item is underlined, blinking, or boldfaced. The user can click on the anchored item to go to another document, which may or may not be stored on the same server as the original document.

XML

HTML adds formatting capability to a document, but it does not define the type of data. For example, HTML can define that a line of text is intended as an item in a list, but it does not define the nature of the item. **Extensible Markup Language (XML)** is a language in which tags can be used to define the content (type) of the text between two tags. In HTML, the tags define the *format* and the text defines the *value*. In XML, the tags define the *type* and the text defines the *value*. Figure 6.31 compares a line of HTML with a corresponding line of XML.

The two tags <LI> and </LI> in HTML are predefined tags for HTML: the two tags <Course> and </Course> in the XML example are user-defined tags

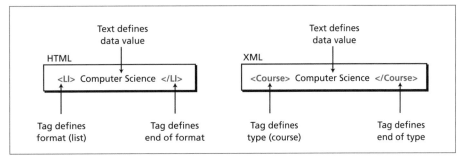

Figure 6.31   Comparing HTML and XML

created for this particular language. Another document can use different tags to denote the same type of data.

In the HTML document, the text "Computer science" can be the name of a course or the name of a computer scientist's dog: HTML cannot tell the difference. In the XML document, by contrast, the same text value is defined as the title of a course by its tags.

Why do we need to define the type of data in a web page? One reason is that it makes searching easier. For example, a search engine such as Google, which needs to find whether a particular university offers computer science courses, needs to look for the text value "Computer science" in the all corresponding HTML documents. The same search engine could limit the search only to lines tagged with <Course> in a corresponding XML document. An XML document is therefore faster to search than an HTML document.

XML also allows different organizations to define their own applications. For example, Chemistry Markup Language, CML, uses a set of tags to define the structures of materials, MathML defines the set of tags to display mathematical symbols and relations, and so on.

Dynamic documents

A **dynamic document** is created by a web server whenever a browser requests the document. When a request arrives, the web server runs an application program that creates the dynamic document. The server returns the output of the program as a response to the browser that requested the document. Because a fresh document is created for each request, the contents of a dynamic document can vary from one request to another. A very simple example of a dynamic document is the retrieval of the time and date from a server. Time and date are dynamic information in that they change from moment to moment. The client can ask the server to run a program such as the date program in UNIX and send the result of the program to the client.

Common Gateway Interface (CGI)

The Common Gateway Interface (CGI) is a technology that creates and handles dynamic documents. CGI is a set of standards that defines how a dynamic document is written, how data is input to the program, and how the output result is used. CGI is not a new language: instead, it allows programmers to use any of several languages such as C, C++, or the Bourne shell, Korn shell, C shell, Tcl, or Perl scripting languages.

Scripting technologies for dynamic documents

The problem with CGI technology is the inefficiency that results if part of the dynamic document that is to be created is fixed and does not change from request to request. For example, assume that we need to retrieve a list of spare parts, their availability, and prices for a specific make of car over the web. Although availability and prices vary from time to time, the name, description, and the picture of the parts are fixed. If we use CGI, the program must create an entire document each time a request is made.

The solution is to create a file containing the fixed part of the document using HTML and embed a script, a type of source code, that can be run by the server to provide the varying availability and price data. Several technologies have been employed to create dynamic documents using scripts. Among the most common are **Hypertext Preprocessor (PHP)**, which uses the Perl language, **Java Server Pages (JSP)**, which uses the Java language for scripting, **Active Server Pages (ASP)**, a Microsoft product which uses Visual Basic language for scripting, and **ColdFusion**, which embeds SQL database queries in the HTML document.

Active documents

For many applications we need to be able to run a program or a script at the client site. These are called **active documents**. For example, suppose we want to run a program that creates animated graphics on the screen, or a program that interacts with the user. The program definitely needs to be run on the client computer where the animation or interaction takes place. When a browser requests an active document, the server sends a copy of the document or a script. The document is then run under the control of the client's browser.

Java applets

One way to create an active document is to use **Java applets**. Java is a combination of a high-level programming language, a runtime environment, and a class library that allows a programmer to write an active document (an applet) and a browser to run it. An applet is a program written in Java and saved on the server, compiled and ready to be run. The document is in byte-code (binary) format. The client process (the browser) creates an instance of this applet and runs it.

A Java applet can be run by the browser in two ways. In the first method, the browser can directly request the Java applet program in the URL and receive the applet in binary form. In the second method, the browser can retrieve and run an HTML file that has embedded the address of the applet as a tag.

JavaScript

The idea of scripts in dynamic documents can also be used for active documents. If the active part of the document is small, it can be written in a scripting language, which is then interpreted and run by the client. The script is in source code (text) and not binary form. The scripting technology used in this case is usually **JavaScript**. JavaScript, which bears a small resemblance to Java, is a very high-level scripting language developed for this purpose.

Other Internet applications

During the last decades other applications have been developed on the Internet. These applications are not as popular as those discussed above, but they are gaining ground. We discuss a few of them here.

Video-conferencing

Videoconferencing can eliminate the cost of traveling, and save time and energy, by providing communication between two or more groups of participants or a set of individual participants (sometimes called *desktop* videoconferencing).

Each participant or group of participants uses a videoconferencing client program. The video and audio data is sent from the clients to the videoconferencing server program, which then redistributes data to all clients, as shown in Figure 6.32.

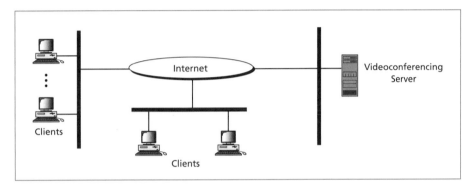

Figure 6.32 Videoconferencing

Group discussion – Listservs

Another popular class of applications is **listservs**, which allow a group of users to discuss a common topic of interest. For example, there could be a group for people interested in seventeenth century Flemish tapestries, or a group of San Francisco Seals fans. One popular use of listservs is the creation of discussion groups for students at colleges and universities, especially for those enrolled in distance learning classes. This is an excellent way for students unable to attend a traditional class to communicate with each other.

Like the others we have discussed, this is also a client-server application. However, there are two server programs running on the server: the subscriber server and the mailer server. Figure 6.33 shows the situation.

Subscribing

The subscriber server accepts membership to a group. A user who wants to be a member of the group sends an e-mail addressed to this server. The e-mail contains a SUBSCRIBE request (command) that is scanned by the subscriber server. The user is then registered if the user has permission to be part of the group. The

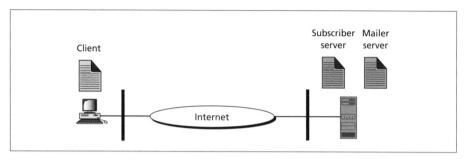

Figure 6.33   Listserver organization

subscriber server informs the user of the registration via return e-mail. A typical subscribe command is shown below:

> **SUBSCRIBE mailer-server-e-mail-address** *user-e-mail-address*

To subscribe, the user sends the request to the subscriber server, not the mailer server.

Sending e-mail

After subscribing, a user can send e-mail to the group. This time, the user sends an e-mail addressed to the mailer server. The mailer server automatically relays the e-mail to every member of the group provided that the e-mail is from a registered user.

Unsubscribing

To cancel a subscription, a user sends an UNSUBSCRIBE command to the subscriber server. A typical unsubscribe command is shown below:

> **UNSUBSCRIBE mailer-server-e-mail-address** *user-e-mail-address*

Chat

Another popular class of Internet application is **chat**. This is a real-time application like videoconferencing, in which two or more parties are involved in an exchange of text and optionally audio and video. The two parties can send text to each other, talk to each other (the same way as they might talk on the phone), and even see each other with suitable cameras.

Chatting works the same way as videoconferencing but on a smaller scale. The two parties each use a client program to send text, audio, or video information to a server. The server receives the information and relays the data with a small delay.

6.5 RECOMMENDED READING

For more details about the subjects discussed in this chapter, the following books are recommended:

❏ Forouzan B: *Data Communication and Networking*, New York: McGraw-Hill College, 2006

❏ Forouzan B: *TCP/IP Protocol Suite*, New York: McGraw-Hill, 2007

❏ Forouzan B: *Local Area Networks*, New York: McGraw-Hill Higher Education, 2003

❏ Kurose J and Ross K: *Computer Networking*, Reading, MA: Addison Wesley, 2007

6.6 KEY TERMS

This chapter has introduced the following key terms, which are listed here with the pages on which they first occur:

active document 178	Active Server Pages 178
application layer 152	backbone 147
best-effort service 161	bus topology 147
chatting 180	client-sever architecture 153
cold fusion 178	Common Gateway Interface 177
congestion control 156	connection-oriented protocol 157
connectionless protocol 157	data link layer 161
data-link layer address 161	demultiplexing 156
domain name 168	Domain Name Server 154
dotted decimal notation 160	dynamic document 177
electronic mail (e-mail) 165	encapsulation 164
Extensive Markup Language 176	frame 161
header 164	hub 147
Hypertext Markup Language 175	Hypertext Preprocessor 178
Hypertext Transfer Protocol 173	Internet
internet 149	Internet Mail Access Protocol 167
Internet Protocol 160	internet service provider 150
internetwork 149	IP address 154
Java Applet 178	Java Server Pages 178
JavaScript 178	listserv 178
local area network 148	medium access control address 163
mesh topology 147	message transfer agent 166
metropolitan area network 149	multidrop connection 147

6.7 SUMMARY

- A network is a combination of hardware and software that sends data from one location to another. We discussed two types of connection in a network: point-to-point and multipoint. We discussed four types of physical topologies in a network: mesh, star, bus, and ring.

- We mentioned three types of networks: LAN, MAN, and WAN. A local area network (LAN) is usually privately owned and links the devices in a single office, building, or campus. A wide area network (WAN) provides long-distance transmission of data, image, audio, and video information over large geographic areas that may comprise a country, a continent, or even the whole world. A metropolitan area network (MAN) is a network with a size between a LAN and a WAN. When two or more networks are connected, they become an internetwork, or an internet.

- The most notable internet is called the Internet (uppercase letter "I"), a collaboration of hundreds of thousands of interconnected networks. Most end users who want Internet connection use the services of Internet service providers (ISPs). The set, or suite, of protocols that controls the Internet today is referred to as the TCP/IP protocol suite. The suite is made up of five layers.

- The application layer enables the user to access the network. It provides support for services such as electronic mail, remote file access and transfer, browsing the World Wide Web, and so on. The addresses on the application layer are specific to the application programs.

- The transport layer is responsible for process-to-process delivery of the entire message; this means that a logical communication is created between the transport layers of the client and the server computer. During the life of the TCP/IP protocol suite, three transport layer protocols have been designed: UDP, TCP, and SCTP.

- The network layer is responsible for the source-to-destination delivery of a packet, possibly across multiple networks. The network layer ensures that each packet gets from its point of origin to its final destination. In the TCP/IP protocol suite, the main protocol at the network layer is Internet Protocol (IP).

- The data-link layer delivers a packet from one node to another. The data-link layer is also responsible for error and flow control between "hops". It uses physical or MAC address to identify the nodes.

- The physical layer coordinates the functions required to carry a bit stream over a physical medium. Although the data-link layer is responsible for moving a frame from one node to another, the physical layer is responsible for moving the individual bits that enable the frame to reach the next node.

- Electronic mail (e-mail) is the most popular application on the Internet. The main protocol used for e-mail is called Simple Mail Transfer Protocol (SMTP). Other protocols used for electronic mail are POP and IMAP.

- File Transfer Protocol (FTP) is the standard mechanism for one of the most common tasks on the Internet, copying a file from one computer to another. FTP differs from other client-server applications in that it establishes two connections: one for data transfer and one for exchanging control commands.

- TELNET is a general-purpose client-server program that lets a user access any application program on a remote computer. In other words, it allows the user to log in to a remote computer. After login, a user can use the services available on the remote computer and transfer the results back to the local computer.

- The World Wide Web (WWW), or web, is a repository of information spread all over the world and linked together. To use the WWW, we need three components: a browser, a web server, and a protocol called Hypertext Transfer Protocol (HTTP).

- Documents on the WWW can be grouped into three broad categories: static, dynamic, and active. The category is based on the time at which the contents of the document are determined. A dynamic document is created by a web server whenever a browser requests the document. An active document is a program that is run at the client site.

- Three other applications were mentioned in this chapter. Videoconferencing can provide communication between two or more groups of participants or a set of individual participants. Listservs allow a group of users to discuss a common topic of interest by using two programs running on the server: the subscriber server and the mailer server. Finally, chat is supported by a class of real-time applications similarly to videoconferencing, in which two or more parties are involved in an exchange of text, audio, and video.

6.8   PRACTICE SET

Review questions

1. What is the difference between a point-to-point and a multipoint connection?
2. List common physical network topologies.
3. Define the three types of network.
4. Distinguish between an internet and the Internet.
5. Name the layers of the TCP/IP protocol suite.
6. What is the main function of the application layer in the TCP/IP protocol suite? What type of addresses are used in this layer?
7. What is the main function of the transport layer in the TCP/IP protocol suite? What type of addresses are used in this layer?
8. What is the main function of the network layer in the TCP/IP protocol suite? What type of addresses are used in this layer?

9. What is the main function of the data-link layer in the TCP/IP protocol suite? What type of addresses are used in this layer?

10. What is the main function of the physical layer in the TCP/IP protocol suite? Why are addresses not used in the physical layer?

11. Define node-to-node delivery. In which layer does this type of delivery take place?

12. Define source-to-destination delivery. In which layer does this type of delivery take place?

13. Define process-to-process delivery. In which layer does this type of delivery take place?

14. What is the purpose of SMTP?

15. What is the purpose of FTP?

16. What is the purpose of TELNET?

17. What is the difference between local login and remote login?

18. Compare and contrast the three Internet document types: static, dynamic, and active.

Multiple-choice questions

19. The TCP/IP model has _____ layers.
    a. five
    b. six
    c. seven
    d. any of the above

20. The _____ layer of the TCP/IP protocol suite provides services for end users.
    a. data-link
    b. transport
    c. application
    d. physical

21. The _____ layer of the TCP/IP protocol suite transmits a bit stream over a physical medium.
    a. physical
    b. data-link
    c. network
    d. transport

22. The _____ layer of the TCP/IP protocol suite is responsible for node-to-node delivery of a frame between two adjacent nodes.
    a. transport
    b. network
    c. data-link
    d. session

23. The _____ layer of the TCP/IP protocol suite is responsible for source-to-destination delivery of the entire message.
    a. transport
    b. network
    c. data-link
    d. session

24. What is the domain name in the e-mail address *kayla@nasa.gov*?
    a. kayla
    b. kayla@nasa.gov
    c. nasa.gov
    d. none of the above

25. Which physical topology uses a hub or switch?
    a. bus
    b. ring
    c. star
    d. all of the above

26. IP addresses are currently _____ bits in length.
    a. 4
    b. 8
    c. 32
    d. any of the above

27. The _____ protocol is one of the protocols in the transport layer.
    a. TCP
    b. UDP
    c. SCTP
    d. all of the above

28. _____ is a protocol for file transfer.
    a. FTP
    b. SMTP
    c. TELNET
    d. HTTP

29. _____ is a protocol for e-mail services.
    a. FTP
    b. SMTP
    c. TELNET
    d. HTTP

30. _____ is a protocol for accessing and transferring documents on the WWW.
    a. FTP
    b. SMTP

c. TELNET

d. HTTP

31. A _____ document has fixed contents.

a. static

b. dynamic

c. active

d. all of the above

Exercises

32. What is the highest TCP/IP layer responsible for each of the following activities:

a. Sending a frame to the next node.

b. Sending a packet from the source to the destination.

c. Delivery of a long message from the source computer to the destination computer.

d. Logging in to a remote computer.

33. A small part of a bus LAN with 200 stations is damaged. How many stations are affected by this damage?

34. A small part of a star LAN with 200 stations is damaged. How many stations are affected by this damage?

35. A small part of a ring LAN with 200 stations is damaged. How many stations are affected by this damage?

36. If you have a square room with a computer in each corner, which topology needs least cabling? Justify your answer.

a. A bus LAN.

b. A ring LAN.

c. A star LAN with a hub in the center of the room.

37. If you have a square room with a computer in each corner, which topology is more reliable? Justify your answer.

a. A bus LAN.

b. A ring LAN.

c. A star LAN with a hub in the center of the room.

38. An engineer notices that the data received by computers at the two ends of a bus LAN contains many errors. What do you think is the problem? What can be done to solve the problem?

39. What is the advantage of having three transport protocols in TCP/IP?

40. Change the following IP addresses from dotted-decimal notation to binary notation:

a. 112.32.7.28

b. 129.4.6.8

c. 208.3.54.12

d. 38.34.2.1

e. 255.255.255.255

41. Change the following IP addresses from binary notation to dotted-decimal notation:

a. 01111110 11110001 01100111 01111111

b. 10111111 11011100 11100000 00000101

c. 00011111 11110000 00111111 11011101

d. 10001111 11110101 11000011 00011101

e. 11110111 10010011 11100111 01011101

42. Explain the client-server model on the Internet. In which layer of the TCP/IP protocol suite is the model implemented?

43. Separate the local part and the domain name in the following e-mail addresses:

a. madeline@belle.gov

b. lindsey@jasmine.com

c. wuteh@hunan.int

d. honoris@queen.org

44. Explain the difference between an e-mail address and an IP address. Is there a one-to-one relationship between the two addresses?

45. Explain the difference between FTP and TELNET. When would you use FTP and when would you use TELNET?

46. A user uses a browser to download a game program. What type of document is downloaded?

47. A user uses a browser to download a technical document. What type of document is downloaded?

48. Write a URL that uses HTTP to access a file with the path */user/general* in a computer with the alias name *www.hadb*.

7
Operating Systems

This is the first chapter in this book to deal with computer software. In this chapter we explore the role of the operating system in a computer.

Objectives

After studying this chapter, the student should be able to:

❏ Understand the role of the operating system in a computer system.

❏ Give a definition of an operating system.

❏ Understand the process of bootstrapping to load the operating system into memory.

❏ List the components of an operating system.

❏ Discuss the role of the memory manager in an operating system.

❏ Discuss the role of the process manager in an operating system.

❏ Discuss the role of the device manager in an operating system.

❏ Discuss the role of the file manager in an operating system.

❏ Understand the main features of three common operating systems: UNIX, Linux, and Windows NT.

A computer is a system composed of two major components: *hardware* and *software*. Computer hardware is the physical equipment. Software is the collection of programs that allows the hardware to do its job. Computer **software** is divided into two broad categories: the *operating system* and *application programs* (Figure 7.1). Application programs use the computer hardware to solve users' problems. The operating system, on the other hand, controls the access to hardware by users.

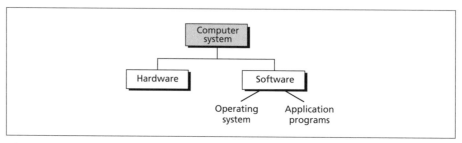

Figure 7.1   A computer system

7.1 INTRODUCTION

An **operating system** is complex, so it is difficult to give a simple universal definition. Instead, here are some common definitions:

❑ An operating system is an interface between the hardware of a computer and the user (programs or humans).

❑ An operating system is a program (or a set of programs) that facilitates the execution of other programs.

❑ An operating system acts as a general manager supervising the activity of each component in the computer system. As a general manager, the operating system checks that hardware and software resources are used efficiently, and when there is a conflict in using a resource, the operating system mediates to solve it.

> **An operating system is an interface between the hardware of a computer and the user (programs or humans) that facilitates the execution of other programs and the access to hardware and software resources.**

Two major design goals of an operating system are:

❑ Efficient use of hardware.

❑ Easy of use of resources.

Bootstrap process

The operating system, based on the above definitions, provides supports for other programs. For example, it is responsible for loading other programs into memory for execution. However, the operating system itself is a program that needs to be loaded into the memory and run. How is this dilemma solved?

The problem can be solved if the operating system is stored (by the manufacturer) in part of memory using ROM technology. The program counter of the CPU (see Chapter 5) can be set to the beginning of this ROM memory. When the computer is turned on, the CPU reads instructions from ROM and executes them. This solution, however, is not very efficient, because a significant part of the memory would need to be composed of ROM and could not therefore be used by other programs. Today's technology needs to allocate just a small part of memory to part of the operating system.

The solution adopted today is a two-stage process. A very small section of memory is made of ROM and holds a small program called the **bootstrap** program. When the computer is turned on, the CPU counter is set to the first instruction of this bootstrap program and executes the instructions in this program. This program is only responsible for loading the operating system itself, or that part of it required to start up the computer, into RAM memory. When loading is done, the program counter in the CPU is set to the first instruction of the operating system in RAM and the operating system is executed. Figure 7.2 illustrates the bootstrap process.

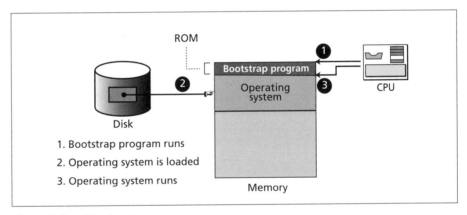

Figure 7.2   The bootstrap process

7.2 EVOLUTION

Operating systems have gone through a long history of evolution, which we summarize next.

Batch systems

Batch operating systems were designed in the 1950s to control mainframe computers. At that time, computers were large machines that used punched cards for input, line printers for output, and tape drives for secondary storage media.

Each program to be executed was called a *job*. A programmer who wished to execute a job sent a request to the operating room along with punched cards for the program and data. The punched cards were fed into the computer by an operator. If the program was successful, a printout of the result was sent to the programmer—if not, a printout of the error was sent.

Operating systems during this era were very simple: they only ensured that all of the computer's resources were transferred from one job to the next.

Time-sharing systems

To use computer system resources efficiently, *multiprogramming* was introduced. The idea is to hold several jobs in memory at a time, and only assign a resource to a job that needs it on the condition that the resource is available. For example, when one program is using an input/output device, the CPU is free and can be used by another program. We discuss multiprogramming later in this chapter.

Multiprogramming brought the idea of **time sharing**: resources could be shared between different jobs, with each job being allocated a portion of time to use a resource. Because a computer is much faster than a human, time sharing is hidden from the user—each user has the impression that the whole system is serving them exclusively.

Multiprogramming, and eventually time sharing, improved the efficiency of computer systems tremendously. However, they required a more complex operating system. The operating system now had to do **scheduling**: allocating resources to different programs and deciding which program should use which resource, and when. During this era, the relationship between a computer and a user also changed. The user could interact with the system directly without going through an operator. A new term was also coined: **process**. A job is a program to be run, while a process is a program that is in memory and waiting for resources.

Personal systems

When personal computers were introduced, there was a need for an operating system for this new type of computer. During this era, **single-user operating systems** such as DOS (Disk Operating System) were introduced.

Parallel systems

The need for more speed and efficiency led to the design of **parallel systems:** multiple CPUs on the same machine. Each CPU can be used to serve one program or a part of a program, which means that many tasks can be accomplished in parallel instead of serially. The operating systems required for this are more complex than those that support single CPUs.

Distributed systems

Networking and internetworking, as we saw in Chapter 6, have created a new dimension in operating systems. A job that was previously done on one computer can now be shared between computers that may be thousands of miles apart. A program can be run partially on one computer and partially on another if they are connected through an internetwork such as the Internet. In addition, resources can be distributed. A program may need files located in different parts of the world.

Distributed systems combine features of the previous generation with new duties such as controlling security.

Real-time systems

A **real-time system** is expected to do a task within specific time constraint. They are used with real-time applications, which monitor, respond to, or control external processes or environments. Examples can be found in traffic control, patient monitoring, or military control systems. The application program can sometimes be an embedded system as a component of a larger system, such as the control system in an automobile.

The requirements for a real-time operating system are often different than those for a general-purpose system. For this reason, we do not discuss them in this chapter.

7.3 COMPONENTS

Today's operating systems are very complex. An operating system needs to manage different resources in a computer system. It resembles an organization with several managers at the top level. Each manager is responsible for managing their department, but also needs to cooperate with others and coordinate activities. A modern operating system has at least four duties: memory manager, process manager, device manager, and file manager. Like many organizations that have a department that is not necessarily under any specific manager, an operating system also has such a component, which is usually called a user interface or a **shell**. The user interface is responsible for communication outside the operating system. Figure 7.3 shows the typical components of an operating system.

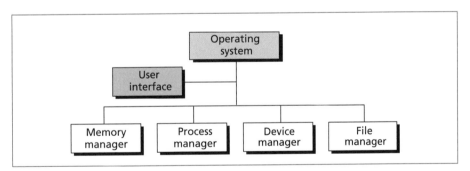

Figure 7.3 Components of an operating system

User interface

Each operating system has a **user interface**, a program that accepts requests from users (processes) and interprets them for the rest of the operating system. A user interface in some operating systems, such as UNIX, is called a **shell**. In others, it is called a **window** to denote that it is menu-driven and has a **GUI (graphical user interface)** component.

Memory manager

One of the responsibilities of a modern computer system is **memory management**. Although the memory size of computers has increased tremendously in recent years, so has the size of the programs and data to be processed. Memory allocation must be managed to prevent applications from running out of memory. Operating systems can be divided into two broad categories of memory management: *monoprogramming* and *multiprogramming*.

Mono-programming

Monoprogramming belongs to the past, but it is worth mentioning because it helps us to understand multiprogramming. In monoprogramming, most of the memory capacity is dedicated to a single program (we consider the data to be processed by a program as part of the program): only a small part is needed to hold the operating system. In this configuration, the whole program is in memory for execution. When the program finishes running, the program area is occupied by another program (Figure 7.4).

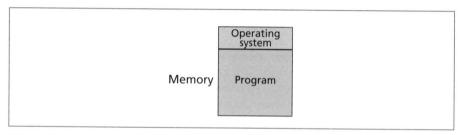

Figure 7.4   Monoprogramming

The job of the memory manager is straightforward here. It loads the program into memory, runs it, and replaces it with the next program. However, there are several problems with this technique:

❑ The program must fit into memory. If the size of memory is less than the size of the program, the program cannot be run.

❑ When one program is being run, no other program can be executed. A program, during its execution, often needs to receive data from input devices and needs to send data to output devices. Input/output devices are slow compared with the CPU, so when input/output operations are being carried out, the CPU is idle. It cannot serve another program because this program is not in memory. This is a very inefficient use of memory and CPU time.

Multi-programming

In **multiprogramming**, more than one program is in memory at the same time, and they are executed concurrently, with the CPU switching rapidly between the programs. Figure 7.5 shows memory in a multiprogramming environment.

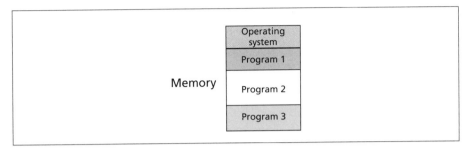

Figure 7.5 Multiprogramming

Since the 1960s, multiprogramming has gone through several improvements that can be seen in the taxonomy in Figure 7.6. We discuss each scheme very briefly in the next few sections. Two techniques belong to the *nonswapping* category, which means that the program remains in memory for the duration of execution. The other two techniques belong to the *swapping* category. This means that, during execution, the program can be swapped between memory and disk one or more times.

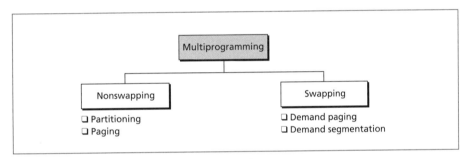

Figure 7.6 Categories of multiprogramming

Partitioning

The first technique used in multiprogramming is called **partitioning**. In this scheme, memory is divided into variable-length sections. Each section or partition holds one program. The CPU switches between programs. It starts with one program, executing some instructions until it either encounters an input/output operation or the time allocated for that program has expired. The CPU then saves the address of the memory location where the last instruction was executed and moves to the next program. The same procedure is repeated with the second program. After all the programs have been served, the CPU moves back to the first program. Priority levels can also be used to control the amount of CPU time allocated to each program (Figure 7.7).

With this technique, each program is entirely in memory and occupying contiguous locations. Partitioning improves the efficiency of the CPU, but there are still some issues:

❑ The size of the partitions has to be determined beforehand by the memory manager. If partition sizes are small, some programs cannot be loaded into

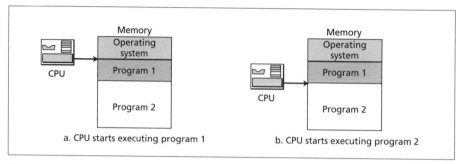

Figure 7.7   Partitioning

memory. If partition sizes are large, there might be some "holes" (unused locations) in memory.

❏ Even if partitioning is perfect when the computer is started, there may be some holes after completed programs are replaced by new ones.

❏ When there are many holes, the memory manager can compact the partitions to remove the holes and create new partitions, but this creates extra overhead on the system.

Paging

Paging improves the efficiency of partitioning. In paging, memory is divided into equally sized sections called **frames**. Programs are also divided, into equally sized sections called **pages**. The size of a page and a frame is usually the same and equal to the size of the block used by the system to retrieve information from a storage device (Figure 7.8).

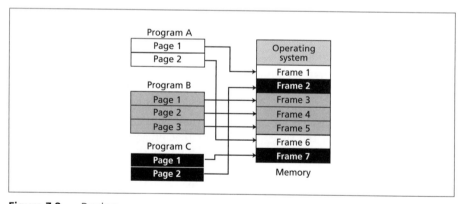

Figure 7.8   Paging

A page is loaded into a frame in memory. If a program has three pages, it occupies three frames in memory. With this technique, the program does not have to be contiguous in memory: two consecutive pages can occupy noncontiguous frames in memory. The advantage of paging over partitioning is that two programs, each using three noncontiguous frames, can be replaced by one program that needs six frames.

There is no need for the new program to wait until six contiguous frames are free before being loaded into memory.

Paging improves efficiency to some extent, but the whole program still needs to be in memory before being executed. This means that a program that needs six frames, for example, cannot be loaded into memory if there are currently only four unoccupied frames.

Demand paging

Paging does not require that the program be in contiguous memory locations, but it does require that the entire program be in memory for execution. Demand paging has removed this last restriction. In **demand paging** the program is divided into pages, but the pages can be loaded into memory one by one, executed, and replaced by another page. In other words, memory can hold pages from multiple programs at the same time. In addition, consecutive pages from the same program do not have to be loaded into the same frame—a page can be loaded into any free frame. An example of demand paging is shown in Exercise 7.9. Two pages from program A, one page from program B, and one page from program C are in the memory.

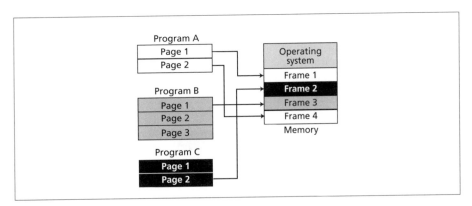

Figure 7.9 Demand paging

Demand segmentation

A technique similar to paging is *segmentation*. In paging, a program is divided into equally sized pages, which is not the way a programmer thinks—a programmer thinks in terms of modules. As we will see in later chapters, a program is usually made up of a main program and subprograms. In **demand segmentation**, the program is divided into segments that match the programmer's view. These are loaded into memory, executed, and replaced by another module from the same or a different program. An example of demand segmentation is shown in Figure 7.10. Since segments in memory are of equal size, part of a segment may remain empty.

Demand paging and segmentation

Demand paging and segmentation can be combined to further improve the efficiency of the system. A segment may be too large to fit any available free space in memory. Memory can be divided into frames, and a module can be divided into

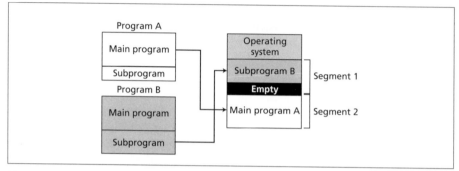

Figure 7.10   Demand segmentation

pages. The pages of a module can then be loaded into memory one by one and executed.

Virtual memory

Demand paging and demand segmentation mean that, when a program is being executed, part of the program is in memory and part is on disk. This means that, for example, a memory size of 10 MB can execute 10 programs, each of size 3 MB, for a total of 30 MB. At any moment, 10 MB of the 10 programs are in memory and 20 MB are on disk. There is therefore an actual memory size of 10 MB, but a **virtual memory** size of 30 MB. Figure 7.11 shows the concept. Virtual memory, which implies demand paging, demand segmentation, or both, is used in almost all operating systems today.

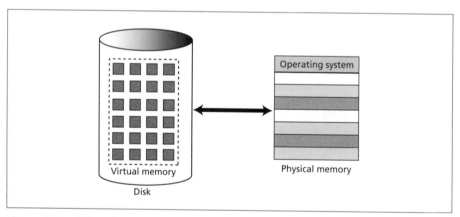

Figure 7.11   Virtual memory

Process manager

A second function of an operating system is process management, but before discussing this concept, we need to define some terms.

Program, job, and process

Modern operating systems use three terms that refer to a set of instructions: *program*, *job*, and *process*. Although the terminology is vague and varies from one operating system to another, we can define these terms informally.

Program

A **program** is a nonactive set of instructions stored on disk (or tape). It may or may not become a job.

Job

A program becomes a **job** from the moment it is selected for execution until it has finished running and becomes a program again. During this time a job may or may not be executed. It may be located on disk waiting to be loaded to memory, or it may be loaded into memory and waiting for execution by the CPU. It may be on disk or in memory waiting for an input/output event, or it may be in memory while being executed by the CPU. The program is a job in all of these situations. When a job has finished executing (either normally or abnormally), it becomes a program and once again resides on the disk. The operating system no longer governs the program. Note that every job is a program, but not every program is a job.

Process

A **process** is a program in execution. It is a program that has started but has not finished. In other words, a process is a job that is being run in memory. It has been selected among other waiting jobs and loaded into memory. A process may be executing or it may be waiting for CPU time. As long as the job is in memory, it is a process. Note that every process is a job, but not every job is a process.

State diagrams

The relationship between a program, a job, and a process becomes clearer if we consider how a program becomes a job and how a job becomes a process. This can be illustrated with a **state diagram** that shows the different states of each of these entities. Figure 7.12 is a state diagram using boundaries between a program, a job, and a process.

A program becomes a job when selected by the operating system and brought to the **hold state**. It remains in this state until it can be loaded into memory. When there is memory space available to load the program totally or partially, the job moves to the **ready state**. It now becomes a process. It remains in memory and in this state until the CPU can execute it, moving to the **running state** at this time. When in the running state, one of three things can happen:

❑ The process executes until it needs I/O resources

❑ The process exhausts its allocated time slot

❑ The process terminates

In the first case, the process goes into the **waiting state** and waits until I/O is complete. In the second case, it goes directly to the ready state. In the third case, it goes into the **terminated state** and is no longer a process. A process can move between the running, waiting, and ready states many times before it goes to the terminated state. Note that the diagram can be much more complex if the system uses virtual memory and swaps programs in and out of main memory.

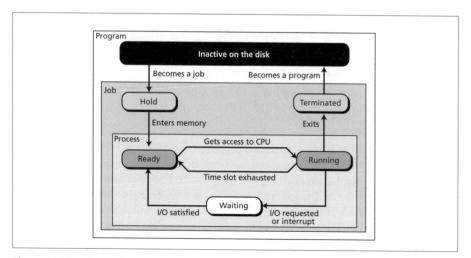

Figure 7.12 State diagram with boundaries between program, job, and process

Schedulers

To move a job or process from one state to another, the process manager uses two **schedulers**: the job scheduler and the process scheduler.

Job scheduler

The **job scheduler** moves a job from the hold state to the ready state or from the running state to the terminated state. In other words, a job scheduler is responsible for creating a process from a job and terminating a process. Figure 7.13 shows the job scheduler.

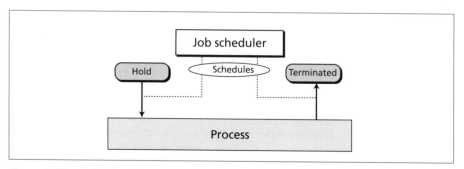

Figure 7.13 Job scheduler

Process scheduler

The **process scheduler** moves a process from one state to another. It moves a process from the running state to the waiting state when the process is waiting for some event to happen. It moves the process from the waiting state to the ready state when the event has occurred. It moves a process from the running state to the ready state if the process' time allotment has expired. When the CPU is ready to run the process, the process scheduler moves the process from the ready state to the running state. Figure 7.14 shows the process scheduler.

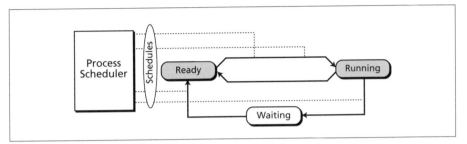

Figure 7.14 Process scheduler

Other schedulers

Some operating systems use other types of schedulers to make switching between processes more efficient.

Queuing

Our state diagram shows one job or process moving from one state to another. In reality, there are many jobs and many processes competing with each other for computer resources. For example, when some jobs are in memory, others must wait until space is available. Or when a process is running using the CPU, others must wait until the CPU is free. To handle multiple processes and jobs, the process manager uses **queues** (waiting lists). A *job control block* or *process control block* is associated with each job or process. This is a block of memory that stores information about that job or process. The process manager stores the job or process control block in the queues instead of the job or process itself. The job or process itself remains in memory or disk, as it is too big to be duplicated in a queue: the job control block or process control block is the representative of the waiting job or process.

An operating system can have several queues. For example, Figure 7.15 shows the circulation of jobs and processes through three queues: the *job queue*, the *ready queue*, and the *I/O queue*. The job queue holds the jobs that are waiting for memory. The ready queue holds the processes that are in memory, ready to be run and waiting for the CPU. The I/O queue holds the processes that are waiting for an I/O device (there can be several I/O queues, one for each input/output device, but we show only one for simplicity).

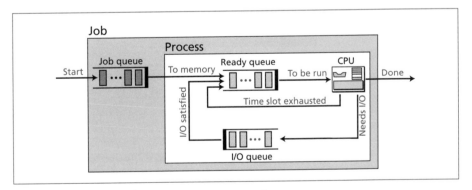

Figure 7.15 Queues for process management

The process manager can have different policies for selecting the next job or process from a queue: it could be first in, first out (FIFO), shortest length first, highest priority first, and so on.

Process synchronization

The whole idea behind process management is to synchronize different processes with different resources. Whenever resources can be used by more than one user (or process, in this case), we can have two problematic situations: *deadlock* and *starvation*. A brief discussion of these two situations follows.

Deadlock

Instead of a formal definition of **deadlock**, we give an example. Assume that there are two processes, A and B. Process A is holding a file File1 (that is, File1 is assigned to A) and cannot release it until it acquires another file, File2 (that is, A has requested File2). Process B is holding File2 (that is, File2 is assigned to B) and cannot release it until it has File1 (that is, B has requested File1). Files in most systems are not sharable—when in use by one process, a file cannot be used by another process. If there is no provision in this situation to force a process to release a file, deadlock is created (Figure 7.16).

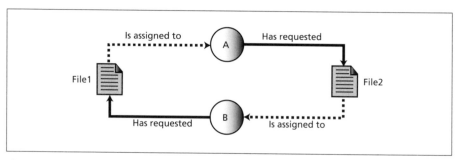

Figure 7.16   Deadlock

As an analogy, Figure 7.17 shows deadlock on a narrow bridge. The situation is similar because the resource (part of the bridge) is held by a vehicle that does not release it until it gets the other part of the bridge, which is held by the other vehicle, and vice versa.

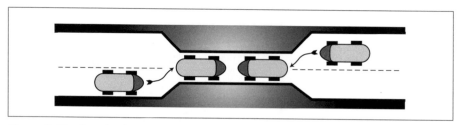

Figure 7.17   Deadlock on a bridge

Deadlock occurs if the operating system allows a process to start running without first checking to see if the required resources are ready, and allows a process to hold a resource as long as it wants. There should be some provision in the system to prevent deadlock. One solution is not to allow a process to start running until the required resources are free, but we will see later that this creates another problem. The second solution is to limit the time a process can hold a resource.

> **Deadlock occurs when the operating system does not put resource restrictions on processes.**

Deadlock does not always occur. There are four necessary conditions for deadlock as shown below:

❑ **Mutual exclusion**. Only one process can hold a resource.

❑ **Resource holding**. A process holds a resource even though it cannot use it until other resources are available.

❑ **No preemption**. The operating system cannot temporarily reallocate a resource.

❑ **Circular waiting**. All processes and resources involved form a loop, as in Figure 7.16.

All four conditions are required for deadlock to occur. However, these conditions are only necessary preconditions, and are not sufficient to cause deadlock of themselves—they must be present for deadlock, but they might not be enough to cause it. If one of these conditions is missing, deadlock cannot occur. This gives us a method for preventing or avoiding deadlock: do not allow one of these conditions to happen.

Starvation

Starvation is the opposite of deadlock. It can happen when the operating system puts too many resource restrictions on a process. For example, imagine an operating system that specifies that a process must have possession of its required resources before it can be run.

In Figure 7.18, imagine that process A needs two files, File1 and File2. File1 is being used by process B and File2 is being used by process E. Process B terminates first and releases File1. Process A cannot be started, because File2 is still not available. At this moment, process C, which needs only File1, is allowed to run. Now process E terminates and releases File2, but process A still cannot run because File1 is unavailable.

A classic starvation problem was introduced by Edsger Dijkstra. Five philosophers are sitting at a round table (Figure 7.19). Each philosopher needs two chopsticks to eat a bowl of rice. However, one or both chopsticks could be used by a neighbor. A philosopher could starve if two chopsticks are not available at the same time.

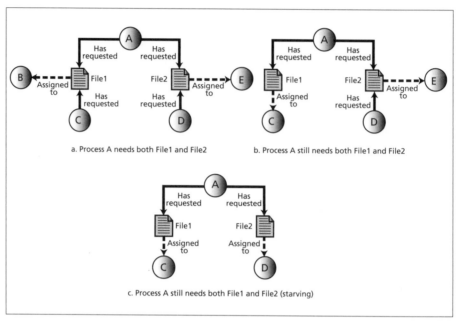

Figure 7.18   Starvation

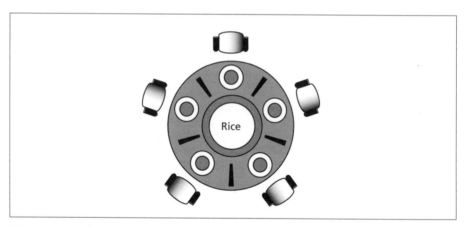

Figure 7.19   The dining philosophers problem

Device manager

The device manager, or input/output manager, is responsible for access to input/output devices. There are limitations on the number and speed of input/output devices in a computer system. Because these devices are slower in speed compared with the CPU and memory, when a process accesses an input/output device, the device is not available to other processes for a period of time. The device manager is responsible for the efficient use of input/output devices.

A detailed discussion of device managers requires advanced knowledge of operating system principles and is beyond the scope of this book. However, we can briefly list the responsibilities of a device manager:

- ❏ The device manager monitors every input/output device constantly to ensure that the device is functioning properly. The manager also needs to know when a device has finished serving one process and is ready to serve the next process in the queue.

- ❏ The device manager maintains a queue for each input/output device or one or more queues for similar input/output devices. For example, if there are two fast printers in the system, the manager can have one queue for each or one queue for both.

- ❏ The device manager controls the different policies for accessing input/output devices. For example, it may use FIFO for one device and shortest length first for another.

File manager

Operating systems today use a file manager to control access to files. A detailed discussion of the file manager also requires advanced knowledge of operating system principles and file access concepts that are beyond the scope of this book. We discuss some issues related to file access in Chapter 13, but this is not adequate to understand the actual operation of a file manager. Here is a brief list of the responsibilities of a file manager:

- ❏ The file manager controls access to files. Access is allowed only by permitted applications and/or users, and the type of access can vary. For example, a process (or a user that calls a process) may be allowed to read from a file but is not allowed to write to it (that is, change it). Another process may be allowed to execute a file and a process, but not allowed to read its contents, and so on.

- ❏ The file manager supervises the creation, deletion, and modification of files.

- ❏ The file manager can control the naming of files.

- ❏ The file manager supervises the storage of files: how they are stored, where they are stored, and so on.

- ❏ The file manager is responsible for archiving and backups.

7.4 A SURVEY OF OPERATING SYSTEMS

In this section we introduce some popular operating systems and encourage you to study them further. We have chosen three operating systems that are familiar to most computer users: UNIX, Linux, and Windows.

UNIX

UNIX was originally developed in 1969 by Thomson and Ritchie of the Computer Science Research Group at Bell Laboratories. UNIX has gone through many versions since then. It has been a popular operating system among computer programmers and computer scientists. It is a very powerful operating system with three outstanding features. First, UNIX is a portable operating system that can be moved from one platform to another without many changes. The reason is that it is written mostly in the C language (instead of a machine language specific to a particular computer system). Second, UNIX has a powerful set of utilities (commands) that can be combined (in an executable file called a *script*) to solve many problems that require programming in other operating systems. Third, it is device-independent, because it includes device drivers in the operating system itself, which means that it can be easily configured to run any device.

UNIX is a multiuser, multiprocessing, portable operating system designed to facilitate programming, text processing, communication, and many other tasks that are expected from an operating system. It contains hundreds of simple, single-purpose functions that can be combined to do virtually every processing task imaginable. Its flexibility is demonstrated by the fact that it is used in three different computing environments: stand-alone personal environments, time-sharing systems, and client–server systems.

> **UNIX is a multiuser, multiprocessing, portable operating system.**
> **It is designed to facilitate programming, text processing, and communication.**

UNIX structure

UNIX consists of four major components: the *kernel*, the *shell*, a standard set of *utilities*, and *application programs*. These components are shown in Figure 7.20.

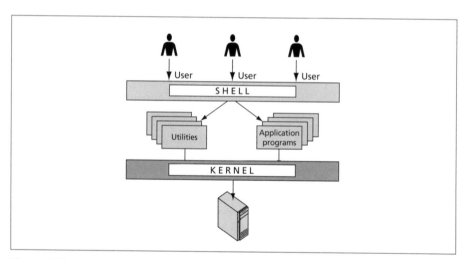

Figure 7.20   Components of the UNIX operating system

The kernel

The **kernel** is the heart of the UNIX system. It contains the most basic parts of the operating system: memory management, process management, device management, and file management. All other components of the system call on the kernel to perform these services for them.

The shell

The shell is the part of UNIX that is most visible to the user. It receives and interprets the commands entered by the user. In many respects, this makes it the most important component of the UNIX structure. It is certainly the part that users get to know best. To do anything in the system, we must give the shell a command. If the command requires a utility, the shell requests that the kernel execute the utility. If the command requires an application program, the shell requests the kernel to run it. Some operating systems, such as UNIX, have several different shells.

Utilities

There are literally hundreds of UNIX utilities. A **utility** is a standard UNIX program that provides a support process for users. Three common utilities are text editors, search programs, and sort programs.

Many of the system utilities are actually sophisticated applications. For example, the UNIX e-mail system is considered a utility, as are the three common text editors, **vi**, **emacs**, and **pico**. All four of these utilities are large systems in themselves. Other utilities are shorter, simpler functions. For example, the list (**ls**) utility displays the files in a disk directory.

Applications

Applications in UNIX are programs that are not a standard part of the operating system distribution. Written by systems administrators, professional programmers, or users, they provide extended capabilities to the system. In fact, many of the standard utilities started out as applications years ago and proved so useful that they are now part of the system.

Linux

In 1991, Linus Torvalds, a Finnish student at the University of Helsinki at the time, developed a new operating system that is known today as **Linux**. The initial kernel, which was similar to a small subset of UNIX, has grown into a full-scale operating system today. The Linux 2.0 kernel, released in 1997, was accepted as a commercial operating system: it has all features traditionally attributed to UNIX.

Components   Linux has the following components.

Kernel

The kernel is responsible for all duties attributed to a kernel, such as memory management, process management, device management, and file management.

System libraries

The system libraries hold a set of functions used by the application programs, including the shell, to interact with the kernel.

System utilities

The system utilities are individual programs that use the services provided by the system libraries to perform management tasks.

Networking capabilities   Linux supports the standard Internet protocols discussed in Chapter 6. It supports three layers: the socket interface, protocol drivers, and network device drivers.

Security
: Linux' security mechanism provides the security aspects defined traditionally for UNIX, such as authentication and access control.

Windows NT/2000/XP

In the late 1980s Microsoft, under the leadership of Dave Cutler, started development of a new single-user operating system to replace **MS-DOS** (Microsoft Disk Operating System). **Windows NT** (NT standing for New Technology) was the result. Several versions of Windows NT followed and the name was changed to **Windows 2000**. Windows XP (XP stands for eXPerience) was released in 2001. We refer to all of these versions as Windows NT or just NT.

Design goals
: Design goals released by Microsoft are *extensibility, portability, reliability, compatibility,* and *performance.*

Extensibility

Windows NT is designed as a modular architecture with several layers. The purpose is to allow the higher layers to be changed with time without affecting the lower layers.

Portability

NT, like UNIX, is mostly is written in C or C++ and the code is independent of the machine language of the computer on which it is running.

Reliability

Windows NT was designed to handle error conditions including protection from malicious software. NT uses a file system called the **NT file system (NTFS)** that recovers from file-system errors.

Compatibility

NT was designed to run programs written for other operating systems and the earlier versions of Windows NT.

Performance

NT was designed to have a fast response time to applications that run on top of the operating system.

Architecture
: NT uses a layered architecture, as shown in Figure 7.21.

HAL

The **hardware abstraction layer (HAL)** hides hardware differences from the upper layers.

Kernel

The kernel is the heart of the operating system. It is an object-oriented piece of software that sees any entity as an object.

Executive

The NT executive provides services for the whole operating system. It is made up of six subsystems: object manager, security reference monitor, process manager,

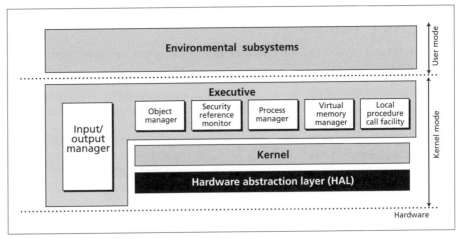

Figure 7.21   The architecture of Windows NT

virtual memory manager, local procedure call facility, and the I/O manager. Most of these subsystems are familiar from our previous discussions of operating subsystems. Some subsystems, like the object manager, are added to NT because of its object-oriented nature. The executive runs in kernel (privileged) mode.

Environmental subsystems

These are subsystems designed to allow NT to run application programs designed for NT, for other operating systems, or for earlier versions of NT. The native subsystem that runs application designed for NT is called Win32. The environment subsystems run in user mode (a non-privileged mode).

7.5 RECOMMENDED READING

For more details about the subjects discussed in this chapter, the following books are recommended:

- Bic L and Shaw A: *Operating Systems Principles*, Upper Saddle River, NJ: Prentice Hall, 2003
- McHoes A and Flynn I: *Understanding Operating Systems*, Boston, MA: Course Technology, 2007
- Nutt G: *Operating Systems: A Modern Perspective*, Reading, MA: Addison Wesley, 2001
- Silberschatz A and Galvin P: *Operating System Concepts*, New York: Wiley, 2004

7.6 KEY TERMS

This chapter has introduced the following key terms, which are listed here with the pages on which they first occur:

batch operating system 189	bootstrap 189
circular waiting 201	deadlock 200
demand paging 195	demand paging and segmentation 195
demand segmentation 195	device manager 202
distributed system 190	frame 194
graphical user interface (GUI) 192	hold state 197
job 197	job scheduler 198
kernel 204	Linux 205
memory management 192	Microsoft Disk Operating System (MS-DOS) 206
monoprogramming 192	multiprogramming 190
mutual exclusion 201	native NT file system (NTFS) 206
no-preemption 201	operating system 188
page 194	paging 194
parallel system 190	partitioning 193
process 190	process scheduler 198
program 197	queuing 199
ready state 197	real-time system 191
resource holding 201	running state 197
scheduler 198	scheduling 190
shell 191	single-user operating system 190
software 188	starvation 201
state diagram 197	terminal state 197
time sharing 190	UNIX 203
user interface 191	utility 205
virtual memory 196	waiting state 197
window 192	Windows 2000 206
Windows NT 206	Windows XP 206

7.7 SUMMARY

- An operating system is an interface between the hardware of a computer and the user that facilitates the execution of programs and access to hardware and software resources. Two major design goals of an operating system are efficient use of hardware and ease of use of resources.

- Operating systems have gone through a long history of evolution: batch systems, time-sharing systems, personal systems, parallel systems, and distributed systems.

- A modern operating system has at least four functional areas: memory manager, process manager, device manager, and file manager. An operating system also provides a user interface.

- The first responsibility of a modern computer system is memory management. Memory allocation must be controlled by the operating system. Memory management techniques can be divided into two categories: monoprogramming and multiprogramming. In monoprogramming, most of the memory capacity is dedicated to one single program. In multiprogramming, more than one program can be in memory at the same time.

- The second responsibility of an operating system is process management. A process is a program in execution. The process manager uses schedulers and queues to manage processes. Process management involves synchronizing different processes with different resources. This may potentially create resource deadlock or starvation. Deadlock occurs when the operating system does not put

resource restrictions on processes: starvation can happen when the operating system puts too many resource restrictions on a process.

- The third responsibility of an operating system is device or input/output management. There are limitations on the number and speed of input/output devices in a computer system. Because these devices are much slower compared with the CPU and memory, when a process accesses an input/output device, it is not available to other processes. The device manager is responsible for the efficient use of input/output devices.

- The fourth responsibility of an operating system is file management. An operating system uses a file manager to control access to files. Access is permitted only by processes or users that are allowed access to specific files, and the type of access can vary.

- Two common operating systems with some similarities are UNIX and Linux. UNIX is a multiuser, multiprocessing, portable operating system made up from four parts: the kernel, the shell, a standard set of utilities, and application programs. Linux has three components: a kernel, system utilities, and a system library.

- A popular family of operating systems from Microsoft is referred to as Windows NT. Windows NT is an object-oriented, multi-layer operating system. It uses several layers, including a hardware abstract layer (HAL), executive layer, and an environment subsystem layer.

7.8 PRACTICE SET

Review questions

1. What is the difference between an application program and an operating system?

2. What are the components of an operating system?

3. What is the difference between monoprogramming and multiprogramming?

4. How is paging different from partitioning?

5. How is demand paging more efficient than regular paging?

6. How is a program related to a job? How is a job related to a process? How is a program related to a process?

7. Where does a program reside? Where does a job reside? Where does a process reside?

8. What is the difference between a job scheduler and a process scheduler?

9. Why does an operating system need queues?

10. How does deadlock differ from starvation?

Multiple-choice questions

11. _____ is a program that facilitates the execution of other programs.
    a. An operating system
    b. Hardware
    c. A queue
    d. An application program

12. _____ supervises the activity of each component in a computer system.
    a. An operating system
    b. Hardware
    c. A queue
    d. An application program

13. Multiprogramming requires a _____ operating system.
    a. batch
    b. time-sharing
    c. parallel
    d. distributed

14. _____ is multiprogramming with swapping.
    a. Partitioning
    b. Paging
    c. Demand paging
    d. Queuing

15. _____ is multiprogramming without swapping.
    a. Partitioning
    b. Virtual memory
    c. Demand paging
    d. Queuing

16. In _____, only one program can reside in memory for execution.
    a. monoprogramming
    b. multiprogramming
    c. partitioning
    d. paging

17. _____ is a multiprogramming method in which multiple programs are entirely in memory with each program occupying a contiguous space.
    a. Partitioning
    b. Paging
    c. Demand paging
    d. Demand segmentation

18. In paging, a program is divided into equally sized sections called _____.
    a. pages
    b. frames
    c. segments
    d. partitions

19. In _____, the program can be divided into differently sized sections.
    a. partitioning
    b. paging
    c. demand paging
    d. demand segmentation

20. In _____, the program can be divided into equally sized sections called pages, but the pages need not be in memory at the same time for execution.
    a. partitioning
    b. paging
    c. demand paging
    d. demand segmentation

21. A process in the _____ state can go to either the ready, terminated, or waiting states.
    a. hold
    b. virtual
    c. running
    d. a and c

22. A process in the ready state goes to the running state when _____.
    a. it enters memory
    b. it requests I/O
    c. it gets access to the CPU
    d. it finishes running

23. A program becomes a _____ when it is selected by the operating system and brought to the hold state.
    a. job
    b. process
    c. deadlock
    d. partition

24. Every process is a _____.
    a. job
    b. program
    c. partition
    d. a and b

25. The _____ scheduler creates a process from a job and changes a process back to a job.
    a. job
    b. process
    c. virtual
    d. queue

26. The _____ scheduler moves a process from one process state to another.
    a. job
    b. process
    c. virtual
    d. queue

27. To prevent _____, an operating system can put resource restrictions on processes.
    a. starvation
    b. synchronization
    c. paging
    d. deadlock

28. _____ can occur if a process has too many resource restrictions.
    a. Starvation
    b. Synchronization
    c. Paging
    d. Deadlock

29. The _____ manager is responsible for archiving and backup.
    a. memory
    b. process
    c. device
    d. file

30. The _____ manager is responsible for access to I/O devices.
    a. memory
    b. process
    c. device
    d. file

Exercises

31. A computer has a monoprogramming operating system. If the size of memory is 64 MB and the memory-resident part of the operating system needs 4 MB, what is the maximum size of program that can be run by this computer?

32. Redo Exercise 31 if the operating system automatically allocates 10 MB of memory to data.

33. A monoprogramming operating system runs programs that on average need 10 microseconds access to the CPU and 70 microseconds access to the I/O devices. What percentage of time is the CPU idle?

34. A multiprogramming operating system uses an apportioning scheme and divides the 60 MB of available memory into four partitions of 10 MB, 12 MB, 18 MB, and 20 MB. The first program to be run needs 17 MB and occupies the third partition. The second program needs 8 MB and occupies the first partition. The third program needs 10.5 MB and occupies the second partition. Finally, the fourth program needs 20 MB and occupies the fourth partition. What is the total memory used? What is the total memory wasted? What percentage of memory is wasted?

35. Redo Exercise 34 if all programs need 10 MB of memory.

36. A multiprogramming operating system uses paging. The available memory is 60 MB divided into 15 frames, each of 4 MB. The first program needs 13 MB. The second program needs 12 MB. The third program needs 27 MB.
    a. How many frames are used by the first program?
    b. How many frames are used by the second program?
    c. How many frames are used by the third program?
    d. How many frames are unused?
    e. What is the total memory wasted?
    f. What percentage of memory is wasted?

37. An operating system uses virtual memory but requires the whole program to be in physical memory during execution (no paging or segmentation). The size of physical memory is 100 MB. The size of virtual memory is 1 GB. How many programs of size 10 MB can be run concurrently by this operating system? How many of them can be in memory at any time? How many of them must be on disk?

38. What is the status of a process in each of the following situations?

    a. The process is using the CPU.

    b. The process has finished printing and needs the attention of the CPU again.

    c. The process has been stopped because its time slot is over.

    d. The process is reading data from the keyboard.

    e. The process is printing data.

39. Three processes (A, B, and C) are running concurrently. Process A has acquired File1, but needs File2. Process B has acquired File3, but needs File1. Process C has acquired File2, but needs File3. Draw a diagram for these processes. Is this a deadlock situation?

40. Three processes (A, B, and C) are running concurrently. Process A has acquired File1. Process B has acquired File2, but needs File1. Process C has acquired File3, but needs File2. Draw a diagram for these processes. Is this a deadlock situation? If your answer is "no", show how the processes can eventually finish their tasks.

8

Algorithms

In this chapter we introduce the concept of algorithms, step-by-step procedures for solving a problem. We then discuss the tools used to develop algorithms. Finally, we give some examples of common iterative and recursive algorithms.

Objectives

After studying this chapter, the student should be able to:

❏ Define an algorithm and relate it to problem solving.

❏ Define three constructs—sequence, selection, and repetition—and describe their use in algorithms.

❏ Describe UML diagrams and how they can be used when representing algorithms.

❏ Describe pseudocode and how it can be used when representing algorithms.

❏ List basic algorithms and their applications.

❏ Describe the concept of sorting and understand the mechanisms behind three primitive sorting algorithms.

❏ Describe the concept of searching and understand the mechanisms behind two common searching algorithms.

❏ Define subalgorithms and their relations to algorithms.

❏ Distinguish between iterative and recursive algorithms.

8.1   CONCEPT

In this section we informally define an **algorithm** and elaborate on the concept using an example.

Informal definition

An informal definition of an algorithm is:

> **Algorithm: a step-by-step method for solving a problem or doing a task.**

In this definition, an algorithm is independent of the computer system. More specifically, we should also note that the algorithm accepts **input data** and creates **output data** (Figure 8.1).

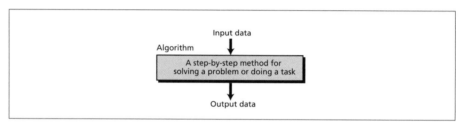

Figure 8.1   Informal definition of an algorithm used in a computer

Example

Let us elaborate on this simple definition with an example. We want to develop an algorithm for finding the largest integer among a list of positive integers. The algorithm should find the largest integer among a list of any values (for example 5, 1000, 10,000, 1,000,000). The algorithm should be general and not depend on the number of integers.

It is obvious that finding the largest integer among many integers is a task that cannot be done in one step, either by a human or a computer. The algorithm needs to test each integer one by one.

To solve this problem, we need an intuitive approach. First use a small number of integers (for example, five), then extend the solution to any number of integers. Our solution for five integers follows the same principles and restrictions for one thousand or one million integers. Assume, even for a five-integer case, that the algorithm handles the integers one by one. It looks at the first integer without knowing the values of the remaining integers. After it handles the first one, it looks at the second integer, and so on. Figure 8.2 shows one way to solve this problem.

We call the algorithm *FindLargest*. Each algorithm has a name to distinguish it from other algorithms. The algorithm receives a list of five integers as input and gives the largest integer as output.

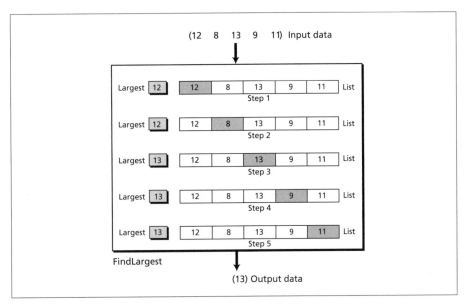

Figure 8.2 Finding the largest integer among five integers

Input

The algorithm accepts the list of five integers as input.

Processing

The algorithm uses the following five steps to find the largest integer:

Step 1

In this step, the algorithm inspects the first integer (12). Since it does not know the values of other integers, it decides that the largest integer (so far) is the first integer. The algorithm defines a data item, called Largest, and sets its value to the first integer (12).

Step 2

The largest integer so far is 12, but the new integer may change the situation. The algorithm makes a comparison between the value of Largest (12) and the value of the second integer (8). It finds that Largest is larger than the second integer, which means that Largest is still holding the largest integer. There is no need to change the value of Largest.

Step 3

The largest integer so far is 12, but the new integer (13) is larger than Largest. This means that the value of Largest is no longer valid. The value of Largest should be replaced by the third integer (13). The algorithm changes the value of Largest to 13 and moves to the next step.

Step 4

Nothing is changed in this step because Largest is larger than the fourth integer (9).

Step 5

Again nothing is changed because Largest is larger than the fifth integer (11).

Output   Because there are no more integers to be processed, the algorithm outputs the value of Largest, which is 13.

Defining actions

Figure 8.2 does not show what should be done in each step. We can modify the figure to show more details. For example, in step 1, set Largest to the value of the first integer. In steps 2 to 5, however, additional actions are needed to compare the value of Largest with the current integer being processed. If the current integer is larger than Largest, set the value of Largest to the current integer (Figure 8.3).

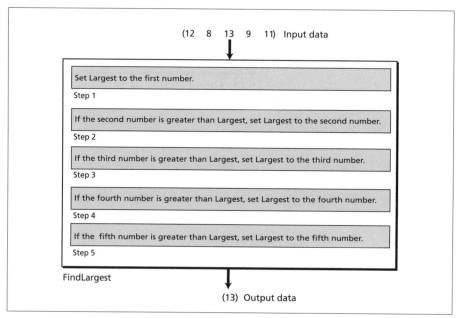

Figure 8.3   Defining actions in FindLargest algorithm

Refinement

This algorithm needs refinement to be acceptable to the programming community. There are two problems. First, the action in the first step is different than those for the other steps. Second, the wording is not the same in steps 2 to 5. We can easily redefine the algorithm to remove these two inconveniences by changing the wording in steps 2 to 5 to "If the current integer is greater than Largest, set Largest to the current integer." The reason that the first step is different than the other steps is because Largest is not initialized. If we initialize Largest to $-\infty$ (minus infinity), then the first step can be the same as the other steps, so we add a new step, calling it step 0 to show that it should be done before processing any integers.

Figure 8.4 shows the result of this refinement. Note that we do not have to show all the steps, because they are now the same.

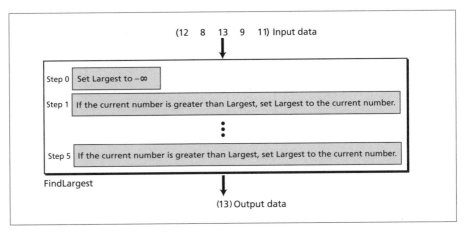

Figure 8.4   FindLargest refined

Generalization

Is it possible to generalize the algorithm? We want to find the largest of *n* positive integers, where *n* can be 1000, 1,000,000, or more. Of course, we can follow Figure 8.4 and repeat each step. But if we change the algorithm to a program, then we need to actually type the actions for *n* steps!

There is a better way to do this. We can tell the computer to repeat the steps *n* times. We now include this feature in our pictorial algorithm (Figure 8.5).

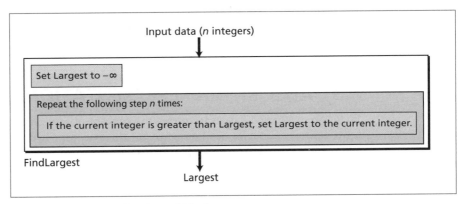

Figure 8.5   Generalization of FindLargest

8.2   THREE CONSTRUCTS

Computer scientists have defined three constructs for a structured program or algorithm. The idea is that a program must be made of a combination of only these three constructs: *sequence*, *decision* (selection), and *repetition* (Figure 8.6). It has been proven there is no need for any other constructs. Using only these constructs makes a program or an algorithm easy to understand, debug, or change.

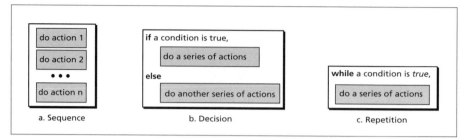

Figure 8.6   Three constructs

Sequence

The first construct is called the **sequence**. An algorithm, and eventually a program, is a sequence of instructions, which can be a simple instruction or either of the other two constructs.

Decision

Some problems cannot be solved with only a sequence of simple instructions. Sometimes we need to test a condition. If the result of testing is true, we follow a sequence of instructions: if it is false, we follow a different sequence of instructions. This is called the **decision (selection)** construct.

Repetition

In some problems, the same sequence of instructions must be repeated. We handle this with the **repetition** or **loop** construct. Finding the largest integer among a set of integers can use a construct of this kind.

8.3   ALGORITHM REPRESENTATION

So far, we have used figures to convey the concept of an algorithm. During the last few decades, tools have been designed for this purpose. Two of these tools, UML and pseudocode, are presented here.

UML

Unified Modeling Language (UML) is a pictorial representation of an algorithm. It hides all the details of an algorithm in an attempt to give the "big picture" and to show how the algorithm flows from beginning to end.

UML is covered in detail in Appendix B. Here we show only how the three constructs are represented using UML (Figure 8.7). Note that UML allows us a lot of flexibility, as shown in Appendix B. For example, the decision construct can be simplified if there are no actions on the *false* part.

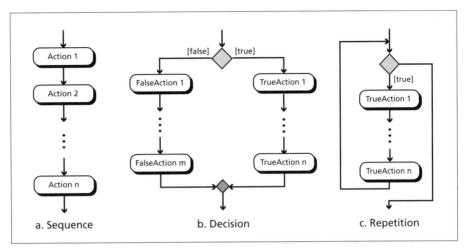

Figure 8.7 UML for three constructs

Pseudocode

Pseudocode is an English-language-like representation of an algorithm. There is no standard for pseudocode—some people use a lot of detail, others use less. Some use a code that is close to English, while others use a syntax like the Pascal programming language.

Pseudocode is covered in detail in Appendix C. Here we show only how the three constructs can be represented by pseudocode (Figure 8.8).

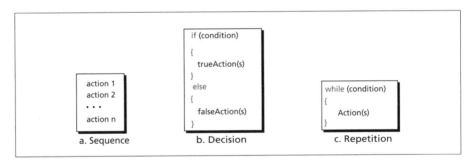

Figure 8.8 Pseudocode for three constructs

Example 8.1

Write an algorithm in pseudocode that finds the sum of two integers.

Solution

This is a simple problem that can be solved using only the sequence construct. Note also that we name the algorithm, define the input to the algorithm, and at the end, we use a return instruction to return the sum.

Algorithm 8.1   Calculating the sum of two integers

Algorithm: **SumOfTwo** (first, second)

Purpose: Find the sum of two integers

Pre: Given: two integers (first and second)

Post: None

Return: The sum value

{

     sum ← first + second
     return *sum*

}

Example 8.2

Write an algorithm to change a numeric grade to a pass/no pass grade.

Solution

This problem cannot be solved with only the sequence construct. We also need the decision construct. The computer is given an integer between 0 and 100. It returns "pass" if the integer is greater than or equal to 70, and returns "no pass" if the integer is less than 70. Algorithm 8.2 shows the pseudocode for this algorithm.

Algorithm 8.2   Assigning pass / no pass grade

Algorithm: **Pass/NoPass** (score)

Purpose: Creates a pass/no pass grade given the score

Pre: Given: the score to be changed to grade

Post: None

Return: The grade

{

     if (*score* ≥ 70)   *grade* ← *"pass"*
     else   *grade* ← *"nopass"*
     return *grade*

}

Example 8.3

Write an algorithm to change a numeric grade (integer) to a letter grade.

Solution

This problem needs more than one decision. The pseudocode in Algorithm 8.3 shows one way to solve the problem—not the best one, but an easy one to understand. Again, an integer is given between 0 and 100, and we want to change it to a letter grade (A, B, C, D, or F).

Algorithm 8.3   Assigning a letter grade

Algorithm: **LetterGrade** (score)

Purpose: Find the letter grade corresponding to the given score

Pre: Given: a numeric score

Post: None

Return: A letter grade

{

       if (100 ≥ *score* ≥ 90)   *grade* ← 'A'
       if (89 ≥ *score* ≥ 80)   *grade* ← 'B'
       if (79 ≥ *score* ≥ 70)   *grade* ← 'C'
       if (69 ≥ *score* ≥ 60)   *grade* ← 'D'
       if (59 ≥ *score* ≥ 0)   *grade* ← 'F'
       return *grade*

}

Note that the decision constructs do not need an *else* section, because we do nothing if the condition is false.

Example 8.4

Write an algorithm to find the largest of a set of integers. We do not know the number of integers.

Solution

We use the concept in Figure 8.5 on page 217 to write an algorithm for this problem (see Algorithm 8.4).

Example 8.5

Write an algorithm to find the largest of the first 1000 integers in a set of integers.

Solution

Here we need a counter to count the number of integers. We initialize the counter to 1 and increment it in each repetition. When the counter is greater than 1000, we exit from the loop (see Algorithm 8.5). Note that there are more than 1000 integers in the list, but we want to find the largest among the first 1000.

Algorithm 8.4   Finding the largest integer among a set of integers

```
Algorithm: FindLargest (list)

Purpose: Find the largest integer among a set of integers

Pre: Given: the set of integers

Post: None

Return: The largest integer
{
        largest ← − ∞
        while (more integers to check)
        {
                current ← next integer
                if (current > largest)          largest ← current

        }
        return largest

}
```

Algorithm 8.5   Finding the largest integer among the first 1000 integers

```
Algorithm: FindLargest2 (list)

Purpose: Find and return the largest integer among the first 1000 integers

Pre: Given: the set of integers with more than 1000 integers

Post: None

Return: The largest integer
{
        largest ← − ∞
        counter ← 1
        while (counter ≤ 1000)
        {
                current ← next integer
                if (current > largest)          largest ← current
                counter ← counter + 1
        }
        return largest

}
```

8.4   A MORE FORMAL DEFINITION

Now that we have discussed the concept of an algorithm and shown its representation, here is a more formal definition.

> **Algorithm:**
> **An ordered set of unambiguous steps that produces a result and**
> **terminates in a finite time.**

Let us elaborate on this definition.

Ordered set

An algorithm must be a well-defined, ordered set of instructions.

Unambiguous steps

Each step in an algorithm must be clearly and unambiguously defined. If one step is to *add two integers*, we must define both "integers" as well as the "add" operation: we cannot for example use the same symbol to mean addition in one place and multiplication somewhere else.

Produce a result

An algorithm must produce a result, otherwise it is useless. The result can be data returned to the calling algorithm, or some other effect (for example, printing).

Terminate in a finite time

An algorithm must terminate (halt). If it does not (that is, it has an infinite loop), we have not created an algorithm. In Chapter 17 we will discuss *solvable* and *unsolvable* problems, and we will see that a solvable problem has a solution in the form of an algorithm that terminates.

8.5   BASIC ALGORITHMS

Several algorithms are used in computer science so prevalently that they are considered "basic". We discuss the most common here. This discussion is very general: implementation depends on the language.

Summation

One commonly used algorithm in computer science is **summation**. We can add two or three integers very easily, but how can we add many integers? The solution is simple: we use the add operator in a loop (Figure 8.9).

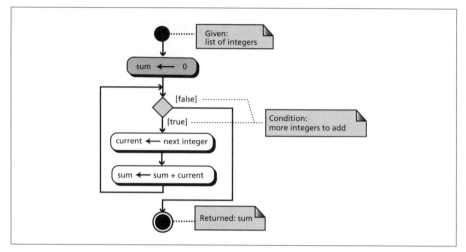

Figure 8.9   Summation algorithm

A summation algorithm has three logical parts:

1. Initialization of the sum at the beginning.
2. The loop, which in each iteration adds a new integer to the sum.
3. Return of the result after exiting from the loop.

Product

Another common algorithm is finding the **product** of a list of integers. The solution is simple: use the multiplication operator in a loop (Figure 8.10). A product algorithm has three logical parts:

1. Initialization of the product at the beginning.
2. The loop, which in each iteration multiplies a new integer with the product.
3. Return of the result after exiting from the loop.

For example, the preceding algorithm can be used to calculate x^n using a minor modification—this is left as an exercise. As another example, the same algorithm can be used to calculate the factorial of an integer, which is discussed later in the chapter.

Smallest and largest

We discussed the algorithm for finding the largest among a list of integers at the beginning of this chapter. The idea was to write a decision construct to find the larger of two integers. If we put this construct in a loop, we can find the largest of a list of integers.

Finding the smallest integer among a list of integers is similar, with two minor differences. First, we use a decision construct to find the smaller of two integers. Second, we initialize with a very large integer instead of a very small one.

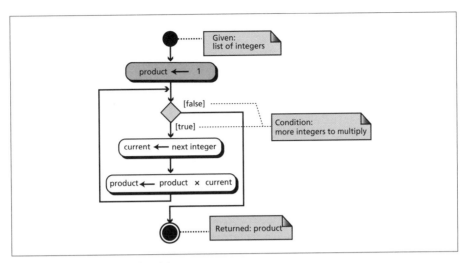

Figure 8.10 Product algorithm

Sorting

One of the most common applications in computer science is **sorting**, which is the process by which data is arranged according to its values. People are surrounded by data. If the data was not ordered, it would take hours and hours to find a single piece of information. Imagine the difficulty of finding someone's telephone number in a telephone book that is not ordered.

In this section, we introduce three sorting algorithms: *selection sort*, *bubble sort*, and *insertion sort*. These three sorting algorithms are the foundation of faster sorting algorithms used in computer science today.

Selection sorts

In a **selection sort**, the list to be sorted is divided into two sublists—sorted and unsorted—which are separated by an imaginary wall. We find the smallest element from the unsorted sublist and swap it with the element at the beginning of the sorted sublist. After each selection and swap, the imaginary wall between the two sublists moves one element ahead, increasing the number of sorted elements and decreasing the number of unsorted ones. Each time we move one element from the unsorted sublist to the sorted sublist, we have completed a **sort pass**. A list of *n* elements requires *n* – 1 passes to completely rearrange the data. Selection sort is presented graphically in Figure 8.11.

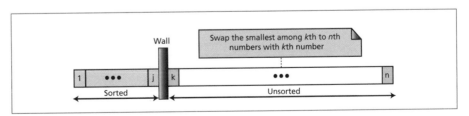

Figure 8.11 Selection sort

Figure 8.12 traces a set of six integers as we sort them.

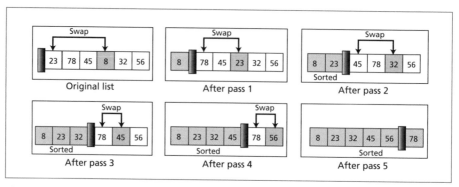

Figure 8.12 Example of selection sort

The figure shows how the wall between the sorted and unsorted sublists moves in each pass. As we study the figure, we will see that the list is sorted after five passes, which is one less than the number of elements in the list. Thus, if we use a loop to control the sorting, the loop will have one less iteration than the number of elements to be sorted.

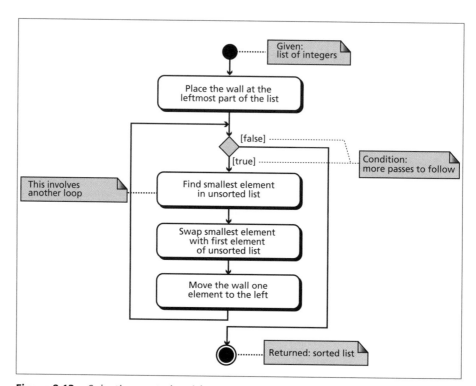

Figure 8.13 Selection sort algorithm

A selection sort algorithm

The algorithm uses two loops, one inside the other. The outer loop is iterated for each pass: the inner loop finds the smallest element in the unsorted list. Figure 8.13 shows the UML for the selection sort algorithm. The inner loop is not explicitly shown in the figure, but the first instruction in the loop is itself a loop. We leave the demonstration of the loop as an exercise.

Bubble sorts   In the **bubble sort** method, the list to be sorted is also divided into two sublists— sorted and unsorted. The smallest element is *bubbled up* from the unsorted sublist and moved to the sorted sublist. After the smallest element has been moved to the sorted list, the wall moves one element ahead, increasing the number of sorted elements and decreasing the number of unsorted ones. Each time an element moves from the unsorted sublist to the sorted sublist, one sort pass is completed (Figure 8.14). Given a list of n elements, bubble sort requires up to $n - 1$ passes to sort the data.

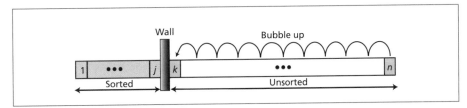

Figure 8.14   Bubble sort

Figure 8.15 shows how the wall moves one element in each pass. Looking at the first pass, we start with 56 and compare it to 32. Since 56 is not less than 32, it is not moved, and we step down one element. No exchanges take place until we compare 45 to 8. Since 8 is less than 45, the two elements are exchanged, and we step down one element. Because 8 was moved down, it is now compared to 78, and these two elements are exchanged. Finally, 8 is compared to 23 and exchanged. This series of exchanges places 8 in the first location, and the wall is moved up one position. The algorithm gets its name from the way in which numbers—in this example, 8—appear to move to the start, or top, of the list in the same way that bubbles rise through water.

Note that we have to stop before the wall moves to the end of the list, because the list is already sorted. We can always included an indicator in the algorithm to stop the passes if no number exchanges occur in a pass. This fact can be used to improve the efficiency of the bubble sort by reducing the number of steps.

The bubble sort was originally written to "bubble down" the highest element in the list. From an efficiency point of view, it makes no difference whether high elements are moved down or low elements are moved up. From a consistency point of view, however, it makes comparisons between the sort algorithms easier if all of them work in the same manner. For that reason, we have chosen to move the lowest value up in each pass.

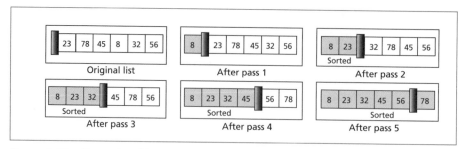

Figure 8.15 Example of bubble sort

A bubble sort algorithm

Bubble sorts also use two loops, one inside the other. The outer loop is iterated for each pass, while each iteration of the inner loop tries to bubble one element up to the top (left). We leave the UML and pseudocode as exercises.

Insertion sorts

The **insertion sort** algorithm is one of the most common sorting techniques, and it is often used by card players. Each card a player picks up is inserted into the proper place in their hand of cards to maintain a particular sequence. (Card sorting is an example of a sort that uses two criteria for sorting: suit and rank.)

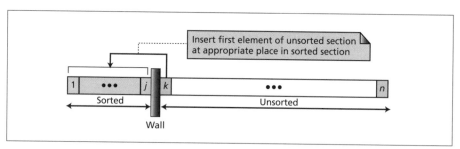

Figure 8.16 Insertion sort

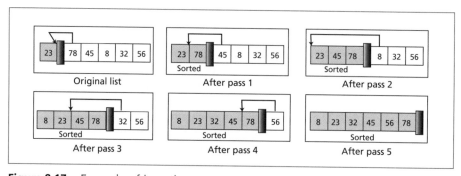

Figure 8.17 Example of insertion sort

In an insertion sort, as in the other two sorting algorithms discussed above, the list is divided into two parts—sorted and unsorted. In each pass, the first element of the unsorted sublist is transferred to the sorted sublist and inserted at the appropriate place (Figure 8.16). Note that a list of *n* elements will take *n* – 1 passes to sort the data.

Figure 8.17 traces an insertion sort through our list of six numbers. The wall moves with each pass as an element is removed from the unsorted sublist and inserted into the sorted sublist.

Insertion sort algorithm

The design of insertion sort follows the same pattern seen in both selection sort and bubble sort. The outer loop is iterated for each pass, and the inner loop finds the position of insertion. We leave the UML diagram and pseudocode as exercises.

Other sorting algorithms
The three sorting algorithms discussed here are the least efficient sorting algorithms, and should not be used if the list to be sorted has more than a few hundred elements. We have discussed these algorithm here for educational purposes, but they are not practical. There are however several reason for discussing these sorting algorithms in an introductory book:

❑ They are the simplest algorithms to understand and analyze.

❑ They are the foundation of more efficient algorithms such as *quicksort*, *heap sort*, *Shell sort*, *bucket sort*, *merge sort*, *radix sort*, and so on.

Most such advanced sorting algorithms are discussed in books on data structures.

We may ask why there are so many sorting algorithms. The reason lies in the type of data that needs to be sorted. One algorithm may be more efficient for a list that is partially sorted, whereas another algorithm may be more efficient for a list that is completely unsorted. To decide which algorithm is best suited for a particular application, a measurement called the *complexity of algorithms* is needed. We discuss this issue in Chapter 17, but a thorough understanding requires additional courses in programming and data structures.

Searching

Another common algorithm in computer science is **searching**, which is the process of finding the location of a target among a list of objects. In the case of a list, searching means that given a value, we want to find the location of the first element in the list that contains that value. There are two basic searches for lists: *sequential search* and *binary search*. Sequential search can be used to locate an item in any list, whereas binary search requires the list first to be sorted.

Sequential search

Sequential search is used if the list to be searched is not ordered. Generally, we use this technique only for small lists, or lists that are not searched often. In other cases, the best approach is to first sort the list and then search it using the binary search discussed later.

In a sequential search, we start searching for the target from the beginning of the list. We continue until we either find the target or reach the end of the list. Figure 8.18 traces the steps to find the value 62. The search algorithm needs to be designed so that the search stops when we find the target or when we reach the end of the list.

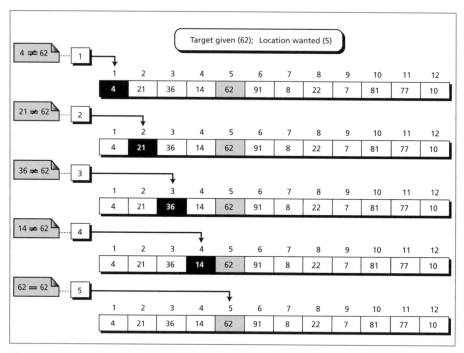

Figure 8.18   An example of a sequential search

Binary search

The sequential search algorithm is very slow. If we have a list of a million elements, we must do a million comparisons in the worst case. If the list is not sorted, this is the only solution. If the list *is* sorted, however, we can use a more efficient algorithm called **binary search**. Generally speaking, programmers use a binary search when a list is large.

A binary search starts by testing the data in the element at the middle of the list. This determines whether the target is in the first half or the second half of the list. If it is in the first half, there is no need to further check the second half. If it is in the second half, there is no need to further check the first half. In other words, we eliminate half the list from further consideration.

We repeat this process until we either find the target or satisfy ourselves that it is not in the list. Figure 8.19 shows how to find the target, 22, in a list of twelve numbers using three references: *first, mid,* and *last.*

1. At the beginning, *first* shows 1 and *last* shows 12. Let *mid* show the middle position, (1 + 12) / 2, or 6 if truncated to an integer. Now compare the target

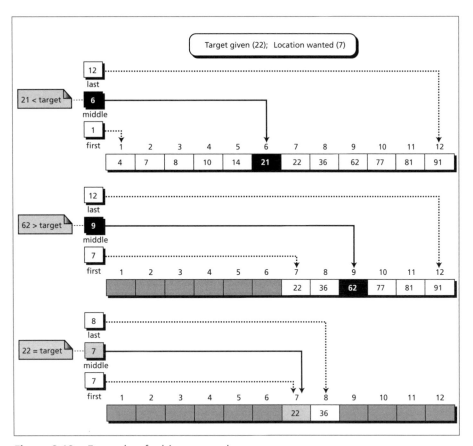

Figure 8.19 Example of a binary search

(22) with data at position 6 (21). The target is greater than this value, so we ignore the first half of the list.

2. Move *first* after *mid*, to position 7. Let *mid* show the middle of the second half, (7 + 12) / 2, or 9. Now compare the target (22) with data at position 9 (62). The target is smaller than this value, so we ignore the integers from this value (62) to the end.

3. Move last before *mid* to position 8. Recalculate *mid* again, (8 + 7) / 2, or 7. Compare the target (22) with the value at this position (22). We have found the target and can quit.

The algorithm for binary search needs to be designed to find the target or to stop if the target is not in the list. It can be shown that if the target is not found in the list, the value of *last* becomes smaller than the value of *first*, an abnormal condition that helps us to know when to come out of the loop.

8.6 SUBALGORITHMS

The three programming constructs described in Section 8.2 allow us to create an algorithm for any solvable problem. The principles of structured programming, however, require that an algorithm be broken into small units called **subalgorithms**. Each subalgorithm is in turn divided into smaller subalgorithms. A good example is the algorithm for the selection sort in Figure 8.13. Finding the smallest integer in the unsorted sublist is an independent task that can be considered as a subalgorithm. (Figure 8.20). The algorithm SelectionSort calls the subalgorithm FindSmallest in each iteration.

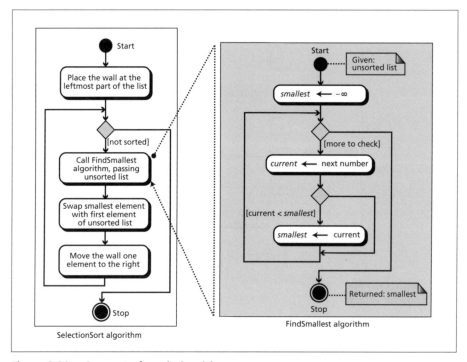

Figure 8.20   Concept of a subalgorithm

Using subalgorithms has at least two advantages:

❑ It is more understandable. Looking at the SelectionSort algorithm, we can immediately see that a task (finding the smallest integer among the unsorted list) is repeated.

❑ A subalgorithm can be called many times in different parts of the main algorithm without being rewritten.

Structure chart

Another tool programmers use is the **structure chart**. A structure chart is a high-level design tool that shows the relationship between algorithms and subalgorithms. It is used mainly at the design level rather than at the programming level. We briefly discuss the structure chart in Appendix D.

8.7 RECURSION

In general, there are two approaches to writing algorithms for solving a problem. One uses iteration, the other uses *recursion*. **Recursion** is a process in which an algorithm calls itself.

Iterative definition

To study a simple example, consider the calculation of a factorial. The factorial of an integer is the product of the integral values from 1 to the integer. The definition is *iterative* (Figure 8.21). An algorithm is iterative whenever the definition does not involve the algorithm itself.

$$\text{Factorial } (n) = \begin{bmatrix} 1 & \text{if } n = 0 \\ n \times (n-1) \times (n-2) \quad \cdots \quad 3 \times 2 \times 1 & \text{if } n > 0 \end{bmatrix}$$

Figure 8.21   Iterative definition of factorial

Recursive definition

An algorithm is defined recursively whenever the algorithm appears within the definition itself. For example, the factorial function can be defined recursively as shown in Figure 8.22.

$$\text{Factorial } (n) = \begin{bmatrix} 1 & \text{if } n = 0 \\ n \times \text{Factorial } (n-1) & \text{if } n > 0 \end{bmatrix}$$

Figure 8.22   Recursive definition of factorial

The decomposition of factorial (3), using recursion, is shown in Figure 8.23. If we study the figure carefully, we will note that the recursive solution for a problem involves a two-way journey. First we decompose the problem from top to bottom, and then we solve it from bottom to top.

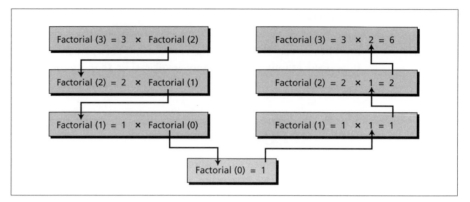

Figure 8.23   Tracing the recursive solution to the factorial problem

Judging by this example, it looks as if the recursive calculation is much longer and more difficult. So why would we want to use the recursive method? Although the recursive calculation looks more difficult when using paper and pencil, it is often a much easier and more elegant solution when using computers. Additionally, it offers a conceptual simplicity to the creator and the reader.

Iterative solution

Let us write an algorithm to solve the factorial problem iteratively. This solution usually involves a loop such as that in Algorithm 8.6.

Algorithm 8.6   An iterative solution to the factorial problem

Algorithm: **Factorial (n)**

Purpose: Find the factorial of a number using a loop

Pre: Given: n

Post: None

Return: $n!$

```
{
        F ← 1
        i ← 1
        while (i ≤ n)
        {
                F ← F × i
                i ← i + 1
        }
        return F
}
```

Recursive solution

The recursive solution to factorials is shown in Algorithm 8.7. It does not need a loop, as the recursion concept itself involves repetition. In the recursive version, we let the algorithm Factorial call itself.

Algorithm 8.7 Pseudocode for recursive solution of factorial problem

Algorithm: **Factorial** (n)

Purpose: Find the factorial of a number using recursion

Pre: Given: n

Post: None

Return: $n!$

```
{
        if (n = 0)          return 1
        else                return n × Factorial (n −1)
}
```

8.8 RECOMMENDED READING

For more details about the subjects discussed in this chapter, the following books are recommended:

❏ Aho A, Hopcroft J, and Ullman J: *The Design and Analysis of Computer Algorithms*, Boston, MA: Addison Wesley, 1974

❏ Cormen T, Leiserson C, and Rivest R: *Introduction to Algorithms*, New York: McGraw-Hill, 2003

❏ Gries D: *The Science of Programming*, New York: Springer, 1998

❏ Tardos E and Kleinberg J: *Algorithm Design*, Boston, MA: Addison Wesley, 2006

❏ Roberts E: *Thinking Recursively*, New York: Wiley, 1998

8.9 KEY TERMS

This chapter has introduced the following key terms, which are listed here with the pages on which they first occur:

algorithm 214	binary search 230
bubble sort 227	decision 218
input data 214	insertion sort 228
loop 218	output data 214
product 224	pseudocode 219
recursion 233	repetition 218
searching 229	selection 218

8.10 SUMMARY

- An algorithm can be informally defined as "a step-by-step method for solving a problem or doing a task". More formally, an algorithm is defined as "an ordered set of unambiguous steps that produces a result and terminates in a finite time".
- Computer scientists have defined three constructs for a structured program or algorithm: *sequence*, *decision* (selection), and *repetition* (loop).
- Several tools have been designed to show an algorithm: UML, pseudocode, and structure charts. UML is a pictorial representation of an algorithm. Pseudocode is an English-language-like representation of an algorithm. A structure chart is a high-level design tool that shows the relationship between algorithms and subalgorithms.
- Several algorithms are used in computer science so prevalently that they are considered basic. We discussed the most common in this chapter: *summation*, *product*, *finding the smallest and largest*, *sorting*, and *searching*.
- One of the most common applications in computer science is sorting, which is the process by which data is arranged according to its value. We introduced three primitive but fundamental, sorting algorithms: *selection sort*, *bubble sort*, and *insertion sort*. These three sorting algorithms are the foundation of the faster sorts used in computer science today.
- Another common algorithm in computer science is searching, which is the process of finding the location of a target among a list of objects. There are two basic searches for lists: *sequential search* and *binary search*. Sequential search can be used to locate an item in any list, whereas binary search requires the list to be sorted.
- The principles of structured programming require that an algorithm be broken into small units called *subalgorithms*. Each subalgorithm is in turn divided into smaller subalgorithms.
- In general, there are two approaches to writing algorithms to solve a problem. One uses *iteration*, the other uses *recursion*. An algorithm is iterative whenever the definition does not involve the algorithm itself. An algorithm is defined recursively whenever the algorithm appears within the definition itself.

8.11 PRACTICE SET

Review questions

1. What is the formal definition of an algorithm?
2. Define the three constructs used in structured programming.
3. How is a UML diagram related to an algorithm?
4. How is pseudocode related to an algorithm?
5. What is the purpose of a sorting algorithm?
6. What are the three basic sorting algorithms discussed in this chapter?
7. What is the purpose of a searching algorithm?
8. What are the two basic searching algorithms discussed in this chapter?
9. Give a definition and an example of an iterative process.

10. Give a definition and an example of a recursive process.

Multiple-choice questions

11. _____ is a step-by-step method for solving a problem or doing a task.
    a. A construct
    b. A recursion
    c. An iteration
    d. An algorithm

12. There are _____ basic constructs in computer science.
    a. one
    b. two
    c. three
    d. four

13. The _____ construct tests a condition.
    a. sequence
    b. decision
    c. repetition
    d. none of the above

14. The _____ construct uses a set of actions one after another.
    a. sequence
    b. decision
    c. repetition
    d. none of the above

15. The _____ construct handles repeated actions.
    a. sequence
    b. decision
    c. repetition
    d. none of the above

16. _____ is a pictorial representation of an algorithm.
    a. A UML digram
    b. A program
    c. Pseudocode
    d. An algorithm

17. _____ is an English-language-like representation of code.
    a. A UML diagram
    b. A program
    c. Pseudocode
    d. An algorithm

18. _____ is a basic algorithm that adds a list of numbers.
    a. Summation
    b. Product
    c. Smallest
    d. Largest

19. _____ is a basic algorithm that multiplies a list of numbers.
    a. Summation
    b. Product
    c. Smallest
    d. Largest

20. _____ is a basic algorithm that arranges data according to its value.
    a. Inquiry
    b. Sorting
    c. Searching
    d. Recursion

21. In _____ sort, the items are divided into two lists: sorted and unsorted.
    a. selection
    b. bubble
    c. insertion
    d. all of the above

22. In _____ sort, the item that goes into the sorted list is always the first item in the unsorted list.
    a. selection
    b. bubble
    c. insertion
    d. all of the above

23. In _____ sort, the smallest item from the unsorted list is swapped with the item at the beginning of the unsorted list.
    a. selection
    b. bubble
    c. insertion
    d. all of the above

24. In _____ sort, the smallest item moves to the beginning of the unsorted list. There is no one-to-one swapping.
    a. selection
    b. bubble
    c. insertion
    d. all of the above

25. _____ is a basic algorithm in which we want to find the location of a target in a list of items.
    a. Sorting
    b. Searching
    c. Product
    d. Summation

26. We use a _____ search for an unordered list.
    a. sequential
    b. binary
    c. bubble
    d. insertion

27. We use a _____ search for an ordered list.
    a. sequential
    b. binary
    c. bubble
    d. insertion

28. _____ is a process in which an algorithm calls itself.
    a. Insertion
    b. Searching
    c. Recursion
    d. Iteration

Exercises

29. Using the summation algorithm, make a table to show the value of the sum after each integer in the following list is processed:

| 20 | 12 | 70 | 81 | 45 | 13 | 81 |

30. Using the product algorithm, make a table to show the value of the product after each integer in the following list is processed:

| 2 | 12 | 8 | 11 | 10 | 5 | 20 |

31. Using the FindLargest algorithm, make a table to show the value of Largest after each integer in the following list is processed:

| 18 | 12 | 8 | 20 | 10 | 32 | 5 |

32. Using the FindSmallest algorithm, make a table to show the value of Smallest after each integer in the following list is processed:

| 18 | 3 | 11 | 8 | 20 | 1 | 2 |

33. Using the selection sort algorithm, manually sort the following list and show your work in each pass using a table:

| 14 | 7 | 23 | 31 | 40 | 56 | 78 | 9 | 2 |

34. Using the bubble sort algorithm, manually sort the following list and show your work in each pass using a table:

| 14 | 7 | 23 | 31 | 40 | 56 | 78 | 9 | 2 |

35. Using the insertion sort algorithm, manually sort the following list and show your work in each pass:

| 7 | 23 | 31 | 40 | 56 | 78 | 9 | 2 |

36. A list contains the following elements. The first two elements have been sorted using the selection sort algorithm. What is the value of the elements in the list after three more passes of the selection sort?

| 7 | 8 | 26 | 44 | 13 | 23 | 98 | 57 |

37. A list contains the following elements. The first two elements have been sorted using the bubble sort algorithm. What is the value of the elements in the list after three more passes of the bubble sort?

| 7 | 8 | 26 | 44 | 13 | 23 | 57 | 98 |

38. A list contains the following elements. The first two elements have been sorted using the insertion sort algorithm. What is the value of the elements in the list after three more passes of the insertion sort?

| 3 | 13 | 7 | 26 | 44 | 23 | 98 | 57 |

39. A list contains the following elements. Using the binary search algorithm, trace the steps followed to find 88. At each step, show the values of *first*, *last*, and *mid*.

| 8 | 13 | 17 | 26 | 44 | 56 | 88 | 97 |

40. A list contains the following elements. Using the binary search algorithm, trace the steps followed to find 20. At each step, show the values of *first*, *last*, and *mid*.

17	26	44	56	88	97

41. Using Figure 8.18 on page 230 (sequential search) show all the steps to try to find a target of 11 (which is not in the list).

42. Using Figure 8.19 on page 231 (binary search) show all the steps to try to find a target of 17 (which is not in the list).

43. Apply the iterative definition of the Factorial algorithm to show the value of F in each step when finding the value of 6! (6 factorial).

44. Apply the recursive definition of the Factorial algorithm to show the value of Factorial in each step when finding the value of 6!

45. Write a recursive algorithm in pseudocode to find the greatest common divisor (gcd) of two integers using the definition in Figure 8.24. In this definition, the expression "$x \bmod y$" means dividing x by y and using the remainder as the result of the operation.

$$\mathbf{gcd}\,(x\,,\;y) = \begin{bmatrix} x & \text{if } y = 0 \\ \gcd(y\,,\,x \bmod y) & \text{otherwise} \end{bmatrix}$$

Figure 8.24 Exercise 45

46. Using the definition of Figure 8.24, find the following:
   a. gcd(7, 41)
   b. gcd(12, 100)
   c. gcd(80, 4)
   d. gcd(17, 29)

47. Write a recursive algorithm in pseudocode to find the combination of n objects taken k at a time using the definition in Figure 8.25.

$$C\,(n\,,\,k) = \begin{bmatrix} 1 & \text{if } k = 0 \text{ or } n = k \\ C(n-1,\,k) + C(n-1,\,k-1) & \text{if } n > k > 0 \end{bmatrix}$$

Figure 8.25 Exercise 47

48. Using the definition in Figure 8.25, find the following:
   a. $C(10, 3)$
   b. $C(5, 5)$
   c. $C(2, 7)$
   d. $C(4, 3)$

49. The Fibonacci sequence, $\text{Fib}(n)$, is used in science and mathematics as shown in Figure 8.26. Write a recursive algorithm in pseudocode to calculate the value of $\text{Fib}(n)$.

$$\text{Fib}\,(n) = \begin{bmatrix} 0 & \text{if } n = 0 \\ 1 & \text{if } n = 1 \\ \text{Fib}(n-1) + \text{Fib}(n-2) & \text{if } n > 1 \end{bmatrix}$$

Figure 8.26 Exercise 49

50. Using the definition of Figure 8.26, find the following:
   a. Fib(2)
   b. Fib(3)
   c. Fib(4)
   d. Fib(5)

51. Draw a UML diagram for the selection sort algorithm that uses two loops. The nested loop is used to find the smallest element in the unsorted sublist.

52. Draw a UML diagram for the bubble sort algorithm that uses two loops. The nested loop is used to swap adjacent items in the unsorted sublist.

53. Draw a UML diagram for the insertion sort algorithm that uses two loops. The nested loop is used to do the insertion into the sorted sublist.

54. Draw a UML diagram for the bubble sort algorithm that uses a subalgorithm. The subalgorithm bubbles the unsorted sublist.

55. Draw a UML diagram for the insertion sort algorithm that uses a subalgorithm. The subalgorithm is used to do the insertion into the sorted sublist.

56. Write an algorithm in pseudocode for the UML diagram in Figure 8.9 on page 224 (summation).

57. Write an algorithm in pseudocode for the UML diagram in Figure 8.10 on page 225 (product).

58. Write an algorithm in pseudocode for the selection sort using two nested loops.

59. Write an algorithm in pseudocode for the selection sort using a subalgorithm to find the smallest integer in the unsorted sublist.

60. Write an algorithm in pseudocode for the bubble sort using two nested loops.

61. Write an algorithm in pseudocode for the bubble sort using a subalgorithm to do bubbling in the unsorted sublist.

62. Write an algorithm in pseudocode for the insertion sort using two nested loops.

63. Write an algorithm in pseudocode for the insertion sort using a subalgorithm to do insertion in the sorted sublist.

64. Write an algorithm in pseudocode for the sequential search algorithm. Include the condition for algorithm termination if the target is found or not found.

65. Write an algorithm in pseudocode for the binary search algorithm. Include the condition for algorithm termination if the target is found or not found.

66. Using the UML diagram for the product algorithm, draw a diagram to calculate the value of x^n, when x and n are two given integers.

67. Write an algorithm in pseudocode to find the value of x^n, when x and n are two given integers (see Exercise 66).

9 Programming Languages

In Chapter 8 we discussed algorithms. We showed how we can write algorithms in UML or pseudocode to solve a problem. In this chapter, we examine programming languages that can implement pseudocode or UML descriptions of a solution in a programming language. This chapter is not designed to teach a particular programming language; it is written to compare and contrast different languages.

Objectives

After studying this chapter, the student should be able to:

- ❏ Describe the evolution of programming languages from machine language to high-level languages.
- ❏ Understand how a program in a high-level language is translated into machine language using an interpreter or a compiler.
- ❏ Distinguish between four computer language paradigms.
- ❏ Understand the procedural paradigm and the interaction between a program unit and data items in the paradigm.
- ❏ Understand the object-oriented paradigm and the interaction between a program unit and objects in this paradigm.
- ❏ Define the functional paradigm and understand its applications.
- ❏ Define a declaration paradigm and understand its applications.
- ❏ Define common concepts in procedural and object-oriented languages.

9.1 EVOLUTION

To write a program for a computer, we must use a computer language. A **computer language** is a set of predefined words that are combined into a program according to predefined rules **(syntax)**. Over the years, computer languages have evolved from *machine language* to *high-level languages*.

Machine languages

In the earliest days of computers, the only programming languages available were **machine languages**. Each computer had its own machine language, which was made of streams of 0s and 1s. In Chapter 5 we showed that in a primitive hypothetical computer, we need to use eleven lines of code to read two integers, add them, and print the result. These lines of code, when written in machine language, make eleven lines of binary code, each of 16 bits, as shown in Table 9.1.

Table 9.1   Code in machine language to add two integers

Hexadecimal	Code in machine language			
$(1FEF)_{16}$	0001	1111	1110	1111
$(240F)_{16}$	0010	0100	0000	1111
$(1FEF)_{16}$	0001	1111	1110	1111
$(241F)_{16}$	0010	0100	0001	1111
$(1040)_{16}$	0001	0000	0100	0000
$(1141)_{16}$	0001	0001	0100	0001
$(3201)_{16}$	0011	0010	0000	0001
$(2422)_{16}$	0010	0100	0010	0010
$(1F42)_{16}$	0001	1111	0100	0010
$(2FFF)_{16}$	0010	1111	1111	1111
$(0000)_{16}$	0000	0000	0000	0000

Machine language is the only language understood by the computer hardware, which is made of electronic switches with two states: off (representing 0) and on (representing (1).

> **The only language understood by a computer is machine language.**

Although a program written in machine language truly represents how data is manipulated by the computer, it has at least two drawbacks. First, it is machine-dependent. The machine language of one computer is different than the machine language of another computer if they use different hardware. Second, it is very tedious to write programs in this language and very difficult to find errors. The era of machine language is now is referred to as the *first generation* of programming languages.

Assembly languages

The next evolution in programming came with the idea of replacing binary code for instructions and addresses with symbols or mnemonics. Because they used symbols, these languages were first known as *symbolic languages*. These mnemonic languages were later referred to as **assembly languages**. The assembly language for our hypothetical computer to replace the machine language in Table 9.2 is shown in Program 9.1.

Table 9.2 Code in assembly language to add two integers

Code in assembly language			Description
LOAD	RF	Keyboard	Load from keyboard controller to register F
STORE	Number1	RF	Store register F into Number1
LOAD	RF	Keyboard	Load from keyboard controller to register F
STORE	Number2	RF	Store register F into Number2
LOAD	R0	Number1	Load Number1 into register 0
LOAD	R1	Number2	Load Number2 into register 1
ADDI	R2	R0 R1	Add registers 0 and 1 with result in register 2
STORE	Result	R2	Store register 2 into Result
LOAD	RF	Result	Load Result into register F
STORE	Monitor	RF	Store register F into monitor controller
HALT			Stop

A special program called an **assembler** is used to translate code in assembly language into machine language.

High-level languages

Although assembly languages greatly improved programming efficiency, they still required programmers to concentrate on the hardware they were using. Working with symbolic languages was also very tedious, because each machine instruction had to be individually coded. The desire to improve programmer efficiency and to change the focus from the computer to the problem being solved led to the development of **high-level languages**.

High-level languages are portable to many different computers, allowing the programmer to concentrate on the application rather than the intricacies of the computer's organization. They are designed to relieve the programmer from the details of assembly language. High-level languages share one characteristic with symbolic languages: they must be converted to machine language. This process is called *interpretation* or *compilation* (described later in the chapter).

Over the years, various languages, most notably BASIC, COBOL, Pascal, Ada, C, C++, and Java, were developed. Program 9.1 shows the code for adding two integers as it would appear in the C++ language. Although the program looks longer, some of the lines are used for documentation (comments).

Program 9.1 Addition program in C++

```
/*      This program reads two integers from the keyboard and prints their
        sum.
        Written by:
        Date:
*/
#include <iostream.h>
using namespace std;
int main (void)
{
        // Local Declarations
        int number1;
        int number2;
        int result;
        // Statements
        cin >> number1;
        cin >> number2;
        result = number1 + number2;
        cout << result;
        return 0;
} // main
```

9.2 TRANSLATION

Programs today are normally written in one of the high-level languages. To run the program on a computer, the program needs to be translated into the machine language of the computer on which it will run. The program in a high-level language is called the **source program**. The translated program in machine language is called the **object program**. Two methods are used for translation: **compilation** and **interpretation**.

Compilation

A **compiler** normally translates the whole source program into the object program.

Interpretation

Some computer languages use an **interpreter** to translate the source program into the object program. Interpretation refers to the process of translating each line of the source program into the corresponding line of the object program and executing the line. However, we need to be aware of two trends in interpretation: that used by some languages before Java and the interpretation used by Java.

First approach to interpretation

Some interpreted languages prior to Java (such as BASIC and APL) used a kind of interpretation process that we refer to as the *first approach* to interpretation for the lack of any other name. In this type of interpretation, each line of the source program is translated into the machine language of the computer being used and executed immediately. If there are any errors in translation and execution, the process displays a message and the rest of the process is aborted. The program needs to be corrected and be interpreted and executed again from the beginning. This first approach was considered to be a slow process, which is why most languages use compilation instead of interpretation.

Second approach to interpretation

With the advent of Java, a new kind of interpretation process was introduced. The Java language is designed to be portable to any computer. To achieve portability, the translation of the source program to the object program is done in two steps: compilation and interpretation. A Java source program is first compiled to create Java **bytecode**, which looks like code in a machine language, but is not the object code for any specific computer: it is the object code for a virtual machine, called the Java Virtual Machine or JVM. The byte code then can be compiled or interpreted by any computer that runs a JVM emulator—that is, the computer that runs the bytecode needs only a JVM emulator, not the Java compiler.

Translation process

Compilation and interpretation differ in that the first translates the whole source code before executing it, while the second translates and executes the source code a line at a time. Both methods, however, follow the same translation process shown in Figure 9.1.

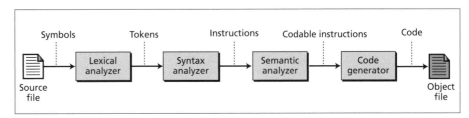

Figure 9.1   Source code translation process

Lexical analyzer

A **lexical analyzer** reads the source code, symbol by symbol, and creates a list of **tokens** in the source language. For example, the five symbols *w, h, i, l, e* are read and grouped together as the token *while* in the C, C++, or Java languages.

Syntax analyzer

The **syntax analyzer** parses a set of tokens to find instructions. For example, the token "*x*", "=", "0" are used by the syntax analyzer to create the assignment statement in the C language "*x* = 0". We will discuss the function of a parser and a syntax analyzer in more detail when we describe language recognition in artificial intelligence in Chapter 18.

Semantic analyzer

The **semantic analyzer** checks the sentences created by the syntax analyzer to be sure that they contain no ambiguity. Computer languages are normally unambiguous, which means that this stage is either omitted in a translator, or its duty is minimal. We also discuss semantic analysis in more details in Chapter 18.

Code generator

After unambiguous instructions are created by the semantic analyzer, each instruction is converted to a set of machine language instructions for the computer on which the program will run. This is done by the **code generator**.

9.3   PROGRAMMING PARADIGMS

Today computer languages are categorized according to the approach they use to solve a problem. A *paradigm*, therefore, is a way in which a computer language looks at the problem to be solved. We divide computer languages into four paradigms: *procedural* (imperative), *object-oriented*, *functional*, and *declarative*. Figure 9.2 summarizes these.

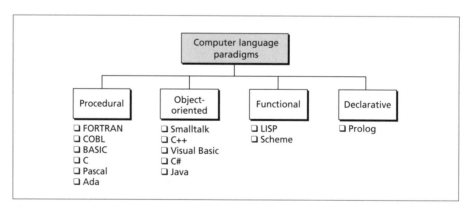

Figure 9.2   Categories of programming languages

The procedural paradigm

In the **procedural paradigm** (or **imperative paradigm**) we can think of a program as an *active agent* that manipulates *passive objects*. We encounter many passive objects in our daily life: a stone, a book, a lamp, and so on. A passive object cannot initiate an action by itself, but it can receive actions from active agents.

A program in a procedural paradigm is an active agent that uses passive objects that we refer to as *data* or *data items*. Data items, as passive objects, are stored in the memory of the computer, and a program manipulates them. To manipulate a piece of data, the active agent (program) issues an action, referred to as a *procedure*. For example, think of a program that prints the contents of a file. To be printed, the file needs to be stored in memory (or some registers that act as memory). The file is a passive object or a collection of passive objects. To print the file, the program uses a procedure, which we call *print*. The procedure print has usually been written previously to include all the actions required to tell the computer how to print each character in the file. The program invokes or *calls* the procedure *print*. In a procedural paradigm, the object (*file*) and the procedure (*print*) are completely separate entities. The object (*file*) is an independent entity that can receive the *print* action, or some other actions, such as *delete*, *copy*, and so on. To apply any of these actions to the file, we need a procedure to act on the file. The procedure *print* (or *copy* or *delete*) is a separate entity that is written and the program only triggers it.

To avoid writing a new procedure each time we need to print a file, we can write a general procedure that can print any file. When we write this procedure, every reference to the file name is replaced by a symbol, such as F, or FILE, or something else. When the procedure is called (triggered), we pass the name of the actual file to be printed to the procedure, so that we can write a procedure called *print* but call it twice in the program to print two different files. Figure 9.3 shows how a program can call different predefined procedures to print or delete different object files.

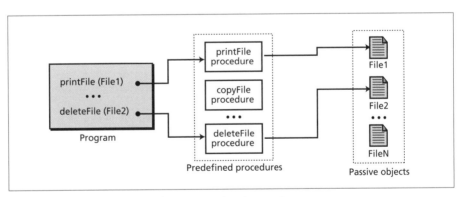

Figure 9.3   The concept of the procedural paradigm

We need to separate the procedure from its triggering by the program. The program does not define the procedure (as explained later), it only triggers or calls the procedure. The procedure must already exist.

When we use a procedural high-level language, the program consists of nothing but a lot of procedure calls. Although it is not immediately obvious, even when we use a simple mathematical operator such as the addition operator (+), we are using a procedure call to a procedure that is already written. For example, when we use the expression A + B and expect the expression to add the value of two objects A and B, we are calling the procedure *add* and passing the name of these two objects to the procedure. The procedure *add* needs two objects to act on. It adds the values of the two objects and returns the result. In other words, the expression A + B is a short cut for *add* (A, B). The designer of the language has written this procedure and we can call it.

If we think about the procedures and the objects to be acted upon, the concept of the procedural paradigm becomes simpler to understand. A program in this paradigm is made up of three parts: a part for object creation, a set of procedure calls, and a set of code for each procedure. Some procedures have already been defined in the language itself. By combining this code, the programmer can create new procedures.

Figure 9.4 shows these three components of a procedural program. There are also extra tokens in the language that are used for delimiting or organizing the calls, but these are not shown in the figure.

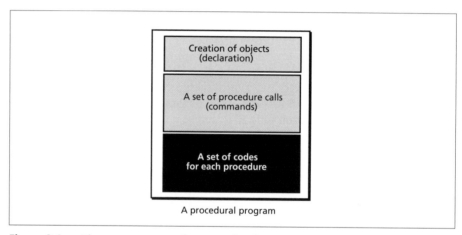

Figure 9.4   The components of a procedural program

Some procedural languages

Several high-level imperative (procedural) languages have been developed over the last few decades, such as FORTRAN, COBOL, Pascal, C, and Ada.

FORTRAN

FORTRAN (FORmula TRANslation), designed by a group of IBM engineers under the supervision of Jack Backus, became commercially available in 1957. FORTRAN was the first high-level language. During the last forty years FORTRAN has gone through several versions: FORTRAN, FORTRAN II, FORTRAN IV, FORTRAN 77, FORTRAN 99, and HPF (High Performance FORTRAN). The newest version (HPF) is used in high-speed multiprocessor computer systems. FORTRAN has some features that, even after four decades, still make it an ideal language for scientific and engineering applications. These features can be summarized as:

- ❏ High-precision arithmetic
- ❏ Capability of handling complex numbers
- ❏ Exponentiation computation (a^b)

COBOL

COBOL (COmmon Business-Oriented Language) was designed by a group of computer scientists under the direction of Grace Hopper of the US Navy. COBOL had a specific design goal: to be used as a business programming language. The problems to be solved in a business environment are totally different from those in an engineering environment. The programming needs of the business world can be summarized as follows:

- ❏ Fast access to files and databases
- ❏ Fast updating of files and databases
- ❏ Large amounts of generated reports
- ❏ User-friendly formatted output

Pascal

Pascal was invented by Niklaus Wirth in 1971 in Zurich, Switzerland. It was named after Blaise Pascal, the 17th century French mathematician and philosopher who invented the Pascaline calculator. Pascal was designed with a specific goal in mind: to teach programming to novices by emphasizing the structured programming approach. Although Pascal became the most popular language in academia, it never attained the same popularity in industry. Today's procedural languages owe a lot to this language.

C

The **C language** was developed in the early 1970s by Dennis Ritchie at Bell Laboratories. It was originally intended for writing operating systems and system software—most of the UNIX operating system is written in C. Later, it became popular among programmers for several reasons:

- ❏ C has all the high-level instructions a structured high-level programming language should have: it hides the hardware details from the programmer.
- ❏ C also has some low-level instructions that allow the programmer to access the hardware directly and quickly: C is closer to assembly language than any other high-level language. This makes it a good language for system programmers.
- ❏ C is a very efficient language: its instructions are short. This conciseness attracts programmers who want to write short programs.

Ada

Ada was named after Augusta Ada Byron, the daughter of Lord Byron and the assistant to Charles Babbage, the inventor of the Analytical Engine. It was created for the US Department of Defense (DoD) to be the uniform language used by all DoD contractors. Ada has three features that make it very popular for the DoD, and industry:

❑ Ada has high-level instructions like other procedural languages.

❑ Ada has instructions to allow real-time processing. This makes it suitable for process control.

❑ Ada has parallel-processing capabilities. It can be run on mainframe computers with multiple processors.

The object-oriented paradigm

The **object-oriented paradigm** deals with active objects instead of passive objects. We encounter many active objects in our daily life: a vehicle, an automatic door, a dishwasher, and so on. The action to be performed on these objects are included in the object: the objects need only to receive the appropriate stimulus from outside to perform one of the actions.

Returning to our example in the procedural paradigm, a file in an object-oriented paradigm can be packed with all the procedures—called **methods** in the object-oriented paradigm—to be performed by the file: printing, copying, deleting, and so on. The program in this paradigm just sends the corresponding request to the object (print, delete, copy, and so on) and the file will be printed, copied, or deleted. Figure 9.5 illustrates the concept.

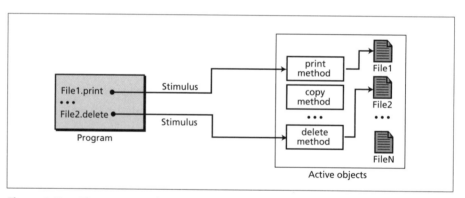

Figure 9.5   The concept of an object-oriented paradigm

The methods are shared by all objects of the same type, and also for other objects that are inherited from these objects, as we discuss later. If the program wants to print File1, it just sends the required stimulus to the active objects and File1 will be printed.

Comparing the procedural paradigm with the object-oriented paradigm (Figure 9.3 and Figure 9.5), we see that the procedures in the procedural paradigm are independent entities, but the methods in the object-oriented paradigm belong to the object's territory.

Classes

As Figure 9.5 shows, objects of the same type (files, for example) need a set of methods that show how an object of this type reacts to stimuli from outside the object's "territories". To create these methods, object-oriented languages such as C++, Java, and C# (pronounced "C sharp") use a unit called a **class**, as shown in Figure 9.6. The exact format of this program unit is different for different object-oriented languages (see Appendix F).

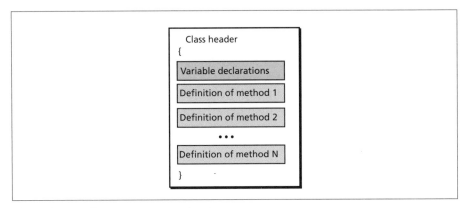

Figure 9.6   The components of a class

Methods

In general, the format of methods are very similar to the functions used in some procedural languages. Each **method** has its header, its local variables, and its statement. This means that most of the features we discussed for procedural languages are also applied to methods written for an object-oriented program. In other words, we can claim that object-oriented languages are actually an extension of procedural languages with some new ideas and some new features. The C++ language, for example, is an object-oriented extension of the C language. The C++ language can even be used as a procedural language with no or minimum use of objects. The Java language is an extension of C++, but it is totally an object-oriented language.

Inheritance

In the object-oriented paradigm, as in nature, an object can inherit from another object. This concept is called **inheritance**. When a general class is defined, we can define a more specific class that inherits some of the characteristics of the general class, but also has some new characteristics. For example, when an object of the type *GeometricalShapes* is defined, we can define a class called *Rectangles*. Rectangles are geometrical shapes with additional characteristics.

Polymorphism

Polymorphism means "many forms". Polymorphism in the object-oriented paradigm means that we can define several operations with the same name that can do different things in related classes. For example, assume that we define two classes, Rectangles and Circles, both inherited from the class GeometricalShapes. We define two operations both named *area*, one in Rectangles and one in Circles, that calculate the area of a rectangle or a circle. The two operations have the same name but do different things, as calculating the area of a rectangle and the area of a circle need different operands and operations.

Some object-oriented languages

Several **object-oriented languages** have been developed. We briefly discuss the characteristics of two: C++ and Java.

C++

The **C++ language** was developed by Bjarne Stroustrup at Bell Laboratory as an improvement of the C language. It uses *classes* to define the general characteristics of similar objects and the operations that can be applied to them. For example, a programmer can define a GeometricalShapes class and all the characteristics common to two-dimensional geometrical shapes, such as center, number of sides, and so on. The class can also define operations (functions or methods) that can be applied to a geometrical shape, such as calculating and printing the area, calculating and printing the perimeter, printing the coordinates of the center point, and so on. A program can then be written to create different objects of type GeometricalShapes. Each object can have a center located at a different point and a different number of sides. The program can then calculate and print the area, perimeter, and the location of the center for each object.

Three principles were used in the design of the C++ language: *encapsulation*, *inheritance*, and *polymorphism*.

Java

Java was developed at Sun Microsystems, Inc. It is based on C and C++, but some features of C++, such as multiple inheritance, are removed to make the language more robust. In addition, the language is totally class-oriented. In C++ one can solve a problem without ever defining a class, but in Java every data item belongs to a class.

A program in Java can either be an application or an **applet**. An application is a complete stand-alone program that can be run independently. An applet, on the other hand, is embedded HTML (see Chapter 6), stored on a server, and run by a browser. The browser can download the applet and run it locally.

In Java, an application program (or an applet) is a collection of classes and instances of those classes. One interesting feature of Java is the *class library*, a collection of classes. Although C++ also provides a class library, in Java the user can build new classes based on those provided by the library.

The execution of a program in Java is also unique. We create a class and pass it to the interpreter, which calls the class methods. Another interesting feature of Java is support for **multithreading**. A thread is a sequence of actions executed one after another. C++ allows only single threading—that is, the whole program is executed as a single process thread—but Java allows the concurrent execution of several lines of code.

The functional paradigm

In the **functional paradigm** a program is considered a mathematical function. In this context, a **function** is a black box that maps a list of inputs to a list of outputs (Figure 9.7).

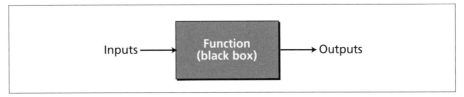

Figure 9.7   A function in a functional language

For example, *summation* can be considered as a function with *n* inputs and only one output. The function takes the *n* inputs, adds them, and creates the sum. A **functional language** does the following:

❑   Predefines a set of primitive (atomic) functions that can be used by any programmer.

❑   Allows the programmer to combine primitive functions to create new functions.

For example, we can define a primitive function called *first* that extracts the first element of a list. It may also have a function called *rest* that extracts all the elements except the first. A program can define a function that extracts the third element of a list by combining these two functions as shown in Figure 9.8.

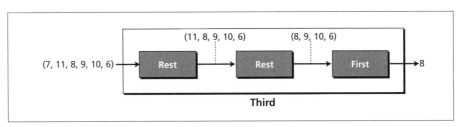

Figure 9.8   Extracting the third element of a list

A functional language has two advantages over a procedural language: it encourages modular programming and allows the programmer to make new functions out of existing ones. These two factors help a programmer create large and less error-prone programs from already-tested programs.

Some functional languages

We briefly discuss LISP and Scheme as examples of functional languages.

LISP

LISP (LISt Programming) was designed by a team of researchers at MIT in the early 1960s. It is a list-processing programming language in which everything is considered a list.

Scheme

The LISP language suffered from a lack of standardization. After a while, there were different versions of LISP everywhere. The de facto standard is the one developed by MIT in the early 1970s called **Scheme**.

The Scheme language defines a set of primitive functions that solves problems. The function name and the list of inputs to the function are enclosed in parentheses. The result is an output list, which can be used as the input list to another function. For example, there is a function, *car*, that extracts the first element of a list. There is a function, called *cdr*, that extracts the rest of the elements in a list except the first one. In other words, we have:

```
(car 2 3 7 8 11 17 20)  → 2
(cdr 2 3 7 8 11 17 20)  →  3 7 8 11 17 20
```

Now we can combine these two functions to extract the third element of any list.

```
(car (cdr (cdr  list)))
```

If we apply the above function to (2 3 7 8 11 17 20), it extracts 7 because the result of the innermost parentheses is 3 7 8 11 17 20. This becomes the input to the middle parentheses, with the result 7 8 11 17 20. This list now becomes the input to the car function, which takes out the first element, 7.

The declarative paradigm

A **declarative paradigm** uses the principle of logical reasoning to answer queries. It is based on formal logic defined by Greek mathematicians and later developed into *first-order predicate calculus.*

Logical reasoning is based on deduction. Some statements (facts) are given that are assumed to be true, and the logician uses solid rules of logical reasoning to deduce new statements (facts). For example, the famous rule of deduction in logic is:

```
If (A is B) and (B is C), then (A is C)
```

Using this rule and the two following facts,

```
Fact 1: Socrates is a human  →  A is B
Fact 2: A human is mortal  →  B is C
```

we can deduce a new fact:

```
Fact 3: Socrates is mortal  →  A is C
```

Programmers study the domain of their subject—that is, know all the facts in the domain—or get the facts from experts in the field. Programmers also need to be expert in logic to carefully define the rules. The program can then deduce and create new facts.

One problem associated with declarative languages is that a program is specific to a particular domain, because collecting all the facts into one program makes it huge. This is the reason why declarative programming is limited so far to specific fields such as artificial intelligence. We discuss logic further in Chapter 18.

Prolog

One of the famous declarative languages is **Prolog (PROgramming in LOGic)**, developed by A. Colmerauer in France in 1972. A program in Prolog is made up of facts and rules. For example, the previous facts about human beings can be stated as:

```
human (John)
mortal (human)
```

The user can then ask:

```
?-mortal (John)
```

and the program will respond with *yes*.

9.4 COMMON CONCEPTS

In this section we conduct a quick navigation through some procedural languages to find common concepts. Some of these concepts are also available in most object-oriented languages because, as we explain, an object-oriented paradigm uses the procedural paradigm when creating methods.

Identifiers

One feature present in all procedural languages, as well as in other languages, is the **identifier**—that is, the name of objects. Identifiers allow us to name objects in the program. For example, each piece of data in a computer is stored at a unique address. If there were no identifiers to represent data locations symbolically, we would have to know and use data addresses to manipulate them. Instead, we simply give data names and let the **compiler** keep track of where they are physically located.

Data types

A **data type** defines a set of values and a set of operations that can be applied to those values. The set of values for each type is known as the *domain* for the type. Most languages define two categories of data types: *simple types* and *composite types*.

Simple data types

A **simple type** (sometimes called an *atomic type, fundamental type, scalar type,* or *built-in type*) is a data type that cannot be broken into smaller data types. Several simple data types have been defined in imperative languages:

❑ An *integer* type is a whole number, that is, a number without a fractional part. The range of values an integer can take depends on the language. Some languages support several integer sizes.

❑ A *real* type is a number with a fractional part.

❑ A *character* type is a symbol in the underlying character set used by the language, for example, ASCII or Unicode.

❑ A *Boolean* type is type with only two values, *true* or *false*.

Composite data types

A **composite type** is a set of elements in which each element is a simple type or a composite type (that is, a recursive definition). Most languages defines the following composite types:

❑ An *array* is a set of elements each of the same type.

❑ A *record* is a set of elements in which the elements can be of different types.

Variables

Variables are names for memory locations. As discussed in Chapter 5, each memory location in a computer has an address. Although the addresses are used by the computer internally, it is very inconvenient for the programmer to use addresses for two reasons. First, the programmer does not know the relative address of the data item in memory. Second, a data item may occupy more than one location in memory. Names, as a substitute for addresses, free the programmer to think at the level at which the program is executed. A programmer can use a variable, such as *score*, to store the integer value of a score received in a test. Since a variable holds a data item, it has a type.

Variable declarations

Most procedural and object-oriented languages required that variables be declared before being used. Declaration alerts the computer that a variable with a given name and type will be used in the program. The computer reserves the required storage area and names it. Declaration is part of the object creation we discussed in the previous section. For example, in C, C++, and Java we can declare three variables of type character, integer, and real as shown below:

```
char C;
int num;
double result;
```

The first line declares a variable C to be of type character. The second declares a variable num to be of type integer. The third line declares a variable named result to be of type real.

Variable initialization

Although the value of data stored in a variable may change during the program's execution, most procedural languages allow the initialization of the variables when they are declared. Initialization stores a value in the variable. The following shows how the variables can be declared and initialized at the same time.

```
char C ='Z';
int num = 123;
double result = 256,782;
```

Literals

A **literal** is a predetermined value used in a program. For example, if we need to calculate the area of a circle when the value of the radius is stored in the variable r, we can use the expression $3.14 \times r^2$, in which the approximate value of π (pi) is used as a literal. In most programming languages we can have integer, real, character, and Boolean literals. In most languages, we can also have string literals. To distinguish the character and string literals from the names of variables and other objects, most languages require that the character literals be enclosed in single quotes, such as 'A', and strings to be enclosed in double quotes, such as "Anne".

Constants

The use of literals are not considered good programming practice unless we are sure that the value of the literal will not change with time (such as the value of π in geometry). However, most literals may change value with time. For example, if a sales tax is 8 percent this year, it may not be the same next year. When we write a program to calculate the cost of items, we should not use the literal in our program.

$$cost \leftarrow price \times 1.08$$

For this reason, most programming languages define **constants**. A constant, like a variable, is a named location that can store a value, but the value cannot be changed after it has been defined at the beginning of the program. However, if next year we want to use the program again, we can change just one line at the beginning of the program, the value of the constant. For example, in a C, or C++ program, the tax rate can be defined at the beginning and used during the program.

```
const float taxMultiplier = 1.08;
...
cost = price * taxMultiplier;
```

Note that a constant, like a variable, has a type that must be defined when the constant is declared.

Input and output

Almost every program needs to read and/or write data. These operations can be quite complex, especially when we read and write large files. Most programming languages use a predefined function for input and output.

Input

Data is **input** by either a statement or a predefined function. The C language has several input functions. For example, the *scanf* function reads data from the keyboard, formats it, and stores it in a variable. The following is an example:

```
scanf ("%d", &num);
```

When the program encounters this instruction, it waits for the user to type an integer. It then stores the value in the variable num. The %d tells the program to expect a decimal integer.

Output

Data is **output** by either a statement or a predefined function. The C language has several output functions. For example, the *printf* function displays a string on the monitor. The programmer can include the value of a variable or variables as part of the string. The following displays the value of a variable at the end of a literal string.

```
printf ("The value of the number is: %d", num);
```

Expressions   An **expression** is a sequence of operands and operators that reduces to a single value. For example, the following is an expression with a value of 13:

```
2 * 5 + 3
```

Operator

An **operator** is a language-specific token that requires an action to be taken. The most familiar operators are drawn from mathematics. For example, multiply (*) is an operator—it indicates that two numbers are to be multiplied together. Every language has operators, and their use is rigorously specified in the syntax, or rules, of the language.

❑   **Arithmetic operators** are used in most languages. Table 9.3 shows some arithmetic operators used in C, C++, and Java.

Table 9.3   Arithmetic operators

Operator	Definition	Example
+	Addition	3 + 5
−	Subtraction	2 − 4
*	Multiplication	Num * 5
/	Division (the result is the quotient)	Sum / Count
%	Division (the result is the remainder)	Count % 4
++	Increment (add 1 to the value of the variable)	Count++
− −	Decrement (subtract 1 from the value of the variable)	Count− −

❏ **Relational operators** compare data to see if a value is greater than, less than, or equal to another value. The result of applying relational operators is a Boolean value (true or false). C, C++, and Java use six relational operators, as shown in Table 9.4:

Table 9.4 Relational operators

Operator	Definition	Example
<	Less than	Num1 < 5
<=	Less than or equal to	Num1 <= 5
>	Greater than	Num2 > 3
>=	Greater than or equal to	Num2 >= 3
==	Equal to	Num1 == Num2
!=	Not equal to	Num1 != Num2

❏ **Logical operators** combine Boolean values (true or false) to get a new value. The C language uses three logical operators, as shown in Table 9.5:

Table 9.5 Logical operators

Operator	Definition	Example
!	Not	! (Num1 < Num2)
&&	And	(Num1 < 5) && (Num2 > 10)
||	Or	(Num1 < 5) || (Num2 > 10)

Operand

An **operand** receives an operator's action. For any given operator, there may be one, two, or more operands. In our arithmetic example, the operands of division are the dividend and the divisor.

Statements A **statement** causes an action to be performed by the program. It translates directly into one or more executable computer instructions. For example, C, C++, and Java define many types of statements. We discuss some of these in this section.

Assignment statements

An **assignment statement** assigns a value to a variable. In other words, it stores the value in the variable, which has already been created in the declaration section. We use the symbol ← in our algorithm to define assignment. Most languages (like C, C++, and Java) use the symbol = for assignment. Other languages such as Ada or Pascal use := for assignment.

Compound statements

A **compound statement** is a unit of code consisting of zero or more statements. It is also known as a *block.* A compound statement allows a group of statements to be treated as a single entity. A compound statement consists of an opening brace, an optional statement section, followed by a closing brace. The following shows the makeup of a compound statement.

```
{
  x = 1;
  y = 20;
}
```

Control statements

A program in a procedural language is a set of statements. The statements are normally executed one after another. However, sometimes it is necessary to change this sequential order, for example to repeat a statement or a set of statements, or two different sets of statements to be executed based on a Boolean value. The instruction provided in the machine languages of computers for this type of deviation from sequential execution is the *jump* instruction we discussed briefly in Chapter 5. Early imperative languages used the *go to* statement to simulate the *jump* instruction. Although the *go to* statement can be found in some imperative languages today, the principle of structured programming discourages its use. Instead, structured programming strongly recommends the use of the three constructs of *sequence, selection*, and *repetition*, as we discussed in Chapter 8. Control statements in imperative languages are related to selection and repetition.

❑ Most imperative languages have two-way and multi-way selection statements. Two-way selection is achieved through the *if-else* statement, multi-way selection through the *switch* (or *case*) statement. The UML diagram and the code for the *if-else* statement is shown in Figure 9.9.

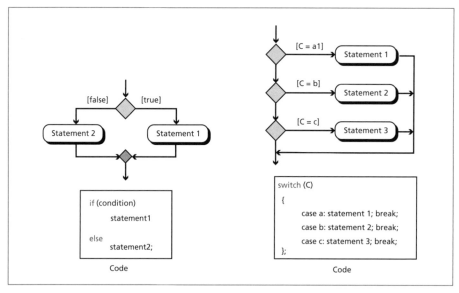

Figure 9.9   Two-way and multi-way decisions

In an *if-else* statement, if the condition is true, statement 1 is executed, while if the condition is false, statement 2 is executed. Both statement 1 and 2 can be any type of statement, including a null statement or a compound statement. Figure 9.9 also shows the code for the *switch* (or *case*) statement. The value of C (a, b, or c) decides which of statement1, statement2, or statement 3 is executed.

❑ We discussed the repetition construct in Chapter 8. Most of the imperative languages define between one and three loop statements that can achieve repetition. C, C++ and Java define three loop statements, but all of them can be simulated using the *while* loop (Figure 9.10).

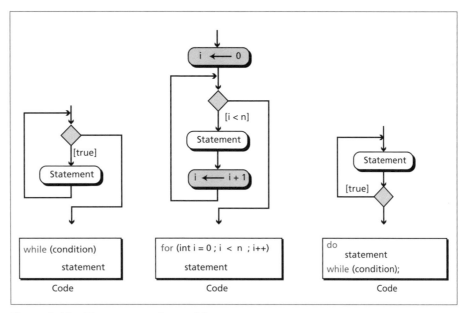

Figure 9.10 Three types of repetition

The main repetition construct in the C language is the *while* loop. A *while* loop is a *pretest* loop: it checks the value of a testing expression. If the value is true, the program goes through one iteration of the loop and tests the value again. The *while* loop is considered an event-controlled loop: the loop continues in iteration until an event happens that changes the value of the test expression from true to false.

The *for* loop is also a pretest loop. However, in contrast to the *while* loop, it is a counter-controlled loop. A counter is set to an initial value and is incremented or decremented in each iteration. The loop is terminated when the value of the counter matches a predetermined value.

The *do* loop is also an event-controlled loop. However, in contrast to the *while* loop, it is a post-test loop. The loop does one iteration and tests the value of an expression. If it is false, it terminates, if true, it does one more iteration and tests again.

Subprograms   In Chapter 8 we showed that a selection sort algorithm can be written as a main program and a **subprogram**. All procedures that are needed to find the smallest item among an unsorted list can be grouped into a subprogram. The idea of subprograms is crucial in procedural languages and to a lesser extent in object-oriented languages. We explained that a program written in a procedural language is a set of procedures that are normally predefined, such as addition, multiplication, and so on. However, sometimes a subset of these procedures to accomplish a single task can be collected and be placed in their own program unit, a subprogram. This is useful because the subprogram makes programming more structural: a subprogram to accomplish a specific task can be written once but called many times, just like predefined procedures in the programming language.

Subprograms also make programming easier: in incremental program development the programmer can test the program step by step by adding a subprogram at each step. This helps to detect errors before the next subprogram is written. Figure 9.11 illustrates the idea of a subprogram.

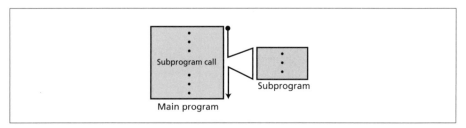

Figure 9.11   The concept of a subprogram

Local variables

In a procedural language, a subprogram, like the main program, can call predefined procedures to operate on local objects. These local objects or **local variables** are created each time the subprogram is called and destroyed when control returns from the subprogram. The local objects *belong* to the subprograms.

Parameters

It is rare for a subprogram to act only upon local objects. Most of the time the main program requires a subprogram to act on an object or set of objects created by the main program. In this case, the program and subprogram use *parameters*. These are referred to as **actual parameters** in the main program and **formal parameters** in the subprogram.

A program can normally pass parameters to a subprogram in either of two ways:

❑   By *value*

❑   By *reference*

These are described below.

Pass by value

In parameter **pass by value**, the main program and the subprogram create two different objects (variables). The object created in the program belongs to the program and the object created in the subprogram belongs to the subprogram. Since the territory is different, the corresponding objects can have the same or different names. Communication between the main program and the subprogram is one-way, from the main program to the subprogram. The main program sends the value of the actual parameter to be stored in the corresponding formal parameter in the subprogram: there is no communication of parameter value from the subprogram to the main program.

Example 9.1

Assume that a subprogram is responsible for carrying out printing for the main program. Each time the main program wants to print a value, it sends it to the subprogram to be printed. The main program has its own variable X, the subprogram has its own variable A. What is sent from the main program to the subprogram is the *value* of variable X. This value is stored in the variable A in the subprogram and the subprogram will then print it (Figure 9.12).

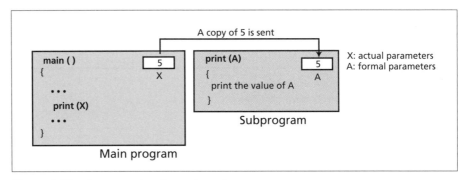

Figure 9.12   An example of pass by value

Example 9.2

In Example 9.1, since the main program sends only a value to the subprogram, it does not need to have a variable for this purpose: the main program can just send a literal value to the subprogram. In other words, the main program can call the subprogram as print (X) or print (5).

Example 9.3

An analogy of pass by value in real life is when a friend wants to borrow and read a valued book that you wrote. Since the book is precious, possibly out of print, you make a copy of the book and pass it to your friend. Any harm to the copy therefore does not affect your book.

Pass by value has an advantage: the subprogram receives only a value. It cannot change, either intentionally or accidentally, the value of the variable in the main program. However, the inability of a subprogram to change the value of the variable in the main program is a disadvantage when the program actually needs the subprogram to do so.

Example 9.4

Assume that the main program has two variables X and Y that needs to swap their values. The main program calls a subprogram called *swap* to do so. It passes the value of X and Y to the subprogram, which are stored in two variables A and B. The *swap* subprogram uses a local variable T (temporary) and swaps the two values in A and B, but the original values in X and Y remain the same: they are not swapped. This is illustrated in Figure 9.13.

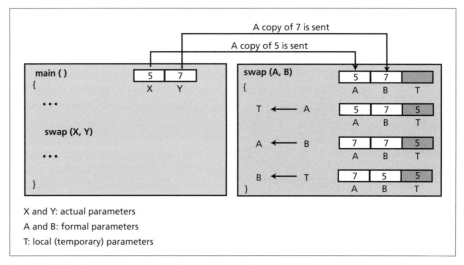

Figure 9.13   An example in which pass by value does not work

Pass by reference

Pass by reference was devised to allow a subprogram to change the value of a variable in the main program. In pass by reference, the variable, which in reality is a location in memory, is shared by the main program and the subprogram. The same variable may have different names in the main program and the subprogram, but both names refer to the same variable. Metaphorically, we can think of pass by reference as a box with two doors: one opens in the main program, the other opens in the subprogram. The main program can leave a value in this box for the subprogram, the subprogram can change the original value and leave a new value for the program in it.

Example 9.5

If we use the same *swap* subprogram but let the variables be passed by reference, the two values in X and Y are actually exchanged, as Figure 9.14 shows.

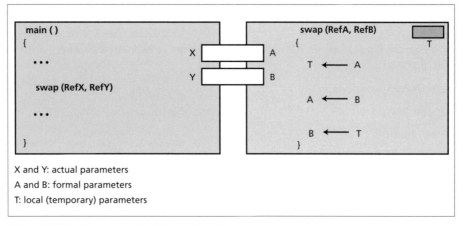

X and Y: actual parameters
A and B: formal parameters
T: local (temporary) parameters

Figure 9.14   An example of pass by reference

Returning values

A subprogram can be designed to return a value or values. This is the way that pre-defined procedures are designed. When we use the expression C ← A + B, we actually call a procedure *add* (A, B) that return a value to be stored in the variable C.

Implementation

The concept of subprogram is implemented differently in different languages. In C and C++, the subprogram is implemented as a **function**.

9.5 RECOMMENDED READING

For more details about the subjects discussed in this chapter, the following books are recommended:

❑   Cooke D A: *Concise Introduction to Computer Languages*, Pacific Grove, CA: Brooks/Cole, 2003

❑   Tucker A and Noonan R: *Programming Languages: Principles and Paradigms*, Burr Ridge, IL: McGraw-Hill, 2002

❑   Pratt T and Zelkowitz M: *Programming Languages, Design and Implementation*, Englewood Cliffs, NJ: Prentice Hall, 2001

❑   Sebesta R: *Concepts of Programming Languages*, Boston, MA: Addison Wesley, 2006

9.6   KEY TERMS

This chapter has introduced the following key terms, which are listed here with the pages on which they first occur:

actual parameter 262	Ada 249
applet 252	arithmetic operator 258
assembler 243	assembly language 243
assignment statement 259	bytecode 245
C language 249	C++ language 252
class 251	code generator 246
COmmon Business-Oriented Language (COBOL) 248	compilation 244
compiler 244	composite type 256
compound statement 259	computer language 242
constant 257	control statement 260
data type 255	declarative paradigm 254
expression 258	formal parameter 262
FORmula TRANslation (FORTRAN) 248	functional language 253
functional paradigm 252	high-level language 243
identifier 255	imperative paradigm 246
inheritance 251	input 258
interpretation 245	interpreter 245
Java 252	lexical analyzer 246
LISt Programming Language (LISP) 253	literal 257
local variable 262	logical operator 259
machine language 242	method 250
multithreading 252	object program 244
object-oriented language 252	object-oriented paradigm 250
operand 259	operator 258
output 258	Pascal 249
pass by reference 263	pass by value 263
polymorphism 251	procedural paradigm 246
Programming in LOGic (PROLOG)254	relational operator 259
semantic analyzer 246	simple type 256
source program 244	statement 259
subprogram 262	syntax 242
syntax analyzer 246	token 246
variable 256	

9.7 SUMMARY

- A computer language is a set of predefined words that are combined into a program according to predefined rules, the language's syntax. Over the years, computer languages have evolved from machine language to high-level languages. The only language understood by a computer is machine language.

- High-level languages are portable to many different computers, allowing the programmer to concentrate on the application rather than the intricacies of the computer's organization.

- To run a program on a computer, the program needs to be translated into the computer's native machine language. The program in the high-level language is called the *source program*. The translated program in machine language is called the *object program*. Two methods are used for translation: *compilation* and *interpretation*. A compiler translates the whole source program into the object program. Interpretation refers to the process of translating each line of the source program into the corresponding object program line by line and executing them.

- The translation process uses a lexical analyzer, a syntax analyzer, a semantic analyzer, and a code generator to create a list of tokens.

- A paradigm describes a way in which a computer language can be used to approach a problem to be solved. We divide computer languages into four paradigms: *procedural*, *object-oriented*, *functional*, and *declarative*.

- The procedural paradigm considers a program as an active agent that manipulates passive objects. FORTRAN, COBOL, Pascal, C, and Ada are examples of procedural languages.

- The object-oriented paradigm deals with active objects instead of passive objects. C++ and Java are common object-oriented languages.

- In the functional paradigm, a program is considered as a mathematical function. In this context, a function is a black box that maps a list of inputs to a list of outputs. LISP and Scheme are common functional languages.

- A declarative paradigm uses the principle of logical reasoning to answer queries. One of the best-known declarative languages is PROLOG.

- Some common concepts in procedural and object-oriented languages are *identifiers*, *data types*, *variables*, *literals*, *constants*, *inputs* and *outputs*, *expressions*, and *statements*. Most languages use two categories of control statements: *decision* and *repetition*. *Subprogramming* is a common concept among procedural languages.

9.8 PRACTICE SET

Review questions

1. Distinguish between machine language and assembly language.

2. Distinguish between assembly language and a high-level language.

3. Which computer language is directly related to and understood by a computer?

4. Distinguish between compilation and interpretation.

5. List four steps in programming language translation.

6. List four common computer language paradigms.

7. Compare and contrast a procedural paradigm with an object-oriented paradigm

8. Define a class and a method in an object-oriented language. What is the relation between these two concepts and the concept of an object?

9. Define a functional paradigm.

10. Define a declarative paradigm.

Multiple-choice questions

11. The only language understood by computer hardware is a _____ language.
    a. machine
    b. symbolic
    c. high-level
    d. none of the above

12. C, C++, and Java can be classified as _____ languages.
    a. machine
    b. symbolic
    c. high-level
    d. natural

13. _____ is a program's code in machine language.
    a. A procedure
    b. An object program
    c. A source program
    d. none of the above

14. FORTRAN is a(n) _____ language.
    a. procedural
    b. functional
    c. declarative
    d. object-oriented

15. Pascal is a(n) _____ language.
    a. procedural
    b. functional
    c. declarative
    d. object-oriented

16. C++ is a(n) _____ language.
    a. procedural
    b. functional
    c. declarative
    d. object-oriented

17. LISP is a(n) _____ language.
    a. procedural
    b. functional
    c. declarative
    d. object-oriented

18. _____ is a common language in the business environment.
    a. FORTRAN
    b. C++

    c. C
    d. COBOL

19. _____ is a popular object-oriented language.
    a. FORTRAN
    b. COBOL
    c. C++
    d. LISP

20. A _____ program can be either an application or an applet.
    a. FORTRAN
    b. C++
    c. C
    d. Java

21. LISP and Scheme are both _____ languages.
    a. procedural
    b. functional
    c. declarative
    d. object-oriented

22. Prolog is an example of a(n) _____ language.
    a. procedural
    b. functional
    c. declarative
    d. object-oriented

Exercises

23. Declare three variables of type integer in the C language.

24. Declare three variables of type real in C and initialize them to three values.

25. Declare three constants in C of type character, integer, and real respectively.

26. Explain why a constant must be initialized when it is declared.

27. Find how many times the *statement* in the following code segment in C is executed:

```
A = 5
while (A < 8)
{
        statement;
        A = A + 2;
}
```

28. Find how many times the *statement* in the following code segment in C is executed:

```
A = 5
while (A < 8)
{
        statement;
        A = A - 2;
}
```

29. Find how many times the *statement* in the following code segment in C is executed:

```
for (int i = 5; i < 20, i++)
{
        statement;
        i = i + 1;
}
```

30. Find how many times the *statement* in the following code segment in C is executed:

```
A = 5
do
{
        statement;
        A = A + 1;
} while (A < 10) ;
```

31. Write the code in Exercise 28 using a *do-while* loop.
32. Write the code in Exercise 29 using a *do-while* loop.
33. Write the code in Exercise 29 using a *while* loop.
34. Write the code in Exercise 30 using a *for* loop.
35. Write the code in Exercise 28 using a *for* loop.
36. Write a code fragment using a *while* loop that never executes its body.
37. Write a code fragment using a *do* loop that never executes its body.

38. Write a code fragment using a *for* loop that never executes its body.
39. Write a code fragment using a *while* loop that never stops.
40. Write a code fragment using a *do* loop that never stops.
41. Write a code fragment using a *for* loop that never stops.
42. In the following code, find all the literal values:

```
C = 12 * A + 4 * (B - 5)
```

43. In the following code, find the variables and literals:

```
Hello = "Hello";
```

44. Change the following segment of code to use a *switch* statement:

```
if (A = = 4) statement1;
else
        if (A == 6) statement 2
        else if (A == 8) statement 3
```

45. If the subprogram *calculate (A, B, S, P)* accepts the value of A and B and calculates their sum S and product P, which variable do you pass by value and which one by reference?
46. If the subprogram *smaller(A, B, S)* accepts the value of A and B and finds the smaller of the two, which variable do you pass by value and which one by reference?
47. If the subprogram *cube (A)* accepts the value of A and calculates its cube (A^3), should you pass A to the subprogram by value or by reference?
48. If the subprogram needs to get a value for A from the keyboard and return it to the main program, should you pass A to the subprogram by value or by reference?
49. If the subprogram needs to display the value of A on the monitor, should you pass A to the subprogram by value or by reference?

10 Software Engineering

In this chapter we introduce the concept of software engineering. We begin with the idea of the software life cycle. We then show two models used for the development process: the *waterfall* model and the *incremental* model. A brief discussion of four phases in the development process follows.

Objectives

After studying this chapter, the student should be able to:

❑ Understand the concept of the software life cycle in software engineering.

❑ Describe two major types of development process, the waterfall and incremental models.

❑ Understand the analysis phase and describe two separate approaches in the analysis phase: procedure-oriented analysis and object-oriented analysis.

❑ Understand the design phase and describe two separate approaches in the design phase: procedure-oriented design and object-oriented design.

❑ Describe the implementation phase and recognize the quality issues in this phase.

❑ Describe the testing phase and distinguish between glass-box testing and black-box testing.

❑ Recognize the importance of documentation in software engineering and distinguish between user documentation, system documentation, and technical documentation.

Software engineering is the establishment and use of sound engineering methods and principles to obtain reliable software. This definition, taken from the first international conference on software engineering in 1969, was proposed thirty years after the first computer was built.

10.1   THE SOFTWARE LIFECYCLE

A fundamental concept in **software engineering** is the **software lifecycle**. Software, like many other products, goes through a cycle of repeating phases (Figure 10.1).

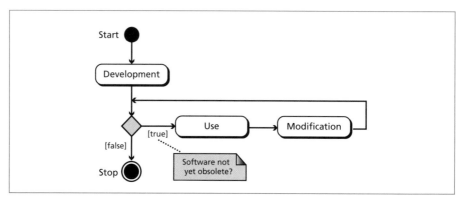

Figure 10.1   The software lifecycle

Software is first developed by a group of developers. Usually it is in use for a while before modifications are necessary. Modification is often needed due to errors found in the software, changes in the rules or laws governing its design, or changes in the company itself. The software therefore needs to be modified before further use. These two steps, *use* and *modify*, continue until the software becomes obsolete. By "obsolete", we mean that the software loses its validity because of inefficiency, obsolescence of the language, major changes in user requirements, or other factors.

Development process models

Although software engineering involves all three processes in Figure 10.1, in this chapter we discuss only the **development process**, which is shown outside the cycle in Figure 10.1. The development process in the software lifecycle involves four phases: analysis, design, implementation, and testing. There are several models for the development process. We discuss the two most common here: the waterfall model and the incremental model.

The waterfall model   One very popular model for the software development process is known as the **waterfall model** (Figure 10.2). In this model, the development process flows in only one direction. This means that a phase cannot be started until the previous phase is completed. For example, the analysis phase of the whole project should be completed before its design phase is started. The entire design phase should be finished before the implementation phase can be started.

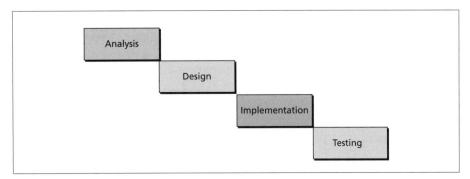

Figure 10.2   The waterfall model

There are advantages and disadvantages to the waterfall model. One advantage is that each phase is completed before the next phase starts. The group that works on the design phase, for example, knows exactly what to do because they have the complete results of the analysis phase. The testing phase can test the whole system because the entire system under development is ready. However, a disadvantage of the waterfall model is the difficulty in locating a problem: if there is a problem in part of the process, the entire process must be checked.

The incremental model

In the **incremental model**, software is developed in a series of steps. The developers first complete a simplified version of the whole system. This version represents the entire system but does not include the details. Figure 10.3 shows the incremental model concept.

In the second version, more details are added, while some are left unfinished, and the system is tested again. If there is a problem, the developers know that the problem is with the new functionality, they do not add more functionality until the existing system works properly. This process continues until all required functionality has been added.

10.2   ANALYSIS PHASE

The development process starts with the **analysis phase**. This phase results in a specification document that shows *what* the software will do without specifying *how* it will be done. The analysis phase can use two separate approaches, depending on whether the implementation phase is done using a procedural programming language or an object-oriented language. We briefly discuss both in this section.

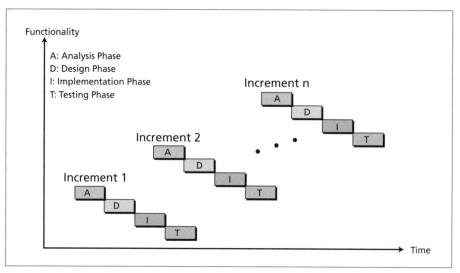

Figure 10.3   The incremental model

Procedure-oriented analysis

Procedure-oriented analysis—also called *structured analysis* or *classical analysis*—is the analysis process used if the system implementation phase will use a procedural language. The specification in this case may use several modeling tools, but we discuss only a few of them here.

Data flow diagrams

Data flow diagrams show the movement of data in the system. They use four symbols: a square box shows the source or destination of data, a rectangle with rounded corners shows the process (the action to be performed on the data), an open-ended rectangle shows where data is stored, and arrows show the flow of data.

Figure 10.4 shows a simplified version of a booking system in a small hotel that accepts reservations from potential guests through the Internet and confirms or denies the reservation based on available vacancies.

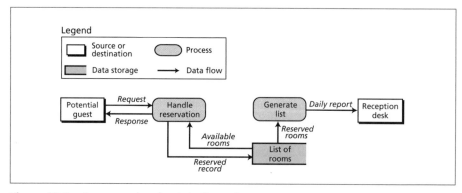

Figure 10.4   An example of a data flow diagram

The only process in this diagram (handle reservation) checks the availability using the reservation file and accepts or rejects a reservation. If the reservation is accepted, it will be recorded in the reservation file.

Entity-relationship diagrams

Another modeling tool used during the analysis phase is the **entity-relationship diagram**. Since this diagram is also used in database design, we discuss it in Chapter 12.

State diagrams

State diagrams (see Appendix B) provide another useful tool that is normally used when the state of the entities in the system will change in response to events. As an example of a state diagram, we show the operation of a one-passenger elevator. When a floor button is pushed, the elevator moves in the requested direction. It does not respond to any other request until it reaches its destination.

Figure 10.5 shows a state diagram for this old-style elevator. The elevator can be in one of three states: moving up, moving down, or parked. Each of these states is represented by a rounded rectangle in the state diagram. When the elevator is in the parked state, it accepts a request. If the requested floor is the same as the current floor, the request is ignored—the elevator remains in the parked state. If the requested floor is above the current floor, the elevator starts moving up. If the requested floor is lower than the requested floor, the elevator starts moving down. Once moving, the elevator remains in one of the moving states until it reaches the requested floor.

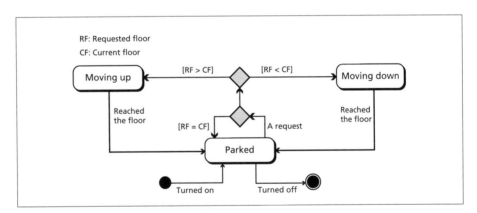

Figure 10.5   An example of a state diagram

Object-oriented analysis

Object-oriented analysis is the analysis process used if the implementation uses an object-oriented language. The specification document in this case may use several tools, but we discuss only a few of them here.

Use case diagrams

A **use-case diagram** gives the user's view of a system: it shows how users communicate with the system. A use-case diagram uses four components: system, use cases, actors, and relationships. A system, shown by a rectangle, performs a function. The

actions in the system are shown by use cases, which are denoted by rounded rectangles. An actor is someone or something that uses the system. Although actors are represented by stick figures, they do not necessarily represent human beings.

Figure 10.6 shows the use case diagram for the old-style elevator for which we gave a state diagram in Figure 10.5. The system in this figure is the elevator. The only actor is the user of the elevator. There are two uses cases: pressing the elevator button (in the hall of each floor) and pressing the floor button inside the elevator. The elevator has only one button on each floor that gives the signal to the elevator to move to that floor.

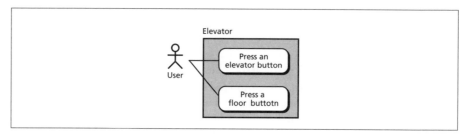

Figure 10.6   An example of use case diagram

Class diagrams

The next step in analysis is to create a **class diagram** for the system. For example, we can create a class diagram for our old-style elevator. To do so, we need to think about the entities involved in the system. In the elevator system we have two classes of entities: the buttons and the elevator itself. At first glance, therefore, it looks as if we have two classes: a button class and an elevator class. However, we have two types of buttons: the elevator buttons in the hallways and the floor buttons inside the elevator. It seems then that we can have a button class and two classes that inherit from the button class: an elevator button class and a floor button class. The first class diagram that we can create for the elevator problem is therefore that shown in Figure 10.7.

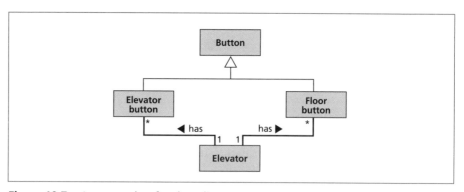

Figure 10.7   An example of a class diagram

Note that the elevator button class and the floor button class are subclasses of the button class. However, the relationship between the elevator class and the two button classes (elevator button and floor button) is a one-to-many relation (see Appendix B). The class diagram for the elevator system can of course be extended, but we leave this to books on software engineering.

State chart   After the class diagram is finalized, a **state chart** can be prepared for each class in the class diagram. A state chart in object-oriented analysis plays the same role as the state diagram in procedure-oriented analysis. This means that for the class diagram of Figure 10.7, we need to have a four-state chart.

10.3   DESIGN PHASE

The **design phase** defines *how* the system will accomplish *what* was defined in the analysis phase. In the design phase, all components of the system are defined.

Procedure-oriented design

In **procedure-oriented design** we have both procedures and data to design. We discuss a category of design methods that concentrate on procedures. In procedure-oriented design, the whole system is divided into a set of procedures or modules.

Structure charts   A common tool for illustrating the relations between modules in procedure-oriented design is a **structure chart**. For example, the elevator system whose state diagram is shown in Figure 10.5 can be designed as a set of modules shown in the structure chart in Figure 10.8. Structure charts are discussed in Appendix D.

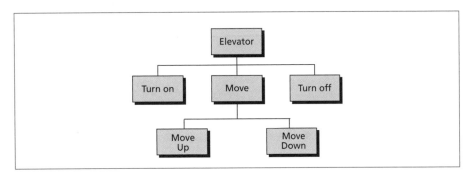

Figure 10.8   A structure chart

Modularity   **Modularity** means breaking a large project into smaller parts that can be understood and handled easily. In other words, modularity means dividing a large task into small tasks that can communicate with each other. The structure chart discussed in the previous section shows the modularity in the elevator system. There are two main concerns when a system is divided into modules: *coupling* and *cohesion*.

Coupling

Coupling is a measure of how tightly two modules are bound to each other. The more tightly coupled, the less independent they are. Since the objective is to make modules as independent as possible, we want them to be loosely coupled. There are at least three reasons why loose coupling is desirable:

❑ Loosely coupled modules are more likely to be reusable.

❑ Loosely coupled modules are less likely to create errors in related modules.

❑ When the system needs to be modified, loosely coupled modules allow us to modify only modules that need to be changed without affecting modules that do not need to change.

> **Coupling between modules in a software system must be minimized.**

Cohesion

Another issue in modularity is cohesion. **Cohesion** is a measure of how closely the modules in a system are related. We need to have maximum possible cohesion between modules in a software system.

> **Cohesion between modules in a software system must be maximized.**

Object-oriented design

In **object-oriented design** the design phase continues by elaborating the details of classes. As we mentioned in Chapter 9, a class is made of a set of variables (attributes) and a set of methods. The object-oriented design phase lists details of these attributes and methods. Figure 10.9 shows an example of the details of our four classes used in the design of the old-style elevator.

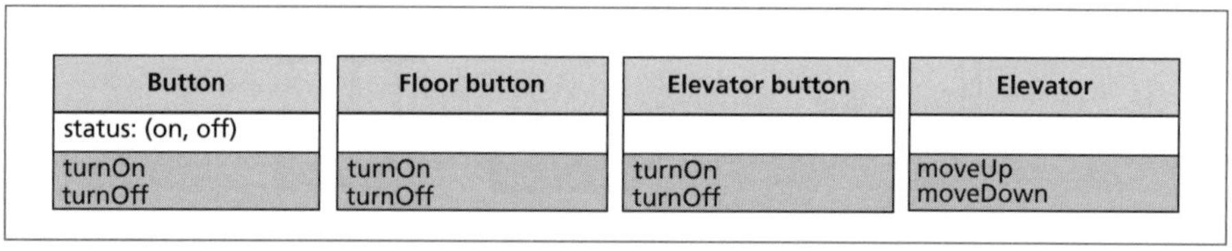

Button	Floor button	Elevator button	Elevator
status: (on, off)			
turnOn turnOff	turnOn turnOff	turnOn turnOff	moveUp moveDown

Figure 10.9   An example of classes with attributes and methods

10.4   IMPLEMENTATION PHASE

In the waterfall model, after the design phase is completed, the **implementation phase** can start. In this phase the programmers write the code for the modules in procedure-oriented design, or write the program units to implement classes in object-oriented design. There are several issues we need to mention in each case.

Choice of language

In a procedure-oriented development, the project team needs to choose a language or a set of languages from among the procedural languages discussed in Chapter 10. Although some languages like C++ are considered to be both a procedural and an object-oriented language, normally an implementation uses a purely procedural language such as C. In the object-oriented case, both C++ and Java are common.

Software quality

The quality of software created at the implementation phase is a very important issue. A software system of high quality is one that satisfies the user's requirements, meets the operating standards of the organization, and runs efficiently on the hardware for which it was developed. However, if we want to achieve a software system of high quality, we must be able to define some attributes of quality.

Software quality factors

Software quality can be divided into three broad measures: *operability, maintainability,* and *transferability*. Each of these measures can be further broken down as shown in Figure 10.10.

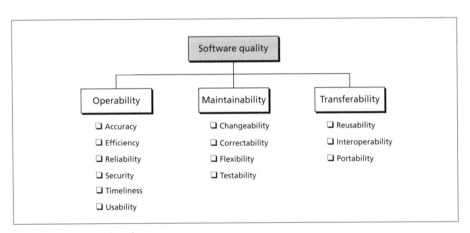

Figure 10.10 Quality factors

Operability

Operability refers to the basic operation of a system. Several measures can be mentioned for operability, as shown in Figure 10.10: *accuracy, efficiency, reliability, security, timeliness,* and *usability*.

❑ A system that is not *accurate* is worse than no system at all. Any system that is developed, therefore, must be thoroughly tested both by a system's test engineer and the user. *Accuracy* can be measured by such metrics as mean time between failures, number of bugs per thousand lines of code, and number of user requests for change.

❑ *Efficiency* is a subjective term. In some cases, the user will specify a performance standard, such as a real-time response that must be received within 1 second 95 percent of the time. This is certainly measurable.

❑ *Reliability* is really the sum of the other factors. If users count on the system to get their job done and are confident in it, then it is most likely reliable. On the other hand, some measures speak directly to a system's reliability, most notably, mean time between failures.

❑ How *secure* a system is refers to how easy it is for unauthorized people to access the system's data. Although this is a subjective area, there are checklists that assist in assessing the system's security. For example, does the system have and require passwords to identify users?

❑ *Timeliness* in software engineering can mean several different things. Does the system deliver its output in a timely fashion? For online systems, does the response time satisfy the users' requirements?

❑ *Usability* is another area that is highly subjective. The best measure of usability is to watch the users and see how they are using the system. User interviews will often reveal problems with the usability of a system.

Maintainability

Maintainability refers to the ease with which a system can be kept up to date and running correctly. Many systems require regular changes, not because they were poorly implemented, but because of changes in external factors. For example, the payroll system for a company might have to be changed often to meet changes in government laws and regulations.

❑ *Changeability* is a subjective factor. Experienced project leaders, however, are able to estimate how long a requested change will take to implement. If too long, it may indicate that the system is difficult to change. This is especially true of older systems. There are software measurement tools in the field today that will estimate a program's complexity and structure.

❑ One measure of *correctability* is *mean time to recovery*, which is the time it takes to get a program back into operation after it fails. Although this is a reactive definition, there are currently no predictors of how long it will take to correct a program when it fails.

❑ Users are constantly requesting changes to systems. *Flexibility* is a qualitative attribute that attempts to measure how easy it is to make these changes. If a program needs to be completely rewritten to effect a change, it is not flexible.

❑ We might think that *testability* is a highly subjective area, but test engineers have checklists of factors that can assess a program's testability.

Transferability

Transferability refers to the ability to move data and/or a system from one platform to another and to reuse code. In many situations this is not an important factor. On the other hand, if we are writing generalized software, it can be critical.

❑ If modules are written so that they can be reused in other systems, then they have a high level of *reusability*. Good programmers build libraries of functions that they can reuse for solving similar problems.

❑ *Interoperability* is the capability of sending data to other systems. In today's highly integrated systems, it is a desirable attribute. In fact, it has become so important that operating systems now support the ability to move data between systems, such as between a word processor and a spreadsheet.

❑ *Portability* is the ability to move software from one hardware platform to another.

10.5 TESTING PHASE

The goal of the **testing phase** is to find errors, which means that a good testing strategy is the one that finds most errors. There are two types of testing: *glass-box* and *black-box* (Figure 10.11).

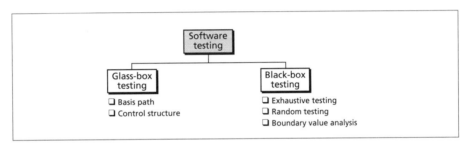

Figure 10.11 Software testing

Glass-box testing

Glass-box testing (or **white-box testing**) is based on knowing the internal structure of the software. The testing goal is to check to determine whether all components of the software do what they are designed to. Glass-box testing assumes that the tester knows everything about the software. In this case, the software is like a glass box in which everything inside the box is visible. Glass-box testing is done by the software engineer or a dedicated team. Glass-box testing that uses the structure of the software is required to guarantee that at least the following four criteria are met:

❑ All independent paths in every module are tested at least once.

❑ All the decision constructs (two-way and multiway) are tested on each branch.

❑ Each loop construct is tested.

❑ All data structures are tested.

Several testing methodologies have been designed in the past. We briefly discuss two of them: *basis path* testing and *control structure* testing.

Basis path testing

Basis path testing was proposed by Tom McCabe. This method creates a set of test cases that executes *every statement* in the software at least once.

> **Basis path testing is a method in which each statement in the software is executed at least once.**

Basis path testing uses *graph theory* (see Chapter 12) and *cyclomatic complexity* to find the independent paths that must be followed to guarantee that each statement is executed at least once.

Example 10.1

To give the idea of basis path testing and finding the independent paths in part of a program, assume that a system is made up of only one program and that the program is only a single loop with the UML diagram shown in Figure 10.12.

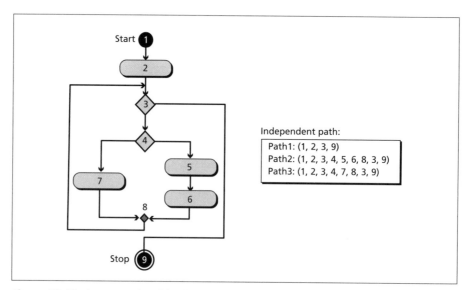

Independent path:

Path1: (1, 2, 3, 9)
Path2: (1, 2, 3, 4, 5, 6, 8, 3, 9)
Path3: (1, 2, 3, 4, 7, 8, 3, 9)

Figure 10.12 An example of basis path testing

In this simple program we have three independent paths. The first path is the case in which the loop is bypassed. The second path is where the loop is executed once through the right branch of the decision construct. The third path is when the loop is executed once but through the left branch of the decision construct. If there are more iterations, the paths created are not independent of these three paths: it is possible to prove this if we change the UML to a flow graph, but we must leave the proof to books on software engineering. The idea is to design test cases that cover all three paths in the basis path set, so that all statements are executed at least once.

Control structure testing

Control structure testing is more comprehensive than basis path testing and includes it. This method uses different categories of tests that are briefly described below.

Condition testing

Condition testing applies to any condition expression in the module. A *simple condition* is a relational expression, while a *compound condition* is a combination of simple conditions and logical operators (see Chapter 9). Condition testing is designed to check whether all conditions are set correctly.

Data flow testing

Data flow testing is based on the flow of data through the module. This type of testing selects test cases that involve checking the value of variables when they are used on the left side of the assignment statement.

Loop testing

Loop testing uses test cases to check the validity of loops. All types of loops (*while*, *do*, and *for*) are carefully tested.

Black-box testing

Black box testing gets its name from the concept of testing software without knowing what is inside it and without knowing how it works. In other words, the software is like a black box into which the tester cannot see. Black-box testing tests the functionality of the software in terms of what the software is supposed to accomplish, such as its inputs and outputs. Several methods are used in black-box testing, discussed below.

Exhaustive testing

The best black-box test method is to test the software for all possible values in the input domain. However, in complex software the input domain is so huge that it is often impractical to do so.

Random testing

In random testing, a subset of values in the input domain is selected for testing. It is very important that the subset be chosen in such a way that the values are distributed over the domain input. The use of random number generators can be very helpful in this case.

Boundary-value testing

Errors often happen when boundary values are encountered. For example, if a module defines that one of its inputs must be greater than or equal to 100, it is very important that module be tested for the boundary value 100. If the module fails at this boundary value, it is possible that some condition in the module's code such as x ≥ 100 is written as x > 100.

10.6 DOCUMENTATION

For software to be used properly and maintained efficiently, **documentation** is needed. Usually, three separate sets of documentation are prepared for software:

user documentation, system documentation, and technical documentation. However, note that documentation is an ongoing process. If the software has problems after release, they must be documented too. If the software is modified, all modifications and their relationship to the original package must also be documented. Documentation only stops when the package becomes obsolete.

> **Documentation is an ongoing process.**

User documentation

To run the software system properly, the users need documentation, traditionally called a *user guide*, that shows how to use the software step by step. User guides usually contains a tutorial section to guide the user through each feature of the software.

A good user guide can be a very powerful marketing tool: the importance of user documentation in marketing cannot be overemphasized. User guides should be written for both the novice and the expert users, and a software system with good user documentation will definitely increase sales.

System documentation

System documentation defines the software itself. It should be written so that the software can be maintained and modified by people other than the original developers. System documentation should exist for all four phases of system development.

In the analysis phase, the information collected should be carefully documented. In addition, the analysts should define the sources of information. The requirements and methods chosen in this phase must be clearly stated with the rationale behind them.

In the design phase, the tools used in the final copy must be documented. For example, if a chart undergoes several changes, the final copy of the chart should be documented with complete explanations.

In the implementation phase, every module of the code should be documented. In addition, the code should be self-documenting as far as possible using comments and descriptive headers.

Finally, the developers must carefully document the testing phase. Each type of test applied to the final product should be mentioned along with its result. Even unfavorable results and the data that produced them must be documented.

Technical documentation

Technical documentation describes the installation and the servicing of the software system. Installation documentation defines how the software should be installed on each computer, for example, servers and clients. Service documentation defines how the system should be maintained and updated if necessary.

10.7 RECOMMENDED READING

For more details about the subjects discussed in this chapter, the following books are recommended:

- ❏ Braude E: *Software Engineering – An Object-Oriented Perspective*, New York: Wiley, 2001
- ❏ Gustafson D: *Software Engineering*, New York: McGraw-Hill, 2002
- ❏ Lethbridge T and Laganiere R: *Object-Oriented Software Engineering*, New York: McGraw-Hill, 2005
- ❏ Pressman R: *Software Engineering: A Practitioner's Approach*, New York: McGraw-Hill, 2005
- ❏ Schach S. *Object-Oriented and Classical Software Engineering*, New York: McGraw-Hill, 2007

10.8 KEY TERMS

This chapter has introduced the following key terms, which are listed here with the pages on which they first occur:

analysis phase 273	basis path testing 282
black-box testing283	class diagram 276
cohesion 278	control structure testing 283
coupling 278	data flow diagram 275
design phase 277	development process 272
documentation 283	entity-relationship diagram 275
glass-box testing 281	implementation phase 278
incremental model 271	maintainability 280
modularity 277	object-oriented analysis 275
object-oriented design 278	operability 279
procedure-oriented analysis 274	procedure-oriented design 277
software engineering 272	software life cycle 272
software quality 279	state chart 277
state diagram 275	structure chart 277
testing phase 281	transferability 280
use case diagram 275	waterfall model 271
white-box testing 281	

10.9 SUMMARY

- The software lifecycle is a fundamental concept in software engineering. Software, like many other products, goes through a cycle of repeating phases.

- The development process in the software lifecycle involves four phases: analysis, design, implementation, and testing. Several models have been used in relation to these phases. We discussed the two most common: the waterfall model and the incremental model.

- The development process starts with the analysis phase. The analyst prepares a specification document that shows *what* the software will do without specifying *how* it will be done. The analysis phase can be done in two ways: procedure-oriented analysis and object-oriented analysis.

- The design phase defines *how* the system will accomplish what was defined in the analysis phase. In procedure-oriented design, the whole project is divided into a set of procedure or modules. In object-oriented design, the design phase continues by elaborating the details of classes.

- Modularity means breaking a large project into smaller parts that can be understood and handled easily. Two issues are important when a system is divided into modules: coupling and cohesion. Coupling is a measure of how tightly two modules are bound to each other. Coupling between modules in a software system must be minimized. Cohesion is a measure of how closely the modules in a system are related. Cohesion between modules in a software system should be maximized.

- In the implementation phase, programmers write the code for the modules in procedure-oriented design, or write the program units to implement classes in the object-oriented design.

- The quality of software is important. Software quality can be divided into three broad measures: operability, maintainability, and transferability.

- The goal of the testing phase is to find errors. There are two types of testing: glass-box and black-box. Glass-box testing (or white-box testing) is based on knowing the internal structure of the software. Glass-box testing assumes that the tester knows everything. Black box testing means testing the software without knowing what is inside it and without knowing how it works.

10.10 PRACTICE SET

Review questions

1. Define "software lifecycle".
2. Distinguish between the waterfall model and the incremental development model.
3. List the four phases in the development process.
4. Define the purpose of the analysis phase and describe two trends in this phase.
5. Define the purpose of the design phase and describe two trends in this phase.
6. Describe modularity and mention two issues related to modularity.
7. Distinguish between coupling and cohesion.
8. Define the purpose of the implementation phase and describe the issue of quality in this phase.
9. Define the purpose of the testing phase and list two categories of testing.
10. Distinguish between glass-box testing and black-box testing.

Multiple-choice questions

11. One phase in system development is _____.
    a. analysis
    b. testing
    c. design
    d. all of the above

12. Defining the users, requirements, and methods is part of the _____ phase.
    a. analysis
    b. design

c. implementation

d. testing

13. In the system development process, writing the program is part of the _____ phase.

   a. analysis

   b. design

   c. implementation

   d. testing

14. In the system development process, structure charts are tools used in the _____ phase.

   a. analysis

   b. design

   c. implementation

   d. testing

15. Testing a software system can involve _____ testing.

   a. black-box

   b. glass-box

   c. neither a nor b

   d. a and b

16. _____ is the breaking up of a large project into smaller parts.

   a. Coupling

   b. Incrementing

   c. Obsolescence

   d. Modularization

17. _____ is a measure of how tightly two modules are bound to each other.

   a. Modularity

   b. Coupling

   c. Interoperability

   d. Cohesion

18. _____ is a measure of how closely the processes in a program are related.

   a. Modularity

   b. Coupling

   c. Interoperability

   d. none of the above

19. _____ between modules in a software system must be minimized.

   a. Coupling

   b. Cohesion

   c. neither a nor b

   d. a and b

20. _____ between modules in a software system must be maximized.

   a. Coupling

   b. Cohesion

   c. neither a nor b

   d. a and b

Exercises

21. In Chapter 9 we explained that the use of constant values are preferred to literals. What it the effect of this preference on the software lifecycle?

22. In Chapter 9 we showed that communication between two modules can take place either by pass-by-value or pass-by-reference. Which method provides less coupling between the two modules?

23. In Chapter 9 we showed that communication between two modules can take place either by pass-by-value or pass-by-reference. Which method provides more cohesion between the two modules?

24. Draw a use case diagram for a simple library.

25. Draw a use case diagram for a small grocery store.

26. Show the data flow diagram for a simple mathematical formula $x + y$.

27. Show the data flow diagram for a simple mathematical formula $x \times y + z \times t$.

28. Show the data flow diagram for a library.

29. Show the data flow diagram for a small grocery store.

30. Create a structure chart for Exercise 28.

31. Create a structure chart for Exercise 29.

32. Show a state diagram for a stack of fixed capacity (see Chapter 12).

33. Show a state diagram for a queue of fixed capacity (see Chapter 12).

34. Create a class diagram for a library.

35. Create a class diagram for a small grocery store.

36. Show the details of classes in Exercise 34.

37. Show the details of classes in Exercise 35.

38. The input data to a program is made up of a combination of three integers in the range 1000 to 1999 (inclusive). Find the number of exhaustive tests to test all combinations of these numbers.

39. List the boundary-value tests required for Exercise 38.

40. A random number generator creates a number between 0 and 0.999. How can this random number generator be used to do random testing for the system described in Exercise 38?

11

Data Structures

In the preceding chapters, we used variables that store a single entity. Although single variables are used extensively in programming languages, they cannot be used to solve complex problems efficiently. In this chapter, we introduce data structures. This chapter is a prelude to the next chapter, in which we introduce abstract data types (ADTs)

Objectives

After studying this chapter, the student should be able to:

❏ Define a data structure.

❏ Define an array as a data structure and how it is used to store a list of data items.

❏ Distinguish between the name of an array and the names of the elements in an array.

❏ Describe operations defined for an array.

❏ Define a record as a data structure and how it is used to store attributes belonging to a single data element.

❏ Distinguish between the name of a record and the names of its fields.

❏ Define a linked list as a data structure and how it is implemented using pointers.

❏ Understand the mechanism through which the nodes in an array are accessed.

❏ Describe operations defined for a linked list.

❏ Compare and contrast arrays, records, and linked lists.

❏ Define the applications of arrays, records, and linked lists.

A **data structure** uses a collection of related variables that can be accessed individually or as a whole. In other words, a data structure represents a set of data items that share a specific relationship. We discuss three data structures in this chapter: *arrays*, *records*, and *linked lists*. Most programming languages have an implicit implementation of the first two. The third, however, is simulated using pointers and records.

11.1 ARRAYS

Imagine that we have 100 scores. We need to read them, process them, and print them. We must also keep these 100 scores in memory for the duration of the program. We can define a hundred *variables*, each with a different name, as shown in Figure 11.1.

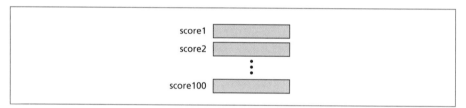

Figure 11.1   A hundred individual variables

But having 100 different names creates other problems. We need 100 references to read them, 100 references to process them, and 100 references to write them. Figure 11.2 shows a diagram that illustrates this problem.

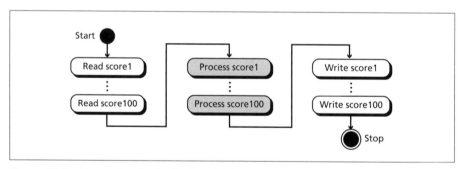

Figure 11.2   Processing individual variables

The number of instructions we need to handle even these relatively small number of scores is unacceptable. To process large amounts of data, we need a data structure such as an array.

An **array** is a sequenced collection of elements, normally of the same data type, although some programming languages accept arrays in which elements are of different types. We can refer to the elements in the array as the first element, the second element, and so forth until we get to the last element. If we were to put our 100 scores into an array, we could designate the elements as scores[1], scores[2], and so on. The **index** indicates the ordinal number of the element, counting from the beginning of the array. The elements of the array are individually addressed through their subscripts (Figure 11.3). The array as a whole has a name, *scores*, but each score can be accessed individually using its subscript.

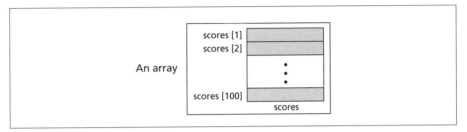

Figure 11.3 Arrays with indexes

We can use loops to read and write the elements in an array. We can also use loops to process elements. Now it does not matter if there are 100, 1000, or 10,000 elements to be processed—loops make it easy to handle them all. We can use an integer variable to control the loop, and remain in the loop as long as the value of this variable is less than the total number of elements in the array (Figure 11.4).

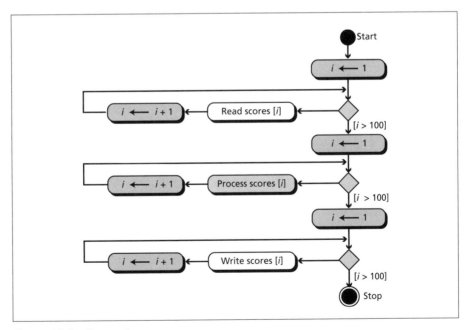

Figure 11.4 Processing an array

> We have used indexes that start from 1; some modern languages such as C,
> C++, and Java start indexes from 0.

Example 11.1

Compare the number of instructions needed to handle 100 individual elements in Figure 11.2 and the array with 100 in Figure 11.4. Assume that processing each score needs only one instruction.

Solution

❑ In the first case, we need 100 instructions to read, 100 instructions to write, and 100 instructions to process. The total is 300 instructions.

❑ In the second case, we have three loops. In each loop we have two instructions, for a total of six instructions. However, we also need three instructions for initializing the index and three instruction to check the value of the index. In total, we have twelve instructions.

Example 11.2

The number of cycles (fetch, decode, and execute phases) the computer needs to perform is not reduced if we use an array. The number of cycles is actually increased, because we have the extra overhead of initializing, incrementing, and testing the value of the index. But our concern is not the number of cycles: it is the number of lines we need to write the program.

Example 11.3

In computer science, one of the big issues is the reusability of programs—for example, how much needs to be changed if the number of data items is changed. Assume we have written two programs to process the scores as shown in Figure 11.2 and Figure 11.4. If the number of scores changes from 100 to 1000, how many changes do we need to make in each program?

In the first program we need to add $3 \times 900 = 2700$ instructions. In the second program, we only need to change three conditions ($I > 100$ to $I > 1000$). We can actually modify the diagram in Figure 11.4 to reduce the number of changes to one.

Array name versus element name

In an array we have two types of identifiers: the name of the array and the name of each individual element. The name of the array is the name of the whole structure, while the name of an element allows us to refer to that element. In the array of Figure 11.3, the name of the array is *scores* and name of each element is the name of the array followed by the index, for example, scores[1], scores[2], and so on. In this chapter, we mostly need the names of the elements, but in some languages, such as C, we also need to use the name of the array.

Multi-dimensional arrays

The arrays discussed so far are known as **one-dimensional arrays** because the data is organized linearly in only one direction. Many applications require that data be stored in more than one dimension. One common example is a table, which is an array that consists of rows and columns. Figure 11.5 shows a table, which is commonly called a **two-dimensional array**.

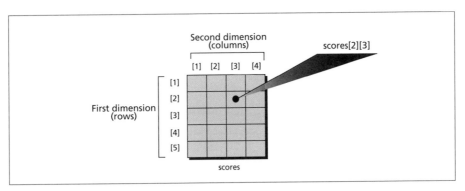

Figure 11.5 A two-dimensional array

The array shown in Figure 11.5 holds the scores of students in a class. There are five students in the class and each student has four different scores for four quizzes. The variable scores[2][3] shows the score of the second student in the third quiz. Arranging the scores in a two-dimensional array can help the teacher to find the average of scores for each student (the average over the row values) and find the average for each quiz (the average over the column values), as well as the average of all quizzes (the average of the whole table).

Multidimensional arrays—arrays with more than two dimensions—are also possible. However, we do not discuss arrays beyond two dimensions in this book.

Memory layout

The indexes in a one-dimensional array directly define the relative positions of the element in actual memory. A two-dimensional array, however, represents rows and columns. How each element is stored in memory depends on the computer. Most computers use **row-major storage**, in which an entire row of an array is stored in memory before the next row. However, a computer may store the array using **column-major storage**, in which the entire column is stored before the next column. Figure 11.6 shows a two-dimensional array and how it is stored in memory using row-major or column-major storage. Row-major storage is more common.

Example 11.4

We have stored the two-dimensional array *students* in memory. The array is 100×4 (100 rows and 4 columns). Show the address of the element *students*[5][3] assuming that the element *student*[1][1] is stored in the memory location with address 1000 and each element occupies only one memory location. The computer uses row-major storage.

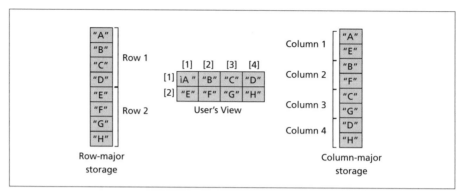

Figure 11.6   Memory layout of arrays

Solution

We can use the following formula to find the location of an element, assuming each element occupies one memory location.

$$y = x + \text{Cols} \times (i-1) + (j-1)$$

where x defines the start address, Cols defines the number of columns in the array, i defines the row number of the element, j defines the column number of the element, and y is the address we are looking for. In our example, x is 1000, Cols is 4, i is 5 and j is 3. We are looking for the value of y.

$$y = x + \text{Cols} \times (i-1) + (j-1) = 1000 + 4\,(5-1) + (3-1) = 1018$$

The answer makes sense because the element is at row 5 and column 3. There are four rows before this element that occupy 16 (4 × 4) memory locations. The previous two elements in row 5 have also occupied two memory locations. This means that all elements before the target elements occupy 18 memory locations. If the first element occupies the location 1000, the target element occupies the location 1018.

Operations on array

Although we can apply conventional operations defined for each element of an array (see Chapter 4), there are some operations that we can define on an array as a data structure. The common operations on arrays as structures are *searching, insertion, deletion, retrieval*, and *traversal*.

Searching for elements   We often need to find the index of an element when we know the value. This type of search was discussed in Chapter 8. We can use sequential search for unsorted arrays or binary search on sorted arrays. Searching is used for the next three operations.

Insertion of elements

Traditionally, computer languages require that the size of an array (the number of elements in the array) be defined at the time the program is written and prevent it from being changed during the execution of the program. Recently, some languages have allowed variable-size arrays (for example, the most recent version of C). Even when the language allows variable-sized arrays, insertion of an element into an array needs careful attention.

Insertion at the end

If the insertion is at the end of an array and the language allows us to increase the size of the array, this can be done easily. For example, if an array has 30 elements, we increase the size of the array to 31 and insert the new item as the 31st item.

Insertion at the beginning or middle

If the insertion is to be at the beginning or in the middle of an array, the process is lengthy and time consuming. This happens when we need to insert an element in a sorted array. We first search the array, as described before. After finding the location of the insertion, we insert the new element. For example, if we want to insert an element as the ninth element in an array of 30 elements, elements 9 to 30 should be shifted one element towards the end of the array to open an empty element at position 9 for insertion. The following shows part of the pseudocode that needs to be applied to the array:

```
i ← 30
while (i ≥ 9)
{
    array[i + 1] ← array[i]
    i ← i − 1
}
array[i] ← newValue
```

Note that the shifting needs to take place from the end of the array to prevent losing the values of the elements. The code first copies the value of the 30th element into the 31st element, then copies the value of the 29th element into the 30th element, and so on. When the code comes of the loop, the ninth element is already copied to the tenth element. The last line copies the value of the new item into the ninth element.

Deletion of elements

Deletion of an element in an array is as lengthy and involved as insertion. For example, if the ninth element should be deleted, we need to shift elements 10 to 30 one position towards the start of the array. We leave the pseudocode for this operation as an exercise, which is similar to the one for addition of an element.

Retrieving elements

Retrieving means randomly accessing an element for the purpose of inspecting or copying the data contained in the element. Unlike insertion and deletion operations, retrieving is an easy operation when a data structure is an array. In fact, an array is a *random-access* structure, which means that each element of the array can be accessed randomly without the need to access the elements before or after it. For example, if we want to retrieve the value of the ninth element in the array, we can do so using a single instruction, as shown below:

RetrievedValue ← array[9]

Traversal of arrays

Array traversal refers to an operation that is applied to all elements of the array, such as reading, writing, applying mathematical operations, and so on.

Algorithm 11.1 gives an example of finding the average of elements in array whose elements are reals. The algorithm first finds the sum of the elements using a loop. After the loop is terminated, the average is calculated, which is the sum divided by the number of elements. Note that for proper calculation of the sum, the sum needs to be set to 0.0 before the loop.

Algorithm 11.1   Calculating the average of elements in an array

Algorithm: **ArrayAverage** (Array, *n*)

Purpose: Find the average value

Pre: Given the array **Array** and the number of elements, *n*

Post: None

Return: The average value

```
{
    sum ← 0.0
    i ← 1
    while (i ≤ n)
    {
        sum ← sum + Array[i]
        i ← i + 1
    }
    average ← sum / n
    Return ( average )
}
```

Application

Thinking about the operations discussed in the previous section gives a clue to the application of arrays. If we have a list in which a lot of insertions and deletions are expected after the original list has been created, we should not use an array. An array is more suitable when the number of deletions and insertions is small, but a lot of searching and retrieval activities are expected.

An array is a suitable structure when a small number of insertions and deletions are required, but a lot of searching and retrieval is needed.

11.2 RECORDS

A **record** is a collection of related elements, possibly of different types, having a single name. Each element in a record is called a *field*. A **field** is the smallest element of named data that has meaning. A field has a type, and exists in memory. Fields can be assigned values, which in turn can be accessed for selection or manipulation. A field differs from a variable primarily in that it is part of a record.

Figure 11.7 contains two examples of records. The first example, fraction, has two fields, both of which are integers. The second example, student, has three fields made up of three different types.

> **The elements in a record can be of the same or different types, but all elements in the record must be related.**

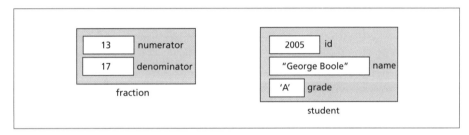

Figure 11.7   Records

The data in a record should all be related to one object. In Figure 11.7, the integers in the fraction both belong to the same fraction, and the data in the second example all relates to one student. (Note that we have placed string data between two double quotes and a single character between two single quotes. This is the convention used in most programming languages.)

Record name *versus* field name

Just like in an array, we have two types of identifier in a record: the name of the record and the name of each individual field inside the record. The name of the record is the name of the whole structure, while the name of each field allows us to refer to that field. For example, in the student record of Figure 11.7, the name of the record is *student*, the name of the fields are *student.id*, *student.name*, and *student.grade*. Most programming languages use a period (.) to separate the name of the structure (record) from the name of its components (fields). This is the convention we use in this book.

Example 11.5
The following shows how the value of fields in Figure 11.7 are stored.

student.id ← 2005   student.name ← "G. Boole"   student.grade ← 'A'

Comparison of records and arrays

We can conceptually compare an array with a record. This helps us to understand when we should use an array and when a record. An array defines a combination of elements, while a record defines the identifiable parts of an element. For example, an array can define a class of students (40 students), but a record defines different attributes of a student, such as id, name, or grade.

Array of records

If we need to define a combination of elements and at the same time some attributes of each element, we can use an array of records. For example, in a class of 30 students, we can have an array of 30 records, each record representing a student. Figure 11.8 shows an array of 30 student records called *students*.

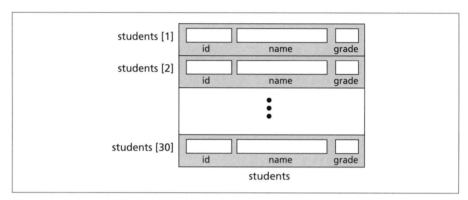

Figure 11.8   Array of records

In an array of records, the name of the array defines the whole structure, the group of students as a whole. To define each element, we need to use the corresponding index. To define the parts (attributes) of each element, we need to use the dot operator. In other words, first we need to define the element, then we can define part of that element. Therefore, the id of the third student is defined as:

(student[3]).id

Note that we use parentheses to emphasize that first a particular student should be chosen, then the id of that student. In other words, the parentheses tell us that the index operator has precedence over the dot operator. In some languages, there is no need to use parentheses, because the precedence is already established in the language itself, but using parentheses always guarantees the precedence.

Example 11.6

The following shows how we access the fields of each record in the students array to store values in them.

(students[1]).id ← 1001	(students[1]).name ← "J. Aron"	(students[1]).grade ← 'A'
(students[2]).id ← 2007	(students[2]).name ← "F. Bush"	(students[2]).grade ← 'F'
...	...	...
(students[30]).id ←3012	(students[30]).name ← "M. Blair"	(students[1]).grade ← 'B'

Example 11.7

However, we normally use a loop to read data into an array of records. Algorithm 11.2 shows part of the pseudocode for this process.

Algorithm 11.2   Part of the pseudocode to read student records

```
i ← 1

while (i < 31)

{

        read (students [i]).id
        read (students [i]).name
        read (students [i]).grade
        i ← i + 1

}
```

Arrays *versus* arrays of records

Both an array and an array of records represent a list of items. An array can be thought of as a special case of an array of records in which each element is a record with only a single field.

11.3   LINKED LISTS

A **linked list** is a collection of data in which each element contains the location of the next element—that is, each element contains two parts: data and **link**. The data part holds the value information: the data to be processed. The link is used to chain the data together, and contains a **pointer** (an address) that identifies the next element in the list. In addition, a pointer variable identifies the first element in the list. The name of the list is the same as the name of this pointer variable.

Figure 11.9 shows a linked list called *scores* that contains four elements. The link in each element, except the last, points to its successor. The link in the last element contains a **null pointer**, indicating the end of the list. We define an empty linked list to be only a null pointer: Figure 11.9 also shows an example of an empty linked list.

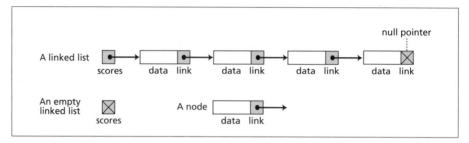

Figure 11.9 Linked lists

The elements in a linked list are traditionally called *nodes*. A **node** in a linked list is a record that has at least two fields: one contains the data, and the other contains the address of the next node in the sequence (the link). Figure 11.9 also shows a node.

Before further discussion of linked lists, we need to explain the notation we use in the figures. We show the connection between two nodes using a line. One end of the line has an arrowhead, the other end has a solid circle. The arrowhead represents a copy of the address of the node to which the arrow head is pointed. The solid circle shows where this copy of the address is stored (Figure 11.10). The figure also shows that we can store a copy of the address in more than one place. For example, Figure 11.10 shows that two copies of the address are stored in two different locations. Understanding these concepts helps us to understand operations on a linked list better.

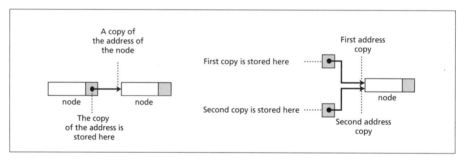

Figure 11.10 The concept of copying and storing pointers

Arrays *versus* linked lists

Both an array and a linked list are representations of a list of items in memory. The only difference is the way in which the items are linked together. In an array of records, the *linking tool* is the index. The element scores[3] is linked to the element scores[4] because the integer 4 comes after the integer 3. In a linked list, the *linking tool* is the link that points to the next element—the pointer or the address of the next element. Figure 11.11 compares the two representations for a list of five integers.

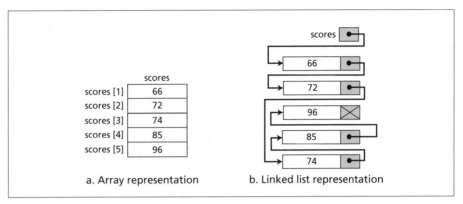

Figure 11.11 Array versus linked list

The elements of an array are stored one after another in the memory without a gap in between: the list is contiguous. The nodes of a linked list can be stored with gaps between them: the link part of the node "glues" the items together. In other words, the computer has the option to store them contiguously or spread the nodes through the whole memory. This has an advantage: insertion and deletion in a linked list is much easier. The only thing that needs to be changed is the pointer to the address of the next element. However, this comes with an overhead: each node of a linked list has an extra field, the address of the next node in memory.

Linked list names *versus* nodes names

As for arrays and records, we need to distinguish between the name of the linked list and the names of the nodes, the elements of a linked list. A linked list must have a name.

The name of a linked list is the name of the head pointer that points to the first node of the list. Nodes, on the other hand, do not have an explicit name in a linked list, just implicit ones. The name of a node is related to the name of the pointer that points to the node. Different languages handle the relation between the pointer and the node to which the pointer points differently. We use the convention used in the C language. If the pointer that points to a node is called **p**, for example, we call the node ***p**. Since the node is a record, we can access the fields inside the node using the name of the node. For example, the data part and the link part of node pointed by a pointer **p** can be called **(*p).data** and **(*p).link**. This naming convention implies that a node can have more than one name. Figure 11.12 shows the name of the linked list and the names of the nodes.

Operations on linked lists

The same operations we defined for an array can be applied to a linked list.

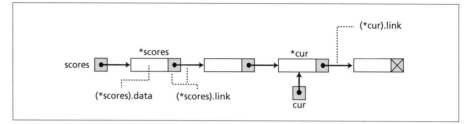

Figure 11.12 The name of a linked list versus the names of nodes

Searching a linked list

The search algorithm for a linked list can only be sequential (see Chapter 8) because the nodes in a linked list have no specific names (unlike the elements in an array) that can be found using a binary search. However, since nodes in a linked list have no names, we use two pointers, *pre* (for previous) and *cur* (for current).

At the beginning of the search, the *pre* pointer is null and the *cur* pointer points to the first node. The search algorithm moves the two pointers together towards the end of the list. Figure 11.13 shows the movement of these two pointers through the list in an extreme case scenario: when the target value is larger than any value in the list. For example, in the five-node list, assume that our target value is 220, which is larger than any value in the list.

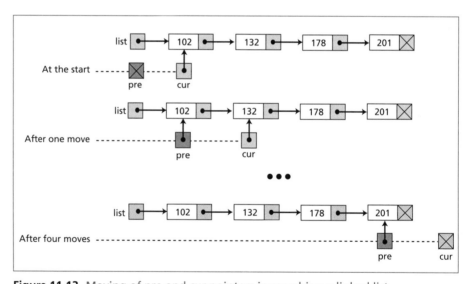

Figure 11.13 Moving of pre and cur pointers in searching a linked list

However, other situations can occur. The value of the target can be less that data value in the first node, or it can be equal to one of the data values in one of the nodes, and so on. In all situations, however, when the search stops, the *cur* pointer points to the node that stops the search and the *pre* pointer points to the previous node. If the target is found, the *cur* pointer points to the node that holds the target value. If the target value is not found, the *cur* pointer points to the node with a value larger than the target value. In other words, since the list is sorted, and may be very long, we never allow the two pointers to reach the end of the list if we are sure that we have passed the target value. The searching algorithm uses a flag (a variable that can take only *true* or *false* values). When the target is found, the flag is set to *true*: when the target is not found, the flag is set to *false*. When the flag is *true* the *cur* pointer points to the target value: when the flag is *false*, the *cur* pointer points to a value larger than the target value.

Figure 11.14 shows some different situations. In the first case, the target is 98.

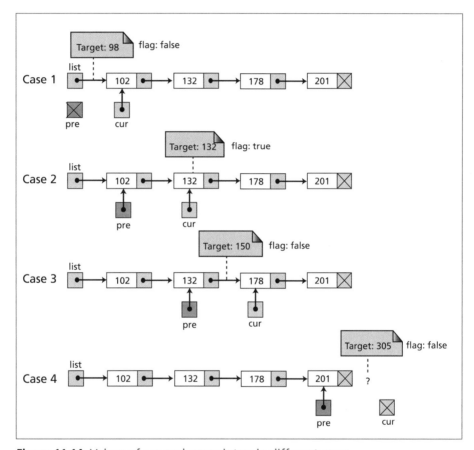

Figure 11.14 Values of *pre* and *cur* pointers in different cases

This value does not exist in the list and is smaller than any value in the list, so the search algorithm stops while *pre* is null and *cur* points to the first node. The value of the flag is false because the value was not found. In the second case, the target is 132, which is the value of the second node. The search algorithm stops while *cur* is pointing to the second node and *pre* is pointing to the first node. The value of the flag is true because the target is found. In the third and the fourth cases, the targets are not found so the value of the flag is *false*.

Algorithm 11.3 shows a simplified algorithm for the search. We need more conditions on the *while* loop, but we leave that for more advanced discussions of linked lists. Note how we move the two pointers forward together. In each move, we have:

$$\text{pre} \leftarrow \text{cur} \qquad \text{and} \qquad \text{cur} \leftarrow (*\text{cur}).\text{link}$$

This guarantees that the two pointers move together. The first assignment makes a copy of *cur* and stores it in *pre*. This means *pre* is taking the previous value of *cur*. In the second assignment, the node pointed to by *cur* is selected and value of its link field is copied and stored in *cur* (see Figure 11.12 for clarification). The search algorithm is used both by the insertion algorithm (if the target is not found) and by the delete algorithm (if the target is found).

Algorithm 11.3 Searching a linked list

Algorithm: **SearchLinkedList** (list, target, **pre, cur, flag**)

Purpose: Search the list using two pointers: **pre** and **cur**

Pre: The linked list (head pointer) and target value

Post: None

Return: The position of **pre** and **cur** pointers and the value of the flag (*true* or *false*)

```
{
     pre ← null
     cur ← list
     while (target < (*cur).data)
     {
          pre ← cur
          cur ← (*cur).link
     }
     if ((*cur).data = target)   flag ← true
     else   flag ← false


}
```

Inserting a node

Before insertion into a linked list, we first apply the searching algorithm. If the flag returned from the searching algorithm is false, we will allow insertion, otherwise we abort the insertion algorithm, because we do not allow data with duplicate values. Four cases can arise:

❏   Inserting into an empty list.

❏   Insertion at the beginning of the list.

❏   Insertion at the end of the list.

❏   Insertion in the middle of the list.

Insertion into an empty list

If the list is empty (list = null), the new item is inserted as the first element. One statement can do the job:

list ← new

Insertion at the beginning

If the searching algorithm returns a flag with a value of *false* and the value of the *pre* pointer is null, the data needs to be inserted at the beginning of the list. Two statements are needed to do the job:

(*new).link ← cur   and   list ← new

The first assignment makes the new node become the predecessor of the previous first node. The second statement makes the newly connected node the first node. Figure 11.15 shows the situation.

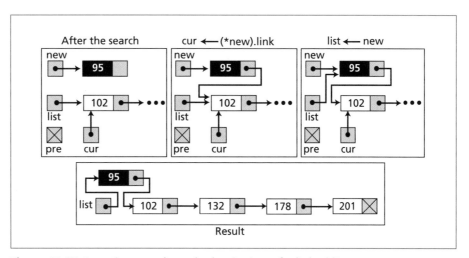

Figure 11.15 Inserting a node at the beginning of a linked list

Insertion at the end

If the searching algorithm returns a flag with a value of *false* and the value of the *cur* pointer is null, the data needs to be inserted at the end of the list. Two statements are needed to do the job:

(*pre).link ← new   and   (*new).link ← null

The first assignment connects the new node to the previous last node. The second statement makes the newly connected node become the last node. Figure 11.16 shows the situation.

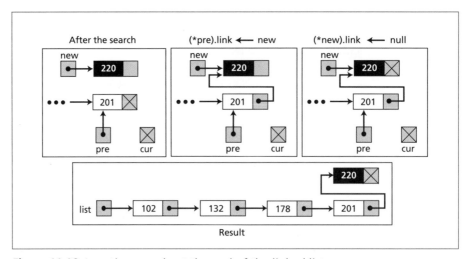

Figure 11.16 Inserting a node at the end of the linked list

Insertion in the middle

If the searching algorithm returns a flag with a value of *false* and none of the returned pointers are null, the new data needs to be inserted in the middle of the list. Two statements are needed to do the job:

(*new).link ← cur   and   (*pre).link ← new

The first assignment connects the new node to its successor. The second statement connects the new node to its predecessor. Figure 11.17 shows the situation.

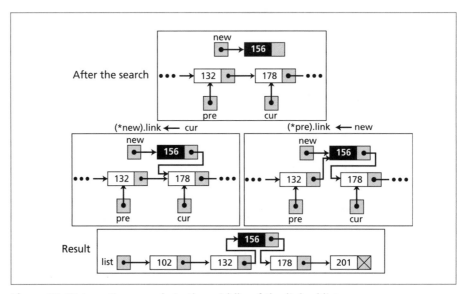

Figure 11.17 Inserting a node in the middle of the linked list

Algorithm 11.4 shows the pseudocode for inserting a new node in a linked list. The first section just adds a node to an empty list.

Algorithm 11.4   Inserting a node in a linked list

Algorithm: **InsertLinkedList** (list, target, new)

Purpose: Insert a node in the linked list after searching the list for the right position

Pre: The linked list and the target data to be inserted

Post: None

Return: The new linked list

```
{
        searchlinkedlist (list, target, pre, cur, flag)
        // Given target and returning pre, cur, and flag

        if (flag = true)   return list              // No duplicate
        if (list = null )                           // Insert into empty list
        {
             list ← new
        }

        if (pre = null)                             // Insertion at the beginning
        {
             (*new).link ← cur
             list ← new
             return list
        }

        if (cur = null)                             // Insertion at the end
        {
             (*pre).link ← new
             (*new).link ← null
             return list
        }

        (*new).link ← cur                           // Insertion in the middle
        (*pre).link ← new
        return list
}
```

Deleting a node

Before deleting a node in a linked list, we apply the search algorithm. If the flag returned from the search algorithm is true (the node is found), we can delete the node from the linked list. However, deletion is simpler than insertion: we have only two cases—deleting the first node and deleting any other node. In other words, the deletion of the last and the middle nodes can be done by the same process.

Deleting the first node

If the *pre* pointer is null, the first node is to be deleted. The *cur* pointer points to the first node and deleting can be done by one statement:

list ← (*cur).link

The statement connects the second node to the list pointer, which means that the first node is deleted. Figure 11.18 (page 308) shows the case.

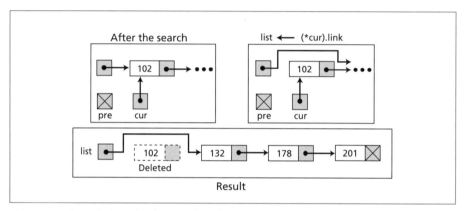

Figure 11.18 Deleting the first node of a linked list

Deleting the middle or the last node

If neither of the pointers are null, the node to be deleted is either a middle node or the last node. The *cur* pointer points to the corresponding node and deleting can be done by one statement:

(*pre).link ← (*cur).link

The statement connects the successor node to the predecessor node, which means that the current node is deleted. Figure 11.19 shows the case.

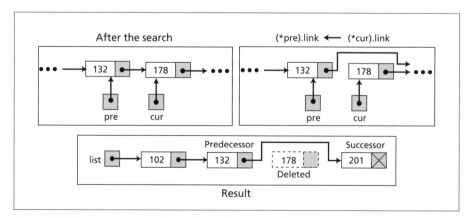

Figure 11.19 Deleting a node at the middle or end of a linked list

Algorithm 11.5 shows the pseudocode for deleting a node. The algorithm is much simpler than the one for inserting. We have only two cases and each case needs only one statement.

Algorithm 11.5   Deleting a node in a linked list

Algorithm: **DeleteLinkedList** (list, target)

Purpose: Delete a node in a linked list after searching the list for the right node

Pre: The linked list and the target data to be deleted

Post: None

Return: The new linked list

```
{
        // Given target and returning pre, cur, and flag
        searchlinkedlist (list, target, pre, cur, flag)
        if (flag = false) return list        // The node to be deleted not found
        if (pre = null)                      // Deleting the first node
        {
                list← (*cur).link
                return list
        }
        (*pre).link ← (*cur).link            // Deleting other nodes
        return list

}
```

Retrieving a node

Retrieving means randomly accessing a node for the purpose of inspecting or copying the data contained in the node. Before retrieving, the linked list needs to be searched. If the data item is found, it is retrieved, otherwise the process is aborted. Retrieving uses only the *cur* pointer, which points to the node found by the search algorithm. Algorithm 11.6 shows the pseudocode for retrieving the data in a node. The algorithm is much simpler than the insertion or deletion algorithm.

Algorithm 11.6   Retrieving a node in a linked list

Algorithm: **RetrieveLinkedList** (list, target)

Purpose: Retrieves the data in a node after searching the list for the right node

Pre: The linked list (head pointer) and the target (data to be retrieved)

Post: None

Return: Return the data retrieved

```
{
        searchlinkedlist (list, target, pre, cur, flag)
        if (flag = false) return error    // The node not found
        return (*cur).data

}
```

Traversing a linked list

To traverse the list, we need a "walking" pointer, which is a pointer that moves from node to node as each element is processed. We start traversing by setting the walking pointer to the first node in the list. Then, using a loop, we continue until all of the data has been processed. Each iteration of the loop processes the current node, then advances the walking pointer to the next node. When the last node has been processed, the walking pointer becomes null and the loop terminates (Figure 11.20).

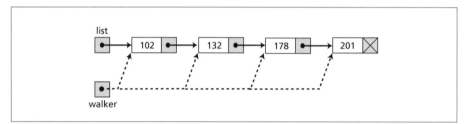

Figure 11.20 Traversing a linked list

Algorithm 11.7 shows the pseudocode for traversing a linked list.

Algorithm 11.7 Traversing a linked list

```
Algorithm: TraverseLinkedList (list)

Purpose: Traverse a linked list and process each data item

Pre: The linked list (head pointer)

Post: None

Return: The list
{
      walker ← list
      while (walker ≠ null)
      {
            Process (*walker).data
            walker ← (*walker).link
      }
      return list
}
```

Applications of linked lists

A linked list is a very efficient data structure for storing data that will go through many insertions and deletions. A linked list is a dynamic data structure in which the list can start with no nodes and then grow as new nodes are needed. A node can be easily deleted without moving other nodes, as would be the case with an array.

For example, a linked list could be used to hold the records of students in a school. Each quarter or semester, new students enroll in the school and some students leave or graduate.

A linked list can grow infinitely and can shrink to an empty list. The overhead is to hold an extra field for each node. A linked list, however, is not a good candidate for data that must be searched often. This appears to be a dilemma, because each deletion or insertion needs a search. We will see that some abstract data types, discussed in the next chapter, have the advantages of an array for searching and the advantages of a linked list for insertion and deletion.

> A linked list is a suitable structure if a large number of insertions and deletions are needed, but searching a linked list is slower that searching an array.

11.4 RECOMMENDED READING

For more details about the subjects discussed in this chapter, the following books are recommended:

- ❑ Gilberg R and Forouzan B: *Data Structures – A Pseudocode Approach with* C, Boston, MA: Course Technology, 2005
- ❑ Goodrich M and Tamassia R: *Data Structures and Algorithms in Java*, New York: Wiley, 2005
- ❑ Neapolitan R and Naimipour K: *Foundations of Algorithms Using* C++ *Pseudocode*, Sudbury, MA: Jones and Bartlett, 2004
- ❑ Main M and Savitch W: *Data Structures and Other Objects Using* C++, Reading, MA: Addison Wesley, 2004
- ❑ Standish T: *Data Structures, Algorithms, and Software Principles*, Reading, MA: Addison Wesley, 1994

11.5 KEY TERMS

This chapter has introduced the following key terms, which are listed here with the pages on which they first occur:

array 290	column-major storage 293
data structure 290	field 297
index 290	link 299
linked list 299	multi-dimensional array 293
node 300	null pointer 299
one-dimensional array 292	pointer 299
record 297	row-major storage 293
two-dimensional array 293	

11.6 SUMMARY

- A data structure uses a collection of related variables that can be accessed individually or as a whole. In other words, a data structure represents a set of data items that share a specific relationship. We discussed three data structures in this chapter: *arrays*, *records*, and *linked lists*.

- An array is a sequenced collection of elements normally of the same data type. We use indexes to refer to the elements of an array. In an array we have two types of identifiers: the name of the array and the name of each individual element.

- Many applications require that data is stored in more than one dimension. One common example is a table, which is an array that consists of rows and columns. Two-dimensional arrays can be stored in memory using either row-major or column-major storage. The first is more common.

- The common operations on arrays as a structure are *searching, insertion, deletion, retrieval,* and *traversal*. An array is a suitable structure in applications where the number of deletions and inser-

tions is small but a lot of searching and retrieval operations are required. An array is normally a static data structure and so is more suitable when the number of data items is fixed.

- A record is a collection of related elements, possibly of different types, having a single name. Each element in a record is called a *field*. A field is the smallest element of named data that has meaning in a record.

- A linked list is a collection of data in which each element contains the location of the next element; that is, each element contains two parts: *data* and *link*. The data part holds the useful information: the data to be processed. The link is used to chain the data together.

- The same operations defined for an array can be applied to a linked list. A linked list is a very efficient structure for data that will go through many insertions and deletions. A linked list is a dynamic data structure in which the list can start with no nodes and grow as new nodes are needed.

11.7 PRACTICE SET

Review questions

1. Name three types of data structures.
2. How is an element in an array different than an element in a record?
3. How is an element in an array different than an element in a linked list?
4. Why should we use indexes rather than subscripts to identify array elements?
5. How are the elements of an array stored in memory?
6. What is the definition of a field in a record?
7. What are the fields of a node in a linked list?
8. What is the function of the pointer in a linked list?
9. How do you point to the first node in a linked list?
10. What is the value of the link field in the last node of a linked list?

Multiple-choice questions

11. A data structure can be _____.
    a. an array
    b. a record
    c. a linked list
    d. all of the above

12. An array that consists of just rows and columns is a _____ array.
    a. one-dimensional
    b. two-dimensional
    c. three-dimensional
    d. multidimensional

13. Each element in a record is called _____.
    a. a variable
    b. an index
    c. a field
    d. a node

14. All the members of a record must be _____.
    a. the same type
    b. related types
    c. integer type
    d. character type

15. _____ is an ordered collection of data in which each element contains the location of the next element.
    a. An array
    b. A record
    c. A linked list
    d. All of the above

16. In a linked list, each element contains _____.
    a. data
    b. a link
    c. a record
    d. a and b

17. The _____ is a pointer that identifies the next element in the linked list.
    a. link
    b. node
    c. array
    d. a or b

18. Given a linked list called *children*, the pointer variable *children* identifies _____ element of the linked list.
    a. the first
    b. the second
    c. the last
    d. any

19. An empty linked list consists of _____.
    a. a node
    b. two nodes
    c. data and a link
    d. a null head pointer

20. To traverse a list, you need a _____ pointer.
    a. null
    b. walking
    c. beginning
    d. insertion

Exercises

21. There are two arrays, A and B, each of 10 integers. Write an algorithm that tests if every element of array A is equal to its corresponding element in array B.

22. Write an algorithm that reverses the elements of an array so that the last element becomes the first, the second to the last becomes the second, and so forth.

23. Write an algorithm to print the contents of a two-dimensional array of R rows and C columns.

24. Write an algorithm to apply sequential search on an array of N elements.

25. Write an algorithm to apply binary search on an array of N elements.

26. Write an algorithm to insert an element into a sorted array. The algorithm must call a search algorithm to find the location for insertion.

27. Write an algorithm to delete an element in a sorted array. The algorithm must call a search algorithm to find the location of insertion.

28. Write an algorithm to multiply each element of an array by a constant.

29. Write an algorithm to add a fraction (Fr1) to another fraction (Fr2).

30. Write an algorithm to subtract a fraction (Fr1) from another fraction (Fr2).

31. Write an algorithm to multiply a fraction (Fr1) by another fraction (Fr2).

32. Write an algorithm to divide a fraction (Fr1) by another fraction (Fr2).

33. Draw a diagram to show a linked list in which the data part is a student record with three fields: *id*, *name*, and *grade*.

34. Show how the delete algorithm for a linked list (Algorithm 11.5, page 309) can delete the only node in a linked list.

35. Show how the insertion algorithm for a linked list (Algorithm 11.4, page 307) can add a node to an empty linked list.

36. Show how we can build a linked list from scratch using the insertion algorithm (Algorithm 11.4, page 307).

37. Write an algorithm to find the average of the numbers in a linked list of numbers.

38. Show what happens if we apply the following statements to the linked list in Figure 11.9, page 300.

> **scores ← (*scores).link**

39. Show what happens if we apply the following statements to the linked list in Figure 11.13, page 302.

> **cur ← (*cur).link   and   pre ← (*pre).link**

12

Abstract Data Types

In this chapter we discuss abstract data types (ADTs), which are data types at a higher level of abstraction than the data structures we discussed in Chapter 11. ADTs use data structures for implementation. We begin this chapter with a brief background on ADTs. We then give a definition and propose a model. The remainder of the chapter discusses various ADTs, such as stacks, queues, general linear lists, trees, binary trees, binary search trees, and graphs.

Objectives

After studying this chapter, the student should be able to:

❑ Define the concept of an abstract data type (ADT).

❑ Define a stack, the basic operations on stacks, their applications, and how they can be implemented.

❑ Define a queue, the basic operations on queues, their applications, and how they can be implemented.

❑ Define a general linear list, the basic operations on lists, their applications, and how they can be implemented.

❑ Define a general tree and its application.

❑ Define a binary tree—a special kind of tree—and its applications.

❑ Define a binary search tree (BST) and its applications.

❑ Define a graph and its applications.

12.1   BACKGROUND

Problem solving with a computer means processing data. To process data, we need to define the data type and the operation to be performed on the data. For example, to find the sum of a list of numbers, we should select the type for the number (integer or real) and define the operation (addition). The definition of the data type and the definition of the operation to be applied to the data is part of the idea behind an **abstract data type** (ADT)—to hide how the operation is performed on the data. In other words, the user of an ADT needs only to know that a set of operations are available for the data type, but does not need to know how they are applied.

Simple ADTs

Many programming languages already define some **simple ADTs** as integral parts of the language. For example, the C language defines a simple ADT called an *integer*. The type of this ADT is an integer with predefined ranges. C also defines several operations that can be applied on this data type (addition, subtraction, multiplication, division, and so on). C explicitly defines these operations on integers and what we expect as the results. A programmer who writes a C program to add two integers should know about the integer ADT and the operations that can be applied to it.

The programmer, however, does not need to know *how* these operations are actually implemented. For example, the programmer uses the expression $z \leftarrow x + y$ and expects the value of x (an integer) to be added to the value of y (an integer) and the result to be named z (an integer). The programmer does not need to know how addition is performed. We learned in previous chapters that the way this addition is done by a computer is to store the two integers in two memory locations in two's complement format, to load them into the CPU register, to add them in binary, and to store the result back to another memory location. The programmer however does not need to know this. An integer in C is a simple abstract data type with predefined operations. How the operations are performed is not a concern for the programmer.

Complex ADTs

Although several simple ADTs, such as integer, real, character, pointer, and so on, have been implemented and are available for use in most language, many useful complex ADTs are not. As we will see in this chapter, we need a list ADT, a stack ADT, a queue ADT, and so on. To be efficient, these ADTs should be created and stored in the library of the computer to be used. The user of a *list*, for example, should only need to know what operations are available for the list, not how these operations are performed.

Therefore, with an ADT, users are not concerned with *how* the task is done, but rather with *what* it can do. In other words, the ADT consists of a set of definitions that allow programmers to use the operation while their implementation is hidden. This generalization of operations with unspecified implementations is known as **abstraction**. We abstract the essence of the process and leave the implementation details hidden.

> **The concept of abstraction means:**
> 1. We know what a data type can do.
> 2. How it is done is hidden.

Definition

Let us now define an ADT. An abstract data type is a data type packaged with the operations that are meaningful for the data type. We then encapsulate the data and the operations on the data and hide them from the user.

> **Abstract data type:**
> 1. Definition of data
> 2. Definition of operations
> 3. Encapsulation of data and operation

Model for an abstract data type

The ADT model is shown in Figure 12.1. The colored area with an irregular outline represents the ADT. Inside the ADT are two different parts of the model: *data structure* and *operations* (public and private). The application program can only access the public operations through the **interface**. An interface is a list of public operations and data to be passed to or returned from those operations. The private operations are for internal use by the ADT. The data structures, such as arrays and linked lists, are inside the ADT and are used by the public and private operations.

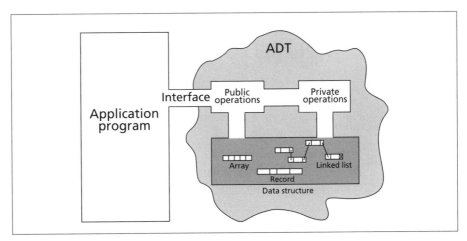

Figure 12.1 The model for an ADT

Although the public operations and the interface should be independent of the implementation, the private operations are dependent on the data structures chosen during the implementation of the ADT. We will elaborate on this issue when we discuss some of the ADTs.

Implementation

Computer languages do not provide ADT packages. To use an ADT, it is first implemented and kept in a library. The main purpose of this chapter is to introduce some common ADTs and their applications. However, we also give a brief discussion of each ADT implementation for the interested reader. We leave the pseudocode algorithms of the implementations as challenging exercises.

12.2   STACKS

A **stack** is a restricted linear list in which all additions and deletions are made at one end, the top. If we insert a series of data items into a stack and then remove them, the order of the data is reversed. Data input as 5, 10, 15, 20, for example, would be removed as 20, 15, 10, and 5. This reversing attribute is why stacks are known as **last in, first out (LIFO)** data structures.

We use many different types of stacks in our daily lives. We often talk of a stack of coins or a stack of books. Any situation in which we can only add or remove an object at the top is a stack. If we want to remove an object other than the one at the top, we must first remove all objects above it. Figure 12.2 shows three representations of stacks.

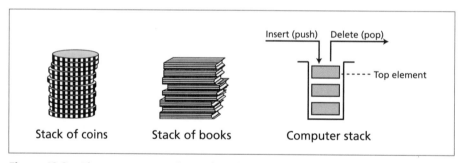

Figure 12.2   Three representations of stacks

Operations on stacks

Although we can define many operations for a stack, there are four basic operations, *stack*, *push*, *pop*, and *empty*, that we define in this chapter.

The stack operation

The stack operation creates an empty stack. The following shows the format.

stack (stackName)

stackName is the name of the stack to be created. This operation returns an empty stack. Figure 12.3 shows the pictorial representation of this operation.

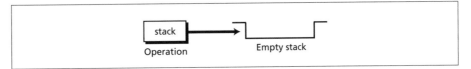

Figure 12.3   Stack operation

The push operation

The **push** operation inserts an item at the top of the stack. The following shows the format.

> **push (stackName, dataItem)**

stackName is the name of the stack and *dataItem* is the data to be inserted at the top of the stack. After the push operation, the new item becomes the top item in the stack. This operation returns the new stack with *dataItem* inserted at the top. Figure 12.4 shows the pictorial representation of this operation.

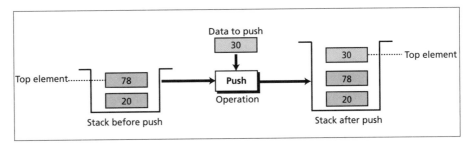

Figure 12.4   Push operation

The pop operation

The **pop** operation deletes the item at the top of the stack. The following shows the format.

> **pop (stackName, dataItem)**

stackName is the name of the stack and *dataItem* is the data that is deleted from the stack. Figure 12.5 shows the pictorial representation of this operation.

The deleted item can be used by the application program or can be just discarded. After the pop operation, the item that was under the top element before the deletion becomes the top element. This operation returns the new stack with one less element.

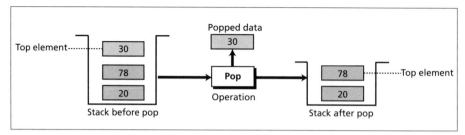

Figure 12.5 Pop operation

The *empty* operation checks the status of the stack. The following shows the format.

> **empty (stackName)**

The *stackName* is the name of the stack. This operation returns *true* if the stack is empty and *false* if the stack is not empty.

Stack ADT

We define a stack as an ADT as shown below:

Stack ADT	
Definition	A list of data items that can only be accessed at one end, called the *top* of the stack.
Operations	**stack:** Creates an empty stack.
	push: Inserts an element at the top.
	pop: Deletes the top element.
	empty: Checks the status of the stack.

Example 12.1

Figure 12.6 shows a segment of an algorithm that applies the previously defined operations on a stack S. The fourth operation checks the status of the stack before trying to pop the top element. The value of the top element is stored in the variable *x*. However, we do not use this value: it will be automatically discarded at the end of the algorithm segment.

Stack applications

Stack applications can be classified into four broad categories: reversing data, pairing data, postponing data usage, and backtracking steps. We discuss the first two in the sections that follow.

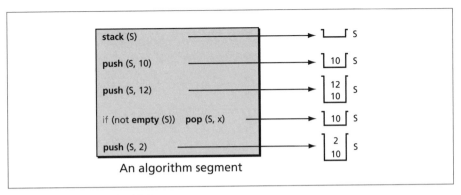

An algorithm segment

Figure 12.6 Example 12.1

Reversing data items

Reversing data items requires that a given set of data items be reordered so that the first and last items are exchanged, with all of the positions between the first and last being relatively exchanged also. For example, the list (2, 4, 7, 1, 6, 8) becomes (8, 6, 1, 7, 4, 2).

Example 12.2

In Chapter 2 (Figure 2.6 on page 27) we gave a simple UML diagram to convert an integer from decimal to any base. Although the algorithm is very simple, if we print the digits of the converted integer as they are created, we will get the digits in reverse order. The print instruction in any computer language prints characters from left to right, but the algorithm creates the digits from right to left. We can use the reversing characteristic of a stack (LIFO structure) to solve the problem.

Algorithm 12.1 shows the pseudocode to convert a decimal integer to binary and print the result. We create an empty stack first. Then we use a *while* loop to

Algorithm 12.1 Example 12.2

```
Algorithm: DecimalToBinary (number)

Purpose: Print the binary equivalent of a given integer (absolute value)

Pre: Given the integer to be converted (number)

Post: The binary integer is printed

Return: None
{
     stack (S)
     while (number ≠ 0)
     {
            remainder ← number mod 2
            push (S, remainder)
            number ← number / 2
     }
```

Algorithm 12.1   Example 12.2 (continued)

```
    while (not empty (S))
    {
            pop (S, x)
            print (x)
    }
    return
}
```

create the bits, but instead of printing them, we push them into the stack. When all bits are created, we exit the loop. Now we use another loop to pop the bits from the stack and print them. Note that the bits are printed in the reverse order to that in which they have been created.

Pairing data items

We often need to pair some characters in an expression. For example, when we write a mathematical expression in a computer language, we often need to use parentheses to change the precedence of operators. The following two expressions are evaluated differently because of the parentheses in the second expression:

$$3 \times 6 + 2 = 20 \qquad\qquad 3 \times (6 + 2) = 24$$

In the first expression, the multiplication operator has precedence over the addition operator—it is calculated first. In the second expression, the parentheses ignore the precedence, so the addition is calculated first. When we type an expression with a lot of parentheses, we often forget to pair the parentheses. One of the duties of a compiler is to do the checking for us. The compiler uses a stack to check that all opening parentheses are paired with a closing parentheses.

Example 12.3

Algorithm 12.2 shows how we can check if all opening parentheses are paired with a closing parenthesis.

Stack implementation

In this section we describe the general ideas behind the implementation of a stack ADT. At the ADT level, we use the stack and its four operations (*stack, push, pop,* and *empty*): at the implementation level, we need to choose a data structure to implement it. Stack ADTs can be implemented using either an array or a linked list. Figure 12.7 shows an example of a stack ADT with five items. The figure also shows how we can implement the stack.

In our array implementation, we have a record that has two fields. The first field can be used to store information about the array: we have used it as the count field, which at each moment shows the number of data item in the stack. The second field is an integer that holds the index of the top element. Note that the array is shown upside down to match the linked list implementation.

Algorithm 12.2   Example 12.3

Algorithm: **CheckingParentheses** (expression)

Purpose: Check the pairing of parentheses in an expression

Pre: Given the expression to be checked

Post: Error messages if unpaired parentheses are found

Return: None
```
{
     stack (S)
     while (more character in the expression)
     {
          Char  ←  next character
          if (Char = '(')             push (S, Char)
          else
          {
               if (Char = ')')
               {
                    if (empty (S))    print (unmatched opening parenthesis)
                    else              pop (S, x)
               }
          }
     }
     if (not empty (S))        print (a closing parenthesis not matched)
     return
}
```

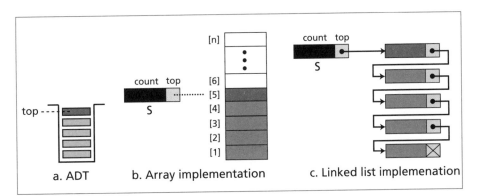

a. ADT   b. Array implementation   c. Linked list implemenation

Figure 12.7   Stack implementations

The linked list implementation is similar: we have an extra node that has the name of the stack. This node also has two fields: a counter and a pointer that points to the top element.

Algorithms   We can write four algorithms in pseudocode for the four operations we defined for stacks in each implementation. We showed algorithms to handle arrays and linked lists in Chapter 11: these algorithms can be modified to create the four operations we defined for stacks: *stack*, *push*, *pop*, and *empty*. These algorithms are even easier than those presented in Chapter 11, because the insertion and deletion is done only at the top of stack. We leave the writing of these algorithms as exercises.

12.3 QUEUES

A **queue** is a linear list in which data can only be inserted at one end, called the **rear**, and deleted from the other end, called the **front**. These restrictions ensure that the data is processed through the queue in the order in which it is received. In other words, a queue is a **first in, first out (FIFO)** structure.

Queues are familiar from everyday life. A line of people waiting for the bus at a bus station is a queue, a list of calls put on hold to be answered by a telephone operator is a queue, and a list of waiting jobs to be processed by a computer is a queue.

Figure 12.8 shows two representations of queues, one a queue of people and the other a computer queue. Both people and data enter the queue at the rear and progress through the queue until they arrive at the front. Once they are at the front of the queue, they leave the queue and are served.

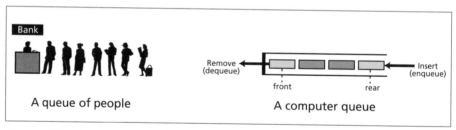

Figure 12.8   Two representations of queues

Operations on queues

Although we can define many operations for a queue, four are basic: *queue*, *enqueue*, *dequeue*, and *empty*, as defined below.

The queue operation   The *queue* operation creates an empty queue. The following shows the format.

queue (queueName)

queueName is the name of the queue to be created. This operation returns an empty queue. Figure 12.9 shows a pictorial representation of this operation.

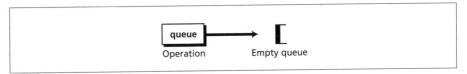

Figure 12.9   The queue operation

The enqueue operation

The **enqueue** operation inserts an item at the rear of the queue. The following shows the format.

enqueue (queueName, dataItem)

queueName is the name of the queue and *dataItem* is the data to be inserted at the rear of the queue. After the enqueue operation, the new item becomes the last item in the queue. This operation returns the new queue with *dataItem* inserted at the rear. Figure 12.10 shows the pictorial representation of this operation.

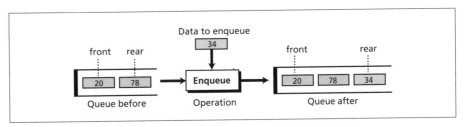

Figure 12.10   The enqueue operation

The dequeue operation

The **dequeue** operation deletes the item at the front of the queue. The following shows the format.

dequeue (queueName, dataItem)

queueName is the name of the queue and *dataItem* is the data that is deleted from the queue. The deleted item can be used by the application program or can be just discarded. After the dequeue operation, the item that followed the front element becomes the front element. This operation returns the new queue with one less element. Figure 12.11 shows the pictorial representation of this operation.

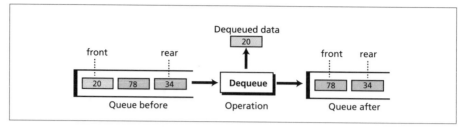

Figure 12.11 The dequeue operation

The *empty* operation checks the status of the queue. The following shows the format.

> **empty (queueName)**

queueName is the name of the queue. This operation returns *true* if the queue is empty and *false* if the queue is not empty.

Queue ADT

We define a queue as an ADT as shown below:

Queue ADT	
Definition	A list of data items in which an item can be deleted from one end, called the *front* of the queue and an item can be inserted at the other end, called the *rear* of the queue.
Operations	**queue:** Creates an empty queue.
	enqueue: Inserts an element at the rear.
	dequeue: Deletes an element from the front.
	empty: Checks the status of the queue.

Example 12.4

Figure 12.12 shows a segment of an algorithm that applies the previously defined operations on a queue Q. The fourth operation checks the status of the queue before trying to dequeue the front element. The value of the front element is stored in the variable *x*. However, we do not use this value—it will automatically be discarded at the end of the algorithm segment.

Queue applications

Queues are one of the most common of all data processing structures. They are found in virtually every operating system and network and in countless other areas. For example, queues are used in online business applications such as processing customer requests, jobs, and orders. In a computer system, a queue is needed to process jobs and for system services such as print spools.

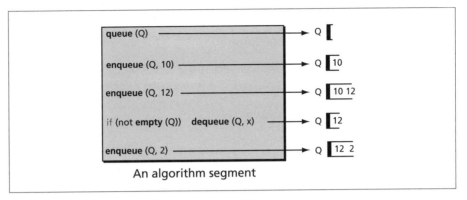

An algorithm segment

Figure 12.12 Example 12.4

Example 12.5

Queues can be used to organize databases by some characteristic of the data. For example, imagine we have a list of sorted data stored in the computer belonging to two categories: less than 1000, and greater than 1000. We can use two queues to separate the categories and at the same time maintain the order of data in their own category. Algorithm 12.3 shows the pseudocode for this operation.

Example 12.6

Another common application of a queue is to adjust and create a balance between a fast producer of data and a slow consumer of data. For example, assume that a CPU is connected to a printer. The speed of a printer is not comparable with the speed of a CPU. If the CPU waits for the printer to print some data created by the CPU, the CPU would be idle for a long time. The solution is a queue. The CPU creates as many chunks of data as the queue can hold and sends them to the queue. The CPU is now free to do other jobs. The chunks are dequeued slowly and printed by the printer. The queue used for this purpose is normally referred to as a *spool queue*.

Queue implementation

At the ADT level, we use the queue and its four operations (*queue, enqueue, dequeue,* and *empty*): at the implementation level, we need to choose a data structure to implement it. A queue ADT can be implemented using either an array or a linked list. Figure 12.13 on page 329 shows an example of a queue ADT with five items. The figure also shows how we can implement it.

In the array implementation we have a record with three fields. The first field can be used to store information about the queue: we have used this as a count field that shows the current number of data items in the queue. The second field is an integer that holds the index of the front element. The third field is also an integer, which holds the index of the rear element.

The linked list implementation is similar: we have an extra node that has the name of the queue. This node also has three fields: a count, a pointer that points to the front element, and a pointer that points to the rear element.

Algorithm 12.3   Example 12.5

```
Algorithm: Categorizer (list)

Purpose: Categorize data into two categories and create two separate lists

Pre: Given: original list

Post: Prints the two lists

Return: None
{
        queue (Q1)
        queue (Q2)
        while (more data in the list)
        {
                if (data < 1000)                    enqueue (Q1, data)
                if (data ≥ 1000)                    enqueue (Q2, data)
        }
        while (not empty (Q1))
        {
                dequeue (Q1, x)
                print (x)
        }
        while (not empty (Q2))
        {
                dequeue (Q2, x)
                print (x)
        }
        return
}
```

Algorithms

We can write four algorithms in pseudocode for the four operations we defined for queues in each implementation. We described algorithms to handle arrays and linked lists in Chapter 11: we can modify those algorithms to create the four algorithms we need for queues: *queue, enqueue, dequeue,* and *empty*. These algorithms are easier than those presented in Chapter 11, because insertion is done only at the end of the queue and deletion is done only at the front of the queue. We leave the writing of these algorithms as exercises.

12.4   GENERAL LINEAR LISTS

Stacks and queues defined in the two previous sections are *restricted linear lists*. A general linear list is a list in which operations, such as insertion and deletion, can be done anywhere in the list—at the beginning, in the middle, or at the end. Figure 12.14 shows a general linear list.

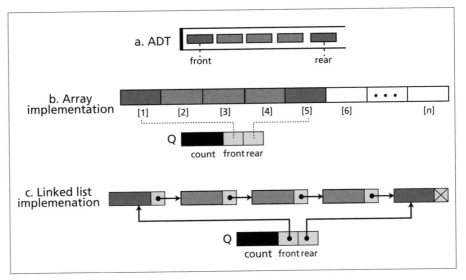

Figure 12.13 Queue implementation

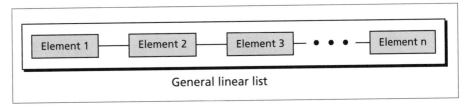

Figure 12.14 General linear list

We define a **general linear list** as a collection of elements with the following properties:

❑ The elements are of the same type.

❑ The elements are arranged sequentially, which means that there is a first element and a last element.

❑ Each element except the first has a unique predecessor, each element except the last has a unique successor.

❑ Each element is a record with a key field.

❑ The elements are sorted based on the key value.

Operations on general linear lists

Although we can define many operations on a general linear list, we discuss only six common operations in this chapter: *list, insert, delete, retrieve, traverse,* and *empty.*

The list operation

The *list* operation creates an empty list. The following shows the format:

list (listName)

listName is the name of the general linear list to be created. This operation returns an empty list.

The insert operation

Since we assume that data in a general linear list is sorted, insertion must be done in such a way that the ordering of the elements is maintained. To determine where the element is to be placed, searching is needed. However, searching is done at the implementation level, not at the ADT level. In addition, we assume for simplicity that duplicate data is not allowed in a general linear list. Therefore we insert an element in a location that preserves the order of the keys. The following shows the format:

insert (listName, element)

Insertion is shown graphically in Figure 12.15.

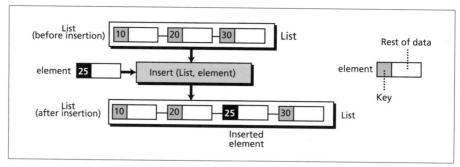

Figure 12.15 The insert operation

The delete operation

Deletion from a general list (Figure 12.16) also requires that the list be searched to locate the data to be deleted. After the location of the data is found, deletion can be done. The following shows the format:

delete (listName, target, element)

target is a data value of the same type as the key of the elements in the list. If an element with the key value equal to the target is found, that element is deleted. The delete operation is shown graphically in Figure 12.16.

Note that this operation returns the deleted element. This is necessary if we want, say, to change the value of some fields and reinsert the item into the list again—we have not defined any operation that changes the value of the fields in the list.

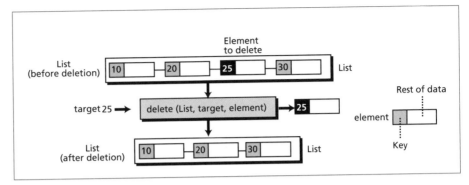

Figure 12.16 The delete operation

The retrieve operation

By retrieval, we mean access of a single element. Like insertion and deletion, the general list should be first searched, and if the data is found, it can be retrieved. The format of the retrieve operation is:

retrieve (listName, target, element)

target is a data value of the same type as the key of the elements in the list. Figure 12.17 shows the retrieve operation graphically. If an element with the key value equal to the target is found, a copy of the element is retrieved, but the element still remains in the list.

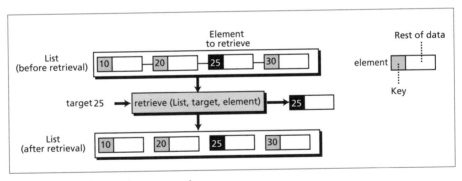

Figure 12.17 The retrieve operation

The traverse operation

Each of the previous operations involves a single element in the list, randomly accessing the list. List traversal, on the other hand, involves sequential access. It is an operation in which all elements in the list are processed one by one. The following shows the format:

traverse (listName, action)

The traverse operation accesses the element of the list sequentially, while the action specifies the operation to be performed on each element. Some examples of actions are printing the data, applying some mathematical operation on the data, and so on.

The empty operation

The *empty* operation checks the status of the list. The following shows the format:

empty (listName)

listName is the name of the list. This operation returns *true* if the list is empty, or *false* if the list is not empty.

General linear list ADT

We define a general linear list as an ADT as shown below:

General linear list ADT

Definition	A list of sorted data items, all of the same type.
Operations	**list:** Creates an empty list.
	insert: Inserts an element in the list.
	delete: Deletes an element from the list.
	retrieve: Retrieves an element from the list.
	traverse: Traverses the list sequentially.
	empty: Checks the status of the list.

Example 12.7

Figure 12.18 shows a segment of an algorithm that applies the previously defined operations on a list *L*. Note that the third operation inserts the new data at the correct position because the insert operation calls the search algorithm at the implementation level to find where the new data should be inserted.

The fourth operation is required to delete the data item 3 from the list. It calls the *empty* operation to be sure that the list is not empty. Since the list is not empty, this operation can proceed, but when it calls the search operation at the implementation level, the data item is not found in the list. The list is therefore returned without a change. Finally the final operation inserts 6 at the appropriate location.

General linear list applications

General linear lists are used in situations in which the elements are accessed randomly or sequentially. For example, in a college a linear list can be used to store information about students who are enrolled in each semester.

Example 12.8

Assume that a college has a general linear list that holds information about the students and that each data element is a record with three fields: *ID*, *Name*, and *Grade*. Algorithm 12.4 shows an algorithm that helps a professor to change the grade for a student. The delete operation removes an element from the list, but

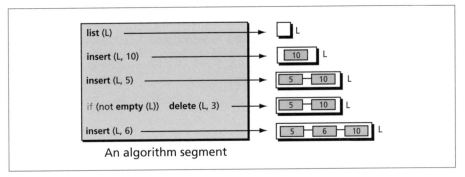

An algorithm segment

Figure 12.18 Example 12.7

makes it available to the program to allow the grade to be changed. The insert operation inserts the changed element back into the list. The element holds the whole record for the student, and the target is the *ID* used to search the list.

Algorithm 12.4 Example 12.8

```
Algorithm: ChangeGrade (StudentList, target, grade)

Purpose: Change the grade of a student

Pre: Given the list of students and the grade

Post: None

Return: None
{
        delete (StudentList, target, element)
        (element.data).Grade ← grade
        insert (StudentList, element)
        return
}
```

Example 12.9

Continuing with Example 12.8, assume that the tutor wants to print the record of all students at the end of the semester. Algorithm 12.5 can do this job.

We assume that there is an algorithm called *Print* that prints the contents of the record. For each node, the list traverse calls the *Print* algorithm and passes the data to be printed to it.

General linear list implementation

At the ADT level, we use the list and its six operations (*list*, *insert*, *delete*, *retrieve*, *traverse*, and *empty*), but at the implementation level we need to choose a data structure to implement it. A general list ADT can be implemented using either an array or a linked list. Figure 12.19 shows an example of a list ADT with five items. The figure also shows how we can implement it.

Algorithm 12.5   Example 12.9

Algorithm: **PrintRecord** (StudentList)

Purpose: Print the record of all students in the StudentList

Pre: Given the list of students

Post: None

Return: None
{
        traverse (StudentList, Print)
        return
}

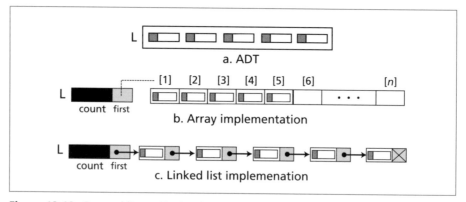

Figure 12.19 General linear list implementation

In our array implementation we have a record with two fields. The first field can be used to store information about the array: we have used it as a count field that shows the current number of data items in a list. The second field is an integer that holds the index of the first element. The linked list implementation is similar: we have an extra node that has the name of the list. This node also has two fields, a counter and a pointer that points to the first element.

Algorithms   We can write six algorithms in pseudocode for the six operations we defined for a list in each implementation. We showed algorithms to handle arrays and linked lists in Chapter 11: these algorithms can be slightly modified to create the algorithms we need for a list. We leave these as an exercise.

12.5 TREES

A **tree** consists of a finite set of elements, called **nodes** (or **vertices**), and a finite set of directed lines, called **arcs**, that connect pairs of the nodes. If the tree is not empty, one of the nodes, called the **root**, has no incoming arcs. The other nodes in a tree can be reached from the root by following a unique **path**, which is a sequence of consecutive arcs. Trees structures are normally drawn upside down with the root at the top.

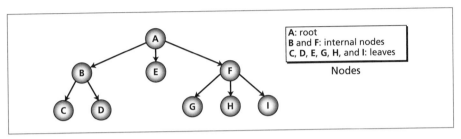

Figure 12.20 Tree representation

We can divided the vertices in a tree into three categories: the root, **leaves**, and the **internal nodes**.

Table 12.1 shows the number of outgoing and incoming arcs allowed for each type of node.

Table 12.1 Number of incoming and outgoing arcs

Type of node	Incoming arc	Outgoing arc
root	0	0 or more
leaf	1	0
internal	1	1 or more

A node that is directly accessible (through a single arc) from a given node is called the **child**: the node from which the child is directly accessible is called a **parent**. Nodes with a common parent are called **siblings**. **Descendents** of a node are all nodes that can be reached by that node, and a node from which all descendents can be reached is called an **ancestor**.

Each node in a tree may have a **subtree**. The subtree of each node includes one of its children and all descendents of that child. Figure 12.21 shows all subtrees for the tree in Figure 12.20.

Although trees have many applications in computer science, such as index files, their study is beyond the scope of this book. We introduce trees as a prelude to discussing one special type of tree, *binary trees*.

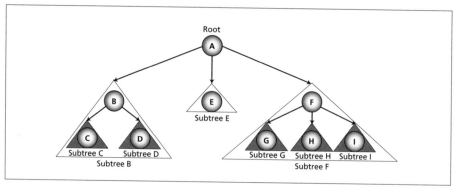

Figure 12.21 Subtrees

12.6 BINARY TREES

A **binary tree** is a tree in which no node can have more than two subtrees. In other words, a node can have zero, one, or two subtrees. These subtrees are designated as the **left subtree** and the **right subtree**. Figure 12.22 shows a binary tree with its two subtrees. Note that each subtree is itself a binary tree.

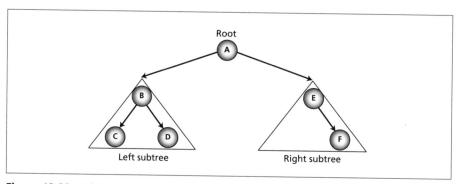

Figure 12.22 A binary tree

Recursive definition of binary trees

In Chapter 8 we introduced the recursive definition of an algorithm. We can also define a structure or an ADT recursively. The following gives the recursive definition of a binary tree. Note that, based on this definition, a binary tree can have a root, but each subtree can also have a root.

Binary tree

Definition   A binary tree is either empty or consists of a node, *root*, with two subtrees, in which each subtree is also a binary tree.

Figure 12.23 shows eight trees, the first of which is an empty binary tree (sometimes called a *null* binary tree).

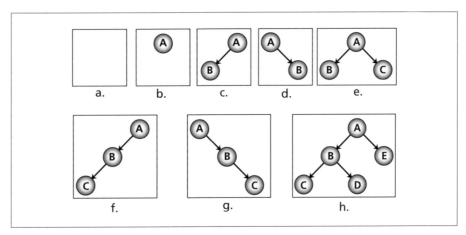

Figure 12.23 Examples of binary trees

Operations on binary trees

The six most common operations defined for a binary tree are *tree* (creates an empty tree), *insert, delete, retrieve, empty* and *traversal.* The first five are complex and beyond the scope of this book. We discuss binary tree traversal in this section.

Binary tree traversals

A *binary tree traversal* requires that each node of the tree be processed once and only once in a predetermined sequence. The two general approaches to the traversal sequence are *depth-first* and *breadth-first* traversal.

Depth-first traversals

Given that a binary tree consists of a root, a left subtree, and a right subtree, we can define six different **depth-first traversal** sequences. Computer scientists have assigned standard names to three of these sequences in the literature: the other three are unnamed but are easily derived. The standard traversals are shown in Figure 12.24.

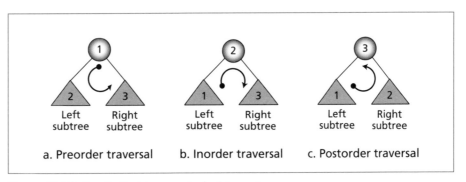

Figure 12.24 Depth-first traversal of a binary tree

☐ **Preorder traversal.** In **preorder traversal** the root node is processed first, followed by the left subtree and then the right subtree. The prefix *pre* indicates that the root node is processed *before* the subtrees.

☐ **Inorder traversal.** In **inorder traversal** the left subtree is processed first, then the root node, and finally the right subtree. The prefix *in* indicates that the root node is processed *between* the subtrees.

☐ **Postorder traversal.** In **postorder traversal** the root node is processed after the left and right subtrees have been processed. The prefix *post* indicates that the root is processed *after* the subtrees.

Example 12.10

Figure 12.25 shows how we visit each node in a tree using preorder traversal. The figure also shows the *walking order*. In preorder traversal we visit a node when we pass from its left side. The nodes are visited in this order: A, B, C, D, E, F.

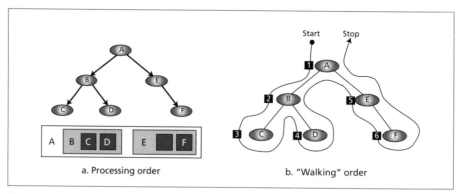

a. Processing order   b. "Walking" order

Figure 12.25 Example 12.10

Breadth-first traversals

In **breadth-first traversal** of a binary tree we process all the children of a node before proceeding with the next generation. As with depth-first traversals, we can trace the traversal with a walk.

Example 12.11

Figure 12.26 shows how we visit each node in a tree using breadth-first traversal. The figure also shows the walking order. The traversal order is A, B, E, C, D, F.

Binary tree applications

Binary trees have many applications in computer science. In this section we mention only two of them: Huffman coding and expression trees.

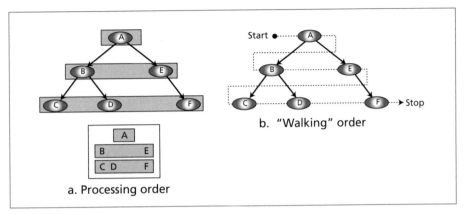

b. "Walking" order

a. Processing order

Figure 12.26 Example 12.11

Huffman coding

Huffman coding is a compression technique that uses binary trees to generate a variable length binary code from a string of symbols. We discuss Huffman coding in detail in Chapter 15.

Expression trees

An arithmetic expression can be represented in three different formats: **infix**, **postfix**, and **prefix**. In an infix notation, the operator comes between the two operands. In postfix notation, the operator comes after its two operands, and in prefix notation it comes before the two operands. These formats are shown below for addition of two operands A and B.

Prefix: + A B	**Infix:** A + B	**Postfix:** A B +

Although we use infix notation in our algorithm and in programming languages, the compiler often changes them to postfix notation before evaluating them. One way to do this conversion is to create an **expression tree**. In an expression tree, the root and the internal nodes are operators and the leaves are the operands. The three standard traversals (preorder, inorder, and postorder: Figure 12.24) then represent the three different expression formats: **infix**, **postfix**, and **prefix**. The inorder traversal produces the infix expression, the postorder traversal produces the postfix expression, and the preorder traversal produces the prefix expression. Figure 12.27 shows an expression and its expression tree. Note that only the infix notation needs parentheses.

Binary tree implementation

Binary trees can be implemented using arrays or linked lists. Linkedd list implementation is more efficient for deletion and insertion and is more prevalent.

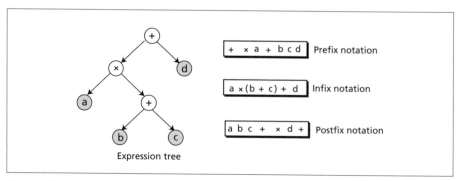

Figure 12.27 Expression tree

12.7   BINARY SEARCH TREES

A **binary search tree (BST)** is a binary tree with one extra property: the key value of each node is greater than the key values of all nodes in each left subtree and smaller than the value of all nodes in each right subtree. Figure 12.28 shows the idea.

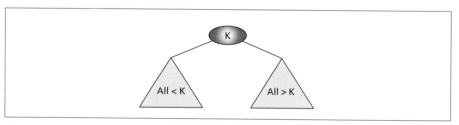

Figure 12.28 Binary search tree (BST)

Example 12.12

Figure 12.29 shows some binary trees that are BSTs and some that are not. Note that a tree is a BST if all its subtrees are BSTs and the whole tree is also a BST.

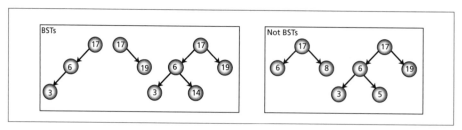

Figure 12.29 Example 12.12

A very interesting property of a BST is that if we apply the inorder traversal of a binary tree, the elements that are visited are sorted in ascending order. For example, the three BSTs in Figure 12.29, when traversed in order, gives the list (3, 6, 17), (17, 19), and (3, 6, 14, 17, 19).

> **An inorder traversal of a BST creates a list that is sorted in ascending order.**

Another feature that makes a BST interesting is that we can use a version of the binary search we used in Chapter 8 for a binary search tree. Figure 12.30 shows the UML for a BST search.

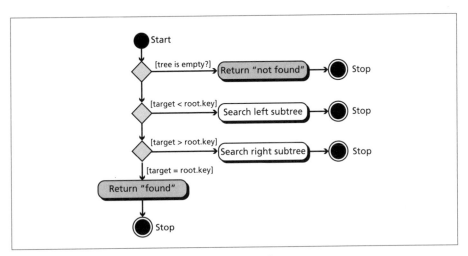

Figure 12.30 Inorder traversal of a binary search tree

Binary search tree ADTs

The ADT for a binary search tree is similar to the one we defined for a general linear list with the same operation. As a matter of fact, we see more BST lists than general linear lists today. The reason is that searching a BST is more efficient than searching a linear list: a general linear list uses sequential searching, but BSTs use a version of binary search.

BST implementation

BSTs can be implemented using either arrays or linked lists. However, linked list structures are more common and more efficient. A linear implementation uses nodes with two pointers, *left* and *right*. The left pointer points to the left subtree and the right pointer points to the right subtree. If the left subtree is empty, the left pointer is null: if the right subtree is empty, the right pointer is null. Like a linked-list implementation of a general linear list, a BST linked list implementation uses a dummy node that has the same name as the BST. The data section of this dummy node can hold information about the tree, such as the number of nodes in the tree. The pointer section points to the root of the tree. Figure 12.31 shows a BST in which the data field of each node is a record.

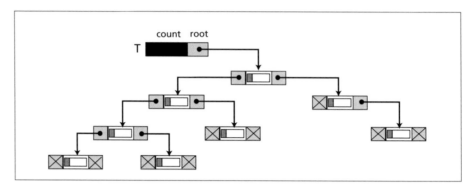

Figure 12.31 A BST implementation

12.8 GRAPHS

A **graph** is an ADT made of a set of nodes, called **vertices**, and set of lines connecting the vertices, called **edges** or **arcs**. Whereas a tree defines a hierarchical structure in which a node can have only one single parent, each node in a graph can have one or more parents. Graphs may be either *directed* or *undirected*. In a **directed graph**, or **digraph**, each edge, which connects two vertices, has a direction (shown in the figure by an arrowhead) from one vertex to the other. In an **undirected graph**, there is no direction. Figure 12.32 shows an example of both a directed graph (a) and an undirected graph (b).

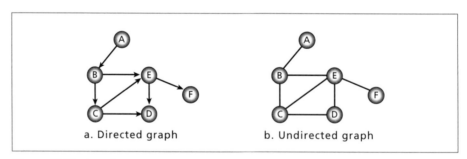

Figure 12.32 Graphs

The vertices in a graph can represent objects or concepts and the edges or arcs can represent a relationship between those objects or concepts. If a graph is directed, the relations are one-way: if a graph is undirected, the relations are two-way.

Example 12.13

A map of cities and the roads connecting the cities can be represented in a computer using an undirected graph. The cities are vertices and the undirected edges are the roads that connect them. If we want to show the distances between the cities, we can use *weighted graphs*, in which each edge has a weight that represents the distance between two cities connected by that edge.

Example 12.14

Another application of graphs is in computer networks (Chapter 6). The vertices can represent the nodes or hubs, the edges can represent the route. Each edge can have a weight that defines the cost of reaching from one hub to an adjacent hub. A router can use graph algorithms to find the shortest path between itself and the final destination of a packet.

12.9 RECOMMENDED READING

For more details about the subjects discussed in this chapter, the following books are recommended:

❑ Gilberg R and Forouzan B: *Data Structures – A Pseudocode Approach with* C, Boston, MA: Course Technology, 2005

❑ Goodrich M and Tamassia R: *Data Structures and Algorithms in Java*, New York: Wiley, 2005

❑ Nyhoff L: *ADTs, Data Structures, and Problem Solving with* C++, Upper Saddle River, NJ: Prentice Hall, 2005

12.10 KEY TERMS

This chapter has introduced the following key terms, which are listed here with the pages on which they first occur:

abstract data type (ADT) 316	ancestor 335
arc 334	binary search tree (BST) 340
binary tree 336	breadth-first traversal
child 335	depth-first traversal 337
dequeue 325	descendent 335
digraph 342	directed graph 342
edge 342	enqueue 325
first in, first out (FIFO)	front 325
general linear list 329	graph 342
Huffman coding 339	infix 339
inorder traversal 338	interface 317
internal node 335	last in, first out (LIFO) 318

12.11   SUMMARY

- Although several simple data types have been implemented in all programming languages, most languages do not define complex data types. An abstract data type (ADT) is a package that defines a new data type, defines operations on that data type, and encapsulates the data and the operations.

- A stack is a restricted linear list in which all additions and deletions are made at one end, called the *top*. If we insert a series of data items into a stack and then remove them, the order of the data is reversed. This reversing attribute is why stacks are known as a last in, first out (LIFO) structure. We defined four basic operations on a stack: *stack*, *push*, *pop*, and *empty*.

- A queue is a linear list in which data can only be inserted at one end, called the *rear*, and deleted from the other end, called the *front*. These restrictions ensure that data is processed through the queue in the order in which it is received. In other words, a queue is a first in, first out (FIFO) structure. We defined four basic operations for a queue: *queue*, *enqueue*, *dequeue*, and *empty*.

- A general linear list is a list in which operations, such as insertion and deletion, can be done anywhere in the list—at the beginning, in the middle, or at the end. We defined six operations for a

general linear list: *list*, *insert*, *delete*, *retrieve*, *traverse*, and *empty*.

- A tree consists of a finite set of elements, called *nodes* (or *vertices*), and a finite set of directed lines, called *arcs*, that connect pairs of nodes. If the tree is not empty, one of the nodes, called the *root*, has no incoming arcs.

- A binary tree is a tree in which no node can have more than two subtrees. In other words, a node can have zero, one, or two subtrees. A binary tree traversal requires that each node of the tree be processed once and only once in a predetermined sequence. The two general approaches to the traversal sequence are *depth first* and *breadth first*.

- A binary search tree (BST) is a binary tree with one extra property: the key value of each node is greater than the key values of all nodes in each left subtree and smaller than the value of all nodes in each right subtree.

- A graph is an ADT made up of a set of nodes, called *vertices*, and a set of lines connecting the vertices, called *edges* or *arcs*. Whereas a tree defines a hierarchical structure in which a node can only have a single parent, each node in a graph can have one or more parents. Graphs may be either directed or undirected.

12.12   PRACTICE SET

Review questions

1. What is an abstract data type? In an ADT, what is known and what is hidden?

2. What is a stack? What are the four basic stack operations defined in this chapter?

3. What is a queue? What are the four basic queue operations defined in this chapter?

4. What is a general linear list? What are the six basic operations defined for a general linear list in this chapter?

5. Define a tree. Distinguish between a tree and a binary tree. Distinguish between a binary tree and a binary search tree.

6. Distinguish between a depth-first traversal and breadth-first traversal of a binary tree.

7. What is a graph? Distinguish between a directed graph and an undirected graph.

8. List some applications of stacks and queues.

9. List some applications of general linear lists.

10. List some applications of binary trees and binary search trees.

Multiple-choice questions

11. In an abstract data type, _____.
    a. the ADT implementation is known
    b. the ADT implementation is hidden
    c. the ADT public operations are hidden
    d. none of the above

12. In an ADT, the _____.
    a. data is defined
    b. public operations are defined
    c. data and operations are encapsulated
    d. all of the above

13. A stack is a _____ structure.
    a. FIFO
    b. LIFO
    c. both a and b

d. none of the above

14. A(n) _____ list is also known as a queue.
    a. LIFO
    b. FIFO
    c. unordered
    d. ordered

15. If A is the first data element input into a stack, followed by B, C, and D, then _____ is the first element to be removed.
    a. A
    b. B
    c. C
    d. D

16. If A is the first data element input into a queue, followed by B, C, and D, then _____ is the first element to be removed.
    a. A
    b. B
    c. C
    d. D

17. The pop operation _____ of the stack.
    a. deletes an item from the top
    b. deletes an item from the bottom
    c. inserts an item at the top
    d. inserts an item at the bottom

18. The push operation _____ of the stack.
    a. deletes an item from the top
    b. deletes an item from the bottom
    c. inserts an item at the top
    d. inserts an item at the bottom

19. In a binary tree, each node has _____ two subtrees.
    a. more than
    b. less than
    c. at most
    d. at least

20. In preorder traversal of a binary tree, the _____ is processed first.
    a. left subtree
    b. right subtree
    c. root
    d. a or b

21. In _____ traversal of a binary tree, the right subtree is processed last.
    a. preorder
    b. inorder
    c. postorder
    d. a or b

22. In postorder traversal of a binary tree, the root is processed _____.
    a. first
    b. second
    c. last
    d. a or b

23. In postorder traversal of a binary tree, the left subtree is processed _____.
    a. first
    b. second
    c. last
    d. a or b

24. In _____ traversal of a binary tree, the left subtree is processed last.
    a. preorder
    b. inorder
    c. postorder
    d. none of the above

25. In an inorder traversal of a binary tree, the root is processed _____.
    a. first
    b. second
    c. last
    d. a or b

Exercises

26. Write an algorithm segment using *while* loops to empty the contents of stack S2.

27. Write an algorithm segment using *while* loops to move the contents of stack S1 to S2. After the operation, stack S1 should be empty.

28. Write an algorithm segment using *while* loops to copy the contents of stack S1 to S2. After the operation, the contents of stacks S1 and S2 should be the same.

29. Write an algorithm segment using *while* loops to concatenate the contents of stack S2 with the contents of stack S1. After the concatenation, the elements of stack S2 should be above the elements of stack S1 and stack S2 should be empty.

30. Show the contents of stack S1 and the value of variables x and y after the following algorithm segment is executed.

```
stack (S1)
push (S1, 5)
push (S1, 3)
push (S1, 2)
if (not empty (S1)) pop (S1, x)
if (not empty (S1)) pop (S1, y)
push (S1, 6)
```

31. A palindrome is a string that can be read backwards and forwards with the same result. For example, the following is a palindrome if we ignore spaces.

> Able was I ere I saw Elba

Write an algorithm in pseudocode using a stack to test whether a string is a palindrome.

32. Write an algorithm in pseudocode to compare the contents of two stacks.

33. Use a *while* loop to empty the contents of queue Q.

34. Use *while* loops to move the contents of queue Q1 to queue Q2. After the operation, queue Q1 should be empty.

35. Use *while* loops to copy the contents of queue Q1 to queue Q2. After the operation, the contents of queue Q1 and queue Q2 should be the same.

36. Use *while* loops to concatenate the contents of queue Q2 and the contents of queue Q1. After the concatenation, the elements of queue Q2

should be at the end of the elements of queue Q1. Queue Q2 should be empty.

37. Write an algorithm to compare the contents of two queues.

38. Find the root of each of the following binary trees:

   a. Tree with postorder traversal: FCBDG
   b. Tree with preorder traversal: IBCDFEN
   c. Tree with postorder traversal: CBIDFGE

39. A binary tree has 10 nodes. The inorder and preorder traversal of the tree are shown below.

Preorder:	Inorder:
JCBADEFIGH	ABCEDFJGIH

   Draw the tree.

40. A binary tree has eight nodes. The inorder and postorder traversal of the tree follow:

Postorder: FECHGDBA   **Inorder:** FECABHDG

   Draw the tree.

41. A binary tree has seven nodes. The following shows the inorder and postorder traversal of a tree. Can we draw the tree? If not, explain why not.

Postorder: GFDABEC   **Inorder:** ABDCEFG

42. Create the ADT package in pseudocode to implement the four operations defined for a stack in this chapter using an array as the data structure.

43. Create the ADT package in pseudocode to implement the four operations defined for a stack in this chapter using a linked list as the data structure.

44. Create the ADT package in pseudocode to implement the four operations defined for a queue in this chapter using an array as the data structure.

45. Create the ADT package in pseudocode to implement the four operations defined for a queue in this chapter using a linked list as the data structure.

46. Create the ADT package in pseudocode to implement the six operations defined for a general linear list in this chapter using an array as the data structure.

47. Create the ADT package in pseudocode to implement the six operations defined for a general linear list in this chapter using a linked list as the data structure.

13

File Structures

In this chapter we discuss file structures. Based on the application, files are stored in auxiliary storage devices using various methods. We also discuss how individual records are retrieved. This chapter is a prelude for the following chapter, which discusses how a collection of related files, called a *database*, is organized and accessed.

Objectives

After studying this chapter, the student should be able to:

- ❏ Define two categories of access methods: sequential access and random access.
- ❏ Understand the structure of sequential files and how they are updated.
- ❏ Understand the structure of indexed files and the relation between the index and the data file.
- ❏ Understand the idea behind hashed files and describe some hashing methods.
- ❏ Describe address collisions and how they can be resolved.
- ❏ Define directories and how they can be used to organize files.
- ❏ Distinguish between text and binary files.

A file is an external collection of related data treated as a unit. The primary purpose of a file is to store data. Since the contents of main memory are lost when the computer is shut down, we need files to store data in a more permanent form. Additionally, the collection of data is often too large to reside entirely in main memory at one time. Therefore, we must have the ability to read and write portions of the data while the rest remains in a file.

Files are stored on **auxiliary** or **secondary storage devices**. The two most common forms of secondary storage are disk and tape. Files in secondary storage can be both read from and written to. Files can also exist in forms that the computer can write to but not read. For example, the display of information on the system monitor is a form of file, as is data sent to a printer. In a general sense, the keyboard is also a file, although it cannot store data.

For our purposes, a file is a collection of data records in which each record consists of one or more fields, as defined in Chapter 11.

13.1   ACCESS METHODS

When we design a file, the important issue is how we will retrieve information (a specific record) from the file. Sometimes we need to process records one after another, whereas sometimes we need to access a specific record quickly without retrieving the preceding records. The **access method** determines how records can be retrieved: *sequentially* or *randomly*.

Sequential access

If we need to access a file sequentially—that is, one record after another, from beginning to end—we use a **sequential file** structure.

Random access

If we need to access a specific record without having to retrieve all records before it, we use a file structure that allows **random access**. Two file structures allow this: *indexed files* and *hashed files*. This taxonomy of file structures is shown in Figure 13.1.

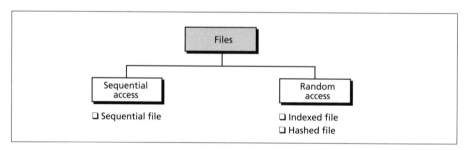

Figure 13.1   A taxonomy of file structures

13.2 SEQUENTIAL FILES

A sequential file is one in which records can only be accessed one after another from beginning to end. Figure 13.2 shows the layout of a sequential file. Records are stored one after another in auxiliary storage, such as tape or disk, and there is an EOF (end-of-file) marker after the last record. The operating system has no information about the record addresses, it only knows where the whole file is stored. The only thing known to the operating system is that the records are sequential.

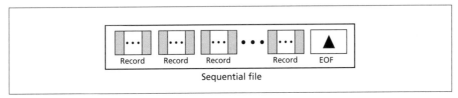

Figure 13.2 A sequential file

Algorithm 13.1 shows how records in a sequential file are processed. We process the records one by one. After the operating system processes the last record, the EOF is detected and the loop is exited.

Algorithm 13.1 Pseudocode for processing records in a sequential file

Algorithm: **SequentialFileProcessing** (file)

Purpose: Process all records in a sequential file

Pre: Given the beginning address of the file on the auxiliary storage

Post: None

Return: None

{

    while (***Not EOF***)

    {

        Read the next record from the auxiliary storage into memory

        Process the record

    }

}

Sequential files are used in applications that need to access all records from beginning to end. For example, if personal information about each employee in a company is stored in a file, we can use sequential access to retrieve each record at the end of the month to print the paychecks. Because we have to process each record, sequential access is more efficient and easier than random access.

However, the sequential file is not efficient for random access. For example, if all customer records in a bank can only be accessed sequentially, a customer who needs to get money from an ATM would have to wait as the system checks each record from the beginning of the file until it reaches the customer's record. If this bank has a million customers, the system, on average, would retrieve half a million records before reaching the customer's record. This is very inefficient.

Updating sequential files

Sequential files must be updated periodically to reflect changes in information. The updating process is very involved because all the records need to be checked and updated (if necessary) sequentially.

Files involved in updating

There are four files associated with an update program: the new master file, the old master file, the transaction file, and the error report file. All these files are sorted based on key values. Figure 13.3 is a pictorial representation of a sequential file update. In this figure, we see the four files discussed above. Although we use the tape symbol for the files, we could just as easily have represented them with a hard disk symbol. Note that after the update program completes, the new master file is sent to off-line storage, where it is kept until needed again. When the file is to be updated, the master file is retrieved from off-line storage and becomes the old master.

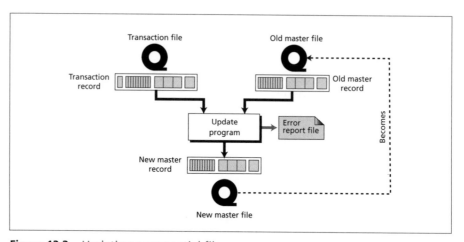

Figure 13.3   Updating a sequential file

❑ **New master file.** The new permanent data file or, as it is commonly known, the **new master file**, contains the most current data.

❑ **Old master file.** The **old master file** is the permanent file that should be updated. Even after updating, the old master file is normally kept for reference.

❑ **Transaction file.** The third file is the **transaction file**. This contains the changes to be applied to the master file. There are three basic types of changes in all file updates. *Add transactions* contain data about a new record to be added to the master file. *Delete transactions* identify records to be deleted from the file. *Change transactions* contain revisions to specific records in the file. To process any of these transactions, we need a *key*. A **key** is one or more fields that uniquely identify the data in the file. For example, in a file of students, the key could be student ID. In an employee file, the key could be social security number.

❑ **Error report file.** The fourth file needed in an update program is an **error report file.** It is very rare that an update process does not produce at least one error. When an error occurs, we need to report it. The *error report* contains a listing of all errors discovered during the update process and is presented for corrective action. The next section describes some cases that can cause errors.

Processing file updates

To make the updating process efficient, all files are sorted on the same key. This updating process is shown in Figure 13.4.

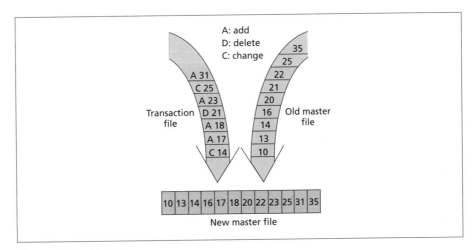

Figure 13.4   Updating process

The update process requires that we compare the keys on the transaction and master files and, assuming that there are no errors, follow one of three actions:

1. If the transaction file key is less than the master file key and the transaction is an add (A), add the transaction to the new master.

2. If the transaction file key is equal to the master file key, either:

    a. Change the contents of the master file data if the transaction is a change (C).

    b. Remove the data from the master file if the transaction is a deletion (D).

3. If the transaction file key is greater than the master file key, write the old master file record to the new master file.

4. Several cases may create an error and be reported in the error file:

   a. If the transaction defines adding a record that already exist in the old master file (same key values).

   b. If the transaction defines deleting or changing a record that does not exist in the old master file.

13.3   INDEXED FILES

To access a record in a file randomly, we need to know the address of the record. For example, suppose a customer wants to check their bank account. Neither the customer nor the teller knows the address of the customer's record. The customer can only give the teller their account number (key). Here, an indexed file can relate the account number (key) to the record address (Figure 13.5).

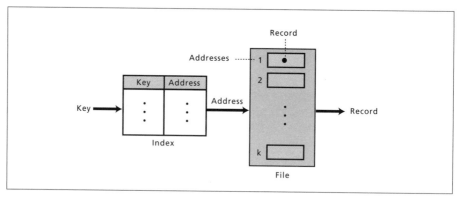

Figure 13.5   Mapping in an indexed file

An **indexed file** is made of a **data file**, which is a sequential file, and an **index**. The index itself is a very small file with only two fields: the key of the sequential file and the address of the corresponding record on the disk. The index is sorted based on the key values of the data files. Figure 13.6 shows the logical view of an indexed file.

   Accessing a record in the file requires these steps:

1. The entire index file is loaded into main memory (the file is small and uses little memory).

2. The index entries are searched, using an efficient search algorithm such as a binary search, to find the desired key.

3. The address of the record is retrieved.

4. Using the address, the data record is retrieved and passed to the user.

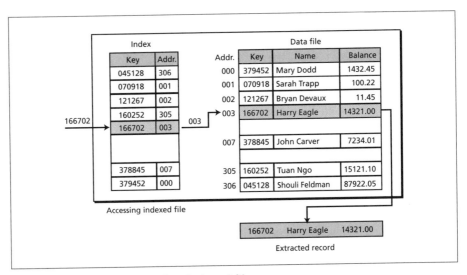

Figure 13.6 Logical view of an indexed file

Inverted files

One of the advantages of indexed files is that we can have more than one index, each with a different key. For example, an employee file can be retrieved based on either social security number or last name. This type of indexed file is usually called an **inverted file**.

13.4 HASHED FILES

In an indexed file, the index maps the key to the address. A **hashed file** uses a mathematical function to accomplish this mapping. The user gives the key, the function maps the key to the address and passes it to the operating system, and the record is retrieved (Figure 13.7).

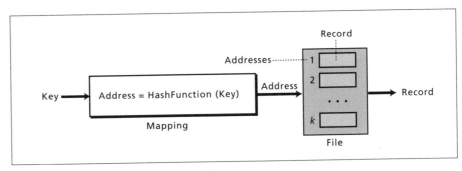

Figure 13.7 Mapping in a hashed file

The hashed file eliminates the need for an extra file (the index). In an indexed file, we must keep the index on file on the disk, and when we need to process the data file, we must first load the index into memory, search it to find the address of the data record, and then access the data file to access the record. In a hashed file, finding the address is done through the use of a function, so there is no need for an index and all of the overhead associated with it. However, we will see that hashed files have their own drawbacks.

Hashing methods

For key-address mapping, we can select one of several **hashing methods**. We discuss a few of them here.

Direct hashing

In **direct hashing**, the key is the data file address without any algorithmic manipulation. The file must therefore contain a record for every possible key. Although situations suitable for direct hashing are limited, it can be very powerful because it guarantees that there are no *synonyms* or *collisions* (discussed later in this chapter), as with other methods.

Let's look at a trivial example. Imagine that an organization has fewer than 100 employees. Each employee is assigned a number between 1 and 100 (their employee ID). In this case, if we create a file of 100 employee records, the employee number can be directly used as the address of any individual record. This concept is shown in Figure 13.8. The record with key 025 (John Carver...) is hashed to address (sector) 025. Note that not every element in the file contains an employee record. Some of the space is wasted.

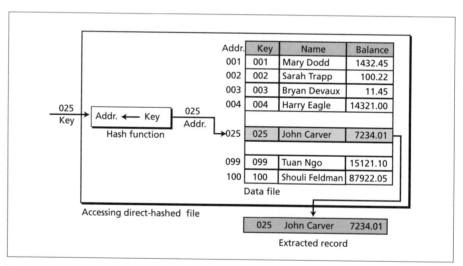

Figure 13.8   Direct hashing

Although this is the ideal method, its application is very limited. For example, it is very inefficient to use long identifiers as keys, because they must have several digits. For example, if the identifier is nine digits, we need a huge file with

999,999,999 records, but we would use less than ·100. Let's turn our attention, therefore, to hashing techniques that map a large population of possible keys to a small address space.

Modulo division hashing

Also known as **division remainder hashing**, the **modulo division** method divides the key by the file size and uses the remainder plus 1 for the address. This gives the simple hashing algorithm that follows, where *list_size* is the number of elements in the file. The reason for adding a 1 to the mod operation result is that our list starts with 1 instead of 0.

address = key **mod** *list_size* + 1

Although this algorithm works with any list size, a list size that is a prime number produces fewer collisions than other list sizes. Therefore, whenever possible, we try to make the file size a prime number.

As our company begins to grow, we realize that soon we will have more than 100 employees. Planning for the future, we create a new employee numbering system that will handle a million employees. We also decide that we want to provide data space for up to 300 employees. The first prime number greater than 300 is 307. We therefore choose 307 as our list (file) size. Our new employee list and some of its hashed addresses are shown in Figure 13.9. In this case, Bryan Devaux, with key 121267, is hashed to address 003 because 121267 mod 307 = 2, and we add 1 to the result to get the address (003).

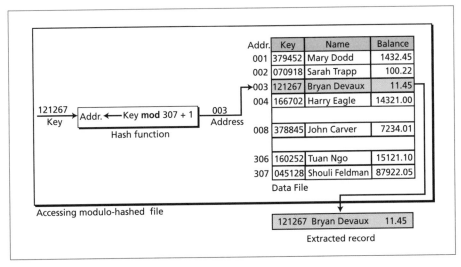

Figure 13.9 Modulo division

Digit extraction hashing

Using **digit extraction hashing**, selected digits are extracted from the key and used as the address. For example, using our six-digit employee number to hash to a three-digit address (000–999), we could select the first, third, and fourth digits (from the left) and use them as the address. Using the keys from Figure 13.9, we hash them to the following addresses:

125870 → 158   122801 → 128   121267 → 112

Other hashing methods

Other popular methods exist, such as the midsquare method, folding methods, the rotational method, and the pseudorandom method. We leave the exploration of these as exercises.

Collision

Generally, the population of keys for a hashed list is greater than the number of records in the data file. For example, if we have a file of 50 students for a class in which the students are identified by the last four digits of their social security number, then there are 200 possible keys for each element in the file (10,000/50). Because there are many keys for each address in the file, there is a possibility that more than one key will hash to the same address in the file. We call the set of keys that hash to the same address in our list **synonyms**. The collision concept is illustrated in Figure 13.10.

In the figure, when we calculate the address for two different records, we obtain the same address (214). Obviously, the two records cannot be stored in the same address. We need to resolve the situation, as discussed in the next section.

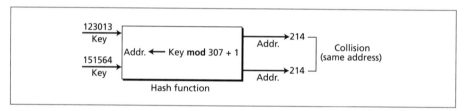

Figure 13.10 Collision

If the actual data that we insert into our list contains two or more synonyms, we will have collisions. A **collision** is the event that occurs when a hashing algorithm produces an address for an insertion key but that address is already occupied. The address produced by the hashing algorithm is known as the **home address**. The part of the file that contains all the home addresses is known as the **prime area**. When two keys collide at a home address, we must resolve the collision by placing one of the keys and its data in another location, outside the prime area.

Collision resolution

With the exception of the direct method, none of the methods we have discussed for hashing creates one-to-one mappings. This means that when we hash a new key to an address, we may create a collision. There are several methods for handling collisions, each of them independent of the hashing algorithm. That is, any hashing method can be used with any **collision resolution** method. In this section, we discuss some of these methods.

Open addressing

The first collision resolution method, **open addressing resolution**, resolves collisions in the prime area. When a collision occurs, the prime area addresses are searched for an open or unoccupied record where the new data can be placed. One simple strategy for data that cannot be stored in the home address is to store it in the next address (home address + 1). Figure 13.11 shows how to solve the collision in Figure 13.10 using this method. The first record is stored in address 214, and the second is stored in address 215 if it is not occupied.

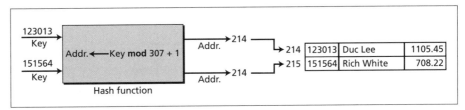

Figure 13.11 Open addressing resolution

Linked list resolution

A major disadvantage of open addressing is that each collision resolution increases the probability of future collisions. This disadvantage is eliminated in another approach to collision resolution, **linked list resolution**. In this method, the first record is stored in the home address, but contains a pointer to the second record. Figure 13.12 shows how to resolve the situation in Figure 13.10.

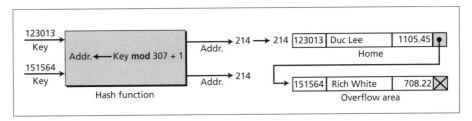

Figure 13.12 Linked list resolution

Bucket hashing

Another approach to handling the problem of collisions is to hash to **buckets**. Figure 13.13 shows how to solve the collision in Figure 13.10 using **bucket hashing**. A bucket is a node that can accommodate more than one record. The disadvantage of this method is that there may be a lot of wasted (unoccupied) locations.

Combination approaches

There are several approaches to resolving collisions. As with hashing methods, a complex implementation will often use multiple approaches.

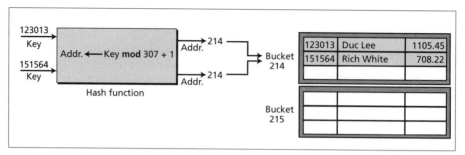

Figure 13.13 Bucket hashing resolution

13.5   DIRECTORIES

Directories are provided by most operating systems for organizing files. A directory performs the same function as a folder in a filing cabinet. However, a directory in most operating systems is represented as a special type of file that holds information about other files. A directory not only serves as a kind of index that tells the operating system where files are located on an auxiliary storage device, but can also contain other information about the files it contains, such as who has the access to each file, or the date when each file was created, accessed, or modified.

Directories in most operating systems are organized like the *tree* abstract data type (ADT) we discussed in Chapter 12, in which each directory except the root directory has a parent. A directory contained in another directory is called a *subdirectory* of the container directory.

Directories in the UNIX operating system

In UNIX the directory system is organized as shown in Figure 13.14. At the top of the directory structure is a directory called the *root*. Although its name is root, in commands related to directories it is typed as one slash (/). In turn, each directory can contain subdirectories and files.

Special directories

There are four special types of directory that play an important role in the directory structure in UNIX: the root directory, home directories, working directories, and parent directories.

Root directory

The **root directory** is the highest level in the file system hierarchy. It is the root of the whole file structure, and therefore does not have a parent directory. In a UNIX environment, the root directory always has several levels of subdirectories. The root directory belongs to the system administrator and can be changed only by the system administrator.

Home directory

We use our **home directory** when we first log into the system. This contains any files we create while in it and may contain personal system files. Our home directory is also the beginning of our personal directory structure. Each user has a home directory.

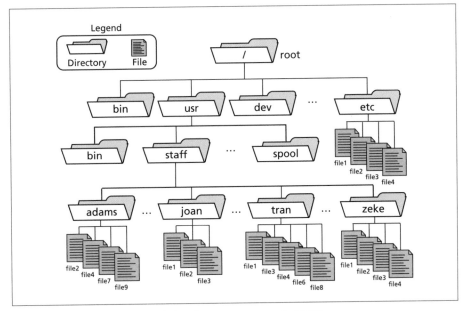

Figure 13.14 An example of the directory system in UNIX

Working directory

The **working directory** (or **current directory**) is the directory we are "in" at any point in a user session. When we first log in, the working directory is our home directory. If we have subdirectories, we will most likely move from our home directory to one or more subdirectories as needed during a session. When we change directory, our working directory changes automatically.

Parent directory

The **parent directory** is the directory immediately above the working directory. When we are in our home directory, its parent is one of the system directories.

Paths and pathnames

Every directory and file in a file system must have a name. If we examine Figure 13.14 carefully, however, we will note that there are some files that have the same names as files in other directories. It should be obvious, therefore, that we need more than just the filename to identify them. To uniquely identify a file, therefore, we need to specify the file's **path** from the root directory to the file. The file's path is specified by its **absolute pathname**, a list of all directories separated by a slash character (/).

The absolute pathname for a file or a directory is like an address of a person. If we know only the person's name, we cannot easily find that person. On the other hand, if we know a person's name, street address, city, state, and country, then we can locate anyone in the world. This full or absolute pathname can get quite long.

For that reason, UNIX also provides a shorter pathname under certain circumstances, known as a **relative pathname**, which is the path relative to the working directory. For example if our working directory in Figure 13.14 is *staff*, the file3 under the *joan* directory can be selected using both relative and absolute pathnames:

Relative pathname:	**joan/file3**
Absolute pathname:	**/usr/staff/joan/file3**

13.6 TEXT VERSUS BINARY

Before closing this chapter, we discuss two terms used to categorize files: *text* files and *binary* files. A file stored on a storage device is a sequence of bits that can be interpreted by an application program as a text file or a binary file, as shown in Figure 13.15.

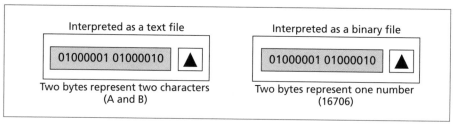

Figure 13.15 Text and binary interpretations of a file

Text files

A **text file** is a file of characters. It cannot contain integers, floating-point numbers, or any other data structures in their internal memory format. To store these data types, they must be converted to their character equivalent formats.

Some files can only use character data types. Most notable are file streams (input/output objects in some object-oriented language like C++) for keyboards, monitors, and printers. This is why we need special functions to format data that is input from or output to these devices.

Let's look at an example. When data (a file stream) is sent to the printer, the printer takes eight bits, interprets them as a byte, and decodes them into the encoding system of the printer (ASCII or EBCDIC). If the character belongs to the printable category, it will be printed, otherwise some other activity takes place, such as printing a space. The printer takes the next eight bits and repeats the process. This is done until the file stream is exhausted.

Binary files

A **binary file** is a collection of data stored in the internal format of the computer. In this definition, data can be an integer (including other data types represented as unsigned integers, such as image, audio, or video), a floating-point number, or any other structured data (except a file).

Unlike text files, binary files contain data that is meaningful only if it is properly interpreted by a program. If the data is textual, one byte is used to represent one character. But if the data is numeric, two or more bytes are considered a data item. For example, assume we are using a personal computer that uses two bytes to store an integer. In this case, when we read or write an integer, two bytes are interpreted as one integer.

13.7 RECOMMENDED READING

For more details about the subjects discussed in this chapter, the following books are recommended:

❏ Forouzan B and Gilberg R: *Computer Science: A Structured Programming Approach Using* C, Boston, MA: Course Technology, 2007

❏ Forouzan B and Gilberg R: *UNIX and Shell Programming*, Pacific Grove, CA: Brooks/Cole, 2003

❏ Gilberg R and Forouzan B: *Data Structures – A Pseudocode Approach with* C, Boston, MA: Course Technology, 2005

13.8 KEY TERMS

This chapter has introduced the following key terms, which are listed here with the pages on which they first occur:

absolute pathname 361	access method 350
auxiliary storage 350	binary file 362
bucket 359	bucket hashing 359
collision 358	collision resolution 358
current directory 361	data file 354
digit extraction method 357	direct hashing 356
directory 360	division remainder method 357
error report file 353	hashed file 355
hashing method 356	home address 358
home directory 360	index 354
indexed file 354	inverted file 355
key 353	linked list resolution 359
modulo division 357	new master file 352
old master file 352	open addressing resolution 359
parent directory 361	path 361
prime area 358	random access 350

13.9   SUMMARY

- A file is an external collection of related data treated as a single unit. The primary purpose of a file is to store data. Since the contents of main memory are lost when the computer is shut down, we need files to store data in a more permanent form. Files are stored in auxiliary or secondary storage devices.

- The access method determines how records can be retrieved: sequentially or randomly. If we need to access a file sequentially, we use a sequential file structure. If we need to access one specific record without having to retrieve all records before it, we use a random file structure.

- A sequential file is one in which records can only be accessed sequentially—one after another—from beginning to end. Sequential files must be updated periodically to reflect changes in information. There are four files associated with an update program: the new master file, the old master file, the transaction file, and the error report file.

- To access a record in a file randomly, we need to know the address of the record. Two types of files are normally used for accessing records randomly: an indexed file and a hashed file.

- An indexed file is made up of a data file, which is a sequential file, and an index. The index itself is a very small file with only two fields: the key of the sequential file and the address of the corre-

sponding record on disk. The index is sorted based on the key values of the data files. In a hashed file, the key is mapped to the record address using a hashing function.

- Several methods have been used for hashing. In the direct method, the key is the address without any algorithmic manipulation. In the modulo division method, the key is divided by the file size and the remainder plus 1 is used for the address. In digit extraction hashing, selected digits are extracted from the key and used as the address.

- In hashing there is a possibility that more than one key will hash to the same address in the file, resulting in a collision. We discussed a few collision resolution methods: open addressing, linked list resolution, and bucket hashing.

- Directories are provided by most operating systems for organizing files. A directory performs the same function as a folder in a filing cabinet. However, a directory in most operating systems is represented as a special type of file that holds information about other files.

- A file stored on a storage device is a sequence of bits that can be interpreted by an application program as a text file or a binary file. A text file is a file of characters. A binary file is a collection of data stored in the internal format of the computer.

13.10   PRACTICE SET

Review questions

1. What are the two general types of file access methods?
2. What is the relationship between the new master file and the old master file?
3. What is the purpose of the transaction file in updating a sequential file?
4. Describe the function of the address in a randomly accessed file.
5. How is the index related to the data file in indexed files?
6. What is the relationship between the key and the address in direct hashing of a file?
7. What is the relationship between the key and the address in modulo division hashing of a file?
8. What is the relationship between the key and the address in digit extraction hashing of a file?
9. List and describe three collision resolution methods.
10. What is the difference between a text file and a binary file?

Multiple-choice questions

11. _____ file can be accessed randomly.
    a. A sequential
    b. An indexed
    c. A hashed
    d. b and c
12. _____ file can be accessed sequentially.
    a. A sequential
    b. An indexed
    c. A hashed
    d. all of the above
13. When a sequential file is updated, the _____ file gets the actual update.
    a. new master
    b. old master
    c. transaction
    d. error report
14. When a sequential file is updated, the _____ file contains a list of all errors occurring during the update process.
    a. new master
    b. old master
    c. transaction
    d. error report
15. When a sequential file is updated, the _____ file contains the changes to be applied.
    a. new master
    b. old master
    c. transaction
    d. error report
16. After a sequential file is updated, the _____ file contains the most current data.
    a. new master
    b. old master
    c. transaction
    d. error report
17. If the transaction file key is 20 and the first master file key is 25, then we _____.
    a. add the new record to the new master file
    b. revise the contents of the old master file
    c. delete the data
    d. write the old master file record to the new master file
18. If the transaction file key is 20 with a delete code and the master file key is 20, then we _____.
    a. add the transaction to the new master file
    b. revise the contents of the old master file
    c. delete the data
    d. write the old master file record to the new master file
19. An indexed file consists of _____.
    a. a sequential data file
    b. an index
    c. a random data file
    d. b and c

20. The index of an indexed file has _____ fields.
    a. two
    b. three
    c. four
    d. any number of
21. In the _____ hashing method, selected digits are extracted from the key and used as the address.
    a. direct
    b. division remainder
    c. modulo division
    d. digit extraction
22. In the _____ hashing method, the key is divided by the file size, and the address is the remainder plus 1.
    a. direct
    b. modulo division
    c. division remainder
    d. digit extraction
23. In the _____ hashing method, there are no synonyms or collisions.
    a. direct
    b. modulo division
    c. division remainder
    d. digit extraction
24. _____ are keys that hash to the same location in the data file.
    a. Collisions
    b. Buckets
    c. Synonyms
    d. Linked lists
25. When a hashing algorithm produces an address for an insertion key and that address is already occupied, it is called a _____.
    a. collision
    b. probe
    c. synonym
    d. linked list
26. The address produced by a hashing algorithm is the _____ address.
    a. probe

b. synonym
c. collision
d. home
27. The _____ area is the file area that contains all the home addresses.
    a. probe
    b. linked
    c. hash
    d. prime
28. In the _____ collision resolution method, we try to put data that cannot be placed in location 123 into location 124.
    a. open addressing
    b. linked list
    c. bucket hashing
    d. a and b

Exercises

29. Given the old master file and the transaction file in Figure 13.16, find the new master file. If there are any errors, create an error file too.

Old master file

Key	Name	Pay rate
14	John Wu	17.00
16	George Brown	18.00
17	Duc Lee	11.00
20	Li Nguyen	12.00
26	Ted White	23.00
31	Joanne King	27.00
45	Brue Wu	12.00
89	Mark Black	19.00
92	Betsy Yellow	14.00

Transaction file

Action	Key	Name	Pay rate
A	17	Martha Kent	17.00
D	20		
C	31		28.00
D	45		
A	90	Orva Gilbert	20.00

Figure 13.16 Exercise 29

30. Create an index file for Table 13.1.

    Table 13.1 Exercise 30

Key	Name	Department
123453	John Adam	CIS
114237	Ted White	MTH
156734	Jimmy Lions	ENG
093245	Sophie Grands	BUS
077654	Eve Primary	CIS
256743	Eva Lindens	ENG
423458	Bob Bauer	ECO

31. A hash file uses a modulo division method with 41 as the divisor. What is the address for each of the following keys?
    a. 14232
    b. 12560
    c. 13450
    d. 15341

32. In the midsquare hashing method, the key is squared and the address is selected from the middle of the result. Use this method to select the address from each of the following keys. Use digits 3 and 4, counting from the left.
    a. 142
    b. 125
    c. 134
    d. 153

33. In the fold shift hashing method, the key is divided into parts. The parts are added to obtain the address. Use this method to find the address from the following keys. Divide the key into two-digit parts and add them to find the address.
    a. 1422
    b. 1257
    c. 1349
    d. 1532

34. In the fold boundary hashing method, the key is divided into parts. The left and right parts are reversed and added to the middle part to obtain the address. Use this method to find the address from the following keys. Divide the key into three two-digit parts, reverse the digits in the first and the third part, and then add the parts to obtain the address.

    a. 142234
    b. 125711
    c. 134919
    d. 153213

35. Find the address of the following keys using the modulo division method and a file of size 411. If there is a collision, use open addressing to resolve it. Draw a figure to show the position of the records.
    a. 10278
    b. 08222
    c. 20553
    d. 17256

36. Redo Exercise 35 using linked list resolution.

37. One common algorithm in file processing is to merge two sequential files sorted on the key values to create a new sequential file, which is also sorted. The merge algorithm can become quite simple if each file has a dummy record at the end with a unique key value that is larger than any key values in either file. The unique key value is referred to as a *sentinel*. In this hypothetical situation, there is no need to check the files for EOF markers. Draw a UML diagram to merge two files for this hypothetical situation.

38. Write an algorithm in pseudocode for Exercise 37.

39. Draw a UML diagram to update a sequential file based on a transaction file if the two files have sentinel values as discussed in Exercise 37.

40. Write an algorithm in pseudocode for Exercise 39.

41. The hypothetical situation of Exercise 37 can be applied to real situations (files with an EOF marker) if we can artificially create the sentinel during the processing. Draw a UML diagram to merge two sequential files with EOF markers but no sentinel.

42. Write an algorithm in pseudocode for Exercise 41.

43. Draw a UML diagram to update a sequential file based on a transaction file if the two files use EOF markers but no sentinel. Use the idea described in Exercise 41.

44. Write an algorithm in pseudocode for Exercise 43.

14

Databases

In this chapter we discuss databases and database management systems (DBMS). We present the three-level architecture for a DBMS, focusing on the relational database model, with examples of its operation. We also discuss a language (Standard Query Language) that operates on relational databases. We briefly touch on the design of the databases, and finally mention other database models.

Objectives

After studying this chapter, the student should be able to:

❑ Define a database and a database management system (DBMS) and describe the components of a DBMS.

❑ Describe the architecture of a DBMS based on the ANSI/SPARC definition.

❑ Define the three traditional database models: hierarchical, networking, and relational.

❑ Describe the relational model and relations.

❑ Understand operations on a relational database based on commands available in SQL.

❑ Describe the steps in database design.

❑ Define ERM and E-R diagrams and explain the entities and relationships in this model.

❑ Define the hierarchical levels of normalization and understand the rationale for normalizing the relations.

❑ List database types other than the relational model.

14.1 INTRODUCTION

Data storage traditionally used individual, unrelated files, sometimes called **flat files**. In the past, each application program in an organization used its own file. In a university, for example, each department might have its own set of files: the record office kept a file about the student information and their grades, the financial aid office kept its own file about students that needed financial aid to continue their education, the scheduling office kept the name of the professors and the courses they were teaching, the payroll department kept its own file about the whole staff (including professors), and so on. Today, however, all of these flat files can be combined in a single entity, the database for the whole university.

Definition

Although it is difficult to give a universally agreed definition of a database, we use the following common definition:

> **Definition:**
> **A database is a collection of related, logically coherent, data used by the application programs in an organization.**

Advantages of databases

Comparing the flat-file system, we can mention several advantages for a database system.

Less redundancy
In a flat-file system there is a lot of redundancy. For example, in the flat file system for a university, the names of professors and students are stored in more than one file.

Inconsistency avoidance
If the same piece of information is stored in more than one place, then any changes in the data need to occur in all places that data is stored. For example, if a female student marries and accepts the last name of her husband, the last name of the student needs to be changed in all files that hold information about the student. Lack of care may create inconsistency in the data.

Efficiency
A database is usually more efficient that a flat file system, because a piece of information is stored in fewer locations.

Data integrity
In a database system it is easier to maintain data integrity (see Chapter 16) because a piece of data is stored in fewer locations.

Confidentiality
It is easier to maintain the confidentiality of the information if the storage of data is centralized in one location.

14.2 DATABASE MANAGEMENT SYSTEMS

A **database management system (DBMS)** defines, creates, and maintains a database. The DBMS also allows controlled access to data in the database. A DBMS is a combination of five components: hardware, software, data, users, and procedures (Figure 14.1).

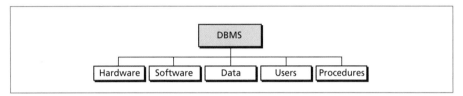

Figure 14.1 DBMS components

Hardware

The **hardware** is the physical computer system that allows access to data. For example, the terminals, hard disk, main computer, and workstations are considered part of the hardware in a DBMS.

Software

The **software** is the actual program that allows users to access, maintain, and update data. In addition, the software controls which user can access which parts of the data in the database.

Data

The data in a database is stored physically on the storage devices. In a database, data is a separate entity from the software that accesses it. This separation allows the organization to change the software without having to change the physical data or the way in which it is stored. If an organization decides to use a DBMS, then all the information needed by the organization should be kept together as one entity, to be accessible by the software in the DBMS.

Users

The term **users** in a DBMS has a broad meaning. We can divide users into two categories: end users and application programs.

End users

End users are those humans who can access the database directly to get information. There are two types of end users: database administrators (DBAs) and normal users. Database administrators have the maximum level of privileges and can control other users and their access to the DBMS, grant some of their privileges to somebody else, but retain the ability to revoke them at any time. A normal user, on the other hand, can only use part of the database and has limited access.

Application programs

The other users of data in a database are **application programs**. Applications need to access and process data. For example, a payroll application program needs to access part of the data in a database to create paychecks at the end of the month.

Procedures The last component of a DBMS is a set of **procedures** or rules that should be clearly defined and followed by the users of the database.

14.3 DATABASE ARCHITECTURE

The American National Standards Institute **Standards Planning and Requirements Committee** (ANSI/SPARC) has established a three-level architecture for a DBMS: internal, conceptual, and external (Figure 14.2).

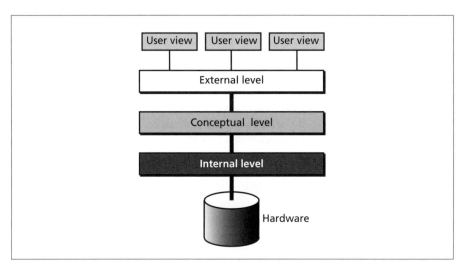

Figure 14.2 Database architecture

Internal level

The **internal level** determines where data is actually stored on the storage devices. This level deals with low-level access methods and how bytes are transferred to and from storage devices. In other words, the internal level interacts directly with the hardware.

Conceptual level

The **conceptual level** defines the logical view of the data. The data model is defined on this level, and the main functions of the DBMS, such as queries, are also on this level. The DBMS changes the internal view of data to the external view that users need to see. The conceptual level is an intermediary and frees users from dealing with the internal level.

External level

The **external level** interacts directly with the user (end users or application programs). It changes the data coming from the conceptual level to a format and view that is familiar to the users.

14.4 DATABASE MODELS

A **database model** defines the logical design of data. The model also describes the relationships between different parts of the data. In the history of database design, three models have been in use: the hierarchical model, the network model, and the relational model.

Hierarchical database model

In the **hierarchical model**, data is organized as an inverted tree. Each entity has only one parent but can have several children. At the top of the hierarchy, there is one entity, which is called the *root*. Figure 14.3 shows a logical view of an example of the hierarchical model. As the hierarchical model is obsolete, no further discussion of this model is necessary.

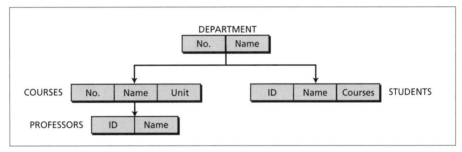

Figure 14.3   An example of the hierarchical model representing a university

Network database model

In the **network model**, the entities are organized in a graph, in which some entities can be accessed through several paths (Figure 14.4). There is no hierarchy. This model is also obsolete and needs no further discussion.

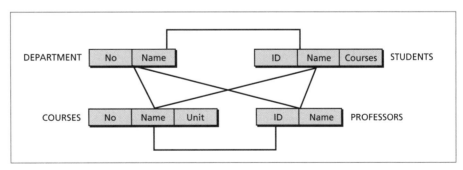

Figure 14.4   An example of the network model representing a university

Relational database model

In the **relational model**, data is organized in two-dimensional tables called *relations*. There is no hierarchical or network structure imposed on the data. The tables or relations are, however, related to each other, as we will see shortly (Figure 14.5).

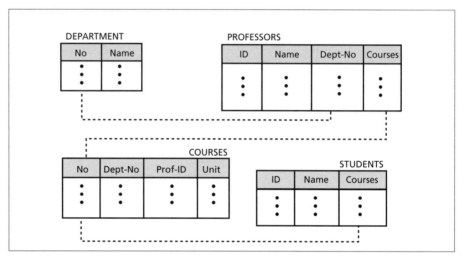

Figure 14.5   An example of the relational model representing a university

The relational model is one of the common models in use today, and we devote most of this chapter to it. In the last section, we briefly discuss the other two common models that are derived from the relational model: the distributed model and the object-oriented model.

14.5   THE RELATIONAL DATABASE MODEL

In the **relational database management system (RDBMS)**, the data is represented as a set of relations.

Relations

A **relation**, in appearance, is a two-dimensional table. The RDBMS organizes the data so that its external view is a set of relations or tables. This does not mean that data is stored as tables: the physical storage of the data is independent of the way in which the data is logically organized. Figure 14.6 shows an example of a relation.
    A relation in an RDBMS has the following features:

❑   **Name**. Each relation in a relational database should have a name that is unique among other relations.

❑   **Attributes**. Each column in a relation is called an **attribute**. The attributes are the column headings in the table in Figure 14.6. Each attribute gives meaning to the data stored under it. Each column in the table must have a name that is

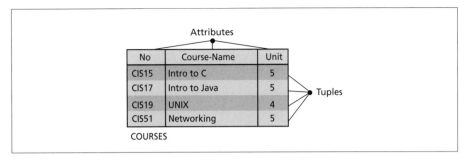

Figure 14.6   An example of a relation

unique in the scope of the relation. The total number of attributes for a relation is called the degree of the relation. For example, in Figure 14.6, the relation has a degree of 3. Note that the attribute names are not stored in the database: the conceptual level uses the attributes to give meaning to each column.

❑ **Tuples**. Each row in a relation is called a **tuple**. A tuple defines a collection of attribute values. The total number of rows in a relation is called the **cardinality** of the relation. Note that the cardinality of a relation changes when tuples are added or deleted. This makes the database dynamic.

14.6   OPERATIONS ON RELATIONS

In a relational database we can define several operations to create new relations based on existing ones. We define nine operations in this section: *insert, delete, update, select, project, join, union, intersection*, and *difference*. Instead of discussing these operations in the abstract, we describe each operation as defined in the database query language SQL (Structured Query Language).

Structured Query Language

Structured Query Language (SQL) is the language standardized by the American National Standards Institute (ANSI) and the International Organization for Standardization (ISO) for use on relational databases. It is a declarative rather than procedural language, which means that users declare what they want without having to write a step-by-step procedure. The SQL language was first implemented by the Oracle Corporation in 1979, with various versions of SQL being released since then.

Insert

The **insert operation** is a unary operation—that is, it is applied to a single relation. The operation inserts a new tuple into the relation. The insert operation uses the following format:

```
insert into   RELATION-NAME
values   (..., ..., ...)
```

The *values* clause defines all the attribute values for the corresponding tuple to be inserted. For example, Figure 14.7 shows how this operation can be applied to a relation. Note that in SQL string values are enclosed in quotation marks, numeric values are not.

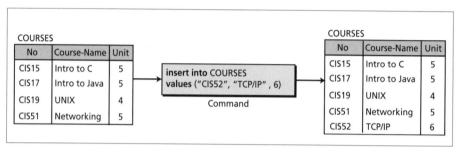

Figure 14.7   An example of an insert operation

Delete

The **delete operation** is also a unary operation. The operation deletes a tuple defined by a criterion from the relation. The delete operation uses the following format:

> **delete from** RELATION-NAME
> **where** criteria

The criteria for deletion are defined in the *where* clause. For example, Figure 14.8 shows how one tuple can be deleted from a relation called COURSES. Note that the criteria is No = "CIS19".

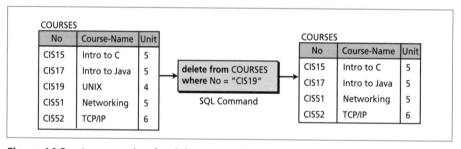

Figure 14.8   An example of a delete operation

Update

The **update operation** is also a unary operation that is applied to a single relation. The operation changes the value of some attributes of a tuple. The update operation uses the following format:

```
update   RELATION-NAME
set attribute1 = value1,   attribute2 = value2, ...
where   criteria
```

The attribute to be changed is defined in the *set* clause and the criteria for updating in the *where* clause. For example Figure 14.9 shows how the number of units in one tuple is updated.

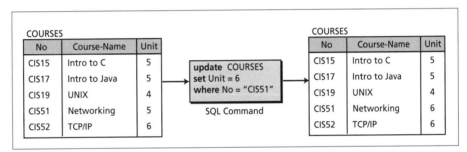

Figure 14.9   An example of an update operation

Select

The **select operation** is a unary operation—that is, is applied to a single relation—and creates another relation. The tuples (rows) in the resulting relation are a subset of the tuples in the original relation. The select operation uses some criteria to select some of the tuples from the original relation. The select operation uses the following format:

```
select    *
from RELATION-NAME
where   criteria
```

The asterisk signifies that all attributes are chosen. Figure 14.10 shows an example of the select operation. In this figure, there is a relation that shows courses offered by a small department. The select operation allows the user to select only the five-unit courses.

Project

The **project** operation is also a unary operation, and creates another relation. The attributes (columns) in the resulting relation are a subset of the attributes in the original relation. The project operation creates a relation in which each tuple has

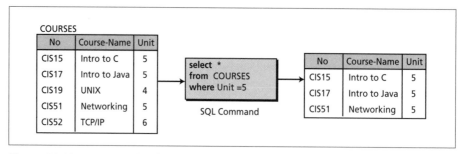

Figure 14.10 An example of a select operation

fewer attributes. The number of tuples (rows) in this operation remains the same. The project operation uses the following format:

select   attribute-list
from RELATION-NAME

The names of the columns for the new relation are explicitly listed. Figure 14.11 shows an example of a project operation that creates a relation with only two columns.

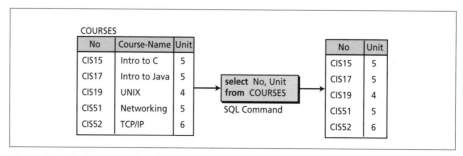

Figure 14.11 An example of a project operation

Join

The **join operation** is a binary operation—it takes two relations and combines them based on common attributes. The join operation uses the following format:

select   attribute-list
from RELATION1, RELATION2
where criteria

The attribute list is the combination of attributes from the two input relations: criteria explicitly define the attributes used as common attributes. The join operation is complex and has many variations. In Figure 14.12, we show a very simple example in which the COURSES relation is combined with the TAUGHT-BY relation to create a new relation that shows full information about the courses, including the names of the professors that teach them. In this case, the common attribute is the course number (No).

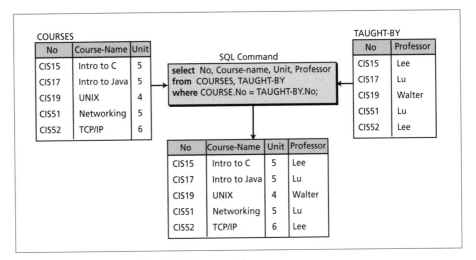

Figure 14.12 An example of a join operation

Union

The **union operation** is also a binary operation, taking two relations and creating a new relation. However, there is a restriction on the two relations: they must have the same attributes. The union operation, as defined in set theory, creates a new relation in which each tuple is either in the first relation, in the second, or in both. The union operation uses the following format:

```
select *
from RELATION1
union
select *
from RELATION2
```

Again, asterisks signify that all attributes are selected. For example, Figure 14.13 shows two relations. On the upper left is the roster for course CIS15, on the upper right is the roster for course CIS52. The result is a relation with information about students that take either CIS15, CIS52, or both.

Intersection

The **intersection operation** is also a binary operation, taking two relations and creating a new relation. Like the union operation, the two relations must have the same attributes. The intersection operation, as defined in set theory, creates a new

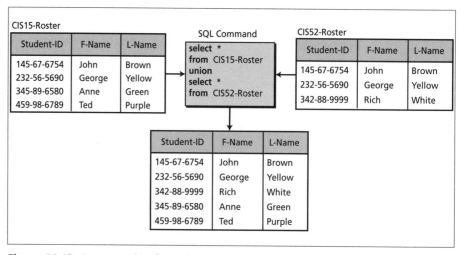

Figure 14.13 An example of a union operation

relation in which each tuple is a member of both relations. The intersection operation uses the following format:

```
select *
from RELATION1
intersection
select *
from RELATION2
```

Again, asterisks signify that all attributes are selected. For example, the intersection operation in Figure 14.14 shows that all attributes are selected. The figure shows two input relations. The result of the intersection operation is a relation with information about students taking both courses CIS15 and CIS52.

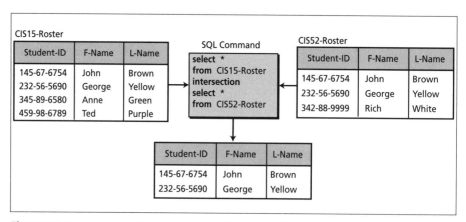

Figure 14.14 An example of an intersection operation

Difference

The **difference operation** is also a binary operation. It is applied to two relations with the same attributes. The tuples in the resulting relation are those that are in the first relation but not the second. The difference operation uses the following format:

```
select *
from RELATION1
minus
select *
from RELATION2
```

Again, asterisks signify that all attributes are selected. For example, Figure 14.15 shows two input relations. The result of the difference operation is a relation with information about students taking course CIS15 but not course CIS52.

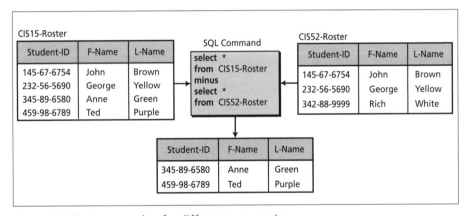

Figure 14.15 An example of a difference operation

Combination of statements The SQL language allows us to combine the foregoing statements to extract more complex information from a database.

14.7 DATABASE DESIGN

The design of any database is a lengthy and involved task that can only be done through a step-by-step process. The first step normally involves a lot of interviewing of potential users of the database, for example in a university, to collect the information needed to be stored and the access requirement of each department. The second step is to build an **entity-relationship model (ERM)** that defines the entities for which some information must be maintained, the attributes of these entities, and the relationship between these entities.

The next step in design is based on the type of database to be used. In a relational database, the next step is to build relations based on the ERM and normalize the relations. In this introductory course, we just give some idea about ERMs and normalization.

Entity-relationship models (ERM)

In this step, the database designer creates an **entity-relationship (E-R)** diagram to show the entities for which information needs to be stored and the relationship between those entities. E-R diagrams use several geometric shapes, but we use only a few of them here:

❑   *Rectangles* represent entity sets
❑   *Ellipses* represent attributes
❑   *Diamonds* represent relationship sets
❑   *Lines* link attributes to entity sets and link entity sets to relationships sets

Example 14.1

Figure 14.16 shows a very simple E-R diagram with three entity sets, their attributes, and the relationship between the entity sets.

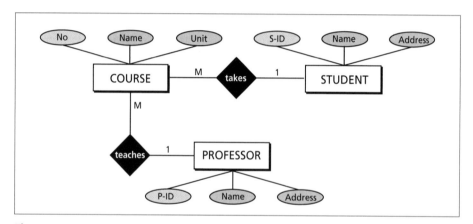

Figure 14.16 Entities, attributes, and relationships in an E-R diagram

The relationships, which are shown by diamonds, can be one-to-one, one-to-many, many-to-one, and many-to-many. In Figure 14.16 the relationship between the STUDENT set and the COURSE set is one-to-many (shown by 1-M in the diagram), which means each student in the set of students can take many courses in the set of courses. If we change the relationship from *takes* to *is taken*, then the relationship between the STUDENT set and the COURSE set can be many-to-one.

   Some of the attributes in Figure 14.16 are shaded. These are attributes in each set that are considered key for that set. Note that the relationship sets can also have some entities, but we have shown no attributes for the relationship set to make the discussion easier.

From E-R diagrams to relations

After the E-R diagram has been finalized, relations (tables) in the relational database can be created.

Relations for entity sets

For each entity set in the E-R diagram, we create a relation (table) in which there are n columns related to the n attributes defined for that set.

Example 14.2

We can have three relations (tables), one for each entity set defined in Figure 14.16, as shown in Figure 14.17.

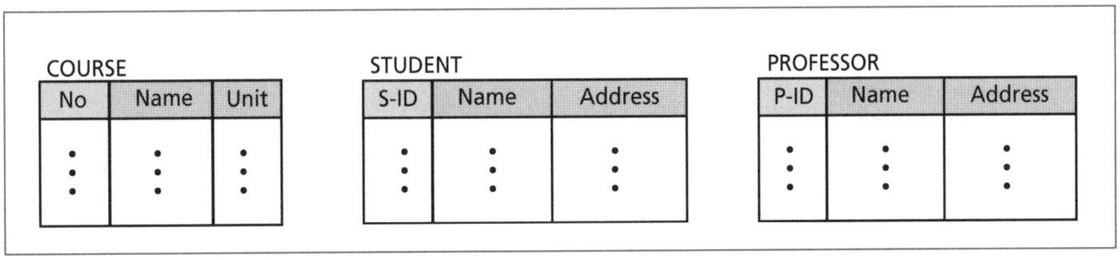

COURSE			STUDENT			PROFESSOR		
No	Name	Unit	S-ID	Name	Address	P-ID	Name	Address
⋮	⋮	⋮	⋮	⋮	⋮	⋮	⋮	⋮

Figure 14.17 Relations for entity set in Figure 14.16

Relations for relationship sets

For each relationship set in the E-R diagram, we create a relation (table). This relation has one column for the key of each entity set involved in this relationship and also one column for each attribute of the relationship itself if the relationship has attributes (not in our case).

Example 14.3

There are two relationship sets in Figure 14.16, *teaches* and *takes*, each connected to two entity sets. The relations for these relationship sets are added to the previous relations for the entity set and shown in Figure 14.18.

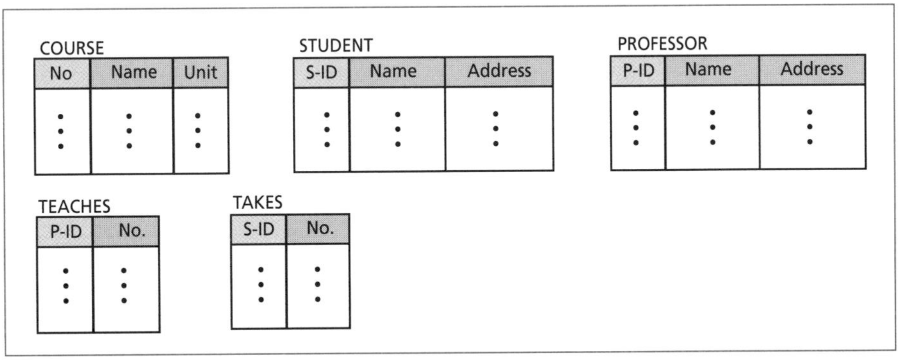

COURSE			STUDENT			PROFESSOR		
No	Name	Unit	S-ID	Name	Address	P-ID	Name	Address
⋮	⋮	⋮	⋮	⋮	⋮	⋮	⋮	⋮

TEACHES		TAKES	
P-ID	No.	S-ID	No.
⋮	⋮	⋮	⋮

Figure 14.18 Relations for E-R diagram in Figure 14.16

Normalization

Normalization is the process by which a given set of relations are transformed to a new set of relations with a more solid structure. Normalization is needed to allow any relation in the database to be represented, to allow a languages like SQL to use powerful retrieval operations composed of atomic operations, to remove anomalies in insertion, deletion, and updating, and reduce the need for restructuring the database as new data type are added.

The normalization process defines a set of hierarchical **normal forms** (NFs). Several normal forms have been proposed, including 1NF, 2NF, 3NF, BCNF (Boyce-Codd Normal Form), 4NF, PJNF (Projection/Joint Normal Form), 5NF, and so on. The discussion of these normal forms (except 1NF) involves the discussion of functional dependencies, a theoretical discipline, which is beyond the scope of this book, although we briefly discuss some of them here for interest. However, one important point that we need to know is that these normal forms form a hierarchical structure. In other words, if the relations in a database are in 3NF, it should have been first in 2NF.

First normal form (1NF)

When we transform entities or relationships into tabular relations, there may be some relations in which there are more values in the intersection of a row or column. For example, in our set of relations in Figure 14.18, there are two relations, *teaches* and *takes*, that are not in first normal form. A professor can teach more than one course, and a student can take more than one course. These two relations can be normalized by repeating the rows in which this problem exists.

Figure 14.19 shows how normalization is done for the relation *teaches*. A relation that is not in the first normal form may suffer from many problems. For example, if the professor with ID 8256 is not teaching the course CIS15, we need to delete only part of the record for this professor in the *teaches* relation. In a database system, we should always delete a whole record, not part of a record.

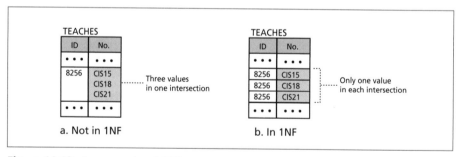

Figure 14.19 An example of 1NF

Second normal form (2NF)

In each relation we need to have a key (called a *primary* key) on which all other attributes (column values) need to depend. For example, if the ID of a student is given, it should be possible to find the student's name. However, it may happen that when relations are established based on the E-R diagram, we may have some composite keys (a combination of two or more keys). In this case, a relation is in second normal form if every non-key attribute depends on the whole composite key.

If some attributes depend on part of the composite key, the relation is not in second normal form. As a simple example, assume that we have a relation in which there are four attributes (Student ID, Course No, Student Grade, and Student Name) in which the first two make up a composite key. The student's grade depends on the whole key, but the name depends on only part of the key. We can apply the 2NF process and divide the relation into two, both in the second normal form.

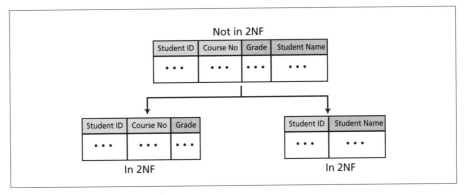

Figure 14.20 An example of 2NF

A relation that is not in second normal form may also suffer from problems. For example, in Figure 14.20, we cannot add a student to the database if the student does not have a grade in at least one course. But if we have two relations, the student can be added to the second relation. The information about this student is added to the first relation when they take a course and complete it with a grade.

Other normal forms

Other normal forms use more complicated dependencies among attributes. We leave these dependencies to books dedicated to the discussion of database topics.

14.8 OTHER DATABASE MODELS

The relational database is not the only database model in use today. Two other common models are *distributed databases* and *object-oriented databases*. We briefly discuss these here.

Distributed databases

The **distributed database** model is not a new model, but is based on the relational model. However, the data is stored on several computers that communicate through the Internet or a private wide area network. Each computer (or *site*) maintains either part of the database or the whole database. In other words, data is either fragmented, with each fragment stored at one site, or data is replicated at each site.

Fragmented distributed databases

In a **fragmented distributed database**, data is localized—locally used data is stored at the corresponding site. However, this does not mean that a site cannot access data stored at another site, but access is mostly local, but occasionally global. Although each site has complete control over its local data, there is global control through the Internet or a wide area network.

For example, a pharmaceutical company may have multiple sites in many countries. Each site has a database with information about its own employees, but a central personnel department could have control of all the databases.

Replicated distributed databases

In a **replicated distributed database**, each site holds an exact replica of another site. Any modification to data stored in one site is repeated exactly at every site. The reason for having such a database is security. If the system at one site fails, users at the site can access data at another site.

Object-oriented databases

The relational database has a specific view of data that is based on the nature of the database's tuples and attributes. The smallest unit of data in a relational database is the intersection of a tuple and an attribute. However, some applications need to look at data in other forms, for example to see data as a structure (see Chapter 11), such as a record composed of fields.

An **object-oriented database** tries to keep the advantages of the relational model and at the same time allows applications to access structured data. In an object-oriented database, objects and their relations are defined. In addition, each object can have attributes that can be expressed as fields.

For example, in an organization, one could define object types for employee, department, and customer. The employee class could define the attributes of an employee object (first name, last name, social security number, salary, and so on) and how they can be accessed. The department object could define the attributes of the department and how they can be accessed. In addition, the database could create a relation between an employee object and a department object to denote that the employee works in that department.

XML

The query language normally used for objected-oriented databases is XML (Extensible Markup Language). As we discussed in Chapter 6, XML was originally designed to add markup information to text documents, but it has also found its application as a query language in databases. XML can represent data with nested structure.

14.9 RECOMMENDED READING

For more details about the subjects discussed in this chapter, the following books are recommended:

- ❏ Alagic S: *Relational Database Technology*, New York: Springer, 1986
- ❏ Dietrich S: *Understanding Relational Database Query Language*, Upper Saddle River, NJ: Prentice Hall, 2001
- ❏ Elmasri R and Navathe S: *Fundamentals of Database Systems*, Reading, MA: Addison Wesley, 2006
- ❏ Mannino M: *Database Application Development and Design*, New York: McGraw-Hill, 2001
- ❏ Ramakrishnan R and Gehrke J: *Database Management Systems*, New York: McGraw-Hill, 2003
- ❏ Silberschatz A, Korth H, and Sudarshan S: *Databases: System Concepts*, New York: McGraw-Hill, 2005

14.10 KEY TERMS

This chapter has introduced the following key terms, which are listed here with the pages on which they first occur:

attribute 374	cardinality 374
conceptual level 372	database 370
database management system (DBMS) 371	database model 373
delete operation 376	difference operation 381
distributed database 385	Entity-Relation (E-R) diagram 382
Entity-Relationship Model (ERM) 381	external level 372
fragmented distributed database 386	hierarchical model 373
insert operation 375	internal level 372
intersection operation 379	join operation 378
network model 373	Normal Form (NF) 384
normalization 384	object-oriented database 386
project operation 377	relation 374
relation database management system (RDBMS) 374	relational model 374
replicated distributed database 386	select operation 377
Structured Query Language (SQL)	tuple 375
union operation 379	update operation 377

14.11 SUMMARY

- A database is a collection of data that is logically, but not necessarily physically, coherent—its various parts can be physically separated. A database management system (DBMS) defines, creates, and maintains a database.

- The American National Standards Institute/Standards Planning and Requirements Committee (ANSI/SPARC) has established a three-level architecture for a DBMS: internal, conceptual, and external. The internal level determines where data is actually stored on storage devices. The conceptual level defines the logical view of the data. The external level interacts directly with the user.

- Traditionally, three types of database model were defined: hierarchical, network, and relational. Only the last, relational model, has survived.

- In the relational model, data is organized in two-dimensional tables called relations. A relation has the following features: name, attributes, and tuples.

- In a relational database we can define several operations to create new relations based on existing ones. We mentioned nine operations in the context of the database query language SQL (Structured Query Language): insert, delete, update, select, project, join, union, intersection, and difference.

- The design of a database, for example for an organization, is often a lengthy task that can only be done through a step-by-step process. The first step often involves interviewing potential users of the database to collect the information that needs to be stored. The second step is to build an Entity-Relationship Model (ERM) that defines the entities for which information must be maintained. The next step is to build relations based on the ERM.

- Normalization is the process by which a given set of relations are transformed to a new set of relations with a more solid structure. Normalization is required to allow any relation in the database to be represented, to allow a query language such as SQL to use powerful retrieval operations composed of atomic operations, to remove anomalies in insertion, deletion, and updating, and to reduce the need for restructuring the database as new data types are to be added.

- The relational database is not the only model of database in use today. The other two common models are distributed databases and object-oriented databases.

14.12 PRACTICE SET

Review questions

1. What are the five necessary components of a DBMS?

2. What are the three database models? Which is the most popular today?

3. What is a relation in a relational database?

4. In a relation, what is an attribute? What is a tuple?

5. List some unary operations in relational databases.

6. List some binary operations in relational databases.

7. What is SQL? What is XML? Which one is a query language for relational databases? Which one is a query language for the objected-oriented language?

Multiple-choice questions

8. In a three-level DBMS architecture, the layer that interacts directly with the hardware is the _____ level.
   a. external
   b. conceptual
   c. internal
   d. physical

9. In a three-level DBMS architecture, the _____ level determines where data is actually stored on the storage devices.
   a. external
   b. conceptual
   c. internal
   d. physical

10. The _____ level of a three-level DBMS architecture defines the logical view of the data.
    a. external
    b. conceptual
    c. internal
    d. physical

11. The data model and the schema of a DBMS are often defined at the _____ level.
    a. external
    b. conceptual
    c. internal
    d. physical

12. In a three-level DBMS architecture, the _____ level interacts directly with the users.
    a. external
    b. conceptual
    c. internal
    d. physical

13. Of the various database models, the _____ model is the most prevalent today.
    a. hierarchical
    b. network
    c. relational
    d. linked list

14. Each column in a relation is called _____.
    a. an attribute
    b. a tuple
    c. a union
    d. an attitude

15. Each row in a relation is called _____.
    a. an attribute
    b. a tuple
    c. a union
    d. an attitude

16. A unary operator is applied to _____ relation(s) and creates an output of _____ relation(s).
    a. one, one
    b. one, two
    c. two, one
    d. two, two

17. A binary operator is applied to _____ relations(s) and creates an output of _____ relation(s).
    a. one, one
    b. one, two
    c. two, one
    d. two, two

18. The unary _____ operation always results in a relation that has exactly one more row than the original relation.
    a. insert
    b. delete
    c. update
    d. select

19. If you want to change the value of an attribute of a tuple, you use the _____ operation.
    a. project
    b. join
    c. update
    d. select

20. The operation that takes two relations and combines them based on common attributes is the _____ operation.
    a. join
    b. project
    c. union
    d. intersection

21. If you need to delete an attribute in a relation, you can use the _____ operation.
    a. join
    b. project
    c. union
    d. intersection

22. You want to create a relation called New that contains tuples that belong to both relation A and relation B. For this, you can use the _____ operation.
    a. select
    b. union
    c. project
    d. intersection

23. Which of the following is a unary operator?
    a. intersection
    b. union
    c. join
    d. project

24. Which of the following is a binary operator?
    a. select
    b. update
    c. difference
    d. all of the above

25. _____ is a declarative language used on relational databases.
    a. PDQ
    b. SQL
    c. LES
    d. PBJ

Exercises

Figure 14.21 is used in Exercise 26 through Exercise 30.

A				B			C		
A1	A2	A3		B1	B2		C1	C2	C3
1	12	100		22	214		31	401	1006
2	16	102		24	216		32	401	1025
3	16	103		27	284		33	405	1065
4	19	104		29	216				

Figure 14.21 Relations for Exercise 26 – Exercise 30

26. You have relations A, B, and C as shown in Figure 14.21. Show the resulting relation if you apply the following SQL statements:

```
select *
from A
where A2 = 16
```

27. You have relations A, B, and C as shown in Figure 14.21. Show the resulting relation if you apply the following SQL statements:

```
select A1 A2
from A
where A2 = 16
```

28. You have relations A, B, and C as shown in Figure 14.21. Show the resulting relation if you apply the following SQL statements:

```
select A3
from A
```

29. You have relations A, B, and C as shown in Figure 14.21. Show the resulting relation if you apply the following SQL statements:

```
select B1
from B
where B2 = 216
```

30. You have relations A, B, and C as shown in Figure 14.21. Show the resulting relation if you apply the following SQL statements:

```
update C
set C1 = 37
where C1 = 31
```

31. Using the model in Figure 14.5 on page 374, show the SQL statement that creates a new relation containing only the course number and the number of units for each course.

32. Using the model in Figure 14.5, show the SQL statement that creates a new relation containing only the student ID and student name.

33. Using the model in Figure 14.5, show the SQL statement that creates a new relation containing only the professor's name.

34. Using the model in Figure 14.5, show the SQL statement that creates a new relation containing only the department name.

35. Using the model in Figure 14.5, show the SQL statement that creates a new relation containing the courses taken by the student with ID 2010.

36. Using the model in Figure 14.5, show the SQL statement that creates a new relation containing the courses taught by Professor Blake.

37. Using the model in Figure 14.5, show the SQL statement that creates a new relation containing only courses that have three units.

38. Using the model in Figure 14.5, show the SQL statement that creates a new relation containing only the name of students taking course CIS015.

39. Using the model in Figure 14.5, show the SQL statement that creates a new relation containing the department number of the Computer Science Department.

40. Is the following relation in first normal form (1NF)? If not, change the table to make it pass 1NF criteria.

A	B	C	D
1	70	65	14
2	25, 32, 71	24	12, 18
3	32	6, 11	18

41. Create an E-R diagram for a public library. Show the outline of the relations that can be created from that diagram.

42. Create an E-R diagram for a real estate company, then show the outline of the relations that can be created from that diagram.

43. Create an E-R diagram for three entities FLIGHT, AIRCRAFT, and PILOT in an airline, then show the outlines of the relations in this company.

44. Use references or the Internet to find some information about third normal form (3NF). What kind of functional dependency is involved in this normal form?

45. Use references or the Internet and find some information about Boyce-Codd Normal Form (BCNF). What kind of functional dependency is involved in this normal form?

15

Data Compression

In recent years technology has changed the way we transmit and store data. For example, fiber-optic cable allows us to transmit data much faster, and DVDs allow us to store huge amounts of data on a physically small medium. However, as in other aspects of life, the rate of demand from the public is ever increasing. Today, we want to download more and more data in a shorter and shorter amount of time. We also want to store more and more data in a smaller space.

Compressing data can reduce the amount of data to be sent or stored by partially eliminating inherent redundancy. Redundancy is created when we produce data. Through data compression, we make transmission and storage more efficient, and at the same time, we preserve the integrity of the data.

Objectives

After studying this chapter, the student should be able to:

❏ Distinguish between lossless and lossy compression.

❏ Describe run-length encoding and how it achieves compression.

❏ Describe Huffman coding and how it achieves compression.

❏ Describe Lempel Ziv encoding and the role of the dictionary in encoding and decoding.

❏ Describe the main idea behind the JPEG standard for compressing still images.

❏ Describe the main idea behind the MPEG standard for compressing video and its relation to JPEG.

❏ Describe the main idea behind the MP3 standard for compressing audio.

Data compression implies sending or storing a smaller number of bits. Although many methods are used for this purpose, in general these methods can be divided into two broad categories: *lossless* and *lossy* methods. Figure 15.1 shows the two categories and common methods used in each category.

We first discuss lossless compression methods, as they are simpler and easier to understand. We then present lossy compression methods.

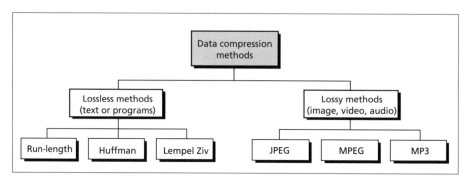

Figure 15.1   Data compression methods

15.1   LOSSLESS COMPRESSION

In **lossless data compression**, the integrity of the data is preserved. The original data and the data after **compression** and **decompression** are exactly the same because, in these methods, the compression and decompression algorithms are exact inverses of each other: no part of the data is lost in the process. Redundant data is removed in compression and added during decompression.

Lossless compression methods are normally used when we cannot afford to lose any data. For example, we must not lose data when we compress a text file or an application program.

We discuss three lossless compression methods in this section: run-length encoding, Huffman coding, and the Lempel Ziv algorithm.

Run-length encoding

Run-length encoding is probably the simplest method of compression. It can be used to compress data made of any combination of symbols. It does not need to know the frequency of occurrence of symbols (as is necessary for Huffman coding) and can be very efficient if data is represented as 0s and 1s.

The general idea behind this method is to replace consecutive repeating occurrences of a symbol by one occurrence of the symbol followed by the number of occurrences. For example, AAAAAAAA can be replaced by A08. Figure 15.2 shows an example of this simple compression method. Note that we use a fixed number of digits (two) to represent the count.

The method can be even more efficient if the data uses only two symbols (for example 0 and 1) in its bit pattern and one symbol is more frequent than the other.

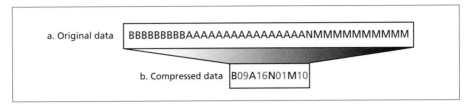

Figure 15.2 Run-length encoding example

For example, let's say we have an image represented by mostly 0s and some 1s. In this case, we can reduce the number of bits by sending (or storing) the number of 0s occurring between two 1s (Figure 15.3).

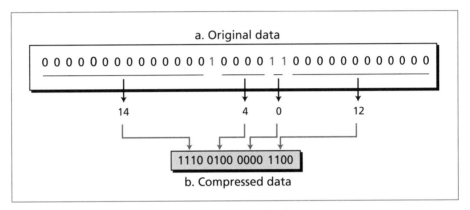

Figure 15.3 Run-length encoding for two symbols

We have represented the counts as a 4-bit binary number (unsigned integer). In an actual situation, we would find an optimal number of bits to avoid introducing extra redundancy. In Figure 15.3, there are fourteen 0s before the first 1. These fourteen 0s are compressed to the binary pattern 1110 (14 in binary). The next set of 0s is compressed to 0100 because there are four 0s. Next we have two 1s in the original data, which are represented by 0000 in the compressed data. Finally, the last twelve 0s in the data are compressed to 1100.

Note that, given a 4-bit binary compression, if there are more than fifteen 0s, they are broken into two or more groups. For example, a sequence of twenty-five 0s is encoded as 1111 1010. Now the question is how the decoding algorithm knows that this consists of twenty-five 0s and not fifteen 0s, then a 1, and then ten 0s. The answer is that if the first count is 1111, the receiver knows the next 4-bit pattern is a continuation of 0s. Now another question is raised: what if there are exactly fifteen 0s between two 1s? In this case, the pattern is 1111 followed by 0000.

Huffman coding

Huffman coding assigns shorter codes to symbols that occur more frequently and longer codes to those that occur less frequently. For example, imagine we have a text file that uses only five characters (A, B, C, D, E). We chose only five characters to make the discussion simpler, but the procedure is equally valid for a smaller or greater number of characters.

Before we can assign bit patterns to each character, we assign each character a weight based on its frequency of use. In this example, assume that the frequency of the characters is as shown in Table 15.1. Character A occurs 17 percent of the time, character B occurs 12 percent of the time, and so on.

Table 15.1   Frequency of characters

Character	A	B	C	D	E
Frequency	17	12	12	27	32

Once the weight of each character is established, we build a tree based on those values. The process for building this tree is shown in Figure 15.4. It follows three basic steps:

1. Put the entire character set in a row. Each character is now a **node** at the lowest level of the tree.

2. Find the two nodes with the smallest weights and join them to form a third node, resulting in a simple two-level tree. The weight of the new node is the combined weights of the original two nodes. This node, one level up from the leaves, is eligible for combination with other nodes. Remember that the sum of the weights of the two nodes chosen must be smaller than the combination of any other possible choices.

3. Repeat step 2 until all of the nodes, on every level, are combined into a single tree.

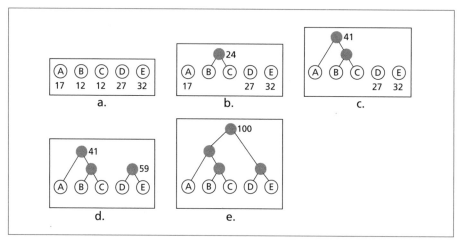

Figure 15.4   Huffman coding

Once the tree is complete, use it to assign codes to each character. First, assign a bit value to each **branch**. Starting from the root (top node), assign 0 to the left branch and 1 to the right branch and repeat this pattern at each node.

A character's code is found by starting at the root and following the branches that lead to that character. The code itself is the bit value of each branch on the path, taken in sequence. Figure 15.5 shows the final tree with bits added to each branch. Note that we moved the leaf nodes to make the tree look like a **binary tree**.

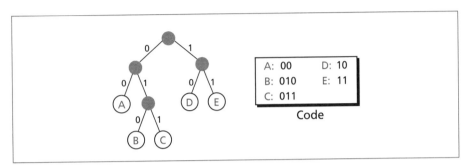

Figure 15.5 Final tree and code

Note these points about the codes. First, the characters with higher frequencies receive a shorter code (A, D, and E) than the characters with lower frequencies (B and C). Compare this with a code that assigns equal bit lengths to each character. Second, in this coding system, no code is a prefix of another code. The 2-bit codes, 00, 10, and 11, are not the prefixes of any of the two other codes (010 and 011). In other words, we do not have a 3-bit code beginning with 00, 10, or 11. This property makes Huffman code an *instantaneous* code. We will explain this property when we discuss encoding and **decoding** in Huffman coding.

Encoding

Let us see how to encode text using the code for our five characters. Figure 15.6 shows the original and the encoded text.

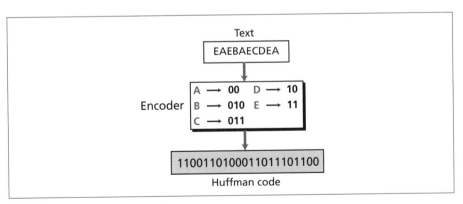

Figure 15.6 Huffman encoding

Two points about this figure are worth mentioning. First, notice that there is a sense of compression even in this small and unrealistic code. If we want to send the text without using Huffman coding, we need to assign a 3-bit code to each character. You would have sent 30 bits, whereas with Huffman coding, we send only 22 bits.

Second, notice that we have not used any delimiters between the bits that encode each character. We write the codes one after another. The beauty of Huffman coding is that no code is the prefix of another code. There is therefore no ambiguity in encoding, so the decoding algorithm can decode the received data without ambiguity.

Decoding

The recipient has a very easy job in decoding the data it receives. Figure 15.7 shows how decoding takes place. When the recipient receives the first 2 bits, it does not have to wait for the next bit to make a decision—it knows that these 2 bits encode the letter E. This is because these 2 bits are not the prefix of any 3-bit code (there is no 3-bit code that starts with 11). Likewise, when the receiver receives the next 2 bits (00), it also knows that the character must be A. The next 2 bits are interpreted the same way (11 must be E). However, when it receives bits 7 and 8, it knows that it must wait for the next bit, because this code (01) is not in the list of codes. After receiving the next bit (0), it interprets the 3 bits together (010) as B. This is why Huffman code is called an instantaneous code—the decoder can unambiguously decode the bits instantaneously, using the minimum number of bits.

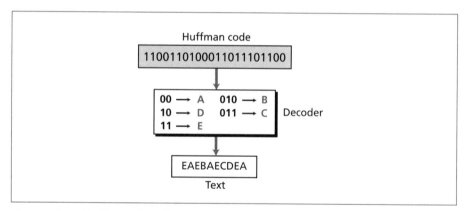

Figure 15.7   Huffman decoding

Lempel Ziv encoding

Lempel Ziv (LZ) encoding, named after its inventors (Abraham Lempel and Jacob Ziv), is an example of a category of algorithms called **dictionary-based encoding**. The idea is to create a dictionary (a table) of strings used during the communication session. If both the sender and the receiver have a copy of the dictionary, then previously-encountered strings can be substituted by their index in the dictionary to reduce the amount of information transmitted.

Although the idea appears simple, several difficulties surface in the implementation. First, how can a dictionary be created for each session? It cannot be universal, due to its length. Second, how can the recipient acquire the dictionary created by the sender—if we send the dictionary, we are sending extra data, which defeats the whole purpose of compression?

The Lempel Ziv (LZ) algorithm is a practical algorithm that uses the idea of adaptive dictionary-based encoding. The algorithm has gone through several versions (LZ77, LZ78). We introduce the basic idea of this algorithm with an example, but do not delve into the details of different versions and implementations. In the example, assume that the following string is to be sent. We have chosen this specific string to simplify the discussion.

BAABABBBAABBBBAA

Using our simple version of the LZ algorithm, the process is divided into two phases: compressing the string and decompressing the string.

Compression   In this phase there are two concurrent events: building an indexed dictionary and compressing a string of symbols. The algorithm extracts the smallest **substring** that cannot be found in the dictionary from the remaining uncompressed string. It then stores a copy of this substring in the dictionary as a new entry and assigns it an index value. Compression occurs when the substring, except for the last character, is replaced with the index found in the dictionary. The process then inserts the index and the last character of the substring into the compressed string. For example, if the substring is ABBB, we search for ABB in the dictionary. You find that the index for ABB is 4, so the compressed substring is therefore 4B.

Figure 15.8 shows the process for our sample string. Let us go through a few steps in this figure:

Step 1

The encoding process extracts the smallest substring from the original string that is not in the dictionary. Because the dictionary is empty, the smallest character is one character (the first character, B). The process stores a copy of it as the first entry in the dictionary with an index of 1. No part of this substring can be replaced with an index from the dictionary, as it is only one character. The process inserts B in the compressed string. So far, the compressed string has only one character, B. The remaining uncompressed string is the original string without the first character.

Step 2

The encoding process extracts the next smallest substring that is not in the dictionary from the remaining string. This substring is the character A, which is not in the dictionary. The process stores a copy of it as the second entry in the dictionary. No part of this substring can be replaced with an index from the dictionary, as it is only one character. The process inserts A in the compressed string. So far, the compressed string has two characters: B and A (we have placed commas between the substrings in the compressed string to show the separation).

Step 3

The encoding process extracts the next smallest substring that is not in the dictionary from the remaining string. This situation differs from the two previous steps:

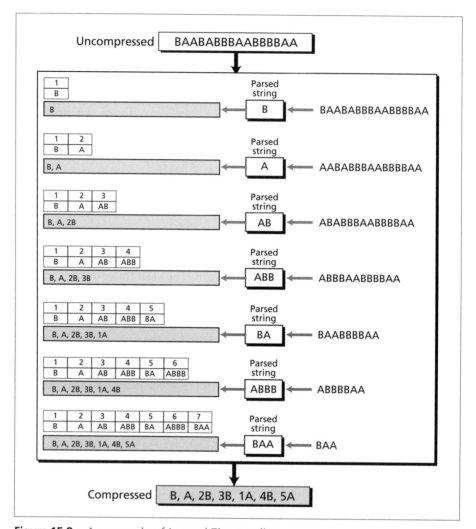

Figure 15.8   An example of Lempel Ziv encoding

the next character (A) *is* in the dictionary, so the process extracts two characters (AB), which are not in the dictionary. The process stores a copy of AB as the third entry in the dictionary. The process now finds the index of an entry in the dictionary that is the substring without the last character (AB without the last character is A). The index for A is 2, so the process replaces A with 2 and inserts 2B in the compressed string.

Step 4

Next the encoding process extracts the substring ABB (because A and AB are already in the dictionary). A copy of ABB is stored in the dictionary with an index of 4. The process finds the index of the substring without the last character (AB), which is 3. The combination 3B is inserted into the compressed string.

You may have noticed that in the three previous steps, we have not actually achieved any compression, because we have replaced one character with one character (A by A in the first step and B by B in the second step) and two characters with two characters (AB by 2B in the third step). But in this step, we have reduced the number of characters (ABB becomes 3B). If the original string has many repetitions (which is true in most cases), we can greatly reduce the number of characters.

The remaining steps are all similar to one of the preceding four steps. Note that the dictionary was only used by the encoding program to find the indexes. It is not sent to the recipient, and the recipient must create the dictionary for itself, as we will see in the next section.

Decompression   Decompression is the inverse of the compression process. The process extracts the substrings from the compressed string and tries to replace the indexes with the corresponding entry in the dictionary, which is empty at first and built up gradually. The idea is that when an index is received, there is already an entry in the dictionary corresponding to that index.

Figure 15.9 shows the decompression process. Let us go through a few steps in the figure:

Step 1

The first substring of the compressed string is examined. It is B without an index. Because the substring is not in the dictionary, it is added to the dictionary. The substring (B) is inserted into the decompressed string.

Step 2

The second substring (A) is examined: the situation is similar to step 1. Now the decompressed string has two characters (BA), and the dictionary has two entries.

Step 3

The third substring (2B) is examined. The process searches the dictionary and replaces the index 2 with the substring A. The new substring (AB) is added to the decompressed string, and AB is added to the dictionary.

Step 4

The fourth substring (3B) is examined. The process searches the dictionary and replaces the index 3 with the substring AB. The substring ABB is now added to the decompressed string, and ABB is added to the dictionary.

We leave exploration of the last three steps as an exercise. As we have noticed, we used a number such as 1 or 2 for the index. In reality, the index is a binary pattern (possibly variable in length) for better efficiency. Also note that LZ encoding leaves the last character uncompressed (which means less efficiency). A version of LZ encoding, called **Lempel Ziv Welch (LZW) encoding**, compresses even this single character. However, we leave the discussion of this algorithm to more specialized textbooks.

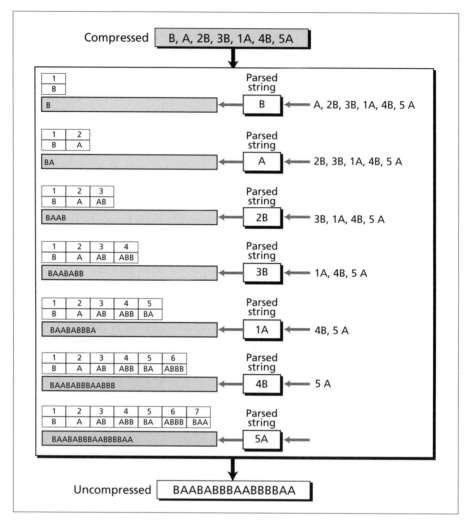

Figure 15.9   An example of Lempel Ziv decoding

15.2 LOSSY COMPRESSION METHODS

Loss of information is not acceptable in a text file or a program file. It is, however, acceptable in an image, video, or audio file. The reason is that our eyes and ears cannot distinguish subtle changes. In such cases, we can use a **lossy data compression** method. These methods are cheaper—they take less time and space when it comes to sending millions of bits per second for images and video.

Several methods have been developed using lossy compression techniques. **JPEG (Joint Photographic Experts Group)** encoding is used to compress pictures and graphics, **MPEG (Moving Picture Experts Group)** encoding is used to compress video, and **MP3 (MPEG audio layer 3)** for audio compression.

Image compression – JPEG encoding

As discussed in Chapter 2, an image can be represented by a two-dimensional array (table) of picture elements (pixels). For example, 640 × 480 = 307,200 pixels. If the picture is grayscale, each pixel can be represented by an 8-bit integer, giving 256 levels of gray. If the picture is color, each pixel can be represented by 24 bits (3 × 8 bits), with each 8 bits representing one of the colors in the RBG color system. To simplify the discussion, we concentrate on a grayscale picture with 640 × 480 pixels. You can see why we need compression. A grayscale picture of 307,200 pixels is represented by 2,457,600 bits, and a color picture is represented by 7,372,800 bits.

In JPEG, a grayscale picture is divided into blocks of 8 × 8 pixel blocks (Figure 15.10). The purpose of dividing the picture into blocks is to decrease the number of calculations because, as we will see shortly, the number of mathematical operations for each picture is the square of the number of units. That is, for the entire image, we need $307,200^2$ operations (94,371,840,000 operations). If we use JPEG, we need 64^2 operations for each block, a total of 64^2 × 80 × 60, or 19,660,800 operations. This decreases by 4800 times the number of operations.

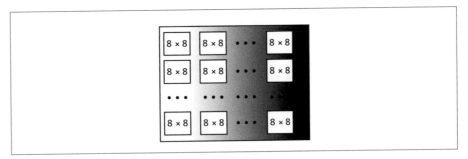

Figure 15.10 JPEG grayscale example, 640 × 480 pixels

The whole idea of JPEG is to change the picture into a linear (vector) set of numbers that reveals the redundancies. The redundancies (lack of changes) can then be removed using one of the lossless compression methods we studied previously. A simplified version of the process is shown in Figure 15.11.

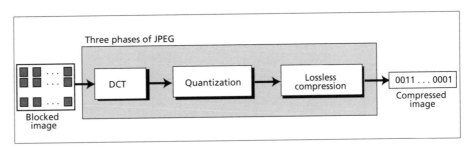

Figure 15.11 The JPEG compression process

Discrete cosine transform (DCT)

In this step, each block of 64 pixels goes through a transformation called the **discrete cosine transform (DCT)**. The transformation changes the 64 values so that the relative relationships between pixels are kept but the redundancies are revealed. The formula is given in Appendix G. $P(x, y)$ defines one value in the block, while $T(m, n)$ defines the value in the transformed block.

To understand the nature of this transformation, let us show the result of the transformations for three cases.

Case 1

In this case, we have a block of uniform grayscale, and the value of each pixel is 20. When we do the transformations, we get a nonzero value for the first element (upper left corner). The rest of the pixels have a value of 0 because, according to the formula, the value of $T(0,0)$ is the average of the other values. This is called the **DC value** (direct current, borrowed from electrical engineering). The rest of the values in $T(m, n)$, called **AC values**, represent changes in the pixel values. But because there are no changes, the rest of the values are 0s (Figure 15.12).

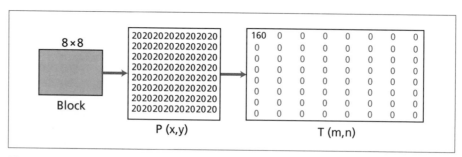

Figure 15.12 Case 1: uniform grayscale

Case 2

In the second case, we have a block with two different uniform grayscale sections. There is a sharp change in the values of the pixels (from 20 to 50). When we do the transformations, we get a DC value as well as nonzero AC values. However, there are only a few nonzero values clustered around the DC value. Most of the values are 0 (Figure 15.13).

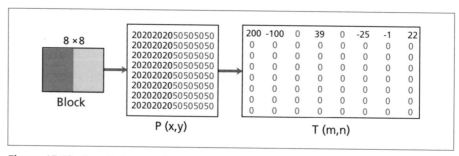

Figure 15.13 Case 2: two sections

Case 3

In the third case, we have a block that changes gradually. That is, there is no sharp change between the values of neighboring pixels. When we do the transformations, we get a DC value, with many nonzero AC values also (Figure 15.14).

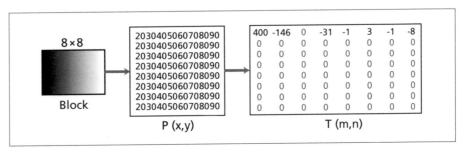

Figure 15.14 Case 3: gradient grayscale

From Figures 15.12, 15.13, and 15.14, we can state the following:

- ❏ The transformation creates table T from table P.
- ❏ The DC value gives the average value of the pixels.
- ❏ The AC values gives the changes.
- ❏ Lack of changes in adjacent pixels creates 0s.

Note that the DCT transformation is reversible. Appendix G also shows the mathematical formula for a reverse transformation.

Quantization After the T table is created, the values are quantized to reduce the number of bits needed for encoding. Quantization divides the number of bits by a constant and then drops the fraction. This reduces the required number of bits even more. In most implementations, a quantizing table (8 by 8) defines how to quantize each value. The divisor depends on the position of the value in the T table. This is done to optimize the number of bits and the number of 0s for each particular application.

Note that the only phase in the process that is not reversible is the quantizing phase. You lose some information here that is not recoverable. The only reason that JPEG is a *lossy* compression method is because of the quantization phase.

Compression After quantization the values are read from the table, and redundant 0s are removed. However, to cluster the 0s together, the process reads the table diagonally in a zigzag fashion rather than row by row or column by column. The reason is that if the picture does not have fine changes, the bottom right corner of the T table is all 0s. Figure 15.15 shows the process. JPEG usually uses run-length encoding at the compression phase to compress the bit pattern resulting from the zigzag linearization.

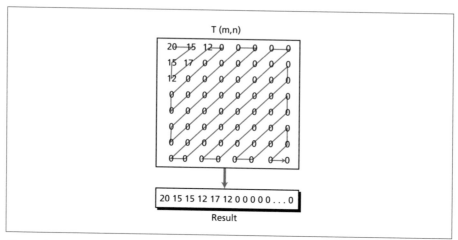

Figure 15.15 Reading the table

Video compression – MPEG encoding

The Moving Picture Experts Group (MPEG) method is used to compress video. In principle, a motion picture is a rapid sequence of a set of frames in which each frame is a picture. In other words, a frame is a spatial combination of pixels, and a video is a temporal combination of frames that are sent one after another. Compressing video, then, means spatially compressing each frame and temporally compressing a set of frames.

Spatial compression

The **spatial compression** of each frame is done with JPEG, or a modification of it. Each frame is a picture that can be independently compressed.

Temporal compression

In **temporal compression**, redundant frames are removed. When we watch television, for example, we receive 30 frames per second. However, most of the consecutive frames are almost the same. For example, in a static scene in which someone is talking, most frames are the same except for the segment around the speaker's lips, which changes from one frame to the next.

A rough calculation points to the need for temporal compression for video. A 20:1 JPEG compression of one frame sends 368,640 bits per frame: at 30 frames per second, this is 11,059,200 bits per second. We need to reduce this number!

To temporally compress data, the MPEG method first divides frames into three categories: I-frames, P-frames, and B-frames.

❑   **I-frames**. An **intracoded frame (I-frame)** is an independent frame that is not related to any other frame—that is, not to the frame sent before or to the frame sent after. They are present at regular intervals (for example, every ninth frame is an I-frame). An I-frame must appear periodically due to some sudden change in the frame that the previous and following frames cannot show. Also, when a video is broadcast, a viewer may tune in their receiver at any time. If there is only one I-frame at the beginning of the broadcast, the viewer who tunes in late will not receive a complete picture. I-frames are independent of other frames and cannot be constructed from other frames.

❑ **P-frames.** A **predicted frame (P-frame)** is related to the preceding I-frame or P-frame. In other words, each P-frame contains only the changes from the preceding frame. The changes, however, cannot cover a big segment of the image. For example, for a fast-moving object, the new changes may not be recorded in a P-frame. P-frames can be constructed only from previous I- or P-frames. P-frames carry much less information than other frame types and carry even fewer bits after compression.

❑ **B-frames.** A **bidirectional frame (B-frame)** is relative to the preceding and following I-frame or P-frame. In other words, each B-frame is relative to the past and the future. Note that a B-frame is never related to another B-frame.

Figure 15.16 shows a sample sequence of frames and how they are constructed. Note that for decoding, the decoding process should receive the P frames before the B frames. For this reason, the order of transmission of frames is different than the order in which they displayed at the receiving application. The frames are sent as I, P, B, B, P, B, B, I.

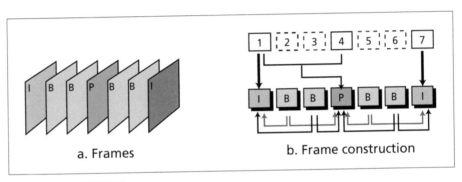

a. Frames   b. Frame construction

Figure 15.16 MPEG frames

Versions

MPEG has gone through several versions. The discussion above is related to MPEG-1. MPEG-2 was introduced in 1991, is more capable than MPEG-1 and can be used for video storage as well as TV broadcasting, including high definition TV (HDTV). A more recent version of MPEG is called MPEG-7, which is named "Multimedia Content Description Interface". MPEG-7 is mostly a standard that uses XML to describe *metadata* (data about data), the description of what is included in the video.

Audio compression

Audio compression can be used for speech or music. For speech we need to compress a 64 kHz digitized signal, while for music we need to compress a 1.411 MHz signal. Two categories of techniques are used for audio compression: predictive encoding and perceptual encoding.

Predictive encoding

In **predictive encoding**, the differences between samples are encoded instead of encoding all the sampled values. This type of compression is normally used for speech. Several standards have been defined such as GSM (13 kbps), G.729 (8 kbps), and G.723.3 (6.4 or 5.3 kbps). Detailed discussions of these techniques are beyond the scope of this book.

Perceptual encoding: MP3

The most common compression technique used to create CD-quality audio is based on the **perceptual encoding** technique. This type of audio needs at least 1.411 Mbps, which cannot be sent over the Internet without compression. MP3 (MPEG audio layer 3), a part of the MPEG standard (discussed in the video compression section), uses this technique.

Perceptual encoding is based on the science of psychoacoustics, which is the study of how people perceive sound. The idea is based on flaws in our auditory system: some sounds can mask other sounds. Masking can happen in both frequency and time. In **frequency masking**, a loud sound in one frequency range can partially or totally mask a softer sound in another frequency range. For example, we cannot hear what our dance partner says in a room in which a loud heavy metal band is performing. In **temporal masking**, a loud sound can reduce the sensitivity of our hearing for a short time even after the sound has stopped.

MP3 uses these two phenomena, frequency and temporal masking, to compress audio signals. The technique analyzes and divides the audio spectrum into several groups. Zero bits are allocated to frequency ranges that are totally masked, a small number of bits are allocated to frequency ranges that are partially masked, and a larger number of bits are allocated to frequency ranges that are not masked.

MP3 produces three data rates: 96 kbps, 128 kbps, and 160 kbps. The rate is based on the range of the frequencies in the original analog audio.

15.3 RECOMMENDED READING

For more details about the subjects discussed in this chapter, the following books are recommended:

❑ Drozdek A: *Elements of Data Compression*, Boston, MA: Course Technology, 2001

❑ Symes P: *Video Compression*, New York: McGraw-Hill, 1998

❑ Haskell B, Puri A, and Netravali A: *Digital Video: An Introduction to MPEG2*, New York: Chapman & Hill, 1997

❑ Pennebaker W and Mitchell J: *JPEG Still Image Data Compression Standard*, New York: Van Nostrand Reinhold, 1993

15.4 KEY TERMS

This chapter has introduced the following key terms, which are listed here with the pages on which they first occur:

AC Value 404	bidirectional frame (B-frame) 407
data compression 394	DC Value 404
dictionary-based encoding 401	Discrete Cosine Transform 404
frequency masking 408	Huffman encoding 395
intracoded frame (I-frame) 406	Joint Photographic Expert Group (JPEG) 402
Lempel Ziv (LZ) encoding 398	Lempel Ziv Welch (LZW) encoding 401
lossless data compression 394	lossy data compression 402
Motion Picture Expert Group (MPEG) 402	MPEG audio layer 3 (MP3) 402
perceptual encoding 408	predicted frame (P-frame) 407
predictive encoding 408	run-length encoding 394
spatial compression 406	temporal compression 406
temporal masking 408	

15.5 SUMMARY

- Data compression methods are either lossless (all information is recoverable) or lossy (some information is lost).
- In lossless compression methods, the received data is an exact replica of the sent data. Three lossless compression methods are run-length encoding, Huffman coding, and Lempel Ziv (LZ) encoding.
- In run-length encoding, repeated occurrences of a symbol are replaced by a symbol and the number of occurrences of the symbol.
- In Huffman coding, the code length is a function of symbol frequency: more frequent symbols have shorter codes than less frequent symbols.
- In LZ encoding, repeated strings or words are stored in memory locations. An index to the memory location replaces the string or word. LZ encoding requires a dictionary and an algorithm at both sender and receiver.

- In lossy compression methods, the received data need not be an exact replica of the sent data. Three lossy compression method were discussed in this chapter: JPEG, MPEG, and MP3.
- JPEG (Joint Photographic Experts Group) compression is a method of compressing pictures and graphics. The JPEG process involves blocking, the discrete cosine transform, quantization, and lossless compression.
- MPEG (Motion Pictures Experts Group) compression is a method of compressing video. MPEG involves both spatial compression and temporal compression. The former is similar to JPEG, while the latter removes redundant frames.
- MP3 (MPEG audio layer 3) is a part of the MPEG standard. MP3 uses perceptual encoding techniques to compress CD-quality audio.

15.6 PRACTICE SET

Review questions

1. What are the two categories of data compression methods?
2. What is the difference between lossless compression and lossy compression?
3. What is run-length encoding?
4. How does Lempel Ziv encoding reduce the amount of bits transmitted?
5. What is Huffman coding?
6. What is the role of the dictionary in LZ encoding?
7. What is the advantage of LZ encoding over Huffman coding?
8. Name three lossy compression methods.
9. When would you use JPEG? When would you use MPEG?
10. How is MPEG related to JPEG?
11. In JPEG, what is the function of blocking?
12. Why is the discrete cosine transform needed in JPEG?
13. How does quantization contribute to compression?
14. What is a frame in MPEG compression?
15. What is spatial compression compared to temporal compression?
16. Discuss the three types of frames used in MPEG.

Multiple-choice questions

17. Data is compressed using a dictionary with indexes to strings. This is _____.
    a. Huffman encoding
    b. Lempel Ziv encoding
    c. Morse coding
    d. lossy coding

18. A string of one hundred 0s is replaced by two markers, a 0, and the number 100. This is _____.
    a. run-length encoding
    b. Morse coding

    c. Huffman encoding
    d. Lempel Ziv encoding

19. _____ is an example of lossy compression.
    a. Huffman encoding
    b. Lempel Ziv encoding
    c. Run-length encoding
    d. JPEG

20. In a _____ data compression method, the received data is an exact copy of the original message.
    a. lossless
    b. lossy
    c. JPEG
    d. MPEG

21. In a _____ data compression method, the received data need not be an exact copy of the original message.
    a. MP3
    b. JPEG
    c. MPEG
    d. all of the above

22. _____ encoding is a lossless data compression method.
    a. Huffman
    b. Run-length
    c. LZ
    d. all of the above

23. In _____ encoding, the more frequently occurring characters have shorter codes than the less frequently occurring characters.
    a. Huffman
    b. run-length
    c. LZ
    d. all of the above

24. In _____ encoding, PPPPPPPPPPPPPP can be replaced by P15.
    a. Huffman
    b. run-length
    c. LZ
    d. all of the above

25. In _____ encoding, a string is replaced by a pointer to the stored string.
   a. Huffman
   b. run-length
   c. LZ
   d. all of the above

26. LZ encoding requires _____.
   a. a dictionary
   b. a buffer
   c. an algorithm
   d. all of the above

27. JPEG encoding involves _____, a process that reveals the redundancies in a block.
   a. blocking
   b. the discrete cosine transform
   c. quantization
   d. vectorization

28. In JPEG encoding, the _____ process breaks the original picture into smaller blocks and assigns a value to each pixel in a block.
   a. blocking
   b. DCT
   c. quantization
   d. vectorization

29. The last step in JPEG, _____, removes redundancies.
   a. blocking
   b. quantization
   c. compression
   d. vectorization

30. _____ is a lossy compression method for pictures and graphics, whereas _____ is a lossy compression method for video.
   a. DCT, MPEG
   b. MPEG, JPEG
   c. JPEG, MPEG
   d. JPEG, DCT

Exercises

31. Encode the following bit pattern using run-length encoding with 5-bit codes:

18 zeros, 11, 56 zeros, 1, 15 zeros, 11

32. Encode the following bit pattern using run-length encoding with 5-bit codes:

1, 8 zeros, 1, 45 zeros, 11

33. Encode the following characters using Huffman coding with the given frequencies:

A (12), B (8), C (9), D (20), E (31), F (14), G (8)

34. Encode the following characters using Huffman coding. Each character has the same frequency (1):

A, B, C, D, E, F, G, H, I, J

35. Can the following be a Huffman code? Explain.

A: 0   B: 10   C:11

36. Can the following be a Huffman code? Explain.

A: 0   B:1   C: 00   D: 01   E: 10   F: 11

37. Encode the message BAABBBBAACAA using the following Huffman code:

A: 0   B: 10   C: 11

38. Decode the message 0101000011110 using the following Huffman code:

A: 0   B: 10   C: 11

39. Encode the message BAABBBBAACAA using the Lempel Ziv method, then decode the encoded message to get the original message.

40. Encode the string AAAABBCCCBBB (part of a message) using the Lempel Ziv method if the dictionary contains ABB. Show the final contents of the dictionary.

41. DCT evaluation requires a lot of calculation and is normally performed using a computer program. Instead of DCT, use the following rule to transform a 2 × 2 table:

$$T(0,0) = (1/16) [P(0,0) + P(0,1) + P(1,0) + P(1,1)]$$

$$T(0,1) = (1/16) [0.95P(0,0) + 0.9P(0,1) + 0.85P(1,0) + 0.80P(1,1)]$$

$$T(1,0) = (1/16) [0.90P(0,0) + 0.85P(0,1) + 0.80P(1,0) + 075P(1,1)]$$

$$T(1,1) = (1/16) [0.85P(0,0) + 0.80P(0,1) + 0.75P(1,0) + 0.70P(1,1)]$$

If $P(0,0) = 64$, $P(0,1) = 32$, $P(1,0) = 128$, and $P(1,1) = 148$, find $T(0,0)$, $T(0,1)$, $T(1,0)$, and $T(1,1)$.

16
Security

We are living in the information age. We need to keep information about every aspect of our lives. Information is an asset that has a value like any other asset. As an asset, information needs to be secured from attack.

Objectives

After studying this chapter, the student should be able to:

❑ Define three security goals—*confidentiality*, *integrity*, and *availability*—and attacks that threatens these security goals.

❑ Define five security services to prevent security attacks—*data confidentiality, data integrity, authentication, nonrepudiation*, and *access control*.

❑ Discuss two techniques for providing security services: *cryptography* and *steganography*.

❑ Distinguish between *symmetric-key cryptography* and *asymmetric-key cryptography* and show how confidentiality can be provided using either symmetric-key or asymmetric-key ciphers.

❑ Show how integrity can be provided using *cryptographic hashing functions*.

❑ Discuss the idea of *digital signatures* and how they can provide message integrity, message authentication, and nonrepudiation.

❑ Briefly discuss entity authentication and categories of witnesses: something known, something possessed, and something inherent.

❑ Discuss four techniques used for entity authentication: *password-based, challenge-response, zero knowledge*, and *biometrics*.

❑ Discuss key management in symmetric-key and asymmetric-key cryptography.

16.1   INTRODUCTION

In this section we describe the general idea behind information security.

Security goals

We will first discuss three **security goals**: confidentiality, integrity, and availability (Figure 16.1).

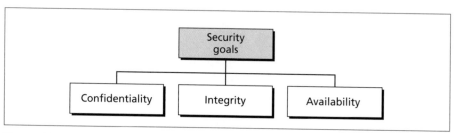

Figure 16.1   Taxonomy of security goals

Confidentiality   **Confidentiality**, keeping information secret from unauthorized access, is probably the most common aspect of information security: we need to protect confidential information. An organization needs to guard against those malicious actions that endanger the confidentiality of its information. In military applications, conceal-ment of sensitive information is the major concern, while in industry, hiding infor-mation from competitors is crucial to the operation of the organization. In banking, customers' accounts need to be kept secret.

Integrity   Information needs to be changed constantly. In a bank, when a customer deposits or withdraws money, the balance of their account needs to be changed. **Integrity** means that changes should be done only by authorized users and through autho-rized mechanisms.

Availability   The third component of information security is **availability**. The information cre-ated and stored by an organization needs to be available to authorized users and applications. Information is useless if it is not available. Information needs to be changed constantly, which means that it must be accessible to those authorized to access it. Unavailability of information is just as harmful to an organization as a lack of confidentiality or integrity. Imagine what would happen to a bank if the custom-ers could not access their accounts for transactions.

Attacks

The three goals of security—confidentiality, integrity, and availability—can be threatened by **security attacks**. Figure 16.2 relates the taxonomy of attack types to security goals.

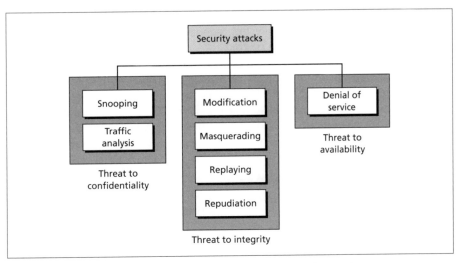

Figure 16.2   Taxonomy of attacks with relation to security goals

Attacks threatening confidentiality   In general, two types of attack threaten the confidentiality of information: **snooping** and **traffic analysis**. Snooping refers to unauthorized access to or interception of data. For example, a file transferred through the Internet may contain confidential information. An unauthorized person could intercept the transmission and use the contents for their own benefit. To prevent snooping, the data can be made unintelligible to the intercepter by using one of the encipherment techniques discussed later in the chapter. Traffic analysis refers to other types of information collected by an intruder by monitoring online traffic. For example, they could find the electronic address (such as the e-mail address) of the sender or the recipient, or collect pairs of requests and responses to help guess the nature of a transaction and so on.

Attacks threatening integrity   The integrity of data can be threatened by several kinds of attack: **modification**, **masquerading**, **replaying**, and **repudiation**. *Modification* refers to a type of attack in which the attacker modifies the information to make it beneficial to themselves. For example, a customer might send a message to a bank to carry out a transaction. The attacker intercepts the message and changes the type of transaction for their own benefit. *Masquerading*, or "spoofing", happens when the attacker impersonates somebody else. For example, an attacker might steal the bank card and PIN of a bank customer and pretend to be that customer.

Replaying is another type of attack: the attacker obtains a copy of a message sent by a user and later tries to replay it. For example, a customer sends a request to their bank to ask for payment to a third party. The third party intercepts the message and sends it again to receive another payment from the bank.

Repudiation is different from other types of attack, because it is performed by one of the two parties in the communication: the sender or the recipient. The sender of the message might later deny having sent the message: the recipient of the message might later deny receiving the message. An example of denial by the sender would be a bank customer asking their bank to send some money to a third party, but later denying having made such a request. An example of denial by the recipient could occur when a person buys a product from a manufacturer and pays for it electronically, but the manufacturer later denies having received the payment and asks again to be paid.

Attacks threatening availability

Denial of service (DoS) attacks may slow down or totally interrupt the service of a system. The attacker can use several strategies to achieve this. They might make the system so busy that it collapses, or they might intercept messages sent in one direction and make the sending system believe that one of the parties involved in the communication or message has lost the message and that it should be resent.

Security services

Standards have been defined for security services to achieve security goals and prevent security attacks. Figure 16.3 shows the taxonomy of the five common services.

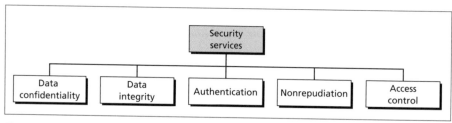

Figure 16.3   Security services

Data confidentiality is designed to protect data from snooping and traffic analysis. **Data integrity** is designed to protect data from modification, insertion, deletion, and replaying by an adversary. It may protect the whole message or part of the message. **Authentication** identifies the party at the other end of the communication. It provides authentication of the sender or recipient during the connection establishment (*peer entity authentication*). It also authenticates the source of the data (*data origin authentication*). **Nonrepudiation** protects against repudiation by either the sender or the recipient of the data. In nonrepudiation with proof of origin, the recipient of the data can later prove the identity of the sender if it is denied. In nonrepudiation with proof of delivery, the sender of data can later prove that the data was delivered to the intended recipient. **Access control** protects against unauthorized access to data. The term *access* in this definition is very broad and can involve reading, writing, modifying, executing programs, and so on.

Techniques

The actual implementation of security goals needs some help from mathematics. Two techniques are prevalent today: one is very general—*cryptography*—and one is specific—*steganography*.

Cryptography

Some security services can be implemented using cryptography. **Cryptography**, a word with Greek origins, means "secret writing". However, we use the term to refer to the science and art of transforming messages to hide their meaning from an intruder. Although in the past *cryptography* referred only to the encryption and decryption of messages using secret keys, today it is defined as involving three distinct mechanisms: **symmetric-key encipherment**, **asymmetric-key encipherment**, and **hashing**. All three will be discussed shortly.

Steganography Although this chapter is based on cryptography as a technique for implementing security services, another technique that was used for secret communication in the past is being revived at present: steganography. The word **steganography**, with origins in Greek, means "covered writing", in contrast to cryptography, which means "secret writing". Cryptography means concealing the contents of a message by enciphering, while steganography means concealing the message itself by covering it with something else.

History is full of facts and myths about the use of steganography. In ancient China war messages were written on thin pieces of silk and rolled into a small ball and swallowed by the messenger. In the Roman and Greek civilizations, messages were carved on pieces of wood that were later dipped in wax to cover the writing. Invisible inks such as onion juice or ammonia salts were also used to write a secret message between the lines of the covering message or on the back of the paper: the secret message was exposed when the paper was heated or treated with another substance.

In recent times other methods have been devised. Some letters in an innocuous message might be overwritten with pencil lead that is visible only when exposed to light at an angle. "Null ciphers" were used to hide a secret message inside an innocuous simple message. For example, the first or second letter of each word in the covering message might compose a secret message. Microdots were also used for this purpose: secret messages were photographed and reduced to a size of a dot (period) and inserted into simple cover messages in place of regular periods at the end of sentences.

Today, any form of data, such as text, image, audio, or video, can be digitized, and it is possible to insert secret binary information into the data during digitization process. Such hidden information is not necessarily used for secrecy—it can also be used to protect copyright, prevent tampering, or add extra information.

16.2   SYMMETRIC-KEY CRYPTOGRAPHY

Figure 16.4 shows the general idea behind **symmetric-key cryptography**. Alice can send a message to Bob over an insecure channel with the assumption that an adversary, Eve, cannot understand the contents of the message by simply eavesdropping on the channel.

The original message from Alice to Bob is referred to as **plaintext**, while the message that is sent through the channel is referred to as the **ciphertext**. To create the ciphertext from the plaintext, Alice uses an **encryption algorithm** and a shared **secret key**. To create the plaintext from the ciphertext, Bob uses a **decryption algorithm** and the same secret key. We refer to encryption and decryption algorithms as **ciphers**. A **key** is a set of values (numbers) on which the cipher, as an algorithm, operates.

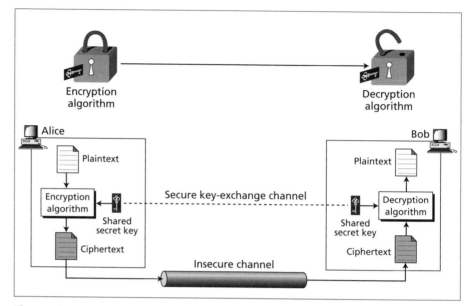

Figure 16.4   The general idea of symmetric-key cryptography

Encryption can be thought of as locking the message in a box, while decryption can be thought of as unlocking the box. In symmetric-key encipherment, the same key locks and unlocks the "box", as shown in Figure 16.4.

Note that symmetric-key encipherment uses a single key for both encryption and decryption. In addition, the encryption and decryption algorithms are inverses of each other. If P is the plaintext, C is the ciphertext, and K is the key, the encryption algorithm $E_K(P)$ creates the ciphertext from the plaintext and the decryption algorithm $D_K(C)$ creates the plaintext from the ciphertext.

We need to emphasize that, according to a very import principle (Kerckhoff's principle), it is better to assume that the adversary knows the algorithm. The only thing that should be kept secret is the key. This means that Alice and Bob need another, secure, channel, to exchange the secret key. Alice and Bob could meet and exchange the key personally: the secure channel here is the face-to-face exchange of the key. They can also trust a third party to give them the same key, or they can create a temporary secret key using another kind of cipher—*asymmetric-key ciphers*—which we will describe later. In this section, we assume that there is an established secret key between Alice and Bob.

Using symmetric-key encipherment, Alice and Bob can use the same key for communication in the other direction, from Bob to Alice. This is why the method is called symmetric.

Another element in symmetric-key encipherment is the number of keys. Alice needs another secret key to communicate with a different person, say David. If there are n people in a group who need to communicate with each other, how many keys are needed? The answer is $(n \times (n - 1))/2$ because each person needs $(n - 1)$ keys to communicate with the rest of the group, but the key between A and B can be used in both directions. We will see later how this problem is handled.

We can divide traditional symmetric-key cryptography into two broad categories: traditional symmetric-key ciphers and modern symmetric-key ciphers.

Traditional ciphers

Traditional ciphers used two techniques for hiding information from an intruder: substitution and transposition.

Substitution ciphers

A **substitution cipher** replaces one symbol with another. If the symbols in the plaintext are alphabetic characters, we replace one character with another. For example, we can replace the letter A with the letter D, and the letter T with the letter Z. If the symbols are digits (0 to 9), we can replace 3 with 7, and 2 with 6.

A substitution cipher replaces one symbol with another.

The simplest substitution cipher is a **shift cipher**. The reason is that the encryption algorithm can be interpreted as "shift *key* characters down" and the decryption algorithm can be interpreted as "shift *key* characters up". For example, if the key = 15, the encryption algorithm shifts each character 15 characters down—toward the end of the alphabet, and the decryption algorithm shifts 15 characters up—toward the beginning of the alphabet. Of course, when we reach the end or the beginning of the alphabet, we wrap around. Julius Caesar used a shift cipher to communicate with his officers. For this reason, shift ciphers are sometimes referred to as **Caesar ciphers**. Julius Caesar used a key of 3 for his communications.

Example 16.1

Use the additive cipher with key = 15 to encrypt the message "hello".

Solution
We apply the encryption algorithm to the plaintext, character by character:

Plaintext: h	→	Shift 15 characters down	→	Ciphertext: w
Plaintext: e	→	Shift 15 characters down	→	Ciphertext: t
Plaintext: l	→	Shift 15 characters down	→	Ciphertext: a
Plaintext: l	→	Shift 15 characters down	→	Ciphertext: a
Plaintext: o	→	Shift 15 characters down	→	Ciphertext: d

The ciphertext is therefore "wtaad". Note that the process is not safe. The key in this case can be only between 0 and 25, so an intruder can intercept the ciphertext and easily use a brute-force attack by trying all possible keys to find a plaintext that makes sense. If the text is long, another attack is to use the frequency of characters in the underlying language, in this case English. The intruder knows that in English the character "e" occurs more frequently than any other character. They find out which character is used most in the text and replace that character with the character "e", thus finding the key.

Transposition ciphers

A **transposition cipher** does not substitute one symbol for another, instead it changes the location of the symbols. A symbol in the first position of the plaintext may appear in the tenth position of the ciphertext, while a symbol in the eighth position in the plaintext may appear in the first position of the ciphertext. In other words, a transposition cipher reorders (transposes) the symbols.

A transposition cipher reorders symbols.

Example 16.2

Alice needs to send the message "Enemy attacks tonight" to Bob. Alice and Bob have agreed to divide the text into groups of five characters and then permute the characters in each group. The following shows the grouping after adding a bogus character (z) at the end to make the last group the same size as the others.

e	n	e	m y	a	t	t	a c	k	s	t	o n	i	g	h t z

The key used for encryption and decryption is a permutation key, which shows how the character are permuted. For this message, assume that Alice and Bob used the following key:

Encryption ↓

3	1	4	5	2
1	2	3	4	5

↑ Decryption

The third character in the plaintext block becomes the first character in the ciphertext block, the first character in the plaintext block becomes the second character in the ciphertext block, and so on. The permutation yields:

e	e	m y	n	t	a	a c	t	t	k	o n	s	h	i	t z g

Alice sends the ciphertext "eemyntaacttkonshitzg" to Bob. Bob divides the ciphertext into five-character groups and, using the key in the reverse order, finds the plaintext.

This primitive method of encipherment is not safe. Although many attacks have been devised for this type of encipherment, the frequency attack mentioned for the previous example can also be used here because the transposition cipher preserves the frequency of characters.

Modern symmetric-key ciphers

Since traditional ciphers are no longer secure, modern symmetric-key ciphers have been developed during the last few decades. Modern ciphers normally use a combination of substitution, transposition, and some other complex transformations to create a ciphertext from a plaintext. Modern ciphers are bit-oriented (instead of character-oriented). The plaintext, ciphertext, and the key are strings of bits.

In this section we briefly discuss two examples of modern symmetric-key ciphers: DES and AES. The coverage of these two ciphers is short: interested readers can consult the references at the end of the chapter for more details.

DES

The **Data Encryption Standard (DES)** is a symmetric-key block cipher published by the **National Institute of Standards and Technology (NIST)** in 1977. DES has been the most widely used symmetric-key block cipher since its publication (Figure 16.5).

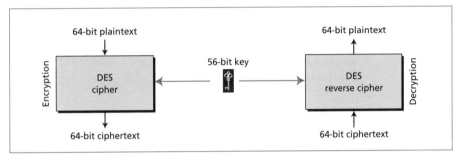

Figure 16.5 Encryption and decryption with DES

At the encryption site, DES takes a 64-bit plaintext and creates a 64-bit ciphertext: at the decryption site, DES takes a 64-bit ciphertext and creates a 64-bit block of plaintext. The same 56-bit cipher key is used for both encryption and decryption. The encryption and decryption ciphers are complex combinations of substitution and transposition units that are repeated ten times.

After its publication DES was severely criticized for two reasons. First, critics questioned the small key length (only 56 bits), which could make the cipher vulnerable to brute-force attack. Second, critics were concerned about possible hidden design behind the internal structure of DES. They were suspicious that some part of its structure might have a hidden "trapdoor" that could allow the US National Security Agency (NSA) to decrypt the messages without the need for the key. Later IBM designers mentioned that the internal structure was designed to prevent some forms of advanced attack.

AES

The **Advanced Encryption Standard (AES)** is a symmetric-key block cipher published by the US National Institute of Standards and Technology (NIST) in 2001 in response to the shortcoming of DES, for example its small key size. See Figure 16.6.

In 1997 the NIST started looking for a replacement for DES. The NIST specifications required a block size of 128 bits and three different key sizes, of 128, 192, and 256 bits. The specifications also required that AES be an open algorithm, available to the public worldwide. The announcement was made internationally to solicit responses from all over the world. After three open conferences, NIST announced that an algorithm called *Rijndael*, (pronounced "Rain Doll"), designed

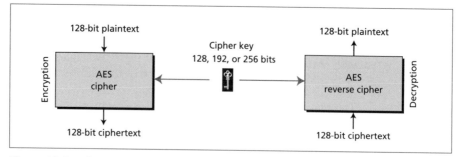

Figure 16.6   The general design of the AES encryption cipher

by Belgian researchers Joan Daemen and Vincent Rijment, was selected as the Advanced Encryption Standard. AES uses a cipher made of 10, 12, or 14 complex rounds in which each round uses three to four transformations. The minimum key size of 128 bits (compared with the 56-bit key of DES) makes AES very secure. It is expected that AES will totally replace DES in the future.

16.3   ASYMMETRIC-KEY CRYPTOGRAPHY

Figure 16.7 shows the general idea of **asymmetric-key cryptography** as used for confidentiality. We will see other applications of asymmetric-key cryptography later in the chapter. The figure shows that, unlike symmetric-key cryptography, there are distinctive keys in asymmetric-key cryptography: a *private key* and a *public key*. If encryption and decryption are thought of as locking and unlocking padlocks with keys, then the padlock that is locked with a public key can be unlocked only with the corresponding private key. The figure shows that if Alice locks the padlock with Bob's public key, then only Bob's private key can unlock it.

Figure 16.7 illustrates several important facts. First, it emphasizes the asymmetric nature of the cryptosystem. The burden of providing security falls mostly on the shoulders of the recipient, in this case Bob. Bob needs to create two keys: one private and one public. He is responsible for distributing the public key to the community. This can be done through a public-key distribution channel. Although this channel is not required to provide secrecy, it must provide authentication and integrity. Eve should not be able to advertise her public key to the community pretending that it is Bob's public key.

Second, asymmetric-key cryptography means that Bob and Alice cannot use the same set of keys for two-way communication. Each individual in the community should create their own private and public keys. Figure 16.7 shows how Alice can use Bob's public key to send encrypted messages to Bob. If Bob wants to respond, Alice needs to establish her own private and public keys.

Third, asymmetric-key cryptography means that Bob needs only one private key to receive messages from anyone in the community, but Alice needs n public keys to communicate with n people in the community, one public key for each person. In other words, Alice needs a ring of public keys.

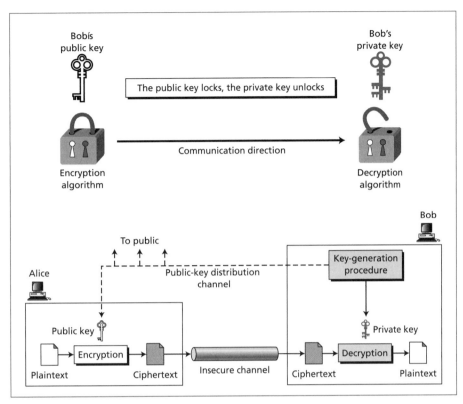

Figure 16.7 The general idea behind asymmetric-key cryptography

Plaintext/ciphertext

Unlike symmetric-key cryptography, plaintext and ciphertext are treated as integers in asymmetric-key cryptography. The message must be encoded as a long integer (or a set of long integers) before encryption: the integer (or the set of integers) must be decoded into the message after decryption. Asymmetric-key cryptography is normally used to encrypt or decrypt small pieces of information.

Encryption/decryption

Encryption and decryption in asymmetric-key cryptography are mathematical functions applied over the numbers representing the plaintext and ciphertext. The ciphertext can be thought of as $C = f(K_{public}, P)$: the plaintext can be thought of as $P = g(K_{private}, C)$ in which f and g are mathematical functions. The decryption function f is used only for encryption and the decryption function g is used only for decryption.

The most common public-key algorithm is the **RSA algorithm**, named after its inventors, Ron Rivest, Aid Shamir, and Leonard Adleman. In the RSA algorithm, Bob selects two prime numbers p and q and creates a modulus $n = p \times q$ (see Appendix G for modular arithmetic). Bob then calculates two exponents e and d using a process that is beyond the scope of this book. Bob's public key is (n and e)

and his private key is (d). If P is the plaintext and C is the ciphertext, encryption and decryption are shown below:

Encryption: $C = P^e \bmod n$ **Decryption:** $P = C^d \bmod n$

Example 16.3

Bob chooses $p = 7$ and $q = 11$ and calculates $n = 7 \times 11 = 77$. Now he chooses two exponents, 13 and 37, using the complex process mentioned before. The public key is ($n = 77$ and $e = 13$) and the private key is ($d = 37$). Now imagine that Alice wants to send the plaintext 5 to Bob. The following shows the encryption and decryption.

Encryption at Alice's site	Decryption at Bob's site
P:5 → $C = 5^{13} = 26 \bmod 77$	C:26 → $P = 26^{37} = 5 \bmod 77$

16.4   COMPARISON OF METHODS

Both symmetric-key and asymmetric-key cryptography will continue to exist in parallel. We believe that they are complements of each other: the advantages of one can compensate for the disadvantages of the other.

The number of secrets

The conceptual differences between the two systems are based on how these systems keep a secret. In symmetric-key cryptography, the secret token must be shared between two parties. In asymmetric-key cryptography, the token is unshared: each party creates its own token.

In symmetric-key cryptography, therefore, a bank with one million customers needs one million shared secret tokens if its customers want to send secret messages to the bank. In asymmetric-key cryptography, only one token is needed for this purpose.

In general, in a community of n people, $n(n - 1)/2$ shared tokens are needed for symmetric-key cryptography; only n tokens are needed in asymmetric-key cryptography. For a community with a population of 1 million, symmetric-key cryptography would require half a billion shared tokens, while asymmetric-key cryptography would require 1 million personal tokens.

> **Symmetric-key cryptography is based on sharing secrecy:**
> **asymmetric-key cryptography is based on personal secrecy.**

A need for both systems

There are other aspects of security besides confidentiality that need asymmetric-key cryptography. These include authentication and digital signatures (discussed later).

Whenever an application is based on a personal secret, we need to use asymmetric-key cryptography.

Whereas symmetric-key cryptography is based on substitution and permutation of symbols (characters or bits), asymmetric-key cryptography is based on applying mathematical functions to numbers. In symmetric-key cryptography, the plaintext and ciphertext are thought of as a combination of symbols. Encryption and decryption permute these symbols or substitute a symbol for another. In asymmetric-key cryptography, the plaintext and ciphertext are numbers: encryption and decryption are mathematical functions that are applied to numbers to create other numbers.

> **In symmetric-key cryptography, symbols are permuted or substituted:**
> **in asymmetric-key cryptography, numbers are manipulated.**

16.5   OTHER SECURITY SERVICES

The cryptography systems we have studied so far provide *secrecy*, or *confidentiality*, but none of the other services we discussed at the beginning of the chapter. In this section, we show how we can create other services.

Message integrity

There are occasions on which we may not even need secrecy but instead must have integrity. For example, Alice may write a will to distribute her estate upon her death. The will does not need to be encrypted: after her death, anyone can examine it. The integrity of the will, however, needs to be preserved: Alice does not want the contents of the will to be changed without her knowledge.

One way to preserve the integrity of a document was traditionally through the use of a *fingerprint*. If Alice needs to be sure that the contents of her document would not be changed, she could put her fingerprint at the bottom of the document. Eve cannot modify the contents of this document or create a false document because she cannot forge Alice's fingerprint. To ensure that the document has not been changed, Alice's fingerprint on the document could be compared to Alice's fingerprint on file. If they are not the same, the document is not from Alice.

The electronic equivalent of the document and fingerprint pair is the *message* and *digest* pair. To preserve the integrity of a message, the message is passed through an algorithm called a **cryptographic hash function**. The function creates a compressed image of the message that can be used like a fingerprint. Figure 16.8 shows the message, cryptographic hash function, and **message digest**.

The two pairs, document/fingerprint and message/message digest, are similar, with some differences. The document and fingerprint are physically linked

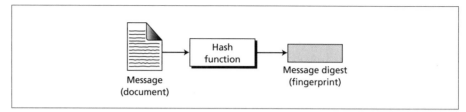

Figure 16.8   Message and digest

together. The message and message digest can be unlinked (or sent) separately, and, most importantly, the message digest needs to be safe from change.

> **The message digest needs to be safe from change.**

Checking integrity

To check the integrity of a message or document, we run the cryptographic hash function again and compare the new message digest with the previous one. If both are the same, we are sure that the original message has not been changed. Figure 16.9 shows the idea.

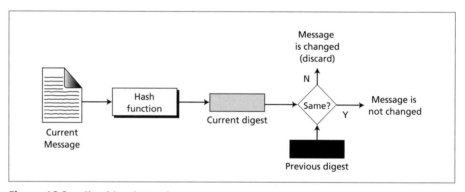

Figure 16.9   Checking integrity

Message authentication

A message digest guarantees the integrity of a message—it guarantees that the message has not been changed. A message digest, however, does not authenticate the sender of the message. When Alice sends a message to Bob, Bob needs to know that the message is really from Alice. To provide message authentication, Alice needs to provide proof that it is she who is sending the message and not an impostor. A message digest per se cannot provide such a proof. The digest created by a cryptographic hash function is normally called a *modification detection code* (MDC). The code can detect any modification in the message. What we need for message authentication (data origin authentication) is a *message authentication code* (MAC).

Message authentication code (MAC)

To ensure the integrity of the message and authenticate its origin—that Alice is the originator of the message and not somebody else—we need to change a modification detection code (MDC) to a **message authentication code (MAC)**. The difference between an MDC and an MAC is that the latter includes a secret between Alice and Bob—for example, some secret key that Eve, an eavesdropper, does not possess. Figure 16.10 shows the idea.

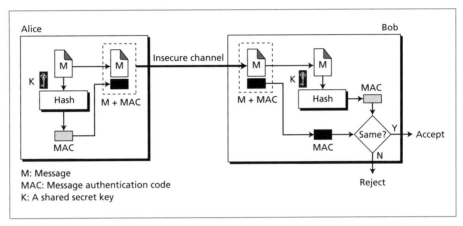

Figure 16.10 Message authentication code

Alice uses a hash function to create an MAC from the concatenation of the key and the message. She sends the message and the MAC to Bob over the insecure channel. Bob separates the message from the MAC. He then makes a new MAC from the concatenation of the message and the secret key. Bob then compares the newly created MAC with the one received. If the two MACs match, the message is authentic and has not been modified by an adversary.

Note that there is no need to use two channels in this case. Both message and the MAC can be sent on the same insecure channel. Eve can see the message, but she cannot forge a new message to replace it because she does not possess the secret key between Alice and Bob. She is unable to create the same MAC as Alice did.

Digital signatures

We are all familiar with the concept of a signature. A person signs a document to show that it originated from them or was approved by them. The signature is proof to the recipient that the document comes from the correct entity. When a customer signs a check, for example, the bank needs to be sure that the check was issued by that customer and nobody else. In other words, a signature on a document, when verified, is a sign of authentication—the document is authentic.

When Alice sends a message to Bob, Bob needs to check the authenticity of the sender: he needs to be sure that the message comes from Alice and not Eve. Bob can ask Alice to sign the message electronically. In other words, an electronic signature can prove the authenticity of Alice as the sender of the message. We refer to this type of signature as a **digital signature**.

There are several differences between a conventional and a digital signature:

- ❑ A conventional signature is included in the document: it is part of the document. When we write a check, the signature is on the check, not a separate document. But when we sign a document digitally, we send the signature as a separate document. The sender sends two documents: the message and the signature. The recipient receives both documents and verifies that the signature belongs to the supposed sender. If this is proven, the message is kept, otherwise it is rejected.

- ❑ The second difference between the two types of signatures is the method of verifying the signature. For a conventional signature, when the recipient receives a document, they compare the signature on the document with the signature on file. If they are the same, the document is authentic. The recipient needs to have a copy of the signature on file for comparison. For a digital signature, the recipient receives the message and the signature. A copy of the signature is not stored anywhere. The recipient needs to apply a verification technique to the combination of the message and the signature to verify the sender's authenticity.

- ❑ A person uses the same signature to sign many documents. Each message has its own digital signature. The digital signature of one message cannot be used in another message. If Bob receives two messages from Alice one after another, he cannot use the digital signature of the first message to verify the second—each message needs a new signature.

- ❑ Another difference between the two types of signatures is a quality called *duplicity*. A conventional signature allows a copy of the signed document to be distinguished from the original one on file. With a digital signature, there is no such distinction unless there is a factor of time (such as a timestamp) on the document. For example, suppose Alice sends a document instructing Bob to pay Eve. If Eve intercepts the document and the signature, she can replay it later to get money again from Bob.

Digital signature process

Figure 16.11 shows the digital signature process. The sender uses a **signing algorithm** to sign the message. The message and the signature are sent to the recipient. The recipient receives the message and the signature and applies the **verifying algorithm** to the combination. If the result is true, the message is accepted, otherwise it is rejected.

The need for keys

A conventional signature is like a private key belonging to the signer of the document. The signer uses it to sign documents: no one else has this signature. The copy of the signature is on file like a public key, so that anyone can use it to verify a document by comparing it to the original signature. With a digital signature, the signer uses his or her private key, applied to a signing algorithm, to sign the document. The verifier, on the other hand, uses the public key of the signer, applied to the verifying algorithm, to verify the document. Note that when a document is signed,

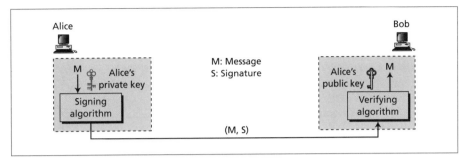

Figure 16.11 The digital signature process

anyone, including Bob, can verify it, because everyone has access to Alice's public key. Alice must not use her public key to sign the document because then anyone could forge her signature.

Can we use a secret (symmetric) key to both sign and verify a signature? The answer is negative for several reasons. First, a secret key is known by only two parties (Alice and Bob in this example). So if Alice needs to sign another document and send it to Ted, she needs to use another secret key. Second, as we will see, creating a secret key for a session involves authentication, which uses a digital signature. We therefore have a vicious circle. Third, Bob could use the secret key between himself and Alice, sign a document, send it to Ted, and pretend that it came from Alice.

> **A digital signature needs a public-key system. The signer signs with their private key, the verifier verifies with the signer's public key.**

We should make a distinction between private and public keys as used in digital signatures and public and private keys as used in a cryptosystem for confidentiality. In the latter, the private and public keys of the recipient are used in the process. The sender uses the public key of the recipient to encrypt and the recipient uses their own private key to decrypt. In a digital signature, the private and public keys of the sender are used. The sender uses his or her private key and the recipient uses the sender's public key.

> **A cryptosystem uses the private and public keys of the recipient: a digital signature uses the private and public keys of the sender.**

Signing the digest

Asymmetric-key cryptosystems are very inefficient when dealing with long messages. In a digital signature system, the messages are normally long, but we have to use asymmetric-key schemes. The solution is to sign a digest of the message, which is much shorter than the message itself. A carefully selected message digest has a one-to-one relationship with the message: the sender can sign the message digest and the recipient can verify the message digest—the effect is the same. Figure 16.12 shows signing of a digest in a digital signature system.

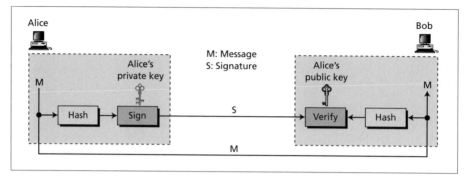

Figure 16.12 Signing the digest

A digest is made from the message at Alice's site. The digest then goes through the signing process using Alice's private key. Alice then sends the message and the signature to Bob.

At Bob's site, using the same public hash function, a digest is first created out of the received message. Calculations are done on the signature and the digest. The verifying process also applies criteria to the result of the calculation to determine the authenticity of the signature. If authentic, the message is accepted, otherwise it is rejected.

Services

A digital signature provides three out of our initial five security services: *message authentication*, *message integrity*, and *nonrepudiation*.

Message authentication

A secure digital signature scheme, like a secure conventional signature—that is, one that cannot be easily copied—can provide message authentication, also referred to as *data-origin authentication*. Bob can verify that the message is sent by Alice because Alice's public key is used in verification. Alice's public key cannot verify the signature signed by Eve's private key.

Message integrity

The integrity of the message is preserved even if we don't sign the whole message, because we cannot extract the same signature if the message is changed. The digital signature schemes today use a hash function in the signing and verifying algorithms that better preserves the integrity of the message.

Nonrepudiation

If Alice signs a message and then denies it, can Bob later prove that Alice actually signed it? For example, if Alice sends a message to a bank (Bob) and asks to transfer $10,000 from her account to Ted's account, can Alice later deny that she sent this message? With the scheme we have presented so far, Bob might have a problem. Bob must keep the signature on file and later use Alice's public key to create the original message to prove the message in the file and the newly created message are the same. This is not feasible, because Alice may have changed her private or public key during this time. She may also claim that the file containing the signature is not authentic.

One solution is a trusted third party. People can create an established trusted center among themselves. In such a scheme, Alice creates a signature from her message (S_A) and sends the message, her identity, Bob's identity, and the signature to the trusted center. The center, after checking that Alice's public key is valid, verifies through Alice's public key that the message came from Alice. The center then saves a copy of the message in its archive with the sender's identity, recipient's identity, and a timestamp. The center uses its private key to create another signature (S_T) from the message. The center then sends the message, the new signature, Alice's identity, and Bob's identity to Bob. Bob verifies the message using the public key of the trusted center: see Figure 16.13.

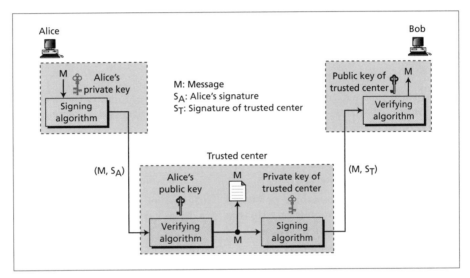

Figure 16.13 Nonrepudiation using digital signatures

If at some time in the future Alice denies that she sent the message, the center can show a copy of the saved message. If Bob's message is a duplicate of the message saved at the center, Alice will lose the dispute. To make everything confidential, a level of encryption and decryption can be added to the scheme.

Confidentiality

A digital signature does not provide confidential communication. If confidentiality is required, the message and the signature must be encrypted using either a secret-key or public-key cryptosystem.

Entity authentication

Entity authentication is a technique designed to let one party prove the identity of another party. An *entity* can be a person, a process, a client, or a server. The entity whose identity needs to be proved is called the *claimant*: the party that tries to prove the identity of the claimant is called the *verifier*. When Bob tries to prove the identity of Alice, Alice is the claimant, and Bob is the verifier.

Data-origin versus entity authentication

There are two differences between *message authentication (data-origin authentication)*, discussed before, and *entity authentication*, discussed in this section.

❑ Message authentication (or data-origin authentication) might not happen in real time, while entity authentication does. In the former, Alice sends a message to Bob. When Bob authenticates the message, Alice may or may not be present in the communication process. On the other hand, when Alice requests entity authentication, no real message communication is involved until Alice is authenticated by Bob. Alice needs to be online and to take part in the process. Only after she is authenticated can messages be communicated between Alice and Bob. Data-origin authentication is required when an e-mail is sent from Alice to Bob. Entity authentication is required when Alice gets cash from an automatic teller machine.

❑ Message authentication simply authenticates one message: the process needs to be repeated for each new message. Entity authentication authenticates the claimant for the entire duration of a session.

Verification categories

In entity authentication, the claimant must identify themselves to the verifier. This can be done with one of three kinds of witnesses: *something known, something possessed*, or *something inherent*.

❑ **Something known**. This is a secret known only by the claimant that can be checked by the verifier. Examples are a password, a PIN, a secret key, and a private key.

❑ **Something possessed**. This is something that can prove the claimant's identity. Examples are a passport, a driver's license, an identification card, a credit card, and a smart card.

❑ **Something inherent**. This is an inherent characteristic of the claimant. Examples are conventional signatures, fingerprints, voice, facial characteristics, retinal pattern, and handwriting.

Passwords

The simplest and oldest method of entity authentication is **password-based authentication**, where the password is something that the claimant *knows*. A password is used when a user needs to access a system to use the system's resources (login). Each user has a user identification that is public and a password that is private.

Challenge-response

In password authentication, the claimant proves their identity by demonstrating that they know a secret, the password. However, because the claimant reveals this secret, it is susceptible to interception by an adversary. In **challenge-response authentication**, the claimant proves that they *know* a secret without revealing it. In other words, the claimant does not send the secret to the verifier, the verifier either has it or finds it.

> **In challenge-response authentication, the claimant proves that they know a secret without revealing it to the verifier.**

The *challenge* is a time-varying value such as a random number or a timestamp that is sent by the verifier. The claimant applies a function to the challenge and sends the result, called a *response*, to the verifier. The response shows that the claimant knows the secret.

Zero-knowledge

In **zero-knowledge authentication**, the claimant does not reveal anything that might endanger the confidentiality of the secret. The claimant proves to the verifier that they know a secret, without revealing it. The interactions are so designed that they cannot lead to revealing or guessing the secret. After exchanging messages, the verifier only knows that the claimant does or does not have the secret, nothing more. The result is a yes/no situation, just a single bit of information.

For example, the claimant may show that they can easily find the square root of the challenge in modular arithmetic ($R = C^{1/2} \bmod n$) to prove that they know how n (a very large number) was originally calculated. Note that if the claimant has chosen two prime numbers p and q such that $n = p \times q$, the claimant knows how to find the square root of C. When the verifier receives R, they can calculate $C = R^2 \bmod n$. If the value of C is the same as the one sent by the verifier, this verifies that the claimant knows their secret (p and q). Note that the claimant never reveals p and q, only shows that they know them.

Biometrics

Biometrics is the measurement of physiological or behavioral features that identify a person—that is, authentication by something inherent. Biometrics measures features that cannot be guessed, stolen, or shared. Several components are needed for biometrics, including capturing devices, processors, and storage devices. Capturing devices such as readers or sensors measure biometric features. Processors change the measured features to the type of data appropriate for saving. Storage devices save the result of processing for authentication.

Before using any biometric techniques for authentication, the corresponding feature of each person in the authorized community must be available in a database. This is referred to as *enrollment*. Authentication is done by verification or identification. In verification, a person's feature is matched against a single record in the database (one-to-one matching) to find if they are who they are claiming to be. This is useful, for example, when a bank needs to verify a customer's signature on a check.

In identification, a person's feature is matched against all records in the database (one-to-many matching) to find if they have a record in the database. This is useful, for example, when a company needs to allow access to its building only to employees.

Techniques

Biometrics techniques can be divided into two broad categories: *physiological* and *behavioral*.

Physiological techniques measure the physical traits of the human body for verification and identification. To be effective, a trait should be unique among all or most of the population. In addition, the feature should be changeable due to aging, surgery, illness, disease, and so on. There are several physiological techniques.

Physiological characteristics that can form a basis of biometric identification include *fingerprint, iris, retina, face, hands, voice,* and *DNA*.

Behavioral techniques measure some human behavior traits. Unlike physiological techniques, behavioral techniques need to be monitored to ensure the claimant behaves normally and does not attempt to impersonate someone else. Among behavioral techniques are *signature* and *keystroke* recognition.

16.6   KEY MANAGEMENT

To use symmetric-key cryptography, a shared secret key needs to be established between the two parties. To use asymmetric-key cryptography, each entity needs to create a pair of keys and distribute the public key securely to the community. Key management defines some procedures to create and distribute keys securely.

Symmetric-key distribution

Symmetric-key cryptography is more efficient than asymmetric-key cryptography for enciphering large messages. Symmetric-key cryptography, however, needs a shared secret key between two parties.

In a community with n entities, $n(n-1)/2$ keys are needed for symmetric-key communication. The number of keys is not the only problem: the distribution of keys is another. If Alice and Bob want to communicate, they need a way to exchange a secret key. If Alice wants to communicate with a million people, how can she exchange a million keys with them? Using the Internet is definitely not a secure method. It is obvious that we need an efficient way to maintain and distribute secret keys.

Key-distribution center: KDC

A practical solution is the use of a trusted third party, referred to as a **key-distribution center (KDC)**. To reduce the number of keys, each person establishes a shared secret key with the KDC.

A secret key is established between the KDC and each member. Alice has a secret key with the KDC which we refer to as K_{Alice}, Bob has a secret key with the KDC which we refer to as K_{Bob}, and so on. Now the question is how Alice can send a confidential message to Bob. The process is as follows:

1. Alice sends a request to the KDC stating that she needs a session (temporary) secret key between herself and Bob.
2. The KDC informs Bob about Alice's request.
3. If Bob agrees, a session key is created between the two.

> **A session symmetric key between two parties is used only once.**

Public-key distribution

In asymmetric-key cryptography, people do not need a symmetric shared key. If Alice wants to send a message to Bob, she only needs to know Bob's public key, which is open to the public and available to everyone. If Bob needs to send a message to Alice, he only needs to know Alice's public key, which is also known to everyone. In public-key cryptography, everyone shields a private key and advertises a public key.

> **In public-key cryptography, everyone has access to everyone's public key – public keys are available to the public.**

Public keys, like secret keys, need to be distributed to be useful. Let us briefly discuss the ways in which public keys can be distributed.

Public announcement

The naive approach is to announce public keys publicly. Bob can put his public key on his web site or announce it in a local or national newspaper. When Alice needs to send a confidential message to Bob, she can obtain Bob's public key from his site or from the newspaper, or even send a message to ask for it.

This approach, however, is not secure—it is subject to forgery. For example, Eve could make such a public announcement. Before Bob can react, damage could be done. Eve could then fool Alice into sending her a message that is intended for Bob. Eve could also sign a document with a corresponding forged private key and make everyone believe it was signed by Bob. The approach is also vulnerable if Alice directly requests Bob's public key. Eve can intercept Bob's response and substitute her own forged public key for Bob's public key.

Trusted center

A more secure approach is to have a trusted center retain a directory of public keys. The directory, like the one used in a telephone system, is dynamically updated. Each user can select a private and public key, keep the private key, and deliver the public key for insertion into the directory. The center requires that each user register in the center and prove their identity. The directory can be publicly advertised by the trusted center. The center can also respond to any inquiry about a public key.

Certification authority

The previous approach can create a heavy load on the center if the number of requests is large. The alternative is to create **public-key certificates**. Bob wants two things: he wants people to know his public key, and he wants no-one to accept a forged public key as his.

Bob can go to a **certification authority (CA)**, a government authority that binds a public key to an entity and issues a certificate. The CA itself has a well-known public key that cannot be forged. The CA checks Bob's identification, for example by using a picture ID along with other proof. It then asks for Bob's public key and writes it on the certificate. To prevent the certificate itself from being forged, the CA signs the certificate with its private key. Now Bob can upload the signed certificate. Anyone who wants Bob's public key downloads the signed certificate and uses the center's public key to extract Bob's public key.

16.7 RECOMMENDED READING

For more details about the subjects discussed in this chapter, the following books are recommended:

❑   Bishop M: *Computer Security*, Reading, MA: Addison Wesley, 2002

❑   Forouzan B: *Cryptography and Network Security*, New York: McGraw-Hill, 2007

❑   Kaufman C, Perlman R, and Speciner M: *Network Security*, Upper Saddle River, NJ: Prentice Hall, 2002

❑   Stallings W: *Cryptography and Network Security*, Upper Saddle River, NJ: Prentice Hall, 2006

16.8 KEY TERMS

This chapter has introduced the following key terms, which are listed here with the pages on which they first occur:

access control 416	Advanced Encryption Standard (AES) 421
asymmetric-key cryptography 421	asymmetric-key encipherment 421
authentication 416	availability 414
biometrics 433	Caesar cipher 419
certification authority 435	cipher 417
ciphertext 417	confidentiality 414
cryptographic hash function 425	cryptography 416
data confidentiality 416	Data Encryption Standard (DES) 421
data integrity 416	decryption algorithm 417
denial of service 416	digital signature 428
encryption algorithm 417	entity authentication 431
hashing 417	integrity 414
key-distribution center 434	masquerading 415
message authentication code 427	message digest 425
modification 415	National Institute of Standards and Technology (NIST) 421
nonrepudiation 416	password-based authentication 432
plaintext 417	public-key certificate 435
replaying 415	repudiation 415
secret key 417	security attack 414
security goal 414	shift cipher 419
snooping 415	something inherent 432
something known 432	something possessed 432

16.9   SUMMARY

- We mentioned three goals of security: *confidentiality*, *integrity*, and *availability*.

- We have divided attacks on security into three categories: attacks threatening confidentiality, attacks threatening integrity, and attacks threatening availability.

- To achieve security goals and prevent the corresponding attacks, the ITU-U (International Telecommunication Union) has defined several services: *data confidentiality*, *data integrity*, *authentication*, *nonrepudiation*, and *access control*.

- Two techniques are used to provide these services: *cryptography* and *steganography*.

- *Symmetric-key cryptography* uses a single key for encryption and decryption. Alice and Bob first agree upon a shared secret, which forms their secret key. To send a message to Bob, Alice encrypts her message using the secret key: to send a message to Alice, Bob encrypts his message using the same secret key.

- Traditional symmetric-key ciphers were character-oriented and used two techniques for hiding information from an intruder: *substitution* and *transposition*.

- Modern symmetric-key ciphers are bit-oriented and use very complex algorithms to encrypt and decrypt blocks of bits.

- *Asymmetric-key cryptography* uses two distinct keys: a private key and a public key. Bob first creates a pair of keys. He keeps the private key and announces the public key. If anyone needs to send a message to Bob, they encrypt the message with Bob's public key. To read the message, Bob decrypts the message with his private key.

- *Integrity* means protecting a message from being modified. To preserve the integrity of a message, the message is passed through an algorithm called a *cryptographic hash function*. The function creates a compressed image of the message called a *message digest*.

- To provide message authentication, a message authentication code (MAC) is needed. An MAC includes a secret shared by the sender and the recipient.

- A digital signature is the process of signing a document electronically. It provides *message integrity*, *message authentication*, and *nonrepudiation*.

- Entity authentication is a technique designed to let one party prove the identity of another party. Entity authentication uses three verification categories: *something known*, *something possessed* and *something inherent*. We mentioned four authentication techniques: *password-based*, *challenge-response*, *zero-knowledge*, and *biometrics*.

- For symmetric-key or asymmetric-key cryptography, the two parties need to exchange keys. Key management methods allow us to do this without the need for face-to-face key exchange. In symmetric-key cryptography, a practical solution is the use of a key-distribution center (KDC). In asymmetric-key cryptography, a practical solution is the use of certificates issued by a certification authority (CA).

16.10 PRACTICE SET

Review questions

1. List and define three security goals discussed in this chapter.
2. List and define five security services discussed in this chapter.
3. Distinguish between cryptography and steganography.
4. Distinguish between a substitution cipher and a transposition cipher.
5. Distinguish between symmetric-key and asymmetric-key cryptography.
6. Distinguish between public and private keys in asymmetric-key cryptography.
7. Distinguish between message integrity and message authentication.
8. Compare and contrast a conventional signature and a digital signature.
9. List the security services provided by a digital signature.
10. List and define three kinds of identification witness in entity authentication.
11. Define a session key and show how a KDC can create a session key between Alice and Bob.
12. Define a certification authority (CA) and its relation to public-key cryptography.

Multiple-choice questions

13. In symmetric-key cryptography, there is (are) _____ key(s).
    a. one secret
    b. one private and one public
    c. either a or b
    d. both a and b
14. In asymmetric-key cryptography, there is (are) only _____ key(s).
    a. one secret
    b. one private and one public
    c. either a or b
    d. both a and b
15. _____ is achieved through encryption/decryption.
    a. Authentication
    b. Integrity

c. Confidentiality
d. Nonrepudiation

16. In symmetric-key cryptography, _____ possession of the secret key.
    a. only the sender has
    b. only the recipient has
    c. both the sender and the recipient have
    d. none of the above
17. To create a digest of a document, you can use _____.
    a. a symmetric-key cipher
    b. an asymmetric-key cipher
    c. a cryptographic hash function
    d. none of the above
18. In the digital signature method, the sender uses their _____ key to sign the message or digest.
    a. public
    b. private
    c. secret
    d. none of the above
19. In the digital signature method, the recipient uses the _____ key of the sender to verify the message.
    a. public
    b. private
    c. secret
    d. none of the above
20. In a digital signature involving a digest, the hash function is needed _____.
    a. only by the recipient
    b. only by the sender
    c. by both the sender and recipient
    d. none of the above
21. The digital signature method does not provide _____.
    a. confidentiality
    b. authentication
    c. integrity
    d. nonrepudiation
22. Snooping is a type of attack that threatens _____.
    a. confidentiality

b. integrity

c. availability

d. none of the above

23. Masquerading is a type of attack that threatens _____.

a. confidentiality

b. integrity

c. availability

d. none of the above

24. Denial of service is a type of attack that threatens _____.

a. confidentiality

b. integrity

c. availability

d. none of the above

25. Repudiation is a type of attack that threatens _____.

a. confidentiality

b. integrity

c. availability

d. none of the above

26. DES is an example of a modern _____.

a. symmetric-key cipher

b. asymmetric-key cipher

c. cryptography hashing function

d. none of the above

27. AES is an example of a modern _____.

a. symmetric-key cipher

b. asymmetric-key cipher

c. cryptography hashing function

d. none of the above

28. In entity authentication, a password is _____.

a. something known

b. something possessed

c. something inherent

d. none of the above

29. In entity authentication, a passport is _____.

a. something known

b. something possessed

c. something inherent

d. none of the above

30. In entity authentication, handwriting is _____.

a. something known

b. something possessed

c. something inherent

d. none of the above

31. A KDC is used for key distribution in _____ cryptography.

a. symmetric-key

b. asymmetric-key

c. both a and b

d. neither a nor b

32. A CA is used for key distribution in _____ cryptography.

a. symmetric-key

b. asymmetric-key

c. both a and b

d. neither a nor b

Exercises

33. Which of cryptography or steganography is used in each of the following cases for confidentiality?

a. A student writes the answers to a test on a small piece of paper, rolls up the paper, inserts it in a ball-point pen, and passes the pen to another student.

b. To send a message, a spy replaces each character in the message with a symbol that was agreed upon in advance as the character's replacement.

c. A company uses special ink on its checks to prevent forgeries.

d. A graduate student uses watermarks to protect their thesis, which is posted on their web site.

34. A small private club has only 100 members. Answer the following questions:

a. How many secret keys are needed if all members of the club need to send secret messages to each other?

b. How many secret keys are needed in the following scenario? Everyone trusts the president of the club. If a member needs to send a message to another member, they first send it to the president, and the president then sends the message to the other member.

c. How many secret keys are needed if the president decides that the two members who need to communicate should contact him first. The president then creates a temporary key to be used between the two. The temporary key is encrypted and sent to both members.

35. Alice often needs to encipher plaintext written in lowercase letters (a to z). If she uses a shift cipher, what is the range of keys from which she can select?

36. In a shift cipher, what is the maximum number of characters that will be changed in the ciphertext if only a single character is changed in the plaintext?

37. In a simple transposition cipher, what is the maximum number of characters that will be changed in the ciphertext if only a single character is changed in the plaintext?

38. Encrypt the message "this is an exercise" using a shift cipher with key 7. Ignore the space between words. Decrypt the message to get the original plaintext.

39. Encrypt the message "this is an exercise" using a simple transposition cipher with the following key:

1	2	3	4
4	3	2	1

Encryption ↓   ↑ Decryption

Ignore the space between words. Decrypt the message to get the original plaintext.

40. To understand the security of the RSA algorithm, find d if you know that $e = 17$ and $n = 187$.

41. In the RSA algorithm, given $e = 13$ and $n = 100$, encrypt the message "HI" using 00 to 25 for letters A to Z.

42. In the RSA algorithm, why can't Bob choose 1 as the public key e?

43. Assume we have a very simple message digest. Our unrealistic message digest is just one number between 0 and 25. The digest is initially set to 0. The cryptographic hash function adds the current value of the digest to the value of the current character (between 0 and 25). Addition is in modulo 26. Find the digest if the message is "HELLO".

44. Fixed and one-time passwords are two extremes. What about frequently changed passwords? How do you think this scheme can be implemented? What are the advantages and disadvantages?

45. How can a system prevent a guessing attack on a password? How can a bank prevent PIN guessing if someone has found or stolen a bank card and tries to use it?

46. Discuss the effectiveness of the Caesar cipher. Can an intruder guess the key by looking only at the ciphertext? If so, how?

47. One of the operations used in a secret key algorithm is the permutation of bits. An 8-bit plaintext is permuted (scrambled). Bit 1 becomes bit 3, bit 2 becomes bit 7, and so on. Draw a diagram to show the encryption and decryption. Choose your own scrambling. What is the key here? What is the encryption algorithm? What is the decryption algorithm?

48. One operation in a secret key algorithm is the XOR operation. A fixed-size bit pattern (plaintext) is XORed with the same size bit pattern (key) to create a fixed-sized ciphertext. What is the encryption algorithm here? What is the decryption algorithm? Use the fact that an XOR algorithm is a reversible algorithm.

49. Use the public key ($n = 15$, $e = 3$) to encrypt the number 7. Use the private key ($d = 11$) to decrypt the result of the previous encryption.

50. Prove that the role of the public key and private key can be changed by repeating the previous exercise, but encrypt the number 7 with the public key ($n = 15$, $e = 11$) and decrypt it with the public key ($d = 3$).

51. Discuss why symmetric-key cryptography cannot be used for nonrepudiation.

52. Discuss why symmetric-key cryptography cannot be used for authentication.

53. Add a layer of symmetric-key encryption/decryption to Figure 16.11 to provide privacy.

54. Add a layer of asymmetric-key encryption/decryption to Figure 16.11 to provide privacy.

17

Theory of Computation

In Chapters 1 through 16, we consider a computer as a problem-solving machine. In this chapter, we answer some questions such as: which problems can be solved by a computer? Is one language superior to another? Before running a program, can it be determined whether the program will halt (terminate) or run forever? How long does it take to solve a problem using a particular language? To answer these questions, we turn to a discipline called the *theory of computation*.

Objectives

After studying this chapter, the student should be able to:

❑ Describe a programming language we call Simple Language and define its basic statements.

❑ Write macros in Simple Language using the combination of simple statements.

❑ Describe the components of a Turing machine as a computation model.

❑ Show how simple statements in Simple Language can be simulated using a Turing machine.

❑ Understand the Church-Turing thesis and its implication.

❑ Define the Gödel number and its application.

❑ Understand the concept of the halting problem and how it can be proved that this problem is unsolvable.

❑ Distinguish between solvable and unsolvable problems.

❑ Distinguish between polynomial and non-polynomial solvable problems.

This chapter is a brief introduction to the *theory of computation*. First, we introduce a language we call Simple Language, to show that the minimum number of statements needed to solve any problem that is solvable by a computer is three. Second, we explain another tool, a computer model called the *Turing machine*, which we introduced in Chapter 1. We show that a problem that can be solved by our Simple Language can also be solved by the Turing machine. Third, we prove that no program can tell whether another program halts or not. This proof is itself an indication that there are problems that cannot be solved by a computer. Finally, we briefly discuss the complexity of algorithms. The ideas represented in this chapter are from pioneers in computer science, such as Alan Turing, Kurt Gödel, Marvin Minsky, Alonzo Church, and Stephen Cole Kleene.

17.1   SIMPLE LANGUAGE

We can define a computer language with only three statements: the **increment statement**, the **decrement statement**, and the **loop statement** (Figure 17.1). In this language, the only data type we use is nonnegative integers. There is no need for any other data type, because the goal of the chapter is merely to demonstrate some ideas in computation theory. The language uses only a few symbols such as "{" and "}".

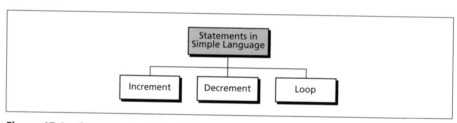

Figure 17.1   Statements in Simple Language

Increment statement

The **increment statement** adds 1 to a variable. The format is shown in Algorithm 17.1.

Algorithm 17.1   The increment statement

```
incr (X)
```

Decrement statement

The **decrement statement** subtracts 1 from a variable. The format is shown in Algorithm 17.2.

Algorithm 17.2   The decrement statement

```
decr (X)
```

Loop statement

The **loop statement** repeats an action (or a series of actions) while the value of the variable is not 0. The format is shown in Algorithm 17.3.

Algorithm 17.3   Loop statement

```
while (X)
{
      decr (X)
      Body of the loop

}
```

The power of the Simple Language

It can be shown that this simple programming language with only three statements is as powerful—although not necessarily as efficient—as any sophisticated language in use today, such as C. To do so, we show how we can simulate several statements found in some popular languages.

Macros in Simple Language

We call each simulation a **macro** and use it in other simulations without the need to repeat code. A *macro* (short for *macroinstruction*) is an instruction in a high-level language that is equivalent to a specific set of one or more ordinary instructions in the same language.

First macro: X ← 0

Algorithm 17.4 shows how to use the statements in Simple Language to assign 0 to a variable X. It is sometimes called *clearing* a variable.

Algorithm 17.4   Macro X ← 0

```
while (X)
{
      decr (X)

}
```

Second macro: X ← n

Algorithm 17.5 shows how to use the statements in Simple Language to assign a positive integer n to a variable X. First clear the variable X, then increment X n times.

Algorithm 17.5   Macro X ← n

```
X ← 0
incr (X)
incr (X)
...
incr (X)                          // The statement incr (X) is repeated n times.
```

Third macro: Y ← X

Algorithm 17.6 simulates the macro Y ← X in Simple Language. Note that we can use an extra line of code to restore the value of X.

Algorithm 17.6   Macro Y ← X

```
Y ← 0
while (X)
{
        decr (X)
        incr (Y)
}
```

Fourth macro: Y ← Y + X

Algorithm 17.7 simulates the macro Y ← Y + X in Simple Language. Again, we can use more code lines to restore the value of X to its original value.

Algorithm 17.7   Macro Y ← Y + X

```
while (X)
{
        decr (X)
        incr (Y)
}
```

Fifth macro: Y ← Y × X

Algorithm 17.8 simulates the macro Y ← Y × X in Simple Language. We can use the addition macro because integer multiplication can be simulated by repeated addition. Note that we need to preserve the value of X in a temporary variable, because in each addition we need the original value of X to be added to Y.

Algorithm 17.8   Macro Y ← Y × X

```
TEMP ← Y
Y ← 0
while (X)
{
        decr (X)
        Y ← Y + TEMP
}
```

Sixth macro: Y ← Y^X

Algorithm 17.9 simulates the macro Y ← Y^X in Simple Language. We do this using the multiplication macro because integer exponentiation can be simulated by repeated multiplication.

Algorithm 17.9 Macro Y ← Y^X

```
TEMP ← Y
Y ← 1
while (X)
{
        decr (X)
        Y ← Y × TEMP
}
```

Seventh macro: if X then A

Algorithm 17.10 simulates the seventh macro in Simple Language. This macro simulates the decision-making (*if*) statement of modern languages. In this macro, the variable X has only one of the two values 0 or 1. If the value of X is not 0, A (an action or a series of actions) is executed in the loop. However, the loop is executed only once because, after the first iteration, the value of X becomes 0 and we come out of the loop. If the value of X is originally 0, the loop is skipped.

Algorithm 17.10 Macro if X then A

```
while (X)
{
        decr (X)
        A
}
```

Other macros

It is obvious that we need more macros to make Simple Language compatible with contemporary languages. Creating other macros is possible, although not trivial.

Input and output

In this simple language the statement *read* X can be simulated using (X ← *n*). We also simulate the output by assuming that the last variable used in a program holds what should be printed. Remember that this is not a practical language, it is merely designed to prove some theorems in computer science.

17.2 THE TURING MACHINE

The **Turing machine** was introduced in 1936 by Alan M. Turing to solve computable problems, and is the foundation of modern computers. In this section we introduce a very simplified version of the machine to show how it works.

Turing machine components

A Turing machine is made of three components: a tape, a controller, and a read/write head (Figure 17.2).

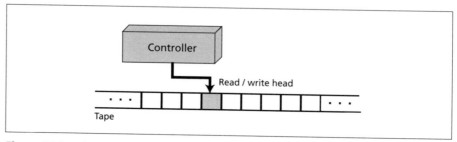

Figure 17.2   The Turing machine

Tape

Although modern computers use a random-access storage device with finite capacity, we assume that the Turing machine's memory is infinite. The **tape**, at any one time, holds a sequence of characters from the set of characters accepted by the machine. For our purpose, we assume that the machine can accept only two symbols: a blank (**b**) and digit 1. Figure 17.3 shows an example of data on a tape in this machine.

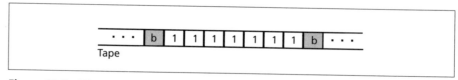

Figure 17.3   The tape in the Turing machine

The left-hand blank defines the beginning of the nonnegative integers stored on the tape. An integer is represented by a string of 1s, and the right-hand blank defines the end of the integer. The rest of the tape contains blank characters. If more than one integer is stored on the tape, they are separated by at least one blank character.

We also assume that the tape processes only positive integer data represented in unary arithmetic. In this arithmetic, a positive integer is made up only of 1s. For example, the integer 4 is represented as 1111 (four 1s) and the integer 7 is represented as 1111111 (seven 1s). The absence of 1s represents 0.

Read/write head

The **read/write head** at any moment points to one symbol on the tape. We call this symbol the *current* symbol. The read/write head reads and writes one symbol at a time from the tape. After reading and writing, it moves to the left or to the right. Reading, writing, and moving are all done under instructions from the controller.

Controller

The controller is the theoretical counterpart of the central processing unit (CPU) in modern computers. It is a finite state automaton, a machine that has a predetermined finite number of **states** and moves from one state to another based on the input. At any moment, it can be in one of these states.

Figure 17.4 shows the transition state diagram for a simple controller as a finite state automaton. In this figure, the automaton has only three states (A, B, and C), although a controller normally has many states. The diagram shows the change of state as a function of the character read. The expression on each line, $x/y/L$, $x/y/R$, and $x/y/N$, shows that if the controller has read the symbol x, it writes the symbol y (overwrites x), and the read/write head moves to the left (L), right (R), or does not move (N). Note that since the symbols on the tape can be only a blank or the digit 1, there should be two paths out of each state: one if the blank symbol is read and one if the digit 1 is read. The beginning of the line (called the *transition* line) shows the current state and the end of the line (arrow head) shows the next state.

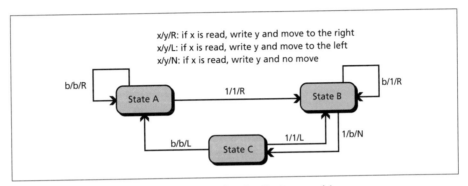

Figure 17.4 Transition state diagram for the Turing machine

We can create a transition table in which each row relates to one state. The table will have five columns: the current state, the symbol that is read, the symbol to write, the direction of movement of the head, and the next symbol. Since the machine can only go through a finite number of states, we can create an instruction set like the one we created for the simple computer in Chapter 5.

Table 17.1 Transition table

Current state	Read	Write	Move	New state
A	b	b	R	A
A	1	1	R	B
B	b	1	R	B
B	1	b	N	C
C	b	b	L	A
C	1	1	L	B

The instructions put together the value of five columns in each row. For this elementary machine, we have only six instructions:

1. (A, b, b, R, A)	3. (B, b, 1, R, B)	5. (C, b, b, L, A)
2. (A, 1, 1, R, B)	4. (B, 1, b, N, C)	6. (C, 1, 1, L, B)

For example, the first instruction says that if the machine is in state A and has read the symbol b, it overwrites the symbol with a new b, moves to the next symbol to the right, and the machine transitions to state A—that is, remains in the same state.

Example 17.1

A Turing machine has only two states and the following four instructions:

1. (A, b, b, L, A)	2. (A, 1, 1, R, B)	3. (B, b, b, L, A)	4. (B, 1, b, R, A)

If the machine starts with the configuration shown in Figure 17.5, what is the configuration of the machine after executing one of the above instructions? Note that the machine can only execute one of the instructions, the one that matches the current state and the current symbol.

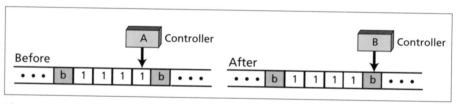

Figure 17.5   Example 17.1

Solution
The machine is in state A and the current symbol is 1, which means that only the second instruction, (A, 1, 1, R, B) can be executed. The new configuration is also shown in Figure 17.5. Note that the state of the controller has been changed to B and the read/write head has moved one symbol to the right.

Simulating Simple Language

We can now write programs that implement the statements of Simple Language. Note that these statements can be written in many different ways: we have chosen the simplest or most convenient for our educational purpose, but they are not necessarily the best ones.

Increment statement

Figure 17.6 shows the Turing machine for the **incr**(X) statement. The controller has four states, S_1 through S_4. State S_1 is the starting state, state S_2 is the moving-right state, state S_3 is the moving-left state, and state 4 is the halting state. If the machine reaches the halting state, it stops: there is no instruction that starts with this state.

Figure 17.6 also shows the program for the **incr** (X) statement. It has only five instructions. The process starts from the blank symbol at the left of X (data to be incremented), moves right over all 1s until it reaches the blank symbol at the right of X. It changes this blank to 1. It then moves left over all 1s until it reaches the blank at the left again. At this point it halts. Note that we have also written the program to move the read/write head back to the blank symbol to the left of X, which is necessary if more operations are to be performed on X.

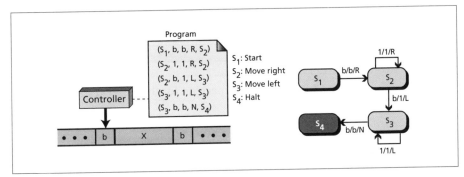

Figure 17.6 The Turing machine for the **incr (X)** statement

Example 17.2
Show how the Turing machine can increment X when X = 2.

Solution
Figure 17.7 shows the solution. The value of X (11 in the unary system) is stored between the two blank symbols. It takes seven steps for the machine to increment X and return the read/write head to its original position. Steps 1 to 4 move the read/write head to the end of X. Steps 5 to 7 change the blank at the end and move the read/write head back to where it was before.

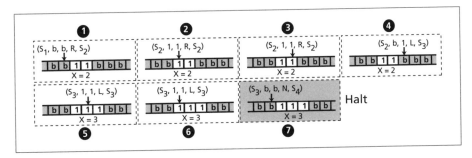

Figure 17.7 Example 17.2

Decrement statement

We implement the **decr** (X) statement using the minimum number of instructions. The reason is that we need to use this statement in the next statement, the *while* loop, which will also be used to implement all macros. Figure 17.8 shows the Turing machine for this statement. The controller has three states, S_1, S_2, and S_3. Statement S_1 is the starting state. State S_2 is the checking statement, which checks to see if the current symbol is 1 or b. If it is b, the statement goes to the halting state: if the next symbol is 1, the second statement changes it to b and goes to the halting state. Figure 17.8 also shows the program for this statement.

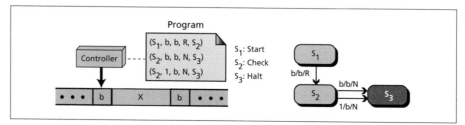

Figure 17.8 The Turing machine for the decr (X) statement

Example 17.3

Show how the Turing machine can decrement X when X = 2.

Solution
Figure 17.9 shows the situation. The machine starts at the blank to the left of the data and changes the next symbol to blank if it is 1. The read/write head stops over the blank character to the left of the resulting data. This is the same arrangement as with the increment statement. Note that we could have moved the read/write head to the end of the data and deleted the last 1 instead of the first one, but that program would be much longer than our version. Since we need this statement in every loop statement, we have used the shorter version to save the number of instructions. We use the short version of this statement in the *while* loop statement that we develop next.

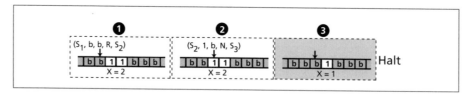

Figure 17.9 Example 17.3

Loop statement

To simulate the loop, we assume that X and the data to be processed by the body of the loop are stored on the tape separated by a single blank symbol. Figure 17.10 shows the table, the program, and the state transition diagram for a general loop statement.

The three states S_1, S_2, and S_3 control the loops by determining X and exiting the loop if X = 0. Compare these three statements to the three statements used in the decrement statement in Figure 17.8. The state M_R moves the read/write head over the blank symbol that defines the start of the data at the beginning of processing

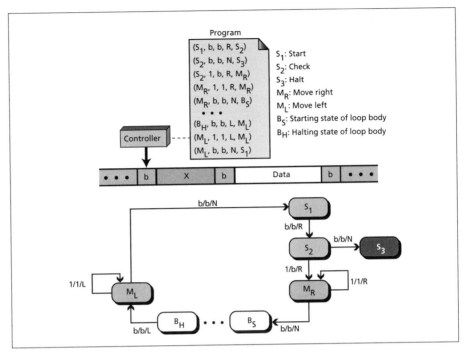

Figure 17.10 The Turing machine for the **while** loop statement

data in each iteration: the state M_L moves the read/write head over the blank symbol defining the start of the X at the end of processing in each iteration. The state B_S (*body start*) defines the beginning state of the body of the loop, while the state B_H (*body halt*) defines the halting state for the body of the loop. The body of the loop may have several states between these two states.

Figure 17.10 also shows the repetitive nature of the statement. The state diagram itself is a loop that is repeated as long as the value of X is not zero. When the value of X becomes 0, the loop stops and state S_3, the halting state, is reached.

Example 17.4

Let us show a very simple example. Suppose we want to simulate the fourth macro, $Y \leftarrow Y + X$ (page 444). As we discussed before, this macro can be simulated using the while statement in Simple Language:

```
while (X)
{
        decr (X)
        incr (Y)
}
```

To make the procedure shorter, we assume that X = 2 and Y = 3, so the result is Y = 5. Figure 17.11 shows the state of the tape before and after applying the macro.

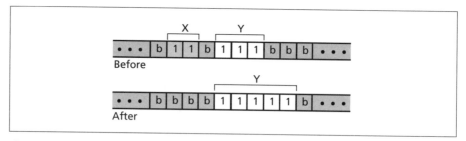

Figure 17.11 Configuration of the tapes for Example 17.4

Note that in this program we erase the value of X to make the process shorter, but the original value of X can be preserved if we allow other symbols on the tape.

Since X = 2, the program goes through two iterations. Figure 17.12 shows the first iteration.

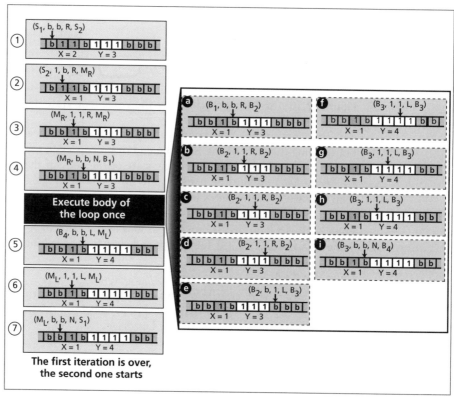

Figure 17.12 First iteration in Example 17.4

At the end of this iteration, the value of X = 1 and the value of Y = 4. Note that the first four steps (1, 2, 3, 4) decrement the value of X and move the read/write head over the blank before the value of Y. At this moment steps *a* to *i* are executed. Steps *a* to *i* correspond to steps B_S and B_H and the states in between in Figure

17.10. Nine steps are needed to increment Y and return the read/write head to its original position. After incrementing Y, the control returns the loop and steps 5, 6. and 7 are executed to move the read/write head to the beginning of X.

Figure 17.13 shows the second iteration.

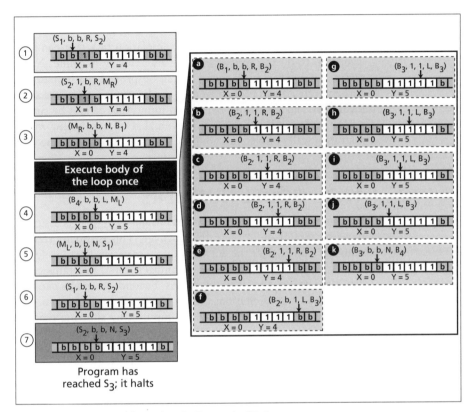

Figure 17.13 Second iteration in Example 17.4

At the beginning of this iteration, the value of X = 1 and the value of Y = 4. At the end of the second iteration, the value of X = 0 and the value of Y = 5. The loop stops and the value of Y is what we expect.

This example definitely shows that the Turing machine is not efficient if it is implemented in the way we have shown in this program. However, the purpose is not to implement the addition of two small integers using the Turing machine: the purpose is to show that Turing machines can solve any problem that a modern program can solve.

The Church–Turing thesis

We have shown that a Turing machine can simulate the three basic statements in Simple Language. This means that the Turing machine can also simulate all the macros we defined for Simple Language. Can the Turing machine therefore solve any problem that can be solved by a computer? The answer to this question can be found in the **Church–Turing thesis**.

The Church–Turing Thesis
If an algorithm exists to do a symbol manipulation task,
then a Turing machine exists to do that task.

Based on this claim, any symbol-manipulation task that can be done by writing an algorithm to do so can also be done by a Turing machine. Note that this is only a *thesis*, not a *theorem*. A theorem can be proved mathematically, a thesis cannot. Although this thesis probably never can be proved, there are strong arguments in its favor. First, no algorithms have been found that cannot be simulated using a Turing machine. Second, it has been proven that all computing models that *have* been mathematically proved are equivalent to the Turing machine model.

17.3 GÖDEL NUMBERS

In theoretical computer science, an unsigned number is assigned to every program that can be written in a specific language. This is usually referred to as the **Gödel number**, named after the Austrian mathematician Kurt Gödel.

This assignment has many advantages. First, programs can be used as a single data item as input to other programs. Second, programs can be referred to by just their integer representations. Third, the numbering can be used to prove that some problems cannot be solved by a computer, by showing that the total number of problems in the world is much larger than the total number of programs that can ever be written.

Different methods have been devised for numbering programs. We use a very simple transformation to number programs written in our Simple Language. Simple Language uses only fifteen symbols (Table 17.2).

Table 17.2 Code for symbols used in Simple Language

Symbol	Hex code	Symbol	Hex code
1	1	9	9
2	2	incr	A
3	3	decr	B
4	4	while	C
5	5	{	D
6	6	}	E
7	7	X	F
8	8		

Note that in this language we use only X, X_1, X_2, ..., X_9 as variables. To encode these variables, we handle X_n as two symbols X and n (X_3 is X and 3). If we have a macro with other variables, they need to be changed to X_n.

Representing a program

Using the table, we can represent any program written in Simple Language by a unique positive integer by following these steps:

1. Replace each symbol with the corresponding hexadecimal code from the table.
2. Interpret the resulting hexadecimal number as an unsigned integer.

Example 17.5

What is the Gödel number for the program **incr** (X)?

Solution
Replace each symbol by its hexadecimal code.

incr X → $(AF)_{16}$ → 175

So this program can be represented by the number 175.

Interpreting a number

To show that the numbering system is unique, use the following steps to interpret a Gödel number:

1. Convert the number to hexadecimal.
2. Interpret each **hexadecimal digit** as a symbol using Table 17.2 (ignore a 0).

Note that while any program written in Simple Language can be represented by a number, not every number can be interpreted as a valid program. After conversion, if the symbols do not follow the syntax of the language, the number is not a valid program.

Example 17.6

Interpret 3058 as a program.

Solution
Change the number to hexadecimal and replace each digit with the corresponding symbol:

3058 → $(BF2)_{16}$ → decr X 2 → **decr** (X_2)

This means that the equivalent code in Simple Language is **decr** (X_2). Note that in Simple Language, each program includes input and output. This means that the combination of a program and its inputs defines the Gödel number.

17.4   THE HALTING PROBLEM

Almost every program written in a programming language involves some form of repetition—loops or recursive functions. A repetition construct may never terminate (halt): that is, a program can run forever if it has an infinite loop. For example, the following program in Simple Language never terminates:

```
X ← 1
while (X)
{

}
```

A classical programming question is:

> **Can we write a program that tests whether or not any program, represented by its Gödel number, will terminate?**

The existence of this program would save programmers a lot of time. Running a program without knowing if it halts or not is a tedious job. Unfortunately, it has now been proven that such a program cannot exist—much to the disappointment of programmers!

The halting problem is not solvable

Instead of saying that the testing program does not exist and can never exist, the computer scientist says "The **halting problem** is not solvable".

Proof

Let us give an informal proof about the nonexistence of this testing program. Our method, called *proof by contradiction*, is often used in mathematics: we assume that the program does exist, then show that its existence creates a contradiction—therefore, it cannot exist. We use three steps to show the proof in this approach.

Step 1

In this step, we assume that a program, called Test, exists. It can accept any program such as P, represented by its Gödel number, as input, and outputs either 1 or 0. If P terminates, the output of Test is 1: if P does not terminate, the output of Test is 0 (Figure 17.14).

Step 2

In this step, we create another program called Strange that is made of two parts: a copy of Test at the beginning and an empty loop—a loop with an empty body—at the end. The loop uses X as the testing variable, which is actually the output of the Test program. This program also uses P as the input. We call this program Strange for the following reason: if P terminates, the first part of Strange, which is a copy of Test, outputs 1. This 1 is input to the loop. The loop does not terminate—it's an infinite loop—and consequently Strange does not terminate. If P does not terminate, the first part of Strange, which is a copy of Test, outputs 0. This 0 is input to

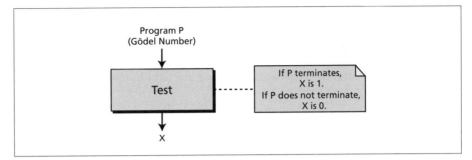

Figure 17.14 Step 1 in the proof

the loop, so the loop does terminate—it's now a finite loop, the loop never iterates—and consequently, Strange does terminate. In other words, we have these strange situations:

If P terminates, Strange does not terminate.
If P does not terminate, Strange terminates.

Figure 17.15 shows step two of the proof.

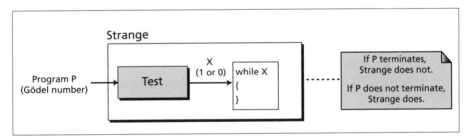

Figure 17.15 Step 2 in the proof

Step 3

Having written the program Strange, we test it with itself (its Gödel number) as input. This is legitimate because we did not put any restrictions on P. Figure 17.16 shows the situation.

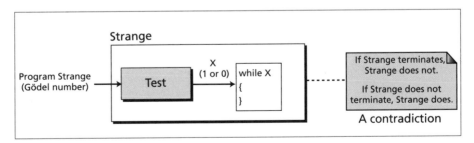

Figure 17.16 Step 3 in the proof

Contradiction

> If we assume that Test exists, we have the following contradictions:
> Strange does not terminate if Strange terminates.
> Strange terminates if Strange does not terminate.

This proves that the Test program cannot exist and that we should stop looking for it, so...

| The halting problem is unsolvable. |

The unsolvability of the halting program has proved that many other programs are also unsolvable, because if they are solvable, then the halting problem is solvable—which it is not.

17.5   THE COMPLEXITY OF PROBLEMS

Now that we have shown that at least one problem is unsolvable by a computer, we'll touch on this important issue a bit more. In computer science, we can say that, in general, problems can be divided into two categories: **solvable problems** and **unsolvable problems**. The solvable problems can themselves be divided into two categories: *polynomial* and *non-polynomial* problems (Figure 17.17).

Unsolvable problems

There is an infinite number of problems that cannot be solved by a computer: one is the halting problem. One method to prove that a problem is not solvable is to show that if that problem is solvable, the halting problem is solvable too. In other words, prove that the solvability of a problem results in the solvability of the halting problem.

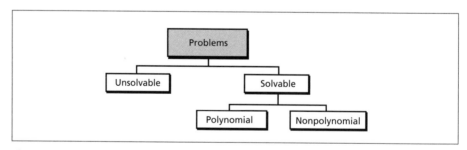

Figure 17.17 Taxonomy of problems

Solvable problems

There are many problems that *can* be solved by a computer. However, we often want to know how *long* it takes for the computer to solve that problem. In other words, how complex is the program?

The complexity of a program can be measured in several different ways, such as its run time, the memory it needs, and so on. One approach is the program's run time—how long does the program take to run?

Complexity of solvable problems

One way to measure the complexity of a solvable problem is to find the number of operations executed by the computer when it runs the program. In this way, the complexity measure is independent of the speed of the computer that runs the program. This measure of complexity can depend on the number of inputs. For example, if a program is processing a list, such as sorting it, the complexity depends on the number of elements in the list.

Big-O notation

With the speed of computers today, we are not as concerned with exact numbers as with general orders of magnitude. For example, if the analysis of two programs shows that one executes fifteen operations (or a set of operations) while the other executes twenty-five, they are both so fast that we can't see the difference. On the other hand, if the numbers are fifteen versus 1500, we should be concerned.

This simplification of efficiency is known as **big-O notation**. We present the idea of this notation without delving into its formal definition and calculation. In big-O notation, the number of operations—or a set of related operations—is given as a function of the number of inputs. The notation $O(n)$ means a program does n operations for n inputs, while the notation $O(n^2)$ means a program does n^2 operations for n inputs.

Example 17.7

Imagine we have written three different programs to solve the same problem. The first one has a complexity of $O(\log_{10} n)$, the second $O(n)$, and the third $O(n^2)$. Assuming 1 million inputs, how long does it take to execute each of these programs on a computer that executes one instruction in 1 microsecond, that is, 1 million instructions per second?

Solution

The following shows the analysis:

1st program:	$n = 1{,}000{,}000$	$O(\log_{10} n) \rightarrow 6$	Time $\rightarrow$ 6 µs
2nd program:	$n = 1{,}000{,}000$	$O(n) \rightarrow 1{,}000{,}000$	Time $\rightarrow$ 1 sec
3rd program:	$n = 1{,}000{,}000$	$O(n^2) \rightarrow 10^{12}$	Time $\rightarrow$ 277 h

Polynomial problems

If a program has a complexity of $O(\log n)$, $O(n)$, $O(n^2)$, $O(n^3)$, $O(n^4)$, or $O(n^k)$, where k is a constant, it is called *polynomial*. With the speed of computers today, we can get solutions to **polynomial problems** with a reasonable number of inputs, for example 1000 to 1 million.

Non-polynomial problems

If a program has a complexity that is greater than a polynomial—for example, $O(10^n)$ or $O(n!)$—it can be solved if the number of inputs is very small, such as fewer than 100. If the number of inputs is large, one could sit in front of the computer for months to see the result of a **non-polynomial problem**. But who knows? At the rate at which the speed of computers is increasing, we may be able to get a result for this type of problem in time.

17.6   RECOMMENDED READING

For more details about the subjects discussed in this chapter, the following books are recommended:

❑   Hennie F: *Introduction to Computability*, Reading, MA: Addison Wesley,1977

❑   Hofstadter D: *Gödel, Escher, Bach: An Eternal Golden Braid*, St. Paul, MN: Vintage, 1980

❑   Hopcroft J, Motwani R, and Ullman J: *Introduction to Automata Theory, Languages, and Computation*, Reading, MA: Addison Wesley, 2006

❑   Kfoury A, Moll R and Michael A: *A Programming Approach to Computability*, New York: Springer, 1982

❑   Minsky M: *Computation: Finite and Infinite Machines*, Engelwood Cliffs, NJ: Prentice-Hall, 1967

❑   Sipser M: *Introduction the Theory of Computation*, Boston, MA: Course Technology, 2005

17.7   KEY TERMS

This chapter has introduced the following key terms, which are listed here with the pages on which they first occur:

big-O notation 459	Church-Turing thesis 454
controller 446	decrement statement 442
finite state automaton 446	Gödel number 454
halting problem 456	increment statement 442
loop statement 442	macro 443
non-polynomial problem 460	polynomial problem 460
read/write head	solvable problem 458
state 447	tape 446
Turing machine 445	unsolvable problem 458

17.8 SUMMARY

- We can define a computer language with only three statements: the *increment* statement, the *decrement* statement, and the *loop* statement. The increment statement adds 1 to a variable, the decrement statement subtracts 1 from a variable, and the loop statement repeats an action or a series of actions while the value of a variable is not 0.

- It can be shown that this simple programming language can simulate several statements found in some popular languages. We call each simulation a *macro* and use it in other simulations without the need to repeat code.

- The Turing machine was designed to solve computable problems. It is the foundation of modern computers. A Turing machine is made of three components: a tape, a controller, and a read/write head.

- Based on the Church-Turing thesis, if an algorithm to do a symbol manipulation task exists, then a Turing machine to do that task also exists.

- In theoretical computer science, an unsigned number is assigned to every program that can be written in a specific language. This is usually referred to as the *Gödel number*.

- A classical programming question is whether a program that can determine if another program halts can be constructed. Unfortunately, it has now been proved that this program cannot exist: the halting problem is not solvable.

- In computer science, problems can be divided into two categories: solvable problems and unsolvable problems. The solvable problems can themselves be divided into two categories: polynomial and non-polynomial problems.

17.9 PRACTICE SET

Review questions

1. Name and describe the functions of the three basic statements that are the foundation of other statements in Simple Language.

2. Show how assigning the value of one variable to another uses the three basic statements.

3. What is the relationship between the Turing machine and our Simple Language?

4. What are the components of the Turing machine and what is the function of each component?

5. Describe one way to delimit the data on a Turing machine's tape.

6. When a read/write head in a Turing machine finishes reading and writing a symbol, what are its next options?

7. How is a transition state diagram related to a Turing machine controller?

8. How is a transition state diagram related to a transition table? Do they have the same information? Which has more information?

9. What is a Gödel number? How do we use a Gödel number to prove that the halting problem is not solvable?

10. Compare and contrast the complexity of a polynomial solvable problem and a non-polynomial solvable problem.

Multiple-choice questions

11. The _____ statement adds 1 to the variable.
    a. increment
    b. decrement
    c. loop
    d. complement

12. The _____ statement repeats one or more actions.
    a. increment
    b. decrement
    c. loop
    d. complement

13. The _____ statement subtracts 1 from the variable.
    a. increment
    b. decrement
    c. loop
    d. complement

14. To clear a variable, we use the _____ statement(s).
    a. increment
    b. decrement
    c. loop
    d. b and c

15. To assign a number to a variable, we use the _____ statement(s).
    a. increment
    b. decrement
    c. loop
    d. all of the above

16. To copy the value of one variable to another, we use the ____ statement(s).
    a. increment
    b. decrement
    c. loop
    d. all of the above

17. A Turing machine has these components: _____.
    a. tape, memory, and read/write head
    b. disk, controller, and read/write head
    c. tape, controller, and read/write head
    d. disk, memory, and controller

18. In a Turing machine, the _____ holds a sequence of characters.
    a. disk
    b. tape
    c. controller
    d. read/write head

19. After reading a symbol, the read/write head _____.
    a. moves to the left
    b. moves to the right
    c. stays in place
    d. any of the above

20. The _____ is the theoretical counterpart of the CPU.
    a. disk
    b. tape
    c. controller
    d. read/write head

21. The controller has _____ states.
    a. three
    b. four
    c. a finite number of
    d. an infinite number of

22. A _____ is a pictorial representation of the states and their relationships to each other.
    a. transition diagram
    b. flowchart
    c. transition table
    d. Turing machine

23. A _____ shows, among other things, the movement of the read/write head, the character read, and the character written.
    a. diagram
    b. flowchart
    c. transition table
    d. Turing machine

24. Based on the definition in this chapter, the Gödel number for **decr** (X) in decimal is _____.
    a. 367
    b. 175
    c. 174
    d. 191

25. Based on the definition in this chapter, the Gödel number for **decr** (X) in hexadecimal is _____.
    a. B C
    b. C B
    c. B F
    d. A F

26. We use _____ to denote a program's complexity.
    a. the Turing number
    b. big-O notation
    c. factorials
    d. the Simple Language

27. The complexity of a problem is $O(\log_{10}n)$ and the computer executes 1 million instructions

per second. How long does it take to run the program if the number of operations is 10,000?

a. 1 microsecond

b. 2 microseconds

c. 3 microseconds

d. 4 microseconds

Exercises

28. Rewrite Algorithm 17.6 ($Y \leftarrow X$) so that it preserves the value of X.

29. Rewrite Algorithm 17.7 so that it calculates $Z \leftarrow Y + X$ while preserving the values of X and Y.

30. Rewrite Algorithm 17.8 so that it calculates $Z \leftarrow Y \times X$ while preserving the values of X and Y.

31. Rewrite Algorithm 17.9 so that it calculates $Z \leftarrow Y^X$ while preserving the values of X and Y.

32. Simulate the following macro using the previously defined statements or macros in Simple Language: $Y \leftarrow Y - X$.

33. Simulate the following macro using the previously defined statements or macros in Simple Language (X can be only 0 or 1):

```
if (X) then
{
            A₁
}
else
{
            A₂
}
```

34. Given a Turing machine with a single instruction (A, 1, b, R, B) and the tape configuration:

show the final configuration of the tape.

35. Given a Turing machine with a single instruction (A, b, b, R, B) and the tape configuration:

show the final configuration of the tape.

36. Given a Turing machine with five instructions (A, b, b, R, B), (B, 1, #, R, B), (B, b, b, L, C), (C, #, 1, L, C), (C, b, b, R, B) and the tape configuration:

show the final configuration of the tape.

37. Show the state diagram of a Turing machine that increments a nonnegative integer represented in the binary system. For example, if the contents of the tape is $(101)_2$, it will be changed to $(110)_2$.

38. Show that the simulation of **incr**(X) in the Turing machine, as defined in this chapter, gives the correct answer when X = 0.

39. Show that the simulation of **decr**(X) in the Turing machine, as defined in this chapter, gives the correct answer when X = 0.

40. Show how the simulation of a loop statement in the Turing machine, as defined in this chapter, can be changed to preserve the original value of X if we allow another symbol such as # to be used by the machine.

41. Give the transition states and the program for the Turing machine that simulates the macro $X \leftarrow 0$.

42. Give the transition states and the program for the Turing machine that simulates the macro $Y \leftarrow X$.

43. A Turing machine uses a single 1 to represent the integer 0. Show how the integer n can be represented in this machine.

44. What is the Gödel number for the macro $X_1 \leftarrow 0$?

45. What is the Gödel number for the macro $X_2 \leftarrow 2$?

46. What is the Gödel number for the macro $X_3 \leftarrow X_1 + X_2$?

18 Artificial Intelligence

In the last chapter of the book, we offer an introduction to artificial intelligence (AI).

The first section is a brief history and an attempt to define artificial intelligence. *Knowledge representation*, a broad and well-developed area in AI, is discussed in the next section. We then introduce *expert systems*, systems that can replace human expertise when it is needed but not available. We then discuss how artificial intelligence can be used to simulate the normal (mundane) behavior of human beings in two areas: *image processing* and *language analysis*. We then show how expert systems and *mundane systems* can solve problems using different searching methods. Finally, we discuss how *neural networks* can simulate the process of learning in an intelligent agent.

Objectives

After studying this chapter, the student should be able to:

❑ Define and give a brief history of artificial intelligence.

❑ Describe how knowledge is represented in an intelligent agent.

❑ Show how expert systems can be used when a human expert is not available.

❑ Show how an artificial agent can be used to simulate mundane tasks performed by human beings.

❑ Show how expert systems and mundane systems can use different search techniques to solve problems.

❑ Show how the learning process in humans can be simulated, to some extent, using neural networks that create the electronic version of a neuron called a *perceptron*.

18.1   INTRODUCTION

In this section we first try to define the term **artificial intelligence (AI)** informally and give a brief history of it. We also define an *intelligent agent* and its two broad categories. Finally, we mention two programming languages that are commonly used in artificial intelligence.

What is artificial intelligence?

Although there is no universally-agreed definition of artificial intelligence, we accept the following definition that matches the topics covered in this chapter:

> **Artificial intelligence is the study of programmed systems that can simulate, to some extent, human activities such as perceiving, thinking, learning, and acting.**

A brief history of artificial intelligence

Although artificial intelligence as an independent field of study is relatively new, it has some roots in the past. We can say that it started 2,400 years ago when the Greek philosopher Aristotle invented the concept of logical reasoning. The effort to finalize the language of logic continued with Leibniz and Newton. George Boole developed Boolean algebra in the nineteenth century (Appendix E) that laid the foundation of computer circuits. However, the main idea of a thinking machine came from Alan Turing, who proposed the Turing test. The term "artificial intelligence" was first coined by John McCarthy in 1956.

The Turing test

In 1950, Alan Turing proposed the **Turing Test**, which provides a definition of *intelligence* in a machine. The test simply compares the intelligent behavior of a human being with that of a computer. An interrogator asks a set of questions that are forwarded to both a computer and a human being. The interrogator receives two sets of responses, but does not know which set comes from the human and which set from the computer. After careful examination of the two sets, if the interrogator cannot definitely tell which set has come from the computer and which from the human, the computer has passed the Turing test for intelligent behavior.

Intelligent agents

An **intelligent agent** is a system that perceives its environment, learns from it, and interacts with it intelligently. Intelligent agents can be divided into two broad categories: *software agents* and *physical agents*.

Software agents

A **software agent** is a set of programs that are designed to do particular tasks. For example, some intelligent systems can be used to organize electronic mail (e-mail). This type of agent can check the contents of received e-mails and classify them into different categories (junk, less important, important, very important, and so on).

Another example of a software agent is a search engine used to search the World Wide Web and find sites that can provide information about a requested subject.

Physical agents

A **physical agent** (robot) is a programmable system that can be used to perform a variety of tasks. Simple robots can be used in manufacturing to do routine jobs such as assembling, welding, or painting. Some organizations use mobile robots that do routine delivery jobs such as distributing mail or correspondence to different rooms. Mobile robots are used underwater to prospect for oil.

A humanoid robot is an autonomous mobile robot that is supposed to behave like a human. Although humanoid robots are prevalent in science fiction, there is still a lot of work to do before such robots that can interact properly with their surroundings and learn from events that occur there exist.

Programming languages

Although some all-purpose languages such as C, C++, and Java are used to create intelligent software, two languages are specifically designed for AI: LISP and PROLOG

LISP

LISP (LISt Programming) was invented by John McCarthy in 1958. As the name implies, LISP is a programming language that manipulates lists. LISP treats data as well as programs as lists, which means that a LISP program can change itself. This feature matches the idea of an intelligent agent that can learn from its environment and improve its behavior.

However, one drawback of LISP is its sluggishness. It is slow if the list to be handled is long. Another drawback is the complexity of its syntax.

PROLOG

PROLOG (PROgramming in LOGic) is a language that can build a database of facts and a knowledge base of rules. A program in PROLOG can use logical reasoning to answer questions that can be inferred from the knowledge base. However, PROLOG is not a very efficient programming language. Some complex problems can be solved more efficiently using other languages such as C, C++, or Java.

18.2 KNOWLEDGE REPRESENTATION

If an artificial agent is supposed to solve some problems related to the real world, it needs to be able to represent knowledge somehow. Facts are represented as data structures that can be manipulated by programs stored inside the computer. In this section, we describe four common methods for representing knowledge: *semantic networks*, *frames*, *predicate logic*, and *rule-based systems*.

Semantic networks

Semantic networks were developed in early 1960s by Richard H. Richens. A semantic network uses directed graphs to represent knowledge. A directed graph as discussed in Chapter 12 is made of vertices (nodes) and edges (arcs). Semantic networks uses vertices to represent concepts and edges (denoted by arrows) to represent the relation between two concepts (Figure 18.1).

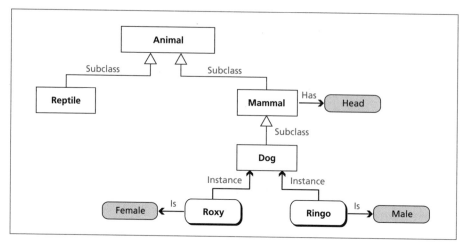

Figure 18.1   A simple semantic network

Concepts

To develop an exact definition of a concept, experts have related the definition of concepts to the theory of sets. A concept, therefore, can be thought of as a set or a subset. For example, *animal* defines the set of all animals, *horse* defines the set of all horses and is a subset of the set *animal*. An object is a member (instance) of a set. Concepts are shown by vertices.

Relations

In a semantic network, relations are shown by edges. An edge can define a *subclass* relation—the edge is directed from the subclass to its superclass. An edge can also define an *instance* relation—the edge is directed from the instance to the set to which it belongs. An edge can also define an *attribute* of an object (color, size, ...). Finally, an edge can define a property of an object, such as possessing another object. One of the most important relations that can be well defined in a semantic network is *inheritance*. An inheritance relation defines the fact that all the attributes of a class are present in an inherited class. This can be used to infer new knowledge from the knowledge represented by the graph.

Frames

Frames are closely related to semantic networks. In semantic networks, a graph is used to represent knowledge: in frames, data structures (records) are used to represent the same knowledge. One advantage of frames over semantic networks is that programs can handle frames more easily than semantic networks. Figure 18.2 shows how a semantic network shown in Figure 18.1 can be implemented using frames.

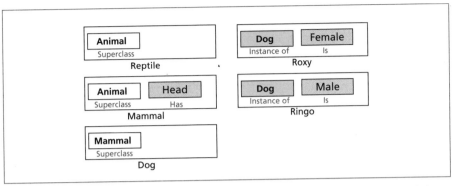

Figure 18.2 A set of frames representing the semantic network in Figure 18.1

Objects

A node in a semantic network becomes an object in a set of frames, so an object can define a class, a subclass, or an instance of a class. In Figure 18.2 reptile, mammal, dog, Roxy, and Ringo are objects.

Slots

Edges in semantic networks are translated into *slots*—fields in the data structure. The name of the slot defines the type of the relationship and the value of the slot completes the relationship. In Figure 18.2, for example, *animal* is a slot in the *reptile* object.

Predicate logic

The most common knowledge representation is **predicate logic**. Predicate logic can be used to represent complex facts. It is a well-defined language developed via a long history of theoretical logic. Although this section defines predicate logic, we first introduce **propositional logic**, a simpler language. We then discuss predicate logic, which employs propositional logic.

Propositional logic

Propositional logic is a language made up from a set of sentences that can be used to carry out logical reasoning about the world.

Operators

Propositional logic uses five operators, as shown below:

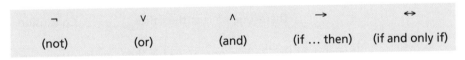

¬	∨	∧	→	↔
(not)	(or)	(and)	(if ... then)	(if and only if)

The first operator is unary—the operator takes only one sentence: the other four operators are binary—they take two sentences. The logical value (*true* or *false*) of each sentence depends on the logical value of the atomic sentences (sentences without no operators) of which the complex sentence is made. Figure 18.3 shows the truth table for each logical operator in propositional logic. Truth tables were introduced in Chapter 4 and are explained in Appendix E.

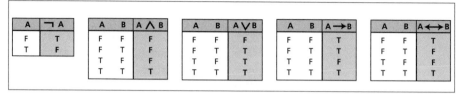

Figure 18.3 Truth table for five operators in propositional logic

Sentence

A sentence in this language is defined recursively as shown below:

1. An uppercase letter, such as A, B, S, or T, that represents a statement in a natural language, is a sentence.
2. Any of the two constant values (*true* and *false*) is a sentence.
3. If P is a sentence, then ¬P is a sentence.
4. If P and Q are sentences, then P ∨ Q, P ∧ Q, P → Q, and P ↔ Q are sentences.

Example 18.1

The following are sentences in propositional language:

    a. Today is Sunday (S).

    b. It is raining (R).

    c. Today is Sunday or Monday (S ∨ M).

    d. It is not raining (¬ R).

    e. If a dog is a mammal then a cat is a mammal (D → C).

Deduction

In AI we need to create new facts from the existing facts. In propositional logic, the process is called *deduction*. Given two presumably true sentences, we can deduce a new true sentence. The first two sentences are called *premises*: the deduced sentence is called the *conclusion*. The whole is called an *argument*. For example:

Either he is at home or at the office	Premise 1:
He is not at home	Premise 2:
Therefore, he is at the office	Conclusion

If we use H for "he is at home", O for "he is at the office", and the symbol |– for the "therefore", then we can show the above argument as:

$$\{H \lor O, \neg H\} \vdash O$$

The question is how we can prove if a deductive argument is *valid*. A valid deductive argument is an argument whose conclusions follow necessarily from its premises. In other words, in a valid deductive argument, it is impossible for the conclusion to be false while its premises all are true.

One way to do this is to create a truth table for the premises and the conclusion. A conclusion is invalid if we can find a *counterexample* case: a case in which both premises are true, but the conclusion is false.

Example 18.2

The validity of the argument $\{H \lor O, \neg H\} \vdash O$ can be proved using the following truth table:

H	O	H ∨ O	¬H	O	
F	F	F	T	F	
F	T	T	T	T	OK
T	F	T	F	F	
T	T	T	F	T	

Premise Premise Conclusion

The only row to be checked is the second row. This row does not show a counterexample, so the argument is valid. There are however arguments that are not logically valid. For example:

If she is rich, she has a car.	Premise 1:
She has a car	Premise 2:
Therefore, she is rich.	Conclusion

It can be seen that even if the first two sentences are true, the conclusion can be false. We can show the above argument as $\{R \rightarrow C, C\} \vdash R$, in which R means "She is rich", and C means "she has a car".

Example 18.3

The argument $\{R \rightarrow C, C\} \vdash R$ is not valid because a counter example can be found:

R	C	R → C	C	R
F	F	T	F	F
F	T	T	T	F
T	F	F	F	T
T	T	T	T	T

Premise Premise Conclusion

Here row 2 and row 4 need to be checked. Although row 4 is ok, row 2 shows a counterexample (two true premises result in a false conclusion). The argument is therefore invalid.

An argument is valid if no counterexample can be found.

Predicate logic

In propositional logic, a symbol that represents a sentence is atomic: it cannot be broken up to find information about its components. For example, consider the sentences:

P_1: "Linda is Mary's mother" P_2: "Mary is Anne's mother"

We can combine these two sentences in many ways to create other sentences, but we cannot extract any relation between Linda and Anne. For example, we cannot infer from the above two sentences that Linda is the grandmother of Anne. To do so, we need predicate logic: the logic that defines the relation between the parts in a proposition.

In predicate logic, a sentence is divided into a predicate and arguments. For example, each of the following propositions can be written as predicates with two arguments:

P_1: "Linda is Mary's mother"	becomes	mother (Linda, Mary)
P_2: "Mary is Anne's mother"	becomes	mother (Mary, Anne)

The relationship of motherhood in each of the above sentences is defined by the predicate *mother*. If the object *Mary* in both sentences refers to the same person, we can infer a new relation between Linda and Anne: grandmother (Linda, Anne). This is the whole purpose of predicate logic.

Sentence

A sentence in predicate language is defined as follows:

1. A predicate with n arguments such as *predicate_name* (*argument$_1$*, ..., *argument$_n$*) is a sentence. The *predicate_name* relates arguments to each other. Each argument can be:

    a. A constant, such as *human, animal, John, Mary*.

    b. A variable, such as *x, y*, and *z*.

    c. A function, such as *mother (Anne)*. Note that a function is a predicate that is used as an argument: a function returns an object that can takes the place of an argument.

2. Any of the two constant values (*true* and *false*) is a sentence.

3. If P is a sentence, then ¬P is a sentence.

4. If P and Q are sentences, then P ∨ Q, P ∧ Q, P → Q, and P ↔ Q are sentences.

Example 18.4

1. The sentence "John works for Ann's sister" can be written as:

$$\text{works[John, sister(Ann)]}$$

   in which the function sister (Ann) is used as an argument.

2. The sentence "John's father loves Ann's sister" can be written as:

$$\text{loves[father(John), sister(Ann)]}$$

Quantifiers

Predicate logic allows us to use **quantifiers**. Two quantifiers are common in predicate logic: ∀ and ∃.

1. The first, ∀, which is read as "for all", is called the *universal quantifier*: it states that something is true for every object that its variable represents.

2. The second, ∃, which is read as "there exists", is called the *existential quantifier*: it states that something is true for one or more objects that its variable represents.

Example 18.5

The following shows how English sentences can be written as sentences in predicate logic (*x* is a placeholder):

1. The sentence "All men are mortals" can be written as:

$$\forall x[\text{man } (x) \rightarrow \text{mortal } (x)]$$

2. The sentence "Frogs are green" can be written as:

$$\forall x[\text{frog } (x) \rightarrow \text{green } (x)]$$

   because the sentence can be written as "All frogs are green" or "Any frog is green". The predicate *greenness* is applied to all frogs.

3. The sentence "Some flowers are red" can be written as:

$$\exists x[\text{flower } (x) \wedge \text{red}(x)]$$

   Note that the operator inside the bracket is ∧ instead of →, but the reason for this is beyond the scope of this book.

4. The sentence "John has a book" can be written as:

$$\exists x[\text{book } (x) \wedge \text{has } (\text{John}, x)]$$

   In other words, the sentence is changed to "There exists a book that belongs to John".

5. The sentence "No frog is yellow" can be written as:

$$\forall x[\text{frog } (x) \rightarrow \neg\text{yellow } (x)] \quad \text{or as} \quad \neg\exists x[\text{frog}(x) \wedge \text{yellow}(x)]$$

   which means that "It is not the case that there exists a frog and it is yellow".

Deduction

In predicate logic, if there is no quantifier, the verification of an argument is the same as that which we discussed in propositional logic. However, the verification becomes more complicated if there are quantifiers. For example, the following argument is completely valid.

All men are mortals	Premise 1:
Socrates is a man	Premise 2:
Therefore, Socrates is mortal	Conclusion

Verification of this simple argument is not difficult. We can write this argument as:

$$\forall x \,[man\,(x) \rightarrow mortal\,(x)]\,,\ man(Socrates)\ |\!-\ mortal\,(Socrates)$$

Since the first premise talks about all men, we can replace one instance of the class man (Socrates) in that premise to get the following argument:

$$man(Socrates) \rightarrow mortal(Socrates)\,,\ man(Socrates)\ |\!-\ mortal\,(Socrates)$$

Which is reduced to $M_1 \rightarrow M_2, M_1 |\!- M_2$, in which M_1 is man (Socrates) and M_2 is mortal (Socrates). The result is an argument in propositional logic and can be easily validated. However, there are many arguments in predicate logic that cannot be validated so easily. We need a set of systematic proofs that are beyond the scope of this book.

Beyond predicate logic

There have been further developments in logic to include the need for logical reasoning. Some examples of these include **high-order logic**, **default logic**, **modal logic**, and **temporal logic**. We briefly mention these topics here only for interest: their discussion is beyond the scope of this book.

High-order logic

High-order logic extends the scope of quantifiers $\forall$ and $\exists$ in predicate logic. These quantifiers in predicate logic bind variables x and y to instances (when instantiating). In high-order logic we can use these quantifiers for binding variables that stand for properties and relations. In this case, during instantiation, these variables are replaced by predicates. For example, we can have $\forall P (Pj \wedge Pa)$, where the subscripts j and a denote John and Anne, which means that John and Anne have exactly the same properties.

Modal logic

One fast-growing trend in logic is **modal logic**, which includes expressions such as "could", "should", "may", "might", "ought", and so on, to express the grammatical mood of a sentence. In this logic, we can have symbols to denote operators such as "it is possible that".

Temporal logic

Temporal logic, like modal logic, extends predicate logic with a set of temporal operators such as "from now on" or "at some point in time" to include the time factor in the validity of the argument.

Default logic

In **default logic**, we assume that the default conclusion of an argument is acceptable if it is consistent with the contents of the knowledge base. For example, we assume that all birds fly unless there is something in the knowledge base that annuls this general fact.

Rule-based systems

A **rule-based system** represents knowledge using a set of rules that can be used to deduce new facts from known facts. The rules express what is true if specific conditions are met. A rule-based database is a set of *if... then...* statements in the form

If A then B   **or**   A → B

in which A is called the *antecedent* and B is called the *consequent*. Note that in a rule-based system, each rule is handled independently without any connection to other rules.

Components A rule-based system is made up of three components: an *interpreter* (or inference engine), a *knowledge base*, and a *fact database*, as shown in Figure 18.4.

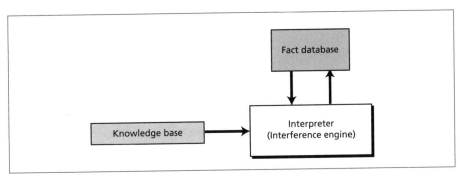

Figure 18.4 The components of a rule-based system

Knowledge base

The knowledge base component in a rule-based system is a database (repository) of rules. It contains a set of pre-established rules that can be used to draw conclusions from the given facts.

Database of facts

The database of facts contains a set of conditions that are used by the rules in the knowledge base.

Interpreter

The interpreter (inference engine) is a processor or controller—a program, for example—that combines rules and facts. Interpreters are of two types: *forward chaining* and *backward chaining*, as we explain shortly.

Forward chaining

Forward chaining is the process in which an interpreter uses a set of rules and a set of facts to perform an action. The action can be just adding a new fact to the base of facts, or issuing some commands, such as start another program or a machine. The interpreter interprets and executes rules until no more rules can be interpreted. Figure 18.5 shows the basic algorithm.

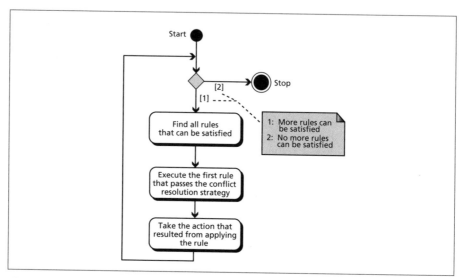

Figure 18.5 Flow diagram for forward chaining

If there is any conflict in which two different rules can be applied to one fact or one rule can be applied to two facts, the system needs to call a conflict resolution procedure to solve the problem. This guarantees that only one of the outputs should be added to the database of facts or only one action should be taken. The discussion of conflict resolution is complex and beyond the scope of this book.

Backward chaining

Forward chaining is not very efficient if the system tries to prove a conclusion. All facts must be checked by all rules to come up with the given conclusion. In this cases, it may be more efficient if backward chaining is used. Figure 18.6 shows the procedure for backward chaining.

The process starts with the conclusion (goal). If the goal is already in the fact database, the process stops and the conclusion is proved. If the goal is not in the fact database, the system finds the rule that has the goal in its conclusion. However, instead of firing that rule, backward chaining is now applied to each fact in the rule (recursion). If all of the facts in that rule are found in the database fact, the original goal is proved.

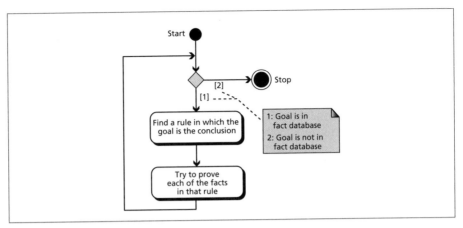

Figure 18.6 Flow diagram for backward chaining

18.3 EXPERT SYSTEMS

Expert systems use the knowledge representation languages discussed in the previous section to perform tasks that normally need human expertise. They can be used in situations in which that expertise is in short supply, expensive, or unavailable when required. For example, in medicine, an expert system can be used to narrow down a set of symptoms to a likely subset of causes, a task normally carried out by a doctor.

Extracting knowledge

An expert system is built on predefined knowledge about its field of expertise. An expert system in medicine, for example, is built on the knowledge of a doctor specialized in the field for which the system is built: an expert system is supposed to do the same job as the human expert. The first step in building an expert system is therefore to extract the knowledge from a human expert. This extracted knowledge becomes the knowledge base we discussed in the previous section.

Knowledge engineering

Extracting knowledge from an expert is normally a difficult task, for several reasons:

❑ The knowledge possessed by the expert is normally heuristic: it is based on probability rather than certainty.

❑ The expert often finds it hard to express their knowledge in such a way that it can be stored in a knowledge base as exact rules. For example, it is hard for an electrical engineer to show how, step by step, a faulty electric motor can be diagnosed: the knowledge is normally intuitive.

❑ Knowledge acquisition can only be done via personal interview with the expert, which can be a tiring and boring task if the interviewer is not an expert in this type of interview.

The knowledge-extraction process is normally done by a *knowledge engineer*, who may not be expert in the field for which the expert system is to be built, but has the expertise to know how to do the interview and how to interpret the answers so that they can be used in building the knowledge base.

Extracting facts

To be able to infer new facts or perform actions, a fact database is needed in addition to the knowledge base for a knowledge representation language. The fact database in an expert system is case-based, in which facts collected or measured are entered into the system to be used by the inference engine.

Architecture

Figure 18.7 shows the general idea behind the architecture of an expert system. As the figure shows, an expert system can have up to seven components: *user, user interface, inference engine, knowledge base, fact database, explanation system*, and *knowledge base editor*.

The inference engine is the heart of an expert system: it communicates with the knowledge base, fact database, and the user interface. Four of the seven components of an expert system—user interface, inference engine, explanation system, and knowledge base editor—can be made once and used for many applications, as they are not dependent on the particular knowledge base or fact database. The figure shows these components in the shaded box, normally called an *expert system shell*.

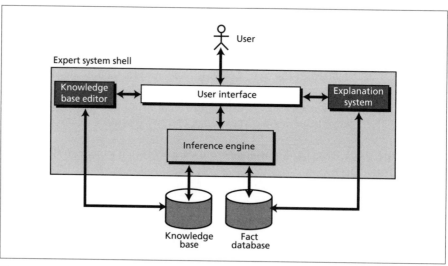

Figure 18.7   The architecture of an expert system

User   The user is the entity that uses the system to benefit from the expertise offered.

User interface	The user interface allows the user to interact with the system. The user interface can accept natural language from the user and interpret it for the system. Most user interfaces also offer a user-friendly menu system.
Inference engine	The inference engine is the heart of the system that uses the knowledge base and the fact database to infer the action to be taken.
Knowledge base	The knowledge base is a collection of knowledge based on interviews with experts in the relevant field of expertise.
Fact database	The fact database in an expert system is case-based. For each case, the user enters the available or measured data into the fact database to be used by the inference engine for that particular case.
Explanation system	The explanation system, which may not be included in all systems, is used to explain the rationale behind the decision made by the inference engine.
Knowledge editor	The knowledge editor, which may not be included in all systems, is used to update the knowledge base if new experience has been obtained from experts in the field.

18.4 PERCEPTION

One of the goals in artificial intelligence is to create a machine that behaves like an expert—an expert system. Another goal is to create a machine that behaves like an ordinary human. One of the meanings of the word "perception" is understanding what is received through the senses—sight, hearing, touch, smell, taste. A human being sees a scene through the eyes, and the brain interprets it to extract the type of objects in the scene. A human being hears a set of voice signals through the ears, and the brain interprets it as a meaningful sentence, and so on.

An intelligent agent should be able to perceive if it needs to act like a human being. AI has been particularly involved in two types of perception, sight and hearing, although other types of perception may be implemented in the future. In this section we briefly discuss these two areas of research.

Image processing

Image processing or *computer vision* is an area of AI that deals with the perception of objects through the artificial eyes of an agent, such as a camera. An image processor takes a two-dimensional image from the outside world and tries to create a description of the three-dimensional objects present in the scene. Although this is an easy tasks for a human being, it turns out to be a difficult task for an artificial agent. The input presented to an image process is one or more images from the scene, while the output is a description of the objects in the scene. The processor uses a database containing the characteristics of objects for comparison (Figure 18.8).

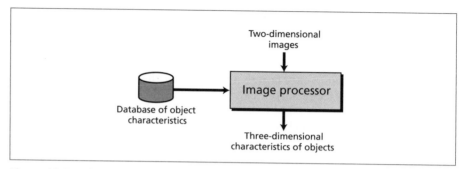

Figure 18.8   The components of an image processor

We need to emphasize that image acquisition uses photography and television technology to create images. The concern of AI is how to interpret the images and extract the characteristics of the objects.

Edge detection

The first stage in image processing is **edge detection**: finding where the edges in the image are. Edges can define the boundaries between an object and its background in the image. Normally there is a sharp contrast between the surfaces belonging to an object and the environment, assuming that there is no camouflage. Edges show discontinuity in surface, in depth, or in illumination. For example, Figure 18.9 shows a very simple image and the intensity of pixels on a scale 0 to 9, where 0 is black and 9 is white. The edges can be detected by finding adjacent pixels with a large difference in intensity.

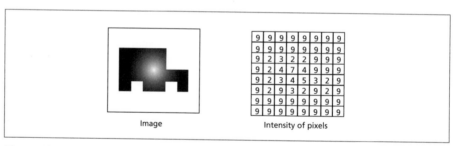

Figure 18.9   The edge-detection process

There are several mathematical methods that use the intensity of the pixels to find the boundary of the objects with respect to the background. The simplest method is to differentiate the matrix of intensities. The areas that have consistent intensity will produce low differentials (0 or 1): the edges will produce greatest differentials. Discussion of these methods is beyond the scope of this book: we recommend the reference books listed at the end of this chapter for further study.

Segmentation

Segmentation is the next stage in image analysis. Segmentation divides the image into homogenous segments or areas. The definition of homogeneity differs in different methods, but in general a homogenous area is an area in which the intensity of pixels varies smoothly. Segmentation is very similar to edge detection. In edge detection, the boundaries of the object and the background are found: in segmentation, the boundaries between different areas inside the object are found. After segmentation, the object is divided into different areas.

Several methods have been used for segmentation. One is called **thresholding**, in which a pixel with a specific intensity is selected and the process tries to find all the pixels with the same or very close intensity. All pixels found in this way make a segment. Another method is called splitting. Splitting takes an area that is not homogenous and divides it into several homogenous areas. Still another method is called **merging**, which can be used to merge areas with the same pixel intensity.

Finding depth

The next step in image analysis is to find the depth of the object or objects in the image. Depth finding can help the intelligent agent to gauge how far the object is from it. Two general methods have been used for this purpose: *stereo vision* and *motion*.

Stereo vision

Stereo vision (sometimes called *stereopsis*) uses the technique deployed by human eyes to find the depth of the object. To have good distance recognition, a human being needs two eyes. If the object is very close, the two images created in our eyes are different, but if the object is far away the two images are almost the same. Without delving into mathematical calculation and proof, we can say that one of the tools for recognizing the distance of objects is to use two eyes or two cameras. The picture created from two cameras can help the intelligent agent to gauge if the object is close or far away.

Motion

Another method that can help to find the distance of objects in an image is to create several images when one or more objects are moving. The relative position of a moving object with respect to other objects in the scene can give a clue to the distance of objects. For example, assume that a video shows a person moving in front of a house. The relative position of the person and house (a close object) will change, but the relative position of the person and a distant mountain will remain the same. The intelligent agent can conclude that the house is close but the mountain is far away.

Finding orientation

Orientation of the object in the scene can be found using two techniques: *shading* and *texture*.

Shading

The amount of light reflected from a surface depends on several factors. If the optical properties of the different surfaces of an object are the same, the amount of reflection depends on the orientation of the surface (its relative position) which reflects the light source. Figure 18.10 shows two drawn objects. The one that is shaded definitely shows the orientation of the object's surfaces more accurately.

Figure 18.10 The effect of shading on orientation finding

Texture

Texture (a regularly repeated pattern) can also help in finding the orientation or the curvature of a surface. If an intelligent agent can recognize the pattern, it can help it to find an object's orientation or curvature.

Object recognition

The last step in image processing is object recognition. To recognize an object, the agent needs to have a model of the object in memory for comparison. However, creating and storing a model for each object in the view is an impossible task. One solution is to assume that the objects to be recognized are compound objects made of a set of simple geometric shapes. These primitive shapes can be created and stored in the intelligent agent's memory, then classes of objects that we need the agent to recognize can be created from a combination of these objects and stored.

When an agent "sees" an object, it tries to decompose the object into a combination of the primitives. If the combination matches one of the classes already known to the agent, the object is recognized. Figure 18.11 shows a small set of primitive geometric shapes.

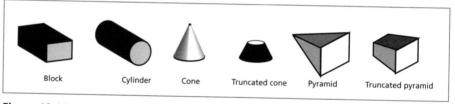

Figure 18.11 Primitive geometric shapes

Applications

One of the areas in which image processing has found application is in manufacturing, particularly on assembly lines. A robot with image processing capability can be used to determine the position of an object on the assembly line. In this environment, where the number of objects to be perceived is limited, an image processor can be very helpful.

Language understanding

One of the inherent capabilities of a human being is to understand—that is, interpret—the audio signal that they perceive. A machine that can understand natural language can be very useful in daily life. For example, it can replace a telephone operator—most of the time. It can also be used on occasions when a system needs a predefined format of queries. For example, the queries given to a database must normally follow the format used by that specific system. A machine that can understand queries in natural language and translate them to formal queries can be very useful.

We can divide the task of a machine that understands natural language into four consecutive steps: *speech recognition*, *syntactic analysis*, *semantic analysis*, and *pragmatic analysis*.

Speech recognition

The first step in natural language processing is **speech recognition**. In this step, a speech signal is analyzed and the sequence of words it contains are extracted. The input to the speech recognition subsystem is a continuos (analog) signal: the output is a sequence of words. The signal needs to be divided into different sounds, sometimes called *phonemes*. The sounds then need to be combined into words. The detailed process, however, is beyond the scope of this book: we leave the task to specialized books in speech recognition.

Syntactic analysis

The **syntactic analysis** step is used to define how words are to be grouped in a sentence. This is a difficult task in a language like English, in which the function of a word in a sentence is not determined by its position in the sentence. For example, in the following two sentences:

> Mary rewarded John.
>
> John was rewarded by Mary.

it is always John who is rewarded, but in the first sentence John is in the last position and Mary is in the first position. A machine that hears any of the above sentences needs to interpret them correctly and come to the same conclusion no matter which sentence is heard.

Grammar

The first tool to correctly analyze a sentence is a well-defined grammar. A fully developed language like English has a very large set of grammatical rules. We assume a very small subset of the English language and define a very small set of rules just to show the idea.

The grammar of a language can be defined using several methods: we use a simple version of BNF (Backus-Naur Form) that is used in computer science to define the syntax of a programming language (Table 18.1).

Table 18.1 A simple grammar

			Rule
1	**Sentence**	→	NounPhrase VerbPhrase
2	**NounPhrase**	→	Noun | Article Noun | Article Adjective Noun
3	**Verb Phrase**	→	Verb | Verb NounPhrase | Verb NounPhrase Adverb
4	**Noun**	→	[home] | [cat] | [water] | [dog] | [John] | [Mary] |
5	**Article**	→	[a] | [the]

Table 18.1   A simple grammar (continued)

	Rule		
6	Adjective	→	[big] | [small] | [tall] | [short] | [white] | [black] |
7	Verb	→	[goes] | [comes] | [eats] | [drinks] | [has] [loves]

The first rule defines a sentence as a noun phrase followed by a verb phrase. The second rule defines three choices for a noun phrase: a single noun, an article followed by a noun, or an article followed by an adjective and a noun. The fourth rule explicitly defines what a noun can be. In our simple language, we have defined only seven nouns: in a language like English the list of nouns is defined in a dictionary. The sixth rule also defines a very small set of adjectives and the seventh rule a small set of verbs.

Although the syntax of our language is very primitive, we can make many sentences out of it. For example, we can have:

> John comes home.
>
> Mary drinks water.
>
> John has a white dog.
>
> John loves Mary.
>
> Mary loves John.

Parser

It should be clear that even a simple grammar as defined in Table 18.1 uses different options. A machine that determines if a sentence is grammatically (syntactically) correct does not need to check all possible choices before rejecting a sentence as an invalid one. This is done by a **parser**. A parser creates a *parse tree* based on the grammar rules to determine the validity of a sentence. Figure 18.12 shows the parse tree for the sentence "John has a white dog" based on our rules defined in Table 18.1.

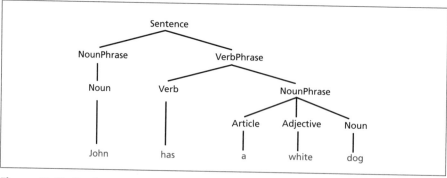

Figure 18.12 Parsing a sentence

Semantic analysis

The **semantic analysis** extracts the meaning of a sentence after it has been syntactically analyzed. This analysis creates a representation of the objects involved in the sentence, their relations, and their attributes. The analysis can use any of the knowledge representation schemes we discussed before. For example, the sentence "John has a dog" can be represented using predicate logic as:

$$\exists\, x \; dog(x) \; has \, (John, x)$$

Pragmatic analysis

The three previous steps—speech recognition, syntax analysis, and semantic analysis—can create a knowledge representation of a spoken sentence. In most cases, another step, **pragmatic analysis**, is needed to further clarify the purpose of the sentence and to remove ambiguities.

Purpose

The purpose of the sentence cannot be found using the three steps listed above. For example, the sentence "Can you swim a mile?" asks about the ability of the hearer. However, the sentence "Can you pass the salt?" is merely a polite request. An English language sentence can have many different purposes, such as informing, requesting, promising, inquiring, and so on. Pragmatic analysis is required to find the purpose of the sentence.

Removing ambiguity

Sometimes a sentence is ambiguous after semantic analysis. Ambiguity can manifest itself in different ways. A word can have more than one function—for example, the word "hard" can be used both as an adjective and an adverb. A word can also have more than one meaning—for example, the word "ball" can mean different things in "football" and "ball room". Two words with the same pronunciation can have different spellings and meanings—a sentence may be syntactically correct, but be nonsense. For example, the sentence "John ate the mountain" can be syntactically parsed as a valid sentence and be correctly analyzed by the semantic analyzer, but it is still nonsense. Another purpose of the pragmatic analyzer is to remove ambiguities from the knowledge representation of sentence if possible.

18.5 SEARCHING

One of the techniques for solving problems in artificial intelligence is *searching*, which is discussed briefly in this section. Searching can be describe as solving a problem using a set of states (a situation). A search procedure starts from an initial state, goes through intermediate states until finally reaching a target state. For example, in solving a puzzle, the initial state is the unsolved puzzle, the intermediate states are the steps taken to solve the puzzle, and the target state is the situation in which the puzzle is solved. The set of all states used by a searching process is referred to as the **search space**.

Figure 18.13 shows an example of a search space with five states. Any of the states can be the initial or the target space. The directed lines show how one can go from one state to another by taking the appropriate action. Note that it may not be possible to go from one state to another if there is no action or series of actions to do so.

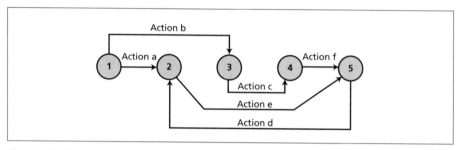

Figure 18.13 An example of a search space

Example 18.6

One example of a puzzle that shows the search space is the famous 8-puzzle. The puzzle is contained in a tray that can be thought of as a grid of nine squares. The tray contains only eight tiles, which means that one of the grids is always empty. The tiles are numbered from 1 to 8. Given an initial random arrangement of the tiles (the initial state), the goal is to rearrange the tiles until an ordered arrangement of the tiles is reached (the target state). The rule of the game is that a tile can be slid into an empty slot. Figure 18.14 shows an instance of the initial and the target states.

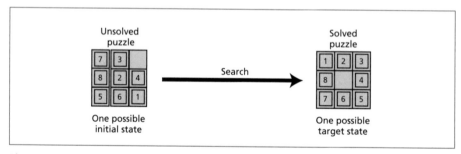

Figure 18.14 The initial and possible states for Example 18.6

Search methods

There are two general search methods: *brute-force* and *heuristic*. The brute force method is itself either breadth-first or depth first

Brute-force search

We use **brute-force search** if we do not have any prior knowledge about the search. For example, consider the steps required to find our way through the maze in Figure 18.15 with points A and T as starting and finishing points respectively. The tree diagram for the maze is shown in Figure 18.16.

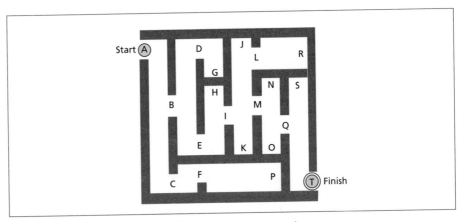

Figure 18.15 A maze used to show brute force search

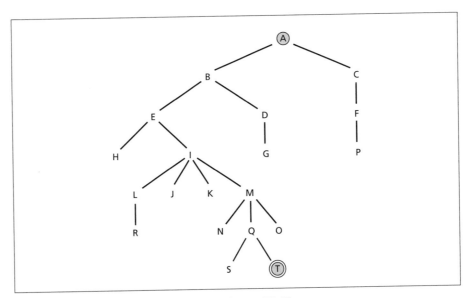

Figure 18.16 The tree for the maze in Figure 18.15

Breadth-first search

In this method we start from the root of the tree and examine all the nodes at each level before we move to the next level. The breadth-first search from left to right for the maze is shown in Figure 18.18. Note that we have to search all nodes before we reach the target state, so the method is very inefficient. If we search from right to left, the number of nodes we need to search may be different.

Depth-first search

In this method we start from the root of the tree and do a forward search until we hit the goal or arrive at a dead end. If we hit a dead end, we backtrack to the nearest branch and do a forward search again. We continue this process until we reach the goal.

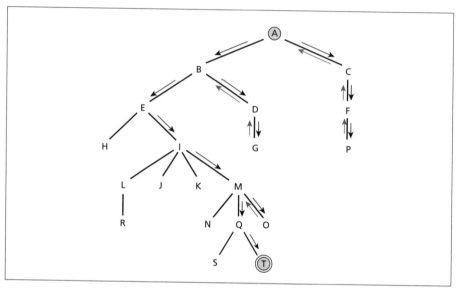

Figure 18.17 Depth-first search of the tree in Figure 18.16

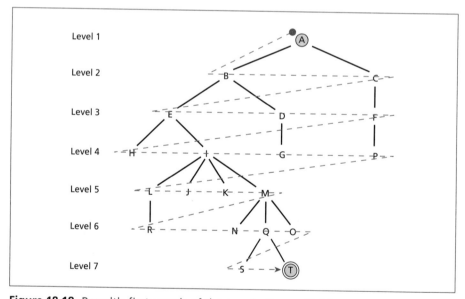

Figure 18.18 Breadth-first search of the tree in Figure 18.16

Figure 18.17 shows the depth-first search from the right for the maze shown in Figure 18.15. The search starts at the root node. The search path ACFP comes to a dead end, so we backtrack to A and continue the search along the path ABDG, which also comes to a dead end. Backtracking to node B and searching along path BEIMO results in another dead end. Backtracking to M and searching along the path MQT, we hit the goal. Note that this method is more efficient than the breadth-first method for the maze problem.

Heuristic search

Using **heuristic search**, we assign a quantitative value called a *heuristic value* (h value) to each node. This quantitative value shows the relative closeness of the node to the goal state. For example, consider solving the 8-puzzle of Figure 18.19.

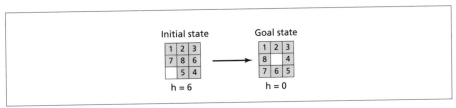

Figure 18.19 Initial and goal states for heuristic search

Assume the initial and goal states of the puzzle are as shown. The heuristic value for each tile is the minimum number of movements the tile must make to come to the goal state. The heuristic value for each state is the sum of the heuristic values of the tiles in that state.

Table 18.2 shows the heuristic value for the initial and the final states of the puzzle.

Table 18.2 Heuristic value

Tile number	1	2	3	4	5	6	7	8	Total
Heuristic value of initial state	0	0	0	1	1	2	1	1	6
Heuristic value of goal state	0	0	0	0	0	0	0	0	0

To start the search, we consider all possible states of the next level and their corresponding heuristic values. For our puzzle a single move results in only two possible states, with the h values shown in Figure 18.20.

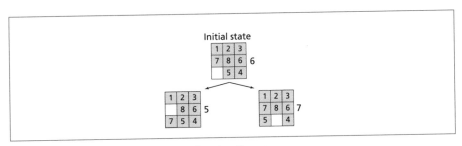

Figure 18.20 The heuristic values for the first step

Next we start with the state with the smaller *h* value and draw the possible states of the next level. We continue this way until we come to the state with an *h* value of zero (the goal state), as shown in Figure 18.21. The route to the puzzle's solution is shown with bold arrows.

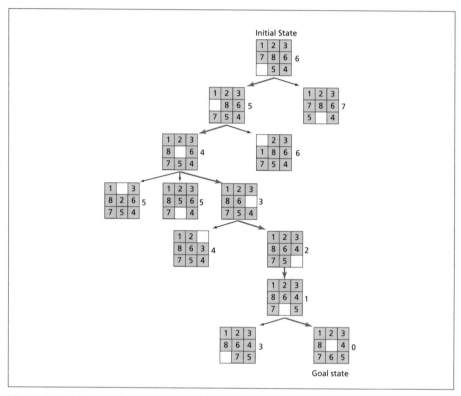

Figure 18.21 Heuristic search for solving the 8-puzzle

18.6   NEURAL NETWORKS

If an intelligent agent is supposed to behave like a human being, it may need to learn. Learning is a complex biological phenomenon that is not even totally understood in humans. Enabling an artificial intelligence agent to learn is definitely not an easy task. However, several methods have been used in the past that create hope for the future. Most of the methods use *inductive learning* or *learning by example*. This means that a large set of problems and their solutions is given to the machine from which to learn. In this section we discuss only one of these methods, which can be describe without complex mathematical concepts: **neural networks**. Neural networks try to simulate the learning process of the human brain using a network of neurons.

Biological neurons

The human brain has billions of processing units, called **neurons**. Each neuron, on average, is connected to several thousand other neurons. A neuron is made of three parts: **soma**, **axon**, and **dendrites**, as shown in Figure 18.22.

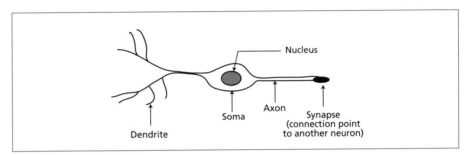

Figure 18.22 A simplified diagram of a neuron

The soma (body) holds the nucleus of the cell: it is the processor. The dendrites act as input devices: each dendrite receives input from another neuron. The axon acts as an output device: it sends the output to other neurons. The **synapse** is the connecting point between the axon of the neuron and dendrites of other neurons. The dendrites collect electrical signals from the neighboring neurons and pass them to the soma. The job of the synapse is to apply a weight to the signal that passes to the neighboring neuron: it acts as strong or weak connection based on the amount of chemical material it produces.

A neuron can be in one of the two states: *excited* or *inhibited*. If the sum of the received signals reaches a threshold, the body is excited and *fires* an output signal that passes to the axon and eventually to other neurons. If the sum of the received signals does not reach the threshold, the neuron remains in the inhibited state: it does not fire or produce an output.

Perceptrons

A **perceptron** is an artificial neuron similar to a single biological neuron. It takes a set of weighted inputs, sums the inputs, and compares the result with a threshold value. If the result is above the threshold value, the perceptron fires, otherwise, it does not. When a perceptron fires, the output is 1: when it does not fire, the output is zero. Figure 18.23 shows a perceptron with five inputs (x_1 to x_5), and five weights (w_1 to w_5). In this perceptron, if T is the value of the threshold, the value of the output is determined as:

$$S = (x_1 . w_1 + x_2 . w_2 + x_3 . w_3 + x_4 . w_4 + x_5 . w_5)$$

If $S > T$, then $y = 1$; else $y = 0$

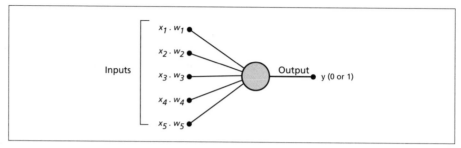

Figure 18.23 A perceptron

Example 18.7

Assume a case study with three inputs and one output. There are already four examples with known inputs and outputs, as shown in the following table:

Inputs			Output
1	0	0	0
0	0	1	0
1	0	1	0
1	1	1	1

This set of inputs is used to train a perceptron with all equal weights ($w_1 = w_2 = w_3$). The threshold is set to 0.8. The original weight for all inputs is 50%. The weights remain the same if the output produced is correct—that is, matches the actual output. The weights are increased by 10% if the output produced is less than the output data: the weights are decreased by 10% if the output produced is greater than the output data. The following table shows the process of applying the previous established examples to train the perceptron.

Inputs			Weight	Weighted sum	Output produced	Actual output	Action
1	0	0	50%	0.5	0	0	None
0	0	1	50%	1	1	0	Decrease
1	0	1	40%	8.0	0	0	None
1	1	1	40%	1.2	1	1	None

Note that the perceptron has been trained even with a small set of available data. In a real situation, a perceptron would be trained with a much larger set of data (100 or 1000 cases). After training, it is ready to accept new input data and produce acceptably correct output.

Multi-layer networks

Several layers of perceptions can be combined to create multilayer neural networks. The output from each layer becomes the input to the next layer. The first layer is called the *input* layer, the middle layers are called the *hidden* layers, and the last layer is called the *output* layer. The nodes in the input layer are not neurons, they are only distributors. The hidden nodes are normally used to impose the weight on the output from the previous layer. Figure 18.24 shows an example of a neural network with three layers.

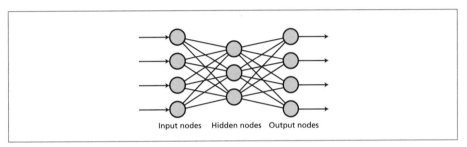

Input nodes   Hidden nodes   Output nodes

Figure 18.24 A multi-layer neural network

Applications

Neural networks can be used when enough pre-established inputs and outputs exist to train the network. Two areas in which neural networks have proved to be useful are optical character recognition (OCR), in which the intelligent agent is supposed to read any handwriting, and credit assignment, where different factors can be weighted to establish a credit rating, for example for a loan applicant.

18.7   RECOMMENDED READING

For more details about the subjects discussed in this chapter, the following books are recommended:

- ❏ Cawsey A: *The Essence of Artificial Intelligence, Upper Saddle River*, NJ: Prentice Hall, 1998
- ❏ Luger G: *Artificial Intelligence: Structures and Strategies for Complex Problem Solving, Reading*, MA: Addison Wesley, 2004
- ❏ Winston P: *Artificial Intelligence*, Reading, MA: Addison Wesley, 1993
- ❏ Coppin B: *Artificial Intelligence Illuminated*, Sudbury, MA: Jones and Bartlett, 2004
- ❏ Russel S and Norvig P: *Artificial Intelligence: A Modern Approach*, Upper Saddle River, NJ: Prentice Hall, 2003
- ❏ Dean T: *Artificial Intelligence: Theory and Practice*, Redwood City, Reading, MA: Addison Wesley, 2002

18.8   KEY TERMS

This chapter has introduced the following key terms, which are listed here with the pages on which they first occur:

artificial intelligence 466	axon 491
brute-force search 486	default logic 475
dendrite 491	edge detection 480
expert system 477	frames 468
heuristic search 489	high-order logic 474
image processing 479	intelligent agent 466
LISP 467	modal logic 474
neural network 490	neuron 491
parser 484	perceptron 491
physical agent 467	pragmatic analysis 485
predicate logic 469	PROLOG 467
propositional logic 469	quantifier 473
rule-based system 475	search space 485
segmentation 480	semantic analysis 485
semantic network 467	software agent 466
soma 491	speech recognition 483
synapse 491	syntactic analysis 483
temporal logic 474	thresholding 481
Turing test 466	

18.9   SUMMARY

- Artificial intelligence is the study of programmed systems that can simulate, to some extent, human activities such as perceiving, thinking, learning, and acting. One way to define artificial intelligence is the Turing Test, which compares the intelligent behavior of a human being with that of a computer.

- An intelligent agent is a system that perceives its environment, learns from it, and interacts with it intelligently. Intelligent agents can be divided into two broad categories: software agents and physical agents.

- Although some all-purpose languages such as C, C++, and Java are used to create intelligent software, two languages are specifically designed for AI: LISP and PROLOG.

- Knowledge representation is the first step in creating an artificial agent. We discussed four common methods for representing knowledge: semantic networks, frames, predicate logic, and rule-based systems. A semantic network uses a directed graph to represent knowledge. Frames are closely related to semantic networks, in which data structures (records) are used to represent the same knowledge. Predicate logic can represent a well-defined language developed during a long history of theoretical logic. A rules-based system represents knowledge using a set of rules that can be used to deduce new facts from known facts.

- One of the goals of AI is to create expert systems to perform tasks that normally need human expertise. It can be used in situations in which that expertise is in short supply, expensive, or unavailable.

- Another goal of AI is to create a machine that behaves like an ordinary human. The first part of this goal involves image processing or computer vision, which is an area of AI that deals with the perception of objects. The second part of this goal is language processing, analyzing and interpreting a natural language.

- In artificial intelligence, one of the techniques for solving problems is searching. Searching can be described as solving a problem using a set of states (situations). Two broad categories of searching are brute-force search and heuristic search.

- If an intelligent agent is supposed to behave like a human being, it may need to learn. Several methods have been used that create hope for the future. Most of the methods use inductive learning or learning by example. One common method involves the use of neural networks that try to simulate the learning process of the human brain using a network of neurons.

18.10 PRACTICE SET

Review questions

1. Describe the Turing test. Do you think this test can be used to define an intelligent system accurately?

2. Define an intelligent system and list two broad categories of agents.

3. Compare and contrast LISP and PROLOG when they are used in artificial intelligence.

4. Describe the need for knowledge representation and list four different methods discussed in this chapter.

5. Compare and contrast predicate logic and propositional logic.

6. Compare and contrast frames and semantic networks.

7. Define a rule-base system and compare it with semantic networks.

8. Compare and contrast expert systems and mundane systems.

9. List the different steps in image processing.

10. List the different steps in language processing.

11. Define a neural network and how it can simulate the learning process in human beings.

12. Define a perceptron.

Multiple-choice questions

13. The main foundation of thinking machines came from:
    a. Sir Isaac Newton
    b. Gottfried W. Leibniz
    c. George Boole
    d. Alan Turing
    e. John McCarthy

14. The term Artificial Intelligence (AI) was first coined by:
    a. Alan Turing
    b. John McCarthy
    c. Steven Spielberg
    d. Richard H. Richen

15. Two programming languages specifically designed for AI are:
    a. C and C++
    b. Java and C++
    c. LISP and PROLOG
    d. FORTRAN and COBOL

16. A node in semantic network becomes:
    a. a slot in frames
    b. an edge in frames
    c. an object in frames
    d. none of the above

17. Which of the following is not a sentence in propositional logic:
    a. Ford is a car.
    b. If John is home then Mary is at work.
    c. True.
    d. Where is John?

18. Which of the following is not an operator in propositional logic:
    a. ¬
    b. v
    c. →
    d. ◆

19. Two quantifiers ∀ and ∃ are used in:
    a. propositional logic
    b. predicate logic
    c. atomic sentences
    d. conclusion of any argument

20. To find the depth of an object, we use:
    a. edge detection
    b. segmentation
    c. stereo vision
    d. shading

21. To find the orientation of an object, we use:
    a. stereo vision
    b. motion
    c. texture
    d. segmentation

22. In language understanding, parsing a sentence is part of:
    a. speech recognition
    b. syntactic analysis
    c. semantic analysis
    d. pragmatic analysis

23. We use brute-force search:
    a. if we have no prior knowledge about the search
    b. if we need to do the search quickly
    c. if we need to do the search thoroughly
    d. after performing heuristic search

24. In a biological neuron, the synapse:
    a. holds the nucleus of the cell
    b. acts as input device
    c. is the connecting point between the axon of the neutron and dendrites of other neutrons

    d. acts as the output device

25. A perceptron:
    a. is a biological neuron
    b. is one of the parts of a biological neuron
    c. is an artificial neuron
    d. applies a weight on signals that pass through the neighboring neuron

Exercises

26. Draw a semantic network to show the relations between the following: medical doctor, family practitioner, gynecologist, intern, engineer, accountant, Dr. Pascal who is a French family practitioner.

27. Represent the semantic network of Exercise 26 as a set of frames.

28. Using the symbol R for the sentence "It is raining" and the symbol S for the sentence "It is sunny", write each of the following English sentences in propositional logic:
    a. It is not raining.
    b. It is not sunny.
    c. It is neither raining nor sunny.
    d. It is raining and sunny.
    e. If it is sunny, then it is not raining.
    f. If it is raining, then it is not sunny.
    g. It is sunny if and only if it is not raining.
    h. It is not true that if it is not raining, it is sunny.

29. If the symbols C, W, and H mean "it is cold", "it is warm", and "it is hot", write the English statements corresponding to the following statements in propositional logic:
    a. ¬H
    b. W v H
    c. W ∧ H
    d. W ∧ (¬ H)
    e. ¬ (W ∧ H)
    f. W → H
    g. (¬C) → W
    h. ¬ (W → H)
    i. H → (¬ W)
    j. ((¬C) ∧ H) v (C ∧ (¬H))

30. Using the symbols Wh, Re, Gr, and Fl for the predicates "is white", "is red", "is green", and

"is a flower" respectively, write the following sentences in predicate logic:

a. Some flowers are white.

b. Some flowers are not red.

c. Not all flowers are red.

d. Some flowers are either red or white.

e. There is not a green flower.

f. No flowers are green.

g. Some flowers are not white.

31. Using the symbols *Has*, *Loves*, *Dog*, and *Cat* for the predicates "has", "loves", "is a dog", and "is a cat" respectively, write the following sentences in predicate logic:

a. John has a cat.

b. John loves all cats.

c. John loves Anne.

d. Anne loves some dogs.

e. Not everything John loves is a cat.

f. Anne does not like some cats.

g. If John loves a cat, Anne loves it.

h. John loves a cat if and only if Anne loves it.

32. Using the symbols *Expensive*, *Cheap*, *Buys*, and *Sells* for the predicates "is expensive", "is cheap", "buys", and "sells" respectively, write the following sentences in predicate logic:

a. Everything is expensive.

b. Everything is cheap.

c. Bob buys everything that is cheap.

d. John sells something expensive.

e. Not everything is expensive.

f. Not everything is cheap.

g. If something is cheap, then it is not expensive.

33. Using the symbol *Identical* for the predicate "is identical to", write the following sentences in predicate logic. Note that the predicate "equal" needs two arguments:

a. John is not Anne.

b. John exists.

c. Anne does not exist.

d. Something exists.

e. Nothing exists.

f. There are at least two things.

34. Use a truth table to find whether the following argument is valid:

$$\{P \rightarrow Q, P\} \mid\text{-} Q$$

35. Use a truth table to find whether the following argument is valid:

$$\{P \vee Q, P\} \mid\text{-} Q$$

36. Use a truth table to find whether the following argument is valid:

$$\{P \wedge Q, P\} \mid\text{-} Q$$

37. Use a truth table to find whether the following argument is valid:

$$\{P \rightarrow Q, Q \rightarrow R\} \mid\text{-} (P \rightarrow R)$$

38. Draw a neural network that can simulate an OR gate.

39. Draw a neural network that can simulate an AND gate.

40. The initial and goal states of an 8-puzzle are shown in Figure 18.25. Draw the heuristic search tree for solving the puzzle.

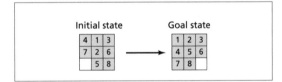

Figure 18.25 Exercise 40

41. Show the breadth-first search for the tree diagram shown in Figure 18.26.

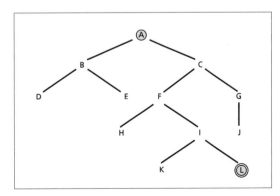

Figure 18.26 Exercise 41

42. Show the depth-first search for the tree diagram of Exercise 41.

43. Draw the tree diagram for the maze shown in Figure 18.27.

44. Draw the tree and show a breadth-first search for Exercise 43.

45. Draw the tree and show a depth-first search for Exercise 43.

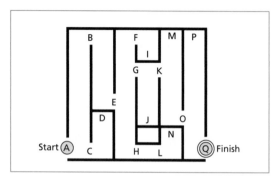

Figure 18.27 Exercise 43

A
Unicode

Computers use numbers. They store characters by assigning a number to each one. The original coding system was called ASCII (American Standard Code for Information Interchange) and had 128 characters (0 to 127) each stored as a 7-bit number. ASCII can satisfactorily handle lowercase and uppercase letters, digits, punctuation characters, and some control characters. An attempt was made to extend the ASCII character set to eight bits. The new code, which was called Extended ASCII, was never internationally standardized.

To overcome the difficulties inherent in ASCII and Extended ASCII—not enough bits to represent characters and other symbols needed for communication in other languages—the Unicode Consortium, a group of multilingual software manufacturers, created a universal encoding system to provide a comprehensive character set, called **Unicode**.

Unicode was originally a 2-byte character set. Unicode version 5, however, is a 4-byte code and is fully compatible with ASCII and Extended ASCII. The ASCII set, which is now called Basic Latin, is Unicode with the upper 25 bits set to zero. Extended ASCII, which is now called Latin-1, is Unicode with the 24 upper bits set to zero. Figure A.1 shows how the different systems are compatible.

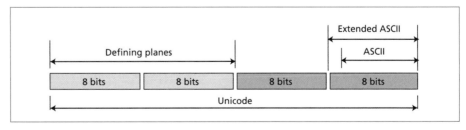

Figure A.1   Unicode compatibility

Each character or symbol in Unicode is defined by a 32-bit number. The code can define up to 2^{32} (4,294,967,296) characters or symbols. The description here uses hexadecimal digits in the following format, in which each X is a hexadecimal digit.

U+XXXXXXXX

A.1 PLANES

Unicode divides the whole code space into planes. The most significant 16 bits define the plane, which means we can have 65,536 (2^{16}) planes. For plane 0, the most significant 16 bits are 0s, $(0000)_{16}$, in plane 1 the bits are $(0001)_{16}$, in plane 2 they are $(0002)_{16}$, and so on until in the plane 65,535, they are $(FFFF)_{16}$. Each plane can define up to 65,536 characters or symbols. Figure A.2 shows the structure of Unicode code spaces and its planes.

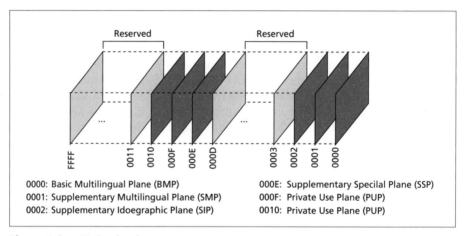

Figure A.2   Unicode planes

Basic multilingual plane (BMP)

The **basic multilingual plane**, plane 0, is designed to be compatible with the previous 16-bit Unicode. The most significant 16 bits in this plane are all zeros. The codes are normally shown as U+XXXX with the understanding that XXXX defines only the least significant 16 bits. This plane mostly defines character sets in different languages, with the exception of some codes used for control or other special characters (for more information, see the Unicode web page).

Other planes

Unicode had other planes:

❑   The **supplementary multilingual plane**, plane $(0001)_{16}$, is designed to provide more codes for multilingual characters that are not included in the BMP plane.

❑   The **supplementary ideographic plane**, plane $(0002)_{16}$, is designed to provide codes for ideographic symbols, any symbol that primarily denotes an idea or meaning in contrast to a sound or pronunciation.

- ❑ The **supplementary special plane**, plane $(000E)_{16}$, is used for special characters not found in the Basic Latin or Basic Latin-1 codes.
- ❑ **Private Use planes**, planes $(000F)_{16}$ and $(0010)_{16}$, are reserved for private use.

A.2 ASCII

Today, ASCII or Basic Latin, is part of Unicode. It occupies the first 128 codes in Unicode (U-00000000 to U-0000007F). Table A.1 contains the hexadecimal codes and symbols. The codes in hexadecimal only define the two least-significant digits in Unicode. To find the actual code, we prepend $(000000)_{16}$ to the code. Explanations of control symbols are given in Table A.2.

Table A.1 ASCII

Code	Symbol	Code	Symbol	Code	Symbol	Code	Symbol
$(00)_{16}$	Null	$(20)_{16}$	Space	$(40)_{16}$	@	$(60)_{16}$	`
$(01)_{16}$	SOH	$(21)_{16}$	!	$(41)_{16}$	A	$(61)_{16}$	a
$(02)_{16}$	STX	$(22)_{16}$	"	$(42)_{16}$	B	$(62)_{16}$	b
$(03)_{16}$	ETX	$(23)_{16}$	#	$(43)_{16}$	C	$(63)_{16}$	c
$(04)_{16}$	EOT	$(24)_{16}$	$	$(44)_{16}$	D	$(64)_{16}$	d
$(05)_{16}$	ENQ	$(25)_{16}$	%	$(45)_{16}$	E	$(65)_{16}$	e
$(06)_{16}$	ACK	$(26)_{16}$	&	$(46)_{16}$	F	$(66)_{16}$	f
$(07)_{16}$	BEL	$(27)_{16}$	'	$(47)_{16}$	G	$(67)_{16}$	g
$(08)_{16}$	BS	$(28)_{16}$	(	$(48)_{16}$	H	$(68)_{16}$	h
$(09)_{16}$	HT	$(29)_{16}$	)	$(49)_{16}$	I	$(69)_{16}$	i
$(0A)_{16}$	LF	$(2A)_{16}$	*	$(4A)_{16}$	J	$(6A)_{16}$	j
$(0B)_{16}$	VT	$(2B)_{16}$	+	$(4B)_{16}$	K	$(6B)_{16}$	k
$(0C)_{16}$	FF	$(2C)_{16}$	,	$(4C)_{16}$	L	$(6C)_{16}$	l
$(0D)_{16}$	CR	$(2D)_{16}$	-	$(4D)_{16}$	M	$(6D)_{16}$	m
$(0E)_{16}$	SO	$(2E)_{16}$	.	$(4E)_{16}$	N	$(6E)_{16}$	n
$(0F)_{16}$	SI	$(2F)_{16}$	/	$(4F)_{16}$	O	$(6F)_{16}$	o
$(10)_{16}$	DLE	$(30)_{16}$	0	$(50)_{16}$	P	$(70)_{16}$	p

Table A.1 ASCII (continued)

Code	Symbol	Code	Symbol	Code	Symbol	Code	Symbol
$(11)_{16}$	DC1	$(31)_{16}$	1	$(51)_{16}$	Q	$(71)_{16}$	q
$(12)_{16}$	DC2	$(32)_{16}$	2	$(52)_{16}$	R	$(72)_{16}$	r
$(13)_{16}$	DC3	$(33)_{16}$	3	$(53)_{16}$	S	$(73)_{16}$	s
$(14)_{16}$	DC4	$(34)_{16}$	4	$(54)_{16}$	T	$(74)_{16}$	t
$(15)_{16}$	NAK	$(35)_{16}$	5	$(55)_{16}$	U	$(75)_{16}$	u
$(16)_{16}$	SYN	$(36)_{16}$	6	$(56)_{16}$	V	$(76)_{16}$	v
$(17)_{16}$	ETB	$(37)_{16}$	7	$(57)_{16}$	W	$(77)_{16}$	w
$(18)_{16}$	CAN	$(38)_{16}$	8	$(58)_{16}$	X	$(78)_{16}$	x
$(19)_{16}$	EM	$(39)_{16}$	9	$(59)_{16}$	Y	$(79)_{16}$	y
$(1A)_{16}$	SUB	$(3A)_{16}$	:	$(5A)_{16}$	Z	$(7A)_{16}$	z
$(1B)_{16}$	ESC	$(3B)_{16}$	;	$(5B)_{16}$	[	$(7B)_{16}$	{
$(1C)_{16}$	FS	$(3C)_{16}$	<	$(5C)_{16}$	\	$(7C)_{16}$		
$(1D)_{16}$	GS	$(3D)_{16}$	=	$(5D)_{16}$	]	$(7D)_{16}$	}
$(1E)_{16}$	RS	$(3E)_{16}$	>	$(5E)_{16}$	^	$(7E)_{16}$	~
$(1F)_{16}$	US	$(3F)_{16}$	?	$(5F)_{16}$	_	$(7F)_{16}$	DEL

Some properties of ASCII

ASCII has some interesting properties that we need to briefly mention here:

1. The first code, $(00)_{16}$, which is non-printable, is the null character. It represents the absence of any character.

2. The last code, $(7F)_{16}$, is the delete character, which is also non-printable. It is used by some programs to delete the current character.

3. The space character, $(20)_{16}$, is a printable character. It prints a blank space.

4. Characters with codes $(01)_{16}$ to $(1F)_{16}$ are control characters: they are not printable. Table A.2 shows their functions. Most of these characters were used in data communication in out-of-date protocols.

5. The uppercase letters start from $(41)_{16}$. The lowercase letters start from $(61)_{16}$. When numerically compared, uppercase letters are smaller than lowercase ones. This means that when we sort a list based on ASCII values, the uppercase letters show before the lowercase letters.

Table A.2 Explanation for control characters

Symbol	Explanation	Symbol	Explanation
SOH	Start of heading	DC1	Device control 1
STX	Start of text	DC2	Device control 2
ETX	End of text	DC3	Device control 3
EOT	End of transmission	DC4	Device control 4
ENQ	Enquiry	NAK	Negative acknowledgment
ACK	Acknowledgment	SYN	Synchronous idle
BEL	Ring bell	ETB	End of transmission block
BS	Backspace	CAN	Cancel
HT	Horizontal tab	EM	End of medium
LF	Line feed	SUB	Substitute
VT	Vertical tab	ESC	Escape
FF	Form feed	FS	File separator
CR	Carriage return	GS	Group separator
SO	Shift out	RS	Record separator
SI	Shift in	US	Unit separator

6. The uppercase and lowercase letters differ by only one bit in the 7-bit code. For example, character A is $(41)_{16}$ and character a is $(61)_{16}$. The difference is bit 6, which is 0 in uppercase letters and 1 in lowercase letters. If we know the code for one case, we can find the code for the other easily by adding or subtracting $(20)_{16}$ in hexadecimal or by flipping the sixth bit. In other words, the code for character A is $(41)_{16} = (1000001)_2$, but the code for character a is $(61)_{16} = (1100001)_2$: the sixth bit in binary notation is flipped from 0 to 1.

7. The uppercase letters are not immediately followed by lowercase letters—there are some punctuation characters in between.

8. Decimal digits (0 to 9) begin at $(30)16$. This means that if we want to change a numeric character to its face value as an integer, we need to subtract $(30)16 = 48$ from it. For example, the code for 8 in ASCII is $(38)_{16} = 56$. To find the face value, we need to subtract 48 from this, or $56 - 48 = 8$.

B
Unified Modeling Language

Unified Modeling Language (UML) is a graphical language used for analysis and design. Through UML we can specify, visualize, construct, and document software and hardware systems using standard graphical notations. UML provides different levels of abstraction, called *views*, as shown in Figure B.1.

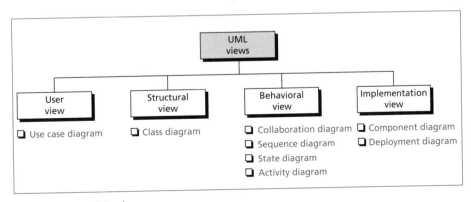

Figure B.1   UML views

The four views are:

1. The *user view*, which shows the interaction of the user with the system. This view is represented by use case diagrams.

2. The *structural view*, which shows the static structure of the system. This view is represented by class diagrams.

3. The *behavioral view*, which shows how the objects in the system behave. This view is represented by collaboration, sequence, state, and activity diagrams.

4. The *implementation view,* which shows how the system is implemented. It contains component and deployment diagrams.

B.1   THE USER VIEW

The user view is a high-level view of the whole system. It shows how a system is organized in general. There is only one type of diagram in user views, the use-case diagram.

Use-case diagrams

A project normally starts with a **use-case diagram**. A use-case diagram gives the user's view of a system: it shows how the users communicate with the system. Figure B.2 shows an example of a use-case diagram. A use-case diagram uses four main components: *system, use cases, actors,* and *relationships*. Each component is explained below.

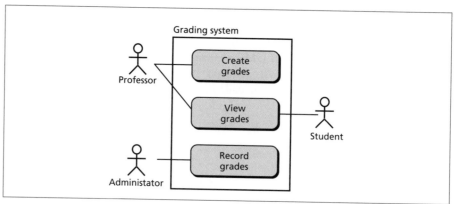

Figure B.2   A use case diagram

System	A system performs a function. We are interested only in a computer system. The computer system in a use-case diagram is shown by a rectangular box with the name of the system outside the box in the top-left corner.

System   A system performs a function. We are interested only in a computer system. The computer system in a use-case diagram is shown by a rectangular box with the name of the system outside the box in the top-left corner.

Use cases   A system contains many actions represented as use cases. Each use case defines one of the actions that can be taken by the users of a system. A use case in a use-case diagram is shown by a rectangle with rounded corners.

Actors   An actor is someone or something that uses the system. Although actors are shown as stick figures, they do not necessarily represent human beings.

Relationships   Relationships are associations between actors and use cases. A relationship is shown as a line connecting actors to use cases. An actor can relate to multiple use cases and a use case can be used by multiple actors.

B.2   THE STRUCTURAL VIEW

The structural view shows the static nature of the system, classes and their relationships. The structural view uses only one type of diagram, class diagrams.

Class diagrams

A **class diagram** manifests the static structure of a system. It shows the characteristics of the classes and the relationships between them. The symbol for a class is a rectangle with the name of the class written inside. Figure B.3 shows three classes, Person, Fraction, and Elevator, belonging to three different systems—that is, there is no relationship between them.

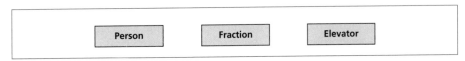

Figure B.3   Symbol for a class

Class diagrams are extended by adding attributes, types, and methods to the diagram. Relationships between classes are shown with association and generalization diagrams.

Attributes and types

A class symbol can include attributes and types in a separate compartment. An attribute is a property of a class and a type is the type of data used to represent that attribute. Figure B.4 shows some attributes of the classes Person and Fraction.

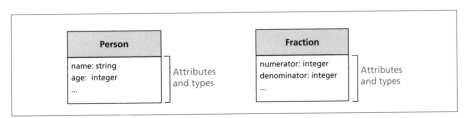

Figure B.4   Attributes added to the class symbols

Methods

A class can also be extended to include methods. A method is a procedure that can be used by an object (an instance of a class) or applied to an object. In other words, an object is either a doer or a receiver. Figure B.5 shows two classes with attributes and methods. The attributes and methods are listed in separate compartments.

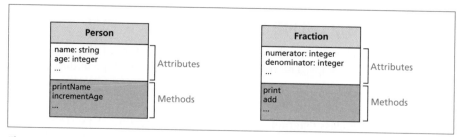

Figure B.5   Attributes and methods added to the class symbols

Association   An association is a conceptual relation between two classes. An association is shown by a solid line between two classes. If a name is given to the association, it is written next to the line with a solid arrow.

An association can be one-to-one, one-to-many, many-to-one or many-to-many. Figure B.6 shows four classes and some association between them. It shows that one professor (an object of the Professor class) can teach from one to five courses (1...5). Conversely, in this example, a course can have only one professor. The university (an object of the University class) can have many professors and many students (objects of the Student class), as indicated by the asterisk (*) on the association line. The figure also shows that a student can take many courses.

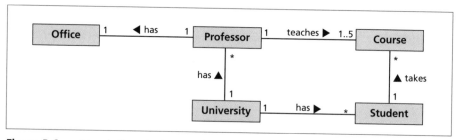

Figure B.6   Associations between classes

Generalization   Generalization organizes classes based on their similarities and differences. Generalization allows us to define *subclasses* and *superclasses*. A subclass inherits characteristics (attributes and methods) of all its superclasses, but it normally has some characteristics (attributes and methods) of its own. Figure B.7 shows single and multiple inheritance.

B.3   THE BEHAVIORAL VIEW

A behavioral view looks at the behavior of objects in a system. Depending on the type of the behavior, we can have four different diagrams: collaboration diagrams, state diagrams, sequence diagrams, and activity diagrams.

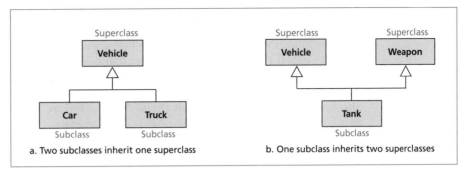

Figure B.7 Generalization (inheritance)

Collaboration diagrams

A collaboration diagram is similar to a class diagram. The difference is that the class diagram shows the relationship between classes, whereas a collaboration diagram shows the relationship between objects (instances of classes).

Any object instantiated from the class can also be shown in a rectangle with the name of the object followed by a colon and the name of the class. For an anonymous object, the name of the object is left out. Figure B.8 shows three objects instantiated from the class Person.

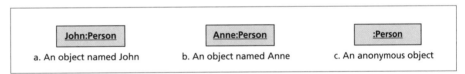

Figure B.8 Three objects instantiated from the same class

Attributes and values An attribute is a property of a class, while a value is a property of an object corresponding to an attribute. An object symbol can include values. Figure B.9 shows some attributes of the classes Person and Fraction with values for attributes within the classes.

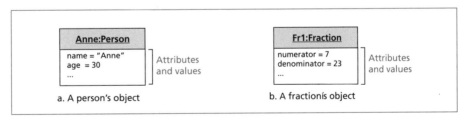

Figure B.9 Examples of attributes and values

Methods and operations Although an object symbol can also include methods and operations, it is not common in a collaboration diagram.

Links   A link in a collaboration diagram is an instance of an association in a class diagram. Objects can be related to each other using links. Two stereotype notations can be used for links: local and parameter. The first shows that one object uses another object as a local variable: the second shows that one object uses another object as a parameter. Multiplicity, as shown in the association between Student and Course in Figure B.6, can also be shown by multiple superimposed objects. Multiplicity can also be shown between objects of the same class. Figure B.10 shows that a Student's object uses multiple Course objects as parameters.

Figure B.10   A link between objects

Messages   An object can send a message to another object. A message can represent an event sent from the first object to the second. A message can also invoke a method in the second object. Finally, an object can create or destroy another object using a message. Messages are shown by an arrow pointing in the direction of the message and are shown over the link between objects. Figure B.11 shows how an Editor object sends a print message to a Printer object.

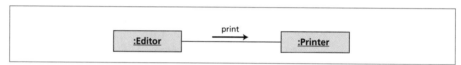

Figure B.11   A message sent from one object to another

State diagrams

A state diagram is used to show changes in the state of a single object. An object may change its state in response to an event. For example, a switch may change its state from *off* to *on* when it is turned on. A washing machine may change its state from *wash* to *rinse* in response to triggers from a timer.

Symbols   A state diagram uses three main symbols, as shown in Figure B.12.

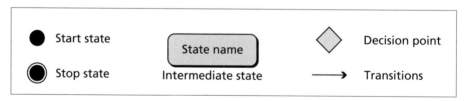

Figure B.12   Symbols used in a state diagram

States

There are three symbols for states: the start state, the stop state, and the intermediate state. The start state, which is drawn as a black circle with its name next to the circle, is allowed only once in the diagram. The stop state, which is drawn as a solid black circle inside another circle, can be repeated in the diagram. The intermediate state is drawn as a rectangle with rounded corner with the name of the state inside the rectangle.

Transitions

In a state diagram, a transition is a movement between states. The transition symbol is an arrowed line between two states. The arrow shows the next state. One or more transition can leave a state: only one transition can arrive at a state.

Decision point

A decision point is shown by a diamond. A transition can take several paths based on data or conditions in the object.

Events

In a state diagram, an object is triggered by an event, which can be external or internal. For example, a switch may move from an *off* state to an *on* state if it is turned on. An event is represented by a string which defines the operation in the class that handles the event. It may have parentheses containing the formal parameters to be passed to the operation. An event can also have a condition enclosed in brackets. The following shows an example of an event:

withdraw(amount)[amount < balance]

An object may or may not move to another state when triggered by an event.

Actions

Although an action may be triggered in several ways, we only mention an action triggered by an event. An action is shown by a string, which normally defines another object and the event that should be invoked for that object. If parameters are needed for the target object they are included in parentheses. The action is separated from the event by using a forward slash. The following shows an example of an action:

deposit(amount)   /   add(balance)

event   action

Example B.1

Figure B.13 shows a simple example of a state diagram. There are six states—start and stop states and four intermediate states—nine events, and four actions.

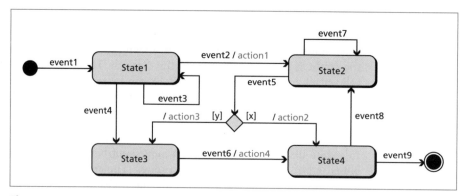

Figure B.13   An example of a state diagram

Sequence diagrams

A sequence diagram shows the interaction between objects (or actors) over time. In a sequence diagram, objects (or actors) are listed as columns and time, which notionally flows downwards, is represented as a vertical broken line.

Symbols

A sequence diagram uses five main symbols, as shown in Figure B.14.

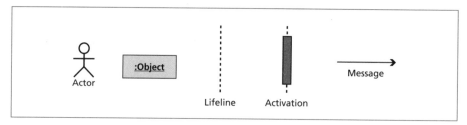

Figure B.14   Symbols used in a sequence diagram

Actor

The symbol for an actor is the same stick figure as we saw in use case diagrams. Since actors can also communicate with objects, they can be part of a sequence diagram.

Object

Objects, as we saw before, are instances of classes. A sequence diagram represents the interaction between the objects.

Lifeline

A lifeline, shown by a solid or dashed vertical line, represents an individual participant in a sequence diagram. It is usually headed by a rectangle that contains the name of the object or actor. The vertical line, which represents the lifespan of the object, extends to the point where the object is no longer active.

Activation

Activation, represented by a solid narrow rectangle, shows the time when an object is involved in an activity, that is, when it is not idle. For example, if an object has sent a message to another object and is waiting for a response, the object is involved during this time.

Message

Messages are shown as horizontal arrowed lines showing the interaction between objects (or actors).

Example B.2

Figure B.15 shows a simple example of a sequence diagram with one actor and three anonymous objects. The diagram also shows concurrency: the first object, after receiving the first message, concurrently sends two messages: one to the actor and one to the second object.

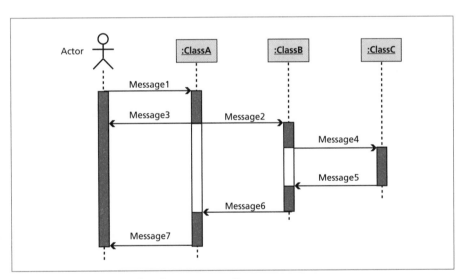

Figure B.15   An example of a sequence diagram

Activity diagrams

An activity diagram shows the breakdown of a complex operation or a process into a set of simpler operations or processes. An activity diagram is more detailed than a sequence diagram. A sequence diagram emphasizes objects, while an activity diagram shows more detailed operations performed by one or more objects. An activity diagram in object-oriented programming replaces a traditional flowchart in procedural programming. However, a traditional flowchart shows only sequential flow control (serial), while an activity diagram can show both sequential and concurrent (parallel) flow control.

Symbols   An activity diagram uses six main symbols, as shown in Figure B.16.

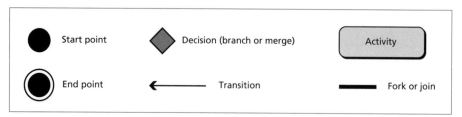

Figure B.16   Symbols used in an activity diagram

Activities

An activity is a step in an activity diagram. We show an activity using a rectangle with rounded corner that contains the name of the activity. The level of detail in an activity should be consistent for the whole diagram. If more detail is needed for one of the activities, a new diagram should be drawn to show it.

Transitions

Similar to a state diagram, a transition in an activity diagram is shown by an arrowed line. The arrow shows the direction of the action.

Start and end points

The start point in an activity diagram is a solid circle with a single outgoing transition: the stop point is a solid circle surrounded by a hollow circle (bull's eye) with a single incoming transition. There can be only one start point. While logically there can be only one end point, multiple end points are allowed to make the diagram easier to read.

Decision and merge

A diamond shows a decision or a merge point. A transition can take several paths based on conditions. When used as a decision point, a diamond symbol can have only one entry, with two or more exits. When used as a merge point, a diamond symbol can have two or more entries but only one exit.

Fork or joint

A thick line shows a fork or join in parallel processing. A fork symbol shows the start of two or more threads of processes: a joint symbol shows the end of the threads.

Example B.3

Figure B.17 shows an example of an activity diagram. Activities 2 and 3 are done concurrently (parallel processing).

Swimlanes

Sometimes operations in an activity diagram are performed by different objects or actors. To show that more than one object or actor is involved, *swimlanes* are added to an activity diagram, as shown in Figure B.18.

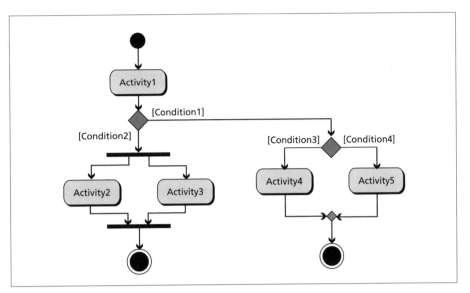

Figure B.17   An example of an activity diagram

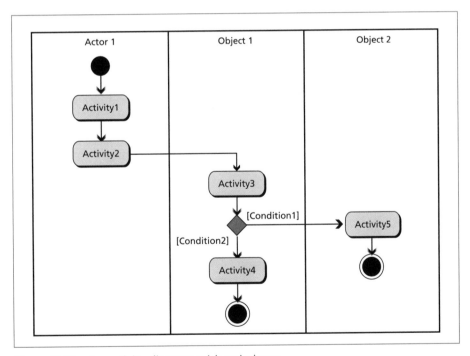

Figure B.18   An activity diagram with swimlanes

B.4   THE IMPLEMENTATION VIEW

An implementation view shows how the final product is implemented. Two types of diagrams are used to show the implementations: component diagrams and deployment diagrams.

Component diagrams

A component diagram shows the software components and the dependencies among them. The components are shown as rectangles with two small rectangles on their left edges. A dependency between the components is shown by a dashed line with an arrow on the end. We can also use stereotyping on the dependency line by including stereotype relations such as **<<report>>**. Figure B.19 shows a component diagram.

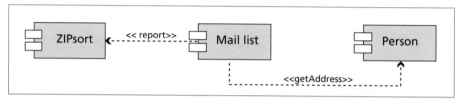

Figure B.19   An example of a component diagram

Deployment diagrams

A deployment diagram shows nodes connected by communication links. A node is shown as a cuboid and the communication association (link) is shown as a line connecting two nodes. A node can also include one or more components. Figure B.20 shows a simple deployment diagram.

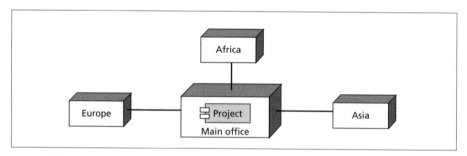

Figure B.20   An example of a deployment diagram

C
Pseudocode

One of the most common tools for defining algorithms is **pseudocode**. Pseudocode is an English-like representation of the code required for an algorithm. It is part English and part structured code. The English part provides a relaxed syntax that is easy to read. The code part consists of an extended version of the basic algorithmic constructs: *sequence*, *selection*, and *loop*. Algorithm C.1 shows an example of pseudocode. We briefly discuss each component in the next section.

C.1 COMPONENTS

An algorithm written in pseudocode can be decomposed into several elements and constructs.

Algorithm header

Each algorithm begins with a header that names it. For example, in Algorithm C.1, the header starts with the word *Algorithm*, which gives the algorithm's title as *FindingSmallest*.

Purpose, conditions, and return

After the header, we normally mention the purpose, the preconditions, postconditions, and the data returned from the algorithm.

Algorithm C.1   Example of pseudocode

```
Algorithm: FindingSmallest (list)

Purpose: Finds the smallest number among a list of numbers

Pre: List of numbers

Post: None

Return: The smallest number in the list
{
        smallest  ←  first number
        Loop (not end of list)
        {
                If (next number < smallest)
                {
                        smallest  ←  second number
                }
        }
        Return value of smallest
}
```

Purpose

The **purpose** is a short statement about what the algorithm does. It needs to describe only the general algorithm processing. It should not attempt to describe all of the processing. In Algorithm C.1 the purpose starts with the word *Purpose* and continues with the goal of the algorithm.

Precondition

The **precondition** lists any precursor requirements. For example, in Algorithm C.1 we require that the list be available to the algorithm.

Postcondition

The **postcondition** identifies any effect created by the algorithm. For example, the algorithm may require the printing of data.

Return

We believe that every algorithm should show what is returned from the algorithm. If there is nothing to be returned, we advise that *null* be specified. In Algorithm C.1, the smallest value that is found is returned.

Statement

Statements are commands such as *assign, input, output, if-then-else,* and *loop,* as shown in Algorithm C.1. Nested statements—statements inside another statement—are indented. The list of nested statement starts with the opening brace (curly bracket) and ends with a closing brace. The whole argument is a list of nested statements inside the algorithm itself. For this reason, we see an opening brace at the beginning and a closing brace at the end.

Statement constructs

When Niklaus Wirth first proposed the structured programming model, he stated that any algorithm could be written with only three programming constructs: *sequence, selection,* and *loop.* Our pseudocode contains only these three basic constructs. The implementation of these constructs relies on the richness of the implementation language. For example, the loop can be implemented as a *while, do-while,* or *for* statement in the C language.

Sequence

A **sequence** is a series of statements that do not alter the execution path within an algorithm. Although it is obvious that statements such as *assign* and *add* are sequence statements, it is not so obvious that a call to other algorithms is also considered a sequence statement. The reason lies in the structured programming concept that each algorithm has only one entry and one exit. Furthermore, when an algorithm completes, it returns to the statement immediately after the call that invoked it. You can therefore properly consider the algorithm call a sequence statement. Algorithm C.2 shows a sequence.

Algorithm C.2 A sequence

```
...
{
    ...
    x   ← first number
    y   ← second number
    z   ← x × y
    call Argument X
    ...
}
```

Selection

Selection statements evaluate one or more alternatives. If true, one path is taken, if false, a different path is taken. The typical selection statement is the two-way selection (*if-else*). Whereas most languages provide for multi-way selections, we provide none in pseudocode. The alternatives of the selection are identified by indentation, as shown in Algorithm C.3.

Algorithm C.3   Example of selection

```
...
{
    ...
    If (x < y)
    {
            Increment x
            Print x
    }
    Else
    {
            Decrement y
            Print y
    }
    ...
}
```

Loop

A **loop** iterates a block of code. The loop in our pseudocode most closely resembles the *while* loop. It is a pretest loop: that is, the condition is evaluated before the body of the loop is executed. If the condition is true, the body is executed. If the condition is false, the loop terminates. Algorithm C.4 shows an example of a loop.

Algorithm C.4   Example of a loop

```
...
{
    ...
    Loop (more line in the file File1?)
    {
            Read next line
            Delete the leading space
            Copy the line to File2
    }
    ...
}
```

D
Structure Charts

The structure chart is the primary tool in a procedure-oriented software design phase. As a design tool, it is created before we start writing our program.

D.1 STRUCTURE CHART SYMBOLS

Figure D.1 shows the various symbols used in a structure chart.

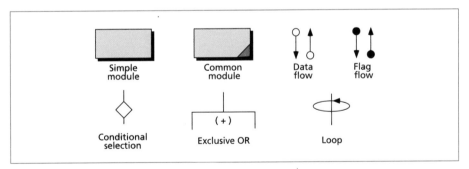

Figure D.1   Structure chart symbols

Module symbol

Each rectangle in a structure chart represents a module. The name in the rectangle is the name you give to the module (Figure D.2).

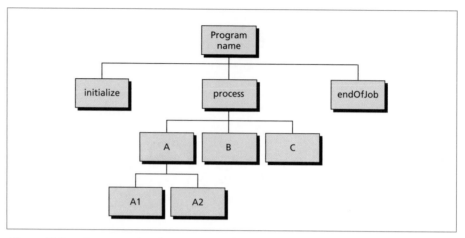

Figure D.2   An example of a structure chart

Selection in structure charts

Figure D.3 shows two symbols for a module that is called by a selection statement: the condition and the exclusive OR.

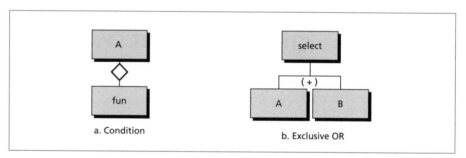

Figure D.3   Selection in a structure chart

In Figure D.3a, the module *A* contains a conditional call to a submodule, *fun*. If the condition is true, we call *fun*. If it is not true, we skip *fun*. This situation is represented in a structure chart as a diamond on the vertical line between the two module blocks.

Figure D.3b represents selection between two different modules. In this example the module *select* chooses between *A* and *B*. One and only one of them will be called each time the selection statement is executed. This is known as an exclusive OR: one of the two alternatives is executed to the exclusion of the other. The exclusive OR is represented by a plus sign between the modules.

Now consider the design of a series of modules that can be called exclusively. This occurs when a multi-way selection contains calls to several different modules.

Figure D.4 contains an example of a selection statement that calls different modules based on color.

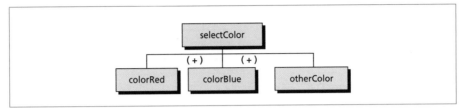

Figure D.4   An example of a selection

Loops in structure charts

Let's look at how loops are shown in a structure chart. The symbols are very simple. Loops go in circles, so the symbol used is a circle. Programmers use two basic looping symbols. The first is a simple loop, shown in Figure D.5a. The other is the conditional loop, shown in Figure D.5b. When the module is called unconditionally, as in a *while* loop, the circle flows around the line above the called module. On the other hand, if the call is conditional, as in a module called in an *if-else* statement inside a loop, then the circle includes a decision diamond on the line.

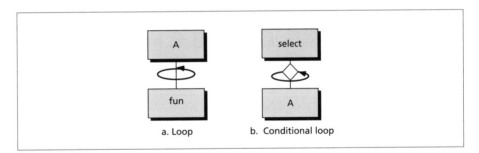

Figure D.5   Loops in a structure chart

Figure D.6 shows the basic structure for a module called *process*. The circle is *below* the module that controls the loop. In this example, the looping statement is contained in *process*, and it calls three modules, *A*, *B*, and *C*. The exact nature of the loop cannot be determined from the structure chart. It could be any of the three basic looping constructs.

D.2 READING STRUCTURE CHARTS

Structure charts are read *top-down* and *left-to-right*. Referring to Figure D.2 (page 522), this rule says that the program (*main*) consists of three submodules: *initialize*, *process*, and *endOfJob*. According to the left-to-right rule, the first call in the

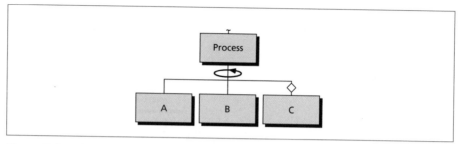

Figure D.6   An example of a loop

program is to *initialize*. After *initialize* is complete, the program calls *process*. When *process* is complete, the program calls *endOfJob*. In other words, the modules on the same level of a structure chart are called in order from left to right.

The concept of top-down is demonstrated by *process*. When *process* is called, it calls *A*, *B*, and *C* in turn. Module *B* does not start running, however, until *A* is finished. While *A* is running, it calls *A1* and *A2* in turn. In other words, all modules in a line from *process* to *A2* must be called before module *B* can start.

Often a program will contain several calls to a common module. These calls are usually scattered throughout the program. The structure chart will show the call wherever it logically occurs in the program. To identify common structures, the lower right corner of the rectangle will contain crosshatching or will be shaded. If the common module is complex and contains submodules, these submodules need to be shown only once. An indication that the incomplete references contain additional structure should be shown. This is usually done with a line below the module rectangle and a cut (~) symbol. This idea is shown in Figure D.7, which uses a common module, *average*, in two different places in the program. Note, however, that we never show a module connected to two calling modules graphically.

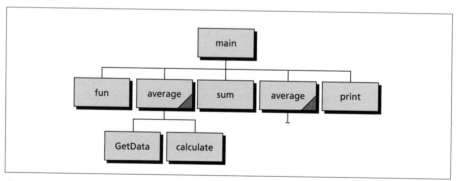

Figure D.7   Several calls to the same module

D.3 RULES OF STRUCTURE CHARTS

We summarize the rules discussed in this section:

- ❑ Each rectangle in a structure chart represents a module.
- ❑ The name in the rectangle is the name that will be used in the coding of the module.
- ❑ The structure chart contains only module flow. No code is indicated.
- ❑ Common modules are indicated by crosshatching or shading in the lower right corner of the module rectangle.
- ❑ Data flows and flags are optional. When used, they should be named.
- ❑ Input flows and flags are shown to the left of the vertical line; output flows and flags are shown to the right.

E
Boolean Algebra and Logic Circuits

E.1 BOOLEAN ALGEBRA

Boolean algebra deals with variables and constants that take only one of two values: 1 or 0. This algebra is a suitable way to represent information in a computer, which is made up of a collection of signals that can be only in one of the two states: on or off.

Constants, variables, and operators

We use constants, variables, and operators in Boolean algebra.

Constants
There are only two constants: 1 and 0. The value of 1 is associated with the logical value *true*: the value 0 is associated with the logical value *false*.

Variables
We use letters such as x, y, and z to represent variables. Boolean variables can take only the values 0 or 1.

Operators
We use three basic operators: NOT, AND, and OR. We use a prime to represent NOT, a dot to represent AND, and a plus sign to represent OR, as shown below:

$$x' \rightarrow \text{NOT } x \qquad x.y \rightarrow x \text{ AND } y \qquad x+y \rightarrow x \text{ OR } y$$

An operator takes one or two values and creates one output value. The first operator, NOT, is a unary operator that takes only one value: the other two, AND and OR, are binary operators that take two values. Note that the choice of operators is arbitrary: we can construct all gates from the NAND gate (explained later).

Expressions

An expression is a combination of Boolean operators, constants, and variables. The following shows some Boolean expressions.

0	**x**	**x . 1**	**x + 0**
x + 1 + y	**x . (y + z)**	**x + y + z**	**x . y . z . t**

Logic gates

A **logic gate** is an electronic device that normally takes 1 to N inputs and creates one output. In this appendix, however, we use gates with only one or two inputs for simplicity. The logical value of the output is determined by the expression representing the gate and the input values. A variety of logic gates are commonly used in digital computers. Figure E.1 shows the symbols for the eight most common gates, their truth tables (see Chapter 4), and the expressions that can be used to find the output when the input or inputs are given.

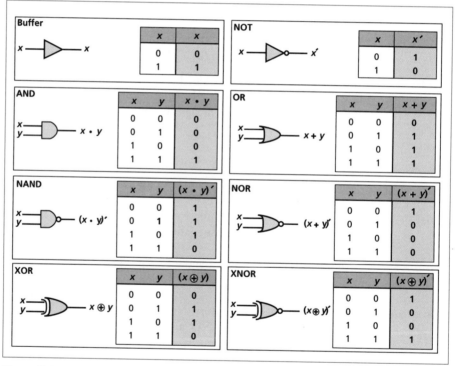

Figure E.1   Symbols and truth tables for common gates

❏   **Buffer.** The first gate is just a buffer, in which the input and the output are the same. If the input is 0, the output is 0: if the input is 1, the output is 1. The buffer only amplifies the input signal.

- ❑ **NOT**. The NOT gate is the implementation of the NOT operator. The output of this gate is the complement of the input. If the input is 1, the output is 0: if the input is 0, the output is 1.

- ❑ **AND**. The AND gate is the implementation of the AND operator. It takes two inputs and creates one output. The output is 1 if both inputs are 1s, otherwise it is 0. Sometimes the AND operator is referred to as *product*.

- ❑ **OR**. The OR gate is the implementation of the OR operator. It takes two inputs and creates one output. The output is 1 if any of the inputs, or both of them, is 1, otherwise it is 0. Sometimes the OR gate is referred to as *sum*.

- ❑ **NAND**. The NAND gate is a logical combination of an AND gate followed by a NOT gate. The reason for its existence can be explained when we discuss the actual implementation of these gates. The output of a NAND gate is the complement of the corresponding AND gate if the inputs to two gates are the same.

- ❑ **NOR**. The NOR gate is a logical combination of an OR gate followed by a NOT gate. The reason for its existence can also be explained when we discuss the actual implementation of these gates. The output of a NOR gate is the complement of the corresponding OR gate if the inputs to two gates are the same.

- ❑ **XOR**. The XOR (exclusive-OR) gate is defined by the expression $(x \cdot y' + x' \cdot y)$, which is normally represented as $(x \oplus y)$. The output of this gate is 1 when the two inputs are different and 0 when the inputs are the same. One can say that this is a more restricted OR gate. The output of an XOR gate is the same as the OR gate except that, if the two inputs are 1s, the output is 0.

- ❑ **XNOR**. The XNOR (exclusive-NOR) gate is defined by the expression $(x \cdot y' + x' \cdot y)'$ which is normally represented as $(x \oplus y)'$. It is the complement of the XOR gate. The output of this gate is 1 when the two inputs are the same and 0 when the inputs are different. One can say that this represents the logical idea of equivalence: only if the two inputs are equal is the output 1.

Implementation of gates

The logic gates discussed in the previous section can be physically implemented using electronic switches (transistors). The most common implementation uses only three gates: NOT, NAND, and NOR. A NAND gate uses less components than an AND gate. This is also true for the NOR gate versus the OR gate. As a result, NAND and NOR gates have become the common standard in the industry. We only discuss these three implementations. Although we show simple switches in this discussion, we need to know that, in practice, switches are replaced by transistors. A transistor, when used in gates, behaves like a switch. The switch can be opened or closed by applying the appropriate voltage to the input. Several different technologies are used to implement these transistors, but we leave this discussion to books on electronics.

Implementation of the NOT gate

The NOT gate can be implemented with an electronic switch, a voltage source, and a resistor, as shown in Figure E.2.

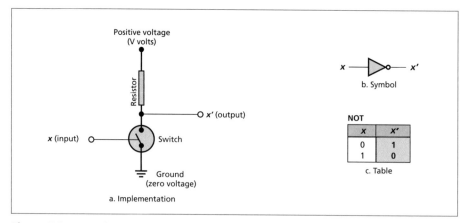

Figure E.2   Implementation of the NOT gate

The input to the gate is a control signal that holds the switch open or closed. An input signal of 0 holds the switch open, while an input signal of 1 closes the switch. The output is the voltage at the point before the switch (output terminal). If the value of this voltage is positive (V volts), the output is interpreted as 1: if the voltage is 0 (or below a threshold), the output is interpreted as 0. When the switch is open, there is no current through the resistor, and therefore no voltage drop. The output voltage is V (interpreted as logic 1). Closing the switch grounds the output terminal and makes its voltage 0 (or almost 0), which is interpreted as logic 0. Note that the behavior of the circuit matches the values shown in the table.

> **To implement a NOT gate, we need only one electronic switch.**

Implementation of the NAND gate

The NAND gate can be implemented using two switches in series (two inputs). For the current to flow through the circuit from the positive terminal to the ground, both switches must be closed—that is, both inputs must be 1s. In this case, the voltage of the output terminal is zero because it is grounded (logic 0). If one of the switches or both switches are open—that is, where the inputs are 00, 01, or 10— no current flows through the resistor. There is thus no voltage drop across the resistor and the voltage at the output terminal is V (logic 1).

Figure E.3 shows the implementation of the NAND gate. The behavior of the circuit matches the values shown in the table. Note that if an AND gate is needed, it can be made from a NAND gate followed by a NOT gate.

> **To implement a NAND gate, we need two electronic switches that are connected in series.**

Implementation of the NOR gate

The NOR gate can be implemented using two switches in parallel (two inputs). If both switches are open, then the current does not flow through the resistor. In this

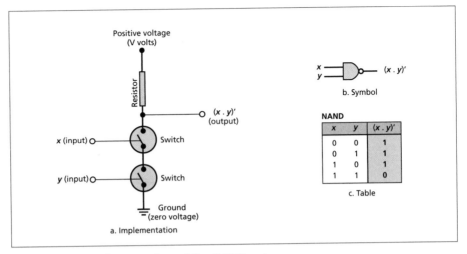

Figure E.3   Implementation of the NAND gate

case, there is no voltage drop across the resistor, which means the output terminal holds the voltage V (logic 1). If either or both of the switches are closed, the output terminal is grounded and the output voltage is zero (logic 0).

Figure E.4 shows the implementation of the NOR gate. The behavior of the circuit matches the values in the table. Note that if an OR gate is needed, it can be simulated using a NOR gate followed by a NOT gate.

To implement a NOR gate, we need two electronic switches that are connected in parallel.

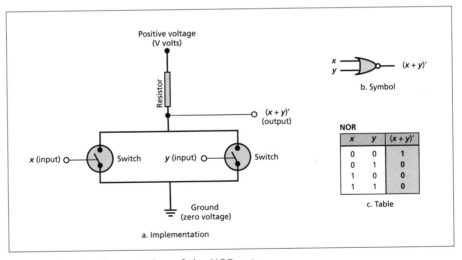

Figure E.4   Implementation of the NOR gate

Axioms, theorems, and Identities

To be able to work with Boolean algebra, we need to have some rules. The rules in Boolean algebra are divided into three broad categories: *axioms*, *theorems*, and *identities*.

Axioms

Boolean algebra, like any other algebra, uses some rules, called **axioms**: they cannot be proved. Table E.1 shows the axioms for Boolean algebra.

Table E.1 Axioms for Boolean algebra

	Related to NOT	Related to AND	Related to OR
1	$x = 0 \;\rightarrow\; x' = 1$		
2	$x = 1 \;\rightarrow\; x' = 0$		
3		$0 \cdot 0 = 0$	$0 + 0 = 0$
4		$1 \cdot 1 = 1$	$1 + 1 = 1$
5		$1 \cdot 0 = 0 \cdot 1 = 0$	$1 + 0 = 0 + 1 = 0$

Theorems

Theorems are rules that we prove using the axioms, although we must leave the proofs to textbooks on Boolean algebra. Table E.2 shows some theorems used in Boolean algebra.

Table E.2 Basic theorems for Boolean algebra

	Related to NOT	Related to AND	Related to OR
1	$(x')' = x$		
2		$0 \cdot x = 0$	$0 + x = x$
3		$1 \cdot x = x$	$1 + x = 1$
4		$x \cdot x = x$	$x + x = x$
5		$x \cdot x' = 0$	$x + x' = 1$

Identities

We can also derive many identities using the axioms and the theorems. We list only the most common in Table E.3, although we must leave the proofs to textbooks on Boolean algebra.

Table E.3 Basic Identities related to OR and AND operators

	Description	Related to AND	Related to OR
1	Commutativity	$x \cdot y = y \cdot x$	$x + y = y + x$
2	Associativity	$x \cdot (y \cdot z) = (x \cdot y) \cdot z$	$x + (y + z) = (x + y) + z$
3	Distributivity	$x \cdot (y + z) = (x \cdot y) + (y \cdot z)$	$x + (y \cdot z) = (x + y) \cdot (y + z)$
4	De Morgan's Rules	$(x \cdot y)' = x' + y'$	$(x + y)' = x' \cdot y'$
5	Absorption	$x \cdot (x' + y) = x \cdot y$	$x + (x' \cdot y) = x + y$

De Morgan's Rules play a very important role in logic design, as we will see shortly. They can be extended to more than one variable. For example, we can have the following two identities for three variables:

$$(x + y + z)' = x' \cdot y' \cdot z' \qquad (x \cdot y \cdot z)' = x' + y' + z'$$

Boolean functions

We define a **Boolean function** as a function with n Boolean input variables and one Boolean output variable, as shown in Figure E.5.

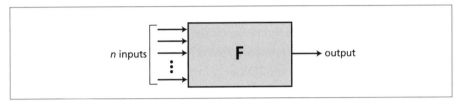

Figure E.5   A Boolean function

A function can be represented either by a truth table or an expression. The truth table for a function has 2^n rows and $n + 1$ columns, in which the first n columns define the possible values of the variables and the last column defines the value of the function's output for the combination of the values defined in the first n columns.

Figure E.6 shows the truth tables and expression representation for two functions F_1 and F_2. Although the truth table representation is unique, a function can be represented by different expressions. We have shown two of the expressions for each function. Note that the second expressions are shorter and simpler. Later we show that we need to simplify the expressions to make the implementation more efficient.

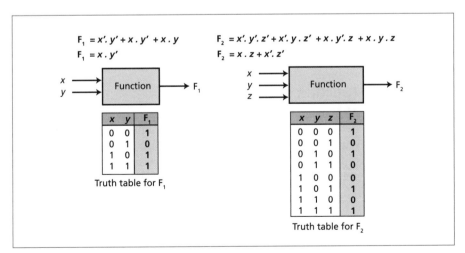

Figure E.6   Examples of table-to-expression transformation

Table-to-expression transformation

The specification of a function is normally given by a truth table (see Chapter 4). To implement the function using logic gates (as discussed earlier), we need to find an expression for the truth table. This can be done in two ways.

Sum of products

The first method of changing a truth table into an expression is referred to as the *sum of products* method. A sum of products representation of a function is made of up to 2^n terms in which each term is called a **minterm**. A minterm is a product (ANDing) of all variables in a function in which each variable appears only once. For example, in a three-variable function, we can have eight minterms, such as x'. y'. z' or x. y'. z'. Each term represents one row in the truth value. If the value of a variable is 0, the complement of the variable appears in the term: if the value of the variable is 1, the variable itself appears in the term. To transform a truth table to a sum of product representation, we use the following strategy:

1. Find the minterms for each row for which the function has a value of 1.
2. Use the sum (ORing) of the terms in step 1.

Product of sums

The second method of changing a truth table to an expression is referred to as the *product of sums* method. A product of sums representation of a function is made of up to 2^n terms in which each term is called a **maxterm**. A maxterm is a sum (ORing) of all variables in a function in which each variable appears only once. For example, in a three-variable function, we can have eight maxterms such as $x' + y' + z'$ or $x + y' + z'$. To transform a truth table to a product of sums representation, we use the following strategy:

1. Find the minterms for each row for which the function has a 0 value.
2. Find the complement of the sum of the terms in step 1.
3. Use De Morgan's rules to change minterms to maxterms.

Example E.1

Figure E.7 shows how we create the sum of products and product of sums for the function F1 and F2 in Figure E.6.

The sum of products is directly made from the table, but the product of sums needs the use of De Morgan's rules. Note that sometimes the first method gives the shorter expression and sometimes the second one.

Function simplification

Although we can implement a Boolean function using the logic gates discussed before, it is normally not efficient. The direct implementation of a function requires more gates. The number of gates could be reduced if we can carry out simplification. Traditionally one uses two methods of simplification: the algebraic method using Karnaugh maps, and the Quine-McCluskey method.

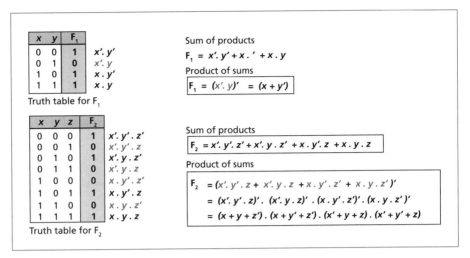

Figure E.7   Example E.1

Algebraic method

We can simplify a function using the axioms, theorems, and identities discussed before. For example, we can simplify the first function (F_1) in Figure E.7 as shown below:

$$
\begin{aligned}
F_1 &= x' \cdot y' + x \cdot y' + x \cdot y & \\
&= (x' + x) \cdot y' + x \cdot y & \text{Identity 3 (distributivity) for AND} \\
&= 1 \cdot y' + x \cdot y & \text{Theorem 5 for OR} \\
&= y' + x \cdot y & \text{Theorem 3 for AND} \\
&= y' + y \cdot x & \text{Theorem 1 (commutativity) for AND} \\
&= y' + x & \text{Identity 5 (absorption)} \\
&= x + y' & \text{Theorem 1 (commutativity) for OR}
\end{aligned}
$$

This means that if the non-simplified version needs eight gates, the simplified version needs only two gates, one NOT and one OR.

Karnaugh map method

Another simplification method involves the use of a **Karnaugh Map**. This method can normally be used for functions of up to four variables. A map is a matrix of 2^n cells in which each cell represents one of the values of the function. The first point that deserves attention is to fill up the map correctly. Contrary to expectations, the map is not always filled up row by row or column by column: it is filled up according to the value of variables as shown on the map. Figure E.8 shows an example where $n = 2$, 3, or 4.

In the truth table, we use the function values from the top to the bottom of the truth table. The map is filled up one by one, but the order of rows is 1, 2, 4, 3. In each row, the columns are filled up one by one, but the order of the columns is 1, 2, 4, 3. The fourth row comes before the third row: the fourth column comes before the third. This arrangement is needed to allow the maximum of simplification.

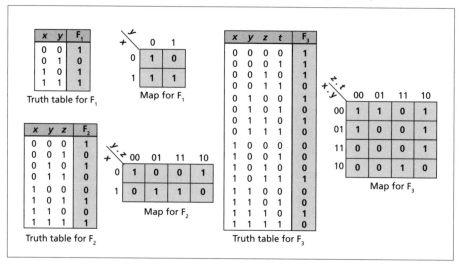

Figure E.8   Construction of Karnaugh Maps

Sum of products

The simplification can be done to create sum of products terms. When we simplify a function in this way we use minterms with value of 1. To create an efficient expression, we first combine adjacent minterm cells. Note that adjacency can also include wrap-around of bits.

Example E.2

Figure E.9 shows the sum of products simplification for our first function. The 1s in the second row comprise the entire x domain. The 1s in the first column comprise the entire y' domain. The resulting simplified function is $F_1 = (x) + (y')$. The figure also shows the implementing using one OR gate and one NOT gate.

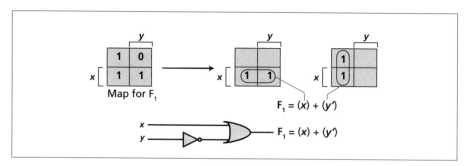

Figure E.9   Example E.2

Example E.3

Figure E.10 shows the sum of products simplification for our second function. The 1s in the second row are the intersection of x and z domains, which is represented as $(x . z)$. The 1s in the first row are the intersection of x' and z' domains, which is represented as $(x' . z')$. The resulting simplified function is $F_2 = (x . z) + (x' . z')$. The figure also shows the implementation using one OR gate, two AND gates, and two NOT gates.

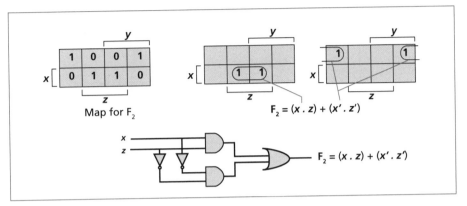

Figure E.10   Example E.3

Product of sums

The simplification can be done using the product of sums methods. When we simplify a function in this way, we need to use maxterms. To create an efficient expression, we first combine the adjacent minterm cells. However, the function obtained in this way is the complement of the function we are looking for: we need to use De Morgan's Rules to find our function.

Example E.4

Figure E.11 shows a product of sums simplification for our first function. Note that in this case the implementation is exactly the same as Figure E.11, but this is not always the case. Also note that our function has only one term: we need no AND gate.

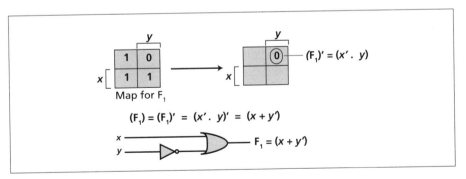

Figure E.11   Example E.4

Example E.5

Figure E.12 shows the product of sums simplification for our second function. Note that the process gives us $(F_2)'$, so we need to apply De Morgan's Rules to find F_2. The figure also shows the implementation using two NOT gates, two OR gates, and one AND gate. This implementation is less efficient than the one we found with minterms. We should always use the implementation that is more efficient.

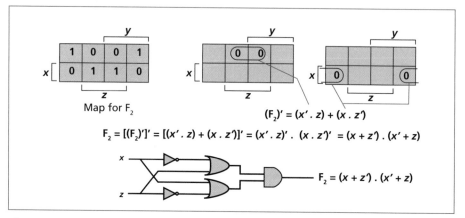

Figure E.12   Example E.5

E.2 LOGIC CIRCUITS

A computer is normally built out of standard components that we collectively refer to as **logic circuits**. Logic circuits are divided into two broad categories, known as *combinational circuits* and *sequential circuits*. We briefly discuss each category here and give some examples.

Combinational circuits

A **combinational circuit** is a circuit made up of a combination of logic gates with n inputs and m outputs. Each output at any time entirely depends on all given inputs.

> **In a combinational circuit, each output at any time depends entirely on all inputs.**

Figure E.13 shows the block diagram of a combinational circuit with n inputs and m outputs. Comparing Figure E.13 and Figure E.5, we can say that a combinational circuit with m outputs can be thought of as m functions, a function for each output.

The outputs of a combinational circuit are normally defined by a truth table. However, the truth table needs to have m outputs.

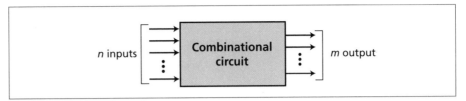

Figure E.13   A combinational circuit

Half adder

A simple example of a combinational circuit is a **half adder**, an adder that can only add two bits. A half adder is a combinational circuit with two inputs and two outputs. The two inputs define the two bits to be added. The first output is the sum of the two bits, while the second output is the carry bit that needs to be propagated to the next adder. Figure E.14 shows a half adder with its truth table and the logic gates used to make the circuit.

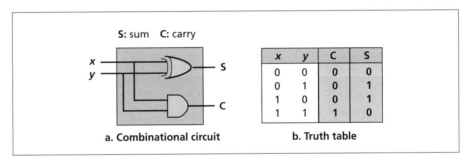

Figure E.14   Half adder

The sum of two bits can be achieved using an XOR gate: the carry can be achieved using an AND gate.

Multiplexer

A **multiplexer** is a combinational circuit with n inputs and only one output. The n inputs are made up of D data inputs and C control inputs ($n = D + C$). At any time, the multiplexer routes one of its D data inputs to its single data output. The selection is based on the value of control bits. To select one of the D data inputs, we need $C = \log_2 D$ control bits. If $D = 2$, at any time only one of the data inputs is routed to the output. The control input is only one bit. If the control input is 0, the first data input is directed to the output: if the control input is 1, the second input is routed to the output.

Figure E.15 shows the truth table and the circuit for a 2 × 1 multiplexer. Note that the circuit actually has three inputs and one output: the control input is considered one of the inputs.

Note that the truth table here is very simplified: the output depends only on the control input but the value of the output, however, is one of the two data inputs.

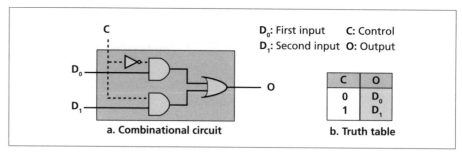

Figure E.15   Multiplexer

Sequential circuits

A combinational circuit is memoryless: it does not remember its previous output. At any moment the output depends on the current input. A **sequential circuit**, on the other hand, includes the concept of memory in the logic. The memory enables the circuit to remember its current state to be used in the future: the future state can be dependent on the current state.

Flip-flops

To add the idea of memory to the combinational circuit, a storage element called a **flip-flop** was invented that can hold one bit of information. A set of flip-flops can be used to hold a set of bits.

SR flip-flops

The simplest type of flip-flop is called an **SR flip-flop**, in which there are two inputs S (set) and R (reset) and two outputs Q and Q', which are always complements of each other. Figure E.16 shows the symbol, the circuit, and the characteristic table of an SR flip-flop. Note that the characteristic table is different from the truth tables we have used for combinational circuits. The characteristic table shows the next output, $Q(t + 1)$ based on the current output, $Q(t)$ and the input.

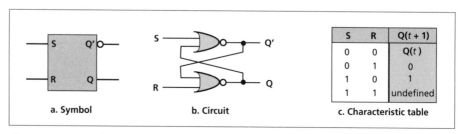

Figure E.16   SR flip-flop

The characteristic table shows that if both S and R are zero, $Q(t + 1) = Q(t)$ and the next output will be the same as the current output. If S is 0 and R is 1, $Q(t + 1) = 0$, which means the output will be reset (R = 1). If S is 1 and R is 0, $Q(t + 1) = 1$, which means that the output will be set. However, if both S and R are 1s, the next output is unpredictable (undefined). Note that we have not shown the value of Q' in the characteristic table, because it is always the complement of Q.

An SR flip-flop can be used as a set-reset device. For example, if the output is connected to an electric sounder, the alarm can be set by letting R = 0 and S = 1. After setting, the alarm continues sounding until it is reset by setting R = 1 and S = 0. The only flaw in this design is that R and S should not simultaneously be 1s.

To understand the behavior of the SR flip-flop we need to create its truth table. However, note that we now have three inputs and one output (Q and Q' are independent). Table E.4 shows the truth table for this flip-flop.

D flip-flop

The SR flip-flop cannot be used as a 1-bit memory, as it needs two inputs instead of one. A small modification to the SR flip-flop can create a **D flip-flop** (D stands for *data*). Figure E.17 shows the symbol and characteristics of a D flip-flop.

Note that the output of D flip-flop is the same as its input. However, the output remains as it is until the new input is given. This means that it memorizes its input states.

JK flip-flop

To remove the undefined state from the SR flip-flop, the **JK flip-flop** was invented (JK stands for Jack Kilby, who invented integrated circuits). Adding two AND gates to an SR flip-flop creates a JK flip-flop that has no undefined state. Figure E.18 shows the JK flip-flop and its characteristic table.

Table E.4   Truth table for an SR flip-flop

S	R	Q(t)	Q(t + 1)
0	0	0	0
0	0	1	1
0	1	0	0
0	1	1	0
1	0	0	1
1	0	1	1
1	1	0	undefined
1	1	1	undefined

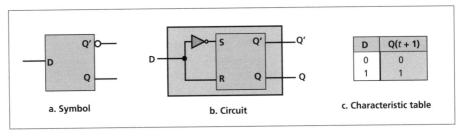

a. Symbol   b. Circuit   c. Characteristic table

Figure E.17   D flip-flop

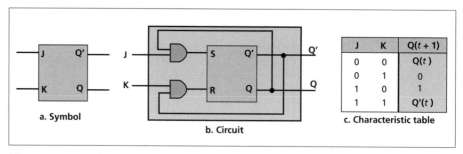

Figure E.18   JK flip-flop

T flip-flop

Another common type of flip-flop is the **T flip-flop** (T stands for *toggle*). This flip-flop can be made by connecting the two inputs of a JK flip-flop together and calling it the T input. This input toggles the state of the flip-flop: if the input is 0, the next state is the same as the current state. If the input is 1, the next state is the complement of current state. Figure E.19 shows the symbol, circuit, and characteristic table of the T flip-flop.

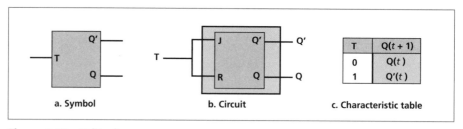

Figure E.19   T flip-flop

Synchronous versus asynchronous

The flip-flops we have discussed so far are all referred to as **asynchronous devices**: the transition from one state to another can happen only when there is a change in the input. Digital computers, on the other hand, are **synchronous devices**. A central clock in the computer controls the timing of all logic circuits. The clock creates a signal—a series of pulses with an exact pulse width—that coordinates all events. A simple event takes place only at the "tick" of this clock signal.

Figure E.20 shows an abstract idea of a clock signal. We call it *abstract* because in reality no electronic circuit can generate a signal with perfectly sharp impulses, but the signal shown here is sufficient for our discussion.

A flip-flop can be synchronous if we add one more input to the circuit: the clock input. The clock input can be ANDed with every input to gate the input so that it is effective only when the clock pulse is present. Figure E.21 shows the symbols for the clocked versions of all four flip-flops types we discussed. Figure E.22 shows the circuit of an SR flip-flop with a clock signal. The other flip-flops have the same additional circuitry.

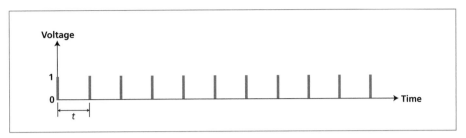

Figure E.20 Clock pulses

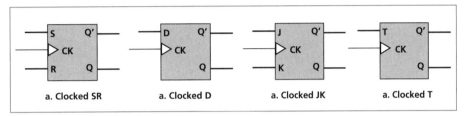

Figure E.21 Clocked flip-flops

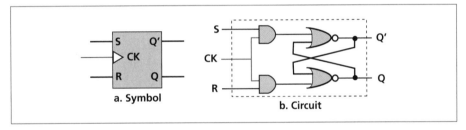

Figure E.22 Circuit of clocked SR flip-flop

Register

As the first application of a synchronous (clocked) sequential circuit, we will introduced a simplified version of a **register**. A register is an n-bit storage device that stores its data between consecutive clock pulses. At the trigger of the clock, the old data is discarded and replaced by the new data.

Figure E.23 shows a 4-bit register in which each cell is composed of a D flipflop. Note that the clock input is common for all cells. We have rotated our previous symbols to make the connections simpler.

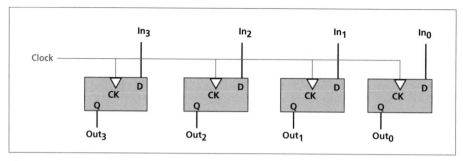

Figure E.23   A 4-bit register

Digital counter

An n-bit **digital counter** counts from 0 to $2^n - 1$. For example, when $n = 4$, the output of the counter is 0000, 0001, 0010, 0011, ..., 1111, so it counts from 0 to 15. An n-bit counter can be made out of n T flip-flops. At the start, the counter represents 0000. The count enable line—see Figure E.24—carries a sequence of 1s: the data (pulse) to be counted. Looking at the sequence of events, we can see that the rightmost bit is complemented with each positive transition of the count enable connection, simulating the arrival of a data item. When the rightmost bit changes from 1 to 0, the next leftmost bit is complemented. The process is repeated for all bits. This observation gives us a clue to the use of a T flip-flop. The characteristic table of this flip-flop shows that each input of value 1 complements the output. Note that this counter can count only up to 15 or $(1111)_2$. The arrival of the sixteenth data item resets the counter back to $(0000)_2$.

Figure E.24 shows the circuit of a 4-bit counter.

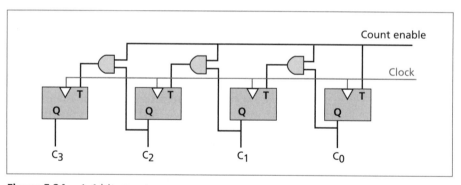

Figure E.24   A 4-bit counter

F

Examples of Programs in C, C++, and Java

In this appendix we present some examples of programs written in three languages: C, C++, and Java, to give a general idea about the structure of these three common languages.

Example 1

This is an example of using a *for* loop and a function in the C language. The program prints a calendar month using a function named *printMonth* that receives only the start day of the month and the number of days in the month. This is all that the program needs to know to print any month of the year. Program F.1 shows the main program, the function, and the result.

Program F.1 Example 1: printing a calendar month

```
/*        Test driver for function to print a calendar month.
          Written by:
          Date:
*/
#include <stdio.h>


// Prototype declarations
void printMonth (int startDay, int days);
int main (void)
{
          // Statements
```

Program F.1   Example 1: printing a calendar month (continued)

```
        printMonth (2, 29);                          // Day 2 is Tuesday
        return 0;
} // main

/*      ==================    printMonth    ==================

        Print one calendar month.

        Pre: startDay is day of week relative to Sunday (0)

        Post: Calendar printed

*/

void printMonth (int startDay, int days)
{
        // Local Declarations
        int weekDay;
        // Statements
        // print day header
        printf ("Sun Mon Tue Wed Thu Fri Sat\n");

        // position first day
        for (weekDay = 0; weekDay < startDay; weekDay++)
                printf ("    ");
        for (int dayCount = 1; dayCount <= days; dayCount++)
        {
                if (weekDay > 6)
                {
                        printf ("\n");
                        weekDay = 1;
                } // if
                else
                        weekDay++;
                printf ("%3d ", dayCount);
        } // for

        return;
} // printMonth
```

Program F.1   Example 1: printing a calendar month (continued)

Sun	Mon	Tue	Wed	Thu	Fri	Sat
		1	2	3	4	5
6	7	8	9	10	11	12
13	14	15	16	17	18	19
20	21	22	23	24	25	26
27	28	29				

Results:

Example 2

This is an example of using a class and three inherited classes in C++. The example shows how a triangular class can inherit from a polygon class (Program F.2).

Program F.2   Example 2: A program in C++

```cpp
class Polygons
{
       protected:
              double area;
              double perimeter;
       public:
              Polygons () {};
              ~Polygons () {};
              void printArea () const;
              void printPeri () const;
}; // Class Polygons
/*    ==================== Polygons :: printArea ====================
       Prints the area of a polygon.
       Pre   area calculated & stored in area
       Post  area printed
*/
void Polygons :: printArea () const
{
       cout << "The area of your polygon is " << area << endl;
       return;
} // Polygons printArea
/*    ==================== Polygons :: printPeri ====================
       Prints the perimeter of a polygon.
```

Program F.2   Example 2: A program in C++ (continued)

```
            Pre   polygon perimeter calculated and stored
            Post  perimeter printed
    */
    void Polygons :: printPeri () const
    {
            cout << "The perimeter of your polygon is " << perimeter << endl;
            return;
    } // Polygons printPeri
```

```
    class Triangle : public Polygons
    {
            private:
                    double sideA;
                    double sideB;
                    double sideC;
                    void calcArea ();
                    void halfPeri ();
            public:
                    // initialization constructor
                    Triangle (double sideAIn, double sideBIn,
                    double sideCIn);
    }; // Class Triangle
```

```
    /*      ==================== Triangle :: Triangle ====================
    Initialization constructor for triangle class.
    Stores sides. Calculates area and perimeter.
    Pre   Given sideA, sideB, and sideC
    Post  data stored; area & perimeter calculated
    */
    Triangle :: Triangle (double sideAIn, double sideBIn, double sideCIn)
    {
            // Verify sides are valid
            if ( ((sideAIn + sideBIn) <= sideCIn) || ((sideBIn + sideCIn) <= sideAIn)
            || ((sideCIn + sideAIn) <= sideBIn) )
            {

                    cout << "Invalid Triangle\n";
                    exit (100);
```

Program F.2 Example 2: A program in C++ (continued)

```
        } // if
        // Valid Triangle
        sideA = sideAIn;
        sideB = sideBIn;
        sideC = sideCIn;
        halfPeri();
        calcArea();
        return;
} // Triangle initialization constructor
/*      ====================== Triangle :: calcArea ====================
        Calculates triangle area & stores in base class area.
        Pre   sideA, sideB, sideC, & perimeter available
        Post  area calculated and stored
*/
void Triangle :: calcArea ()
{

        double halfPeri = perimeter / 2;
        area = ( halfPeri * (halfPeri - sideA) * (halfPeri - sideB) * (halfPeri - sideB)
            * (halfPeri - sideC) );
        area = sqrt(area);
        return;
} // Triangle calcArea
/*      ====================== Triangle :: halfPeri ====================
        Calculates perimeter & stores in base class area.
        Pre   sideA, sideB, & sideC available
        Post  perimeter calculated and stored
*/
void Triangle :: halfPeri ()
{
        perimeter = sideA + sideB + sideC;
        return;
} // Triangle halfPeri
/*
```

Program F.2   Example 2: A program in C++ (continued)

```
        Demonstrate use of inheritance.
        Written by:
        Date:
 */

#include <iostream>
#include <cmath>
#include <cstdlib>
using namespace std;
#include "p12-03.h"                                    // Polygon class

#include "p12-04.h"                                    // Triangle class

int main ()
{

        cout << "Start Polygon Demonstration\n\n";
        Triangle tri (3, 4, 5);
        tri.printPeri();
        tri.printArea();
        cout << "\nEnd Polygon Demonstration\n";
        return 0;
} // main
```

Results

Start Polygon Demonstration

The perimeter of your polygon is 12
The area of your polygon is 6

End Polygon Demonstration

Example 3

This is an example of calculating tax for an imaginary family. The program is written in Java to show the format and the classes normally present in a Java program. (Program F.3).

Program F.3 Example 3: Calculation of tax in Java

```
/* The program calculates the tax for a family based on the following formula:

    1. For each dependent deduct $1,000 from income.

    2. Determine tax rate from the following brackets:

    bracket taxable income      tax rate

    1        < 10001            2%

    2        10001 - 20000   5%

    3        20001 - 30000   7%

    4        30001 - 50000   10%

    5        > 50001            15%

    Then print the amount of tax or the refund.

    Written by:

    Date:

*/
import java.io.*;
class Taxes
{
        static final double LOWEST  = 0000000.00;
        static final double HIGHEST = 1000000.00;
        static final double LIMIT1  = 10000.00;
        static final double LIMIT2  = 20000.00;
        static final double LIMIT3  = 30000.00;
        static final double LIMIT4  = 50000.00;
        static final int RATE1 = 02;
        static final int RATE2   = 05;
        static final int RATE3   = 07;
        static final int RATE4   = 10;
        static final int RATE5   = 15;
        static final double DEDN_PER_DPNDNT = 1000.00;
        public static void main (String [] args) throws IOException
        {
```

Program F.3   Example 3: Calculation of tax in Java (continued)

```java
            // Local Declaration
                int numOfDpndnts;
            double taxDue =0.0;
            double taxPaid;
            double totalIncome;
            double taxableIncome = 0.0;
            double totalTax = 0.0;
            // Instantiation of streams
            InputStreamReader isr = new InputStreamReader (System.in);
            BufferedReader br = new BufferedReader (isr);
            //Statements
            System.out.println("Enter your total income for last year: ");
            totalIncome = Double.parseDouble (br.readLine ());
            System.out.println("Enter total payroll deductions: ");
            taxPaid = Double.parseDouble (br.readLine ());
            System.out.println("Enter the number of dependents ");
            numOfDpndnts = Integer.parseInt (br.readLine ());
            taxableIncome = calcTaxableInc (totalIncome, numOfDpndnts,
            taxableIncome );
            totalTax = calcTotalTax ( taxableIncome, totalTax);
            taxDue = calcTaxDue (totalTax, taxPaid, taxDue);
            printInformation (totalIncome,  taxableIncome, numOfDpndnts,
            totalTax, taxPaid,  taxDue);
} // main


/*      ================ calcTaxableInc ========================
This function calculates the taxable income.
        Pre:   Given-income, numOfDpndnts
        Post:  Returns the taxable income.
*/
public static double calcTaxableInc (double  totInc, int    numOfDpndnts,
double  taxableInc)
{
        //      Statements
        taxableInc = totInc - (numOfDpndnts * DEDN_PER_DPNDNT);
        return taxableInc;
} // calcTaxableInc
```

Program F.3   Example 3: Calculation of tax in Java (continued)

```
/*      ================ calcTotalTax =========================
        This function calculates the total tax.
        Pre: Given-income
        Post: returns the total tax.
*/
public static double calcTotalTax (double  taxableInc, double totalTax)
{
        // Statements
        totalTax = bracketTax(taxableInc, LOWEST, LIMIT1, RATE1) +
        bracketTax(taxableInc, LIMIT1, LIMIT2, RATE2) +
        bracketTax(taxableInc, LIMIT3, LIMIT4, RATE4) +
        bracketTax(taxableInc, LIMIT4, HIGHEST, RATE5);
        return totalTax;
} // calcTotalTax
/*      ================ calcTaxDue =========================
        This function calculates the tax due.
        Pre    Given- tax paid and total tax
        Post   returns the total tax due
*/
public static double calcTaxDue (double  totTax, double taxPaid, double
taxDue)
{
        // Statements
        taxDue = totTax - taxPaid;
        return taxDue;
} // calcTaxDue
/*
                This function prints a table showing all information.
                Pre    The parameter list.
        Post   Prints the table.
*/
public static void printInformation (double  totalIncome, double
taxableIncome, double  taxableIncome, int     numDpndnts, double
totalTax, double  taxPaid, double  taxDue)
```

Program F.3   Example 3: Calculation of tax in Java (continued)

```java
      {
            // Statements
            System.out.println("\nTotal income : " + totalIncome);
            System.out.println("Number of dependents: " + numDpndnts);
            System.out.println("Taxable income: " + taxableIncome);
            System.out.println("Total tax: " + totalTax);
            System.out.println("Tax already paid: " + taxPaid);
            if (taxDue > 0.0)
                    System.out.println("\nTax due : " + taxDue);
            else
                    System.out.println("Refund: " + -taxDue);
      } // printInformation


      /*    ================== bracketTax ========================
                    Calculates the tax for a particular bracket.
            Pre    The taxableIncome.
            Post   Returns the tax for a particular bracket.
       */
      public static double bracketTax (double  taxableIncome, double
      startLimit, double  startLimit, double  stopLimit, int  rate)
      {
            // Local Declarations
                double tax;
            // Statements
                    if (taxableIncome <= startLimit)
                    tax = 0.0;
            else
                    if (taxableIncome > startLimit  && taxableIncome <=
                    stopLimit)
                            tax = (taxableIncome - startLimit) * rate / 100.00;
                    else

                            tax = (stopLimit - startLimit) * rate / 100.00;
            return tax;
      } // bracketTax
} //class Tax
```

Program F.3 Example 3: Calculation of tax in Java (continued)

Results:

    Enter your total income for last year: 54000

    Enter total of payroll deductions: 3250

    Enter the number of dependents: 3

    Total income: 54000.00

    Number of dependents: 3

    Taxable income : 51000.00

    Total tax: 3550.00

G

Mathematical Review

In this appendix we review some mathematical concepts that may aid in understanding the topics covered in the book. We first give a brief treatment of exponential and logarithmic functions. We then discuss modular arithmetic. Finally, we give the formulas for the discrete cosine transforms that are used in data compression.

G.1   EXPONENT AND LOGARITHM

In solving some of the problems in this book, we often need to know how to handle exponential and logarithmic functions. This section briefly reviews these two concepts.

Exponential functions

The exponential function with **base** a is defined as a^x. If x is an integer, this is interpreted as multiplying a by itself x times. Normally we can use a calculator to find the value of y.

Example G.1
Calculate the value of the following exponential functions.

   a. 3^2

   b. 5.2^6

Solution
Using the interpretation of exponentiation, we can find:

   a. $3^2 = 3 \times 3 = 9$

   b. $5.2^6 = 5.2 \times 5.2 \times 5.2 \times 5.2 \times 5.2 \times 5.2 = 19{,}770.609664$

Example G.2

Calculate the value of the following exponential functions:

    a. $3^{2.2}$

    b. $5.2^{6.3}$

Solution

These problems can be done more easily using a calculator—we can find:

    a. $3^{2.2} \approx 11.212$

    b. $5.2^{6.3} \approx 32,420.60$

Three common bases

In the expression a^b, we call a the base and b the exponent. Three bases are very common: base 10, base e, and base 2.

❑ Base 10 is the base of the decimal system. Most calculators have a 10^x key.

❑ The base used in science and mathematics is the **natural base e**, which has the value 2.71828183... Most calculators have an e^x key. This base is used in science because some phenomenon, such as radioactive decay, can be best described using this base.

❑ The base which we normally need in computer science is base 2. Most calculators have no 2^x key, but we can always use the general x^y key and set $x = 2$.

Example G.3

Calculate the value of the following exponential functions:

    a. e^4

    b. $e^{6.3}$

    c. $10^{3.3}$

    d. $2^{6.3}$

    e. 2^{10}

Solution

    a. $e^4 \approx 54.60$

    b. $e^{6.3} \approx 544.57$

    c. $10^{3.3} \approx 1995.26$

    d. $2^{6.3} \approx 78.79$

    e. $2^{10} = 1024$

Example G.4

In computer science the dominant base is 2. It is a good practice for us to know the powers of 2 for some common exponents. We often need to remember that:

$2^0 = 1$	$2^1 = 2$	$2^2 = 2$	$2^3 = 8$	$2^4 = 16$	$2^5 = 32$	$2^6 = 64$
$2^7 = 128$	$2^8 = 256$	$2^9 = 512$	$2^{10} = 1024$			

Properties of the exponential function

Exponential functions have several properties, and some are useful to us:

1. $a^0 = 1$
2. $a^1 = a$
3. $a^{-x} = 1/(a^x)$
4. $a^{x+y} = a^x \times a^y$
5. $a^{x-y} = a^x/a^y$
6. $(a^x)^y = a^{x \times y}$

Example G.5

Examples using these properties are:

a. $5^0 = 1$
b. $6^1 = 6$
c. $2^{-4} = 1/2^4 = 1/16 = 0.0625$
d. $2^{5+3} = 2^5 \times 2^3 = 32 \times 8 = 256$
e. $3^{2-3} = 3^2/3^3 = 9 \times 27 = 1/3 \approx 0.33$
f. $(10^4)^2 = 10^{4 \times 2} = 10^8 = 100,000,000$

Logarithmic function

A logarithmic function is the inverse of an exponential function, as shown below.

$$y = a^x \quad \leftrightarrow \quad x = \log_a y$$

Just as in the exponential function, a is called the *base* of the logarithmic function. In other words, if x is given, we can calculate y by using the exponential function: if y is given, we can calculate x by using the logarithmic function.

Exponential and logarithmic functions are the inverse of each other.

Logarithms facilitate calculations in arithmetic because they convert multiplication into addition and exponentiation into multiplication.

Example G.6

Calculate the values of the following logarithmic functions:

a. $\log_3 9$
b. $\log_2 16$
c. $\log_{10} 0$
d. $\log_2(-2)$

Solution

We have not yet shown how to calculate the log function in different bases, but we can solve this problem intuitively.

a. Because $3^2 = 9$, $\log_3 9 = 2$, using the fact that the two functions are the inverse of each other.
b. Similarly, because $2^4 = 16$, then $\log_2 16 = 4$.

c. Since there is no finite number x such that $10^x = 0$, then $\log_{10}0$ is undefined or mathematically negative infinity.

d. A negative number in real number mathematics does not have a logarithm. However, in the domain of complex numbers we can have the logarithm of a negative number, but we leave this to books on complex number theory.

Three common bases

As in the case of exponentiation, there are three common bases in logarithms: base 10, base e, and base 2. Logarithms in base e are normally shown as *ln* (natural logarithm), and logarithms in base 10 as *log* (omitting the base). Not all calculators have logarithms in base 2. We show how to handle this base shortly.

Example G.7
Calculate the value of the following logarithmic functions:

   a. log233

   b. ln45

Solution
For these two bases we can use a calculator:

   a. $\log233 \approx 2.367$

   b. $\ln45 \approx 3.81$

Base transformation

We often need to find the value of a logarithmic function in a base other than e or 10. If the available calculator cannot give the result in our desired base, we can use a fundamental property of the logarithm, base transformation, as shown:

$$\log_a y = \frac{\log_b y}{\log_b a}$$

Note that the right-hand side shows two log functions with base b, which is different than the base a on the left-hand side. This means that we can choose a base that is available in our calculator (base b) and find the log of a base that is not available (base a).

Example G.8
Calculate the value of the following logarithmic functions:

   a. $\log_3 810$

   b. $\log_5 600$

   c. $\log_2 1024$

   d. $\log_2 600$

Solution
These bases are normally not available on most calculators, but we can use base 10, which is available.

   a. $\log_3 810 = \log810 / \log3 = 2.908 / 0.477 \approx 6.095$

b. $\log_5 600 = \log 600 / \log 5 = 2.778 / 0.699 \approx 3.975$

c. $\log_2 1024 = \log 1024 / \log 2 = 3.01 / 0.301 = 10$

d. $\log_2 600 = \log 600 / \log 2 \approx 2.778 / 0.301 \approx 9.223$

Example G.9

Base 2 is very common in computer science. Since we know that $\log_{10} 2 \approx 0.301$, it is very easy to calculate (approximately) the log of this base. We find the log of the corresponding number in base 10 and divide it by 0.301. Alternatively, we can multiply the corresponding log in base 10 by 3.332 ($\approx 1/0.301$).

a. $\log_2 600 \approx 3.322 \times \log_{10} 600 \approx 3.322 \times 2.778 \approx 9.228$

b. $\log_2 2048 \approx 3.322 \times \log_{10} 2048 \approx 3.322 \times 2.778 = 11$

Properties of logarithmic functions

Logarithmic functions have six useful properties, each related to the corresponding property of the exponential function mentioned earlier.

1. $\log_a 1 = 0$	4. $\log_a(x \times y) = \log_a x + \log_a y$
2. $\log_a a = 1$	5. $\log_a(x/y) = \log_a x - \log_a y$
3. $\log_a(1/x) = -\log_a x$	6. $\log_a x^y = y \times \log_a x$

Example G.10

Calculate the value of the following logarithmic functions:

a. $\log_3 1$

b. $\log_3 3$

c. $\log(1/10)$

d. $\log_a(x \times y)$ if we know that $\log_a x = 2$ and $\log_a y = 3$

e. $\log_a(x / y)$ if we know that $\log_a x = 2$ and $\log_a y = 3$

f. $\log_2(1024)$ without using a calculator

Solution

We use the property of log functions to solve the problems:

a. $\log_3 1 = 0$

b. $\log_3 3 = 1$

c. $\log(1/10) = \log 10^{-1} = -\log 10 = -1$

d. $\log_a(x \times y) = \log_a x + \log_a y = 2 + 3 = 5$

e. $\log_a(x / y) = \log_a x - \log_a y = 2 - 3 = -1$

f. $\log_2(1024) = \log_2(2^{10}) = 10 \times \log_2 2 = 10 \times 1 = 10$

G.2 MODULAR ARITHMETIC

In integer arithmetic, if we divide a by n, we can get q and r. The relationship between these four integers can be shown as $a = q \times n + r$. In this relation, a is called the dividend, q the quotient, n the divisor, and r the residue. Since an operation is normally defined with one single output, this is not an operation. We can call it the *division relation*.

Example G.11

Assume that $a = 214$ and $n = 13$. We can find $q = 16$ and $r = 6$ using the division algorithm we learned in arithmetic, as shown in Figure G.1.

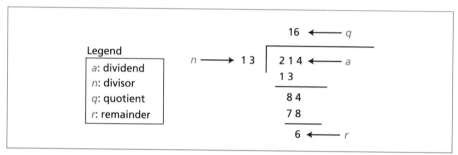

Figure G.1   Integer division

Most computer languages can find the quotient and the residue using language-specific operators. For example, in the C language, the division operator (/) can find the quotient and the modulo operator (%) can find the residue.

The modulo operator

In modular arithmetic we are interested in only one of the outputs, the remainder, r. We don't care about the quotient, q. In other words, we want to know what is the value of r when we divide a by n. This implies that we can change the above relation into a binary operator with two inputs a and n and one output r. The binary operator is then called the **modulo operator** and is shown as *mod*. The second input (n) is called the **modulus** and the output r is called the **residue**. Figure G.2 shows the division relation compared with the modulo operator.

The modulo operator (**mod**) takes an integer (a) a modulus (n). The operator creates a residue (r). Although a and r can be any integer, n cannot be 0 because it implies division by zero, which yields an undefined value or infinity. However, in practice we need the value of n to be non-negative. For this reason, the values of a and r should be between 0 and $n - 1$.

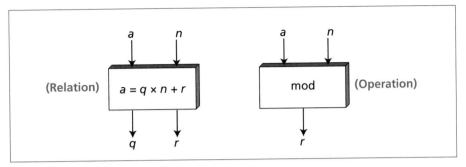

Figure G.2   Division relation versus modulo operator

Example G.12
A very good example of the use of modular arithmetic is our clock system. The clock is based on modulo 12 arithmetic. However, the integer 12 in our clock should actually be 0 to make it conformant with modulo arithmetic.

Example G.13
Find the result of the following operations:

a. 28 mod 6

b. 32 mod 12

c. 19 mod 15

d. 7 mod 11

Solution
We are looking for the residue r. We can divide a by n and find q and r. We can then disregard q and keep r.

a. Dividing 28 by 6 results in $r = 4$. This means that 28 mod 6 = 4.

b. Dividing 32 by 12 results in $r = 8$. This means that 32 mod 12 = 8.

c. Dividing 19 by 15 results in $r = 4$. This means that 19 mod 15 = 4.

d. Dividing 7 by 11 results in $r = 7$. This means that 7 mod 11 = 4.

Arithmetic operations

The three binary operations (addition, subtraction, and multiplication) that we discussed for integers can also be defined for modular arithmetic. We may need to normalize the result (apply the mod operation and use the residue) if the result is greater than $n - 1$, as shown in Figure G.3.

Actually, two sets of binary operators are used here. The first set is one of the binary operators $(+, -, \times)$ and the second is the mod operator. We need to use parentheses to emphasize the order of operations. If at any time during calculation we find a negative value for r, the value should be normalized. We need to add the modulus to the result as many time as is necessary to make it positive.

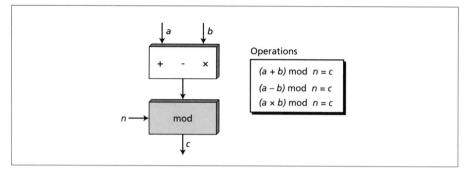

Figure G.3   Three operations in modular arithmetic

Example G.14

Perform the following operations:

    a. Add 7 to 14 using modulo 15.

    b. Subtract 11 from 7 using modulo 13.

    c. Multiply 11 by 7 using modulo 20.

Solution

The following shows the two steps involved in each case:

(14 + 7) mod 15	→	(21) mod 15 = 6
(7 − 11) mod 13	→	(−4) mod 13 = −4 + 13 = 9
(7 × 11) mod 20	→	(77) mod 20 = 17

Example G.15

Perform the following operations:

    a. Add 17 to 27 using modulo 14.

    b. Subtract 43 from 12 using modulo13

    c. Multiply 123 by −10 using modulo 19.

Solution

Note that the integers in these examples are sometimes out of the range of 0 to $n - 1$. We can normalize them either before applying the operation or after applying the operation. We show the second choice: you try the first choice. The result should be the same.

(17 + 27) mod 14	→	(44) mod 14 = 2
(12 − 43) mod 15	→	(−31) mod 15 = −1 + 15 = 14
(123 × −10) mod 20	→	(−1230) mod 19 = −14 + 19 = 5

Modulo-2 arithmetic

Modulo-2 arithmetic is of particular interest. As the modulus is 2, we can use only the values 0 and 1. Operations in this arithmetic are very simple. The following shows how we can add or subtract 2 bits.

Adding:	(0 + 0) mod 2 = 0	(0 + 1) mod 2 = 1
	(1 + 0) mod 2 = 1	(1 + 1) mod 2 = 0
Subtracting:	(0 – 0) mod 2 = 0	(0 – 1) mod 2 = 1
	(1 – 0) mod 2 = 1	(1 – 1) mod 2 = 0

Notice particularly that addition and subtraction gives the same results. In this arithmetic we use the XOR (exclusive OR) operation for both addition and subtraction. The result of an XOR operation is 0 if two bits are the same and 1 if two bits are different. Figure G.4 shows this operation.

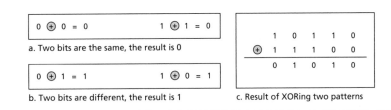

Figure G.4   XORing of two single bits or two words

G.3 DISCRETE COSINE TRANSFORM

In this section we give the mathematical background for the discrete cosine and inverse discrete cosine transforms that are used for data compression, as discussed in Chapter 15.

The discrete cosine transform

The discrete cosine transform (DCT) changes each block of 64 pixels so that the relative relationship between pixels is preserved but redundancies are revealed. The formula follows. $P(x, y)$ defines one particular value in the picture block, while $T(m, n)$ defines one value in the transformed block.

$$T(m, n) = 0.25c(m)c(n) \sum_{x=0}^{7} \sum_{y=0}^{7} P(x, y) \cos\left[\frac{(2x + 1)m\pi}{16}\right] \cos\left[\frac{(2y + 1)n\pi}{16}\right]$$

$$\text{where} \qquad c(i) = \begin{cases} 1/\sqrt{2} & \text{if } i = 0 \\ 1 & \text{otherwise} \end{cases}$$

The inverse discrete cosine transform

The inverse transform is used to create the $P(x, y)$ table from the $T(m, n)$ table.

$$P(x, y) = 0.25c(x)c(y) \sum_{m=0}^{7} \sum_{n=0}^{7} T(m, n)\cos\left[\frac{(2m+1)x\pi}{16}\right]\cos\left[\frac{(2n+1)y\pi}{16}\right]$$

where
$$c(i) = \begin{cases} 1/\sqrt{2} & \text{if } i = 0 \\ 1 & \text{otherwise} \end{cases}$$

Example G.16

Evaluate $T(0, 0)$ and $T(0, 1)$ if $P(x, y) = 20$ for all x and y.

Solution

$$T(0, 0) = 0.25c(0)c(0) \sum_{x=0}^{7} \sum_{y=0}^{7} 20\cos\left[\frac{(2x+1)0\pi}{16}\right]\cos\left[\frac{(2y+1)0\pi}{16}\right]$$

$$= 0.25\frac{1}{\sqrt{2}} \cdot \frac{1}{\sqrt{2}} \sum_{x=0}^{7} \sum_{y=0}^{7} 20\cos 0\cos 0 = \frac{1}{8} \sum_{x=0}^{7} \sum_{y=0}^{7} 20 = \frac{1}{8} \cdot (20 \cdot 8 \cdot 8) = 160$$

$$T(0, 1) = 0.25c(0)c(1) \sum_{x=0}^{7} \sum_{y=0}^{7} 20\cos\left[\frac{(2x+1)0\pi}{16}\right]\cos\left[\frac{(2y+1)\pi}{16}\right]$$

$$= 0.25\frac{1}{\sqrt{2}} \cdot 1 \sum_{x=0}^{7} \sum_{y=0}^{7} 20\cos 0\cos\left[\frac{(2y+1)\pi}{16}\right]$$

$$= \frac{1}{4\sqrt{2}} \sum_{x=0}^{7} \sum_{y=0}^{7} 20\left[\cos\frac{\pi}{16} + \cos\frac{3\pi}{16} + \dots + \cos\frac{13\pi}{16} + \cos\frac{15\pi}{16}\right] = 0$$

Using sum-to-product identity $\cos x + \cos y = 2[\cos (x + y)/2] [\cos (x - y)/2]$, we can show that the sum of all cosine terms are 0.

H
Error Detection and Correction

When data is transferred from one place to another, or moved from one device to another, the accuracy of the data must be checked. For most applications, a system must guarantee that the data received is identical to the data transmitted. Some applications, on the other hand, can tolerate a small level of error. For example, random errors in audio or video transmissions may be tolerable, but when we transfer text, we expect a very high level of accuracy. We only discuss errors in transition: errors due to data corruption in storage are treated in the same way.

H.1 INTRODUCTION

We first discuss some issues related to error detection and correction.

Types of errors

Whenever bits flow from one place to another they are subject to unpredictable changes because of **interference** in the transmission medium, such as crosstalk, external electromagnetic fields, and so on. This is illustrated by Figure H.1.

In a *single-bit error*, a 0 is changed to a 1 or a 1 to a 0. In a *burst error* multiple bits are changed. The term **single-bit error** means that only 1 bit of a given data unit, such as a byte, character, or packet, is changed from 1 to 0 or from 0 to 1. The term **burst error** means that two or more bits in the data unit have changed from 1 to 0 or from 0 to 1.

Redundancy

The central concept in correcting errors is **redundancy**. To be able to correct errors, we need to send extra bits with our data. These redundant bits are added by the

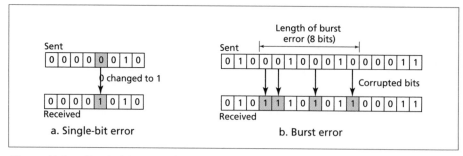

Figure H.1   Single-bit versus burst errors

sender and removed by the receiver. Their presence allows the receiver to correct corrupted bits.

> **To correct errors, we need to send extra (redundant) bits with data.**

Detection versus correction

The correction of errors is more difficult than the detection. In **error detection**, we are looking only to see if an error has occurred. The answer is a simple yes or no. We are not even interested in the number of errors: a single-bit error is the same for us as a burst error.

In **error correction**, we need to know the exact number of bits that are corrupted—and more importantly, their location in the message. The number of errors and the size of the message are important factors. If we need to correct a single error in an 8-bit data unit, we need to consider eight possible error locations: if we need to correct two errors in a data unit of the same size, we need to consider 28 (7 + 6 + ... + 1) possibilities. You can imagine the receiver's difficulty in finding ten errors in a data unit of 1000 bits.

Forward error correction versus retransmission

There are two main methods of error correction. **Forward error correction** is the process in which the receiver tries to guess the message by using redundant bits. This is possible, as we will see later, if the number of errors is small. Correction by **retransmission** is a technique in which the receiver detects the occurrence of an error and asks the sender to resend the message. Re-sending is repeated until a message arrives that the receiver believes is error-free: usually, not all errors can be detected.

Coding

Redundancy is achieved through various coding schemes. The sender adds redundant bits through a process that creates a relationship between the redundant bits and the actual data bits. The receiver checks the relationships between the two sets of bits to detect or correct the errors. The ratio of redundant bits to data bits and the robustness of the process are important factors in any coding scheme. Figure H.2 shows the general idea of coding.

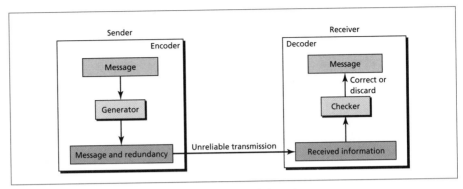

Figure H.2   The structure of an encoder and decoder

We can divide coding schemes into two broad categories: **block coding** and **convolution coding**. In this appendix, we concentrate on block coding: convolution coding is more complex and beyond the scope of this book.

> **We only concentrate on block codes:**
> **we leave convolution codes to advanced texts.**

Block coding uses modular arithmetic, as discussed in Appendix G.

H.2 BLOCK CODING

In block coding we divide a message into blocks, each of k bits, called **datawords**. We add r redundant bits to each block to make the length $n = k + r$. The resulting n-bit blocks are called **codewords**. How the extra r bits are chosen or calculated is something we discuss later. For the moment, it is important to know that we have a set of datawords, each of size k, and a set of codewords, each of size of n.

With k bits, we can create a combination of 2^k datawords: with n bits, we can create a combination of 2^n codewords. Since $n > k$, the number of possible codewords is larger than the number of possible datawords. The block coding process is one-to-one: the same dataword is always encoded as the same codeword. This means that we have $2^n - 2^k$ codewords that are not used. We call these codewords *invalid* or *illegal*. Figure H.3 shows the situation.

Example H.1

Let us assume our message is made up of a single block of 8 bits ($k = 8$). There are $2^8 = 256$ possible combination of datawords. If we add two redundant bits ($r = 1$), then each possible codeword is 10 bits ($n = 10$) and the total number of possible codewords is $2^{10} = 1024$. This means that we have $1024 - 256 = 768$ codewords

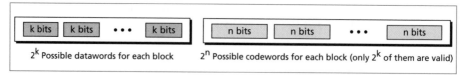

Figure H.3   Datawords and codewords in block coding

that are invalid. If one of these invalid codewords is received, the receiver knows that the codeword is corrupted.

Error detection

How can errors be detected by using block coding? If the following two conditions are met, the receiver detects a change in the original codeword.

1. The receiver has (or can find) a list of valid codewords.

2. The original codeword has changed to an invalid one.

Figure H.4 shows the role of block coding in error detection.

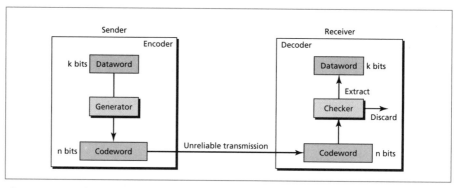

Figure H.4   The process of error detection in block coding

The sender creates codewords out of datawords by using a generator that applies the rules and procedures of encoding (discussed later). Each codeword sent to the receiver may change during transmission. If the received codeword is the same as one of the valid codewords, the word is accepted and the corresponding dataword is extracted for use. If the received codeword is not valid, it is discarded.

However, if the codeword is corrupted during transmission, but the received word still matches a valid codeword, the error remains undetected. This type of coding can therefore detect only single errors: two or more errors in the same codeword may remain undetected.

Example H.2

Let us assume that $k = 2$ and $n = 3$. Table H.1 shows the list of datawords and defined codewords, which is agreed between the sender and the receiver. Later we will see how to derive a codeword from a dataword.

Table H.1 A code for error detection (Example H.2)

Datawords	Codewords
00	000
01	011
10	101
11	110

Assume that the sender encodes the dataword 01 as 011 and sends it to the receiver. Consider the following cases:

1. The receiver receives 011. It is a valid codeword. The receiver extracts the dataword 01 from it.

2. The codeword is corrupted during transmission, and 111 is received—that is, the leftmost bit is corrupted. This is not a valid codeword, so it is discarded.

3. The codeword is corrupted during transmission, and 000 is received—that is, the right two bits are corrupted. This is a valid codeword. The receiver incorrectly extracts the dataword 00. Two corrupted bits have made the error undetectable.

> **An error-detecting code can detect only the types of errors for which it is designed: other types of errors may remain undetected.**

Error correction

Error correction is much more difficult than error detection. In error detection, the receiver needs to know only that the received codeword is invalid: in error correction, the receiver needs to find (or guess) the original codeword sent. We need more redundant bits for error correction than for error detection. Figure H.5 shows the role of block coding in error correction. We can see that the idea is the same as error detection, but the generator and checker functions are much more complex.

Example H.3

Let us add more redundant bits to Example 10.2 to see if the receiver can correct an error without knowing what was actually sent. We add three redundant bits to the 2-bit dataword to make 5-bit codewords. Again, later we will show how we

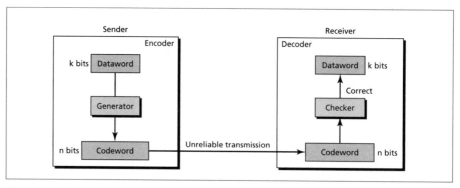

Figure H.5   The structure of encoder and decoder in error correction

chose the redundant bits. For the moment let us concentrate on the error correction concept. Table H.2 shows the datawords and codewords.

Table H.2   A code for error correction (Example 10.3)

Dataword	Codeword	Dataword	Codeword
00	00000	10	10101
01	01011	11	11110

Assume the dataword is 01. The sender consults the table (or uses an algorithm) to create the codeword 01011. The codeword is corrupted during transmission, and 01001 is received—an error in the second bit from the right. First, the receiver finds that the received codeword is not in the table. This means an error has occurred. (Detection must come before correction.) The receiver, assuming that only 1 bit is corrupted, uses the following strategy to guess the correct dataword.

1. Comparing the received codeword with the first codeword in the table (01001 versus 00000), the receiver decides that the first codeword is not the one that was sent because there are two different bits.

2. By the same reasoning, the original codeword cannot be the third or fourth one in the table.

3. The original codeword must be the second one in the table, because this is the only one that differs from the received codeword by 1 bit. The receiver replaces 01001 with 01011 and consults the table to find the dataword 01.

H.3   LINEAR BLOCK CODES

Almost all block codes used today belong to a subset called **linear block codes**. The use of nonlinear block codes for error detection and correction is not as widespread, because their structure makes theoretical analysis and implementation difficult. We therefore concentrate on linear block codes.

The formal definition of linear block codes requires a knowledge of abstract algebra (particularly Galois fields) which is beyond the scope of this book. We therefore give an informal definition. For our purposes, a linear block code is a code in which the exclusive OR (modulo-2 addition, discussed in Appendix G) of two valid codewords creates another valid codeword.

> **In a linear block code, the exclusive OR (XOR) of any two valid codewords creates another valid codeword.**

Example H.4

Let us see if the two codes we defined in Table H.1 and Table H.2 belong to the class of linear block codes.

❑ The scheme in Table H.1 is a linear block code because the result of XORing any codeword with any other codeword is a valid codeword. For example, XORing of the second and third codewords creates the fourth one.

❑ The scheme in Table H.2 is also a linear block code. We can create all four codewords by XORing two other codewords.

Some linear block codes

Let us now show some linear block codes. These codes are trivial because we can easily find the encoding and decoding algorithms and check their performance.

Simple parity-check code

Perhaps the most familiar error-detecting code is the **simple parity-check code**. In this code, a k-bit dataword is changed to an n-bit codeword, where $n = k + 1$. The extra bit, called the *parity bit*, is added to a predefined position. It is selected to make the total number of 1s in the codeword even. Although some implementations specify an odd number of 1s, we discuss the even number case.

> **A simple parity-check code is a single-bit error-detecting code in which $n = k + 1$.**

Our first code (Table H.1) is a parity-check code with $k = 2$ and $n = 3$. The code in Table H.3 is also a parity-check code with $k = 4$ and $n = 5$.

Table H.3   Simple parity-check code C(5, 4)

Datawords	Codewords	Datawords	Codewords
0000	00000	1000	10001
0001	00011	1001	10010
0010	00101	1010	10100
0011	00110	1011	10111

Table H.3   Simple parity-check code C(5, 4) (continued)

Datawords	Codewords	Datawords	Codewords
0100	01001	1100	11000
0101	01010	1101	11011
0110	01100	1110	11101
0111	01111	1111	11110

Figure H.6 shows a possible structure of an encoder (at the sender) and a decoder (at the receiver).

The encoder uses a generator that takes a copy of a 4-bit dataword (a_0, a_1, a_2, and a_3) and generates a parity bit r_0. The dataword bits and the **parity bit** create the 5-bit codeword. The parity bit that is added makes the number of 1s in the codeword even. This is normally done by adding the 4 bits of the dataword (modulo-2): the result is the parity bit. In other words:

$$r_0 = a_3 + a_2 + a_1 + a_0 \quad \text{(modulo-2)}$$

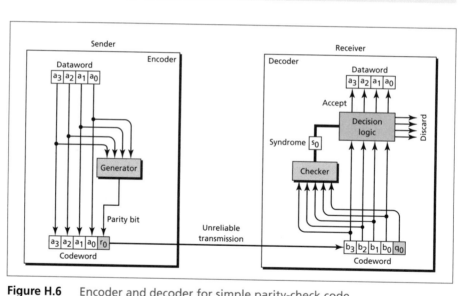

Figure H.6   Encoder and decoder for simple parity-check code

If the number of 1s is even, the result is 0: if the number of 1s is odd, the result is 1. In both cases, the total number of 1s in the codeword is even.

The sender sends the codeword, which may be corrupted during transmission. The receiver receives a 5-bit word. The checker at the receiver does the same thing as the generator in the sender with one exception: the addition is done over all five bits. The result, which is called the **syndrome**, is just 1 bit. The syndrome is 0 when the number of 1s in the received codeword is even, otherwise, it is 1.

$$s_0 = b_3 + b_2 + b_1 + b_0 + q_0 \quad \text{(modulo-2)}$$

A syndrome is the output of a checking process that is fed into the decision logic of a receiver in order to decide what to do with the data portion of the code word. The decision may be to accept it, to reject it, or (for correcting code) to modify it before accepting it. In this case, the syndrome is passed to the *decision logic analyzer*. If there is no error in the codeword, the syndrome is 0 and the decision logic accepts the data portion of the codeword as the actual dataword. If the syndrome is 1, there must be an error in the codeword, and so the decision logic discards the data portion of the codeword: the dataword is not created.

Example H.5

Let us look at some transmission scenarios. Assume that the sender sends the dataword 1011. The parity bit is $(1 + 0 + 1 + 1)$ mod 2 = 1, which is appended to the right of the dataword. The codeword created from this dataword is therefore 10111, which is sent to the receiver. We examine five cases:

1. No error occurs: the received codeword is 10111. The syndrome is 0. The dataword 1011 is created.

2. A single-bit error changes a_1. The received codeword is 10011. The syndrome is 1. No dataword is created.

3. A single-bit error changes the parity bit r_0. The received codeword is 10110. The syndrome is 1. No dataword is created. Note that although none of the dataword bits are corrupted, no dataword is created because the code is not sophisticated enough to show the position of the corrupted bit.

4. An error changes r_0 and a second error changes a_3. The received codeword is 00110. The syndrome is 0. The dataword 0011 is created at the receiver. Note that here the dataword is wrongly created due to the syndrome value: the simple parity-check decoder cannot detect an even number of errors. The errors cancel each other out and give the syndrome a value of 0.

5. Three bits—a_3, a_2, and a_1—are changed by errors. The received codeword is 01011. The syndrome is 1. The dataword is not created. This shows that the simple parity check, guaranteed to detect a single error, can also find any odd number of errors.

A simple parity-check code can detect an odd number of errors.

Hamming codes

Hamming codes are a subset of linear block codes that follow two criteria:

$$n = k + r \quad \text{and} \quad n = 2^r - 1$$

in which k is the number of bits in the dataword, r is the number of redundant bits, and n is the number of bits in the codeword. These codes can detect up to $r - 1$ bits of error and can correct up to $(r - 1)/2$ bits of error.

Example H.6

A code with $k = 4$, $r = 3$, and $n = 7$ satisfies the two conditions of a Hamming code, because we have $7 = 4 + 3$ and $7 = 2^3 - 1$. This code can detect only $(3 - 1) = 2$ bits of error and correct only $(3 - 1) / 2 = 1$ bit of error.

The theory of Hamming codes in general is beyond the scope of this book. For more information, see *Data Communication and Networking*, by Behrouz Forouzan, McGraw-Hill, New York, 2006. In the next section, we discuss a subset of Hamming codes called *cyclic codes*.

H.4   CYCLIC CODES

Cyclic codes are special linear block codes with one extra property. In a **cyclic code**, if a codeword is cyclically shifted (rotated), the result is another codeword. For example, if 1011000 is a codeword and we cyclically left-shift it, then 0110001 is also a codeword.

Cyclic redundancy check

We can create cyclic codes to correct errors. However, the theoretical background required is beyond the scope of this appendix. In this section, we simply discuss a category of cyclic codes called the **cyclic redundancy checks (CRC)** that are used in networks such as LANs and WANs.

Table H.4 shows an example of a CRC code. We can see both the linear and cyclic properties of this code.

Table H.4   A CRC code with k = 4, n = 7, and r = 3

Dataword	Codeword	Dataword	Codeword
0000	0000000	1000	1000101
0001	0001011	1001	1001110
0010	0010110	1010	1010011
0011	0011101	1011	1011000
0100	0100111	1100	1100010
0101	0101100	1101	1101001
0110	0110001	1110	1110100
0111	0111010	1111	1111111

Figure H.7 shows one possible design for the encoder and decoder.

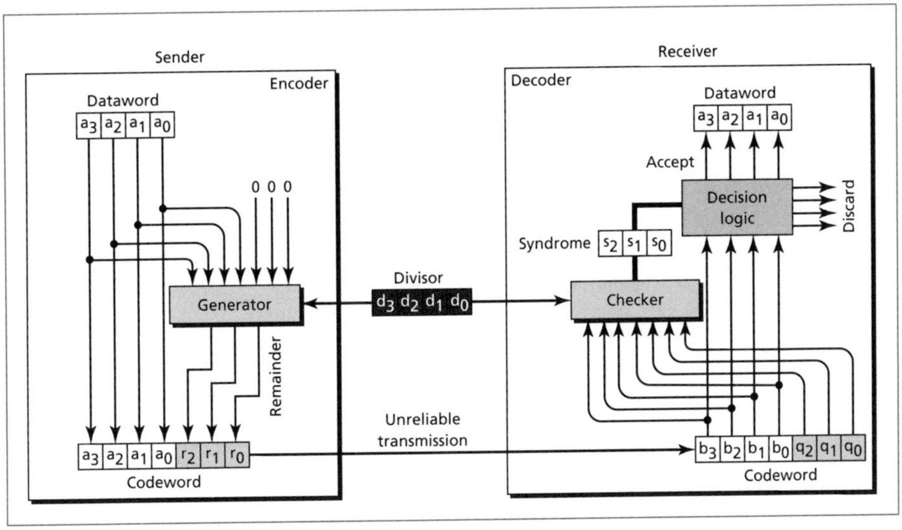

Figure H.7   CRC encoder and decoder

In the encoder in Figure H.7, the dataword has k bits (4 here) and the codeword has n bits (here 7). The size of the dataword is augmented by adding $n - k$ (here 3) 0s to the right-hand side of the word. The n-bit result is fed into the generator. The generator uses a predefined divisor of size $n - k + 1$ (here 4). The generator divides the augmented dataword by the divisor using modulo-2 division. The quotient of the division is discarded: the remainder $(r_2 r_1 r_0)$ is appended to the dataword to create the codeword.

The decoder receives the codeword, which could be corrupted. A copy of all n bits is fed to the checker, which is a replica of the generator. The remainder produced by the checker is a syndrome of $n - k$ (here 3) bits, which is fed to the decision logic analyzer. The analyzer has a simple function: if the syndrome bits are all 0s, the 4 leftmost bits of the codeword are accepted as the dataword (interpreted as no error), otherwise, the 4 bits are discarded (error).

Encoder

Let us take a closer look at the encoder. The encoder takes the dataword and augments it with $n - k$ number of 0s. It then divides the augmented dataword by the divisor, as shown in Figure H.8.

Note that this is not the regular binary *division*—obviously the result of dividing 72 by 11 is not the quotient of 10 and the remainder of 6. This is binary division in modulo 2 arithmetic, as we discussed in Appendix G. In this division, adding and subtracting is the same (it is the XOR operation discussed in Appendix E), which means that we do not subtract, but add. A better explanation of this division is that we treat the binary word as a polynomial with a coefficient in modulo 2 arithmetic—only 0 or 1. For more information, we refer the interested reader to *finite field theory* (Galois fields) and books on error detection and correction.

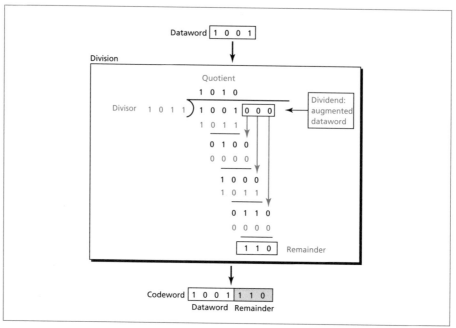

Figure H.8   Division in a CRC encoder

In each step, a copy of the divisor is XORed with the 4 bits of the dividend. The result of the XOR operation (remainder) is 3 bits (in this case), which is used for the next step after 1 extra bit is carried down—see Figure H.8—to make it 4 bits long. There is one important point we need to remember in this type of division. If the leftmost bit of the dividend (or the part used in each step) is 0, the corresponding bit in the quotient is 0.

When there are no bits left to pull down, we have a result. The 3-bit remainder forms the check bits (r_2, r_1, and r_0). These are appended to the dataword to create the codeword. Note also that we are not interested in the quotient, as only the remainder is used in cyclic codes.

Decoder   The codeword can change during transmission. The decoder does the same division process as the encoder. The remainder of the division is the syndrome. If the syndrome is all 0s, there is no error: the dataword is separated from the received codeword and accepted. Otherwise, everything is discarded. Figure H.9 shows two cases. The left-hand figure shows the value of the syndrome when no error has occurred: the syndrome is 000. The right-hand part of the figure shows the case in which there is a single error: the syndrome is not all 0s (it is 011).

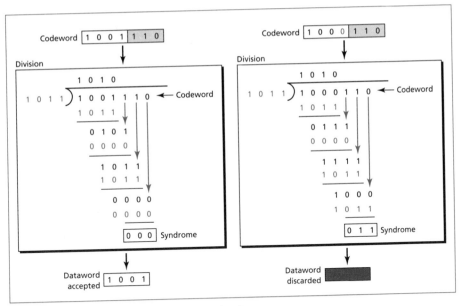

Figure H.9   Division in the CRC decoder for two cases

Divisor

You may be wondering how the divisor 1011 is chosen. This needs abstract algebra and theory of finite field to explain, which we leave to the book specialized in this area.

Performance of cyclic codes

We have seen that cyclic codes have a very good performance in detecting single-bit errors, double errors, an odd number of errors, and burst errors. They can easily be implemented in hardware and software. They are especially fast when implemented in hardware. This has made cyclic codes good candidates for many networks.

H.5 CHECKSUM

The last error detection method we discuss here is called the **checksum**. The checksum is used in the Internet by several protocols. Like linear and cyclic codes, the checksum is based on the concept of *redundancy*.

Checksum concept

The concept of the checksum is not difficult. Let us illustrate it with a few examples.

Example H.7

Suppose our data is a list of five 4-bit numbers that we want to send to some destination. In addition to sending these numbers, we send the sum of the numbers. For example, if the set of numbers is (7, 11, 12, 0, 6), we send (7, 11, 12, 0, 6, 36), where 36 is the sum of the original numbers. The receiver adds the five numbers and compares the result with the sum. If the two are the same, the receiver assumes no error, accepts the five numbers, and discards the sum. Otherwise, there is an error somewhere and the data is not accepted.

Example H.8

We can make the job of the receiver easier if we send the negative (complement) of the sum, called the *checksum*. In this case, we send (7, 11, 12, 0, 6, −36). The receiver can add all the numbers received (including the checksum). If the result is 0, it assumes no error, otherwise there is an error.

One's complement

The previous example has one major drawback. Our data can be written as 4-bit words (they are all less than 15) except for the checksum. One solution is to use **one's complement** arithmetic. as discussed in Chapter 3.

Example H.9

Let us redo Example H.8 using one's complement arithmetic. Figure H.10 shows the process at the sender and at the receiver.

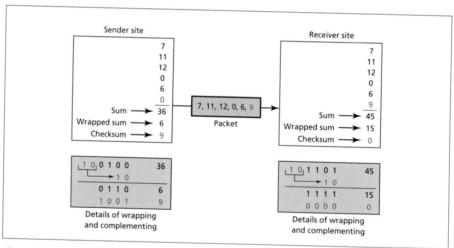

Figure H.10 Example I.7

The sender initializes the checksum to 0 and adds all data items and the checksum (the checksum is considered as one data item and is shown in color). The result is 36. However, 36 cannot be expressed in 4 bits. The extra two bits are wrapped and added with the sum to create the wrapped sum value 6. In the figure, we have shown the details in binary. The sum is then complemented, resulting in the checksum value 9 (15 − 6 = 9). The sender now sends six data items to the receiver, including the checksum 9. The receiver follows the same procedure as the sender.

It adds all data items (including the checksum): the result is 45. The sum is wrapped and becomes 15. The wrapped sum is complemented and becomes 0. Since the value of the checksum is 0, this means that the data is not corrupted. The receiver drops the checksum and keeps the other data items. If the checksum is not zero, the entire packet is dropped and must be retransmitted.

Internet checksum

Traditionally, the Internet (IP protocol) has used a 16-bit checksum. The sender and receiver use the following procedures:

Sender side

- ❏ A 16-bit checksum is set to zero and added to the message.
- ❏ The new message is divided into 16-bit words.
- ❏ All words are added using one's complement addition.
- ❏ The sum is complemented and replaces the previous checksum.

Receiver side

- ❏ The received message (including the checksum) is divided into 16-bit words.
- ❏ All words are added using one's complement addition.
- ❏ The sum is complemented.
- ❏ If the complemented sum is 0, the message is accepted, otherwise it is rejected.

Example H.10

Let us calculate the checksum for a text word of eight characters ("Forouzan") as shown in Figure H.11.

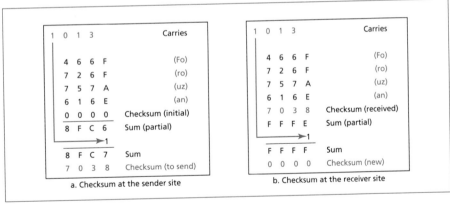

Figure H.11 An example of a checksum calculation

The text needs to be divided into 2-byte (16-bit) words. We use ASCII encoding (see Appendix A) to change each byte to a two-digit hexadecimal number. For example, "F" is represented as $(46)_{16}$ and "o" is represented as $(6F)_{16}$. In Figure H.11.a, the value of the partial sum for the first column is $(36)_{16}$. We keep the rightmost digit (6) and insert the leftmost digit (3) as the carry in the second column. The process is repeated for each column. The checksum is calculated and transmitted with the data to the receiver. The receiver performs the same operations, Figure H.11.b. If there is any corruption, the checksum recalculated by the receiver is not all 0s.

Performance   The traditional checksum uses a small number of bits (16) to detect errors in a message of any size (sometimes thousands of bits). However, it is not as strong as the CRC in its error-checking capability. For example, if the value of one word is incremented and the value of another word is decremented by the same amount, the two errors cannot be detected because the sum and checksum remain the same. Also if the values of several words are incremented but the total change is a multiple of 65535 ($2^{16}-1$), the sum and the checksum remain the same and the error goes undetected.

Acronyms and Glossary

Acronyms

ADT	Abstract data type
AES	Advanced Encryption Standard
ALU	Arithmetic logic unit
ANSI	American National Standards Institute
ASCII	American Standard Code for Information Interchange
B-frame	Bidirectional frame
bit	Binary digit
BST	Binary search tree
CA	Certification authority
CD-R	Compact disc recordable
CD-ROM	Compact disc read-only memory
CD-RW	Compact disc rewritable
CGI	Common Gateway Interface
CISC	Complex instruction set computer
COBOL	COmmon Business-Oriented Language
CPU	Central processing unit
DBMS	Database management system
DCT	Discrete cosine transform
DES	Data Encryption Standard

digraph	Directed graph
DMA	Direct memory access
DRAM	Dynamic RAM
DVD	Digital versatile disk
EBCDIC	Extended Binary Coded Decimal Interchange Code
EEPROM	Electronically erasable programmable read-only memory
EPROM	Erasable programmable read-only memory
E-R	Entity-Relationship
FIFO	First in, first out
FORTRAN	FORmula TRANslation
FTP	File Transfer Protocol
GIF	Graphic Interchange Format
GUI	Graphical user interface
HTML	Hypertext Markup Language
HTTP	Hypertext Transfer Protocol
I-frame	Intracoded frame
IMAP	Internet Mail Access Protocol
IP	Internet Protocol
ISO	International Organization For Standardization
ISP	Internet service provider
JPEG	Joint Photographic Experts Group
KDC	Key distribution center
LAN	Local area network
LIFO	Last in, first out
LZ	Lempel Ziv
LZW	Lempel Ziv Welch
MAC	Media access control, *or* Message authentication code
MAN	Metropolitan area network
MIME	Multipurpose Internet Mail Extension
MP3	MPEG audio layer 3
MPEG	Motion Pictures Experts Group
MS-DOS	Microsoft Disk Operating System
MTA	Message transfer agent
NF	Normal Form
NTFS	NT file system

P-frame	Predicted frame
POP	Post Office Protocol
PROM	Programmable read-only memory
RAM	Random access memory
RDBMS	Relational database management system
RGB	Red, green, blue
RISC	Reduced instruction set computer
ROM	Read-only memory
RSA	Rivest-Shamir-Adleman
SCSI	Small computer system interface
SCTP	Stream Control Transmission Protocol
SMTP	Simple Mail Transfer Protocol
SQL	Structured Query Language
SRAM	Static RAM
TCP	Transmission Control Protocol
TCP/IP	Transmission Control Protocol/Internet Protocol
TELNET	Terminal Network
UDP	User Datagram Protocol
UML	Unified Modeling Language
URL	Uniform Resource Locator
USB	Universal serial bus
WAN	Wide area network
WORM	Write once, read many
WWW	World Wide Web
XML	Extensible Markup Language
XOR	Exclusive OR

Definition of terms

absolute pathname	In UNIX or Linux, a path name that starts from the root.
abstract data type (ADT)	A data declaration packaged together with operations that are meaningful on the data type.
access method	A technique for reading data from a secondary (auxiliary) storage device.
active document	On the World Wide Web, a document executed at the local site using Java.

actual parameters The parameters in the function calling statement that contain the values to be passed to the function. Contrast with *formal parameters*.

Ada A high-level concurrent programming language developed by the US Department of Defense.

address bus The part of the system bus used for address transfer.

address space A range of addresses.

Advanced Encryption Standard (AES) A symmetric-key block cipher that uses a block size and a cipher key of 128 bits.

algorithm The logical steps necessary to solve a problem with a computer.

American National Standards Institute (ANSI) An organization that creates standards in programming languages, electrical specifications, communication protocols, and so on.

American Standard Code for Information Interchange (ASCII) An encoding scheme that defines control and printable characters for 128 values.

analog A continuously varying entity.

analysis phase A phase in the software system lifecycle that defines requirements that specify what the proposed system is to accomplish.

ancestor Any node in the path from the current node to the root of a tree.

AND operation One of the bit-level operations: the result of the operation is 1 only if both bits are 1s, otherwise it is 0.

applet A computer program written in Java that creates an active web document.

application layer The seventh layer in the TCP/IP model: provides access to network services.

arc A directed line in a graph. Contrast with *edge*.

arithmetic logic unit (ALU) The part of a computer system that performs arithmetic and logic operations on data.

arithmetic operation An operation that takes two numbers and creates another number.

arithmetic operator The operator used in an arithmetic operation.

arithmetic shift operation A shift operation in which the sign of the number is preserved.

array A fixed-sized, sequenced collection of elements of the same data type.

artificial intelligence The study of computer systems that simulate the intelligence of the human mind.

assembler System software that converts a source program into executable object code. Traditionally associated with an assembly language program. See also *compiler*.

assembly language	A programming language in which there is a one-to-one correspondence between the computer's machine language and the symbolic instruction set of the language.
assignment statement	The statement that assigns a value to a variable.
asymmetric-key cryptography	A type of cryptography that uses two different keys: a public key for encryption and a private key for decryption.
asymmetric-key encryption	Encryption using a public key.
attribute	In a relational database, each column in a relation.
audio	Recording or transmission of sound or music.
authentication	Verification of the sender of a message.
auxiliary storage	Any storage device outside main memory: permanent data storage. external storage; secondary storage.
availability	The component of information security that requires that information created and stored by an organization be available to authorized entities.
axon	The part of a neuron in the human body that provides output to other neurons via a synapse.
basis path testing	A white-box test method that creates a set of test cases that executes every statement in the software at least once.
batch operating system	The operating system used in early computers, in which jobs were grouped before being served.
bidirectional frame (B-frame)	In MPEG, a frame that is related to both the preceding and following frames.
big-O notation	A measure of the efficiency of an algorithm with only the dominant factor considered.
binary digit (bit)	The smallest unit of information (0 or 1).
binary file	A collection of data stored in the internal format of the computer. Contrast with *text file*.
binary operation	An operation that needs two input operands.
binary search	A search algorithm in which the search value is located by repeatedly dividing the list in half.
binary search tree (BST)	A binary tree in which the keys of the left subtrees are all less than the root key, the keys of all right subtrees are greater than or equal to the root key, and each subtree is itself a binary search tree.
binary system	A numbering system that uses two symbols (0 and 1).
binary tree	A tree in which each node has zero, one, or two subtrees.
biometrics	The measurement of physiological or behavioral features that identify a person.

bit	Acronym for *binary digit*. In a computer, the basic storage unit with a value of either 0 or 1.
bit depth	The number of bits representing a sample in a sampling process.
bit pattern	A sequence of bits (0s and 1s).
bit rate	The number of bits transmitted per second.
bitmap graphic	A graphic representation in which a combination of pixels defines the image.
black box testing	Testing based on the system requirements rather than a knowledge of the program.
Boolean algebra	An algebra for manipulation of objects that can take one only two values: true or false.
bootstrap	The process in which the operating system is loaded into main memory when the computer is turned on.
breadth-first traversal	A graph traversal method in which nodes adjacent to the current node are processed before their descendants.
browser	An application program that displays a WWW document.
brute-force search	A search method that examines every path in a search tree until it finds the goal.
bubble sort	A sort algorithm in which each pass through the data moves (bubbles) the lowest element to the beginning of the unsorted portion of the list.
bucket	In a hashing algorithm, a location that can accommodate multiple data units.
bucket hashing	A hashing method that uses buckets to reduce collision.
bus	The physical channel that links hardware components in a computer: the shared physical medium used in a bus-topology network.
bus topology	A network topology in which all computers are attached to a shared medium.
byte	A unit of storage, usually 8 bits.
bytecode	A machine language into which a Java source program is compiled.
C language	A procedural language developed by Dennis Ritchie.
C++ language	An object-oriented language developed by Bjarne Stroustrup.
cache memory	A small, fast memory used to hold data items that are being processed.
Caesar cipher	A shift cipher used by Julius Caesar.
central processing unit (CPU)	The part of a computer that contains the control components to interpret instructions. In a personal computer, a microchip containing a control unit and an arithmetic logic unit.
certification authority (CA)	An organization that binds a public key to an entity and issues a certificate.

chatting	An application program available on the Internet.
child	A node in a tree or graph that has a predecessor.
Church-Turing thesis	In computability theory, a combined hypothesis about the nature of computable functions by recursion (Church's Thesis) and by mechanical devices equivalent to a Turing machine.
cipher	An encryption decryption algorithm.
ciphertext	Encrypted data.
circular shift operation	A shift operation in which dropped bits from one end of a binary word are inserted at the other end.
circular waiting	A condition in an operating system in which all processes and resources involved form a loop.
class	The combination of data and functions joined to form a type.
class diagram	A diagram in object-oriented program that shows the relationship between objects.
class diagram	A diagram that manifests the relationship between classes in a system.
client-server architecture	The model of interaction between two application programs in which a program at one end (client) requests a service from a program at the other end (server).
code	A set of bit patterns designed to represent text symbols.
code generator	A process in a compiler or interpreter that creates the machine language code.
cohesion	The attribute of a module that describes how closely the processes in a module are related to one another.
cold fusion	A dynamic web technology that allows the fusion of data items coming from a conventional database.
collision	In hashing, an event that occurs when a hashing algorithm produces an address for an insertion, and that address is already occupied.
collision resolution	An algorithmic process that determines an alternative address after a collision.
color depth	The number of bits used to represent the color of a pixel.
column-major storage	A method of storing two-dimensional arrays in which the elements are stored column by column.
COmmon Business-Oriented Language (COBOL)	A business programming language developed by Grace Hopper.
Common Gateway Interface (CGI)	A standard for communication between HTTP servers and executable programs used in creating dynamic documents.
compact disc	A direct access optical storage medium.

compact disc read-only memory (CD-ROM)	A compact disc in which data is written to the disc by the manufacturer and can only be read by the user.
compact disc recordable (CD-R)	A compact disc that a user can write to only once, but read from many times.
compact disc rewritable (CD-RW)	A compact disc that can be written to many times and read from many times
compilation	The process of translating the whole source program written in a high-level language into machine language before executing the program.
compiler	System software that converts a source program into executable object code: traditionally associated with high-level languages. See also *assembler*.
complex instruction set computer (CISC)	A computer that defines an extensive set of instructions, even those that are used less frequently.
composite type	A data type that is composed of two or more simple types.
compound statement	In some programming languages, a collection of statements (instructions) treated as one by the language.
computer language	Any of the syntactical languages used to write programs for computers, such as machine language, assembly language, C, COBOL, and FORTRAN.
conceptual level	Relating to the logical structure of a database. It deals with the meaning of the database, not its physical implementation.
confidentiality	A security goal that defines procedures to hide information from an unauthorized entity.
congestion control	Any method to control excessive network or internetwork traffic causing a general degradation of service.
connectionless protocol	A protocol for data transfer without connection establishment or termination.
connection-oriented protocol	A protocol for data transfer that establishes connection before transferring data.
constant	A data value that cannot change during the execution of the program. Contrast with *variable*.
control bus	The bus that carries information between computer components.
control statement	A statement that alters the sequential flow of control in a source program.
control structure testing	A white-box test method that uses different categories of tests: conditional testing, dataflow testing, and loop testing.
control unit	The component of a CPU that interprets the instructions and controls the flow of data.
controller	A component of a Turing machine that is equivalent to a computer's CPU.

coupling	A measure of the interdependence between two separate functions. See also *content coupling, control coupling, data coupling, global coupling,* and *stamp coupling*
cryptographic hash function	A function that creates a message digest from a message.
cryptography	The science and art of transforming messages to make them secure and immune to attack.
current directory	In UNIX and Linux, the directory that a user is in at the present time.
cycle	A graph path with a length greater than 1 that starts and ends at the same vertex.
data bus	The bus inside a computer used to carry data between components.
data compression	Reduction of the volume of data without significant loss.
data confidentiality	A security service designed to protect data from disclosure attacks, snooping, and traffic analysis.
data encryption standard (DES)	The US government encryption method for nonmilitary and non-classified use.
data file	A file that contains only data, not programs.
data flow diagram	A diagram that shows the movement of data in the system.
data integrity	A security service designed to protect data from modification, insertion, deletion, and replaying.
data link layer	The second layer in the TCP/IP data model responsible for node-to-node delivery.
data link layer address	The address used in the data link layer, sometimes called the MAC address, sometimes the physical address.
data processor	An entity that inputs data, processes it, and outputs the result.
data structure	The syntactical representation of data organized to show the relationship among the individual elements.
data type	A named set of values and operations defined to manipulate them, such as character and integer.
database	A collection of organized information.
database management system (DBMS)	A program or a set of programs that manipulates a database.
database model	A model that defines the logical design of data.
datagram	The packet sent by the IP protocol.
data-link layer	The second layer in the OSI model, responsible for node-to-node delivery of data.
DC value	A value that does not change with time.
deadlock	A situation in which the resources needed by one job to finish its task are held by other jobs.

decimal digit	A symbol in the decimal system.
decimal system	A method of representing numbers using ten symbols (0 to 9).
declarative language	A computer language that uses the principle of logical reasoning to answer queries.
declarative paradigm	A paradigm that uses the principle of logical reasoning to answer queries.
decrement statement	A statement that subtracts 1 from the value of a variable.
decryption	Recovery of the original message from encrypted data. See *encryption*.
default logic	A logic in which the default conclusion of an argument is acceptable if it is consistent with the contents of knowledge base.
delete operation	In a relational database, the operation that deletes a tuple from the relation.
demand paging	A memory allocation method in which a page of a program is loaded into memory only when it is needed.
demand paging and segmentation	A memory allocation method in which a page or a segment of a program is loaded into memory only when it is needed.
demand segmentation	A memory allocation method in which a segment of a program is loaded into memory only when it is needed.
demultiplexing	Separating multiplexed data.
dendrite	In a neuron, the section that acts as the input device.
denial of service	The only attack on the availability goal of security that may slow down or interrupt the system.
depth-first traversal	A traversal method in which all of a node's descendants are processed before any adjacent nodes (siblings).
dequeue	Deleting an element from a queue.
descendant	Any node in the path from the current node to a leaf.
design phase	A phase in the software system lifecycle that defines how the system will accomplish what was defined in the analysis phase.
development process	The process of creating software that is outside the system lifecycle.
device manager	A component of an operating system that controls access to the input/output devices.
dictionary-based encoding	A compression method in which a dictionary is created during the session.
difference operation	An operation on two sets, the result of which is the first set minus the common elements in the two sets, or an operator in a relational database that is applied to two relations with the same attributes. The tuples in the resulting relation are those that are in the first relation but not the second.
digit extraction method	A hashing method that uses digit extraction.
digital	A discrete (noncontinuous) entity.

digital divide	A social issue that divides people in society into two groups: those who are electronically connected to the rest of society and those who are not.
digital signature	A method used to authenticate the sender of a message and to preserve the integrity of its data.
digital versatile disk (DVD)	A direct access optical storage medium.
digraph	A directed graph.
direct hashing	A hashing method in which the key is obtained without algorithmic modification.
direct memory access (DMA)	A form of I/O in which a special device controls the exchange of data between memory and I/O devices.
directed graph	A graph in which the direction is indicated on the lines (arcs).
directory	A file that contains the names and addresses of other files.
discrete cosine transform (DCT)	A mathematical transformation used in JPEG encoding.
distributed database	A database in which data is stored on several computers.
distributed system	An operating system that controls resources located in computers at different sites.
division remainder method	A type of hashing in which the key is divided by a number and the remainder is used as the address.
domain name	In DNS, a sequence of labels separated by dots.
Domain Name Server (DNS)	A computer that holds information about Internet domain names.
dotted-decimal notation	The notation devised to make IP addresses easier to read: each byte is converted to a decimal number, numbers are separated by a dot.
dynamic document	A web document created by running a program at a server site.
dynamic RAM (DRAM)	RAM in which the cells use capacitors. DRAM must be refreshed periodically to retain its data.
edge	A graph line that has no direction.
edge detection	A method of image processing that finds the edges in an image by looking at areas with change in color or texture.
electronic mail (e-mail)	A method of sending messages electronically based on a mailbox address rather than host-to-host exchange.
electronically erasable programmable read-only memory (EEPROM)	Programmable read-only memory that can be programmed and erased using electronic impulses without being removed from the computer.
encapsulation	The software engineering design concept in which data and their operations are bundled together and maintained separately from the application using them.
encryption	Converting a message into a form that is unreadable unless decrypted.

enqueue	Inserting an element into a queue.
entity authentication	A technique designed to let one party prove the identity of another party.
entity-relationship (E-R) diagram	A diagram used in entity-relationship modeling.
entity-relationship (E-R) model	A model that defines the entities and their relationship in a relational database.
erasable programmable read-only memory (EPROM)	Programmable read-only memory that can be programmed. Erasing EPROM requires removing it from the computer.
error report file	In a file update process, a report of errors detected during the update.
Excess representation	A number representation method used to store the exponential value of a fraction.
Excess_1023	The high-precision IEEE standard for representation of floating point numbers.
Excess_127	The low-precision IEEE standard for representing floating-point numbers.
exclusive OR (XOR)	A binary logical operation in which the result is true only if one of the operands is true and the other is false.
expert system	A system that uses knowledge representation to perform tasks that normally need human expertise.
expression	A sequence of operators and operands that reduces to a single value.
Extended Binary Coded Decimal Interchange Code (EBCDIC)	A character set designed by IBM for its large computer systems.
Extensible Markup Language (XML)	A language that allows a user to describe the contents of a document. Also used as a query language in an object-oriented language.
external level	The part of the database that interacts with the user.
fetch	The part of the instruction cycle in which the instruction to be executed is brought in from memory.
field	The smallest named unit of data that has meaning in describing information. A field may be either a variable or a constant.
File Transfer Protocol (FTP)	An application-layer service in TCP/IP for transferring files from and to a remote site.
FireWire	An I/O device controller with a high-speed serial interface that transfers data in packets.
first in, first out (FIFO)	An algorithm in which the first data item that is added to a list is removed from the list first.
fixed-point representation	Representation of numbers in a computer in which the position of the decimal point is fixed (normally at the leftmost or rightmost). Normally used to represent integers.

floating-point representation	A number representation in which the position of the decimal point is floated to create better precision. Normally used to represent real numbers in a computer.
formal parameters	The parameter declaration in a function to describe the type of data to be passed to the function.
FORmula TRANslation (FORTRAN)	A high-level procedural language used for scientific and engineering applications.
fragmented distributed database	A distributed database in which data is localized.
frame	A data unit at the data-link layer.
frames	A method similar to semantic networks for knowledge representation.
front	The next element in a queue that is deleted by the dequeue operation.
functional language	A programming language in which a program is considered to be a mathematical function.
functional paradigm	A paradigm in which a program is considered a mathematical function.
general linear list	A list in which data can be inserted or deleted anywhere in the list.
glass-box testing	See *white-box testing*.
Gödel number	A number assigned to every program that can be written in a specific language.
graph	A collection of nodes, called vertices, and line segments, called edges or arcs, connecting pairs of nodes.
Graphic Interchange Format (GIF)	An 8-bit per pixel bitmap image.
graphical user interface (GUI)	A user interface that defines icons and operations on icons.
halting problem	Writing a program that tests whether or not any program, represented as its Gödel number, will terminate.
hardware	Any of the physical components of a computer system, such as a keyboard or a printer.
hashed file	A file that is searched using one of the hashing methods.
hashing method	A method to access a hashed file.
header	The information added to the beginning of a packet for routing and other purposes.
heuristic search	A search in which a rule or a piece of information is used to make the search more efficient.
hexadecimal digit	A symbol in the hexadecimal system.
hexadecimal system	A numbering system with base 16. Its digits are 0, 1, 2, 3, 4, 5, 6, 7, 8, 9, A, B, C, D, E, and F.

hierarchical model	A database model that organizes data in a treelike structure that can be searched from top to bottom.
high-level language	A (portable) programming language designed to allow the programmer to concentrate on the application rather than the structure of a particular computer or operating system.
high-order logic	A logic that extends the scope of quantifiers $\forall$ and $\exists$ in predicate logic to bind predicates as well as variables.
hold state	The state of a job that is waiting to be loaded into memory.
home address	In a hashed list, the first address produced by the hashing algorithm.
home directory	In UNIX or Linux, a directory that a user is in when first logged in.
home page	The main page of a hypertext document available on the web.
hub	A device that connects other devices in a network.
Huffman coding	A statistical compression method using variable-length code.
hypertext	A document containing embedded links to other documents.
Hypertext Markup Language (HTML)	The computer language for specifying the contents and format of a web document: allows text to include fonts, layouts, embedded graphics, and links to other documents.
Hypertext Transfer Protocol (HTTP)	The protocol that is used to retrieve web pages on the Internet.
identifier	The name given to an object in a programming language.
image processing	An area of artificial intelligence that deals with the perception of objects—the artificial eyes of an agent.
imperative language	Another name for a procedural language.
imperative paradigm	Another name for a procedural paradigm.
implementation phase	A phase in the software system lifecycle in which the actual programs are created.
increment statement	In C or C++, the statement that adds 1 to an integer value.
incremental model	A model in software engineering in which the entire package is constructed with each module consisting of just a shell: modules gain complexity with each iteration of the package.
index	The address of an element in an array.
indexed color	A technique in raster graphic that uses only a portion of True-Color to encode colors in each application.
indexed file	A file that uses an index for random access.
infix	An arithmetic notation in which the operator is placed between two operands.
inheritance	The ability to extend a class to create a new class while retaining the data objects and methods of the base class and adding new data objects and methods.

inorder traversal	A binary tree traversal method in which the root is traversed after the left subtree and before the right subtree.
input data	User information that is submitted to a computer to run a program.
input/output (I/O) controller	A device that controls access to input/output devices.
input/output subsystem	The part of the computer's organization that receives data from the outside and sends data to the outside.
insert operation	An operation in a relational database that inserts a tuple in a relation.
insertion sort	A sort algorithm in which the first element from the unsorted portion of the list is inserted into its proper position in the sorted portion of the list.
instruction	A command that tells a computer what to do.
instruction register	A register in the CPU that holds the instruction before being interpreted by the control unit.
integer	An integral number, a number without a fractional part.
integrated circuit	Transistors, wiring, and other components on a single chip.
integrity	A security goal to protect data from modification, insertion, deletion, or replaying.
intelligent agent	An agent that perceives its environment, learns from it, and interacts with it intelligently.
internal level	The part of the database that defines where data is actually stored.
internal node	Any tree node except the root and the leaves: a node in the middle of a tree.
International Organization For Standardization (ISO)	A worldwide organization that defines and develops standards for a variety of topics.
internet	Abbreviation for *internetwork*.
Internet	The global internet that uses the TCP/IP protocol suite.
Internet address	A 32-bit address used to define a computer uniquely on the Internet
Internet Mail Access Protocol (IMAP)	A protocol that transfers e-mails from an e-mail server to the station of the e-mail recipient.
Internet Protocol (IP)	The network-layer protocol in the TCP/IP protocol responsible for transmitting packets from one computer to another across the Internet.
internet service provider (ISP)	An organization that provides Internet services.
Internet static document	On the WWW, a fixed-content document that is created and stored on the server.
internetwork	A network of networks.
interpreter	A program that translates a source program in a high-level language line by line and executes each line immediately.

interrupt driven I/O	A form of I/O in which the CPU, after issuing an I/O command, continues serving other processes until it receives an interrupt signal that the I/O operation is completed.
intersection operation	An operation on two sets in which the result is a set with the elements common to the two sets.
intersector gap	The gap between sectors on a disk.
intertrack gap	The gap between tracks on a tape.
intracoded frame (I-frame)	In MPEG, an independent frame.
inverted file	A file sorted according to a second key.
IP address	See *Internet address*.
IP datagram	The data unit in the network layer.
isolated I/O	A method of addressing an I/O module in which the instructions used to read/write memory are totally different than the instructions used to read/write to input/output devices.
Java	An object-oriented programming language for creating stand-alone programs or dynamic documents on the Internet.
job	A program becomes a job when it is selected for execution.
job scheduler	A scheduler that selects a job for processing from a queue of jobs waiting to be moved to memory.
join operation	An operation in a relational database that takes two relations and combines them based on common attributes.
Joint Photographic Experts Group (JPEG)	A standard for compressing images.
kernel	The main part of an operating system.
key	One or more fields used to identify a record (structure).
key-distribution center (KDC)	A trusted third party that established a shared secret key between two parties.
land	On an optical disc, an area not hit by the laser in the translation of a bit pattern. Usually represents a bit.
last in, first out (LIFO)	An algorithm in which the last data item that is added to a list is removed from the list first.
leaf	A graph or tree node with one incoming arc and no outgoing arcs.
Lempel Ziv (LZ) encoding	A compression algorithm that uses a dictionary.
Lempel Ziv Welch (LZW) encoding	An enhanced version of LZ encoding.
lexical analyzer	A program used in a translation process that reads the source code symbol by symbol and creates a list of tokens.

linear list	A list structure in which each element except the last has a unique successor.
link	In a list structure, the field that identifies the next element in the list.
linked list	A linear list structure in which the ordering of the elements is determined by link fields.
linked list resolution	A collision resolution method in hashing that uses a separate area for synonyms, which are maintained in a linked list.
linked list traversal	A traversal method in which every element of a linked list is processed in order.
Linux	An operating system developed by Linus Torvalds to make UNIX more efficient when run on an Intel microprocessor.
LISP	A list processing programming language in which everything is considered a list.
list	An ordered set of data contained in main memory. Contrast with *file*.
listserv	An application program in the Internet.
literal	A constant used in a program.
loader	The operating system function that fetches an executable program into memory for running.
local area network (LAN)	A network connecting devices inside a limited area.
local login	A login to a computer attached directly to the terminal.
local variable	A variable defined within a block or a module.
logical address	An address defined at the network layer.
logical data	Data with a value of either true or false.
logical operation	An operation in which the result is a logical value (true or false).
logical shift operation	A shift operation that does not preserve the sign of the number.
loop	In a program, a structured programming construct that causes one or more statements to be repeated. In a graph, a line that starts and ends with the same vertex.
loop statement	A statement that causes the program to iterate a set of statements.
lossless data compression	Data compression in which no data is lost. Used for compressing text or programs.
lossy data compression	Data compression in which some data is allowed to be lost. Used for image, audio, or video compression.
machine language	Instructions native to the central processor of a computer that are executable without assembly or compilation.
macro	A custom-designed procedure that can be used repeatedly.
magnetic disk	A storage medium with random access capability.

magnetic tape	A storage medium with sequential access capability.
main memory	The primary memory of a computer, consisting of medium speed random access memory. Contrast with *cache memory*.
maintainability	A quality that refers to keeping a system running correctly and up to date.
mantissa	The part of a floating-point number that shows the number's significant digits.
mask	A variable or constant that contains a bit configuration used to control the setting of bits in a bitwise operation.
masquerading	A type of attack on integrity of information in which the attacker impersonates somebody else.
master file	A permanent file that contains the most current data regarding an application.
medium access control (MAC) address	See *data link layer address*.
memory	The main memory of a computer consisting of random access memory (RAM) and read-only memory (ROM), used to store data and program instructions.
memory management	The component of the operating system that controls the use of main memory.
memory-mapped I/O	A method of addressing an I/O module in a single address space, used for both memory and I/O devices.
merging	A method used in image segmentation in which pixel with the same intensity are merged together.
mesh topology	A topology in which each device is connected to every other device.
message authentication code (MAC)	A message digest that includes a secret between two parties.
message digest	The fixed-length string created from applying a hash function to a message.
message transfer agent (MTA)	An SMTP program that transfers a message across the Internet.
method	A function in an object-oriented language.
metropolitan area network (MAN)	A network that can span a city or a town.
microcomputer	A computer small enough to fit on a desktop.
Microsoft Disk Operating System (MS-DOS)	The operating system based on DOS and developed by Microsoft.
modal logic	An extension to logic that includes certainty and possibility.
modularity	Breaking a large project into small parts that can be understood and handled easily.

module	A small part created from applying modularity to a project.
modulo division	Dividing two numbers and keeping the remainder.
monoprogramming	The technique that allows only one program to be in memory at a time.
Motion Pictures Experts Group (MPEG)	A lossy compression method for compressing video (and audio).
MPEG audio layer (MP3)	A standard used for compression audio based on MPEG.
multidimensional array	An array with elements having more than one level of indexing.
multidrop connection	See *multipoint connection*.
multiplexing	The process of combining signals or data from multiple sources for transmission.
multipoint connection	A connection in which two or more devices share the capacity of a link.
multiprogramming	A technique that allows more than one program to reside in memory while being processed.
Multipurpose Internet Mail Extension (MIME)	A supplement to SMTP that allows non-ASCII data to be sent through SMTP.
multithreading	Parallel processing supported by some languages such as Java.
mutual exclusion	A condition imposed by an operating system in which only one process can hold a resource.
network	A system of connected nodes that can share resources.
network layer	The third layer in the TCP/IP model, responsible for delivery of packets from the original host to the final destination.
network model	A database model in which a record can have more than one parent record.
neural network	A network of neurons which is modeled on the human brain.
neuron	The individual cells that are responsible for transmitting information in the human brain and nervous system.
new master file	The master file that is created from an old master file when the file is updated.
no preemption	A condition in which the operating system cannot temporarily allocate a resource.
node	In a data structure, an element that contains both data and structural elements used to process the data structure.
node-to-node delivery	The delivery of data from one node to the next.
non-polynomial problem	A problem that cannot be solved with polynomial complexity.
nonpositional number system	A number system in which the position of symbols does not define the value of the symbol.

nonrepudiation	A quality of a received message that does not allow the sender to deny sending it.
Normal Form (NF)	A step in the normalization process of a relational database.
normalization	In a relational database, the process of applying normal forms to a relational model.
NOT operation	The operation that changes a 0 bit to 1 or a 1 bit to 0.
NT file system (NTFS)	The standard file system of Windows NT and later versions.
null pointer	A pointer that points to nothing.
null tree	A tree with no nodes.
number system	A system that uses a set of symbols to define a value.
object program	The machine language code created from a compiler or an interpreter.
object-oriented analysis	The analysis phase of a developmental process in which the implementation uses an object-oriented language.
object-oriented database	A database in which data is treated as structures (objects).
object-oriented language	A programming language in which the objects and the operations to be applied to them are tied together.
object-oriented paradigm	A paradigm in which a program acts on active objects.
octal system	A numbering system with a base of 8: the octal digits are 0 to 7.
old master file	The master file that is processed in conjunction with the transaction file to create the new master file.
one's complement	A bitwise operation that reverses the value of the bits in a variable.
one's complement representation	A method of integer representation in which a negative number is represented by complementing the positive number.
one-dimensional array	An array with only one level of indexing.
open addressing resolution	A collision resolution method in which the new address is in the home area.
operability	The quality factor that addresses the ease with which a system can be used.
operand	An object in a statement on which an operation is performed. Contrast with *operator*.
operating system	The software that controls the computing environment and provides an interface to the user.
operator	The syntactical token representing an action on data (the operand). Contrast with *operand*.
optical storage device	An I/O device that uses (laser) light to store and retrieve data.
OR operation	A binary operation resulting in an output of 0 only if the two inputs are 0s, otherwise 1.

output data	The results of running a computer program.
output device	A device that can be written to but not read from.
overflow	The condition that results when there are insufficient bits to represent a number in binary.
page	One of a number of equally sized sections of a program.
paging	A multiprogramming technique in which memory is divided into equally sized sections called *frames*.
palette color	See *indexed color*.
parallel system	An operating system with multiple CPUs on the same machine.
parameter	A value passed to a function.
parameter list	A list of values passed to a function.
parent	A tree or graph node with one or more child nodes.
parsing	A process that breaks data into pieces or tokens.
partitioning	A technique used in multiprogramming that divides the memory into variable-length sections.
Pascal	A programming language designed with the goal of teaching programming to novices by emphasizing the structured programming approach.
pass by reference	A parameter passing technique in which the called function refers to a passed parameter using an alias name.
pass by value	A parameter passing technique in which the value of a variable is passed to a function.
passive hub	A type of connecting device that does not regenerate data.
password-based authentication	The simplest and oldest method of entity authentication, in which a password is used to identify the claimant.
path	A sequence of nodes in which each vertex is adjacent to the next.
perceptron	A simple neuron-like element that is used in neural networks.
PERL	A high-level language (with a syntax similar to C) using regular expressions that allow the parsing of a string of characters into components.
physical address	The address of a device at the data-link layer.
physical agent	A programmable system (robot) that can be used to perform a variety of tasks.
physical layer	The first layer in the TCP/IP model, responsible for signaling and transmitting bits across the network.
picture element (pixel)	The smallest unit of an image.
pit	On an optical disc, an area struck by the laser in the translation of a bit pattern, which usually represents a 0 bit.
pixel	See *picture element*.

place value	The value related to a position in the positional number system.
plaintext	Text before being encrypted.
pointer	A constant or variable that contains an address that can be used to access data stored elsewhere.
point-to-point connection	A dedicated transmission link between two devices.
polycarbonate resin	In CD-ROM production, a material injected into a mold.
polymorphism	In C++, defining several operations with the same name that can do different things in related classes.
polynomial problem	A problem that can be solved in an acceptable time by a computer.
pop	The stack delete operation.
port address	See *port number*.
port number	The address used in TCP and UDP to distinguish one process from another.
portability	The quality factor relating to the ease with which a system can be moved to other hardware environments.
positional number system	A number system in which the position of a symbol in a number defines its value.
Post Office Protocol (POP)	A popular mail access protocol that transfers e-mails from an e-mail server to the station of the e-mail recipient.
postfix	An arithmetic notation in which the operator is placed after its operands.
postorder traversal	A binary tree traversal method in which the left subtree is processed first, then the right subtree, then the root.
pragmatic analysis	The analysis of a sentence to find the real meaning of words by removing the ambiguities.
predicate logic	A logic system in which quantifiers can be applied to terms but not to predicates.
predicted frame (P-frame)	In MPEG, a frame that is related to the preceding I-frame or B-frame.
prefix	An arithmetic notation in which the operator is placed before the operands.
preorder traversal	A binary tree traversal in which the left subtree is traversed first, the root is traversed next, and the right subtree is traversed last.
prime area	In a hashed list, the memory that contains the home address.
private key	One of the two keys used in public key encryption.
probe	In a hashing algorithm, the calculation of an address and test for success. In a search algorithm, one iteration of the loop that includes the test for the search argument.
procedural language	A computer language in a procedural paradigm.

procedural paradigm	A paradigm in which a program acts on passive objects using procedures.
procedure	Another term for a subalgorithm.
procedure-oriented analysis	The analysis phase of a developmental process in which the implementation uses a procedural language.
procedure-oriented design	The design phase of developmental process when the implementation uses a procedural language
process	A program in execution.
process manager	An operating system component that controls the processes.
process scheduler	An operating system mechanism that dispatches the processes waiting to get access to the CPU.
process synchronization	An operating system mechanism that controls the access of a resource by more than one process.
process-to-process communication	Communication between two computers at the transport layer.
process-to-process delivery	Delivery of a packet from the transport layer of the source computer to the transport layer of the destination computer.
program	A set of instructions.
program counter	A register in the CPU that holds the address of the next instruction in memory to be executed.
programmable data processor	A machine that takes input data and a program to produce output data.
programmable read-only memory (PROM)	Memory with contents electrically set by the manufacturer that may be reset by the user.
programmed I/O	A form of I/O in which the CPU must wait for the I/O operation to be completed.
programming language	A language with limited words and limited rules designed to solve problems on a computer.
project operation	An operation in a relational database in which a set of columns is selected based on a criterion.
Prolog	A high-level programming language based on formal logic.
PROLOG	A programming language that can build a database of facts and a knowledge base of rules.
propositional logic	A logic system based on logical operators and propositional terms.
protocol	A set of rules for data exchange between computers.
pseudocode	English-like statements that follow a loosely defined syntax and are used to convey the design of an algorithm or function.
public key	One of the keys in a public key encryption, revealed to the public.
public key encryption	An encryption method using two keys, private and public. The private key is kept secret, the public key is revealed.

public-key certificate	A certificate that binds an entity to its public key.
push	The stack insert operation.
quantifier	Two operators used in predicate logic: ∀ and ∃.
quantization	Assigning a value from a finite set of values.
queue	A linear list in which data can only be inserted at one end, called the rear, and deleted from the other end, called the front.
radix	The base in a positional number system.
random access	A storage method that allows data to be retrieved in an arbitrary order.
random access memory (RAM)	The main memory of the computer that stores data and programs.
raster graphic	See *bitmap graphic*.
read/write head	The device in a hard disk that reads or writes data.
read-only memory (ROM)	Permanent memory with contents that cannot be changed.
ready state	In process management, the state of processing in which the process is waiting to get the attention of the CPU.
real	A number with both integral and fractional parts.
real-time system	An operating system that is expected to do a task within specific time constraints.
rear	The last element inserted into a queue using the enqueue operation.
record	Information related to one entity.
recursion	A function design in which the function calls itself.
reduced instruction set computer (RISC)	A computer that uses only frequently used instructions.
register	A fast stand-alone storage location that holds data temporarily.
relation	A table in a relational database.
relational database	A database model in which data is organized in related tables called relations.
relational database management system (RDBMS)	A set of programs that handles relations in a relational database model.
relational model	See *relational database*.
relational operator	An operator that compares two values.
reliability	The quality factor that addresses the confidence or trust in a system's total operation.
remote login	Logging on to a remote computer that is connected to the local computer.
repetition	One of the three constructs in structural programming.

replaying	A type of attack on information integrity in which the attacker intercepts the message and resends it again.
replicated distributed database	A database in which each site holds a replica of another site.
repudiation	A type of attack on information integrity that can be launched by one of the two parties in the communication: the sender or the receiver.
reserved words	The set of words in a language that has a predetermined interpretation and cannot be user-defined.
resolution	The scanning rate in image processing: the number of pixels per unit measure.
resource holding	A condition in which a process holds a resource but cannot use it until all other resources are available.
restricted list	A list in which data can only be added or deleted at the ends of the list and processing is restricted to operations on the data at the ends.
retrieval	The location and return of an element in a list.
RGB	A color system in which tints are represented by a combination of red, green, and blue primary colors.
ring topology	A topology in which the devices are connected in a ring. Each device receives a data unit from one neighbor and sends it to its other neighbor.
Rivest-Shamir-Adleman (RSA)	A popular public key encryption/decryption method.
Roman number system	The non-positional number system used by the Romans.
root	The first node of a tree.
rotational speed	The spin rate of a magnetic disk.
router	A device operating at the first three TCP/IP layers that connects independent networks. A router routes a packet based on its destination address.
routing	The process performed by a router.
routing table	The table used by a router to route a packet.
row-major storage	A method of storing array elements in memory in which the elements are stored row by row.
row-major storage	A method of storing two-dimensional arrays in which the elements are stored row by row.
ruled-based system	A knowledge representation system that uses a set of rules that can be used to deduce new facts from known facts.
run-length encoding	A lossless compression method in which a sequence of the same symbols is replaced by the symbol and the number of repetitions.
running state	In process management, a state in which a process is using the CPU.
sampling	Taking measurements at equal intervals.

sampling rate	The number of samples obtained per second in the sampling process.
scanning	Converting an image into digital data by sampling its density and color at evenly-spaced points.
scheduler	A program to move a job from one state to another.
scheduling	Allocating the resources of an operating system to different programs and deciding which program should use which resource, and when.
scheme	The de facto standard of the LISP language.
search space	The set of possible situations that can be examined by a search method to find a solution.
searching	The process that examines a list to locate one or more elements containing a designated value known as the search argument.
secondary storage device	See *auxiliary storage*.
secret key	A key that is shared by two participants in secret key encryption.
sector	A part of a track on a disk.
security	The quality factor that addresses the ease or difficulty with which an unauthorized user can access data.
security attack	An attack threatening the security goals of a system.
security goal	One of the three goals of information security: confidentiality, integrity, and availability.
seek time	In disk access, the time required to move the read/write head over the track that holds the required data.
segmentation	A step in image processing that divides the image into homogenous segments or areas.
select operation	An operation in a relational database that selects a set of tuples.
selection	One of the three constructs in structure programming.
selection sort	A sort algorithm in which the smallest value in the unsorted portion of the list is selected and placed at the end of the sorted portion of the list.
self-referential record	A record in which part of the record is used to point to another record of the same type.
semantic analysis	Analysis of the meaning of words in a sentence or tokens in a statement.
semantic network	A graph in which the nodes represents objects and the edges represent relationships between objects.
sequence	One of the three constructs in structure programming.
sequential access	An access method in which the records in a file are accessed serially beginning with the first element.
sequential file	A file structure in which data must be processed sequentially from the first element in the file.

sequential search	A search technique used with a linear list in which searching begins at the first element and continues until the value of an element equal to the value being sought is located, or until the end of the list is reached.
server	In a client-server system, the centralized computer that provides auxiliary services (server programs).
shell	A user interface in some operating systems, such as UNIX.
shift cipher	A type of substitution cipher in which the key defines shifting of characters toward the end of the alphabet.
siblings	Nodes in a tree with the same parent.
side effect	A change in a variable that results from the evaluation of an expression: any input/output performed by a called function.
sign-and-magnitude representation	A method of integer representation in which 1 bit represents the sign of the number and the remaining bits represent the magnitude.
Simple Mail Transfer Protocol (SMTP)	The TCP/IP protocol for e-mail service.
simple type	An atomic data type such as integer or real.
single-user operating system	An operating system in which only one program can be in memory at a time.
small computer system interface (SCSI)	An I/O device controller with a parallel interface.
snooping	Unauthorized access to confidential information
software	The application and system programs necessary for computer hardware to accomplish a task.
software agent	In artificial intelligence applications, a set of programs that are designed to do particular tasks.
software engineering	The design and writing of structured programs.
software lifecycle	The life of a software package.
solvable problem	A problem that can be solved by a computer.
soma	The body of a neuron that holds the nucleus of the cell.
something inherent	A characteristic of the claimant, such as conventional signature, fingerprint, voice, and so on, used for entity authentication.
something known	A secret known by the claimant that can be used by the verifier in entity authentication.
something possessed	Something belonging to the claimant that can prove the claimant's identity.
sort pass	One loop during which all elements are tested by a sorting program.
sorting	The process that orders a list or file.

source program	The file that contains program statements written by a programmer before they are converted into machine language: the input file to an assembler or compiler.
source-to-destination delivery	The delivery of a data packet from the source to the destination.
spatial compression	Compression done on a frame by the JPEG encoding process.
speech recognition	The first step in natural language processing (in AI) in which the speech signal is analyzed and the sequence of words it contains are extracted.
spoofing	See *masquerading*.
stack	A restricted data structure in which data can be inserted and deleted only at one end, called the top.
star topology	A topology in which all computers are connected to a common hub.
starvation	A problem in the operation of an operating system in which processes cannot get access to the resources they need.
state chart	A diagram, similar to a state diagram, but used in object-oriented software engineering.
state diagram	A diagram that shows the different states of a process.
statement	A syntactical construct in C that represents one operation in a function.
static document	A web page that is created at the remote site and retrieved by the local site. Contrast with *dynamic document*.
static RAM (SRAM)	A technology that uses traditional flip-flop gates (a gate with two states, 0 and 1) to hold data.
statistical compression	A compression method in which encoding is based on the frequency of symbols.
steganography	A security technique in which a message is concealed by covering it with something else.
storage device	An I/O device that can store large amounts of information for retrieval at a later time.
Stream Control Transmission Protocol (SCTP)	The transport layer protocol designed for Internet telephony and related applications.
structure chart	A design and documentation tool that represents a program as a hierarchical flow of functions.
Structured Query Language (SQL)	A database language that includes statements for database definition, manipulation, and control.
subalgorithm	A part of an algorithm that is independently written and is executed when called inside the algorithm.
subprogram	A smaller program called by the main program.
subroutine	See *subalgorithm*.

substitution cipher	A cipher that replaces one symbol with another.
subtree	Any connected structure below the root of a tree.
summation	Addition of a series of numbers.
symbolic language	A computer language, one level removed from machine language, that has a mnemonic identifier for each machine instruction and can use symbolic data names.
symmetric-key cryptography	A type of cryptography in which a single secret key is used for both encryption and decryption.
symmetric-key encryption	Encryption using a symmetric-key cipher.
synapse	A connection between two neurons in the human nervous system.
syndrome	A sequence of bits generated by applying an error-checking function to a code word.
synonym	In a hashed list, two or more keys that hash to the same home address.
syntactic analysis	The analysis of a sentence to check for grammar.
syntax	The grammatical rules of a language.
syntax analyzer	The process that checks the grammar of a sentence.
system development lifecycle	A sequence of steps required to develop software, which starts with the need for the software and concludes with its implementation.
system documentation	A formal structured record of a software package.
TCP/IP protocol suite	A five-layer protocol suite that defines the exchange of transmission across the Internet
TELNET (Terminal Network)	A general-purpose client-server program that allows remote login.
temporal compression	Compression done by MPEG on frames.
temporal logic	A type of logic that includes change and the effect of time in reasoning.
terminal state	The last state in a state diagram.
terminated state	In process management, a state in which a process has finished executing.
testability	An attribute of software that measures the ease with which the software can be tested as an operational system.
testing phase	A phase in the software lifecycle in which experiments are carried out to prove that a software package works.
text	Data stored as characters.
text editor	Software that creates and maintains text files, such as a word processor or a source program editor.
text file	A file in which all data is stored as characters. Contrast with *binary file*.
thresholding	A method used in image segmentation in which a pixel with a specific intensity is selected and the method tries to find all the pixels with the same intensity.

time sharing	An operating system concept in which more than one user has access to a computer at the same time.
token	A syntactical construct that represents an operation, a flag, or a piece of data.
topology	The structure of a network, including the physical arrangement of devices.
track	A part of a disk.
traffic analysis	A type of attack on confidentiality in which the attacker obtains some information by monitoring online traffic.
trailer	Control information appended to a data unit.
transaction file	A file containing relatively transient data that are used to change the contents of a master file.
transfer time	The time to move data from the disk to the CPU/memory.
transferability	A quality in software systems that refers to the ability to move the system from one platform to another.
translator	A generic term for any of the language conversion programs. See also *assembler* and *compiler*.
Transmission Control Protocol (TCP)	One of the transport-layer protocols in the TCP/IP protocol suite.
Transmission Control Protocol / Internet Protocol (TCP/IP)	The official protocol of the Internet, composed of five layers.
transmission rate	The number of bits sent per second.
transport layer	The fourth layer in the TCP/IP model, responsible for end-to-end delivery of the whole message.
transposition cipher	A cipher that transposes symbols in the plaintext to create the ciphertext and vice versa.
traversal	An algorithmic process in which each element in a structure is processed once and only once.
tree	A set of connected nodes structured so that each node has only one predecessor.
True-Color	A technique in raster graphic that uses 24 bits to represent a color.
truncation error	The error that occurs when a number is stored using floating-point represenation. The value of the number stored may not be exactly as expected.
truth table	A table listing all the possible logical input combinations with the corresponding logical output.
tuple	In a relational database, a record (a line) in a relation.
Turing machine	A computer model with three components (tape, controller, and read/write head) that can implement statements in a computer language.

Turing model	A computer model based on Alan Turing's theoretical definition of a computer.
Turing test	A test devised by Alan Turing to determine whether a computer can be said to be truly intelligent.
two's complement	A representation of binary numbers in which the complement of a number is found by complementing all bits and adding a 1 after that.
two's complement representation	A method of integer representation in which a negative number is represented by leaving all the rightmost 0s and the first unchanged and complementing the remaining bits.
two-dimensional array	An Array with elements having two levels of indexing. See also *multidimensional array.*
type	A set of values and a set of operations that can be applied on these values.
unary operation	An operation that needs only one input operand.
underflow	An event that occurs when an attempt is made to delete data from an empty data structure.
undirected graph	A graph consisting only of edges—that is, a graph in which there is no indication of direction on the lines.
Unicode	A 32-bit code that includes the symbols and alphabets from most languages in the world.
Unified Modeling Language (UML)	A graphical language used for analysis and design.
Uniform Resource Locator (URL)	A string of characters that defines a page on the Internet.
union operation	An operation on two sets in which the result contains all the elements from both sets without duplicates.
universal serial bus (USB)	A serial I/O device controller that connects slower devices such as the keyboard and mouse to a computer.
UNIX	A popular operating system among computer programmers and computer scientists.
unsigned integer	An integer without a sign whose value ranges between and positive infinity.
unsolvable problem	A problem that cannot be solved by a computer.
update operation	An operation in a relational database in which the operation about one tuple is changed.
use case diagram	A diagram showing the user view of a system in UML.
user agent (UA)	An SMTP component that prepares the message, creates the envelope, and puts the message in the envelope.
user datagram	The data unit used by the UDP protocol.
User Datagram Protocol (UDP)	One of the transport-layer protocols in the TCP/IP protocol suite.

user interface	A program that accepts requests from users (processes) and interprets them for the rest of the operating system.
utility	An application program in UNIX.
variable	A memory storage object whose value can be changed during the execution of a program. Contrast with *constant*.
vector graphic	A type of graphics file format in which lines and curves are defined using mathematical formulas.
verifying algorithm	The algorithm that verifies the validity of a digital signature.
vertex	A node in a graph.
video	A representation of images (called *frames*) in time.
videoconferencing	An application program on the Internet.
virtual memory	A form of memory organization that allows swapping of programs between memory and magnetic storage to give the impression of a larger main memory than really exists.
von Neumann model	A computer model (consisting of memory, arithmetic logic unit, control unit, and input/output subsystems) upon which the modern computer is based.
waiting state	A state in which a process is waiting to receive the attention of the CPU.
waterfall model	A software development model in which each module is completely finished before the next module is started.
Web	See *World Wide Web*.
Web page	A unit of hypertext or hypermedia available on the web.
white box testing	Program testing in which the internal design of the program is considered. Also known as *glass box testing*. Contrast with *black box testing*.
wide area network (WAN)	A network that spans a large geographical distance.
Windows 2000	A version of the Windows NT operating system.
Windows NT	An operating system devised by Microsoft to replace MS-DOS
Windows XP	A version of the Windows NT operating system.
World Wide Web (WWW)	A multimedia Internet service that allows users to traverse the Internet by moving from one document to another via links.
write once, read many (WORM)	Another name for a CD-R.
XOR operation	A bitwise operation in which the result of the operation is 1 only if one of the operands is 1.
zero-knowledge authentication	An entity authentication method in which the claimant does not reveal anything that might endanger the confidentiality of the secret.

Index